Dormac Easy English Dictionary

Dorothee Baker

Constance Bettino

Edited By

Dorothy J. McCarr

James E. McCarr

Lucille Eckert

Sara Natwick

Illustrated by Carol Webb Atherly
Renae Winters

Dormac, Inc.

Acknowledgement

Pronunciation key and diacritical marks are from *Scott, Foresman Advanced Dictionary* by Thorndike/Barnhart. Copyright © 1983 by Scott, Foresman and Company. Reprinted by permission.

 Dormac, Inc.
P.O. Box 270459
San Diego, California 92128

ISBN 0-86575-598-1
Printed in U.S.A.

Key to Symbols and Abbreviations

Pronounciation Symbols

a	cat, bad	o	pot, rock		a in about	
ā	ate, day	ō	old, low		e in oven	
ä	car, father	ô	or, all	ə =	i in pencil	
		oi	oil, boy		o in memory	
b	baby, tub	ou	out, town		u in circus	
ch	chop, church					
d	dad, red					

p	puppy, stop
r	red, car
s	see, ice
sh	she, fish
t	too, it
th	three, bath
ŦH	there, smooth

e	set, bed
ē	equal, eat
ėr	germ, learn
f	fat, if
g	go, bag
h	hot, he

u	cut, puppy
u̇	book, pull
ü	blue, shoe

i	sit, big
ī	lie, ice
j	judge, job
k	kite, cook

v	very, move
w	was, we
y	yes, you
z	zoo, easy
zh	treasure, garage

l	long, pool
m	mom, woman
n	no, on
ng	song, bank

Abbreviations

abbrev.	abbreviation
adj.	adjective
adv.	adverb
aux.	auxiliary
comp.	comparative
conj.	conjunction
contrac.	contraction
interj.	interjection
n.	noun
part.	participle
pl.	plural
prep.	preposition
pres.	present
pron.	pronoun
pt.	past
superl.	superlative
v.	verb

Introduction

Purpose

The *Dormac Easy English Dictionary* is designed as a simple dictionary with a basic vocabulary and fundamental language structures. The dictionary, therefore, provides for the special needs of hearing and language-impaired students and for those learning English as a second language.

The *Dormac Easy English Dictionary* is not intended to be a complete dictionary. The publishers rather have endeavored to provide a dictionary with a clarity of format that employs the simplest language possible, eliminating non-essentials and thereby best serving its target users.

The approximately 5,000 entry words in the *Dormac Easy English Dictionary* include, with few exceptions, all of the vocabulary in Dormac's basic reading series, *Reading Milestones*. Although this makes the dictionary the perfect supplemental tool for users of *Reading Milestones*, these entries include a basic vocabulary that has a wider applicability than *Reading Milestones* itself.

Not all possible meanings of a word are given; for the sake of clarity and ease of use, only those meanings used in *Reading Milestones* are offered. The definitions and sample sentences reflect the language controls of *Reading Milestones*. For the student, this simplifies the task of learning to use a dictionary.

To enhance comprehension and to facilitate the development of dictionary skills of students with special needs, the following have not been included: 1) the distinction between proper and common nouns; 2) secondary accent marks; 3) the terms transitive and intransitive; 4) all possible meanings and uses for each entry word; and 5) the days of the week, months of the year, colors, numbers, and cities and states within the United States.

We at Dormac are sure that you will find the *Dormac Easy English Dictionary* a helpful and easy-to-use reference guide.

Features

- Simply worded definitions given in an easy-to-read format with large type
- Approximately 5,000 entry words listed
- Illustrations on each page
- Syllabicated forms follow entry words
- Thorndike markings used as a pronunciation guide in all entries
- Definitions written in simple language structures
- Contextual use shown for each meaning
- Part of speech identified for each meaning
- Many irregular verb forms listed as separate entries
- Regular and irregular verb forms completely spelled out in boldface and followed by syllabicated forms
- Regular and irregular plurals of nouns completely spelled out in boldface and followed by syllabicated forms
- Comparative and superlative forms of adjectives and adverbs with **-er** and **-est** endings completely spelled out in boldface and followed by syllabicated forms
- Two-word verbs included as entry words
- Words identical in spelling but different in pronunciation or stress entered separately
- Easy-to-find key to pronunciation and abbreviations located on the first page of the dictionary
- Abbreviated pronunciation key listed on every odd-numbered page
- Idiomatic expressions included as entry words

Guide to the Dictionary

Guide Words

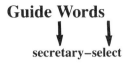

secretary–select

You will find guide words at the top of every page. The guide words help you find the word you are looking for.

All the words in the dictionary are alphabetized. That means they are in A-B-C order. Suppose you are looking for the word **seed.** You will find it on the page that has the guide words **secretary–select**, because **seed** is between **secretary** and **select** in alphabetical order.

Entry Word

↓

sparkle spar·kle (spär′kəl) **1.** to give off a glitter or spark of light; to shine with flashes of light.
    The stars will sparkle in the sky tonight.
    v. **sparkled, sparkled, sparkling** spar·kled, spar·kling
    2. a bright, quick light; something that gives off a quick light.
    We knew she was excited when we saw the sparkle in her eyes.
    n. pl. **sparkles** spar·kles

An entry word is any word that is explained in the dictionary. The entry words are listed in alphabetical order.

Superscript Numbers

↓

close[1] (klōz) **1.** to shut.
    Please close the door when you come into the house. *v.*
    2. not to allow to use.
    The police closed the road because the snow was too deep to drive through.
    v. **closed, closed, closing** clos·ing

↓

close[2] (klōs) **1.** near.
    These chairs are too close. *adj.*
    2. dear; special.
    The women had been close friends for many years.
    adj. **closer, closest** clos·er, clos·est

Sometimes two words are spelled the same but have different pronunciations. These words will be listed as different entry words. They will have superscript numbers [1], [2] next to them to show you that more than one word has this spelling.

Syllabication

sparkle spar·kle (spär⸍kəl) **1.** to give off a glitter or spark of light;
to shine with flashes of light.

The stars will sparkle in the sky tonight.

v. **sparkled, sparkled, sparkling** spar·kled, spar·kling

2. a bright, quick light; something that gives off a quick light.

We knew she was excited when we saw the sparkle in her eyes.

n. pl. **sparkles** spar·kles

The dictionary tells you where you may hyphenate words by using a bullet (·).

Pronunciation

sparkle spar·kle (spär⸍kəl) **1.** to give off a glitter or spark of light;
to shine with flashes of light.

The stars will sparkle in the sky tonight.

v. **sparkled, sparkled, sparkling** spar·kled, spar·kling

2. a bright, quick light; something that gives off a quick light.

We knew she was excited when we saw the sparkle in her eyes.

n. pl. **sparkles** spar·kles

The dictionary uses symbols to show you how to say each entry word. The first page of the dictionary has a guide that shows all the symbols. Also, every odd-numbered page has a short guide that you can refer to.

For words that are pronounced more than one way, more than one pronunciation is shown.

sparkle spar·kle (spär⸍kəl)

The stress mark (′) shows you which syllable is pronounced louder.

Numbers in a Definition

sparkle spar·kle (spär⸍kəl) **1.** to give off a glitter or spark of light;
to shine with flashes of light.

The stars will sparkle in the sky tonight.

v. **sparkled, sparkled, sparkling** spar·kled, spar·kling

2. a bright, quick light; something that gives off a quick light.

We knew she was excited when we saw the sparkle in her eyes.

n. pl. **sparkles** spar·kles

Many words have more than one meaning. In the dictionary each different meaning has a number.

Sample Sentences

sparkle spar·kle (spär‡kəl) **1.** to give off a glitter or spark of light;
to shine with flashes of light.
➤ The stars will sparkle in the sky tonight.
v. **sparkled, sparkled, sparkling** spar·kled, spar·kling
2. a bright, quick light; something that gives off a quick light.
➤ We knew she was excited when we saw the sparkle in her eyes.
n. pl. **sparkles** spar·kles

For each meaning there is a sample sentence. The sample sentence will help you understand how to use the word.

Part-of-Speech Labels

sparkle spar·kle (spär‡kəl) **1.** to give off a glitter or spark of light;
to shine with flashes of light.
The stars will sparkle in the sky tonight.
➤ *v.* **sparkled, sparkled, sparkling** spar·kled, spar·kling
2. a bright, quick light; something that gives off a quick light.
We knew she was excited when we saw the sparkle in her eyes.
➤ *n. pl.* **sparkles** spar·kles

Many words can be used as different parts of speech. Each different part of speech is listed in the dictionary as a separate meaning.

Here is a list of the parts of speech used in the dictionary:

adj.	adjective
adv.	adverb
aux.	auxiliary
conj.	conjunction
interj.	interjection
n.	noun
prep.	preposition
pron.	pronoun
v.	verb

A list of the parts of speech can also be found on the first page of the dictionary.

Plurals of Nouns

sparkle   spar·kle (spär′kəl)   **1.** to give off a glitter or spark of light;
to shine with flashes of light.
The stars will sparkle in the sky tonight.
v. **sparkled, sparkled, sparkling** spar·kled, spar·kling
2. a bright, quick light; something that gives off a quick light.
We knew she was excited when we saw the sparkle in her eyes.
n. pl. **sparkles** spar·kles

In this dictionary, the plural of each noun is given to show you how to spell it. Some words do not have any plural, for example **flour**. These words are marked *no pl.* in the dictionary. Other words are always plural. An example is the word **clothes**. These words are marked *plural n.*

Comparison of Adjectives and Adverbs

cold   (kōld)   **1.** not hot.
It was very cold at the top of the mountain.
adj. **colder, coldest** cold·er, cold·est

Comparative   Superlative

The comparative and superlative forms of adjectives and adverbs are given. These words show you the correct form to use. They also show you how to spell the **-er** or **-est** form of the word.

Principal Parts of Verbs

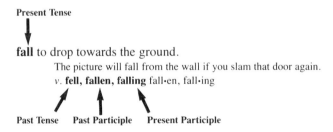

Present Tense

fall to drop towards the ground.
The picture will fall from the wall if you slam that door again.
v. **fell, fallen, falling** fall·en, fall·ing

Past Tense   Past Participle   Present Participle

Many irregular verb forms are included as entry words. The part-of-speech label will tell you the form of the verb. Then you will be referred to the root word. If there is a number in parentheses after the root word, that tells you to look at that definition number. Here is an example:

fell   (fel)   *v. pt. t.* See **fall** (2).

This entry shows you that **fell** is the past tense form of **fall** as used in the second meaning listed for that entry.

Two-word Verbs

Two-word verbs consist of a verb and a preposition or adverb and have a separate meaning from the meaning of the verb by itself or with other prepositions and adverbs. Two-word verbs are listed as separate entries. Here is an example:

> **try on** (trī ôn) to put on some piece of clothing to see if
> it fits or looks right.
>> I want to try on this blue shirt. *v.* **tried on, tried on, trying on** try·ing on

Phrases

Entries that are phrases do not have a part of speech listed, because each word in the phrase is a different part of speech.

> **shaving cream** shav·ing cream (shā′ving krēm) a foamy lotion or
> cream that is put on hair before shaving.
>> My father puts shaving cream on his face before he shaves.

Phrases that include words that are part of an entry phrase and that change according to context are indicated with a dash ___. For example, the entry **change ___ mind** can be used in a sentence as "Sue may change *her* mind." or "I may change *my* mind."

Phrases whose meaning is not clear from the meanings of the separate words in the phrase are marked *idiom*. For example, here are the meanings for three separate words:

> **come** (kum) to go forward.
>> Please come here. *v.* **came, come, coming** com·ing

> **in** (in) inside; within.
>> I put the cat in the box. *prep.*

> **handy** hand·y (han′dē) easy to find; near to the hand.
>> *adj.* **handier, handiest** hand·i·er, hand·i·est

Now, here is the meaning of the phrase **come in handy**:

> **come in handy** come in hand·y (kum in han′dē) to be useful.
>> A towel will come in handy after we swim. *idiom*

↑

The meaning of **come in handy** is not clear from the definitions of **come**, **in** or **handy**. When a phrase has a different meaning from the separate words in the phrase, it is listed separately and is marked *idiom*.

Aa

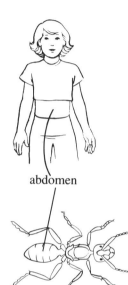

abdomen

Abominable Snowman

a (ə *or* ā) **1.** one; any.
A lady rode a camel at the circus. *indefinite article*
2. a top grade or mark in school.
Jane got an A in math. *n. pl.* **A's** *or* **As.**

A.D. (ā dē) after the birth of Christ.
Columbus discovered America in A.D. 1492. *abbrev.*

A.M. (ā em) before noon; in the morning.
School begins at 9:00 A.M. *abbrev.*

abdomen ab·do·men (ab′də·mən *or* ab′dō·mən) the part of the body between the chest and the hipbones; the lower part of an insect's body.
The horse kicked Mike in the abdomen. *n. pl.* **abdomens** ab·do·mens

ability a·bil·i·ty (ə·bil′ə·tē) skill or power to do something.
Joyce has the ability to write well. *n. pl.* **abilities** a·bil·i·ties

able a·ble (ā′bəl) can do something.
The monkey is able to climb. *adj.* **abler, ablest** a·bler, a·blest

abominable a·bom·i·na·ble (ə·bom′ə·nə·bəl) terrible; very unpleasant.
Murder is an abominable crime. *adj.*

Abominable Snowman a·bom·i·na·ble snow·man (ə·bom′ə·nə·bəl snō′man) a large animal that looks like an ape.
Some people believe they saw an Abominable Snowman.

aborigine ab·o·rig·i·ne (ab·ə·rij′ə·nē) a person whose family always lived in the country.
An Indian is an aborigine of America. *n. pl.* **aborigines** ab·o·rig·i·nes

about a·bout (ə·bout′) **1.** almost.
Our hen lays about 200 eggs a year. *adv.*
2. having to do with something.
Jim read a book about dogs. *prep.*
3. almost ready to; going to.
The cat was about to jump on the mouse. *prep.*

a	cat	i	sit	oi	oil	ch	chop		a in about
ā	ate	ī	lie	ou	out	ng	song		e in oven
ä	car	o	pot	u	cut	sh	she	ə =	i in pencil
e	set	ō	old	u̇	book	th	three		o in memory
ē	equal	ô	or	ü	blue	ŦH	there		u in circus
ėr	germ					zh	treasure		

above   a·bove (ə·buv′)   **1.** in a higher place than something.
There is a light above the door. *prep.*
2. at a higher place; in the sky.
He saw the moon above. *adv.*

absent-minded   ab·sent-mind·ed (ab′sənt-mīn′did)   not
remembering; often forgetting.
The absent-minded man lost his keys. *adj.*

absorb   ab·sorb (ab·sôrb′ *or* ab·zôrb′)   to take in or soak up.
The paper towel absorbed the water.
v. **absorbed, absorbed, absorbing** ab·sorbed, ab·sorb·ing

absorb

accept   ac·cept (ak·sept′)   **1.** to be happy to try something
new or different.
All the students accepted the new class schedule. *v.*
2. to agree to.
I accepted the invitation to Jack's birthday party. *v.*
3. to take or receive.
Mom accepted the package from the mailman.
v. **accepted, accepted, accepting** ac·cept·ed, ac·cept·ing

accident   ac·ci·dent (ak′sə·dənt)   something that happens
but is not planned.
The car accident happened on an icy road. *n. pl.* **accidents** ac·ci·dents

accidentally   ac·ci·den·tal·ly (ak·sə·den′tl·ē)   happening
without being planned.
Karen accidentally bumped into Kathy. *adv.*

accurate   ac·cur·ate (ak′yər·it)   correct; no mistakes.
Sue's math is accurate. *adj.*

accurately   ac·cur·ate·ly (ak′yər·it·lē)   correctly; without mistakes.
Tim's watch tells the time accurately. *adv.*

accident

ache   (āk)   **1.** a pain.
Bob has an ache in his back. *n. pl.* **aches**
2. to hurt.
My tooth aches. *v.* **ached, ached, aching** ach·ing

acid   ac·id (as′id)   something that tastes sour; a chemical used in
garden supplies or house cleaners.
Strong acid can burn your skin. *n. pl.* **acids** ac·ids

acre   a·cre (ā′kər)   a measure of land; 43,560 square feet
or 160 square rods make an acre.
Uncle Al has 260 acres on his farm. *n. pl.* **acres** a·cres

across   a·cross (ə·krôs′ *or* ə·kros′)   from one side to the other.
Jennie walked across the street. *prep.*

actor

actress

ad

act (akt) **1.** to pretend.
The two children acted like they were adults. *v.*
2. to behave.
Sue acted bravely when she went to the dentist.
v. **acted, acted, acting** act·ed, act·ing
3. a part of a play.
I cried during Act II of the play *Cinderella. n. pl.* **acts**

acting act·ing (ak′ting) pretending to be a character in a movie or a play.
John Wayne is famous for acting in cowboy movies. *n. no pl.*

action ac·tion (ak′shən) **1.** movement.
Marcia's pictures showed the action of the runners. *n.*
2. working parts of a machine.
Steve checked the action of his gun. *n. pl.* **actions** ac·tions

active ac·tive (ak′tiv) moving quickly; not resting.
The new puppy is very active. *adj.*

activity ac·tiv·i·ty (ak·tiv′ə·tē) something a person or group does.
Next week we will visit the museum for a Girl Scout activity.
n. pl. **activities** ac·tiv·i·ties

actor ac·tor (ak′tər) a man or boy who acts in a movie or a play.
Jonathan was the actor who played the hero in the school play.
n. pl. **actors** ac·tors

act out (akt out) to pretend to be someone or something in a story.
The first grade children acted out the story of *The Three Bears.*
v. **acted out, acted out, acting out** act·ed out, act·ing out

actress ac·tress (ak′tris) a girl or woman who acts in a movie or play.
Sally Field won the Oscar award for best actress.
n. pl. **actresses** ac·tress·es

actual ac·tu·al (ak′chü·əl) real; true.
Jenny's birthday party is on Saturday but her actual birthday is on Friday. *adj.*

actually ac·tu·al·ly (ak′chü·ə·lē) really.
Bob was not dreaming. He actually won the race. *adv.*

ad (ad) *abbrev. pl.* **ads.** See **advertisement.**

a	cat	i	sit	oi	oil	ch	chop		a in about
ā	ate	ī	lie	ou	out	ng	song		e in oven
ä	car	o	pot	u	cut	sh	she	ə = {	i in pencil
e	set	ō	old	u̇	book	th	three		o in memory
ē	equal	ô	or	ü	blue	ŦH	there		u in circus
ėr	germ					zh	treasure		

add (ad) **1.** to find the sum of.
If you add 2 and 5, you will have 7. *v.*
2. to put one thing with another; to increase.
Scott added chocolate chips to the cookie mix. *v.*
3. to say or write more.
Mom told Kevin to take a bath. Then she added that he should
wash behind his ears. *v.* **added, added, adding** add·ed, add·ing

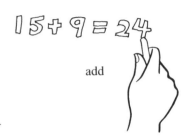

add

additional ad·di·tion·al (ə·dish′ə·nəl) more; extra.
I have additional homework because I missed class yesterday. *adj.*

additive ad·di·tive (ad′ə·tiv) something added to something else
to keep it fresh or make it more powerful.
The bread had additives of vitamins A and D. *n. pl.* **additives** ad·di·tives

address[1] ad·dress (ə·dres′) **1.** a place where a person or business
receives mail.
What is the address of your home? *n.*
2. the writing on an envelope or package that tells
where to send the package or envelope.
Sue wrote the wrong address on the envelope. *n. pl.* **addresses** ad·dress·es

address[2] ad·dress (ad′res) to write the name, street number,
city and state of a person or business on something in
order to mail it.
Cary addressed the package to his aunt.
v. **addressed, addressed, addressing** ad·dressed, ad·dress·ing

address

admire ad·mire (ad·mīr′) to think someone or something
is very nice, good or wonderful.
We admired the policeman's bravery.
v. **admired, admired, admiring** ad·mired, ad·mir·ing

admit ad·mit (ad·mit′) **1.** to let a person or thing come in.
The movie theater admitted the children for half price. *v.*
2. to agree to; to say "yes" to.
I admitted that it was a beautiful, sunny day. *v.*
3. to tell that you did something.
Betti admitted that she broke the vase.
v. **admitted, admitted, admitting** ad·mit·ted, ad·mit·ting

adopt a·dopt (ə·dopt′) to accept as your own.
The Smith family adopted the little boy when his parents died.
v. **adopted, adopted, adopting** a·dopt·ed, a·dopt·ing

adult a·dult (ə·dult′ *or* ad′ult) a grown-up person.
A person becomes an adult at 21 years old. *n. pl.* **adults** a·dults

advance ad·vance (ad·vans′) move toward something.
The family advanced slowly through the woods on their hike.
v. **advanced, advanced, advancing** ad·vanced, ad·vanc·ing

adult

advanced ad·vanced (ad·vanst′) more difficult; a high level.
Marilyn is in the advanced math class. *adj.*

advantage ad·van·tage (ad·van′tij) something that is good,
helpful or useful.
Carla was not sleepy during the long evening meeting because she had
the advantage of a nap after lunch. *n. pl.* **advantages** ad·van·tag·es

adventure ad·ven·ture (ad·ven′chər) **1.** excitement.
The boys are always looking for adventure. *n. no pl.*
2. an exciting experience; a fun time.
Going to the zoo is an adventure. *n. pl.* **adventures** ad·ven·tures
3. exciting.
I read adventure stories. *adj.*

adventurer ad·ven·tur·er (ad·ven′chər·ər) a person who looks
for excitement; a person who likes to try new things.
Jill is an adventurer who likes to eat food from other countries.
n. pl. **adventurers** ad·ven·tur·ers

advertise ad·ver·tise (ad′vər·tīz) to use the newspaper, radio or
television to tell people about something that is for sale.
The store will advertise the new purple shirts.
v. **advertised, advertised, advertising** ad·ver·tised, ad·ver·tis·ing

advertisement ad·ver·tise·ment (ad·vər·tīz′mənt *or*
ad·ver′tis·mənt) something that tells people
about a product or an event.
We saw the advertisement on television.
n. pl. **advertisements** ad·ver·tise·ments

advertisement

advertising ad·ver·tis·ing (ad·vər·tī′zing) advertisements;
things that tell people about a product or an event.
The store is spending a lot of money on advertising. *n. no pl.*

advice ad·vice (ad·vīs′) a suggestion; a shared idea; an opinion.
Mother gave me advice about studying. *n. no pl.*

advise ad·vise (ad·vīz′) to give suggestions; to share
ideas; to give an opinion.
She will advise me about making new friends.
v. **advised, advised, advising** ad·vised, ad·vis·ing

affect af·fect (ə·fekt′) to cause a change or reaction;
to make something happen.
The rain will affect the number of people who come to the party.
v. **affected, affected, affecting** af·fect·ed, af·fect·ing

a	cat	i	sit	oi	oil	ch	chop		a in about
ā	ate	ī	lie	ou	out	ng	song		e in oven
ä	car	o	pot	u	cut	sh	she	ə =	i in pencil
e	set	ō	old	u̇	book	th	three		o in memory
ē	equal	ô	or	ü	blue	ŦH	there		u in circus
ėr	germ					zh	treasure		

5

afford af·ford (ə·fôrd´) to have enough money to buy something; to be able to buy something.
I can afford to buy Mother a birthday gift.
v. **afforded, afforded, affording** af·ford·ed, af·ford·ing

afraid a·fraid (ə·frād´) scared; frightened; full of fear.
I was afraid of the stranger. *adj.*

Africa Af·ri·ca (af´rə·kə) a large continent that is south of Europe.
Elephants can be found in Africa. *n.*

African Af·ri·can (af´rə·kən) being from or about Africa.
The Congo is an African river. *adj.*

after af·ter (af´tər) **1.** later than; at a later time than.
I will come to your house after school. *prep.*
2. following an event or a time.
We will go home after I buy a pair of shoes. *conj.*

after all af·ter all (af´tər ôl) in the end; anyway.
We found that we could be friends after all.

afternoon af·ter·noon (af·tər·nün´) **1.** the time of day between noon and evening.
We went to the zoo this afternoon. *n. pl.* **afternoons** af·ter·noons
2. being the time of day between noon and evening.
Grandmother takes an afternoon walk every day. *adj.*

again a·gain (ə·gen´ *or* ə·gān´) **1.** a repeated time; once more.
I want to go to the zoo again. *adv.*
2. back to the way it was before; to return to the way it was.
He wants to be a baby again. *adv.*

against a·gainst (ə·genst´ *or* ə·gānst´) **1.** as a protection from something or someone.
The shot will protect me against the flu. *prep.*
2. opposed to something; not wanting something.
She is against our going camping. *prep.*
3. in the direction of and touching.
The tree fell against the fence. *prep.*

age (āj) the number of years that something has been alive.
My age is ten. *n. pl.* **ages** ag·es

ago a·go (ə·gō´) in the past.
Dinosaurs lived on Earth a long time ago. *adv.*

agree a·gree (ə·grē´) to have the same idea or thought; to like the same things as someone else; to decide on the same thing.
We will agree on one kind of ice cream.
v. **agreed, agreed, agreeing** a·greed, a·gree·ing

afford

afraid

Africa

ahead   a·head (ə·hed′)   **1.** forward.
It will hurt, but go ahead and pull the bandage off. *adv.*
2. in the future; still to come.
We have a long trip ahead of us. *adv.*
3. before the others; in the lead.
I will go ahead and get a table in the diner. *adv.*
4. in front of.
John is standing ahead of Jill in line. *adv.*

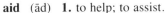

aid   (ād)   **1.** to help; to assist.
The nurse will aid the sick person. *v.* **aided, aided, aiding** aid·ed, aid·ing
2. the act of helping; the help that is given.
The nurse will give aid to the sick. *n. no pl.*
3. a tool or machine that helps a person to do something.
I wear a hearing aid. *n. pl.* **aids**

airplane

aim   (ām)   to point something toward a place.
I will aim the gun at the target. *v.* **aimed, aimed, aiming** aim·ing

air   (er *or* ar)   **1.** the area over you; the sky.
The kite is in the air. *n. no pl.*
2. the oxygen that is in the area over you; the gases that people breathe.
I filled my lungs with air. *n. no pl.*
3. having to do with the oxygen that people breathe; having to do with the sky.
Sue blew air bubbles into her milk with a straw. *adj.*

airfield   air·field (er′fēld *or* ar′fēld)   a place where airplanes take off and land; a small airport.
The small plane landed at the airfield. *n. pl.* **airfields** air·fields

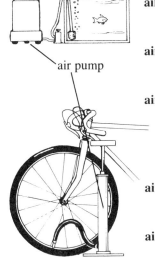

air pump

airplane   air·plane (ər′plān *or* ar′plān)   a vehicle that has wings and that flies in the air.
I flew in an airplane to Chicago. *n. pl.* **airplanes** air·planes

airport   air·port (er′pôrt *or* er′pōrt *or* ar′pôrt *or* ar′pōrt)   **1.** a place where people get on and off airplanes; a place where airplanes take off and land.
Father took us to the airport to catch our airplane. *n. pl.* **airports** air·ports
2. having to do with the place where people catch airplanes.
The airport bus took us to our gate. *adj.*

air pump   (er pump *or* ar pump)   a machine that puts air into things.
We put an air pump on the aquarium.

airway   air·way (er′wā *or* ar′wā)   a tube or passage for air.
Your throat is an airway to your lungs. *n. pl.* **airways** air·ways

a	cat	i	sit	oi	oil	ch	chop		a in about
ā	ate	ī	lie	ou	out	ng	song		e in oven
ä	car	o	pot	u	cut	sh	she	ə =	i in pencil
e	set	ō	old	u̇	book	th	three		o in memory
ē	equal	ô	or	ü	blue	ŦH	there		u in circus
ėr	germ					zh	treasure		

aisle (īl) the path or space between rows of seats; a walkway between rows of seats.
The people walked down the aisle of the theater. *n. pl.* **aisles**

aisle

alarm a·larm (ə·lärm′) **1.** having to do with giving a warning or a signal; having to do with making noise that gives a warning or a signal.
We went outside when the fire alarm bell rang. *adj.*
2. a signal or warning.
The smoke alarm warned the people of the fire. *n. pl.* **alarms** a·larms

alarm clock a·larm clock (ə·lärm′ klok) a timepiece that rings a bell, flashes a light or starts a buzzer when it is time to wake up; a clock that gives a warning or a signal at a certain time.
I set the alarm clock for seven o'clock.

album al·bum (al′bəm) a book in which people save things.
I put the pictures of the party in the photo album. *n. pl.* **albums** al·bums

alcohol al·co·hol (al′kə·hôl *or* al′kə·hol) a liquid that is made by fermenting grain and that is used in drugs and liquor.
Wine and beer have alcohol in them. *n. no pl.*

alarm clock

alert a·lert (ə·lėrt′) **1.** awake; watchful; ready for action.
The soldier was alert to danger. *adj.*
2. to warn someone of danger or possible harm; to give a signal.
Jane will alert us when the teacher is coming into the room.
v. **alerted, alerted, alerting** a·lert·ed, a·lert·ing

Aleut Al·e·ut (al′ē·üt) a member of a people who are from western Alaska.
The Aleut was born in the Aleutian Islands. *n. pl.* **Aleuts** Al·e·uts

algae al·gae (al′jē) plants that live in water or in damp places; small water plants.
The fish ate the algae. *plural n.*

alike a·like (ə·līk′) being the same as another; looking or acting the same; similar.
The two sisters look alike. *adj.*

alive a·live (ə·līv′) having life; not dead; breathing.
Her grandmother is dead, but her grandfather is alive. *adj.*

all (ôl) **1.** the whole number; everybody or everything.
All the students in my class went on the trip to the zoo. *pron.*
2. the whole amount; the whole number.
I waited all day for her to arrive. *adj.*
3. completely; alone.
I made the bed all by myself. *adv.*

album

allergic

allowance

allergic al·ler·gic (ə·lėr′jik) having a reaction to something; unable to be near or to eat something.
I am allergic to chocolate. *adj.*

all of a sudden all of a sud·den (ôl əv ā sud′n) in an instant; quickly; suddenly.
It was very quiet, and then all of a sudden there was a loud noise outside. *idiom*

all over all o·ver (ôl ō′vər) in every place in an area; covering the whole area.
There were flowers all over the yard. *adv.*

all over again all o·ver a·gain (ôl ō′vər ə·gen′) happening once more.
The noise stopped and then started all over again. *idiom*

allow al·low (ə·lou′) **1.** to permit; to let do something; to give permission.
Mother will allow me to go to the movie. *v.*
2. to make able; to let something happen.
The gills on the fish allow the fish to breathe in the water.
v. **allowed, allowed, allowing** al·lowed, al·low·ing

allowance al·low·ance (ə·lou′əns) money that is given to a person every week; money that is set aside for something certain.
Father gave me my two dollars' allowance. *n. pl.* **allowances** al·low·anc·es

all right (ôl rīt) without a problem or a disease; in good health; not sick.
The doctor said that I am all right. *adj.*

all the time (ôl ŦHə tīm) every minute; without stopping.
The dog will sleep all the time if we let her.

all year round (ôl yir round) every day of the year; from January through December.
It is warm in southern California all year round.

almost al·most (ôl′mōst *or* ôl·mōst′) nearly; close but not quite.
I almost have enough money to buy a new bicycle. *adv.*

aloha a·lo·ha (ə·lō′ə *or* ä·lō′hä) Hawaiian word for "hello" or "good-bye."
The people said aloha when we got off the plane in Hawaii.
n. pl. **alohas** a·lo·has

Aloha State A·lo·ha State (ə·lō′ə stāt *or* ä·lō′hä stāt) the nickname for the state of Hawaii.
Everyone calls Hawaii the Aloha State.

a	cat	**i**	sit	**oi**	oil	**ch**	chop
ā	ate	**ī**	lie	**ou**	out	**ng**	song
ä	car	**o**	pot	**u**	cut	**sh**	she
e	set	**ō**	old	**u̇**	book	**th**	three
ē	equal	**ô**	or	**ü**	blue	**ŦH**	there
ėr	germ					**zh**	treasure

ə = { a in about / e in oven / i in pencil / o in memory / u in circus }

alone a·lone (ə·lōn′) by oneself; without other people nearby.
I stayed alone until Mother got home. *adv.*

along a·long (ə·lông′ *or* ə·long′) **1.** on or near the line of.
I walked along the path to the lake. *prep.*
2. forward.
He rides along on his bicycle. *adv.*

ABCDEFGHIJKLM
NOPQRSTUVWXYZ
alphabet

aloud a·loud (ə·loud′) using one's voice so that others can hear.
I will read the report aloud. *adv.*

alphabet al·pha·bet (al′fə·bet) **1.** the letters used to write words.
I can say the alphabet from A to Z. *n. no pl.*
2. having to do with the letters that are used to write words.
I like alphabet soup. *adj.*

alphabetical order al·pha·bet·i·cal or·der (al·fə·bet′ə·kəl ôr′dər)
a listing of words organized in the order of the alphabet.
The words in a dictionary are in alphabetical order.

alpine al·pine (al′pīn) having to do with high mountains;
having to do with the Alps in Switzerland.
We stayed in the alpine area of the country. *adj.*

Alps (alps) large mountains in southern Europe.
Many people go skiing in the Alps. *plural n.*

Alps

already al·read·y (ôl·red′ē) by this time; before this time.
Father is already home; he is early tonight. *adv.*

also al·so (ôl′sō) in addition; too.
Father is already home; Mother is also home. *adv.*

although al·though (ôl·ŦHō′) even if; different from what a
person would think to be true or right.
Although he was sick, Jim went to the movie. *conj.*

altimeter al·tim·e·ter (al·tim′ə·tər) a machine or tool that measures
how high something is; an instrument that measures the height
of something above the Earth.
The pilot read the airplane's altimeter. *n. pl.* **altimeters** al·tim·e·ters

altitude al·ti·tude (al′tə·tüd *or* al′tə·tyüd) the height above
the Earth something is; the distance from the ground.
The altitude of the mountain is 3,400 feet. *n. pl.* **altitudes** al·ti·tudes

altogether al·to·geth·er (ôl·tə·geŦH′ər) everything included;
considering everything.
Altogether, we are glad we moved to New York. *adv.*

aluminum a·lu·mi·num (ə·lü′mə·nəm) a soft, silver-colored metal.
The frying pan is made of aluminum. *n. no pl.*

altimeter

always al·ways (ôl′wiz *or* ôl′wāz) every time; at all times.
I always want chocolate. *adv.*

am (am *or* əm) *v. pres. t.* See **be.**

amaze a·maze (ə·māz′) to cause surprise; to cause wonder.
The high ropewalker will amaze you.
v. **amazed, amazed, amazing** a·mazed, a·maz·ing

ambulance

amazing a·maz·ing (ə·mā′zing) surprising; filling with wonder.
The amazing high ropewalker entertained us. *adj.*

ambition am·bi·tion (am·bish′ən) something one wishes
to do or to become; a goal.
His ambition is to become a doctor. *n. pl.* **ambitions** am·bi·tions

ambulance am·bu·lance (am′byə·ləns) an emergency
vehicle; a vehicle that brings medical help.
The ambulance took the sick man to the hospital.
n. pl. **ambulances** am·bu·lanc·es

amen a·men (ā′men′ *or* ä′men′) Hebrew word that means "so be
it," used as the last word of a prayer.
We said "amen" after the priest said the prayer. *interj.*

America A·mer·i·ca (ə·mer′ə·kə) the United States of America.
It is great to live in America. *n.*

American A·mer·i·can (ə·mer′ə·kən) having to do with the people
and the country of the United States.
The Fourth of July is an American holiday. *adj.*

am going to am go·ing to (am gō′ing tü) *v.* See **be going to.**

ammonia am·mo·nia (ə·mō′nyə *or* ə·mō′nē·ə) a chemical
that has a strong smell.
Some people use ammonia for cleaning. *n. no pl.*

among a·mong (ə·mung′) with; surrounded by; in with.
I was among the students who went to the museum. *prep.*

amount a·mount (ə·mount′) quantity; how many; how
much; the sum of numbers or coins.
The amount of the bill was $16.00. *n. pl.* **amounts** a·mounts

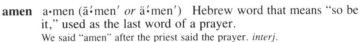

America
Washington, D.C.

a	cat	i	sit	oi	oil	ch	chop		a in about
ā	ate	ī	lie	ou	out	ng	song		e in oven
ä	car	o	pot	u	cut	sh	she	ə =	i in pencil
e	set	ō	old	u̇	book	th	three		o in memory
ē	equal	ô	or	ü	blue	ŦH	there		u in circus
ėr	germ					zh	treasure		

11

amputate am·pu·tate (am′pyə·tāt) to cut off an arm or a leg.
  The doctor must amputate the man's leg.
    v. **amputated, amputated, amputating** am·pu·tat·ed, am·pu·tat·ing

amusement a·muse·ment (ə·myüz′mənt) having to do with having
  a good time; fun; excitement.
    We went to the amusement park and rode the exciting rides. *adj.*

an (an *or* ən) one; any. Use **an** before the sounds *a, e, i, o* or *u.*
    I ate an orange, and he ate a pear. *indefinite article.*

ancestor an·ces·tor (an′ses·tər) a person in a family who lived
  a long time ago.
    The old man in the picture is an ancestor of my father's.
    n. pl. **ancestors** an·ces·tors

anchor

anchor an·chor (ang′kər) **1.** a heavy weight that a person uses
  to keep a ship or boat in a place.
    We put the boat's anchor in the water. *n. pl.* **anchors** an·chors
    2. to keep in place; to hold a boat so it will not move
  from its place.
    We will anchor the boat in the harbor.
    v. **anchored, anchored, anchoring** an·chored, an·chor·ing

ancient an·cient (ān′shənt) long ago; in a time long past; very old.
    In ancient times people did not move far from their families. *adj.*

and (and *or* ənd) also; too; in addition; plus.
    Jim and Jean are going sailing. *conj.*

Andes An·des (an′dēz) a large mountain range on the continent
  of South America.
    People travel great distances to climb the Andes. *n.*

Andes

angel an·gel (ān′jəl) a being who lives in Heaven; a good person;
  a heavenly spirit.
    She put an angel at the top of the Christmas tree. *n. pl.* **angels** an·gels

anger an·ger (ang′gər) **1.** a strong feeling of displeasure.
    The man felt anger when the robber stole his money. *n. no pl*
    2. to become angry; to cause someone to become angry.
    The broken vase will anger Mother.
    v. **angered, angered, angering** an·gered, an·ger·ing

angrily an·gri·ly (ang′grə·lē) in a way that shows anger; violently.
    He spoke angrily to the naughty children. *adv.*

angry an·gry (ang′grē) feeling anger; full of anger;
  feeling displeasure.
    Mother was angry because we broke the vase.
    adj. **angrier, angriest** an·gri·er, an·gri·est

angel

animal   an·i·mal (an'ə·məl)   **1.** a living thing that breathes oxygen and eats food.
A dog is an animal. *n. pl.* **animals** an·i·mals
2. having to do with a living thing that breathes oxygen and eats food.
We heard animal noises in the forest. *adj.*

animated   an·i·mat·ed (an'ə·mā·tid)   looking alive; appearing to be real.
The animated cartoon character in the movie was a mouse. *adj.*

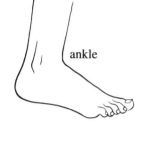

ankle

ankle   an·kle (ang'kəl)   the part of the body between the leg and the foot; the movable joint that attaches the foot to the leg.
The girl hurt her ankle when she kicked the football. *n. pl.* **ankles** an·kles

anniversary   an·ni·ver·sar·y (an·ə·vėr'sər·ē)   **1.** the yearly celebration of something that happened on a certain date.
Tomorrow is the twentieth anniversary of my parents' wedding day.
n. pl. **anniversaries** an·ni·ver·sar·ies
2. having to do with the yearly celebration of an event.
We are having an anniversary party. *adj.*

announce   an·nounce (ə·nouns')   to tell people something; to let people know something.
The radio will announce the scores of all the games.
v. **announced, announced, announcing** an·nounced, an·nounc·ing

announcement   an·nounce·ment (ə·nouns'mənt)   something that is told to the public.
The announcement was made at ten o'clock.
n. pl. **announcements** an·nounce·ments

announcer

announcer   an·nounc·er (ə·noun'sər)   a person who talks on radio or television and who gives information to the public.
The announcer said that Mr. Jones had won the election.
n. pl. **announcers** an·nounc·ers

annoy   an·noy (ə·noi')   to cause trouble; to make someone feel angry or troubled.
Our dog's barking annoys our neighbors.
v. **annoyed, annoyed, annoying** an·noyed, an·noy·ing

annoying   an·noy·ing (ə·noi'ing)   causing trouble; giving a feeling of anger; bothersome, irritating.
The man has an annoying habit of eating with his mouth open. *adj.*

a	cat	**i**	sit	**oi**	oil	**ch**	chop	a in about
ā	ate	**ī**	lie	**ou**	out	**ng**	song	e in oven
ä	car	**o**	pot	**u**	cut	**sh**	she	i in pencil
e	set	**ō**	old	**ú**	book	**th**	three	o in memory
ē	equal	**ô**	or	**ü**	blue	**ŦH**	there	u in circus
ėr	germ					**zh**	treasure	

ə = { a in about / e in oven / i in pencil / o in memory / u in circus }

annual an·nu·al (anʹyü·əl) **1.** a plant that lives for only
a year or one season.
A petunia is an annual. *n. pl.* **annuals** an·nu·als
2. coming every year.
Christmas is an annual holiday. *adj.*

another an·oth·er (ə·nuŦHʹər) **1.** a different one.
I will take this box and you take another. *pron.*
2. one more.
I want another cookie. *adj.*

answer an·swer (anʹsər) **1.** the reply to a question; the
solution to a problem.
I did not know the answer to the question. *n. pl.* **answers** an·swers
2. to give a reply to a question; to give the
solution to a problem.
I will answer the question. *v.*
3. to pick up a telephone that is ringing; to reply to a bell.
I will answer the telephone.
v. **answered, answered, answering** an·swered, an·swer·ing

ant (ant) a small insect that lives in a group and that lives in wood
or in the ground.
The ant walked across the picnic table. *n. pl.* **ants**

ant

Antarctica Ant·arc·ti·ca (ant·ärkʹtə·kə) the cold continent
that surrounds the South Pole.
Antarctica is covered with snow and ice all year round. *n.*

antelope an·te·lope (anʹtl·ōp) a graceful and fast animal that looks
like a deer.
The antelope can run very fast. *n. pl.* **antelopes** *or* **antelope** an·te·lopes

antenna an·ten·na (an·tenʹə) **1.** the long narrow feeler on an
insect's head that helps the insect in finding food.
This bee has only one antenna.
n. pl. **antennae** *or* **antennas** an·ten·nae *or* an·ten·nas
2. high metal bar or bars that pick up radio
and television signals.
We have a TV antenna on our house. *n. pl.* **antennas** an·ten·nas

South Pole

Antarctica

anthropologist an·thro·pol·o·gist (an·thrə·polʹə·jist) a person
who studies people of different countries and cultures.
The anthropologist can tell us about the cave men.
n. pl. **anthropologists** an·thro·pol·o·gists

anthropology an·thro·pol·o·gy (an·thrə·polʹə·jē) the study of
people, their habits and their cultures.
We learn about other countries through anthropology. *n. no pl.*

anti- an·ti- (anʹtī *or* anʹtē) prefix to words to mean "against,"
for example, antiwar means "against war," antigravity
means "against gravity." *prefix*

antelope

antibiotic an·ti·bi·ot·ic (an·ti·bī·ot·′ik)   a medicine or
drug that fights against diseases.
The doctor gave me an antibiotic to cure my sore throat.
n. pl. **antibiotics** an·ti·bi·ot·ics

anticipate an·tic·i·pate (an·tis′·ə·pāt)   expect; await;
look forward to.
We eagerly anticipated Christmas Day.
v. **anticipated, anticipated, anticipating** an·tic·i·pat·ed, an·tic·i·pat·ing

anticipated an·tic·i·pat·ed (an·tis′·ə·pā·tid)   expected; awaited;
looked forward to.
Jack and Mary Jean were happy when the anticipated day for
their trip arrived. *adj.*

anxious anx·ious (angk′·shəs *or* ang′·shəs)   nervous;
eager; worried; concerned.
I felt anxious about meeting the new teacher. *adj.*

anxiously anx·ious·ly (angk′·shəs·lē *or* ang′·shəs·lē)   in a nervous
way; eagerly; in a worried way; full of concern.
I anxiously waited for the doctor to come. *adv.*

antenna

any an·y (en′·ē)   one or some of a kind.
I don't have any clean socks. *adj.*

anymore an·y·more (en′·ē·môr′ *or* en′·ē-mōr′)   never again;
no longer; now.
I don't like her anymore. *adv.*

anyone an·y·one (en′·ē·wun *or* en′·ē·wən)   any person at all.
Is there anyone at home? *pron.*

anyplace an·y·place (en′·ē·plās)   in whatever spot or location;
in an unnamed place or spot.
My lost ring could be anyplace on the farm. *adv.*

anything an·y·thing (en′·ē·thing)   a thing of any kind.
Is there anything in that box? *n. no pl.*

anything else an·y·thing else (en′·ē·thing els)   something
more; more things.
Do we need anything else?

anytime an·y·time (en′·ē·tīm)   some time;
at some time.
I can go anytime. *adv.*

a	cat	i	sit	oi	oil	ch	chop		a in about
ā	ate	ī	lie	ou	out	ng	song		e in oven
ä	car	o	pot	u	cut	sh	she	ə =	i in pencil
e	set	ō	old	ù	book	th	three		o in memory
ē	equal	ô	or	ü	blue	ŦH	there		u in circus
ėr	germ					zh	treasure		

anyway an·y·way (en⸍ē·wā) even if it is not wanted or allowed.
Mother said no, but I took a cookie anyway. *adv.*

anywhere an·y·where (en⸍ē·hwer) in any place; to any place.
We can go anywhere we want today. *adv.*

apart a·part (ə·pärt′) **1.** not together; separated by distance.
The family lives apart. *adv.*
2. into pieces.
The man took the watch apart. *adv.*

apartment house

apartment a·part·ment (ə·pärt⸍mənt) **1.** a group of rooms in
which a person lives; a group of rooms that a person rents.
I do not live in a house; I live in an apartment.
n. pl. **apartments** a·part·ments
2. having to do with a group of rooms in which people live.
I live in a large apartment house. *adj.*

ape (āp) an animal with long arms that looks like a monkey
without a tail.
We saw an ape in the zoo. *n. pl.* **apes**

ape

Appalachian Mountains Ap·pa·la·chian Moun·tains (ap·ə·lā⸍chən
moun⸍tənz) a long range of mountains in the eastern
United States.
The Appalachian Mountains run through many eastern states.

appear ap·pear (ə·pir′) to come into sight.
The sun will appear over the mountain soon.
v. **appeared, appeared, appearing** ap·peared, ap·pear·ing

appearance ap·pear·ance (ə·pir⸍əns) the way a person looks.
The girl worried about her appearance. *n. pl.* **appearances** ap·pear·anc·es

Appalachian Mountains

apple ap·ple (ap⸍əl) **1.** a round fruit that has a red, green or yellow
skin and that grows on a tree.
I ate an apple for lunch. *n. pl.* **apples** ap·ples
2. being made of apples.
Mother made an apple pie. *adj.*

application ap·pli·ca·tion (ap·lə·kā⸍shən) a piece of paper that a
person uses to give information when asking for a job.
I gave the store my application for the sales job.
n. pl. **applications** ap·pli·ca·tions

appreciate ap·pre·ci·ate (ə·prē⸍shē·āt) **1.** to enjoy; to like.
I am learning to appreciate art. *v.*
2. to be thankful for.
I appreciate your help. *v.* **appreciated, appreciated,
appreciating** ap·pre·ci·at·ed, ap·pre·ci·at·ing

approximately ap·prox·i·mate·ly (ə·prok⸍sə·mət·lē) nearly;
almost; a little more or a little less than.
I am approximately 5 feet tall. I am really 4 feet and 11 inches tall. *adv.*

apple

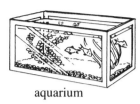

aquarium

Arabia

Arctic

apron   a·pron (ā′prən *or* ā′pərn)   a piece of clothing that a person wears over other clothes to protect them from dirt.
Bill wore an apron when he cooked the chicken. *n. pl.* **aprons** a·prons

apt.   a·part·ment (ə·pärt′mənt)   *abbrev.* See **apartment.** *pl.* **apts.**

aquarium   a·quar·i·um (ə·kwer′ē·əm)   a glass container in which fish are kept as pets.
We put the goldfish in the aquarium. *n. pl.* **aquariums** a·quar·i·ums

Arabia   A·ra·bi·a (ə·rā′bē·ə)   a peninsula in Asia made up of many countries.
Much of the world's oil comes from Arabia. *n.*

Arabian   A·ra·bi·an (ə·rā′bē·ən)   **1.** having to do with the people and the countries of Arabia.
The Arabian governments get money from the export of oil. *adj.*
2. a kind of horse that began in Arabia.
The Arabian is a fast and graceful horse. *n. pl.* **Arabians** A·ra·bi·ans

Arabic   Ar·a·bic (ar′ə·bik)   the language of the people from Arabia.
Arabic is a difficult language to learn. *n. no pl.*

architect   ar·chi·tect (är′kə·tekt)   a person who draws the plans for new buildings; a person who designs buildings.
A famous architect designed this house. *n. pl.* **architects** ar·chi·tects

architecture   ar·chi·tec·ture (är′kə·tek·chər)   the style of a building or a house; the kind of building or house.
A house made of clay bricks is an example of Indian architecture.
n. pl. **architectures** ar·chi·tec·tures

Arctic   Arc·tic (ärk′tik *or* ar′tik)   the area near and around the North Pole.
The Arctic is very cold all year long. *n.*

are   (är *or* ər)   *v. pres. t.* See **be.**

area   ar·e·a (er′ē·ə *or* ar′ē·ə)   place; space; the land around something; the surface of a place.
The playground is a large area with swings, slides and a ball field.
n. pl. **areas** ar·e·as

arena   a·re·na (ə·rē′nə)   a place with walls and seats where games or sporting events happen.
The basketball game will be in the new arena. *n. pl.* **arenas** a·re·nas

a	cat	i	sit	oi	oil	ch	chop		a in about
ā	ate	ī	lie	ou	out	ng	song		e in oven
ä	car	o	pot	u	cut	sh	she	ə =	i in pencil
e	set	ō	old	u̇	book	th	three		o in memory
ē	equal	ô	or	ü	blue	ᵀH	there		u in circus
ėr	germ					zh	treasure		

17

Argentina   Ar·gen·ti·na (är·jən·tē′nə)   a country in South America; its capital is Buenos Aires.
> Many ranchers raise cattle in Argentina. *n.*

argue   ar·gue (är′gyü)   to tell someone that you do not agree with his ideas or decisions; to talk angrily with someone.
> Sometimes our friends argue about what program to watch.
> *v.* **argued, argued, arguing** ar·gued, ar·gu·ing

argument   ar·gu·ment (är′gyə·mənt)   a fight with words only; a verbal disagreement.
> The teams had an argument about the score. *n. pl.* **arguments** ar·gu·ments

arithmetic   a·rith·me·tic (ə·rith′mə·tik)   math; adding, subtracting, multiplying and dividing numbers.
> My brother is very good in arithmetic. *n. no pl.*

arm   (ärm)   **1.** the part of the body between the shoulder and the hand.
> The boy put his arm out of the window. *n.*
> **2.** a mechanical device that works like the arm of a body.
> The arm of the machine picks the apples from the tree. *n.*
> **3.** having to do with the part of the body between the shoulder and the hand.
> The man wore an arm band. *adj.*

armor *or* **armour**   ar·mor (är′mər)   a suit of clothing worn by knights that is made of metal and used to protect the body.
> The armor protected the knight from the point of the arrow. *n. no pl.*

armour   ar·mour (är′mər)   *n.* See **armor.**

army   ar·my (är′mē)   a group of soldiers.
> The army attacked the fort. *n. pl.* **armies** ar·mies

around   a·round (ə·round′)   **1.** in the opposite direction; toward the back; behind.
> I turned around to see the car behind us. *adv.*
> **2.** here and there in a circle.
> The dog jumps around when we come home. *adv.*
> **3.** near; in the area; at home.
> There was no one around when I fell down the stairs. *adv.*

around in circles   a·round in cir·cles (ə·round′ in sėr′kəlz)   being busy but getting nothing done; working without a purpose; not organized.
> The man runs around in circles and gets nothing finished. *idiom*

around the world   a·round the world (ə·round′ ᴛʜə wėrld)   in many countries; in many different places.
> People around the world like ice cream.

Buenos Aires

Argentina

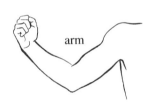

arm

armor or armour

arrangement

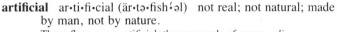

arrow

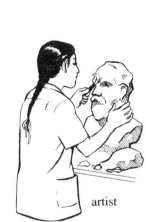

artist

arrangement   ar·range·ment (ə·rānj'mənt)   things put together in order; a display of things.
The florist made a beautiful flower arrangement for the table.
n. pl. **arrangements** ar·range·ments

arrest   ar·rest (ə·rest')   to catch and take to jail; to take to jail for breaking the law.
The police will arrest the robber.
v. **arrested, arrested, arresting** ar·rest·ed, ar·rest·ing

arrive   ar·rive (ə·rīv')   to reach a place; to get to a location.
The airplane will arrive at ten o'clock.
v. **arrived, arrived, arriving** ar·rived, ar·riv·ing

arrow   ar·row (ar'ō)   a stick with a sharp, pointed end that a person shoots with a bow.
The arrow hit the center of the target. *n. pl.* **arrows** ar·rows

art   (ärt)   **1.** paintings, drawings, sculpture, music or dance.
I went to the gallery to see the new art. *n. no pl.*
2. having to do with painting, drawing, sculpting, dancing or music.
I am taking an art class. *adj.*
3. Old English word meaning "are," used with "thou" (you).
"Thou art kind and good," the maiden said to the knight. *v.*

artificial   ar·ti·fi·cial (är·tə·fish'əl)   not real; not natural; made by man, not by nature.
Those flowers are artificial; they are made of paper. *adj.*

artist   ar·tist (är'tist)   a person who has skill in painting, drawing, sculpting, music or dancing.
The artist drew a picture of my mother in ten minutes. *n. pl.* **artists** ar·tists

artistic   ar·tis·tic (är·tis'tik)   having skills in art; being creative.
Mary is very artistic. She paints beautiful pictures. *adj.*

artwork   art·work (ärt'wėrk)   a painting; picture; a work of art.
The teacher will give a prize for the best artwork. *n. no pl.*

as   (az *or* əz)   **1.** in the same way.
Danny is as tall as his brother. *conj.*
2. while.
As I was walking home, it started to rain. *conj.*

as far as   (az   fär   əz)   that; to the degree or extent that.
As far as I know, no one else is coming. *idiom*

a	cat	**i**	sit	**oi**	oil	**ch**	chop		a in about
ā	ate	**ī**	lie	**ou**	out	**ng**	song		e in oven
ä	car	**o**	pot	**u**	cut	**sh**	she	ə =	i in pencil
e	set	**ō**	old	**ú**	book	**th**	three		o in memory
ē	equal	**ô**	or	**ü**	blue	**ŦH**	there		u in circus
ėr	germ					**zh**	treasure		

ash (ash) the remains of something that has burned.
The ash of the log was still in the fireplace. *n. pl.* **ashes** ash·es

ashamed a·shamed (ə·shāmd′) embarrassed; feeling
shame for something that one has done.
I was ashamed that I forgot her birthday. *adj.*

ashore a·shore (ə·shôr′) on land; to land.
The sailors left the ship to go ashore. *adv.*

ashes

Asia A·sia (ā′zhə) the largest continent on Earth.
China is part of Asia. *n.*

ask (ask) to question; to request information or help.
I will ask the teacher for more time. *v.* **asked, asked, asking** ask·ing

ask for (ask fôr) to request something; to use words to
try to get something.
The teacher will ask for our homework before lunchtime.
v. **asked for, asked for, asking for** ask·ing for

asleep a·sleep (ə·slēp′) sleeping; not awake.
The baby is asleep again. *adj.*

asphalt as·phalt (as′fôlt) a dark substance that is
used to pave roads.
The workers spread the asphalt on the road. *n. no pl.*

aspirin as·pir·in (as′pər·ən) a small pill that people use
as medicine for fevers, colds and headaches.
Mother gave me an aspirin before I went to bed.
n. pl. **aspirin** *or* **aspirins** as·pir·in *or* as·pir·ins

Asia

assistant as·sist·ant (ə·sis′tənt) **1.** a helper; a person
who helps another person.
The teacher has an assistant during science class.
n. pl. **assistants** as·sist·ants
2. helping.
The assistant coach worked with us today. *adj.*

assure as·sure (ə·shùr′) to tell another person that something
is right; to promise that something is true
or that something will happen.
I will assure the coach that we will be at practice.
v. **assured, assured, assuring** as·sured, as·sur·ing

astonish as·ton·ish (ə·ston′ish) to surprise someone;
to amaze someone.
I will astonish Mother by cleaning my bedroom.
v. **astonished, astonished, astonishing** as·ton·ished, as·ton·ish·ing

astonished as·ton·ished (ə·ston′isht) surprised; stunned; amazed.
Mother was astonished when she saw my room. *adj.*

asleep

astronaut

astronaut as·tro·naut (as′trə·nôt) **1.** a person who goes into outer space; a person who rides in a rocket or spaceship.
The astronaut walked on the moon. *n. pl.* **astronauts** as·tro·nauts
2. having to do with a person who goes into outer space.
I want to go to astronaut school. *adj.*

astronomer as·tron·o·mer (ə·stron′ə·mər) a person who studies the stars and the planets.
The astronomer looked through the telescope to see Mars.
n. pl. **astronomers** as·tron·o·mers

astronomy as·tron·o·my (ə·stron′ə·mē) the study of the stars and the planets.
I studied astronomy and learned about the planets. *n. no pl.*

as well (az wel) in addition; too.
John is going as well. *adv.*

as well as (az wel az) in addition to; plus.
I could see as well as feel the rain. *conj.*

at (at *or* ət *or* it) **1.** during an event or a time.
I get home at three o'clock. *prep.*
2. in a location or a place.
I will see you at school. *prep.*
3. to; toward; near.
The bird flew at the scarecrow. *prep.*

at all (at ôl) none; in any way.
There was no milk at all. *adv.*

ate (āt) *v. pt. t.* See **eat.**

Athens Ath·ens (ath′ənz) the capital city of the country of Greece.
People once believed that gods lived in Athens. *n.*

athlete ath·lete (ath′lēt) a person who plays sports.
A football player is an athlete. *n. pl.* **athletes** ath·letes

athletic ath·let·ic (ath·let′ik) having to do with sports or the skills to play sports.
Because Ann is athletic, she can play many sports very well. *adj.*

Atlantic Ocean At·lan·tic O·cean (at·lan′tik ō′shən)
the large body of water between the eastern United States and western Europe.
The ship sailed in the Atlantic Ocean.

astronomer

Atlantic Ocean

a	cat	**i**	sit	**oi**	oil	**ch**	chop	a in about
ā	ate	**ī**	lie	**ou**	out	**ng**	song	e in oven
ä	car	**o**	pot	**u**	cut	**sh**	she	ə = i in pencil
e	set	**ō**	old	**u̇**	book	**th**	three	o in memory
ē	equal	**ô**	or	**ü**	blue	**TH**	there	u in circus
ėr	germ					**zh**	treasure	

at last (at last) finally; after a long time.
> We waited and waited. The airplane landed at last! *idiom*

atom at·om (at⋅əm) the smallest part or particle
of a thing or a chemical.
> We cannot see an atom with our eye alone. *n. pl.* **atoms** at·oms

atomic a·tom·ic (ə·tom⋅ik) having to do with small
particles or pieces of things; having to do with atoms.
> Some power plants use atomic energy to make electricity. *adj.*

attach at·tach (ə·tach′) to put a thing onto another thing in a way
that they will not come apart.
> I will attach the string to the kite.
> *v.* **attached, attached, attaching** at·tached, at·tach·ing

attack at·tack (ə·tak′) to try to hurt; to start a battle or a fight.
> The soldiers will attack the enemy.
> *v.* **attacked, attacked, attacking** at·tacked, at·tack·ing

attempt at·tempt (ə·tempt′) to try.
> I will attempt to climb the tree.
> *v.* **attempted, attempted, attempting** at·tempt·ed, at·tempt·ing

attention at·ten·tion (ə·ten⋅shən) the act of listening or looking;
the act of being alert to something.
> Please give me your attention for a minute. *n. no pl.*

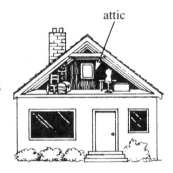

attic

attic at·tic (at⋅ik) **1.** the upper part of a house that is just
under the roof.
> I like to look in the boxes in the attic. *n. pl.* **attics** at·tics

2. having to do with the upper part of a house.
> I forgot to turn off the attic light. *adj.*

attract at·tract (ə·trakt′) **1.** to cause interest in; to be pleasing to.
> Adventure books attract me. *v.*

2. to draw toward.
> The light will attract the bugs.
> *v.* **attracted, attracted, attracting** at·tract·ed, at·tract·ing

attraction at·trac·tion (ə·trak⋅shən) things that happen that interest
people; something that people come to see; something that
brings people to a place.
> The polar bear is the main attraction at the zoo.
> *n. pl.* **attractions** at·trac·tions

auction auc·tion (ôk⋅shən) a sale where people tell how much
money they will give for the things they want to buy.
> I bought the horse at the auction for only one hundred dollars.
> *n. pl.* **auctions** auc·tions

audience

auditorium

audience au·di·ence (ô′dē·əns) a group of people who watch or listen to something.
The audience clapped their hands when the singer finished her song.
n. pl. **audiences** au·di·enc·es

auditorium au·di·to·ri·um (ô·də·tôr′ē·əm) a large theater room; a large room in a building where many people can be seated.
The play was held in the school auditorium.
n. pl. **auditoriums** au·di·to·ri·ums

aunt (ant) the sister of a father or a mother.
My aunt is my mother's sister. *n. pl.* **aunts**

Australia Aus·tral·ia (ô·strā′lyə) **1.** an island continent that is south of Asia.
Many strange animals live in Australia. *n.*
2. a country that includes the continent of Australia and Tasmania; its capital is Canberra.
Kangaroos live in Australia. *n.*

Australian Aus·tral·ian (ô·strā′lyən) having to do with the country, the continent and the people of Australia.
The kangaroo is an Australian animal. *adj.*

Austria Aus·tri·a (ô′strē·ə) a small country in Europe; its capital is Vienna.
Many famous musicians came from Austria. *n.*

author au·thor (ô′thər) a person who writes stories, books, reports or songs.
I want to be an author of children's stories.
n. pl. **authors** au·thors

autobiography au·to·bi·og·ra·phy (ô·tə·bī·og′rə·fē) a story written by a person about his or her own life.
If I become famous, I will write my autobiography.
n. pl. **autobiographies** au·to·bi·og·ra·phies

automatic au·to·mat·ic (ô·tə·mat′ik) moving or happening without help; operating by itself.
The heart is an automatic muscle. *adj.*

available a·vail·a·ble (ə·vā′lə·bəl) near; ready to use or have.
The maid was not available, so I answered the telephone. *adj.*

average av·er·age (av′ər·ij) something that most people do; typical; not different but like most people or things.
I am not real tall; I am average. *adj.*

Australia

Canberra

Vienna

Austria

a	cat	i	sit	oi	oil	ch	chop		a in about
ā	ate	ī	lie	ou	out	ng	song		e in oven
ä	car	o	pot	u	cut	sh	she	ə =	i in pencil
e	set	ō	old	u̇	book	th	three		o in memory
ē	equal	ô	or	ü	blue	ŦH	there		u in circus
ėr	germ					zh	treasure		

avoid a·void (ə·void′) **1.** to miss; to not hit.
You must avoid the flowers when you walk through the garden. *v.*
2. to stay away from.
Because I am angry with Betty, I will avoid her today.
v. **avoided, avoided, avoiding** a·void·ed, a·void·ing

awake

awake a·wake (ə·wāk′) to wake up; to come out of a sleep.
I will awake before sunrise. *v.* **awoke** *or* **awaked, awaked,
awaking** a·woke *or* a·waked, a·wak·ing

awaken a·wak·en (ə·wā′kən) to wake up; to cause to wake up.
I will awaken my sister.
v. **awakened, awakened, awakening** a·wak·ened, a·wak·en·ing

award a·ward (ə·wôrd′) something that a person receives
for good actions; a prize.
I won an award for my painting of the ocean. *n. pl.* **awards** a·wards

away a·way (ə·wā′) in a different place; in the opposite direction.
Mother is away on business. *adj.*

away from a·way from (ə·wā′ from *or* ə·wā′ frum *or* ə·wā′ frəm)
in another direction; not in the same place; at a distance.
Please stay away from her while she is sick.

awful aw·ful (ô′fəl) terrible; very bad.
She has an awful cold. *adj.*

awhile a·while (ə·hwīl′) a short time; a period of time.
Jim watched TV awhile before he went to bed. *adv.*

awkward awk·ward (ôk′wərd) not comfortable;
not evenly balanced; difficult.
I felt awkward meeting my stepmother. *adj.*

award

awoke a·woke (ə·wōk′) *v. pt. t.* See **awake.**

ax (aks) a sharp tool that people use to cut trees or wood.
I cut down the tree with an ax. *n. pl.* **axes** ax·es

axe (aks) *n.* See **ax.**

Aztec Az·tec (az′tek) a member of an Indian tribe that
lived in Mexico.
The vase was made by an Aztec. *n.*

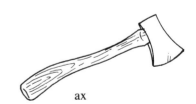
ax

Bb

baby

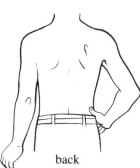

back

backboard

B.C. (bē cē) before Christ; before the birth of Jesus Christ.
Julius Caesar died in 44 B.C. *abbrev.*

babble bab·ble (bab′əl) to make sounds that cannot be
understood; to make sounds that are not words.
The baby babbles, and we pretend that she is talking.
v. **babbled, babbled, babbling** bab·bled, bab·bling

baby ba·by (bā′bē) **1.** a young child; a child that
does not yet walk or talk.
We put the baby in the crib. *n. pl.* **babies** ba·bies
2. having to do with a young child.
Mom gave our baby clothes away. *adj.*

babysit ba·by·sit (bā′bē·sit) to watch a young child
while the parents are not at home.
I will babysit for the people next door.
v. **babysat, babysat, babysitting** ba·by·sat, ba·by·sit·ting

back (bak) **1.** to the place a thing or person started from.
The astronauts came back to Earth yesterday. *adv.*
2. in the rear; at the rear; to the rear.
I sat in the back of the room. *adv.*
3. away from; in the opposite direction.
I jumped back when I saw the spider. *adv.*
4. in return for something.
He gave me a quarter and I gave him back a candy bar. *adv.*
5. having to do with something in the rear of something.
The dog hurt his back leg on the fence. *adj.*
6. the rear part of the body between the head and the waist.
I covered my back with a shawl. *n. pl.* **backs**

back and forth (bak ən fôrth) up and down over the same area
or path; to move over the same area or path again and again.
I walked back and forth in the hall waiting for Mother to get home. *adv.*

backboard back·board (bak′bôrd) the rectangular piece of
material to which a basketball hoop is attached.
The ball hit the backboard and went through the basket.
n. pl. **backboards** back·boards

a	cat	i	sit	oi	oil	ch	chop		a in about
ā	ate	ī	lie	ou	out	ng	song		e in oven
ä	car	o	pot	u	cut	sh	she	ə =	i in pencil
e	set	ō	old	ů	book	th	three		o in memory
ē	equal	ô	or	ü	blue	ŦH	there		u in circus
ėr	germ					zh	treasure		

background back·ground (bak′ground) **1.** the information that explains what happened before; facts given before a story is told.
The teacher gave us the background of the author's life.
n. pl. **backgrounds** back·grounds
2. having to do with the sounds or pictures that are seen and heard in a movie but are not part of the story.
The background music helps to set the mood of the movie. *adj.*

backpack back·pack (bak′pak) a bag or sack that a person wears on the back and uses to carry things.
Every boy scout has a backpack. *n. pl.* **backpacks** back·packs

backpacker back·pack·er (bak′pak·ər) a person who hikes and wears a backpack.
The backpacker climbed the hill easily.
n. pl. **backpackers** back·pack·ers

backpack

back seat (bak sēt) the seat in the rear or the back of a car.
I sat in the back seat, and my brother sat in the front.

backward back·ward (bak′wərd) away from the front; toward the rear.
He walked backward into the wall. *adv.*

backyard back·yard (bak·yärd′) the area behind a house; the land in the rear of a house.
We keep the dog in the backyard. *n. pl.* **backyards** back·yards

bacon ba·con (bā·kən) thin slices of pork that people often eat for breakfast.
Our family ate bacon and eggs this morning. *n. no pl.*

bacon

bacteria bac·ter·i·a (bak·tir′ē·ə) very tiny organisms or plants that can cause disease or that can cure disease.
When you cough, you may be spreading many bacteria. *plural n.*

bad (bad) **1.** evil; not good; not pleasant.
The bad witch turned the man into a frog. *adj.*
2. not delicious; not pleasant to the taste.
The cake tasted bad. *adj.*
3. sorry; regretful.
I felt bad about breaking the vase. *adj.*
4. rainy; stormy; not pretty and clear.
The weather was too bad to play outside. *adj.* **worse, worst**

badge (baj) a patch of material that a person wears on clothing and that is earned for learning to do something well (for example, a scouting award).
I earned a badge for learning to tie knots. *n. pl.* **badges** badg·es

badly bad·ly (bad′lē) not in a good way; seriously; very much.
The boy was hurt badly when he fell. *adv.*

badges

Baffin Island

Baffin Island Baf·fin Is·land (baf'ən ī'lənd) a large island that belongs to Canada and that is near Greenland.
Leif Ericson discovered Baffin Island.

bag (bag) **1.** a sack made of paper and used for carrying things.
The man put the groceries in the bag. *n.*
2. a suitcase that is used for carrying clothes.
I lost my bag on the airplane. *n. pl.* **bags**

Bagdad Bag·dad (bag'dad) a city in Arabia where Sinbad the Sailor lived.
Sinbad returned to Bagdad after his journeys. *n.*

bagpipe bag·pipe (bag'pīp) a musical instrument that has pipes connected to a bag filled with air.
The man who played the bagpipe is from Scotland.
n. pl. **bagpipes** bag·pipes

bake (bāk) to cook in an oven.
Mother will bake a cake for my birthday. *v.* **baked, baked, baking** bak·ing

bake sale (bāk sāl) an event where sweet treats are sold to earn money.
Our class had a bake sale to earn money for a class trip.

balance bal·ance (bal'ənts) the act of standing up without falling; an evenness of weight that allows something to stand without falling or tipping.
The dinosaur used its tail for balance as it stood. *n. no pl.*

bald (bôld) without hair or having little hair.
The bald man had just a little hair on his head. The man was bald.
adj. **balder, baldest** bald·er, bald·est

bald eagle bald ea·gle (bôld ē'gəl) a very large bird that has white feathers on its head and neck.
The bald eagle is a symbol of strength.

bale (bāl) a large package or bundle of something; hay, grass, straw or wool that is tied together in a bundle.
We picked up the bale of hay. *n. pl.* **bales**

baleen ba·leen (bə·lēn') **1.** a thin, curved growth that fills the mouth of some kinds of whales.
Baleen was once used in women's underclothes. *n. no pl.*
2. having to do with the kind of whale that has the thin, curved substance in its mouth.
Baleen whales do not chew their food. *adj.*

bagpipe

bald eagle

a	cat	**i**	sit	**oi**	oil	**ch**	chop
ā	ate	**ī**	lie	**ou**	out	**ng**	song
ä	car	**o**	pot	**u**	cut	**sh**	she
e	set	**ō**	old	**ú**	book	**th**	three
ē	equal	**ô**	or	**ü**	blue	**ŦH**	there
ėr	germ					**zh**	treasure

ə = { a in about, e in oven, i in pencil, o in memory, u in circus }

Balestrand Bal·e·strand (bäl′ə·strand) a town in Norway.
Balestrand is a mountain town. *n.*

ball (bôl) **1.** a round toy that can be thrown, bounced or hit.
We threw the ball to the baby. *n.*
2. something that is shaped like a circle; a circular shape.
We rolled the candy into a ball. *n.*
3. a large, elegant dance.
Everyone danced at the king's ball. *n. pl.* **balls**

ballet bal·let (bal′ā *or* ba·lā′) a kind of dance where the dancers
stand on their toes and their dancing tells a story.
I went to the ballet to watch the dancers. *n. pl.* **ballets** bal·lets

ballet

balloon bal·loon (bə·lün′) an object that is filled with
air and that floats.
Mother blew up the balloon. *n. pl.* **balloons** bal·loons

balloon fish bal·loon fish (bə·lün′ fish) a kind of fish
that fills its body with air when afraid.
The balloon fish swam by the diver.

balloon fish

ballpark ball·park (bôl′pärk) a field where teams get together
to compete in a ball game.
We practiced baseball in the ballpark. *n. pl.* **ballparks** ball·parks

Baltic Sea Bal·tic Sea (bôl′tik sē) a large body of water in Europe.
The Baltic Sea is south of Sweden.

Baltic Sea

banana ba·nan·a (bə·nan′ə) a long fruit with a yellow skin
that must be removed before eating.
I put a banana in my cereal. *n. pl.* **bananas** ba·nan·as

banana split ba·nan·a split (bə·nan′ə split) a dessert made
of ice cream, syrups, nuts, whipped cream and a banana.
I cannot eat a whole banana split.

band (band) a group of people that play music together.
The high school band will play during the football game. *n. pl.* **bands**

bandage band·age (ban′dij) a cover for an injury or cut.
I put a bandage on my finger. *n. pl.* **bandages** band·ag·es

bang (bang) to make noise by hitting something.
I will bang on the wall when I hear your radio.
v. **banged, banged, banging** bang·ing

bank (bangk) **1.** a building where people put money to keep it safe.
I took my money to a bank. *n.*
2. a container in which money is saved.
I put my pennies into a bank in my room. *n. pl.* **banks**

banana

barbecue

banker bank·er (bang'kər) a person who owns or runs a bank.
The banker cashed my check. *n. pl.* **bankers** bank·ers

banquet ban·quet (bang'kwit) a large meal with many different
things to eat; a feast.
The king had a banquet for his returning soldiers. *n. pl.* **banquets** ban·quets

bar (bär) **1.** a rectangular-shaped object that is thick or wide.
I opened a new bar of soap. *n.*
2. a long, heavy piece of metal that is used to make a fence or
cage to keep animals or people from getting away.
A bar on the jail's window is broken. *n. pl.* **bars**

barbecue bar·be·cue (bär'bə·kyü) **1.** to cook meat outside
on a grill or an open fire.
We will barbecue hamburgers on the grill.
v. **barbecued, barbecued, barbecuing** bar·be·cued, bar·be·cu·ing
2. a large meal that is cooked outside for many people.
Our town has a barbecue on the Fourth of July.
n. pl. **barbecues** bar·be·cues

bare (ber *or* bar) uncovered; unclothed.
The man did not wear a hat. His head was bare.
adj. **barer, barest** bar·er, bar·est

bareback bare·back (ber'bak) without a saddle.
That woman does bareback riding in the circus. *adj.*

bark (bärk) **1.** to make a loud, short sound like a dog.
The dog will bark when a stranger comes near.
v. **barked, barked, barking** bark·ing
2. the thick brown covering of a tree trunk.
The bark is peeling off the apple tree. *n. no pl.*

barley bar·ley (bär'lē) **1.** a grain that people use in foods.
This cereal has barley in it. *n. no pl.*
2. having to do with a kind of grain that is used
for making cereals and other foods.
Mother made barley soup. *adj.*

barley

barley corn bar·ley corn (bär'lē kôrn) a unit of measure used long
ago that equaled one-third of an inch.
The farmer's knife is 15 barley corns long.

a	cat	i	sit	oi	oil	ch	chop		a in about
ā	ate	ī	lie	ou	out	ng	song		e in oven
ä	car	o	pot	u	cut	sh	she	ə =	i in pencil
e	set	ō	old	u̇	book	th	three		o in memory
ē	equal	ô	or	ü	blue	ŦH	there		u in circus
ėr	germ					zh	treasure		

barn (bärn) a building on a farm that farmers use to store hay or to keep animals.
The cow is in the barn. *n. pl.* **barns**

barn

barnacle bar·na·cle (bär′nə·kəl) a small sea animal with a hard shell that lives on ships, rocks or piers.
Barnacles covered the bottom of the ship. *n. pl.* **barnacles** bar·na·cles

barnyard barn·yard (bärn′yärd) the land around a barn, where farm animals are kept.
The chickens are in the barnyard. *n. pl.* **barnyards** barn·yards

barrel bar·rel (bar′əl) **1.** the long, round part of a gun through which the bullet travels.
The hunter cleaned the barrel of his gun. *n.*
2. a round, wooden container.
The pickles are in the barrel. *n. pl.* **barrels** bar·rels
3. having to do with a round, wooden container.
We had a barrel race at the picnic. *adj.*

barrel

barrier bar·ri·er (bar′ē·ər) something that is in the way; something that stops someone or something from moving forward.
The police put a barrier in the road to stop the cars. *n. pl.* **barriers** bar·ri·ers

baseball base·ball (bās′bôl) **1.** a ball made of cork and rubber and covered with leather that is used in the game of baseball.
I threw the baseball to Jim. *n. pl.* **baseballs** base·balls
2. a game that two teams play with a bat and ball.
I want to learn to play baseball. *n. no pl.*
3. having to do with the game that is played with a bat and a ball.
I will be on the school's baseball team. *adj.*

baseball

basement base·ment (bās′mənt) the bottom part of a house or building, usually below the ground; the cellar.
We keep our tools in the basement. *n. pl.* **basements** base·ments

basic ba·sic (bā′sik) being the most needed; the necessary part; having to do with the base or foundation of something.
Addition is basic math. *adj.*

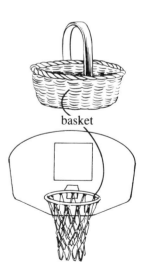
basket

basin ba·sin (bā′sn) a bowl or sink in which people wash themselves.
I brushed my teeth in the basin. *n. pl.* **basins** ba·sins

basket bas·ket (bas′kit) **1.** a container that is made by weaving pieces of wood or grass together.
The farmer put the eggs in the basket. *n.*
2. the net through which a basketball is thrown.
The ball fell through the basket before the buzzer sounded.
n. pl. **baskets** bas·kets

basketball

basketball bas·ket·ball (bas′kit·bôl) **1.** a game that two teams play with a large ball and a hoop on a high backboard.
I will play basketball with you. *n. no pl.*
2. the large ball that is used in the game of basketball.
I dribbled the basketball. *n. pl.* **basketballs** bas·ket·balls
3. having to do with the game that uses a large ball and a hoop on a high backboard.
I saw the basketball team practice. *adj.*

bass (bās) having a low, deep sound.
One person in the band plays a bass drum. *adj.*

baster bast·er (bāst′ər) a tool or utensil used to put fatty juices onto meat when cooking.
Mom used the baster to put liquid on the turkey. *n. pl.* **basters** bast·ers

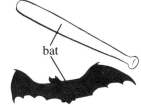

bat

bat (bat) **1.** a long wooden stick that is used to hit the ball in the game of baseball.
I missed the ball with the bat. *n.*
2. an animal that has wings and that flies at night.
There is a bat in the barn. *n. pl.* **bats**

bath (bath) **1.** a container in which people or animals wash; a room in which people wash.
We have a bath downstairs. *n.*
2. the act of washing.
I take a bath every night. *n. pl.* **baths**

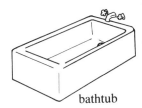

bathtub

bathe (bāŦH) to wash the body in a container with water in it.
Mother will bathe the baby in the tub. *v.* **bathed, bathed, bathing** bath·ing

bathroom bath·room (bath′rüm *or* bath′rủm) **1.** a room that has a sink, a toilet and a shower or a bathtub.
Mother is in the bathroom. *n. pl.* **bathrooms** bath·rooms
2. having to do with the room with a toilet, sink and tub.
The towels are under the bathroom sink. *adj.*

bathtub bath·tub (bath′tub) a container that is filled with water for bathing.
I like to take a bath in the bathtub. *n. pl.* **bathtubs** bath·tubs

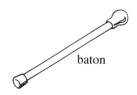

baton

baton ba·ton (ba·ton′) a stick made of wood or metal that people can twirl and spin.
The girl threw the baton in the air. *n. pl.* **batons** ba·tons

a	cat	i	sit	oi	oil	ch	chop		⎧ a in about
ā	ate	ī	lie	ou	out	ng	song		e in oven
ä	car	o	pot	u	cut	sh	she	ə =	i in pencil
e	set	ō	old	ủ	book	th	three		o in memory
ē	equal	ô	or	ü	blue	ŦH	there		⎩ u in circus
êr	germ					zh	treasure		

batter bat·ter (bat'ər) **1.** a mixture of flour, eggs
and other ingredients before it is cooked.
I poured the cake batter into the pan. *n.*
2. in baseball, the person who is hitting the ball with a bat.
The batter swung at the ball. *n. pl.* **batters** bat·ters

battery

battery bat·ter·y (bat'ər·ē) an object that contains electrical
cells that store electricity.
The flashlight needs a new battery. *n. pl.* **batteries** bat·ter·ies

battle bat·tle (bat'l) a fight; an event where soldiers fight;
a fight between two armies.
Our army lost the last battle. *n. pl.* **battles** bat·tles

bay window bay win·dow (bā win'dō) a window that goes
out beyond the wall to make extra space in a room.
We have a seat in the bay window in the living room.

beach

be (bē) **1.** to exist; to have life; to have presence.
You have to be a good girl. *v.*
2. to act like; to represent.
I will be a princess in the play. *v.*
3. to become; to change from one thing to another.
I will be twelve years old tomorrow.
v. **was** *or* **were, been, being** be·ing

beach (bēch) **1.** the land near a body of water;
the sandy area near a lake or an ocean.
I went to the beach yesterday. *n. pl.* **beaches** beach·es
2. having to do with the land near a body of water.
My beach towel got wet. *adj.*

beach ball beach ball (bēch bôl) a large air-filled ball
with which people play at the beach.
The beach ball rolled into the water. *n. pl.* **beach balls**

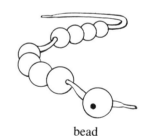
bead

bead (bēd) a small, round piece of glass, metal or
wood that is used for decoration.
I put the bead on the string. *n. pl.* **beads**

beaked whale (bēkt hwāl) a kind of whale that has
a slightly pointed nose.
A beaked whale has teeth.

beaked whale

beam (bēm) to make a big smile.
The little girl will beam when she sees her new bike.
v. **beamed, beamed, beaming** beam·ing

bean

bean (bēn) **1.** a seed from a plant that is eaten.
The bean fell when I picked it off the vine. *n.*
2. the seed of a coffee plant.
The coffee bean is picked when it is red. *n. pl.* **beans**

beanstalk bean·stalk (bēn‑stôk) the stem on which beans grow.
The beanstalk grew very tall. *n. pl.* **beanstalks** bean·stalks

bear (ber *or* bar) **1.** a large furry animal with a short tail.
The bear looked at the ranger and then ran away. *n. pl.* **bears**
2. having to do with the large furry animal with a short tail.
He caught his foot in the bear trap. *adj.*
3. to give life to; to produce a new life or a child.
The cow will bear a calf today. *v.* **bore, born** *or* **borne, bearing** bear·ing

bear

beard (bird) the hair that grows on the chin and
cheeks of a man's face.
Santa Claus has a long white beard. *n. pl.* **beards**

bearer bear·er (ber‑ər *or* bar‑ər) a person who holds something;
a person who carries something.
The bearer of the winning ticket will get a prize. *n. pl.* **bearers** bear·ers

beast (bēst) a large animal.
A lion is a beast. *n. pl.* **beasts**

beastie beas·tie (bēs‑tē) an old word meaning "beast."
The English called him a beastie. *n. pl.* **beasties** beas·ties

beat (bēt) **1.** to win at a game; to defeat another player
or team in a game.
Our basketball team beat your team. *v.*
2. to have a regular movement.
Your heart will beat faster after you run. *v.*
3. to hit hard again and again; to continue to hit.
The bully will beat you if he catches you.
v. **beat, beaten** *or* **beat, beating** beat·en, beat·ing

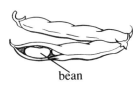

beard

beat up (bēt up) to hurt someone or something by hitting
again and again.
I can beat up my brother. *v.* **beat up, beaten up** *or* **beat up,
beating up** beat·en up, beat·ing up

beautiful beau·ti·ful (byü‑tə‑fəl) very pretty; very pleasing.
The song was beautiful. *adj.*

a	cat	i	sit	oi	oil	ch	chop		a in about
ā	ate	ī	lie	ou	out	ng	song		e in oven
ä	car	o	pot	u	cut	sh	she	ə =	i in pencil
e	set	ō	old	ù	book	th	three		o in memory
ē	equal	ô	or	ü	blue	ŦH	there		u in circus
ėr	germ					zh	treasure		

beautifully beau·ti·ful·ly (byü′tə·fəl·lē) in a very pretty
way; in a very pleasing way.
She sang the song beautifully. *adv.*

beauty beau·ty (byü′tē) the prettiness of something; good looks.
We wake up early to enjoy the beauty of the sunrise.
n. pl. **beauties** beau·ties

beaver bea·ver (bē′vər) an animal with soft fur and a wide
tail that builds dams in water.
The beaver built a dam in the river. *n. pl.* **beavers** bea·vers

beaver

became be·came (bi·kām′) *v. pt. t.* See **become.**

be careful be care·ful (bē ker′fəl *or* bē kar′fəl) to take care not
to get hurt; to try not to hurt or harm oneself or others.
Be careful when you cross the street.

because be·cause (bi·kôz′) since; for this reason.
I was punished because I was late. *conj.*

because of be·cause of (bi·kôz′ əv) due to; by the
action of; by the reason that.
The game ended because of darkness. *adv.*

become be·come (bi·kum′) to change into something else;
to get to be something.
I want to become a doctor. *v.* **became, become,**
becoming be·came, be·come, be·com·ing

bed (bed) **1.** the place where a person or animal sleeps;
a piece of furniture that is used for sleeping.
I like to read in bed. *n.*
2. an area where plants are planted.
We have a flower bed in the front yard. *n. pl.* **beds**

bedspread

bedroom bed·room (bed′rüm *or* bed′rüm) a room in a
house where someone sleeps.
My sister and I share a bedroom. *n. pl.* **bedrooms** bed·rooms

bedspread bed·spread (bed′spred) a pretty cover that goes
over the blankets on a bed.
We each have a flowered bedspread. *n. pl.* **bedspreads** bed·spreads

bedtime bed·time (bed′tīm) the time that a person
goes to bed to go to sleep.
My bedtime is nine o'clock. *n. pl.* **bedtimes** bed·times

bee (bē) an insect that makes honey from the pollen of flowers.
The bee stung the puppy. *n. pl.* **bees**

bee

beef (bēf) the meat that comes from cattle.
We eat beef only once a week. *n. no pl.*

been (bin) *v. pt. part.* See **be.**

beet (bēt) a red vegetable that is the root of a plant.
Mother put a beet in the salad. *n. pl.* **beets**

beetle bee·tle (bē′tl) an insect with wings and a hard shell.
The ladybug is a beetle. *n. pl.* **beetles** bee·tles

beet

before be·fore (bi·fôr′) **1.** in the past; previously.
Man has not been on Jupiter before. *adv.*
2. earlier than.
Joan finished her homework before me. *prep.*
3. in front of.
The teacher stood before the class. *prep.*
4. sooner than.
I will be home before you leave. *conj.*

beg (beg) to ask for; to plead.
I beg your forgiveness for breaking the vase.
v. **begged, begged, begging** beg·ging

began be·gan (bi·gan′) *v. pt. t.* See **begin.**

begin be·gin (bi·gin′) to start.
I will begin dinner tonight. *v.* **began, begun,
beginning** be·gan, be·gun, be·gin·ning

beetle

beginner be·gin·ner (bi·gin′ər) a person who is starting to learn
something; a person who tries a new activity.
John is learning to swim. He is a beginner. *n. pl.* **beginners** be·gin·ners

beginning be·gin·ning (bi·gin′ing) **1.** the start of something;
the first part of something.
I missed the beginning of the movie. *n. pl.* **beginnings** be·gin·nings
2. having to do with the first part or the start of something.
He is taking beginning lessons. *adj.*
3. *v. pres. part.* See **begin.**

be going to be go·ing to (bē gō′ing tü) shows future time.
I am going to watch TV later, but Billy is going to play basketball.
v. **am/is/are/was/were going to**

begun be·gun (bi·gun′) *v. pt. part.* See **begin.**

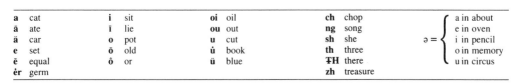

a	cat	i	sit	oi	oil	ch	chop		a in about
ā	ate	ī	lie	ou	out	ng	song		e in oven
ä	car	o	pot	u	cut	sh	she	ə =	i in pencil
e	set	ō	old	u̇	book	th	three		o in memory
ē	equal	ô	or	ü	blue	ŦH	there		u in circus
ėr	germ					zh	treasure		

behave be·have (bi·hāv′) to act in a certain way; to do something in a specific manner.
We will watch the way the owls behave in the dark.
v. **behaved, behaved, behaving** be·haved, be·hav·ing

behavior be·hav·ior (bi·hā′vyər) the way a person acts; actions.
John's behavior has been bad all day. *n. pl.* **behaviors** be·hav·iors

behind be·hind (bi·hīnd′) **1.** in the back of; to the rear.
I sat behind her on the bus. *prep.*
2. late; farther back; slow.
I am behind in my work. *adv.*

be in charge (bē ən chärj) to control; to manage; to be the boss for a time.
Jill will be in charge while the teacher is out of the room.

being be·ing (bē′ing) *v. pres. part.* See **be.**

Belgium Bel·gium (bel′jəm) a country in Europe; its capital is Brussels.
Belgium is between France and West Germany. *n.*

Brussels •
Belgium

belief be·lief (bi·lēf′) something that a person or people think is true; an opinion; something that is believed.
Long ago, people had the belief that the world was flat.
n. pl. **beliefs** be·liefs

believe be·lieve (bi·lēv′) to think something is true; to have faith in something or someone; to trust.
I believe him when he says that he did not break the vase.
v. **believed, believed, believing** be·lieved, be·liev·ing

bell

bell (bel) **1.** a bowl-shaped musical instrument made of metal that makes a chiming sound when hit with a stick, hand or hammer.
The bell on the church rings every hour. *n. pl.* **bells**
2. having to do with a bowl-shaped musical instrument.
The man jumped from the bell tower. *adj.*

belladonna bel·la·don·na (bel·ə·don′ə) a beautiful plant that is poisonous.
The red flowers on the belladonna are very dangerous. *n. no pl.*

bellow bel·low (bel′ō) to make a loud noise with the voice; to shout loudly; to make a deep, low sound.
The bull will bellow when it is angry. *v.* **bellowed, bellowed, bellowing** bel·lowed, bel·low·ing

belly bel·ly (bel′ē) stomach.
The fat man has a big belly. *n. pl.* **bellies** bel·lies

belladonna

belly

bend over

Bering Strait

belong be·long (bi·lông′) **1.** to be owned by.
That car should belong to me. *v.*
2. to have a place.
The book belongs on the bookshelf. *v.* **belonged,**
belonged, belonging be·longed, be·long·ing

below be·low (bi·lō′) **1.** under; underneath; lower than.
Put the desk below the window. *prep.*
2. to or in a lower place.
When we climbed the tree, we could see the people below. *adv.*

belt (belt) a strap of leather or material that goes around a person's
waist and is often used to keep clothes on or closed.
My dress has a blue belt. *n. pl.* **belts**

bend (bend) **1.** to fold over; to fold back; to curve.
I will bend the bush back so you can walk by.
v. **bent, bent, bending** bend·ing
2. a curve in a road.
The truck came around the bend at 40 m.p.h. *n. pl.* **bends**

bend over bend o·ver (bend ō′vər) to curve the body
from the waist towards the toes.
Please bend over and pick up the piece of paper. *v.* **bent over,**
bent over, bending over bent o·ver, bend·ing o·ver

Bengal Ben·gal (beng·gôl′) a country that is now divided into West
Bengal (a part of India) and Bangladesh (a country).
The tiger comes from Bengal. *n.*

bent (bent) *v. pt. t., pt. part.* See **bend** (1).

Bergen Ber·gen (bėr′gən) **1.** a city on the coast of the North Sea
in the country of Norway.
Bergen is near the mountains and the ocean. *n.*
2. having to do with the seaport city in Norway.
We rode the Bergen Railroad. *adj.*

Bering Strait Ber·ing Strait (ber′ing strāt) the narrow body of
water between Alaska and the part of Asia that is Russia.
Many ships go through the Bering Strait.

berry ber·ry (ber′ē) a small, round, juicy fruit that has many seeds.
I picked the berry from the bush. *n. pl.* **berries** ber·ries

beside be·side (bi·sīd′) next to; in the place near something.
I sat beside her in the front seat. *prep.*

a	cat	i	sit	oi	oil	ch	chop		a in about
ā	ate	ī	lie	ou	out	ng	song		e in oven
ä	car	o	pot	u	cut	sh	she	ə =	i in pencil
e	set	ō	old	ú	book	th	three		o in memory
ē	equal	ô	or	ü	blue	ᵀH	there		u in circus
ėr	germ					zh	treasure		

besides be·sides (bi·sīdz′) also; in addition to.
>There will be two other people besides me who will go with you. *prep.*

best (best) **1.** most; to the greatest extent or degree.
>I like ice cream, but I like chocolate best. *superl. adv.* See **well.**
>**2.** better than all the rest.
>Lisa is the best singer in the class. *superl. adj.* See **good.**

bet (bet) to wager; to promise to give something or to do something if one person is wrong or loses a game; to gamble money on the end result of something.
>I will bet you two dollars that my dog runs faster than your dog.
>*v.* **bet** *or* **betted, bet** *or* **betted, betting** bet·ted, bet·ting

bib

better bet·ter (bet′ər) **1.** of greater value, worth or use.
>Vegetables are a better food than candy. *comp. adj.* See **good.**
>**2.** in a greater degree.
>I like carrots better than beets. *adv.* See **well.**

between be·tween (bi·twēn′) **1.** in the area that separates two things or people.
>I sat between Mother and Father at the movie. *prep.*
>**2.** from one place or thing to another.
>There is a path between the house and the forest. *prep.*
>**3.** from one to the other of.
>Is there a difference between jelly and jam? *prep.*

Bible

be up (bē up) to stay awake; to not go to sleep.
>I want to be up when Dad comes home. *idiom*

beyond be·yond (bi·yond′) past a certain place or point; at a farther distance than.
>The school is a half mile beyond the stoplight. *prep.*

bib (bib) a covering worn by a baby to keep food off its clothing.
>Mother put a bib on the baby. *n. pl.* **bibs**

Bible Bi·ble (bī′bəl) **1.** a holy book of writings about God and religion.
>My mother reads the Bible every night. *n.*
>**2.** having to do with the religious book.
>She read me a Bible story. *adj.*

Biblical Bib·li·cal (bib′lə·kəl) having to do with the writings and stories in the Bible; having to do with the times written about in the Bible.
>In Biblical times people did not travel by airplane. *adj.*

bicycle

bicycle bi·cy·cle (bī′sik·əl *or* bī′sə·kəl) a two-wheeled vehicle; a bike.
>My sister has a new red bicycle. *n. pl.* **bicycles** bi·cy·cles

Big Dipper

bighorn sheep

bill

billboard

biennial bi·en·ni·al (bī·en′·ē·əl) a plant that lives for only two years.
A cabbage plant is a biennial. *n. pl.* **biennials** bi·en·ni·als

big (big) **1.** large; not small; having great size or height.
An elephant is a big animal. *adj.*
2. important.
Today is a big day for her. It is her birthday. *adj.*
3. older; more grown up.
My big brother is in college. *adj.* **bigger, biggest** big·ger, big·gest

Big Dipper Big Dip·per (big dip′·ər) a group of seven stars in the sky that make the shape of a water dipper.
You can often see the Big Dipper without a telescope.

Bigfoot Big·foot (big′·fůt) a large animal or creature believed to live in the western and northern United States.
Not many people have seen Bigfoot. *n.*

bighorn sheep big·horn sheep (big′·hôrn shēp) a large grey sheep that lives in the Rocky Mountains of America.
The bighorn sheep can easily climb the mountain.

bike (bīk) a two-wheeled vehicle; a bicycle.
I fell off of my bike. *n. pl.* **bikes**

bill (bil) **1.** a request for money that a person owes.
I got a bill from the bicycle shop for fixing my bicycle. *n.*
2. the beak or mouth of a bird; the hard, pointed part of a bird's face.
The bird had a worm in its bill. *n.*
3. a piece of paper money; a paper money unit.
The man gave me a five dollar bill for finding his wallet. *n. pl.* **bills**

billboard bill·board (bil′·bôrd) a large sign or advertisement by the side of a road or a highway; a board with an advertisement that is on a building.
The man is changing an advertisement on the billboard.
n. pl. **billboards** bill·boards

bin (bin) a container or box used for storing things.
The kitchen cabinet has a flour bin in it. *n. pl.* **bins**

bind (bīnd) to tie together; to put into a bundle.
I will bind the sticks together with rope.
v. **bound, bound, binding** bind·ing

a	cat	i	sit	oi	oil	ch	chop		a in about
ā	ate	ī	lie	ou	out	ng	song		e in oven
ä	car	o	pot	u	cut	sh	she	ə =	i in pencil
e	set	ō	old	ů	book	th	three		o in memory
ē	equal	ô	or	ü	blue	ŦH	there		u in circus
ėr	germ					zh	treasure		

biographical bi·o·graph·i·cal (bī·ə·graf′ə·kəl) having to do with the facts in the story of a person's life; having to do with a person's life story.
The author got the biographical information from other books. *adj.*

biography bi·og·ra·phy (bī·og′rə·fē) a story about a person's life.
I read a biography about Abraham Lincoln.
n. pl. **biographies** bi·og·ra·phies

bird (bėrd) **1.** an animal with wings, feathers and a beak.
I watched the bird fly away. *n. pl.* **birds**
2. having to do with the animal with wings, feathers and a beak.
We found an egg in the bird nest. *adj.*

bird

birdhouse

birdbath bird·bath (bėrd′bath) a container of water in which birds drink and bathe.
We have a birdbath in our front yard. *n. pl.* **birdbaths** bird·baths

birdhouse bird·house (bėrd′hous) a tiny box in which birds are able to build a nest.
We built a birdhouse. *n. pl.* **birdhouses** bird·hous·es

birth (bėrth) the act of being born.
We watched the birth of the puppies. *n. pl.* **births**

birthdate birth·date (bėrth′dāt) the date on which a person was born.
My birthdate is June 1, 1978. *n. pl.* **birthdates** birth·dates

birthday birth·day (bėrth′dā) **1.** the anniversary of the date that a person was born; the day that a person gets older each year.
My birthday is June 1. *n. pl.* **birthdays** birth·days
2. having to do with the date on which a person was born.
Joe used his birthday money to buy a radio. *adj.*

birdbath

bit (bit) **1.** *v. pt. t., pt. part.* See **bite** (1).
2. a small piece.
I want a little bit of that cake. *n. no pl.*
3. the piece of metal on a bridle that goes into the horse's mouth.
The man put the bit into the horse's mouth. *n. pl.* **bits**

bite (bīt) **1.** to put teeth into something; to cut with the teeth.
Do not bite your fingernails! *v.* **bit, bitten** *or* **bit, biting** bit·ten, bit·ing
2. the marks left when an animal or person puts teeth into something or someone.
The dog bite still hurts. *n. pl.* **bites**

bitter bit·ter (bit′ər) not sweet; a sharp, unpleasant taste.
The aspirin tastes bitter. *adj.*

bit

blackbird

blab (blab) to talk without control; to tell what should not be told.
Do not tell your secret to Mary. She will blab it to everyone.
v. **blabbed, blabbed, blabbing** blab·bing

black (blak) a person who has dark-colored skin.
The book is about a black family. *adj.*

blackbird black·bird (blak´bėrd) any of several American birds
that have mostly black feathers.
The male blackbird has more black feathers than the female blackbird.
n. pl. **blackbirds** black·birds

Blackfoot Black·foot (blak´fůt) an Indian tribe from the western
United States and Canada.
The Blackfoot lived on the prairie. *n.*

Black Hills

Black Hills (blak hilz) a mountain range in the states
of South Dakota and Wyoming.
Many Indians once lived in the Black Hills.

blacksmith black·smith (blak´smith) a person who makes things
with metal by heating and bending it.
The blacksmith made a shoe for the horse.
n. pl. **blacksmiths** black·smiths

black widow black wid·ow (blak wid´ō) a kind of spider;
the female is dangerous and poisonous.
I never want to see a black widow.

black widow

blade (blād) a thin, sharp object that cuts; a thin,
sharp piece of metal that cuts.
I cut the beef with the blade of the knife. *n. pl.* **blades**

blame (blām) to give fault to someone; to accuse someone of doing
something; to hold someone responsible for something bad.
He will blame me for breaking the bicycle.
v. **blamed, blamed, blaming** blam·ing

blanket blan·ket (blang´kit) a cover used to keep warm; a
cover for a bed.
I have a homemade blanket on my bed. *n. pl.* **blankets** blan·kets

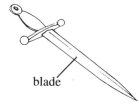

blade

blast-off (blast´ôf) the taking off of a rocket; the launching
of a rocket or a spaceship.
The blast-off to the moon will be at ten o'clock tomorrow. *n. pl.* **blast-offs**

a	cat	**i**	sit	**oi**	oil	**ch**	chop	a in about
ā	ate	**ī**	lie	**ou**	out	**ng**	song	e in oven
ä	car	**o**	pot	**u**	cut	**sh**	she	ə = i in pencil
e	set	**ō**	old	**ů**	book	**th**	three	o in memory
ē	equal	**ô**	or	**ü**	blue	**ŦH**	there	u in circus
ėr	germ					**zh**	treasure	

blaze (blāz) to burn brightly; to give off light while burning.
>The fire will blaze in the fireplace. *v.* **blazed, blazed, blazing** blaz·ing

bleach (blēch) a liquid chemical that is used to make clothes white.
>Mother put some bleach in the washer. *n. no pl.*

bleak (blēk) cold; miserable; without hope or happiness.
>The winter day was very bleak. *adj.* **bleaker, bleakest** bleak·er, bleak·est

bleed (blēd) to have blood come out of the body.
>Your finger will bleed if you cut it. *v.* **bled, bled, bleeding** bleed·ing

bless (bles) to say a prayer for; to pray over; to make holy.
>The minister will bless the new baby.
>*v.* **blessed** *or* **blest, blessed** *or* **blest, blessing** bless·ing

blew (blü) *v. pt. t.* See **blow.**

blind (blīnd) unable to see; without eyesight.
>The man is blind and uses a cane. *adj.* **blinder, blindest** blind·er, blind·est

blinding blind·ing (blīn′ding) being so bright that it is difficult to see.
>The blinding snow made it hard to drive the car. *adj.*

blizzard bliz·zard (bliz′ərd) a bad snowstorm with a lot of wind.
>There was a blizzard in the mountains. *n. pl.* **blizzards** bliz·zards

block (blok) **1.** a piece of wood or other material that has six sides and that children use for building.
>The baby dropped the block on the floor. *n.*
>**2.** anything that has six sides; an object that is shaped like a cube.
>I put a block of wood under the table. *n.*
>**3.** the land between two streets; the area between two streets.
>Joe lives in the next block. *n.*
>**4.** a movement to prevent someone from hitting a person.
>The boy used a karate block to stop the attacker. *n. pl.* **blocks**

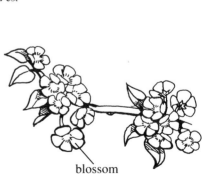

block

blond *or* **blonde** (blond) having yellow-colored hair.
>The little girl is blond. *adj.* **blonder, blondest** blond·er, blond·est

blood (blud) the liquid in the body that carries oxygen to parts of the body.
>I cut my finger. The blood fell on the floor. *n. no pl.*

bloom (blüm) **1.** to have flowers grow and open.
>The tree will bloom in the spring.
>*v.* **bloomed, bloomed, blooming** bloom·ing
>**2.** the open flower on a plant or a tree.
>I like the smell of the rose bloom. *n. pl.* **blooms**

blossom blos·som (blos′əm) the flower on a tree or a plant; a bloom.
>I like the smell of the blossom. *n. pl.* **blossoms** blos·soms

blossom

blueberry

blow (blō) to make air move; to give out air.
The wind will blow very hard during a storm.
v. **blew, blown, blowing** blow·ing

blowhole blow·hole (blō′hōl) the opening to a whale's lungs that is on its back.
I could see the whale breathe through its blowhole.
n. pl. **blowholes** blow·holes

blown (blōn) *v. pt. part.* See **blow.**

blow up (blō up) to fill with air; to put air into.
I will blow up the balloon. *v.* **blew up, blown up, blowing up** blow·ing up

blubber blub·ber (blub′ər) the fat of a whale, used to make oil.
The whale's blubber is very thick. *n. no pl.*

blue (blü) sad; unhappy.
The rain makes me feel blue. *adj.* **bluer, bluest,** blu·er, blu·est

blueberry blue·ber·ry (blü′ber·ē) a kind of fruit that is round, small, sweet and blue.
I picked a blueberry from the bush. *n. pl.* **blueberries** blue·ber·ries

board

board (bôrd) **1.** a flat piece of wood.
We painted a sign on the board. *n.*
2. a piece of strong, stiff paper on which a game is played.
I cannot find the board for the game of checkers. *n. pl.* **boards**

boat (bōt) **1.** a vehicle that floats on water; a small ship.
I took a ride in his boat. *n. pl.* **boats**
2. having to do with a vehicle that floats on the water.
We left the boat dock before it got dark. *adj.*

boat

body bod·y (bod′ē) **1.** the whole of a person, thing or animal; the parts of a person, animal or thing together.
I can see someone's body through the window. *n.*
2. the main part of a letter.
I started a letter but have not finished the body. *n.*
3. a gathering or collection of something.
The ocean is a body of water. *n. pl.* **bodies** bod·ies
4. having to do with the whole of a person, thing or animal.
Our normal body temperature is 98.6°. *adj.*

a	cat	**i**	sit	**oi**	oil	**ch**	chop		a in about
ā	ate	**ī**	lie	**ou**	out	**ng**	song		e in oven
ä	car	**o**	pot	**u**	cut	**sh**	she	**ə =**	i in pencil
e	set	**ō**	old	**u̇**	book	**th**	three		o in memory
ē	equal	**ô**	or	**ü**	blue	**T̶H**	there		u in circus
ėr	germ					**zh**	treasure		

boil   (boil)   to make water so hot that it bubbles and makes steam.
I will boil water and make us some tea. *v.* **boiled, boiled, boiling** boil·ing

boiler   boil·er (boi⋅lər)   a tank that is used to heat water so hot that it makes steam, which is used to heat a building.
The boiler at school makes heat for the classrooms. *n. pl.* **boilers** boil·ers

bold   (bōld)   without fear; unafraid.
Be bold, and don't let that boy bully you.
adj. **bolder, boldest** bold·er, bold·est

bomb   (bom)   to attack with things that explode; to drop explosives.
The airplane will bomb the ship. *v.* **bombed, bombed, bombing** bomb·ing

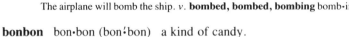

bomb

bonbon   bon·bon (bon⋅bon)   a kind of candy.
I would like a chocolate bonbon. *n. pl.* **bonbons** bon·bons

bone   (bōn)   **1.** a hard substance or thing to which the muscles of the body are attached; one of the pieces that make up the skeleton.
I broke a bone in my leg. *n. pl.* **bones**
2. having to do with the hard substance to which muscles are attached in the body.
My dog likes his bone treat. *adj.*

bonnet   bon·net (bon⋅it)   a kind of hat worn by women and children that is tied under the chin.
My mother wore a bonnet when she was small. *n. pl.* **bonnets** bon·nets

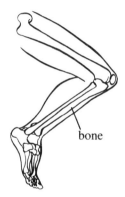
bone

book   (bùk)   **1.** many pages bound together; pages of paper that are put together.
I have a new book. *n. pl.* **books**
2. having to do with pages of paper that are bound together.
I joined a book club. *adj.*

bookmark   book·mark (bùk⋅märk)   a piece of paper, metal, plastic or other material that is used to show where a person stopped reading in a book.
I put my bookmark between pages 40 and 41.
n. pl. **bookmarks** book·marks

bookshelf   book·shelf (bùk⋅shelf)   a place where books are kept; a ledge for books.
I put the vase on the bookshelf. *n. pl.* **bookshelves** book·shelves

bookstore   book·store (bùk⋅stôr)   a store that sells books; a place where books are sold.
I like to go into a bookstore. *n. pl.* **bookstores** book·stores

boom   (büm)   **1.** a loud noise.
I heard the boom of the thunder. *n.*
2. a long arm or pole that sticks out of a machine.
The man lowered the boom to the ground. *n. pl.* **booms**

bonnet

bookmark

book

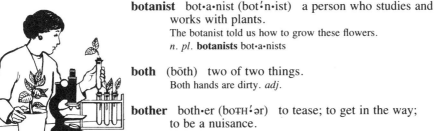

boot

botanist

boot (büt) a covering for the foot that is made of leather or rubber and is worn to keep the foot dry and warm.
I have a hole in my boot. *n. pl.* **boots**

Bordeaux Bor·deaux (bôr·dō′) a city in the country of France.
There are many vineyards in Bordeaux. *n.*

border bor·der (bôr′dər) the edge of a country; the dividing line between countries.
The northern border of the United States touches the country of Canada. *n. pl.* **borders** bor·ders

bored (bôrd) having no interest in something; having nothing to do.
I am so bored. I really want something different to do. *adj.*

boring bor·ing (bôr′ing) dull; not exciting; not interesting.
This story is boring. *adj.*

born (bôrn) **1.** started life.
The baby was born yesterday. *adj.*
2. *v. pt. part.* See **bear** (3).

borrow bor·row (bor′ō) to use something that belongs to another person for a short time.
I need to borrow your dictionary.
v. **borrowed, borrowed, borrowing** bor·rowed, bor·row·ing

boss (bôs) **1.** the person who is in control of an office, a business or other groups; the leader; the person who tells other people what to do.
The boss will decide what we must do next. *n. pl.* **bosses** boss·es
2. to tell what to do; to nag someone to do something.
You cannot boss me around! *v.* **bossed, bossed, bossing** boss·ing

botanist bot·a·nist (bot′n·ist) a person who studies and works with plants.
The botanist told us how to grow these flowers.
n. pl. **botanists** bot·a·nists

both (bōth) two of two things.
Both hands are dirty. *adj.*

bother both·er (boŦH′ər) to tease; to get in the way; to be a nuisance.
Please don't bother me when I am working.
v. **bothered, bothered, bothering** both·ered, both·er·ing

a	cat	i	sit	oi	oil	ch	chop		a in about
ā	ate	ī	lie	ou	out	ng	song		e in oven
ä	car	o	pot	u	cut	sh	she	ə =	i in pencil
e	set	ō	old	ù	book	th	three		o in memory
ē	equal	ô	or	ü	blue	ŦH	there		u in circus
ėr	germ					zh	treasure		

bottle bot·tle (bot⁴l) **1.** a tall container made of glass.
I bought a bottle of milk from the store. *n.*
2. a container from which a baby drinks liquids.
We gave the baby a bottle before she went to bed. *n. pl.* **bottles** bot·tles

bottle-nosed bot·tle-nosed (bot⁴l-nōzd) having a narrow nose that looks like the neck of a bottle.
The bottle-nosed dolphins are very friendly. *adj.*

bottom bot·tom (bot⁴əm) **1.** the lowest part; the floor of something.
Some fish live on the bottom of the sea. *n. pl.* **bottoms** bot·toms
2. being the lowest part or thing.
I ate the bottom layer of the cake. *adj.*

botulism bot·u·lism (boch⁴ə·liz·əm) food poisoning that is caused by bacteria that grow on foods.
The boy got botulism from eating food that was full of harmful bacteria. *n. no pl.*

bought (bôt) *v. pt. t., pt. part.* See **buy.**

bouillon bouil·lon (bul⁴yon) **1.** a clear soup made from chicken or beef.
I added carrots to some chicken bouillon. *n. no pl.*
2. being made from chicken or beef and able to make soup.
I made soup with bouillon cubes. *adj.*

boulder boul·der (bōl⁴dər) a large rock.
The boulder fell from the mountaintop. *n. pl.* **boulders** bould·ers

bounce (bouns) to hit something and then move back; to move up and down after being hit; to cause something to move up and down by hitting it.
I will bounce the ball off the wall.
v. **bounced, bounced, bouncing** bounc·ing

boundary bound·ar·y (boun⁴dər·ē) having to do with the border of something; having to do with the limit or the extent.
The boundary lines are clear on the map. *adj.*

bouquet bou·quet (bō·kā′ *or* bü·kā′) a group of many cut flowers.
I gave Mother a bouquet of flowers to put on the dinner table.
n. pl. **bouquets** bou·quets

boutonniere bou·ton·niere (büt·n·ir′ *or* büt·n·yer′) a single flower worn in a buttonhole or a hole in the lapel of a coat.
The man wore a boutonniere. *n. pl.* **boutonnieres** bou·ton·nieres

bow¹ (bou) to bend from the waist; to give a greeting by bending the body from the waist.
I will bow when I meet the queen.
v. **bowed, bowed, bowing** bow·ing

bottle

boulder

bouquet

boutonniere

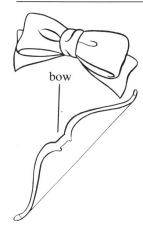

bow

bowline knot

bow² (bō) **1.** a weapon that shoots arrows.
He Indian hunted with a bow and arrows. *n.*
2. the tied ribbon on a package; the looped ribbon
on a package or in the hair.
I put a yellow bow on her birthday present. *n. pl.* **bows**

bowl (bōl) a deep, round dish.
Mother mixed the cookies in a bowl. *n. pl.* **bowls**

bowline knot bow·line knot (bō‑lən not *or* bō‑līn not) a knot
tied to form a tight loop.
Father fastened the sail with a bowline knot.

bow-wow (bou-wou) the sound that a dog makes.
"Bow-wow!" said the dog. *n. no pl.*

box (boks) **1.** a rectangular container.
The salesman put my shoes in a box. *n.*
2. a rectangular shape drawn on paper.
The teacher drew a box around the right answer. *n. pl.* **boxes** box·es
3. to fight with fists.
The teacher taught the children how to box in gym class yesterday.
v. **boxed, boxed, boxing** box·ing

boxer box·er (bok‑sər) a person who fights with the fists.
The boxer with the blue shorts won the fight. *n. pl.* **boxers** box·ers

boy (boi) a young male.
The boy helped his parents by cleaning his bedroom. *n. pl.* **boys**

boyhood boy·hood (boi‑hůd) the stage or time of being a boy.
He has wonderful memories of his boyhood.
n. pl. **boyhoods** boy·hoods

boy scout (boi skout) a member of a club that teaches
boys about camping.
John will become a boy scout this year.

Boy Scouts (boi skouts) world-wide organization that
teaches good habits to boys and young men.
Many boys join the Boy Scouts.

brag (brag) to talk a lot about skills or possessions.
My brothers brag about their cars all the time.
v. **bragged, bragged, bragging** brag·ging

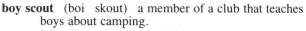

boxer

a	cat	i	sit	oi	oil	ch	chop		a in about
ā	ate	ī	lie	ou	out	ng	song		e in oven
ä	car	o	pot	u	cut	sh	she	ə =	i in pencil
e	set	ō	old	ů	book	th	three		o in memory
ē	equal	ô	or	ü	blue	ŦH	there		u in circus
ėr	germ					zh	treasure		

Brahma Brah•ma (brä′mə) a kind of cattle that was first raised in India.
The Brahma bull chased the bullfighter. *adj.*

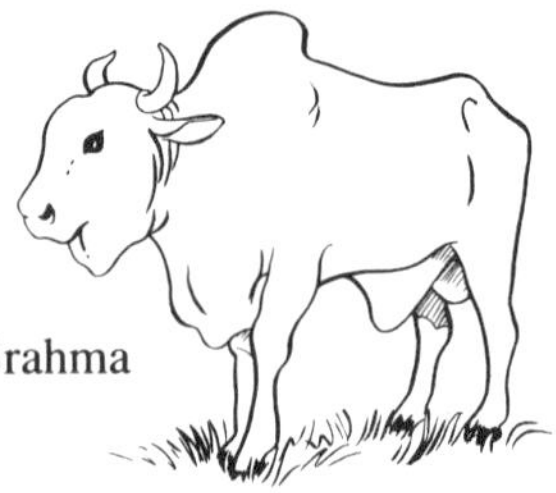
Brahma

braid (brād) **1.** to weave hair together.
The twins braid their long hair every summer.
v. **braided, braided, braiding** braid•ed, braid•ing
2. woven hair.
The girl's long braid hung to the middle of her back. *n.*
3. decorative, twisted ribbon.
The high school band uniforms have gold braid on the shoulders and the sleeves. *n. pl.* **braids**

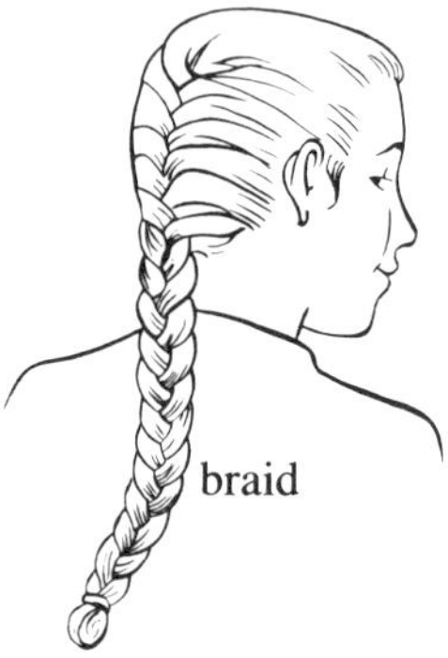
braid

brain (brān) the matter inside the head of a person or animal, which thinks and controls other body actions.
When you are thinking, you are using your brain. *n. pl.* **brains**

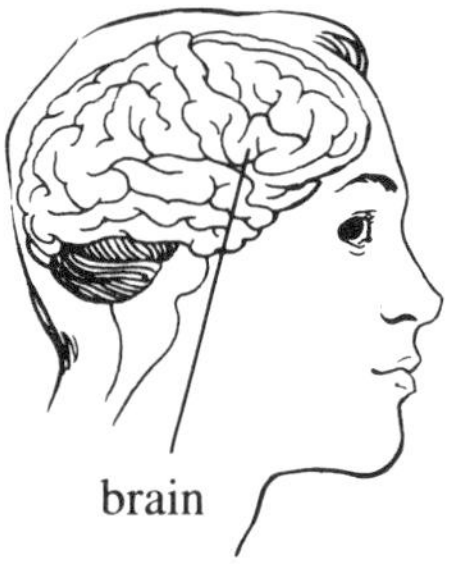
brain

brake (brāk) the part of a car, truck, bicycle or other vehicle that slows or stops it.
Joe ran into the rosebush when his bicycle brake didn't work. *n. pl.* **brakes**

bran (bran) the outer covering of grains like wheat.
Many people like muffins that are made with bran. *n. no pl.*

branch (branch) **1.** a limb of a tree.
Lightning struck a large branch of the oak tree. *n.*
2. a division of a family or a business.
One branch of my family lives in Italy. *n. pl.* **branches** branch•es

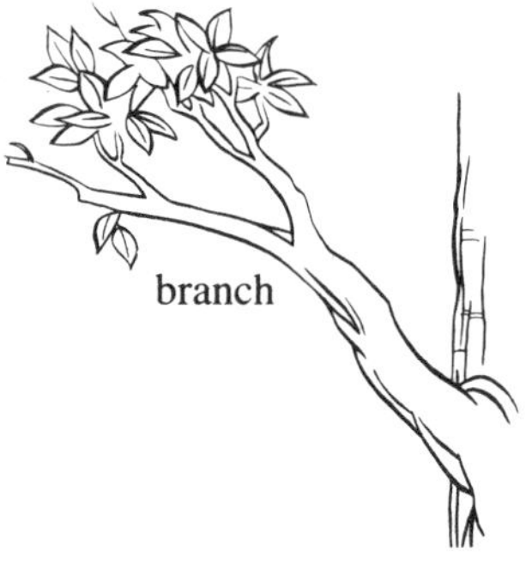
branch

brand (brand) a kind of product; the name of a commercial product.
Mother tried a new brand of soap but did not like the way it cleaned. *n. pl.* **brands**

brat (brat) a bad child.
Katie is a brat. She won't share anything with me. *n. pl.* **brats**

brave (brāv) being without fear.
John was brave as he waited for the dentist to pull his tooth.
adj. **braver, bravest** brav•er, brav•est

bravely brave•ly (brāv′lē) without fear.
John waited bravely for the dentist to pull his tooth. *adv.*

bravery brav•er•y (brā′vər•ē) a characteristic that makes a person unafraid; courage.
The soldier was given a medal for his bravery during the war.
n. pl. **braveries** brav•er•ies

Brazil Bra•zil (brə•zil′) a country in South America; its capital is Brasilia.
Corn, cotton and coffee grow in Brazil. *n.*

bread (bred) a food made of flour and liquid, formed into dough and then baked.
I ate toasted wheat bread for breakfast. *n. pl.* **breads**

Brazil

Brasilia

bread crumb (bred krum) a tiny piece of bread.
Mother feeds bread crumbs to the birds in the backyard.

break (brāk) **1.** to disobey.
People who break the law often go to jail. *v.*
2. to divide into pieces.
Please don't break that glass vase.
v. **broke, broken, breaking** bro·ken, brea·king
3. a short rest period.
The office secretaries take a coffee break at 10:15 A.M.
every day. *n. pl.* **breaks**

breakfast break·fast (brek′fəst) the first meal of the day.
I eat cereal for breakfast every morning. *n. pl.* **breakfasts** break·fasts

breast (brest) the front part of a body from the neck to the stomach.
My favorite part of a roasted chicken is the breast. *n. pl.* **breasts**

breath (breth) air pulled in and out of the lungs.
The doctor said, "Take a deep breath and say 'ah.'" *n. pl.* **breaths**

breathe (brēŦH) to pull air into the lungs and to let air
out of the lungs.
Fish do not breathe through their mouths but through
their gills. *v.* **breathed, breathed, breathing** breath·ing

breathtaking breath·ta·king (breth′tā·king) exciting.
The boat ride was breathtaking. *adj.*

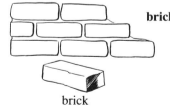

bread

breed (brēd) **1.** to raise animals.
My uncle will breed poodles this year.
v. **bred, bred, breeding** breed·ing
2. a group of animals that look the same.
A collie is one breed of dog. *n. pl.* **breeds**

breeze (brēz) a light wind.
We couldn't fly the kite because the breeze was not strong enough.
n. pl. **breezes** breez·es

brick (brik) **1.** a block made of hardened clay that is used
to build things.
The man bought brown bricks for his new house. *n. pl.* **bricks**
2. something made of brick.
I live in a brick house. *adj.*

brick

a	cat	i	sit	oi	oil	ch	chop		a in about
ā	ate	ī	lie	ou	out	ng	song		e in oven
ä	car	o	pot	u	cut	sh	she	ə =	i in pencil
e	set	ō	old	u̇	book	th	three		o in memory
ē	equal	ô	or	ü	blue	ŦH	there		u in circus
ėr	germ					zh	treasure		

bricklayer brick·lay·er (brik′lā·ər) a person who builds with bricks.
> The bricklayer built the house with red bricks.
> *n. pl.* **bricklayers** brick·lay·ers

bride (brīd) a woman who is getting married.
> The bride wore a long white gown and carried yellow daisies. *n. pl.* **brides**

bride

bridge (brij) something built over a road, river or railroad tracks so that people can cross to the other side.
> Dad drove across the bridge. *n. pl.* **bridges** bridg·es

bright (brīt) **1.** filled with light.
> My bedroom is very bright in the morning. *adj.*
> **2.** vivid in color.
> My favorite color is bright blue.
> *adj.* **brighter, brightest** bright·er, bright·est

bright and early bright and ear·ly (brīt and ėr′lē) in the first part of the morning.
> We are going fishing bright and early tomorrow. *idiom*

brightly bright·ly (brīt′lē) in a bright way.
> The sun shines brightly in California. *adv.*

bridge

brilliant bril·liant (bril′yənt) **1.** being very smart.
> The contest winner is a brilliant young man. *adj.*
> **2.** shining or sparkling.
> Her diamond ring is brilliant. *adj.*

bring (bring) **1.** to carry something to a place.
> The teacher asked me to bring cookies to school tomorrow. *v.*
> **2.** to come with someone.
> I will bring my father to the meeting tonight.
> *v.* **brought, brought, bringing** bring·ing

briquet bri·quet (bri·ket′) a piece of charcoal used to start a fire.
> We need another briquet on the fire in the barbecue.
> *n. pl.* **briquets** bri·quets

briquet

Britain Brit·ain (brit′n) another name for England, Scotland and Wales; a country in Europe, often called Great Britain.
> Elizabeth II is Queen of Britain. *n.*

British Brit·ish (brit′ish) **1.** the people who live in or who were born in Great Britain.
> The British once had a large navy. *plural n.*
> **2.** having to do with the people and the customs of Great Britain.
> John speaks English with a British accent. *adj.*

British Columbia Brit·ish Co·lum·bi·a (brit′ish kə·lum′bē·ə) a province (state) of Canada; its capital is Victoria.
> My dad and uncle go fishing in British Columbia every year.

broccoli

bronco

brook

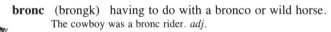

broom

broad (brôd) wide.
The new bridge is very broad. *adj.* **broader, broadest** broad·er, broad·est

broccoli broc·co·li (brok′ə·lē) a green vegetable with stems and flowerettes.
My favorite vegetable is broccoli. *n. pl.* **broccoli** broc·co·li

broke (brōk) *v. pt. t.* See **break** (1, 2).

broken bro·ken (brō′kən) *v. pt. part.* See **break** (1, 2).

broken-down bro·ken-down (brō′kən-doun) worn-out; ruined.
The farmhouse was broken-down and decayed. *adj.*

broker bro·ker (brō′kər) a person who buys and sells stocks and bonds.
My father is a broker in San Francisco. *n. pl.* **brokers** bro·kers

brokerage bro·ker·age (brō′kər·ij) **1.** a business that buys and sells stocks and bonds for people.
My father works for a brokerage in San Francisco.
n. pl. **brokerages** bro·ker·ag·es
2. having to do with a business that buys and sells stocks and bonds.
New York City has many brokerage houses. *adj.*

bronc (brongk) having to do with a bronco or wild horse.
The cowboy was a bronc rider. *adj.*

bronco bron·co (brong′kō) a wild pony.
The cowboy rode a spirited bronco. *n. pl.* **broncos** bron·cos

bronze (bronz) **1.** a brownish-colored metal.
The statue in the park is made of bronze. *n. no pl.*
2. being made of a brownish-colored metal.
There is a bronze statue of Abraham Lincoln in the park. *adj.*

brook (brùk) a small stream.
We waded across the brook carrying our shoes. *n. pl.* **brooks**

broom (brüm *or* brùm) a tool made of a wooden pole with a plastic or straw brush at one end that is used for sweeping.
Mom uses the broom to sweep the kitchen floor. *n. pl.* **brooms**

brother broth·er (bruTH′ər) a male with the same mother and father as another.
Susan's brother, Rob, is a teacher. *n. pl.* **brothers** broth·ers

a	cat	**i**	sit	**oi**	oil	**ch**	chop	
ā	ate	**ī**	lie	**ou**	out	**ng**	song	
ä	car	**o**	pot	**u**	cut	**sh**	she	
e	set	**ō**	old	**ù**	book	**th**	three	
ē	equal	**ô**	or	**ü**	blue	**ŦH**	there	
ėr	germ					**zh**	treasure	

ə = {
a in about
e in oven
i in pencil
o in memory
u in circus

brotherhood broth·er·hood (bruᴛʜ′ər·hùd) a feeling of being brothers; a feeling of being in a family.
   When John joined the troop, he became part of the brotherhood of scouts.
   n. pl. **brotherhoods** broth·er·hoods

brought (brôt) *v. pt. t., pt. part.* See **bring.**

brow (brou) **1.** another name for the forehead; the upper part of the face between the eyes and the hair.
   The man had dirt on his brow and cheeks. *n.*
   2. the part of the horse bridle that fits across the horse's forehead.
   The brow was tight, and it broke. *n. pl.* **brows**

brush

brush (brush) **1.** a tool with bristles that people use for cleaning or painting.
   Dad used a brush to clean the floor. *n.*
   2. a tool with bristles that people use on hair.
   Jill uses a large brush on the horse's mane. *n. pl.* **brushes** brush·es
   3. to use a tool with bristles on the hair.
   Mother will brush my hair before I go to the party.
   v. **brushed, brushed, brushing** brush·ing

brush away brush a·way (brush ə·wā′) to sweep something away with a brush or hand.
   Mary will brush away the dirt from her coat.
   v. **brushed away, brushed away, brushing away** brush·ing a·way

bubble

bubble bub·ble (bub′əl) **1.** a hollow shape that looks like a ball.
   John blew a bubble with his gum. *n.*
   2. a thing made of soapy liquid and filled with air.
   John made a bubble in the bathtub. *n. pl.* **bubbles** bub·bles
   3. being made of soapy liquid and air.
   I take a bubble bath every Sunday afternoon. *adj.*

bubonic plague bu·bon·ic plague (byü·bon′ik plāg) a terrible sickness that usually kills a person who gets it.
   Rats carry the fleas that cause the bubonic plague.

buck (buk) to jump up and down with the back curved.
   The horse will buck to throw off the rider.
   v. **bucked, bucked, bucking** buck·ing

bucket

bucket buck·et (buk′it) a pail that people use for carrying liquids.
   Joan poured the water in the bucket onto the floor. *n. pl.* **buckets** buck·ets

buckle buck·le (buk′əl) the metal part of a belt or strap that joins the two ends together.
   Sally broke the buckle on her shoe. *n. pl.* **buckles** buck·les

bud (bud) a flower that has not yet opened.
   The rosebush has a new bud on it. *n. pl.* **buds**

buckle

buffalo

Buddha   Bud·dha (bü′də *or* bùd′ə)   the man who started the religion of Buddhism in India centuries ago.
Buddha taught people how to be happy and to be kind to other people. *n.*

buffalo   buf·fa·lo (buf′ə·lō)   a large ox-like animal.
The Indians would kill a buffalo for food and then make clothes from the buffalo's fur.
n. pl. **buffalos** *or* **buffaloes** *or* **buffalo**
buf·fa·los *or* buf·fa·loes *or* buf·fa·lo

bug   (bug)   **1.** a small insect.
I saw a bug crawling on the wall. *n. pl.* **bugs**
2. to tease or bother.
Please don't bug me today. *v.* **bugged, bugged, bugging** bug·ging

buggy   bug·gy (bug′ē)   a carriage with one seat and pulled by one horse.
The farmer had a buggy to ride to church. *n. pl.* **buggies** bug·gies

buggy

build   (bild)   to make something out of many parts.
Donald will build a new house with brick and wood.
v. **built, built, building** build·ing

builder   build·er (bil′dər)   a person who makes things out of many parts.
Donald is a house builder. *n. pl.* **builders** build·ers

building   build·ing (bil′ding)   a structure that can hold people or things.
The hotel is a very large building. *n. pl.* **buildings** build·ings

bulb

build up   (bild up)   to make bigger, higher or stronger.
Tom will build up the blocks to make a tower.
v. **built up, built up, building up** build·ing up

built   (bilt)   *v. pt. t., pt. part.* See **build.**

bulb   (bulb)   a round, hollow end of a tool that has a long, thin body.
I squeezed the bulb of the eyedropper to fill it with the eye medicine.
n. pl. **bulbs**

a	cat	i	sit	oi	oil	ch	chop		a in about
ā	ate	ī	lie	ou	out	ng	song		e in oven
ä	car	o	pot	u	cut	sh	she	ə =	i in pencil
e	set	ō	old	ù	book	th	three		o in memory
ē	equal	ô	or	ü	blue	ŦH	there		u in circus
ėr	germ					zh	treasure		

bulge   (bulj)   **1.** to grow outward.
> I ate so much that my stomach began to bulge. *v.*
> **2.** to make something push outward.
> The strong man bent his arm and bulged his muscles.
> *v.* **bulged, bulged, bulging** bul·ging
> **3.** a bump; an outward curve.
> There was a bulge on Ed's head after he bumped it against the wall.
> *n. pl.* **bulges** bul·ges

bull

bull   (bùl)   the male of the cattle family.
> The farmer took the bull out of the barn. *n. pl.* **bulls**

bulldozer   bull·doz·er (bùl'dō·zər)   a large machine that pushes dirt and rocks.
> Bob used a bulldozer to move the pile of dirt. *n. pl.* **bulldozers** bull·doz·ers

bullet   bul·let (bùl'it)   the piece of metal that is fired from a gun.
> He put a bullet in the gun. *n. pl.* **bullets** bul·lets

bully   bul·ly (bùl'ē)   a mean person who scares other people.
> Justin is a bully. He is always trying to start a fight. *n. pl.* **bullies** bul·lies

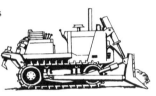
bulldozer

bump   (bump)   **1.** a lump or a swelling.
> Troy got a bump on his head when he fell. *n. pl.* **bumps**
> **2.** to hit against something.
> Do not leave your bicycle in the driveway. I might bump it with the car.
> *v.* **bumped, bumped, bumping** bump·ing

bump into   bump in·to (bump in'tü)   hit against something.
> The car bumped into the bicycle.
> *v.* **bumped into, bumped into, bumping into** bump·ing in·to

bun   (bun)   a small, shaped bread.
> Katie likes her hot dog without a bun. *n. pl.* **buns**

bullet

bunch   (bunch)   a group or set of like things.
> Mom bought a bunch of bananas at the grocery store.
> *n. pl.* **bunches** bunch·es

bundle   bun·dle (bun'dl)   things tied together.
> Tom brought a bundle of sticks for the fire. *n. pl.* **bundles** bun·dles

bunk bed   (bungk bed)   a small bed that can be set on top of another small bed.
> Brent sleeps in the bottom bunk bed, and Justin sleeps in the top bunk bed.

bunny   bun·ny (bun'ē)   a baby rabbit.
> Mom bought Cathy a bunny for Easter. *n. pl.* **bunnies** bun·nies

buried   bur·ied (ber'ēd)   *v. pt. t., pt. part.* See **bury.**

bunk beds

bunny

burn (bėrn) **1.** a hurt caused by heat.
Brent got a burn when he touched the hot stove. *n. pl.* **burns**
2. to damage something with fire.
Be careful not to burn yourself on the candle.
v. **burned** *or* **burnt, burned** *or* **burnt, burning** burn·ing

burn up (bėrn up) to destroy something with fire.
The fire burned up the whole house.
v. **burned up** *or* **burnt up, burned up**
or **burnt up, burning up** burn·ing up

burp (bėrp) a sound made when air is let out of the stomach through the mouth.
The man said "excuse me" when he let out a burp. *n. pl.* **burps**

burst (bėrst) to break open suddenly.
When the bubble hits the grass, it will burst.
v. **burst, burst, bursting** burst·ing

bus

burst into burst in·to (bėrst in´tü) to enter a place suddenly; to start something suddenly.
Do not burst into the room; knock on the door before you come in.
v. **burst into, burst into, bursting into** burst·ing in·to

bury (ber´ē) to place in the ground and cover with dirt.
The dogs bury bones in our backyard.
v. **buried, buried, burying** bur·ied, bur·y·ing

bus (bus) a big vehicle with many seats that is used for carrying many people from place to place.
Sharon rides the school bus every day. *n. pl.* **buses** bus·es

bush (bush) a plant with many branches near the ground.
The bush has many buds on it. *n. pl.* **bushes** bush·es

bush

bushy (bush´ē) being full and shaped like a bush.
Santa Claus wears a white, bushy beard.
adj. **bushier, bushiest** bush·i·er, bush·i·est

busiest bus·i·est (biz´ē·ist) *superl. adj.* See **busy.**

busily bus·i·ly (biz´ə·lē) in an active way.
The woman was busily working at her desk. *adv.*

a	cat	i	sit	oi	oil	ch	chop		a in about
ā	ate	ī	lie	ou	out	ng	song		e in oven
ä	car	o	pot	u	cut	sh	she	ə =	i in pencil
e	set	ō	old	u̇	book	th	three		o in memory
ē	equal	ô	or	ü	blue	ᵺH	there		u in circus
ėr	germ					zh	treasure		

business busi·ness (biz·nis) **1.** work or job.
John's business is building airplanes. *n.*
2. a company.
Nat's mother works for a computer business. *n. pl.* **businesses** busi·ness·es

businessman busi·ness·man (biz·nis·man) a man who works in or for a business.
Donald is a businessman; he owns a pet shop.
n. pl. **businessmen** busi·ness·men

busperson bus·per·son (bus·per·sən) someone who clears off the table in a restaurant.
Brad is working as a busperson at Denny's. *n. pl.* **buspersons** bus·per·sons

busperson

bus stop (bus stop) a place where a bus stops so that people can get on and off the bus.
Mother waits for Sharon at the bus stop.

busy bus·y (biz·ē) having many things to do.
Carol is busy getting ready for the party.
adj. **busier, busiest** bus·i·er, bus·i·est

but (but *or* bət) **1.** however.
I wanted to go to the movie, but Mother said I could not go. *conj.*
2. except.
The teacher gave homework to everyone but me. *prep.*

butcher butch·er (büch·ər) a person who cuts meat as a job.
Mother asked the butcher for a three-pound roast. *n. pl.* **butchers** butch·ers

bus stop

butt (but) to hit something with the head.
The angry bull was ready to butt the barn door when we came inside.
v. **butted, butted, butting** butt·ed, butt·ing

butter but·ter (but·ər) **1.** a food made from the fat in milk.
Jean puts a lot of butter on her toast. *n. no pl.*
2. to put butter on something.
I will butter my toast myself.
v. **buttered, buttered, buttering** but·tered, but·ter·ing

butterfly but·ter·fly (but·ər·flī) an insect with four large wings.
Ellen caught a butterfly with her net. *n. pl.* **butterflies** but·ter·flies

button but·ton (but·n) **1.** a switch that makes something start or stop.
Push that red button to turn on the TV. *n.*
2. something used on clothes to keep them closed.
I lost a button from my dress. *n. pl.* **buttons** but·tons
3. to close a piece of clothing.
Don't forget to button your coat.
v. **buttoned, buttoned, buttoning** but·toned, but·ton·ing

butcher

butterfly

button

buy (bī) to get something by paying money.
> Martha will buy a new car soon. *v.* **bought, bought, buying** buy·ing

buyer buy·er (bī⸱ər) a person who gets something
by paying money.
> He is a buyer for Macy's department store. *n.* **buyers** buy·ers

buying buy·ing (bī⸱ing) *v. pres. part.* See **buy.**

buzz (buz) to make a noise that sounds like z-z-z-z.
> The bee buzzed around the flowers. v. **buzzed, buzzed, buzzing** buzz·ing

buzzer buzz·er (buz⸱ər) something that makes a z-z-z-z sound.
> The clock's buzzer started at 7:00 A.M. *n. pl.* **buzzers** buz·zers

by (bī) **1.** near.
> The dog sits by the chair. *prep.*

2. through the use of.
> We go to school by bus. *prep.*

3. past.
> We didn't see the girls when they walked by us. *prep.*

bye-bye (bī-bī) good-bye.
> "Bye-bye!" said the baby. *interj.*

by themselves by them·selves (bī ᴛʜem·selvz′) they did
something alone, without help.
> They took the bus by themselves.

a	cat	i	sit	oi	oil	ch	chop		a in about
ā	ate	ī	lie	ou	out	ng	song		e in oven
ä	car	o	pot	u	cut	sh	she	ə =	i in pencil
e	set	ō	old	u̇	book	th	three		o in memory
ē	equal	ô	or	ü	blue	ᴛʜ	there		u in circus
ėr	germ					zh	treasure		

Cc

C. (sē) centigrade; Celsius.
The thermometer read 38° C. *abbrev.*

¢ (sent) cent(s).
I had 1¢ in my pocket. *abbrev.* See **cent.**

cabin cab·in (kab´ən) a small house or hut.
We like to visit the cabin in the woods. *n. pl.* **cabins** cab·ins

cabin

cable ca·ble (kā´bəl) **1.** a thick wire.
The repairman changed the electric cable. *n. pl.* **cables** ca·bles
2. to send a message over wires.
We will cable you when we get to Rome.
v. **cabled, cabled, cabling** ca·bled, ca·bling

cable car ca·ble car (kā´bəl kär) a kind of streetcar that is moved
by a motor-driven cable.
We rode in a cable car in San Francisco.

cable TV ca·ble TV (ka´bəl tē·vē) a way of sending television
programs through thick wires.
We pay $25.00 a month for cable TV.

cactus cac·tus (kak´təs) a plant that grows in the desert
and needs little water.
We saw a flowering cactus in the desert.
n. pl. **cactuses** *or* **cacti** cac·tus·es *or* cac·ti

cable car

cage (kāj) a small box or room with bars on every side, used
for holding animals.
Ellen has to clean the bird cages every day. *n. pl.* **cages** ca·ges

cake (kāk) a dessert made with flour, sugar, eggs and other things.
Mom baked Lisa a birthday cake. *n. pl.* **cakes**

calendar cal·en·dar (kal´ən·dər) paper that shows the months,
weeks and days of a year.
This calendar begins with January 1. *n. pl.* **calendars** cal·en·dars

calf (kaf) a baby cow, bull, whale, seal, deer or elephant.
The calf was one hour old and trying to stand up. *n. pl.* **calves**

cactus

cage

call (kôl) **1.** to telephone someone.
I will call you tomorrow. *v.*
2. to shout; to yell; to speak loudly.
Mother will call me when dinner is ready. *v.*
3. to name something or someone.
We will call my new brother Danny. *v.* **called, called, calling** call·ing
4. a talk with someone on a telephone.
I got a call from Cindy yesterday. *n.*
5. an animal noise.
The man heard the call of the owl. *n. pl.* **calls**

call for (kôl fôr) to ask someone or something to come.
The principal will call for me when she wants me in the office.
v. **called for, called for, calling for** call·ing for

call on (kôl ôn *or* kôl on) to visit for a short time.
Mother will call on your mother tomorrow.
v. **called on, called on, calling on** call·ing on

call up (kôl up) to telephone.
Please call up the store and order a cake.
v. **called up, called up, calling up** call·ing up

calm (käm *or* kälm) quiet; without a lot of activity.
The ocean is very calm today. *adj.* **calmer, calmest** calm·er, calm·est

calves (kavz) *n. pl.* See **calf.**

came (kām) *v. pt. t.* See **come.**

camera cam·er·a (kam'ər·ə) a machine that makes photographs.
Joyce took a picture of Ken with her camera. *n. pl.* **cameras** cam·er·as

camera

camp (kamp) **1.** a place with many tents or cabins.
Joe is going to Boy Scout camp in July. *n. pl.* **camps**
2. to sleep in a tent or cabin.
We will camp at Lake Ben this summer.
v. **camped, camped, camping** camp·ing

campaign cam·paign (kam·pān') to ask for votes or
support in an election.
The mayor will campaign downtown on Saturday. *v.* **campaigned,
campaigned, campaigning** cam·paigned, cam·paign·ing

campfire

campfire camp·fire (kamp'fīr) an outdoor fire.
We will cook hot dogs over the campfire. *n. pl.* **campfires** camp·fires

a	cat	**i**	sit	**oi**	oil	**ch**	chop	⎧ a in about
ā	ate	**ī**	lie	**ou**	out	**ng**	song	⎪ e in oven
ä	car	**o**	pot	**u**	cut	**sh**	she	ə = ⎨ i in pencil
e	set	**ō**	old	**u̇**	book	**th**	three	⎪ o in memory
ē	equal	**ô**	or	**ü**	blue	**TH**	there	⎩ u in circus
ėr	germ					**zh**	treasure	

can (kan) **1.** to be able to.
I can ride a bicycle. *aux. pt. t.* **could**
2. to put food in jars or metal containers and cook it so it will not spoil.
Grandmother will can beans this summer.
v. **canned, canned, canning** can·ning
3. a metal container.
The can of peas is on the table. *n. pl.* **cans**

can

Canada Can·a·da (kan′·ə·də) the country north of the United States.
My uncle goes fishing in Canada every year. *n.*

cancer can·cer (kan′sər) a disease.
People who smoke cigarettes sometimes get cancer of the lungs.
n. pl. **cancers** can·cers

candidate can·di·date (kan′də·dāt) a person who is trying to get a job in the government by winning an election.
Mr. Jones is a candidate for mayor. *n. pl.* **candidates** can·di·dates

candies can·dies (kan′dēz) *n. pl.* See **candy.**

candle can·dle (kan′dl) a piece of wax with a wick (string) in the center that burns and gives light.
We will light the candle on the table. *n. pl.* **candles** can·dles

candlemaker can·dle·ma·ker (kan′dl·mā·kər) the person who forms wax into candles.
The candlemaker melted the wax for the candle.
n. pl. **candlemakers** can·dle·ma·kers

Canada

Ottawa

candy can·dy (kan′dē) a small, sweet dessert or treat made with sugar.
Chocolate candy is my favorite dessert. *n. pl.* **candies** can·dies

candy bar can·dy bar (kan′dē bär) a sweet dessert or treat that has a rectangular shape.
My favorite candy bar is a Snickers.

candymaker can·dy·ma·ker (kan′dē·mā·kər) a person who cooks sugar into sweet desserts.
The candymaker cooked the fudge and then poured it on a marble table.
n. pl. **candymakers** can·dy·ma·kers

canned (kand) put into cans or jars and cooked so it will not spoil.
I like canned peas. *adj.*

cannery can·ner·y (kan′ər·ē) a place of business that puts food into jars or cans.
My uncle works in a fish cannery. *n. pl.* **canneries** can·ner·ies

candy bar

cannon

cannon can•non (kan′ən) **1.** a gun that is too large to carry by hand.
The soldiers fired the cannon. *n.*
2. a bone in the lower leg of a horse.
The doctor checked the horse's cannon to be sure it was not broken.
n. pl. **cannons** can•nons

cannot *or* **can not** can•not (kan′ot *or* ka•not′) to be unable to; to be not able.
I cannot find my ring. *aux. pt. t.* **could not**

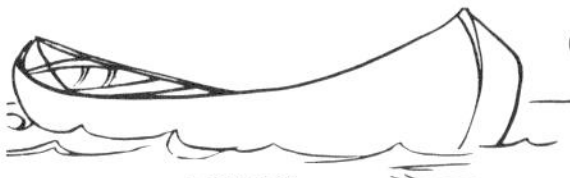
canoe

canoe ca•noe (kə•nü′) a boat built with light material and pointed at both ends.
Indians have used canoes for many years.
n. pl. **canoes** ca•noes

can't (kant) to be not able to.
I can't reach the book. *contrac.* **cannot**

cantle
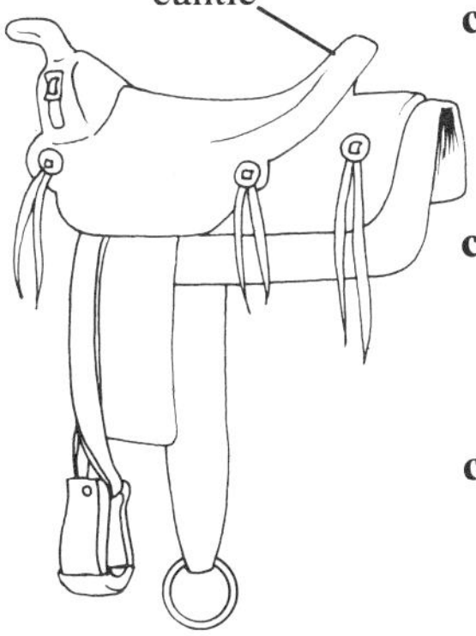

cantle can•tle (kan′təl) the highest part of the back of a horse saddle.
The cantle helps to support the rider's back.
n. pl. **cantles** can•tles

canton can•ton (kan′tən *or* kan′ton) the upper quarter of a flag next to the pole.
There are fifty stars in the canton of the American flag.
n. pl. **cantons** can•tons

canvas can•vas (kan′vəs) **1.** a kind of heavy cloth that people use for making tents, sails and clothes.
The coat was made of canvas. *n. pl.* **canvases** can•vas•es
2. being made of this heavy cloth.
The canvas tent was very heavy. *adj.*

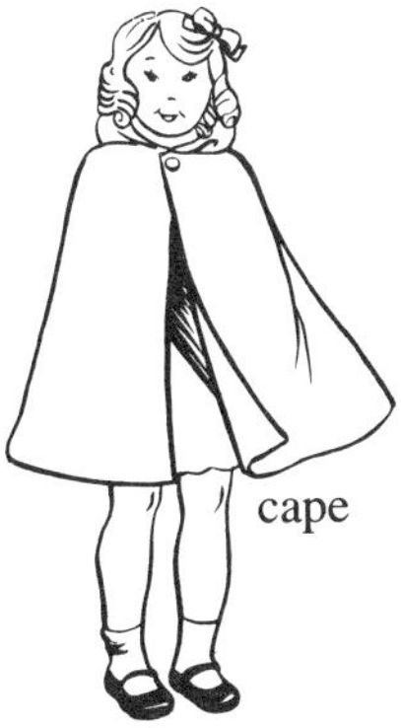
cape

cap (kap) a kind of small hat.
Matthew wears a baseball cap to school. *n. pl.* **caps**

capable ca•pa•ble (kā′pə•bəl) having the ability to do something; being able.
George is a capable ball player. *adj.*

cape (kāp) a coat that does not have sleeves.
Little Red Riding Hood wore a red cape. *n. pl.* **capes**

caper ca•per (kā′pər) a flower bud that is used in cooking to flavor things.
I put some green capers on the fish. *n. pl.* **capers** ca•pers

a	cat	**i**	sit	**oi**	oil	**ch**	chop	ə =	a in about
ā	ate	**ī**	lie	**ou**	out	**ng**	song		e in oven
ä	car	**o**	pot	**u**	cut	**sh**	she		i in pencil
e	set	**ō**	old	**u̇**	book	**th**	three		o in memory
ē	equal	**ô**	or	**ü**	blue	**ŦH**	there		u in circus
ėr	germ					**zh**	treasure		

capillary cap·il·lar·y (kap⁴ə·ler·ē) a tiny vessel (tube) in the body that holds blood.
> She cut a capillary in her finger. *n. pl.* **capillaries** cap·il·lar·ies

capital cap·i·tal (kap⁴ə·təl) a city that is the center of government of a state or country.
> Washington, D.C., is the capital of the United States.
> *n. pl.* **capitals** cap·i·tals

capitol

capitol cap·i·tol (kap⁴ə·təl) the building that holds the government offices.
> The capitol in Charleston, West Virginia, has a gold dome.
> *n. pl.* **capitols** cap·i·tols

captain cap·tain (kap⁴tən) the person who is the leader of a team, of a group or of soldiers.
> Jill is the captain of her basketball team. *n. pl.* **captains** cap·tains

capture cap·ture (kap⁴chər) to take someone or something by force.
> The boy will capture the rabbit. *v.* **captured, captured, capturing**
> cap·tured, cap·tur·ing

car

car (kär) a motor vehicle.
> We bought a new car. *n. pl.* **cars**

caramel car·a·mel (kar⁴ə·məl *or* kär⁴məl) a kind of candy made with brown sugar.
> Mrs. Jones gave me a caramel for Halloween. *n. pl.* **caramels** car·a·mels

carbon dioxide car·bon di·ox·ide (kär⁴bən dī·ok⁴sīd) a gas in the air.
> Carbon dioxide is used by plants. ·

carbon monoxide car·bon mon·ox·ide (kär⁴bən mo·nok⁴sīd) a dangerous gas.
> People should not breathe carbon monoxide.

card (kärd) **1.** one of a set that is used for playing games.
> He dealt one card at a time. *n.*
> **2.** a piece of paper that shows that you joined a club, organization or service group.
> Sarah showed her library card to the librarian and then took a book home. *n.*
> **3.** a paper that tells a message.
> Cynthia sent me a birthday card. *n. pl.* **cards**
> **4.** having to do with the pieces of paper used for playing games.
> I like to play card games. *adj.*
> **5.** to clean wool with a wire brush.
> Uncle John will card the wool that he cut from his sheep.
> *v.* **carded, carded, carding** card·ed, card·ing

card

cardboard   card·board (kärd·bôrd)   **1.** a kind of heavy paper.
The box is made of cardboard. *n. no pl.*
2. made of a heavy paper.
The cardboard box has candy in it. *adj.*

cardinal   car·di·nal (kärd‡n·əl)   a kind of bird.
The male cardinal is a bright red, but the female cardinal is brown.
n. pl. **cardinals** car·di·nals

cardinal

carding   card·ing (kärd‡ing)   the way of cleaning a sheep's fleece
before making it into yarn.
After the carding, wool is made into yarn. *n. no pl.*

card shop   (kärd shop)   a store that sells birthday cards, wedding
cards and other kinds of cards.
I bought her birthday card at the card shop.

care   (ker *or* kar)   **1.** attention; help.
The boy with a broken leg needs a lot of care. *n. no pl.*
2. to help; to give attention.
I will care for your dog while you are on vacation.
v. **cared, cared, caring** car·ing

carefree   care·free (ker‡frē *or* kar‡frē)   happy; without a worry.
I sing a lot when I feel carefree. *adj.*

careful   care·ful (kar‡fəl *or* ker‡fəl)   trying to do something
in a safe way.
Todd is a careful camper. *adj.*

carefully   care·ful·ly (kar‡fə·lē *or* ker‡fə·lē)   doing something in a
safe way.
I carefully put the vase on the table. *adv.*

careless   care·less (kar‡lis *or* ker‡lis)   not worrying about safety.
A careless driver often has accidents. *adj.*

carelessness   care·less·ness (ker‡lis·nəs)   the act of not paying
attention to safety or to what one is doing.
The boy's carelessness with the matches caused the forest fire. *n. no pl.*

cargo   car·go (kär‡gō)   things that are carried on a
plane, train or ship.
The men loaded the cargo onto the plane.
n. pl. **cargoes** *or* **cargos** car·goes *or* car·gos

carol   car·ol (kar‡əl)   a happy song.
Mother sang a Christmas carol in church. *n. pl.* **carols** car·ols

a cat	**i** sit	**oi** oil	**ch** chop		a in about	
ā ate	**ī** lie	**ou** out	**ng** song		e in oven	
ä car	**o** pot	**u** cut	**sh** she	ə =	i in pencil	
e set	**ō** old	**u̇** book	**th** three		o in memory	
ē equal	**ô** or	**ü** blue	**ŦH** there		u in circus	
ėr germ			**zh** treasure			

carpenter car·pen·ter (kär′pən·tər)   a person who makes
   things with wood.
   Mr. Hill is a carpenter who makes tables. *n. pl.* **carpenters** car·pen·ters

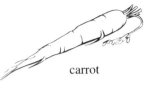
carrot

carriage car·riage (kar′ij)   a vehicle with four wheels that a
   horse can pull or a person can push.
   We rode a carriage around the park. *n. pl.* **carriages** car·riag·es

carried car·ried (kar′ēd)   *v. pt. t., pt. part.* See **carry.**

carrot car·rot (kar′ət)   a long orange vegetable.
   My rabbit eats a carrot every day. *n. pl.* **carrots** car·rots

carry car·ry (kar′ē)   to hold something while moving it from one
   place to another.
   Bill will carry your suitcase to the car.
   v. **carried, carried, carrying** car·ried, car·ry·ing

cart (kärt)   a wagon used to carry heavy things and pulled by an
   animal.
   The milkman would bring milk to Grandmother's house in a cart.
   n. pl. **carts**

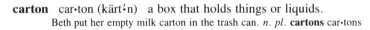
cart

carton car·ton (kärt′n)   a box that holds things or liquids.
   Beth put her empty milk carton in the trash can. *n. pl.* **cartons** car·tons

cartoon car·toon (kär·tün′)   a funny drawing, picture or movie.
   Chuck drew a cartoon of his teacher, Mrs. Byrd. *n. pl.* **cartoons** car·toons

carve (kärv)   **1.** to form something with a knife.
   David will carve a doll out of that piece of wood. *v.*
   2. to cut something with a knife.
   Father will carve the turkey. *v.* **carved, carved, carving** carv·ing

carving carv·ing (kär′ving)   something formed from wood with a
   knife.
   David's doll was the best carving in the woodcarving show.
   n. pl. **carvings** carv·ings

castle cas·tle (kas′əl)   a large house where the king and queen live.
   Susan's house looks like a castle. *n. pl.* **castles** cas·tles

castle

cat (kat)   an animal with whiskers on its face and a long tail.
   My cat has a white spot on its back. *n. pl.* **cats**

catch (kach)   **1.** to get hold of.
   Can you catch the ball? *v.* **caught, caught, catching** catch·ing
   2. a game played with a ball.
   Tony is playing catch with Lee. *n. no pl.*
   3. all the things one has gotten hold of at one time.
   Tom's catch was eight trout. *n. pl.* **catches** catch·es

cat

catch a bus (kach ə bus)   to meet and get on a bus.
   You may catch a bus home from the movie. *idiom*

caterpillar

catfish

cauliflower

cedar

catcher   catch·er (kach′ər)   in baseball, the person who catches balls not hit by the batter.
Brad was the catcher in yesterday's baseball game.
n. pl. **catchers** catch·ers

caterpillar   cat·er·pil·lar (kat′ər·pil·ər)   an insect that looks like a furry worm and that turns into a butterfly or a moth.
The caterpillar will soon become a beautiful butterfly.
n. pl. **caterpillars** cat·er·pil·lars

catfish   cat·fish (kat′fish)   a fish that has long feelers near the mouth.
Catfish keep the aquarium clean. *n. pl.* **catfishes** or **catfish** cat·fish·es

cat stance   (kat stants)   a way to stand that keeps the body balanced while doing Kung Fu.
We practice the cat stance in Kung Fu class.

cattle   cat·tle (kat′l)   **1.** a name for cows and bulls together.
Boys and girls are children; bulls and cows are cattle. *plural n.*
2. having to do with cows and bulls.
My uncle works on a cattle farm. *adj.*

caught   (kôt)   *v. pt. t., pt. part.* See **catch** (1).

cauliflower   cau·li·flow·er (kô′lə·flou·ər)   a white vegetable that grows in a large head.
My sister likes cauliflower, but I like broccoli. *n. pl.* **cauliflower**

cause   (kôz)   **1.** to make something happen.
You will cause a fight if you don't give Katie her ball.
v. **caused, caused, causing** caus·ing
2. the reason something happened.
Mary's teasing was the cause of the fight. *n. pl.* **causes** caus·es

cave   (kāv)   a deep opening or hole in a mountain or hill.
The boys played in the cave. *n. pl.* **caves**

cave man   (kāv man)   a person who lived in a cave many years ago.
The cave man learned to start a fire so he could keep warm.

cedar   ce·dar (sē′dər)   a kind of tree with red wood and a good smell.
The closet in Mother's bedroom is made of cedar. *n. pl.* **cedars** ce·dars

a	cat	i	sit	oi	oil	ch	chop		a in about
ā	ate	ī	lie	ou	out	ng	song		e in oven
ä	car	o	pot	u	cut	sh	she	ə = {	i in pencil
e	set	ō	old	u̇	book	th	three		o in memory
ē	equal	ô	or	ü	blue	TH	there		u in circus
ėr	germ					zh	treasure		

ceiling ceil·ing (sē′ling) the top of a room.
Dad painted my bedroom ceiling white. *n. pl.* **ceilings** ceil·ings

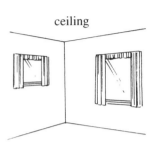
ceiling

celebrate cel·e·brate (sel′ə·brāt) **1.** to keep a day or event special with a ceremony.
We celebrate Independence Day on July 4th. *v.*
2. to have a party or ceremony.
We will celebrate her birthday on Saturday. *v.* **celebrated, celebrated, celebrating** cel·e·brat·ed, cel·e·brat·ing

celebration cel·e·bra·tion (sel·ə·brā′shən) a party or ceremony on a special day.
The celebration of Independence Day always includes a picnic and fireworks. *n. pl.* **celebrations** cel·e·bra·tions

cell (sel) the smallest part of animals and plants.
We cannot see a cell with our eyes. We must use a microscope. *n. pl.* **cells**

cellar cel·lar (sel′ər) the room or rooms under a house or building.
Our cellar is dark and cold. *n. pl.* **cellars** cel·lars

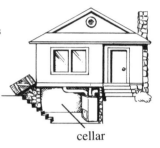
cellar

Celt (selt *or* kelt) the name of the group of people who live in Ireland, Scotland and Wales.
Charles lived in Scotland, so he is a Celt. *n. pl.* **Celts**

cement ce·ment (sə·ment′) **1.** a soft, wet substance made of limestone and sand that becomes hard when it dries.
The sidewalk and the driveway are made of cement. *n. no pl.*
2. to glue things together with a paste that is soft and wet and that becomes hard when it dries.
The bricklayer will cement the bricks together. *v.* **cemented, cemented, cementing** ce·ment·ed, ce·ment·ing

cent (sent) penny.
Jill has only 1 cent in her pocket. *n. pl.* **cents**

cent

centennial cen·ten·ni·al (sen·ten′ē·əl) **1.** a celebration of 100 years of being.
We had our church centennial last week. *n. no pl.*
2. being or talking about something that is 100 years old.
This year our town will have its centennial celebration. *adj.*

center cen·ter (sen′tər) **1.** the middle of something.
Mom put the table in the center of the living room. *n. pl.* **centers** cen·ters
2. to put something in the middle.
Please center the vase on the table. *v.* **centered, centered, centering** cen·tered, cen·ter·ing

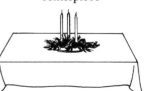
centerpiece

centerpiece cen·ter·piece (sen′tər·pēs) something placed in the middle of the table to decorate it.
The Christmas centerpiece was made of pine branches, pine cones and candles. *n. pl.* **centerpieces** cen·ter·piec·es

Central America

centimeter cen·ti·me·ter (sen⸍tə·mē·tər) a measurement of distance, smaller than an inch.
One centimeter is ¹⁄₁₀₀ of a meter. *n. pl.* **centimeters** cen·ti·me·ters

central cen·tral (sen⸍trəl) being near the middle; being in the center.
Iowa is in the central part of the United States. *adj.*

Central America Cen·tral A·mer·i·ca (sen⸍trəl ə·mer⸍ə·kə) the group of countries between North and South America.
The seven countries in Central America are Belize, Costa Rica, El Salvador, Guatemala, Honduras, Nicaragua and Panama.

century cen·tur·y (sen⸍chər·ē) one hundred years.
Our church has been here for one century, so we had a centennial celebration. *n. pl.* **centuries** cen·tur·ies

ceramics ce·ram·ics (sə·ram⸍iks) **1.** the making of pottery.
Virginia took a class in ceramics. *plural n.*
2. made of clay; pottery.
The ceramic vase is very pretty. *adj.*

cereal cer·e·al (sir⸍ē·əl) a food made from a grain and usually eaten for breakfast.
My favorite cereal is Cheerios. *n. pl.* **cereals** cer·e·als

cereal

ceremony cer·e·mo·ny (ser⸍ə·mō·nē) certain actions done on or for a special event.
The wedding ceremony ended with the bride kissing the groom. *n. pl.*
ceremonies cer·e·mo·nies

certain cer·tain (sėrt⸍n) **1.** sure.
I am certain John is coming home today. *adj.*
2. something that cannot be changed.
The table must be set a certain way, or Mother will ask us to do it again. *adj.*

cetacean ce·ta·cean (sə·tā⸍shən) a name for the mammals that live in the ocean.
A cetacean can be a whale, a dolphin or a porpoise. *n. pl.* **cetaceans** ce·ta·ceans

a	cat	**i**	sit	**oi**	oil	**ch** chop
ā	ate	**ī**	lie	**ou**	out	**ng** song
ä	car	**o**	pot	**u**	cut	**sh** she
e	set	**ō**	old	**u̇**	book	**th** three
ē	equal	**ô**	or	**ü**	blue	**ŦH** there
ėr	germ					**zh** treasure

ə = { a in about / e in oven / i in pencil / o in memory / u in circus }

chair (cher *or* char) a piece of furniture made for people to sit on.
My chair is next to the window. *n. pl.* **chairs**

chairman chair·man (cher′mən) a person who is the leader of a meeting or in a group.
Susie is the chairman of the bake sale committee.
n. pl. **chairmen** chair·men

chair

chalk (chôk) the thing that one uses to write on blackboards.
The teacher gave Alice a piece of chalk so she could write on the chalkboard. *n. pl.* **chalk**

chalkboard chalk·board (chôk′bôrd) a hard surface that one can write or draw on in a classroom; a blackboard.
Alice wrote her name on the chalkboard. *n. pl.* **chalkboards** chalk·boards

challenge chal·lenge (chal′ənj) **1.** something that is hard to learn or get.
Science is a challenge for Jeff. *n. pl.* **challenges** chal·leng·es
2. to call to a game or contest.
I challenge you to a dart game.
v. **challenged, challenged, challenging** chal·lenged, chal·leng·ing

chalk

champion cham·pi·on (cham′pē·ən) **1.** the winner of a race or contest.
Jack is the bowling champion this year. *n. pl.* **champions** cham·pi·ons
2. being good at a sport or activity.
Jack is a champion bowler. *adj.*

championship cham·pi·on·ship (cham′pē·ən·ship) the honor given to the winner of a race.
He won the race car championship. *n. pl.* **championships**
cham·pi·on·ships

chance (chants) a possibility; something that may happen.
I have a chance to go to New York for Christmas. *n. pl.* **chances** chanc·es

chalkboard

change (chānj) **1.** to make or do something different.
I want to change the color of my bedroom. *v.*
2. to take something off and put on something different.
Don will change his pants after school.
v. **changed, changed, changing** chang·ing
3. a difference.
There is a change in the way Sandy is wearing her hair.
n. pl. **changes** chang·es
4. money gotten when more money than the cost is given.
Your change is 52 cents. *n. no pl.*
5. coins.
Every day Dad puts the change from his pockets into my bank. *n. no pl.*

change back to (chānj bak tü) to become something that was before.

A butterfly cannot change back to a caterpillar. *v.* **changed back to, changed back to, changing back to** chang·ing back to

change into (chānj in⌐tü) to become something else.

The caterpillar will change into a butterfly. *v.* **changed into, changed into, changing into** changed in·to, chang·ing in·to

change ___ mind (chānj ___ mīnd) to decide something different from what was first decided.

Yesterday, Sam wanted to be a policeman. Today, he wants to be a doctor. He changes his mind often. *idiom*

character char·ac·ter (kar⌐ik·tər) **1.** a person in a play, story, movie or poem.

The main character in the book is an old man. *n. pl.* **characters** char·ac·ters

2. something about a person that makes them special.

Jan has an open and honest character. *n. no pl.*

chariot

characteristic char·ac·ter·is·tic (kar·ik·tə·ris⌐tik) the things about a person that people can talk about and that make the person different.

Matt has these characteristics: he is tall and thin, has brown hair and green eyes and is cheerful and honest. *n. pl.* **characteristics** char·ac·ter·is·tics

charge (chärj) **1.** the cost of something.

The charge for changing my tire was only $10.00. *n. pl.* **charges** charg·es

2. to run toward something and try to hit it.

The bull is going to charge the barn door. *v.*

3. to buy something now but pay for it later.

I will charge the shoes now and give the store money next week.

v. **charged, charged, charging** charg·ing

chart

chariot char·i·ot (char⌐ē·ət) a two-wheeled wagon pulled by horses that was used centuries ago.

The Roman soldier rode the chariot through the streets.

n. pl. **chariots** char·i·ots

charming charm·ing (chär⌐ming) pleasant; nice.

The new teacher is charming. *adj.*

chart (chärt) a map.

This chart shows all the buildings in Washington, D.C. *n. pl.* **charts**

a	cat	**i**	sit	**oi**	oil	**ch**	chop		a in about
ā	ate	**ī**	lie	**ou**	out	**ng**	song		e in oven
ä	car	**o**	pot	**u**	cut	**sh**	she	ə =	i in pencil
e	set	**ō**	old	**u̇**	book	**th**	three		o in memory
ē	equal	**ô**	or	**ü**	blue	**ŦH**	there		u in circus
ėr	germ					**zh**	treasure		

chase (chās) to run after someone or something.
> The cat will chase the mouse into the hole.
> *v.* **chased, chased, chasing** chas·ing

chat (chat) **1.** a friendly talk.
> We had a nice chat with our new neighbors. *n. pl.* **chats**
> **2.** to have a friendly talk.
> We can chat on the way to school.
> *v.* **chatted, chatted, chatting** chat·ted, chat·ting

cheat (chēt) **1.** to play or do business in a way that is wrong or not honest.
> John will cheat while playing cards, so watch him carefully.
> *v.* **cheated, cheated, cheating** cheat·ed, cheat·ing
> **2.** someone who tricks people.
> John is a cheat. *n. pl.* **cheats**

checkers

check (chek) **1.** to look to see if everything is all right or correct.
> The doctor will go and check on the sick children. *v.* **checked, checked, checking** check·ing
> **2.** a piece of paper given in place of money.
> Mother wrote a check for $15.00 to pay for the shoes. *n. pl.* **checks**

checkbook check·book (chek′bùk) a book of pieces of paper from a bank, which people use in place of money.
> Mother has two more checks in her checkbook.
> *n. pl.* **checkbooks** check·books

checkered check·ered (chek′ərd) a design or pattern of small squares.
> Todd has a new checkered coat. *adj.*

cheek

checkers check·ers (chek′ərz) **1.** a game played on a black and red checkered board.
> My father beat me at checkers. *plural n.*
> **2.** the pieces used while playing the game.
> My father plays the red checkers, and I play the black checkers. *plural n.*

checkup (chek′up) the name for having a doctor look at a person to make sure the person is not sick.
> Dad gets a checkup from Dr. Smith every year. *n. pl.* **checkups**

cheek (chēk) the part of the face between the nose and the ear.
> Aunt Rita kissed Jill on her cheek. *n. pl.* **cheeks**

cheer (chir) **1.** to shout; scream happily.
> We will cheer for our team. *v.* **cheered, cheered, cheering** cheer·ing
> **2.** a happy shout.
> Sue will lead us in a cheer for our team. *n. pl.* **cheers**
> **3.** joy.
> He is full of cheer. *n. no pl.*

cheese

cherry

cheerfully   cheer·ful·ly (chir′fə·lē)   joyfully; gladly.
He cheerfully gave his book to me. *adv.*

cheer up   (chir up)   **1.** to become happy.
Mother will cheer up when she sees the roses. *v.*
2. to make someone happy.
The roses will cheer up Mother.
v. **cheered up, cheered up, cheering up** cheer·ing up

cheese   (chēz)   a food made from milk.
I ate some cheese and crackers before dinner.
n. pl. **cheeses** chees·es

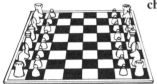
chess

chemical   chem·i·cal (kem′ə·kəl)   **1.** having to do with the science of mixing and changing substances.
There is a chemical business in our city. *adj.*
2. a substance that is made or used in the science of chemistry.
Acid is a chemical that can burn a person's skin.
n. pl. **chemicals** chem·i·cals

chemistry   chem·is·try (kem′ə·strē)   the study of chemicals and the ways they work together.
We will take a class in chemistry when we go to high school.
n. pl. **chemistries** chem·is·tries

Cherokee   Cher·o·kee (cher′ə·kē)   **1.** the name of an Indian tribe.
The Cherokee lived on this land many years ago. *plural n.*
2. a person who belongs to this Indian tribe.
He is a Cherokee. *n. pl.* **Cherokees** Cher·o·kees

chest

cherry   cher·ry (cher′ē)   a small red fruit that grows on a tree and has a small pit (seed) in its center.
I picked a cherry from the tree. *n. pl.* **cherries** cher·ries

chess   (ches)   a game played on a checkered board.
Chess is a hard game to learn. *n. no pl.*

chest   (chest)   **1.** a large box used for keeping things.
Mother puts clothes in the cedar chest. *n.*
2. the front part of the body of a person or animal between the neck and the stomach.
Our hearts are in our chests. *n. pl.* **chests**

chew   (chü)   to cut up food into small pieces with the teeth.
We must chew our food with our mouths closed.
v. **chewed, chewed, chewing** chew·ing

a	cat	i	sit	oi	oil	ch	chop		a in about
ā	ate	ī	lie	ou	out	ng	song		e in oven
ä	car	o	pot	u	cut	sh	she	ə =	i in pencil
e	set	ō	old	u̇	book	th	three		o in memory
ē	equal	ô	or	ü	blue	ŦH	there		u in circus
ėr	germ					zh	treasure		

chewing tobacco chew·ing to·bac·co (chü′ing tə·bak′ō) tobacco leaves prepared for chewing.
The cowboy has chewing tobacco in his mouth while he works.

chick (chik) a baby chicken.
The chick had tiny, soft, white feathers. *n. pl.* **chicks**

chicken chick·en (chik′ən) **1.** a kind of bird raised for food.
The chicken pecked the corn. *n. pl.* **chickens** chick·ens
2. the cooked meat of a chicken.
We ate chicken for dinner last night. *n. no pl.*
3. something made with this bird.
We made chicken soup. *adj.*
4. afraid.
He is chicken about the visit to the dentist. *adj.*

chick   chicken

chide (chīd) to scold someone for doing something wrong.
Mother will chide me because I broke that vase. *v.* **chided** *or* **chid, chided** *or* **chid, chiding** chid·ed *or* chid, chid·ing

chief (chēf) leader of a tribe or a group.
The chief of police caught the robbers. *n. pl.* **chiefs**

child (chīld) **1.** young boy or girl.
The child learned to ride her new bike. *n.*
2. son or daughter.
Bobby is our friend's child. *n. pl.* **children** chil·dren

chimney

children chil·dren (chil′drən) *n. pl.* See **child.**

chill (chil) a deep coldness; a sudden coldness.
A fire in the fireplace will take the chill out of the house. *n. pl.* **chills**

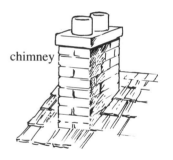

chilly chill·y (chil′ē) cold; uncomfortably cool.
Today is a rainy, chilly day. *adj.* **chillier, chilliest** chill·i·er, chill·i·est

chime (chīm) **1.** to sound like a bell.
The clock will chime at noon. *v.*
2. to say happily.
"Hurray!" we all chimed when Dad brought in the ice cream.
v. **chimed, chimed, chiming** chim·ing

chimney chim·ney (chim′nē) an object made of brick, stone or metal that directs the smoke away from a fire.
The smoke went up the chimney. *n. pl.* **chimneys** chim·neys

chimpanzee chim·pan·zee (chim·pan·zē′ *or* chim·pan′zē) a small ape.
The chimpanzee climbed the tree in its cage.
n. pl. **chimpanzees** chim·pan·zees

chimpanzee

chin

chin (chin)   the bottom part of the face under the mouth.
The man's beard covers his chin. *n. pl.* **chins**

China   Chi·na (chī́nə)   a large country in Asia; its capital is Peking.
Rice is an important crop in China. *n.*

Chinese   Chi·nese (chī·nēz′)   **1.** the people who live in or who were born in China.
The Chinese invented gunpowder many years ago. *plural n.*
2. having to do with China, its people or their language.
We ate dinner at a Chinese restaurant. *adj.*

chip   (chip)   **1.** to cut or break off in small pieces.
Dad will chip the ice off the sidewalk.
v. **chipped, chipped, chipping** chip·ping
2. small pieces broken off something larger.
There are bark chips under the playground equipment. *n. pl.* **chips**

Peking

China

Chippewa   Chip·pe·wa (chiṕpə·wä)   **1.** the name of a tribe of American Indians.
The Chippewa are very proud people. *plural n.*
2. a person who belongs to this Indian tribe.
Some Chippewas live on reservations.
n. pl. **Chippewas** Chip·pe·was

chirp   (chėrp)   **1.** sound made by small birds or insects.
We heard the chirp of the bird in its nest. *n. pl.* **chirps**
2. to make a sound like a small bird or insect.
The crickets chirp at night. *v.* **chirped, chirped, chirping** chirp·ing

chocolate   choc·o·late (chôḱlit *or* chôḱə·lit)   **1.** a flavoring made from cacao seeds.
Mother put the melted chocolate into the cake batter. *n. no pl.*
2. a drink made by mixing hot water or milk with sugar and chocolate.
After playing in the snow, we drank hot chocolate. *n. no pl.*
3. candy made with chocolate.
Mother got a box of chocolates for Valentine's Day.
n. pl. **chocolates** choc·o·lates
4. tasting like chocolate.
She bought chocolate brownies at the bake sale. *adj.*

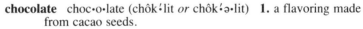

chocolate

choice   (chois)   **1.** the act of picking or selecting.
You have the choice to go to school or go to work. *n.*
2. what or whom a person picks or selects.
Chocolate ice cream is my first choice for dessert. *n. pl.* **choices** choic·es

a	cat	**i**	sit	**oi**	oil	**ch**	chop	
ā	ate	**ī**	lie	**ou**	out	**ng**	song	a in about
ä	car	**o**	pot	**u**	cut	**sh**	she	e in oven
e	set	**ō**	old	**u̇**	book	**th**	three	ə = { i in pencil
ē	equal	**ô**	or	**ü**	blue	**ŦH**	there	o in memory
ėr	germ					**zh**	treasure	u in circus

choose (chüz) to pick out; to select from many.
Choose which coat you want to wear today.
v. **chose, chosen, choosing** cho·sen, choos·ing

chop (chop) **1.** to cut with something sharp.
Dad will chop the wood with his ax.
v. **chopped, chopped, chopping** chop·ping
2. sound made by hitting with something sharp.
I heard the chop of the ax as Father cut the wood. *n. pl.* **chops**

chopine cho·pine (sho·pēn′ *or* cho·pēn′) a kind of woman's shoe with a very high sole.
The chopine was worn over three centuries ago. *n. pl.* **chopines** cho·pines

chopine

chore (chôr) small, daily job.
The little boy's chore was to feed the dog. *n. pl.* **chores**

chorus cho·rus (kôr·əs) **1.** a group of singers.
The school chorus sang at the Spring Concert. *n. pl.* **choruses** cho·rus·es
2. say or sing together as a group.
"Let's go to the beach," chorused the children.
v. **chorused, chorused, chorusing** cho·rused, cho·rus·ing

chorus

chose (chōz) *v. pt. t.* See **choose.**

Christ (krīst) name for Jesus, founder of the Christian religion.
Christ was born in Bethlehem. *n.*

Christian Chris·tian (kris·chən) **1.** person who believes in the teachings of Jesus Christ.
Christians study the Bible. *n. pl.* **Christians** Chris·tians
2. having to do with the teachings of Jesus Christ.
The Christian religion is almost 2000 years old. *adj.*

Christmas Christ·mas (kris·məs) **1.** Christian holiday celebrating the birth of Jesus Christ; December 25th.
Christmas is a time for peace and joy. *n. pl.* **Christmases** Christ·mas·es
2. having to do with the holiday celebrating the birth of Jesus.
The decorations on the Christmas tree are beautiful. *adj.*

chuckle chuck·le (chuk·əl) to laugh softly.
Dad chuckled when Joe told a joke.
v. **chuckled, chuckled, chuckling** chuck·led, chuck·ling

chunk (chungk) a big piece of something.
Mary cut the pineapple into chunks and shared it with her friends. *n. pl.* **chunks**

church

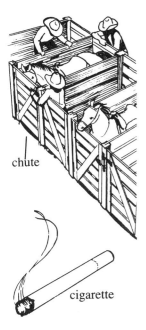

chute

church (chėrch) a building or place to worship.
On Sunday morning the church is full of people. *n. pl.* **churches** church·es

chute (shüt) a small fenced area used for holding an animal at a rodeo or on a ranch.
When the chute opened, the bull ran out. *n. pl.* **chutes**

cigarette cig·a·rette (sig·ə·ret′) tobacco wrapped in paper for smoking.
The man smoked a cigarette after dinner. *n. pl.* **cigarettes** cig·a·rettes

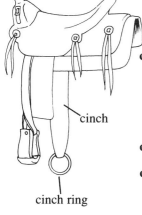

cigarette

cinch (sinch) a strap for fastening a saddle onto a horse.
The cowboy tightened the cinch before getting on the horse. *n. pl.* **cinches** cinch·es

cinch ring (sinch ring) the part of a saddle used to fasten the cinch.
The cowboy could not use the saddle because the cinch ring was broken.

cinder cin·der (sin′dər) large, hard ashes left after a fire.
Cleaning the cinders from the fireplace is a dirty job. *n. pl.* **cinders** cin·ders

Cinderella Cin·der·el·la (sin·də·rel′lə) name of a famous fairy tale.
Our teacher read *Cinderella* to the class. *n.*

circle cir·cle (sėr′kəl) **1.** a round shape.
The clown painted circles on his face. *n. pl.* **circles** cir·cles
2. draw a line around.
Circle the correct answer in your book. *v.*
3. to go around in a circle.
The bee circled the flower before flying away.
v. **circled, circled, circling** cir·cled, cir·cling

circus cir·cus (sėr′kəs) **1.** a traveling show usually performed in a tent with wild animals, clowns, acrobats and horses.
The children laughed at the bears and the clowns at the circus.
n. pl. **circuses** cir·cus·es
2. having to do with the circus.
The circus animals were in colorful cages. *adj.*

cinch

cities cit·ies (sit′ēz) *n. pl.* See **city** (1).

citizen cit·i·zen (sit′ə·zən) a person who is born in or chooses to live in a certain city, state or country.
The citizens had a meeting at the town hall. *n. pl.* **citizens** cit·i·zens

cinch ring

a	cat	**i**	sit	**oi**	oil	**ch**	chop	a in about
ā	ate	**ī**	lie	**ou**	out	**ng**	song	e in oven
ä	car	**o**	pot	**u**	cut	**sh**	she	ə = { i in pencil
e	set	**ō**	old	**u̇**	book	**th**	three	o in memory
ē	equal	**ô**	or	**ü**	blue	**TH**	there	u in circus
ėr	germ					**zh**	treasure	

city cit·y (sit′ē) **1.** a large town.
   The farmer brought vegetables into the city. *n. pl.* **cities** cit·ies
   2. describing something within a city.
   My family had a picnic at the city park. *adj.*

city hall cit·y hall (sit′ē   hôl) a city's government building.
   The mayor's office is in the city hall.

city-wide cit·y-wide (sit′ē-wīd) involving all of the city.
   Many students competed in the city-wide track meet. *adj.*

civil war civ·il war (siv′əl   wôr) **1.** war between groups of people
   in the same country.
   The countries in South America were fighting civil wars.
   2. Civil War; a war in the United States between the northern
   and southern states fought from 1861 to 1865.
   My great-grandfather fought in the Civil War.

clap

claim (klām) **1.** to say strongly that something is true.
   She claimed that her homework was finished.
   v. **claimed, claimed, claiming** claim·ing
   2. a right to something.
   The miners filed their claim for the gold mine. *n. pl.* **claims**

clang (klang) to make a sound like a large bell.
   The bell on the fire engine clanged as the truck raced through the streets.
   v. **clanged, clanged, clanging** clang·ing

clap (klap) to make a noise by hitting one's flat hands together.
   The children clapped at the end of the movie.
   v. **clapped, clapped, clapping** clap·ping

clarinet clar·i·net (klar·ə·net′) a musical instrument.
   Ben played his clarinet in the band. *n. pl.* **clarinets** clar·i·nets

clarinet

class (klas) **1.** group of students learning together.
   The class worked on a science project together. *n.*
   2. a subject that is studied.
   Ten students took the sign language class after school. *n.*
   3. a group of animals or plants that are alike in some way.
   Ants and beetles belong to the class of insects. *n. pl.* **classes** class·es
   4. having to do with a class.
   Everyone participated in the class discussion. *adj.*

classical clas·si·cal (klas′ə·kəl) music of the kind played in Europe
   about 200 years ago.
   There was a classical music concert Sunday night. *adj.*

classified advertisement clas·si·fied ad·ver·tise·ment (klas′ə·fīd
   ad′vər·tīz·mənt *or* klas′ə·fīd ad·vėr′tis·mənt) the section of
   a newspaper that lists job openings, services or sales.
   Dad put a classified advertisement in the newspaper to sell the car.

740 Ford
'75 FORD MAVERICK. Stk #7648.
4 Door, great work car. Only —
pure price — $712. 644-0694 Dlr

classified advertisement

claw

classmate   class•mate (klas´māt)   a student in the same class at school as another.
The little boy invited his classmate to his birthday party.
n. pl. **classmates** class•mates

classroom   class•room (klas´rüm)   place where a class meets.
We decorated our classroom for the Halloween party.
n. pl. **classrooms** class•rooms

claw   (klô)   **1.** a hard, sharp nail on the foot of a bird or animal.
The cat broke one claw when it fell. *n.*
2. a foot that has sharp nails.
The owl grabbed the mouse with its claw. *n. pl.* **claws**
3. to tear or scratch with claws or hands.
Mother was angry when the kitten clawed the curtains.
v. **clawed, clawed, clawing** claw•ing

clay   (klā)   **1.** soft, sticky kind of earth that can be shaped.
The potter made a bowl from clay. *n. no pl.*
2. having to do with something made of clay.
The children planted red flowers in the clay pots. *adj.*

clean   (klēn)   **1.** not dirty.
Jennifer put on a clean dress. *adj.* **cleaner, cleanest** clean•er, clean•est
2. to prepare for cooking.
I will clean the chicken before baking it. *v.*
3. to take off or remove dirt.
Susan will clean the kitchen. *v.* **cleaned, cleaned, cleaning** clean•ing

clay

cleaner   clean•er (klē´nər)   **1.** person whose job is to clean.
The window cleaner sometimes works on tall buildings. *n.*
2. anything used to remove dirt.
He had to use two cans of oven cleaner to get the oven clean.
n. pl. **cleaners** clean•ers

cleaning   clean•ing (klē´ning)   *v. pres. part.* See **clean** (2,3).

cleanliness   clean•li•ness (klen´lē•nis)   the act of being careful to keep things clean and neat.
Cleanliness is important for good health. *n. no pl.*

clean off   (klēn ôf)   to remove objects or dirt from the surface of something.
John cleaned off the table after dinner.
v. **cleaned off, cleaned off, cleaning off** clean•ing off

clean up   (klēn up)   to make neat.
In the spring, we clean up the yard.
v. **cleaned up, cleaned up, cleaning up** clean•ing up

a	cat	i	sit	oi	oil	ch	chop		a in about
ā	ate	ī	lie	ou	out	ng	song		e in oven
ä	car	o	pot	u	cut	sh	she	ə =	i in pencil
e	set	ō	old	u̇	book	th	three		o in memory
ē	equal	ô	or	ü	blue	ŦH	there		u in circus
ėr	germ					zh	treasure		

clear   (klir)   **1.** without color.

Most windows are made with clear glass. *adj.*

2. not raining or cloudy.

Everyone hoped it would be a clear day for the parade. *adj.*

3. easy to understand.

The teacher made the math assignment very clear. *adj.*

4. easy to see.

The sign was not clear because we were too far away. *adj.*

5. easy to hear.

We enjoyed listening to the clear voices of the children singing. *adj.*

6. transparent; easy to see through.

The Easter baskets were wrapped in clear yellow paper.

adj. **clearer, clearest** clear·er, clear·est

clear away   clear a·way (klir   ə·wā′)   to remove; to make a clear space.

After the storm, we had to clear away the branches from the driveway.

v. **cleared away, cleared away, clearing away** clear·ing a·way

clearly   clear·ly (klir′lē)   without difficulty; plainly.

We saw the mountain clearly in the distance. *adv.*

clear off   (klir   ôf)   to take things off the top of something.

Mary cleared off the table and put the dishes in the sink.

v. **cleared off, cleared off, clearing off** clear·ing off

clerk   (klėrk)   salesperson in a shop or store.

The clerk put the toys in a bag and gave Mother the change. *n. pl.* **clerks**

clerk

clever   clev·er (klev′ər)   skillful; smart.

The clever magician pulled a rabbit out of his hat. *adj.*

click   (klik)   **1.** a sudden, short sound.

We could hear the click of her high-heeled shoes as she walked down the hall. *n. pl.* **clicks**

2. to make a sudden, short sound.

Linda clicked the TV dial as she changed the station.

v. **clicked, clicked, clicking** click·ing

cliff   (klif)   a steep, high hill.

The boys climbed carefully down the cliff to the beach below. *n. pl.* **cliffs**

climate   cli·mate (klī′mit)   the kind of weather an area has.

Hawaii's climate is sunny and warm. *n. pl.* **climates** cli·mates

cliff

climb   (klīm)   **1.** to go up.

The monkey climbed the tree. *v.* **climbed, climbed, climbing** climb·ing

2. act of going up.

The climb up the mountainside was hard for the children. *n. pl.* **climbs**

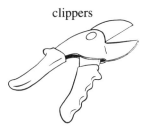

clippers

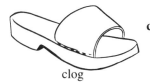

clog

closet

clinic clin·ic (klin‹ik) a place where a person can get medical help.
The doctor saw nine children with sore throats at the clinic today.
n. pl. **clinics** clin·ics

clippers clip·pers (klip‹ərs) cutting tool.
Dad cut the rosebush with his new clippers. *plural n.*

clock (klok) instrument for showing the time of the day.
The kitchen clock is five minutes slow. *n. pl.* **clocks**

clog (klog) a shoe with a heavy wooden sole.
Mary's feet were tired after wearing her new clogs all day. *n. pl.* **clogs**

clone (klōn) **1.** animal or plant produced from only one parent.
All the plants in the class science project were clones of the teacher's plant.
n. pl. **clones**
2. to produce an animal or plant from only one parent.
The frog that the scientist cloned was identical to the parent frog.
v. **cloned, cloned, cloning** clon·ing

close[1] (klōz) **1.** to shut.
Please close the door when you come into the house. *v.*
2. not to allow to use.
The police closed the road because the snow was too deep to drive through.
v. **closed, closed, closing** clos·ing

close[2] (klōs) **1.** near.
These chairs are too close. *adj.*
2. dear; special.
The women had been close friends for many years.
adj. **closer, closest** clos·er, clos·est

closed (klōzd) not open.
The closed door will not open without a key. *adj.*

closely close·ly (klōs‹lē) in a careful, alert way.
The children watch the instructor closely before trying to dive. *adv.*

closet clos·et (kloz‹it) a little room for storing clothing or household things.
All our winter jackets are in the hall closet. *n. pl.* **closets** clos·ets

closing clos·ing (klō‹zing) the end of a letter.
Always sign your name after the closing of a letter. *n. pl.* **closings** clos·ings

a	cat	i	sit	oi	oil	ch	chop		a in about
ā	ate	ī	lie	ou	out	ng	song		e in oven
ä	car	o	pot	u	cut	sh	she	ə =	i in pencil
e	set	ō	old	u̇	book	th	three		o in memory
ē	equal	ô	or	ü	blue	ŦH	there		u in circus
ėr	germ					zh	treasure		

cloth (klôth) **1.** fabric such as cotton or wool; material.
Shine the car with a soft cloth. *n. pl.* **cloths**
2. made of fabric.
The baby's favorite toy was the cloth bunny. *adj.*

clothesline

clothes (klōz) **1.** things to wear.
The boy fell down and got his clothes dirty. *plural n.*
2. having to do with clothes.
Hang your coat in the clothes closet. *adj.*

clothesline clothes·line (klōz′līn) wire or rope on which clothes are
hung to dry.
Mother hung the wet sheets on the clothesline to dry.
n. pl. **clotheslines** clothes·lines

clothes washer clothes wash·er (klōz wosh′ər) a machine for
cleaning clothes.
I took the towels out of the clothes washer and put them in the dryer.

cloud (kloud) a fluffy pile of water droplets floating in the air that
are white, gray or black in color.
The airplane flew through the clouds. *n. pl.* **clouds**

cloud

cloudy cloud·y (klou′dē) having clouds in the sky.
John wore a jacket at the beach because it was a cloudy day.
adj. **cloudier, cloudiest** cloud·i·er, cloud·i·est

clove (klōv) a strong-smelling spice made from a tropical plant.
The chef stuck cloves into the ham before baking it. *n. pl.* **cloves**

clown (kloun) a person who wears funny clothes, does funny things
and makes people laugh.
The circus clown wore a big red nose and funny clothes. *n. pl.* **clowns**

club (klub) **1.** a thick, heavy, wooden stick.
The cave man hit the bear with a club. *n.*
2. a group of people with the same interest who meet together.
The swim club meets at the pool after school. *n. pl.* **clubs**

clubhouse club·house (klub′hous) a building used by a club.
Dad and Jeff drank pop in the clubhouse after playing tennis.
n. pl. **clubhouses** club·hous·es

clown

clue (klü) a hint that helps one find an answer.
The policeman needed a clue to find the missing dog. *n. pl.* **clues**

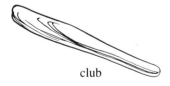

clumsy clum·sy (klum′zē) awkward; not graceful.
Mary felt very clumsy when she bumped the table and broke the
pretty bowl. *adj.* **clumsier, clumsiest** clum·si·er, clum·si·est

club

Clydesdale Clydes·dale (klīdz′dāl) a kind of strong workhorse.
Six Clydesdales pulled the heavy wagon. *n. pl.* **Clydesdales** Clydes·dales

coach

coach (kōch) **1.** a person who teaches or trains someone in sports, acting or singing.
The baseball coach showed the team how to bat. *n.*
2. a fancy carriage.
The king and queen rode to the castle in a beautiful coach. *n.*
3. a train car for passengers.
The train conductor walked from coach to coach as he collected tickets. *n. pl.* **coaches** coach·es
4. to teach or help a team play a game.
Eddy coached the high school basketball team.
v. **coached, coached, coaching** coach·ing

coal (kōl) **1.** black mineral used for burning.
The men shoveled coal into the furnace. *n.*
2. a small piece of burning wood or coal.
Joe burned himself when he touched a hot coal in the fireplace. *n. pl.* **coals**

coast (kōst) the land along the ocean shore.
The waves from the storm hit the coast. *n. pl.* **coasts**

coastal coast·al (kō′stl) at, along or near a coast.
Coastal towns have many visitors in the summer. *adj.*

coastline coast·line (kōst′līn) the place where water and land meet along the ocean.
The coastline in Maine is very rocky. *n. pl.* **coastlines** coast·lines

cobra

coat (kōt) **1.** warm outer clothing with sleeves.
You will be warmer if you button your coat. *n.*
2. animal covering; fur, skin or hair.
We brushed the dog's coat until it shined. *n. pl.* **coats**
3. having to do with a coat.
Kevin put a nickel in his coat pocket. *adj.*

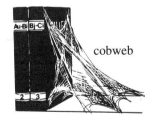

cobweb

cobra co·bra (kō′brə) a kind of large poisonous snake.
The cobra flattens its head and neck when it is angry. *n. pl.* **cobras** co·bras

cobweb cob·web (kob′web) a spider web.
There were cobwebs in the corners of the old house.
n. pl. **cobwebs** cob·webs

a	cat	**i**	sit	**oi**	oil	**ch**	chop		a in about
ā	ate	**ī**	lie	**ou**	out	**ng**	song		e in oven
ä	car	**o**	pot	**u**	cut	**sh**	she	ə =	i in pencil
e	set	**ō**	old	**u̇**	book	**th**	three		o in memory
ē	equal	**ô**	or	**ü**	blue	**ŦH**	there		u in circus
ėr	germ					**zh**	treasure		

cockroach cock·roach (kok⸍rōch) a kind of insect often found in dark, damp places.
> Cockroaches are usually seen at night. *n. pl.* **cockroaches** cock·roach·es

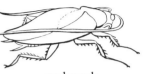
cockroach

cocoa co·coa (kō⸍kō) **1.** a powder tasting like chocolate.
> The brownie recipe called for 1 cup of cocoa. *n. no pl.*
> **2.** a drink made with cocoa, sugar and milk.
> We love to drink hot cocoa on a cold day. *n. no pl.*

coconut co·co·nut (kō⸍kə·nut *or* kō⸍kə·nət) a tropical fruit that grows on palm trees.
> The coconut has a very hard shell. *n. pl.* **coconuts** co·co·nuts

codfish cod·fish (kod⸍fish) a fish that lives in cold parts of the ocean.
> My father's fishing boat catches codfish.
> *n. pl.* **codfishes** *or* **codfish** cod·fish·es *or* cod·fish

coconut

coffee cof·fee (kô⸍fē *or* kof⸍ē) **1.** a brown drink made from the beans of a coffee plant.
> Betty served coffee with the cake. *n. no pl.*
> **2.** roasted seeds of the coffee plant.
> The clerk in the shop measured one pound of coffee. *n. no pl.*
> **3.** having to do with coffee.
> Mother kept the old coffee pot in the camper. *adj.*

coin (koin) **1.** a piece of money made from metal.
> I put a coin in the pay telephone. *n. pl.* **coins**
> **2.** having to do with coins.
> Mary saved pennies, nickels, dimes and quarters in her coin bank. *adj.*
> **3.** to make up a new word or phrase.
> J. R. R. Tolkien coined the word "hobbit" to name the creatures in his book. *v.* **coined, coined, coining** coin·ing

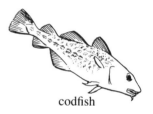
codfish

coining coin·ing (koi⸍ning) *v. pres. part.* See **coin** (3).

cold (kōld) **1.** not hot.
> It was very cold at the top of the mountain.
> *adj.* **colder, coldest** cold·er, cold·est
> **2.** an illness that often causes a runny nose and a sore throat.
> It is wise to stay in bed when you have a cold. *n. pl.* **colds**
> **3.** weather that has low or freezing temperatures.
> The children came in out of the cold and warmed their hands by the fire.
> *n. no pl.*

cold-blooded cold-blood·ed (kōld-blud⸍id) having blood at the temperature of the surrounding air or water.
> Snakes and turtles are cold-blooded animals. *adj.*

coins

collect   col·lect (kə·lekt′)   to gather together.
The Boy Scouts collected newspapers for the paper drive.
v. **collected, collected, collecting** col·lect·ed, col·lect·ing

collecting   col·lect·ing (kə·lek′ting)   *v. pres. part.* See **collect.**

collection   col·lec·tion (kə·lek′shən)   a group of gathered items.
Billy took his rock collection to school. *n. pl.* **collections** col·lec·tions

collector   col·lec·tor (kə·lek′tər)   a person who collects things.
A coin collector always looks for rare coins. *n. pl.* **collectors** col·lec·tors

coin collection

college   col·lege (kol′ij)   **1.** a school for learning more after high school.
John plans to attend college to earn a degree in business.
n. pl. **colleges** col·leg·es
2. having to do with a college.
Jason bought three books at the college bookstore. *adj.*

colonist   col·o·nist (kol′ə·nist)   a person who helps to start or who lives in a colony.
The American colonists lived in log cabins and used candles for light.
n. pl. **colonists** col·o·nists

colony   col·o·ny (kol′ə·nē)   a settlement made by a group of people from another country.
The British started thirteen colonies when they came to North America.
n. pl. **colonies** col·o·nies

color   col·or (kul′ər)   **1.** shades of red, yellow or blue, or any combination of these.
Jeff painted all the colors of the rainbow on his paper. *n. pl.* **colors** col·ors
2. to give something color.
Michelle colored the picture in the book.
v. **colored, colored, coloring** col·ored, col·or·ing

colored   col·ored (kul′ərd)   having color.
The teacher used colored chalk on the chalkboard. *adj.*

a	cat	i	sit	oi	oil	ch	chop		a in about
ā	ate	ī	lie	ou	out	ng	song		e in oven
ä	car	o	pot	u	cut	sh	she	ə =	i in pencil
e	set	ō	old	u̇	book	th	three		o in memory
ē	equal	ô	or	ü	blue	ŦH	there		u in circus
ėr	germ					zh	treasure		

colorful col·or·ful (kul′ər·fəl) having many bright colors.
  The sky was full of colorful kites. *adj.*

color guard col·or guard (kul′ər gärd) a group that
  carries the flag in a ceremony.
  The color guard carried the flags into the room.

coloring col·or·ing (kul′ə·ring) **1.** something added to food
  to give it color.
  Mother put five drops of red food coloring into the frosting.
  n. pl. **colorings** col·or·ings
  2. *v. pres. part.* See **color** (2).

colorless col·or·less (kul′ər·lis) clear; having no color.
  The air around us is a colorless gas. *adj.*

colors col·ors (kul′ərs) the flag of a country.
  The Girl Scouts carried the colors at the beginning of the game. *plural n.*

Christopher Columbus

Columbus, Christopher Co·lum·bus, Chris·to·pher (kə·lum′bəs,
  kris′tə·fər) an explorer who sailed to America in 1492.
  Columbus was surprised when he found America.

column col·umn (kol′əm) **1.** a pillar, usually made of wood,
  stone or metal.
  Many old buildings in Greece have beautiful stone columns. *n.*
  2. slender and upright in shape.
  We saw a column of smoke rising from the factory's smokestack. *n.*
  3. lines or blank spaces that divide a page from top to bottom.
  The coach listed his players' names in two columns.
  n. pl. **columns** col·umns

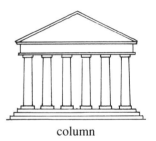

column

comb (kōm) **1.** an object made of metal or plastic that has teeth and
  is used to arrange or fix hair.
  My sister used the blue comb to fix my hair. *n. pl.* **combs**
  2. to straighten or smooth out hair or fiber.
  John combed his hair neatly before school.
  v. **combed, combed, combing** comb·ing

combination com·bi·na·tion (kom·bə·nā′shən) the joining of two
  or more things.
  A combination of lettuce, radishes, celery and tomatoes makes a good
  salad. *n. pl.* **combinations** com·bi·na·tions

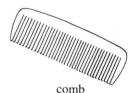

comb

combine[1] com·bine (kəm·bīn′) to join together.
The art teacher combined blue and yellow paint to make green.
v. **combined, combined, combining** com·bined, com·bin·ing

combine[2] com·bine (kom′bīn) a farm machine that cuts and separates grains and other crops.
The farmer used the combine to harvest his crops.
n. pl. **combines** com·bines

combine

come (kum) **1.** to go toward.
Please come here. *v.*
2. to take place; happen.
Christmas comes in December. *v.*
3. to arrive; reach.
The school bus comes every day at 3:00. *v.*
4. become.
The hinges on the door come loose often, but Sue can fix them.
v. **came, come, coming** com·ing

come and get it (kum ənd get it) a call to eat a meal.
The cook yelled to the ranchers, "Come and get it."

comedy com·e·dy (kom′ə·dē) an amusing or funny movie or play.
We chose to see the movie because it was a comedy.
n. pl. **comedies** com·e·dies

come from (kum from *or* kum frum) to start; to begin.
Where does paper come from?
v. **came from, come from, coming from** com·ing from

come in (kum in) **1.** to enter.
Linda invited her friends to come in and play.
v. **came in, come in, coming in** com·ing in
2. to make contact by radio.
The captain on the ship called the Coast Guard saying, "This is Captain Jones. Come in, please." *idiom*

come in handy come in hand·y (kum in han′dē) to be useful.
A towel will come in handy after we swim. *idiom*

come on (kum ôn) **1.** to begin to do something.
The clock radio will come on at 7 o'clock.
v. **came on, come on, coming on** com·ing on
2. to urge someone to hurry; to advise or warn someone to do something.

a	cat	**i**	sit	**oi**	oil	**ch**	chop
ā	ate	**ī**	lie	**ou**	out	**ng**	song
ä	car	**o**	pot	**u**	cut	**sh**	she
e	set	**ō**	old	**u̇**	book	**th**	three
ē	equal	**ô**	or	**ü**	blue	**TH**	there
ėr	germ					**zh**	treasure

ə = {
a in about
e in oven
i in pencil
o in memory
u in circus

come out (kum out) to release or let loose; to exit.
The baby chick came out of the egg.
v. **came out, come out, coming out** com·ing out

come over come o·ver (kum ō·'vər) **1.** to visit.
Aunt Jane will come over for dinner tonight. *v.*
2. to approach or come near.
Mike wants to come over to Janet and ask her to dance. *v.* **came over, come over, coming over** came o·ver, come o·ver, com·ing o·ver

come true (kum trü) to become real.
Sometimes dreams come true.
v. **came true, come true, coming true** com·ing true

come up (kum up) to approach or move towards.
Please come up to the chalkboard and write your name.
v. **came up, come up, coming up** com·ing up

comfort com·fort (kum·'fərt) **1.** any person or thing that brings about good feelings or makes life easier.
The beach cabin had all the comforts of home. *n.*
2. freedom from pain or hard work.
He has a lot of money and lives in comfort.
n. pl. **comforts** com·forts

comfortable com·fort·a·ble (kum·'fər·tə·bəl) **1.** good; adequate; making life easier.
Dad makes a comfortable income at his job. *adj.*
2. feeling good.
I feel comfortable when I'm with my friends. *adj.*

coming com·ing (kum·'ing) *v. pres. part.* See **come.**

command com·mand (kə·mand') **1.** an order.
Not one of the soldiers questioned their leader's command.
n. pl. **commands** com·mands
2. to give orders.
The police chief commanded the officers to surround the building.
v. **commanded, commanded, commanding** com·mand·ed, com·mand·ing

commander com·mand·er (kə·man·'dər) a person who leads; a person who gives orders; a chief or boss.
The commander of the ship gave the order to drop anchor.
n. pl. **commanders** com·mand·ers

commander

commercial com·mer·cial (kə·mėr·'shəl) **1.** an advertisement on radio or TV.
During the TV commercial, Mom made popcorn.
n. pl. **commercials** com·mer·cials
2. being from or paid for by a company.
The commercial radio program has many advertisements. *adj.*

committee

committee com·mit·tee (kə·mit‹ē) a group of persons who work together on special projects.
The fund-raising committee meets every Friday afternoon.
n. pl. **committees** com·mit·tees

common com·mon (kom‹ən) **1.** not pretty; plain.
The dress was not fancy, but common. *adj.*
2. happens often.
It is common for Dad to drive Susan to school. *adj.*
3. usual; natural.
Mountains are common in the Northwest. *adj.*

communicate com·mu·ni·cate (kə·myü‹nə·kāt) to share ideas or thoughts by speaking or writing.
My pen pal and I communicate by letter. *v.* **communicated, communicated, communicating** com·mu·ni·cat·ed, com·mu·ni·cat·ing

communication com·mu·ni·ca·tion (kə·myü·nə·kā‹shən) **1.** a sharing of information between living things.
Scientists study the communication of animals. *n.*
2. information shared.
The President and Vice-President of the United States must have close communication. *n. pl.* **communications** com·mu·ni·ca·tions

community com·mu·ni·ty (kə·myü‹nə·tē) **1.** people living in the same area.
The mayor spoke to the community at the town meeting.
n. pl. **communities** com·mu·ni·ties
2. having to do with a group of people living in the same area.
The community fair will take place in July. *adj.*

company com·pa·ny (kum‹pə·nē) all the people involved in the running of a business or a factory; a group of people that run a business, make a product or do an activity.
Spalding is the company that made my baseball.
n. pl. **companies** com·pa·nies

compare com·pare (kəm·per′ *or* kem·par′) to find or point out what is the same or different between persons, places or things.
Mother compared prices while shopping.
v. **compared, compared, comparing** com·pared, com·par·ing

comparison com·par·i·son (kəm·par‹ə·sən) the act of finding out likenesses and differences.
We studied the comparison of man and ape in science class.
n. pl. **comparisons** com·par·i·sons

a	cat	i	sit	oi	oil	ch	chop		a in about
ā	ate	ī	lie	ou	out	ng	song		e in oven
ä	car	o	pot	u	cut	sh	she	ə =	i in pencil
e	set	ō	old	u̇	book	th	three		o in memory
ē	equal	ô	or	ü	blue	ŦH	there		u in circus
ėr	germ					zh	treasure		

compete com·pete (kəm·pēt′) to try hard to win; to take part in a contest.
> John will compete against four other runners in the race. *v.* **competed, competed, competing** com·pet·ed, com·pet·ing

competition com·pe·ti·tion (kom·pə·tish′ən) a race or contest.
> David won second place in the swimming competition.
> *n. pl.* **competitions** com·pe·ti·tions

competitor com·pet·i·tor (kəm·pet′ə·tər) a person who takes part in a contest.
> There were twelve competitors in the race.
> *n. pl.* **competitors** com·pet·i·tors

complain com·plain (kəm·plān′) to say that something is wrong.
> The students complained that the gym was too hot. *v.* **complained, complained, complaining** com·plained, com·plain·ing

complaint com·plaint (kəm·plānt′) the words used to express one's dislike for something; the words used to say that something is wrong.
> The cook got a complaint about his chili. *n. pl.* **complaints** com·plaints

complete com·plete (kəm·plēt′) done; finished; needing no more work.
> We will finish the work today, and the fence will be complete. *adj.*

completely com·plete·ly (kəm·plēt′lē) entirely; fully.
> The milk jug was completely empty. *adv.*

complex com·plex (kəm·pleks′) difficult; hard to understand.
> The instructions for knitting the sweater were very complex. *adj.*

composer com·pos·er (kəm·pō′zər) a person who writes music.
> Mozart was a famous child composer. *n. pl.* **composers** com·pos·ers

compromise com·pro·mise (kom′prə·mīz) to reach a decision by each side agreeing to give up part of what it wants.
> While planning the party, the students compromised on the menu.
> *v.* **compromised, compromised, compromising** com·pro·mised, com·pro·mis·ing

composer (Mozart)

concentrate con·cen·trate (kon′sən·trāt) to pay close attention.
> The students concentrated on their math facts. *v.* **concentrated, concentrated, concentrating** con·cen·trat·ed, con·cen·trat·ing

concentration con·cen·tra·tion (kon·sən·trā′shən) the act of thinking hard; close attention.
> The computer game required much concentration.
> *n. pl.* **concentration**

concerned con·cerned (kən·sėrnd′) full of worry; anxious; worried.
> I was concerned about my sick dog. *adj.*

condenser con·dens·er (kən·den′sər) the part of a car that changes gas or vapor to a liquid.
The mechanic repaired the condenser on the car.
n. pl. **condensers** con·dens·ers

condition con·di·tion (kən·dish′ən) the way a person or thing is.
The condition of the old car was excellent.
n. pl. **conditions** con·di·tions

cone (kōn) **1.** an object that has a flat, round base and comes to a point at the top.
The math problem asked which cone was the largest. *n.*
2. anything shaped like a cone.
You can buy ice cream in a dish or in a cone. *n.*
3. the part of an evergreen tree that holds the seeds.
We started the campfire with dry pine cones. *n. pl.* **cones**

cones

cone-shaped (kōn-shāpt) having the shape of a cone.
The witch's cone-shaped hat was black. *adj.*

confident con·fi·dent (kon′fə·dənt) feeling sure about oneself or one's abilities.
The soccer team felt confident that their team would win. *adj.*

confuse con·fuse (kən·fyüz′) to make unsure.
All the different road signs can confuse strangers.
v. **confused, confused, confusing** con·fused, con·fus·ing

confused con·fused (kən·fyüzd′) uncertain; not sure.
The confused boy asked the policeman for help. *adj.*

confusing con·fus·ing (kən·fyü′zing) making a person feel uneasy and embarrassed or uncertain.
Entering college can be an exciting but confusing experience. *adj.*

Congo River Con·go Ri·ver (kong′gō riv′ər) a river in Central Africa.
People in Africa travel on the Congo River.

congratulate con·grat·u·late (kən·grach′ə·lāt) to wish a person happiness and good luck in the future; to praise a person for an honor or an award.
We will congratulate the bride and groom after the wedding.
v. **congratulated, congratulated, congratulating** con·grat·u·lat·ed, con·grat·u·lat·ing

a	cat	i	sit	oi	oil	ch	chop		a in about
ā	ate	ī	lie	ou	out	ng	song		e in oven
ä	car	o	pot	u	cut	sh	she	ə =	i in pencil
e	set	ō	old	u̇	book	th	three		o in memory
ē	equal	ô	or	ü	blue	ŦH	there		u in circus
ėr	germ					zh	treasure		

congratulations con·grat·u·la·tions (kən·grach·ə·lā′shənz) the expression of pleasure or happiness at another person's joy or good fortune.
Please accept my congratulations on your new job! *plural n.*

Congress Con·gress (kong′gris) the national lawmaking unit of the United States, which includes the House of Representatives and the Senate.
Congress passed many laws this year. *n. no pl.*

congressman con·gress·man (kong′gris·mən) an elected member of the House of Representatives.
Each area elects a congressman to go to Washington, D.C.
n. pl. **congressmen** con·gress·men

congressman

connect con·nect (kə·nekt′) **1.** to attach.
Billy will connect the leash to the dog's collar. *v.*
2. to join things together.
The boys will connect the caboose to the end of the toy train. *v.* **connected, connected, connecting** con·nect·ed, con·nect·ing

conquer con·quer (kong′kər) to overcome by force or in war.
The Roman Empire conquered its enemies.
v. **conquered, conquered, conquering** con·quered, con·quer·ing

conservation con·ser·va·tion (kon·sər·vā′shən) **1.** protection from loss or harm.
Conservation of electricity is important to our country. *n. no pl.*
2. having to do with protection from loss or harm.
The conservation report was given by the forest ranger. *adj.*

conserve con·serve (kən·sėrv′) to preserve or keep from loss or being used up.
We conserve our water when we are in the desert.
v. **conserved, conserved, conserving** con·served, con·serv·ing

consider con·sid·er (kən·sid′ər) **1.** to think.
Many people consider all snakes to be poisonous. *v.*
2. to think about something before making a choice.
Jane should consider her future before taking a new job.
v. **considered, considered, considering** con·sid·ered, con·sid·er·ing

constant con·stant (kon′stənt) always happening; never stopping.
The constant flow of the water made the river rocks smooth. *adj.*

constantly con·stant·ly (kon′stənt·lē) at all times; without stopping.
The lawn is constantly growing and always needs mowing. *adv.*

The Constitution

constitution con·sti·tu·tion (kon·stə·tǘ·shən *or* kon·stə·tyǘ·shən)
1. the basic beliefs that guide the leaders of a country, state or society.
The school student council developed its constitution.
n. pl. **constitutions** con·sti·tu·tions
2. the Constitution; the written beliefs that guide the United States government.
The Constitution was written in 1787. *n.*

construct con·struct (kən·strukt́) to build.
My brother will construct a new house. *v.* **constructed, constructed, constructing** con·struct·ed, con·struct·ing

construction con·struc·tion (kən·struḱ·shən) **1.** the building of things.
The construction of the new school building was behind schedule.
n. pl. **constructions** con·struc·tions
2. having to do with building.
The construction workers wore yellow hard hats when working. *adj.*

contact con·tact (koń·takt) seeing and talking with someone; spending time together.
My contact with my grandmother gives me an opportunity to learn about the past. *n. pl.* **contacts** con·tacts

contain con·tain (kən·tāń) to include; to have inside it; to have as a part of itself.
The Halloween bag contained all of their treats.
v. **contained, contained, containing** con·tained, con·tain·ing

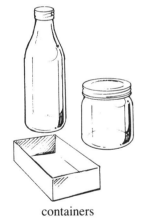

containers

container con·tain·er (kən·tā́·nər) anything like a can, jar or bottle that a person can put things into.
The farmer filled the containers with fresh milk.
n. pl. **containers** con·tain·ers

content con·tent (kən·tent́) happy; satisfied; needs no more.
On a cold day, the children are content to play inside. *adj.*

contentedly con·tent·ed·ly (kən·teń·tid·lē) in a satisfied way.
The dog slept contentedly after eating. *adv.*

contest con·test (koń·test) a comparing of skills to see who will win or who is the best; a competition.
Billy entered the pie-eating contest at the fair.
n. pl. **contests** con·tests

a	cat	i	sit	oi	oil	ch	chop		a in about
ā	ate	ī	lie	ou	out	ng	song		e in oven
ä	car	o	pot	u	cut	sh	she	ə =	i in pencil
e	set	ō	old	u̇	book	th	three		o in memory
ē	equal	ô	or	ü	blue	ṮH	there		u in circus
ėr	germ					zh	treasure		

contestant con·test·ant (kən·tes′tənt) a person who enters a contest.
The contestants for the 50-yard dash were at the starting line.
n. pl. **contestants** con·test·ants

continent con·ti·nent (kon′tə·nənt) one of the seven large land
areas on the Earth.
The United States is on the continent of North America.
n. pl. **continents** con·ti·nents

continue con·tin·ue (kən·tin′yü) to go on doing something
after stopping.
Dad will continue reading the story tomorrow night.
v. **continued, continued, continuing** con·tin·ued, con·tin·u·ing

continuous con·tin·u·ous (kən·tin′yü·əs) not ending; unbroken.
One week of continuous rain flooded the river. *adj.*

control con·trol (kən·trōl′) **1.** to direct or have power
over something.
The engineer must control the train. *v.*
2. to manage or handle.
The trainer can control the dogs.
v. **controlled, controlled, controlling** con·trolled, con·trol·ling

conversation con·ver·sa·tion (kon·vər·sā′shən) a friendly
talk or discussion.
Annie had a nice conversation with Aunt Meg.
n. pl. **conversations** con·ver·sa·tions

conveyor *or* **conveyer** con·vey·or *or* con·vey·er (kən·vā′ər)
something or someone that carries people, things
or information.
The mailman was the conveyor of good news. *n. pl.* **conveyors** *or*
conveyers con·vey·ors *or* con·vey·ers

conveyor belt con·vey·or belt (kən·vā′ər belt) long, wide moving
band that carries things from one place to another.
The conveyor belt moved the cans from the labeler to the box.

cook

convince con·vince (kən·vins′) to make a person agree or believe.
Jack convinced his father to keep the puppy.
v. **convinced, convinced, convincing** con·vinced, con·vinc·ing

cook (kůk) **1.** to prepare food to eat by heating.
Mom will cook hot dogs for lunch. *v.* **cooked, cooked, cooking** cook·ing
2. person who cooks food.
The cook fixed a big dinner for the men. *n. pl.* **cooks**

cookbook cook·book (kůk′bůk) a book of recipes and directions
for making different foods.
Joe used his new cookbook to make bread. *n. pl.* **cookbooks** cook·books

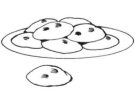
cookies

cop

coral

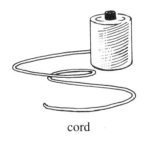

cord

core

cookie cook·ie (kụk′ē) **1.** small, sweet, flat dessert.
The cookies smelled good. *n. pl.* **cookies** cook·ies
2. describing something made with cookies.
The class made cookie flowers for their mothers. *adj.*

cooking cook·ing (kụk′ing) **1.** food that someone prepares for eating.
I love my mother's cooking. *n. no pl.*
2. having to do with preparing food.
Put on the cooking apron before mixing the batter. *adj.*

cool (kül) **1.** between warm and cold.
The cool breeze felt good after a hot day.
adj. **cooler, coolest** cool·er, cool·est
2. to make less hot.
Cool the soup before you eat it.
v. **cooled, cooled, cooling** cool·ing

cop (kop) police officer.
The cop stopped the car for speeding. *n. pl.* **cops**

Copenhagen Co·pen·ha·gen (kō·pən·hā′gən) capital city of Denmark.
The harbor in Copenhagen is busy. *n.*

Copernicus Co·per·ni·cus (kə·pėr′nə·kəs) a famous Polish astronomer who showed that the Earth revolves around the sun.
Copernicus enjoyed watching the stars at night.

copper cop·per (kop′ər) **1.** a soft, reddish metal.
Many electrical wires are made of copper. *n. no pl.*
2. being made of copper.
The water heated quickly in the copper kettle. *adj.*

coral co·ral (kôr′əl) **1.** small, colorful ocean animal.
We saw some coral in the ocean. *n. no pl.*
2. hard skeletons of coral, often used in jewelry.
The pink coral was made into a beautiful necklace. *n. no pl.*
3. having to do with something made of coral.
The ship sank when it hit the sharp coral reef. *adj.*

cord (kôrd) a thin, light rope.
The store clerk used a strong cord to tie up the box. *n. pl.* **cords**

core (kôr) the center part of fruit, containing the seeds.
When you are finished eating the pear, please put the core in the garbage.
n. pl. **cores**

a	cat	**i**	sit	**oi**	oil	**ch**	chop	
ā	ate	**ī**	lie	**ou**	out	**ng**	song	a in about
ä	car	**o**	pot	**u**	cut	**sh**	she	e in oven
e	set	**ō**	old	**ụ**	book	**th**	three	ə = i in pencil
ē	equal	**ô**	or	**ü**	blue	**TH**	there	o in memory
ėr	germ					**zh**	treasure	u in circus

corn (kôrn) **1.** a kind of cereal plant that grows on large ears.
We grow corn in our garden. *no pl.*
2. small, hard seed.
The corn was ground into cereal. *n. pl.* **corns**
3. having to do with or made from corn.
We ate corn chips during the game. *adj.*

corn

cornbread (kôrn⸍bred) bread made from corn meal.
Cornbread and chili make a great meal. *n. no pl.*

corner cor·ner (kôr⸍nər) **1.** the place where two streets meet.
The policeman stood on the corner to direct traffic. *n.*
2. a place where two surfaces meet.
The dog slept in the corner of the room. *n. pl.* **corners** cor·ners

corn syrup corn syr·up (kôrn sir⸍əp *or* kôrn sėr⸍əp) sweet, thick liquid made from corn.
The children made popcorn balls by pouring corn syrup over the warm popcorn.

corral cor·ral (kə·ral′) a fenced area for large animals.
The horses ran around inside the corral. *n. pl.* **corrals** cor·rals

correct cor·rect (kə·rekt′) **1.** right; without mistakes.
Mother showed Johnny the correct way to make a bed. *adj.*
2. to mark errors; to make right.
The teacher corrected the math papers during recess.
v. **corrected, corrected, correcting** cor·rect·ed, cor·rect·ing

correctly cor·rect·ly (kə·rekt′lē) in the right way.
If you ride your bicycle correctly, you will not get hurt. *adv.*

corsage cor·sage (kôr·säzh′) flowers worn on a dress.
All the girls wore beautiful corsages to the dance. *n. pl.* **corsages** cor·sag·es

corsage

cost (kôst) **1.** to be bought at the price of.
The doll cost $8.00. *v.* **cost, cost, costing** cost·ing
2. the amount of money needed to buy something.
The cost of the coat was too high. *n. pl.* **costs**

costume cos·tume (kos⸍tüm *or* kos⸍tyüm) **1.** clothes worn in a play or performance or at a party.
The ballet dancer had to change her costume quickly between dances.
n. pl. **costumes** cos·tumes
2. having to do with a costume.
We went to a costume party at Halloween. *adj.*

cottage cot·tage (kot⸍ij) a small house.
The three bears lived in a cottage in the woods. *n. pl.* **cottages** cot·tag·es

cottage

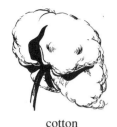

cotton

cotton cot·ton (kot′n) **1.** a tall plant that has white, fluffy fibers around its seeds; the fibers from this plant.
Cotton grows on large farms in the South. *n. no pl.*
2. a type of fabric.
The blouse was made of cotton. *n. no pl.*
3. describing something having to do with or made of cotton.
The cotton balls were very soft. *adj.*

couch (kouch) a long piece of furniture used for sitting or resting; a sofa.
Dad stretched out and took a nap on the couch. *n. pl.* **couches** couch·es

couch

cough (kôf) **1.** to force air from the lungs through the mouth suddenly and loudly.
Mother knew the baby was sick when he coughed all night.
v. **coughed, coughed, coughing** cough·ing
2. a loud, sudden noise coming from the mouth.
Pete had a bad cough with his cold. *n. pl.* **coughs**

cough out (kôf out) force something out of the throat by coughing.
The cat coughed out the fur ball.
v. **coughed out, coughed out, coughing out** cough·ing out

could (kůd) *aux. pt. t.* See **can** (1).

count (kount) **1.** to find how many.
The man at the gate counted the people as they entered the ball park. *v.*
2. to say numbers in order.
The teacher and the children counted from one to twenty.
v. **counted, counted, counting** count·ed, count·ing

countdown count·down (kount′doun) the calling out of the time before launch of a missile or rocket.
Stormy weather delayed the rocket countdown.
n. pl. **countdowns** count·downs

counter

counter coun·ter (koun′tər) a long board or table in a store, bank, restaurant or kitchen.
Service is faster when you sit at the counter in a restaurant.
n. pl. **counters** coun·ters

countless count·less (kount′lis) too many to count.
The author worked countless hours writing his first book. *adj.*

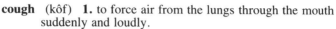

a	cat	**i**	sit	**oi**	oil	**ch**	chop		a in about
ā	ate	**ī**	lie	**ou**	out	**ng**	song		e in oven
ä	car	**o**	pot	**u**	cut	**sh**	she	ə = { i in pencil
e	set	**ō**	old	**ů**	book	**th**	three		o in memory
ē	equal	**ô**	or	**ü**	blue	**ŦH**	there		u in circus
ėr	germ					**zh**	treasure		

country coun·try (kun⸍trē) **1.** land or area of a nation.
The United States is a very large country. *n. pl.* **countries** coun·tries
2. rural land; the area not in cities or towns.
On Sunday afternoon, the family went for a drive in the country. *n. no pl.*
3. having to do with rural areas.
Country life is slower than city life. *adj.*

country gentleman coun·try gen·tle·man (kun⸍trē jen⸍tl·mən)
a rich man in a rural area.
The country gentleman went horseback riding before breakfast.

countryside coun·try·side (kun⸍trē·sīd) a rural area; land outside
of cities or towns.
The countryside was beautiful in the fall. *n. no pl.*

couple cou·ple (kup⸍əl) **1.** a pair; two things.
Grandmother brought us a couple of spoons so we could eat the ice cream.
n. no pl.
2. husband and wife.
Mr. and Mrs. Jones are the new couple who bought the house next door. *n.*
3. two people paired together.
When the music ended, the couples left the dance floor.
n. pl. **couples** coup·les

coupler cou·pler (kup⸍lər) a device that joins two objects together.
Because the coupler was broken, the old TTY did not work.
n. pl. **couplers** cou·plers

courage cour·age (kėr⸍ij) bravery; the ability to face danger.
It took great courage to climb Mt. Everest. *n. no pl.*

court (kôrt) **1.** an area marked off for a game.
We had to wait for our turn on the tennis court. *n.*
2. a place where people receive judgments or answers to
questions about the law.
The judge asked for quiet in the court. *n. pl.* **courts**

courteous cour·te·ous (kėr⸍tē·əs) polite; considerate.
The waitress was courteous to the guests in the restaurant. *adj.*

courthouse court·house (kôrt⸍hous) the building that houses the
city or county government; the building in which
trials take place.
The judge works in the courthouse. *n. pl.* **courthouses** court·hous·es

courthouse

courtyard court·yard (kôrt⸍yärd) an area with walls around it that
is next to or surrounded by a building.
There was a beautiful fountain in the palace courtyard.
n. pl. **courtyards** court·yards

courtyard

cousin cous·in (kuz⸍n) child of one's uncle or aunt.
At the family picnic the children played with their cousins.
n. pl. **cousins** cous·ins

coverall

cover cov·er (kuv′ər) **1.** to spread over a surface.
After the storm, leaves covered the lawn. *v.*
2. to put something over a person or thing.
Mother will cover the cake with thick chocolate frosting.
v. **covered, covered, covering** cov·ered, cov·er·ing
3. anything that covers.
Jack put the cover on the coffee pot. *n. pl.* **covers** cov·ers

coveralls cov·er·alls (kuv′ər·ôls) a piece of clothing worn to protect other clothes while working.
The mechanic spilled grease on his coveralls. *plural n.*

covered cov·ered (kuv′ərd) *v. pt. t., pt. part.* See **cover** (1, 2).

covering cov·er·ing (kuv′ə·ring) something that covers.
Make sure you put coverings over the sofa and chairs before painting the living room. *n. pl.* **coverings** cov·er·ings

cow (kou) the full-grown female of cattle.
The farmer milked the cow. *n. pl.* **cows**

coward cow·ard (kou′ərd) a person who is afraid.
When Ed refused to fight, the bullies called him a coward.
n. pl. **cowards** cow·ards

cowardly cow·ard·ly (kou′ərd·lē) **1.** in a frightened way.
The children acted cowardly in the haunted house. *adv.*
2. timid.
The cowardly lion was afraid of the mouse. *adj.*

cowbell cow·bell (kou′bel) the bell around the neck of a cow, which makes a noise that helps to find where the cow is.
Listening to the cowbell, Jack found the lost cow. *n. pl.* **cowbells** cow·bells

cow

cowboy cow·boy (kou′boi) **1.** a man or boy who works with cattle on a ranch.
The cowboys herded the cattle into the corral.
n. pl. **cowboys** cow·boys
2. having to do with a cowboy.
Max bought a new cowboy hat. *adj.*

cowgirl cow·girl (kou′gėrl) **1.** a woman or girl who works with cattle on a ranch.
The cowgirl roped the calf. *n. pl.* **cowgirls** cow·girls
2. having to do with a cowgirl.
Betsy wore a cowgirl suit for Halloween. *adj.*

a	cat	**i**	sit	**oi**	oil	**ch**	chop		a in about
ā	ate	**ī**	lie	**ou**	out	**ng**	song		e in oven
ä	car	**o**	pot	**u**	cut	**sh**	she	ə =	i in pencil
e	set	**ō**	old	** u̇**	book	**th**	three		o in memory
ē	equal	**ô**	or	**ü**	blue	**TH**	there		u in circus
ėr	germ					**zh**	treasure		

coyote coy·o·te (kī·ō′tē *or* kī′ōt) small wolf-like animal.
　　The coyote howled at the full moon.
　　n. pl. **coyotes** *or* **coyote** coy·o·tes *or* coy·o·te

cozy co·zy (kō′zē) warm and comfortable.
　　The cat curled up by the cozy fire.
　　adj. **cozier, coziest** co·zi·er, co·zi·est

crab (krab) a sea animal with a hard shell and pinchers.
　　We ate crab for dinner at the beach. *n. pl.* **crabs**

crabby crab·by (krab′ē) irritable or grouchy.
　　The little boy was crabby because he needed a nap.
　　adj. **crabbier, crabbiest** crab·bi·er, crab·bi·est

crack (krak) **1.** tiny break.
　　There was a crack in the old plate. *n. pl.* **cracks**
　　2. to break.
　　The candy cane cracked when Bill dropped it. *v.*
　　3. to break open.
　　Father and the children will crack the nuts.
　　v. **cracked, cracked, cracking** crack·ing

cracker crack·er (krak′ər) crisp baked dough in a
　　small thin shape, for eating.
　　There was a plate of cheese and crackers at the party.
　　n. pl. **crackers** crack·ers

cradle cra·dle (krā′dl) a small baby bed that rocks.
　　Mother rocked the baby to sleep in the cradle.
　　n. pl. **cradles** cra·dles

craft (kraft) **1.** a skill to make something.
　　The woodcarver made the chair with great craft. *n.*
　　2. art resulting from skilled work.
　　There are many unusual crafts at the art show. *n. pl.* **crafts**

crash (krash) **1.** to hit hard.
　　The bicycle crashed into the tree. *v.* **crashed, crashed, crashing** crash·ing
　　2. a sudden hitting of one object into another.
　　Everyone drove carefully around the car crash. *n.*
　　3. a sound made by two things hitting together.
　　The crash of cymbals ended the parade song. *n. pl.* **crashes** crash·es

crater cra·ter (krā′ter) a deep, bowl-shaped hole.
　　The surface of the moon is covered with craters.
　　n. pl. **craters** cra·ters

crawl (krôl) to move along on hands and knees.
　　The baby crawled around the room.
　　v. **crawled, crawled, crawling** crawl·ing

coyote

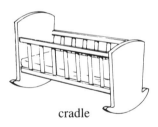
crab

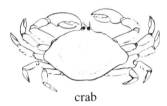
cradle

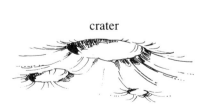
crater

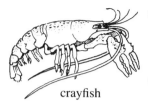

crayfish

crayfish cray·fish (krā′fish) a type of freshwater animal that looks like a little lobster.
Sarah caught ten crayfish in the lake.
n. pl. **crayfish** *or* **crayfishes** cray·fish *or* cray·fish·es

crayon cray·on (krā′on *or* krā′ən) sticks of colored wax that a person uses for coloring or drawing.
The class used crayons to color the big picture for the wall.
n. pl. **crayons** cray·ons

crayon

crazy cra·zy (krā′zē) **1.** insane; difficult to understand.
People thought that she was crazy when she began doing strange things. *adj.*
2. silly or foolish.
The crazy dog chased the fly.
adj. **crazier, craziest** cra·zi·er, cra·zi·est

cream (krēm) rich, oily part of milk.
Grandfather liked cream in his coffee. *n. no pl.*

crease (krēs) a sharply folded edge.
The soldier's pants had a neat crease in them.
n. pl. **creases** creas·es

crease

create cre·ate (krē·āt′) **1.** to make; to produce; to cause to be.
The flowing of the Colorado River created the Grand Canyon. *v.*
2. to make for the very first time.
The artist Leonardo DaVinci created the famous painting *Mona Lisa*.
v. **created, created, creating** cre·at·ed, cre·at·ing

creation cre·a·tion (krē·ā′shən) a thing that is newly made.
The chef's dessert was a tasty creation.
n. pl. **creations** cre·a·tions

creative cre·a·tive (krē·ā′tiv) able to create; imaginative.
John's picture was the most creative. *adj.*

creature crea·ture (krē′chər) a living or imaginary person or animal.
The creature in the scary movie was tall, green and very mean.
n. pl. **creatures** crea·tures

a	cat	i	sit	oi	oil	ch	chop		a in about
ā	ate	ī	lie	ou	out	ng	song		e in oven
ä	car	o	pot	u	cut	sh	she	ə =	i in pencil
e	set	ō	old	u̇	book	th	three		o in memory
ē	equal	ô	or	ü	blue	ŦH	there		u in circus
ėr	germ					zh	treasure		

creek (krēk *or* krik) a small stream.
On a hot day there were many children wading in the creek. *n. pl.* **creeks**

creep (krēp) to move slowly near the ground or floor.
The boys will creep along the floor when they pretend to be snakes.
v. **crept, crept, creeping** creep·ing

crept (krept) *v. pt. t., pt. part.* See **creep.**

crest (krest) a raised bit of hair or feathers on the head of a bird or animal.
The tropical bird had a crest of colorful feathers on its head. *n. pl.* **crests**

Crete (krēt) a Greek island in the Mediterranean Sea.
The warm climate and ancient ruins make Crete a popular vacation spot. *n.*

creek

crew (krü) **1.** people who work together on a boat, airplane or train.
The crew tied the ship to the dock. *n.*
2. a group of people who work together.
The logging crew cut down the trees and loaded them on the truck.
n. pl. **crews**

crib (krib) a small bed for a baby that has bars around the sides.
The baby was safe in its crib. *n. pl.* **cribs**

cried (krīd) *v. pt. t., pt. part.* See **cry** (1, 2).

Crimea Cri·me·a (krī·mē′a) an area in the southwest part of the Soviet Union.
Many ships sail to and from Crimea. *n.*

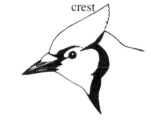

crest

criminal crim·i·nal (krim′ə·nəl) a person who breaks the law.
The judge sent the criminal to jail for 50 years for robbing the bank.
n. pl. **criminals** crim·i·nals

crippled crip·pled (krip′əld) having to do with a person or animal with an injured or deformed arm or leg.
The nurse helped the crippled man into a wheelchair. *adj.*

crisp (krisp) **1.** being firm, thin and easy to break.
Father likes crisp bacon. *adj.*
2. fresh; not stale.
Put the celery and carrot sticks in ice water to keep them crisp. *adj.*
3. brisk, cool weather.
Because it was a crisp fall day, Julie wore her warm jacket.
adj. **crisper, crispest** crisp·er, crisp·est

crib

criticize crit·i·cize (krit′ə·sīz) to disapprove of; to judge in a negative way.
Father criticized Jeff for forgetting to put away the tools.
v. **criticized, criticized, criticizing** crit·i·cized, crit·i·ciz·ing

crocodile croc·o·dile (krok′ə·dīl) a large lizard-like reptile.
The crocodile swam through the warm, marshy water.
n. pl. **crocodiles** croc·o·diles

crocodile

crooked crook·ed (krük′id) bent; twisted; curved; not straight.
The hiker used a crooked stick as a walking cane. *adj.*

crop (krop) food that farmers grow.
The corn crop was ready to pick in July. *n. pl.* **crops**

cross (krôs *or* kros) **1.** two pieces of wood or metal in the shape of an X or T.
The woman wore a gold cross around her neck.
n. pl. **crosses** cross·es
2. to go from one side to the other.
The boy crossed the street at the stoplight. *v.*
3. to put something over something else, forming an X shape.
She crossed her fingers and made a wish.
v. **crossed, crossed, crossing** cros·sing
4. shaped like an X.
The children sat cross-legged on the floor. *adj.*

cross

crossbones cross·bones (krôs′bōnz) two bones placed across each other to form an X.
A picture of a skull and crossbones on a bottle means that there is poison in the bottle. *plural n.*

cross ___ arms (krôs ___ ärms) to fold one arm over the other arm and place them against the chest.
The teacher crossed her arms and waited for the children to stop talking. *idiom*

cross-country cross-coun·try (krôs-kun′trē) going across open country rather than by road.
The cross-country skiers followed a trail through the woods. *adj.*

crossbones

a	cat	i	sit	oi	oil	ch	chop		a in about
ā	ate	ī	lie	ou	out	ng	song		e in oven
ä	car	o	pot	u	cut	sh	she	ə =	i in pencil
e	set	ō	old	ù	book	th	three		o in memory
ē	equal	ô	or	ü	blue	ŦH	there		u in circus
ėr	germ					zh	treasure		

croup (krüp) the back end of a four-legged animal.
The rider hit the horse's croup to get it to run
faster. *n. no pl.*

croup

crowd (kroud) **1.** a large group of people standing or sitting close
together.
The crowd watched the circus parade. *n. pl.* **crowds**
2. to come together around someone or something.
Crowd around the table so that I can show all of you how to work the
camera. *v.* **crowded, crowded, crowding** crowd·ed, crowd·ing

crown (kroun) an object worn on the head of a king or queen.
The king's crown is made of gold and many jewels.
n. pl. **crowns**

Crown Jewels Crown Jew·els (kroun jü·əls) the valuable stones
that belong to a king and queen.
Only the king and the queen can wear the Crown Jewels.

cruel cru·el (krü'əl) very mean.
Cinderella's stepmother was cruel to Cinderella. *adj.* **crueler** *or* **crueller,**
cruelest *or* **cruellest** cru·el·er *or* cru·el·ler, cru·el·est *or* cru·el·lest

crown

cruelly cru·el·ly (krü'ə·lē) acting in a very mean way.
The stepmother treated Cinderella cruelly. *adv.*

crumb (krum) a very small piece broken off of a food like bread,
crackers or cake.
Tom cleaned the bread crumbs off the table. *n. pl.* **crumbs**

crumble crum·ble (krum'bəl) to break into very small pieces.
The old building is starting to crumble.
v. **crumbled, crumbled, crumbling** crum·bled, crum·bling

crunch (krunch) **1.** a noise made when something crisp is eaten or
broken.
We heard the crunch of the apple when the horse ate it.
n. pl. **crunches** crunch·es
2. to make noise when breaking something
or eating something.
The leaves crunched under their feet as they walked through the forest.
v. **crunched, crunched, crunching** crunch·ing

crush (krush) **1.** to change the shape of something by pressing on it.
He will crush the tin cans. *v.*
2. to hurt someone's feelings.
It will crush him when you leave. *v.*
3. to break into very small pieces.
He will crush the rock and make gravel.
v. **crushed, crushed, crushing** crush·ing

crush

Havana

Cuba

crust (krust) **1.** the outside of the Earth.
The Earth's crust is very deep.
2. the outside of bread.
The bread crust is hard and dry. *n. pl.* **crusts**

cry (krī) **1.** to have tears come from the eyes when sad or angry.
I will cry if you do not give me my doll. *v.*
2. to call loudly.
The baby will cry "mama" when she sees her mother.
v. **cried, cried, crying** cry·ing
3. the noise or call of an animal.
We heard the cry of a fox in the forest. *n. pl.* **cries**

crystal crys·tal (kris⸍tl) **1.** a kind of rock that gives off beautiful colors when the sun shines on it.
The miner dug for the crystal. *n. pl.* **crystals** crys·tals
2. drinking glasses made of a special glass.
The crystal is in the cabinet in the dining room. *n. no pl.*
3. made of a special kind of glass.
Mother put the crystal vase on the table. *adj.*

Cuba Cu·ba (kyü⸍bə) an island country that is southeast of Florida; its capital is Havana.
Many people come from Cuba in boats. *n.*

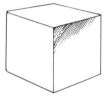

cube

cube (kyüb) a solid with six equal sides.
The waiter put an ice cube into my soda. *n. pl.* **cubes**

cub scout (kub skout) a young boy in a club that teaches about camping.
John is now a cub scout.

Cub Scouts (kub skouts) a club for young boys that teaches them about camping.
First young boys join the Cub Scouts; when they are older, they can join the Boy Scouts.

cultivate cul·ti·vate (kul⸍tə·vāt) to make ground ready for planting seeds by turning the dirt over.
The farmer will cultivate his field before planting the corn seeds.
v. **cultivated, cultivated, cultivating** cul·ti·vat·ed, cul·ti·vat·ing

cub scout

culture cul·ture (kul⸍chər) the set of beliefs, habits and activities that a certain group of people have in common.
The Roman culture greatly influenced the way the American courts were set up. *n. pl.* **cultures** cul·tures

a cat	**i** sit	**oi** oil	**ch** chop		a in about	
ā ate	**ī** lie	**ou** out	**ng** song		e in oven	
ä car	**o** pot	**u** cut	**sh** she	ə =	i in pencil	
e set	**ō** old	**u̇** book	**th** three		o in memory	
ē equal	**ô** or	**ü** blue	**ŦH** there		u in circus	
ėr germ			**zh** treasure			

cup (kup) a small bowl-shaped container, often with a handle, used for drinking.

Mother poured hot milk into my favorite cup. *n. pl.* **cups**

cupboard cup·board (kub′ərd) the closet in the kitchen where people keep dishes or food.

Susie put the clean dishes in the cupboard.

n. pl. **cupboards** cup·boards

cupboard

cupcake cup·cake (kup′kāk) a small cake baked in a cup.

On my birthday Mother made a cupcake for everyone in my class. *n. pl.* **cupcakes** cup·cakes

cupid cu·pid (kyü′pid) **1.** a child-like character who has wings and is used to show love.

The card shop had a large cupid in the window on Valentine's Day.

n. pl. **cupids** cu·pids

2. Cupid; the name of the Greek god of love.

The Greeks believed that Cupid made people fall in love. *n.*

curb strap (kėrb strap) the piece of leather on a horse bridle that tightens the bit, putting pressure in the horse's mouth.

The curb strap helps the rider control the horse.

cure (kyůr) **1.** to make free of a disease or illness.

The doctor cured the sick man. *v.* **cured, cured, curing** cur·ing

2. the treatment for a disease.

Doctors are looking for the cure for cancer. *n. pl.* **cures**

cupid

curious cur·i·ous (kyůr′ē·əs) willing and eager to learn.

He is curious about biology. *adj.*

curiously cur·i·ous·ly (kyůr′ē·əs·lē) with willingness and eagerness to learn.

He is curiously reading the biology book. *adv.*

curl (kėrl) **1.** a piece of hair or string in the shape of a circle.

This curl keeps falling into my eyes. *n. pl.* **curls**

2. to make hair or string look like circles.

Mother will curl my hair before I go to school.

v. **curled, curled, curling** curl·ing

curly cur·ly (kėr′lē) to have many curls.

Lisa's hair is very curly.

adj. **curlier, curliest** curl·i·er, curl·i·est

current cur·rent (kėr′ənt) the flow or movement of water, air or electricity.

The river's current helps the boats move down the river.

n. pl. **currents** cur·rents

curl

curtain

curtain cur·tain (kėrt'n) a cloth that covers a window or a theater stage.
Please open the curtain and let the sunshine into the room.
n. pl. **curtains** cur·tains

curve (kėrv) **1.** to have a bend.
The steps curve up to the second floor.
v. **curved, curved, curving** curv·ing
2. a bend in something.
Drive slowly around this curve. *n. pl.* **curves**

curvy curv·y (kėr'vē) with many bends.
The curvy road goes past my house.
adj. **curvier, curviest** curv·i·er, curv·i·est

cushiony cush·ion·y (kùsh'ə·nē) looks or feels soft.
The sky has many cushiony clouds. *adj.*

Custer, George Armstrong Cus·ter, George Arm·strong (kus'tər, jôrj ärm'strông) a United States general who died in a battle with Indians.
General George Armstrong Custer fought in the United States Civil War.

curve

custom cus·tom (kus'təm) a special action or habit of a country or a family.
An Italian custom is to eat the salad after dinner, not before.
n. pl. **customs** cus·toms

customer cus·tom·er (kus'tə·mər) a person who shops at a store.
The grocery store clerk knows the name of every customer that shops in the store. *n. pl.* **customers** cus·tom·ers

cut (kut) **1.** to divide something into two or more pieces or parts with a knife, scissors or other sharp tool.
He will cut us a piece of the birthday cake. *v.*
2. to hurt someone or something with a sharp tool.
Be careful not to cut yourself with the knife. *v.* **cut, cut, cutting** cut·ting
3. the injury or hurt made with a sharp tool.
The cut on his finger is not big. *n. pl.* **cuts**

cut

cut down (kut doun) to cause to fall to the ground by cutting.
Dad will cut down the dead tree.
v. **cut down, cut down, cutting down** cut·ting down

cute (kyüt) pretty.
The puppy is cute. *adj.* **cuter, cutest** cut·er, cut·est

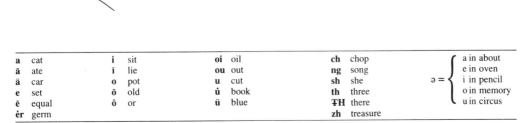

a	cat	**i**	sit	**oi**	oil	**ch**	chop
ā	ate	**ī**	lie	**ou**	out	**ng**	song
ä	car	**o**	pot	**u**	cut	**sh**	she
e	set	**ō**	old	**ù**	book	**th**	three
ē	equal	**ô**	or	**ü**	blue	**ŦH**	there
ėr	germ					**zh**	treasure

ə = {
a in about
e in oven
i in pencil
o in memory
u in circus

cut off (kut   ôf)   to take part of something away by cutting.
> Father will cut off the dead branch of the apple tree.
> *v.* **cut off, cut off, cutting off** cut·ting off

cut out (kut   out)   to take a part out of something by cutting.
> Mother will cut out the recipe from the newspaper.
> *v.* **cut out, cut out, cutting out** cut·ting out

cutout cut·out (kut‹out)   the piece that one takes away after cutting out.
> They pinned the cutout of the donkey on the wall.
> *n. pl.* **cutouts** cut·outs

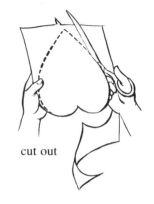

cut out

cut out of (kut   out   əv)   to cut a shape from.
> The dolls will be cut out of paper.
> *v.* **cut out of, cut out of, cutting out of** cut·ting out of

cutter cut·ter (kut‹ər)   a tool that cuts things.
> The paper cutter is sharp. *n. pl.* **cutters** cut·ters

cutter bar cut·ter bar (kut‹ər   bär)   the part of a reaper (a machine used for cutting wheat) that is sharp and that cuts.
> The cutter bar must be sharpened often so that it cuts the wheat.
> *n. pl.* **cutter bars** cut·ter bars

cycle cy·cle (sī‹kəl)   the order that something happens again and again in the same way.
> The seasons of the year always follow this cycle: spring, summer, fall and winter. *n. pl.* **cycles** cy·cles

czar (zär)   **1.** a king in Russia.
> Ivan was a czar in Russia centuries ago. *n. pl.* **czars**
> **2.** Czar; the title of respect given to a Russian king.
> Czar Ivan ruled Russia centuries ago. *n. no pl.*

Czech (chek)   the language of a person who lives in or was born in Czechoslovakia, a country in Europe whose capital is Prague.
> The bus driver speaks Czech, which he learned while living in Prague.
> *n. no pl.*

Dd

daisy

dad (dad) father.
My dad works in a grocery store. *n. pl.* **dads**

daddy dad·dy (dad′ē) child's name for father.
I gave my daddy a tie for Father's Day. *n. pl.* **daddies** dad·dies

daily dai·ly (dā′lē) **1.** every day.
The milkman brings milk to our house daily. *adv.*
2. happening every day.
The daily newspaper comes to the house every day. *adj.*

dairy dair·y (der′ē) **1.** the place where milk is kept and made into cheese or butter.
Her father works in a dairy. *n. pl.* **dairies** dair·ies
2. having to do with cows.
The dairy farm made the cheese that we ate for lunch. *adj.*

daisy dai·sy (dā′zē) a kind of flower that has petals and a yellow center.
The little girl picked a wild daisy for her mother. *n. pl.* **daisies** dai·sies

dam

dam (dam) a wall that stops or controls the flow of a river.
The workers built a dam on the river. *n. pl.* **dams**

damage dam·age (dam′ij) **1.** to break or harm something.
The hard rain will damage the flowers.
v. **damaged, damaged, damaging** dam·aged, dam·ag·ing
2. the harm or injury to something.
The damage caused by the flood was great. *n. pl.* **damages** dam·ag·es

damp (damp) slightly wet; wet but not full of water.
The grass was damp from the dew.
adj. **damper, dampest** damp·er, damp·est

dance (dants) **1.** to move to music.
Katie will dance in the school play. *v.* **danced, danced, dancing** danc·ing
2. steps or other movements to music.
Her dance is a ballet. *n.*
3. a party where people move to music.
I am going to a dance tonight. *n. pl.* **dances** danc·es

dance

a	cat	**i**	sit	**oi**	oil	**ch**	chop		a in about
ā	ate	**ī**	lie	**ou**	out	**ng**	song		e in oven
ä	car	**o**	pot	**u**	cut	**sh**	she	**ə =**	i in pencil
e	set	**ō**	old	** u̇**	book	**th**	three		o in memory
ē	equal	**ô**	or	**ü**	blue	**ŦH**	there		u in circus
ėr	germ					**zh**	treasure		

dancer   danc·er (dan⸴sər)   a person who moves to music.
  Katie is a dancer. *n. pl.* **dancers** danc·ers

dandelion   dan·de·li·on (dan⸴dl·ī·ən)   a yellow flower that
  grows in the grass.
  The farmer pulled the dandelion from the garden.
  n. pl. **dandelions** dan·de·li·ons

Dane   (dān)   a person who lives or was born in Denmark.
  The bakery is owned by a Dane who moved here from Denmark in 1977.
  n. pl. **Danes**

danger   dan·ger (dān⸴jər)   something that may not be safe and that
  could hurt someone or something.
  There is great danger in driving a car too fast. *n. pl.* **dangers** dan·gers

dangerous   dan·ger·ous (dān⸴jər·əs)   unsafe or harmful.
  Driving a car too fast is dangerous. *adj.*

Danish   Dan·ish (dā⸴nish)   **1.** people who live in or who were born
  in Denmark.
  The Danish came to America many years ago. *plural n.*
  2. about or from Denmark.
  The bakery has many Danish desserts. *adj.*

dare   (der *or* dar)   **1.** to try to do something.
  He will dare to ride the bucking horse. *v.*
  2. to try to make someone do something.
  She dared him to ride the horse. *v.* **dared, dared, daring** dar·ing

dark   (därk)   **1.** not having light or sunshine.
  The cave in the hill is very dark. *adj.*
  2. a shade of a color.
  Her new dress is dark blue. *adj.* **darker, darkest** dark·er, dark·est
  3. the time of day when there is no sunshine.
  I must be back home by dark. *n. no pl.*
  4. blackness; without light.
  At night, I sometimes am afraid of the dark. *n. no pl.*

date   (dāt)   **1.** the time in month, day and year.
  The date of this old letter from Grandmother is June 1, 1985. *n. pl.* **dates**
  2. to put the time in month, day and year.
  He dated the check January 15, 1986.
  v. **dated, dated, dating** dat·ed, dat·ing

daughter   daugh·ter (dô⸴tər)   the girl child of a parent.
  Her daughter will be nine years old tomorrow. *n. pl.* **daughters** daugh·ters

Davis Strait   Da·vis Strait (dā⸴vis strāt)   the body of water between
  the countries of Canada and Greenland.
  Ships travel through the Davis Strait on their way from Canada to
  Greenland.

dancer

dandelion

Davis Strait

daydream

dawn (dôn) **1.** the time of day when the sun first begins to shine.
The birds start to sing at dawn each day. *n. pl.* **dawns**
2. to grow light; to begin to shine.
The sun will dawn at 5:45 a.m. tomorrow.
v. **dawned, dawned, dawning** dawn·ing

day (dā) **1.** twenty-four hours.
It rained for one day. *n.*
2. the time between sunrise and sunset.
My father works during the day, and your father works
during the night. *n. pl.* **days**

day after day (dā af′tər dā) every day.
Day after day I wait for a letter from Grandmother.

daydream day·dream (dā′drēm) **1.** to think about something nice
and see it in your mind.
I like to daydream about going to Hawaii. *v.* **daydreamed, daydreamed,**
daydreaming day·dreamed, day·dream·ing
2. the picture in the mind when thinking of something nice.
My daydream is about going to Hawaii. *n. pl.* **daydreams** day·dreams

daylight day·light (dā′līt) **1.** the time between sunrise and sunset.
Daylight begins at dawn each day. *n.*
2. the light of the sun.
Plants need daylight to grow. *n. no pl.*

daytime day·time (dā′tīm) when the sun shines.
I never watch TV in the daytime. *n. no pl.*

dazzling daz·zling (daz′ling) shining; very bright.
She wore a dazzling diamond ring to the party. *adj.*

dead (ded) without life.
We found a dead fish in the river. *adj.*

deadline dead·line (ded′līn) the time by which something
must be finished.
The deadline for the science project is tomorrow.
n. pl. **deadlines** dead·lines

Dead or Alive Dead or A·live (ded or ə·līv′) a saying on old
western posters that meant that the person pictured on the
poster was wanted by the sheriff, breathing or not breathing.
The bank robber's picture was on the poster that read "Dead or Alive,
$1,000 Reward." *idiom*

a	cat	i	sit	oi	oil	ch	chop		a in about
ā	ate	ī	lie	ou	out	ng	song		e in oven
ä	car	o	pot	u	cut	sh	she	ə =	i in pencil
e	set	ō	old	u̇	book	th	three		o in memory
ē	equal	ô	or	ü	blue	ŦH	there		u in circus
ėr	germ					zh	treasure		

deaf (def) cannot hear.
> The little girl could not hear the barking dog because she is deaf.
> *adj.* **deafer, deafest** deaf·er, deaf·est

deal (dēl) a business action.
> I am making a deal to buy a new bicycle. *n. pl.* **deals**

dear (dir) **1.** loved or loving.
> He is a dear man. *adj.*
> **2.** the first word in a letter, used to show how much the writer
> of the letter thinks of the person who is getting the letter.
> My letter started with "Dear Sara." *adj.* **dearer, dearest** dear·er, dear·est

dearly dear·ly (dir′lē) loved greatly.
> She dearly loves her Aunt Daisy. *adv.*

death (deth) the end of life.
> The dog's death made her very sad. *n. pl.* **deaths**

debt (det) **1.** something that is owed.
> I will pay my $36.00 debt to the shoe store today. *n.*
> **2.** owing a lot of money and not having the money to pay it.
> He is in debt to the bank for $10,000. *n. pl.* **debts**

debtor debt·or (det′ər) a person who owes someone something.
> The debtor paid the bank for his loan. *n. pl.* **debtors** debt·ors

decide de·cide (di·sīd′) to make up one's mind about something.
> I will decide if I am going to the party tonight.
> *v.* **decided, decided, deciding** de·cid·ed, de·cid·ing

decide against de·cide a·gainst (di·sīd′ ə·genst′) to make up one's
> mind not to do something.
> I might decide against going to the party. *v.* **decided against, decided**
> **against, deciding against** de·cid·ed a·gainst, de·cid·ing a·gainst

decision de·ci·sion (di·sizh′ən) what a person decides to do.
> My decision is to go to the party. *n. pl.* **decisions** de·ci·sions

deck (dek) **1.** the top floor on a ship or a building.
> We waved to the people on the deck of the ship. *n.*
> **2.** an outside floor of a house.
> We often sit on the deck in the summertime. *n. pl.* **decks**

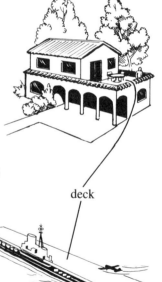

deck

declaration   dec·la·ra·tion (dek·lə·rā′shən)   something important said to the people.
The mayor made the declaration that he would not run for mayor again.
n. pl. **declarations** dec·la·ra·tions

Declaration of Independence   Dec·la·ra·tion of In·de·pend·ence (dek·lə·rā′shən əv in·di·pen′dəns)   an important paper written by the early leaders of the United States. It told England that the United States wanted to be free and would not obey the laws of England any more.
The Declaration of Independence was signed on July 4, 1776.

declare   de·clare (di·kler′ *or* di·klar′)   to tell people something important.
The mayor will declare that he is not going to run for mayor again.
v. **declared, declared, declaring** de·clared, de·clar·ing

decoration

decorate   dec·o·rate (dek′ə·rāt)   to make something look pretty by using party things.
We will decorate the Christmas tree with white lights.
v. **decorated, decorated, decorating** dec·o·rat·ed, dec·o·rat·ing

decoration   dec·o·ra·tion (dek·ə·rā′shən)   something that makes a place look special or party-like.
We put a Christmas decoration in the window.
n. pl. **decorations** dec·o·ra·tions

decorative   dec·o·ra·tive (dek′rə·tiv)   having the look and feel of a party.
The classroom looks so decorative in December. *adj.*

dedicate   ded·i·cate (ded′ə·kāt)   to do something special to make sure that something or someone is remembered.
We will dedicate our school to Abraham Lincoln.
v. **dedicated, dedicated, dedicating** ded·i·cat·ed, ded·i·cat·ing

dedication   ded·i·ca·tion (ded·ə·kā′shən)   a ceremony done to remember someone or something.
The dedication of our school was on June 1, 1985.
n. pl. **dedications** ded·i·ca·tions

a	cat	i	sit	oi	oil	ch	chop		a in about
ā	ate	ī	lie	ou	out	ng	song		e in oven
ä	car	o	pot	u	cut	sh	she	ə =	i in pencil
e	set	ō	old	u̇	book	th	three		o in memory
ē	equal	ô	or	ü	blue	ŦH	there		u in circus
ėr	germ					zh	treasure		

deep (dēp) **1.** far into something.
  The little boy had walked deep into the forest. *adv.*
  2. a long way down from the top.
  The water is very deep. *adj.*
  3. very strong.
  I have deep feelings for my brother.
  adj. **deeper, deepest** deep·er, deep·est

deeply deep·ly (dēp′lē) strongly.
  I was deeply hurt when my brother left home. *adv.*

deer (dir) an animal with horns, called antlers, that lives in the
  forest.
  We saw a deer run out of the forest. *n. pl.* **deer**

deer

deerfly deer·fly (dir′flī) an insect that usually lives on the skin of
  deer.
  The deerfly flew away as the deer started to run. *n. pl.* **deerflies** deer·flies

defeat de·feat (di·fēt′) to win or beat someone in a game, war or
  contest.
  I will defeat you in this game of cards.
  v. **defeated, defeated, defeating** de·feat·ed, de·feat·ing

definition def·i·ni·tion (def·ə·nish′ən) the meaning of a word.
  The teacher asked the class to find the definition of the word "funnel" in
  the dictionary. *n. pl.* **definitions** def·i·ni·tions

deerfly

delegate del·e·gate (del′ə·git *or* del′ə·gāt) a person who takes the
  place of a group of people and votes for what the group wants.
  Mr. Jones is the delegate to the House of Representatives from our state.
  n. pl. **delegates** del·e·gates

delicious de·li·cious (di·lish′əs) tastes good.
  The cherry pie is delicious. *adj.*

delight de·light (di·līt′) **1.** to make someone happy.
  The roses will delight Mother.
  v. **delighted, delighted, delighting** de·light·ed, de·light·ing
  2. a joy.
  It is a delight to see you again. *n. pl.* **delights** de·lights

delighted de·light·ed (di·lī′tid) **1.** very happy.
  I am delighted to see you again. *adj.*
  2. *v. p. t., p. p.* See **delight** (1).

deliver de·liv·er (di·liv′ər) **1.** to bring something to someone.
  Tom will deliver the newspaper to Sara. *v.*
  2. to save from harm or injury.
  The prince said to the princess, "I will deliver you from the evil king."
  v. **delivered, delivered, delivering** de·liv·ered, de·liv·er·ing

den

demand de·mand (di·mand′) **1.** to make someone do something.
He will demand that you give him the money.
v. **demanded, demanded, demanding** de·mand·ed, de·mand·ing
2. an order.
The bank robbers' demand was for all the money in the bank.
n. pl. **demands** de·mands

demonstrate dem·on·strate (dem′ən·strāt) to show how to
do something.
The teacher will demonstrate how to change a tire. *v.* **demonstrated,
demonstrated, demonstrating** dem·on·strat·ed, dem·on·strat·ing

demonstration dem·on·stra·tion (dem·ən·strā′shən) showing how
something is done.
The teacher's demonstration included taking off the tire and using the jack.
n. pl. **demonstrations** dem·on·stra·tions

Denmark

Copenhagen

den (den) an animal's home.
The bear's den is in that cave. *n. pl.* **dens**

denim den·im (den′əm) **1.** a material that is made of a heavy
cotton.
Your blue jeans are made of denim. *n. no pl.*
2. being made of a heavy cotton material.
Your denim coat is in the closet. *adj.*

Denmark Den·mark (den′märk) a country in northern Europe; its
capital is Copenhagen.
The people who live in Denmark are called Danes. *n.*

dense (dens) being close together or crowded.
The dense forest had no more room for new trees. *adj.*

dentist den·tist (den′tist) a doctor who takes care of people's teeth.
The dentist cleaned and polished my teeth. *n. pl.* **dentists** den·tists

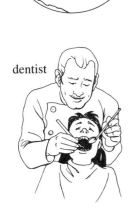

dentist

department de·part·ment (di·pärt′mənt) **1.** a part of a city, state or
county government that does something for the people.
Our city has a water department, a fire department, a police department and
a health department. *n.*
2. an area in a business or an area of a business.
John works in the shoe department. *n. pl.* **departments** de·part·ments

dependable de·pend·a·ble (di·pen′də·bəl) **1.** something that you
can be sure of.
The weather is not dependable. *adj.*
2. someone that you can trust to do something.
Joe is dependable, so he will be here if he said he would be. *adj.*

a	cat	i	sit	oi	oil	ch	chop		a in about
ā	ate	ī	lie	ou	out	ng	song		e in oven
ä	car	o	pot	u	cut	sh	she	ə =	i in pencil
e	set	ō	old	u̇	book	th	three		o in memory
ē	equal	ô	or	ü	blue	ŦH	there		u in circus
ėr	germ					zh	treasure		

depend on de·pend on (di·pend′ ôn) **1.** to need.
The plants depend on water to grow. *v.*
2. to know that someone will do something or that something will happen.
She will depend on me for a ride to school. *v.* **depended on, depended on, depending on** de·pend·ed on, de·pend·ing on

deposit de·pos·it (di·poz′it) **1.** to put money in the bank for savings or for writing checks.
Dad will deposit his paycheck tomorrow.
v. **deposited, deposited, depositing** de·pos·it·ed, de·pos·it·ing
2. money put in the bank for savings or for writing checks.
Mother makes a bank deposit every Friday. *n. pl.* **deposits** de·pos·its

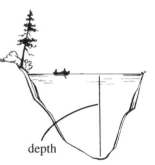

depressed de·pressed (di·prest′) sad.
He is depressed because his dog is lost. *adj.*

depth (depth) the distance (how far) from the top to the bottom of something.
The depth of the river is 75 feet. *n. no pl.*

depth

descendant de·scend·ant (di·sen′dənt) a person who comes from a certain family and is the child, grandchild or great-grandchild of a person in that family.
Jim is a descendant of President Andrew Jackson.
n. pl. **descendants** de·scend·ants

describe de·scribe (di·skrīb′) to tell about someone or something by giving details of how a person looks or what happened.
The woman can describe the bank robber.
v. **described, described, describing** de·scribed, de·scrib·ing

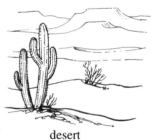

description de·scrip·tion (di·skrip′shən) the details of how a person or a thing looks or of something that has happened.
This is the robber's description: He has brown hair, brown eyes, white eyeglasses and a pointed chin, and he was wearing a blue shirt.
n. pl. **descriptions** de·scrip·tions

desert

desert des·ert (dez′ərt) **1.** an area that is very hot and dry.
Cactuses can grow in the desert because they do not need a lot of water.
n. pl. **deserts** des·erts
2. having to do with a part of the country that is very hot and dry.
The desert flowers are very pretty in the spring. *adj.*

deserve de·serve (di·zèrv′) to have a right to something.
John will deserve a star if he gets all of his math right.
v. **deserved, deserved, deserving** de·served, de·serv·ing

designer

desk

design de·sign (di·zīn′) **1.** the shape or pattern of something.
The design of the lamp is very modern. *n.*
2. a plan.
The design of the house is two stories with three bedrooms and three bathrooms. *n. pl.* **designs** de·signs
3. to make a plan for something.
Donald will design a house for our family.
v. **designed, designed, designing** de·signed, de·sign·ing

designer de·sign·er (di·zī′nər) the person who makes a plan for something.
Donald is the designer of that new house. *n. pl.* **designers** de·sign·ers

desire de·sire (di·zīr′) **1.** to wish for something.
I desire a trip to Hawaii.
v. **desired, desired, desiring** de·sired, de·sir·ing
2. a wish.
My desire is to go on a trip to Hawaii. *n. pl.* **desires** de·sires

dessert

desk (desk) a table that is used for writing.
The school desk is too small for me now. *n. pl.* **desks**

dessert des·sert (di·zėrt′) the last part of a meal, often sweet.
It is difficult for me to pick a dessert because I like cakes, pies and candies.
n. pl. **desserts** des·serts

destroy de·stroy (di·stroi′) to damage something so that it cannot be used.
If the rain does not stop soon, it will destroy the wheat.
v. **destroyed, destroyed, destroying** de·stroyed, de·stroy·ing

detergent

destruction de·struc·tion (di·struk′shən) damage; ruin; destroying of something.
The flood caused a lot of destruction. *n. no pl.*

detail de·tail (di·tāl′ *or* dē′tāl) a small piece of information.
The woman forgot one detail of the robber's description.
n. pl. **details** de·tails

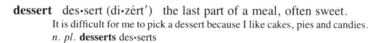

detergent de·ter·gent (di·tėr′jənt) soap.
The dish detergent is under the kitchen sink. *n. pl.* **detergents** de·ter·gents

determine de·ter·mine (di·tėr′mən) to decide; to find an answer.
I will determine what we will do with the puppy.
v. **determined, determined, determining** de·ter·mined, de·ter·min·ing

a	cat	i	sit	oi	oil	ch	chop		a in about
ā	ate	ī	lie	ou	out	ng	song		e in oven
ä	car	o	pot	u	cut	sh	she	ə =	i in pencil
e	set	ō	old	u̇	book	th	three		o in memory
ē	equal	ô	or	ü	blue	ŦH	there		u in circus
ėr	germ					zh	treasure		

develop de·vel·op (di·vel'əp) to grow; to come into being.
   The seeds will develop into beautiful plants in the spring.
   v. **developed, developed, developing** de·vel·oped, de·vel·op·ing

devil dev·il (dev'əl) **1.** an evil, mean spirit who people believe lives in hell.
   Pictures of the devil show him to have a long tail and a red suit.
   n. pl. **devils** dev-ils
   2. to prepare food with strong spices.
   The cook deviled the eggs for the party.
   v. **deviled** *or* **devilled, deviled** *or* **devilled, deviling** *or* **devilling** dev·iled *or* dev·illed, dev·il·ing *or* dev·il·ling

devil

dew (dü *or* dyü) the water on the grass in the morning.
   The dew dries as soon as the sun warms the grass. *n. no pl.*

dial di·al (dī'əl) **1.** the front part of a telephone that turns, or the front part of a watch that has the numbers and the hands on it.
   The numbers on the dial of my watch glow in the dark. *n. pl.* **dials** di·als
   2. to use the numbers on a telephone.
   Please dial the store for me. *v.* **dialed, dialed, dialing** di·aled, di·al·ing

dial

diamond dia·mond (dī'mənd *or* dī'ə·mənd) **1.** a stone that is clear and very valuable.
   The diamond in the ring is not big. *n.*
   2. a shape that has four sides.
   The teacher asked the class to draw a square, a circle and a diamond.
   n. pl. **diamonds** dia·monds
   3. having to do with a clear stone.
   The diamond ring is dazzling. *adj.*

diaper dia·per (dī'pər *or* dī'ə·pər) a soft piece of cloth used as underpants for a baby.
   Mother put a clean diaper on the baby. *n. pl.* **diapers** dia·pers

diamonds

dictionary dic·tion·ar·y (dik'shə·ner·ē) a book that contains an alphabetical listing of words, with the meaning, pronunciation, and other information for each word.
   The teacher told us to use the dictionary to find the definitions of the words on the list. *n. pl.* **dictionaries** dic·tion·ar·ies

did (did) *v. pt. t.* See **do.**

die (dī) to stop living.
   The fish will die without food. *v.* **died, died, dying** dy·ing

die out (dī out) not to be on Earth any more.
   No one knew that the dinosaurs would die out.
   v. **died out, died out, dying out** dy·ing out

diaper

difference dif·fer·ence (dif'ər·əns) something that is not the same.
   The difference between my sister and me is our ages.
   n. pl. **differences** dif·fer·enc·es

different dif·fer·ent (dif′ər·ənt) not the same.
You look different today! Is your hair different? *adj.*

differently dif·fer·ent·ly (dif′ər·ənt·lē) not in the same way.
I am combing my hair differently today. *adv.*

difficult dif·fi·cult (dif′ə·kult) hard to do, not easy.
Math is difficult for me to learn. *adj.*

difficulty dif·fi·cul·ty (dif′ə·kul·tē) a problem.
The biggest difficulty in learning math is remembering the times table.
n. pl. **difficulties** dif·fi·cul·ties

dig (dig) to make a hole in the dirt.
The dog will dig a hole for his bone. *v.* **dug, dug, digging** dig·ging

digestive di·ges·tive (də·jes′tiv *or* dī·jes′tiv) having to do with the changing of food for the body to use.
The digestive system includes the stomach, the large intestine and the small intestine. *adj.*

dig

digger dig·ger (dig′ər) a person or thing that makes holes in the dirt.
Her Uncle Tim is a digger with the water department.
n. pl. **diggers** dig·gers

digging dig·ging (dig′ing) *v. pres. part.* See **dig.**

dig up (dig up) to bring out of the ground something that has been buried.
The dog will dig up the bone he buried yesterday.
v. **dug up, dug up, digging up** dig·ging up

dim (dim) not bright; with little light.
We need to turn on the light because it is dim in this room.
adj. **dimmer, dimmest** dim·mer, dim·mest

dime

dime (dīm) a United States coin; a piece of money worth ten cents.
I put five dimes into the candy machine. *n. pl.* **dimes**

din (din) noise that lasts a long time and is very loud.
There was such a din in the room with the band that I had to turn off my hearing aid. *n. no pl.*

dine (dīn) to eat dinner.
We will dine with Grandmother on Sunday.
v. **dined, dined, dining** din·ing

a	cat	**i**	sit	**oi**	oil	**ch**	chop	a in about
ā	ate	**ī**	lie	**ou**	out	**ng**	song	e in oven
ä	car	**o**	pot	**u**	cut	**sh**	she	i in pencil
e	set	**ō**	old	**u̇**	book	**th**	three	ə = o in memory
ē	equal	**ô**	or	**ü**	blue	**ŦH**	there	o in memory
ėr	germ					**zh**	treasure	u in circus

ding   (ding)   the sound of a bell.
>The ding of the bell is very soft. *n. pl.* **dings**

dinner   din·ner (din′ər)   the last meal of the day.
>We eat dinner when Dad and Mother get home from work.
>*n. pl.* **dinners** din·ners

dinosaur   di·no·saur (dī′nə·sôr)   a large animal that lived on Earth before the cave men.
>The dinosaur died out hundreds of years ago. *n. pl.* **dinosaurs** di·no·saurs

dinner

dip   (dip)   to put something quickly in water or another liquid and take it out again.
>The man will dip the diamond ring in the silver detergent to get it clean.
>*v.* **dipped, dipped, dipping** dip·ping

diplomat   dip·lo·mat (dip′lə·mat)   a person who solves problems between his country and other countries.
>The man is a United States diplomat who lives and works in France.
>*n. pl.* **diplomats** dip·lo·mats

dipper   dip·per (dip′ər)   **1.** a long-handled cup.
>Mother used a dipper to serve the soup. *n. pl.* **dippers** dip·pers
>**2.** Dipper; a set of stars that looks like a dipper.
>The Big Dipper and the Little Dipper can be seen in the sky on a clear night. *n.*

dinosaur

direction   di·rec·tion (də·rek′shən *or* dī·rek′shən)   the way to move; north, south, east or west.
>The wind blew in a westerly direction. *n. pl.* **directions** di·rec·tions

directions   di·rec·tions (də·rek′shəns *or* dī·rek′shəns)   a set of steps that tell how to go somewhere or do something.
>She read the directions and put the bike together. *plural n.*

directly   di·rect·ly (də·rekt′lē *or* dī·rekt′lē)   in a straight line.
>The new house is directly behind the school. *adv.*

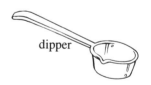

dipper

director   di·rec·tor (də·rek′tər *or* dī·rek′tər)   **1.** a person who tells people what to do; a boss.
>Her uncle is the director of the water department. *n.*
>**2.** a person who tells the actors in a play, TV show or movie what to do.
>Paul was the director of our school play. *n. pl.* **directors** di·rec·tors

Little Dipper

dirt   (dėrt)   loose earth or pieces of ground.
>The dog dug a hole in the dirt. *plural n.*

Big Dipper

dirty   dir·ty (dėr′tē)   **1.** not clean.
>The dog rolled in the mud and is very dirty.
>*adj.* **dirtier, dirtiest** dir·ti·er, dir·ti·est
>**2.** to get dirt on something.
>The baby will dirty her knees crawling in the dirt.
>*v.* **dirtied, dirtied, dirtying** dirt·ied, dirt·y·ing

dirty

dirty trick dir·ty trick (dėr‡tē trik) a bad joke or prank.
Throwing his shoes in the swimming pool was a dirty trick.
n. pl. **dirty tricks** dir·ty tricks *idiom*

disappear dis·ap·pear (dis·ə·pir′) to go without being seen.
The lion will disappear when the magician waves his wand. *v.*
disappeared, disappeared, disappearing dis·ap·peared, dis·ap·pear·ing

disappoint dis·ap·point (dis·ə·point′) to make someone feel
unhappy by not doing what was expected.
If you forget her birthday, you will disappoint Mother. *v.* **disappointed,
disappointed, disappointing** dis·ap·point·ed, dis·ap·point·ing

disappointed dis·ap·point·ed (dis·ə·poin‡tid) being sad about
something that was expected.
Mother felt disappointed because you forgot her birthday. *adj.*

disaster dis·as·ter (də·zas‡tər) a very bad, terrible happening.
A flood is a disaster because it causes a lot of damage.
n. pl. **disasters** dis·as·ters

disciple dis·ci·ple (də·sī‡pəl) **1.** a person who believes in the
teachings of a leader.
Reverend Billy Graham has many disciples. *n.*
2. one of the first believers in Jesus Christ.
Saint Paul was a disciple of Jesus Christ. *n. pl.* **disciples** dis·ci·ples

discipline dis·ci·pline (dis‡ə·plin) to punish; to teach someone to
control himself or herself.
The teacher will discipline the boy who is always talking in class.
v. **disciplined, disciplined, disciplining** dis·ci·plined, dis·ci·plin·ing

discourage dis·cour·age (dis·kėr‡ij) **1.** to make someone feel like
not doing something.
She will discourage you from going on the camping trip. *v.*
2. to take away someone's hope.
Losing the game discouraged the team. *v.*
discouraged, discouraged, discouraging dis·cour·aged, dis·cour·ag·ing

discouraged dis·cour·aged (dis·kėr‡ijd) being without hope or
without a feeling of success.
Joe felt discouraged after he got an F on his report card. *adj.*

discover dis·cov·er (dis·kuv‡ər) to find something or someone.
America was discovered in 1492.
v. **discovered, discovered, discovering** dis·cov·ered, dis·cov·er·ing

a	cat	i	sit	oi	oil	ch	chop	⎰ a in about
ā	ate	ī	lie	ou	out	ng	song	e in oven
ä	car	o	pot	u	cut	sh	she	ə = i in pencil
e	set	ō	old	u̇	book	th	three	o in memory
ē	equal	ô	or	ü	blue	ŦH	there	⎱ u in circus
ėr	germ					zh	treasure	

discovery dis·cov·er·y (dis·kuv′ər·ē) **1.** something that is found.
That chest of gold was a valuable discovery. *n.*
2. the finding of something.
The discovery of America made Columbus famous.
n. pl. **discoveries** dis·cov·er·ies

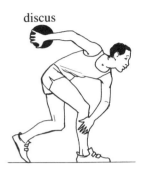

discus

discus dis·cus (dis′kəs) a heavy round dish that athletes throw in
track and field games.
The Greeks had contests to see who could throw the discus the longest
distance. *n. pl.* **discuses** dis·cus·es

discuss dis·cuss (dis·kus′) to talk about.
Today we will discuss the discovery of America.
v. **discussed, discussed, discussing** dis·cussed, dis·cuss·ing

disease dis·ease (də·zēz′) sickness.
Cancer is a disease. *n. pl.* **diseases** dis·eas·es

disguise dis·guise (dis·gīz′) **1.** a way of changing the way one
looks so that people will not know who it is.
John wore a Superman disguise to the Halloween party.
n. pl. **disguises** dis·guis·es
2. to change the way one looks so that people will not know
who it is.
The robber will disguise himself with brown hair and a beard.
v. **disguised, disguised, disguising** dis·guised, dis·guis·ing

disgusted dis·gust·ed (dis·gus′tid) having a strong feeling of not
liking; to dislike greatly.
Joe is disgusted with math. *adj.*

dish (dish) **1.** something that a person puts food on or in; a plate.
The dish was too small for all the food that Jim wanted to eat. *n.*
2. a food.
Mother made a new chicken dish for dinner. *n. pl.* **dishes** dish·es
3. to put food on a plate.
Mother will dish the chicken. *v.* **dished, dished, dishing** dish·ing

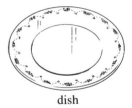

dish

dishwasher dish·wash·er (dish′wosh·ər *or* dish′wôsh·ər) **1.** a
person who cleans the plates.
Dolly is a dishwasher at the restaurant this summer. *n.*
2. a machine that cleans dirty plates.
Mother is getting a new dishwasher for the kitchen.
n. pl. **dishwashers** dish·wash·ers

dishwashing dish·wash·ing (dish′wosh·ing *or* dish′wôsh·ing)
having to do with cleaning plates.
The dishwashing detergent is under the kitchen sink. *adj.*

dismayed dis·mayed (dis·mād′) a sudden feeling of fear and not
knowing what to do.
Mary is dismayed about the spelling contest. *adj.*

dishwasher

dismount dis·mount (dis·mount′) to get off something.
Grace will dismount from the horse near the gate.
v. **dismounted, dismounted, dismounting** dis·mount·ed, dis·mount·ing

display dis·play (dis·plā′) **1.** to set things in a way that shows them to people.
Tom will display his Boy Scout medals at the meeting.
v. **displayed, displayed, displaying** dis·played, dis·play·ing
2. a show where things are set up for people to look at.
The display was in the school. *n. pl.* **displays** dis·plays

distance dis·tance (dis′təns) the space between things or persons.
The distance from my house to the school is two miles.
n. pl. **distances** dis·tanc·es

distress dis·tress (dis·tres′) to make someone feel pain or sadness.
You will distress your mother if you get hurt on the bicycle.
v. **distressed, distressed, distressing** dis·tressed, dis·tress·ing

distressed dis·tressed (dis·trest′) a feeling of great sadness.
He is distressed about the game. *adj.*

distributor dis·trib·u·tor (dis·trib′yə·tər) the part of the car that moves the electric energy from the battery to the spark plugs.
Dad replaced the broken distributor in the car.
n. pl. **distributors** dis·trib·u·tors

disturb dis·turb (dis·tėrb′) to break the quiet or calmness.
The noise of the cars will disturb the deer in the forest.
v. **disturbed, disturbed, disturbing** dis·turbed, dis·turb·ing

ditch (dich) a long hole in the ground.
The man dug a ditch in the road for a new pipe. *n. pl.* **ditches** dit·ches

dive (dīv) **1.** to go into water headfirst.
The boy will dive from the board into the pool. *v.*
2. to jump from an airplane.
The skyjumper will dive from that airplane.
v. **dived** *or* **dove, dived, diving** div·ing
3. a jump.
The boy did the swan dive into the pool. *n. pl.* **dives**

diver di·ver (dī′vər) a person who goes underwater with a tank of air that lets him breathe.
The diver is looking for lost treasure. *n. pl.* **divers** di·vers

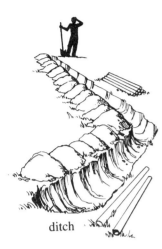

ditch

dive

diver

a	cat	i	sit	oi	oil	**ch**	chop		a in about
ā	ate	ī	lie	ou	out	**ng**	song		e in oven
ä	car	o	pot	u	cut	**sh**	she	ə =	i in pencil
e	set	ō	old	u̇	book	**th**	three		o in memory
ē	equal	ô	or	ü	blue	**ŦH**	there		u in circus
ėr	germ					**zh**	treasure		

divide   di·vide (də·vīd′)   to separate into two or more parts.
Mother will divide the pie into eight pieces.
v. **divided, divided, dividing** di·vid·ed, di·vid·ing

dividend   div·i·dend (div′ə·dend)   money earned on invested
money.
The company paid Dad a $50.00 dividend for his $800.00 investment.
n. pl. **dividends** div·i·dends

divorce   di·vorce (də·vôrs′)   **1.** the ending of a marriage.
She will get a divorce from her husband. *n. pl.* **divorces** di·vorc·es
2. to end a marriage.
She will divorce her husband.
v. **divorced, divorced, divorcing** di·vorced, di·vorc·ing

dock

dizzy   diz·zy (diz′ē)   feeling that one is going around in circles; not
steady on one's feet.
I felt dizzy when we got off the ride in the park.
adj. **dizzier, dizziest** diz·zi·er, diz·zi·est

do   (dü)   **1.** to act or work.
I will do the dishes tonight. *v.*
2. to finish an action.
I will do the painting of the fence. *v.*
3. a word used in a sentence to make the action word stronger.
Yes, I do help with the dishes. *aux.* **did, done, doing** do·ing

dock   (dok)   **1.** a place in the water where people keep boats.
We are going to the dock to meet John's ship. *n. pl.* **docks**
2. to bring a boat or ship to land.
John's ship will dock on Saturday. *v.* **docked, docked, docking** dock·ing

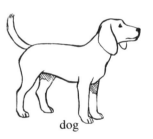
dog

doctor   doc·tor (dok′tər)   a person who helps people who are sick.
The doctor gave me a pill for my cold. *n. pl.* **doctors** doc·tors

document   doc·u·ment (dok′yə·mənt)   an important piece of paper.
This document proves that Mother and Father own the house.
n. pl. **documents** doc·u·ments

does   (duz)   *v. pres. t.* See **do.**

doesn't   does·n't (duz′nt)   does not.
Jim doesn't want his cake. *contrac.*

dog   (dôg)   an animal with four legs that people keep as a pet.
My dog is a collie, but there are many other kinds of dogs. *n. pl.* **dogs**

doghouse   dog·house (dôg′hous)   a small home for a dog.
We made a doghouse for our collie. *n. pl.* **doghouses** dog·hous·es

dog show   (dôg shō)   a contest where people display dogs.
My dog won first place at the dog show. *n. pl.* **dog shows**

doghouse

dolphin

dog sled (dôg sled) a snow vehicle that dogs pull.
Some Eskimos in Alaska have dog sleds. *n. pl.* **dog sleds**

doll (dol) a toy that looks like a baby or an older person.
The doll has brown hair and green eyes. *n. pl.* **dolls**

dollar dol·lar (dol′ər) United States money worth 100 cents.
The wooden doll cost a dollar. *n. pl.* **dollars** dol·lars

dollar bill dol·lar bill (dol′ər bil) paper money worth 100 cents.
The dollar bill fell out of his pocket. *n. pl.* **dollar bills** dol·lar bills

dollhouse doll·house (dol′hous) a small house in which children
play with dolls; a toy that looks like a small house.
I got a dollhouse for Christmas. *n. pl.* **dollhouses** doll·hous·es

dolphin dol·phin (dol′fən) an animal that lives in the ocean and has
a long pointed nose.
The dolphin jumped out of the water as the boat passed.
n. pl. **dolphins** dol·phins

donkey

dome (dōm) a round roof or ceiling.
The capitol has a gold dome. *n. pl.* **domes**

done (dun) **1.** finished.
The work on the house is done. *adj.*
2. *v. pres. part.* See **do.**

donkey don·key (dong′kē) an animal that looks like a horse
with long ears.
The donkey will not move until it is ready to move.
n. pl. **donkeys** don·keys

don't (dōnt) do not.
We don't want to go to school. *contrac.*

door (dôr) the part of a house, vehicle, building or room that opens
and closes for people to go in and out.
Knock on the door and see if they are home. *n. pl.* **doors**

doorbell

doorbell door·bell (dôr′bel) a bell or buzzer that makes a noise
inside a house when someone pushes a button outside the door.
The mailman rang the doorbell, but no one came to the door.
n. pl. **doorbells** door·bells

doorknob

doorknob door·knob (dôr′nob) the part of the door that people use
to open and close the door.
The doorknob on the new door is gold. *n. pl.* **doorknobs** door·knobs

a	cat	i	sit	oi	oil	ch	chop		a in about
ā	ate	ī	lie	ou	out	ng	song		e in oven
ä	car	o	pot	u	cut	sh	she	ə =	i in pencil
e	set	ō	old	u̇	book	th	three		o in memory
ē	equal	ô	or	ü	blue	TH	there		u in circus
ėr	germ					zh	treasure		

doorway   door·way (dôr′wā)   the opening into a room, which may have a door that opens and closes.
>The doorway into our dining room does not have a door on it.
>*n. pl.* **doorways** door·ways

dormant   dor·mant (dôr′mənt)   not active; sleeping.
>Many trees are bare and dormant in the winter. *adj.*

double   dou·ble (dub′əl)   twice as large.
>I ate a double ice cream cone. *adj.*

double-seater   dou·ble-seat·er (dub′əl-sēt′ər)   a car that has only two seats in it.
>That old car is a double-seater. *n. pl.* **double-seaters** dou·ble-seat·ers

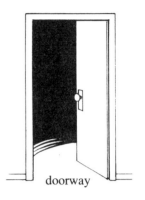
doorway

dough   (dō)   a thick batter made of flour, fat and water or some other liquid.
>The bread dough rises for one hour before we bake it in the oven. *n. pl.* **dough**

dove   (duv)   a small bird.
>The white dove flew over the house. *n. pl.* **doves**

dove   (dōv)   *v. pt. t.* See **dive** (1, 2).

down   (doun)   **1.** away from the top.
>The diver went down into the water. *adv.*
>**2.** toward the bottom.
>The girls walked down the stairs. *adv.*
>**3.** away from the beginning.
>The boat moved down the river. *adv.*
>**4.** lower or behind.
>We stood down the line from the boys. *adv.*

dove

downstairs   down·stairs (doun′sterz)   on a lower floor of a building.
>We keep the bicycles downstairs. *adv.*

downtown   down·town (doun·toun)   the part of a city that has stores and offices.
>We went downtown to buy shoes. *adv.*

downward   down·ward (doun′wərd)   to a lower place, direction or number.
>The baby cried as the elevator moved downward. *adv.*

doze   (dōz)   to take a nap.
>Dad will doze when you turn the news on the television.
>*v.* **dozed, dozed, dozing** doz·ing

dozen   doz·en (duz′n)   twelve things in a group.
>We buy eggs by the dozen. *n. pl.* **dozens** doz·ens

draft horse

Dr.   (dok′tər)   the title for a person who helps sick people.
>Dr. Bob gave me some medicine for my sore throat.
>*abbrev.* See **doctor.**

draft horse (draft hôrs) a large horse used for pulling.
> The draft horse pulls Grandfather's plow.

drag (drag) to pull something across the ground.
> You will get your coat dirty if you drag it on the ground.
> *v.* **dragged, dragged, dragging** drag·ging

dragon drag·on (drag′ən) **1.** an imaginary animal that has wings, a long tail and fire coming from its mouth.
> The dragon looked like a monster. *n. pl.* **dragons** drag·ons
> **2.** being about an animal with wings, a long tail and fire coming from its mouth.
> The boy carried his dragon doll everywhere. *adj.*

dragon

drama dra·ma (drä′mə *or* dram′ə) a play about life's problems.
> Mother wants to see a drama, but Father wants to see a comedy so he can laugh. *n. pl.* **dramas** dra·mas

drank (drangk) *v. pt. t.* See **drink** (1).

draw (drô) to use a pencil, pen or crayon to make a picture.
> The teacher asked us to draw a picture of a tree.
> *v.* **drew, drawn, drawing** draw·ing

drawer

drawer (drôr) a box that has a handle and slides out of a table, dresser, or other piece of furniture.
> I keep my sweaters in the top drawer of the dresser. *n. pl.* **drawers**

drawer draw·er (drô′ər) a person who uses a pen, pencil or crayon to make a picture.
> The drawer of the picture is a nine-year-old boy. *n. pl.* **drawers** draw·ers

drawing draw·ing (drô′ing) **1.** a picture that a person makes with a pen, pencil, or crayon.
> Katie made that drawing on my desk. *n. pl.* **drawings** draw·ings
> **2.** *v. pres. part.* See **draw.**

drawn (drôn) *v. pt. part.* See **draw.**

dream (drēm) **1.** a picture or story that is in the mind while sleeping.
> I had a dream about going to Hawaii. *n. pl.* **dreams**
> **2.** to see pictures in the mind while sleeping.
> I dream about boats several times a month.
> *v.* **dreamed** *or* **dreamt, dreamed** *or* **dreamt, dreaming** dream·ing

a	cat	**i**	sit	**oi**	oil	**ch**	chop	a in about
ā	ate	**ī**	lie	**ou**	out	**ng**	song	e in oven
ä	car	**o**	pot	**u**	cut	**sh**	she	ə = i in pencil
e	set	**ō**	old	**u̇**	book	**th**	three	o in memory
ē	equal	**ô**	or	**ü**	blue	**ŦH**	there	u in circus
ėr	germ					**zh**	treasure	

dress (dres) **1.** a piece of clothing that women or girls wear.
Katie wore a new dress today. *n. pl.* **dresses** dress·es
2. to put on clothes.
I can dress myself. *v.* **dressed, dressed, dressing** dress·ing

drew (drü) *v. pt. t.* See **draw.**

dried (drīd) **1.** without water; not wet.
Cows eat dried grass. *adj.*
2. *v. pt. t., pt. part.* See **dry.**

dress

drift (drift) **1.** a pile of something that the wind blows together.
Drifts of snow were piled as high as the car. *n. pl.* **drifts**
2. to move slowly without knowing where you are going.
Sometimes I drift towards the park when I take a walk. *v.*
3. to float in the air.
The leaves will drift to the ground in the fall.
v. **drifted, drifted, drifting** drift·ed, drift·ing

drill (dril) a practice session where you do the same thing
again and again.
The teacher gave us a math drill this afternoon. *n. pl.* **drills**

drink (dringk) **1.** to swallow a liquid.
We drink milk with our lunch every day.
v. **drank, drunk, drinking** drink·ing
2. a liquid that can be swallowed.
Milk is her favorite drink. *n. pl.* **drinks**

drip (drip) **1.** to fall in drops.
The rain will drip from the leaves.
v. **dripped, dripped, dripping** drip·ping
2. a small drop of liquid.
The drip moved down the window. *n. pl.* **drips**

drive (drīv) **1.** to steer or guide a vehicle such as a car, bus or truck.
I will learn to drive a car when I am sixteen. *v.*
2. to take someone somewhere in a car, bus or truck.
Dad will drive me to school today.
v. **drove, driven, driving** driv·en, driv·ing
3. a street.
I live at 146 Powers Drive. *n.*
4. a ride in a car.
My family takes a drive every Sunday. *n. pl.* **drives**

drive ___ crazy drive ___ cra·zy (drīv ___ krā⸍zē) to
make someone angry; to annoy.
The music you listen to on the radio will drive me crazy. *idiom*

driven driv·en (driv⸍ən) *v. pt. part.* See **drive** (1, 2).

driver dri·ver (drī⸍vər) a person who guides or steers a vehicle
such as a car, bus or truck.
The driver of the bus shouted at the children. *n. pl.* **drivers** dri·vers

driver

driveway   drive·way (drīv⸍wā)   the road that goes from the street to the garage of a house.
Dad asked me to move my bicycle out of the driveway.
n. pl. **driveways** drive·ways

driveway

drone   (drōn)   a bee whose only job is to mate with the queen bee.
The drone will die after mating with the queen. *n. pl.* **drones**

droop   (drüp)   **1.** to become sad or discouraged.
The boys' feelings will droop if they lose this game. *v.*
2. to sag or hang down.
The boy's mouth began to droop when he thought he was not going with his parents. *v.* **drooped, drooped, drooping** droop·ing

droopy   droop·y (drü⸍pē)   sagging; hanging down.
The party decorations are old and droopy.
adj. **droopier, droopiest** droop·i·er, droop·i·est

drop   (drop)   **1.** to let fall.
Be careful not to drop that vase.
v. **dropped, dropped, dropping** drop·ping
2. a small amount of liquid.
A drop of water fell on my head. *n. pl.* **drops**

drop

drop in   (drop in)   **1.** to let something fall into something.
You will need to drop in the film before using the camera. *v.*
2. to visit someone's home unexpectedly.
Please drop in and see me when you are in town.
v. **dropped in, dropped in, dropping in** drop·ping in

drop out   (drop out)   to leave before one is finished.
I had to drop out of the game early.
v. **dropped out, dropped out, dropping out** drop·ping out

dropping   drop·ping (drop⸍ing)   *v. pres. part.* See **drop** (1).

drove   (drōv)   *v. pt. t.* See **drive** (1, 2).

drown   (droun)   to die from water filling the lungs.
You need to learn to swim so that you do not drown.
v. **drowned, drowned, drowning** drown·ing

a	cat	i	sit	oi	oil	ch	chop		a in about
ā	ate	ī	lie	ou	out	ng	song		e in oven
ä	car	o	pot	u	cut	sh	she	ə =	i in pencil
e	set	ō	old	ù	book	th	three		o in memory
ē	equal	ô	or	ü	blue	ŦH	there		u in circus
ėr	germ					zh	treasure		

drug (drug) a substance used as medicine, taken to cure a sickness or to make one feel better.
It is dangerous to take a drug that a doctor did not give to you. *n. pl.* **drugs**

drum (drum) **1.** a musical instrument that is tapped or beaten to make a sound.
John plays a drum in the high school band. *n. pl.* **drums**
2. to tap or beat a drum or other object to make a sound.
Peter always drums on the table at dinnertime.
v. **drummed, drummed, drumming** drum·ming
3. having to do with a musical instrument that is tapped or beaten to make music.
John is a drum player. *adj.*

drum

drumbeat drum·beat (drum·bēt) the sound made by hitting a drum.
The drumbeat is very loud. *n. pl.* **drumbeats** drum·beats

drumming drum·ming (drum·ing) *v. pres. part.* See **drum** (2).

drumstick drum·stick (drum·stik) the stick that a person uses to tap or beat a drum.
John has a drumstick in each hand when he plays the drum.
n. pl. **drumsticks** drum·sticks

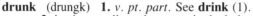
drumsticks

drunk (drungk) **1.** *v. pt. part.* See **drink** (1).
2. having swallowed too much alcohol.
People who are drunk should not drive a car. *adj.*

dry (drī) **1.** to take away water.
Susie will dry the dishes. *v.*
2. to save food by taking the water out of it.
Mother will dry the apricots, and we will have them at Thanksgiving.
v. **dried, dried, drying** dry·ing
3. not wet.
The dishes are dry so you can put them in the cabinet. *adj.*
4. empty of water.
The river is now dry, but last year the water was very deep.
adj. **drier, driest** dri·er, dri·est

dryer dry·er (drī·ər) a machine that takes the water out of something by using heat or hot air.
The hair dryer makes as much noise as the clothes dryer.
n. pl. **dryers** dry·ers

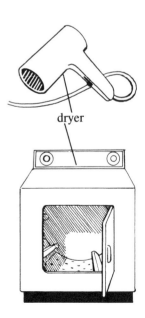
dryer

dry up (drī up) to become empty of water.
The river will dry up again if it does not rain soon.
v. **dried up, dried up, drying up** dry·ing up

128

duck

duck (duk) **1.** a bird that has webbed feet, short legs and a flat bill and that swims in water.
We threw bread crumbs to the duck in the lake. *n. pl.* **ducks**
2. having to do with a bird that has webbed feet, short legs and a flat bill and that swims in water.
The duck pond is in the back of Grandfather's farm. *adj.*

duckbill duck·bill (duk′bil) **1.** an animal that lives in water and has a nose that looks like a duck's bill.
The duckbill lives in Australia. *n.*
2. a kind of shoe whose toes are wide like a duck's bill.
The duckbill is a silly-looking shoe. *n. pl.* **duckbills** duck·bills

duck-like (duk-līk) looking or acting like a web-footed bird.
Craig has a duck-like walk. *adj.*

duckbill

duckling duck·ling (duk′ling) a baby duck.
We watched as the duckling walked behind the mother duck.
n. pl. **ducklings** duck·lings

duct (dukt) a pipe or tube that carries air or some liquid from one place to another place.
The heating duct brings the warm air from the furnace to my bedroom. *n. pl.* **ducts**

duel du·el (dü′əl *or* dyü′əl) a fight between two people with guns or swords.
Aaron Burr shot Alexander Hamilton in a duel. *n. pl.* **duels** du·els

duckling

duffel bag duf·fel bag (duf′əl bag) a sack made from canvas and used to carry clothes.
Each boy scout is allowed to take one duffel bag on the camping trip.

dug (dug) *v. pt. t., pt. part.* See **dig.**

dull (dul) **1.** not exciting; boring.
TV can be dull sometimes. *adj.*
2. not sharp or pointed.
The dull knife will not cut the bread.
adj. **duller, dullest** dull·er, dull·est

dumbwaiter dumb·wait·er (dum′wā·tər) a box that is pulled up and down a tube or a tunnel and is used to bring food from the kitchen.
The hotel uses a dumbwaiter to bring food to your room.
n. pl. **dumbwaiters** dumb·wait·ers

duffel bag

a cat	**i** sit	**oi** oil	**ch** chop		a in about
ā ate	**ī** lie	**ou** out	**ng** song		e in oven
ä car	**o** pot	**u** cut	**sh** she	ə =	i in pencil
e set	**ō** old	** u̇** book	**th** three		o in memory
ē equal	**ô** or	**ü** blue	**ŦH** there		u in circus
ėr germ			**zh** treasure		

dump (dump) **1.** to let fall in a pile.
The truck will dump the dirt in the backyard. *v.*
2. to throw something away.
Mother will dump your toys in the garbage if you don't pick them up.
v. **dumped, dumped, dumping** dump·ing

dunk (dungk) to put a basketball through the hoop by pushing it
down from above the rim.
The basketball team is learning to dunk the ball.
v. **dunked, dunked, dunking** dunk·ing

during dur·ing (dùr′ing *or* dyùr′ing) **1.** at the same time as
something else is happening.
The boys had a fight during the baseball game. *prep.*
2. throughout a certain time.
Men wore long hair during the 1960s. *prep.*

dust

dust (dust) **1.** very tiny pieces of dirt.
The dust went all over the house when the truck dumped the dirt. *plural n.*
2. to clean away the very tiny pieces of dirt.
Mother asked me to dust the furniture.
v. **dusted, dusted, dusting** dust·ed, dust·ing

dusty dust·y (dus′tē) covered with very tiny pieces of dirt.
The house got dusty when the truck dumped the dirt.
adj. **dustier, dustiest** dust·i·er, dust·i·est

Dutch (duch) **1.** the people who live in or who were born
in the Netherlands.
The Dutch were the first people to grow tulips. *plural n.*
2. the language spoken by the people of the Netherlands.
Our gardener speaks Dutch because he was born in the Netherlands.
n. no pl.
3. being from the Netherlands.
My grandmother bought some Dutch tulips. *adj.*

dwarf

dwarf (dwôrf) a person, plant, or animal that does not grow
to a normal size.
The man in the circus was a dwarf who was only three feet
tall. *n. pl.* **dwarfs**

dye (dī) **1.** to color material with a coloring liquid.
Mother will dye my old white dress blue.
v. **dyed, dyed, dyeing** dye·ing
2. the liquid used to color material.
Be careful not to spill the dye on you because it does
not come off. *n. pl.* **dyes**

dying dy·ing (dī′ing) *v. pres. part.* See **die.**

130

Ee

eagle

each (ēch) **1.** every one of several or many.
Each student in our class has a new desk. *adj.*
2. every single one.
Each of the students was asked to join the club. *pron.*
3. for one.
The shirts were ten dollars each. *adv.*

each other each oth·er (ēch uᴛʜ⁄ər) one person to another person.
The teacher asked the students to help each other with the work.

eager ea·ger (ē⁄gər) excited; greatly wanting something.
Jill is eager to go to camp. *adj.*

eagerly ea·ger·ly (ē⁄gər·lē) in an excited way.
She is eagerly waiting for Saturday. *adv.*

eagle ea·gle (ē⁄gəl) **1.** a large bird with strong wings and very good eyesight.
The bald eagle is the national bird of the United States. *n. pl.* **eagles** ea·gles
2. having to do with the large bird with strong wings and very good eyesight.
"Eagle eyes" is a name for people who can see things far away. *adj.*

ear

eaglet ea·glet (ē⁄glit) a baby eagle.
The eaglet flew out of the nest after the mother eagle. *n. pl.* **eaglets** ea·glets

ear (ir) **1.** the part of the body that hears sound.
She cannot hear from her left ear. *n.*
2. the part of a cereal plant that has seeds and can be eaten.
I like to eat an ear of corn. *n. pl.* **ears**

early ear·ly (ėr⁄lē) **1.** at the start of something.
We like to watch the stars come out in the early evening. *adj.*
2. happening before the usual time.
My mother got married at an early age.
adj. **earlier, earliest** ear·li·er, ear·li·est
3. before the usual time.
I came to school early this morning. *adv.*

earmuffs ear·muffs (ir⁄mufs) a pair of ear coverings that keep the ears warm.
My ears are cold because I lost my earmuffs. *plural n.*

earmuffs

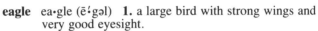

a	cat	i	sit	oi	oil	ch	chop		a in about
ā	ate	ī	lie	ou	out	ng	song		e in oven
ä	car	o	pot	u	cut	sh	she	ə =	i in pencil
e	set	ō	old	ủ	book	th	three		o in memory
ē	equal	ô	or	ü	blue	ᴛʜ	there		u in circus
ėr	germ					zh	treasure		

earn (ėrn) **1.** to get money for doing work.
I will earn three dollars by cutting the grass. *v.*
2. to work hard for something.
Sue will earn a gold star if she gets all of her math correct.
v. **earned, earned, earning** earn·ing

earth (ėrth) **1.** dirt, ground.
The bulldozer moved the earth and rocks. *n. no pl.*
2. Earth; the planet on which we live.
The Earth moves around the sun and our moon moves around the Earth. *n. no pl.*

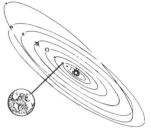
Earth

earthquake earth·quake (ėrth⸴kwāk) a movement of the ground
caused when the crust of the Earth slides.
California had an earthquake last year. *n. pl.* **earthquakes** earth·quakes

earth-year (ėrth-yir) 365 days.
Most people call 365 days a year, but a scientist calls 365 days an earth-year. *n. pl.* **earth-years**

easier eas·i·er (ē⸴zē·ər) *comp. adj.* See **easy.**

easily eas·i·ly (ē⸴zə·lē) without trouble or difficulty.
Dad can easily drive the new car. *adv.*

east (ēst) the direction of the sunrise.
We see the sun dawn in the east every day. *n. no pl.*

Easter Eas·ter (ē⸴stər) a holiday celebrated to remember the day
that Jesus Christ came back from the dead.
Easter is celebrated in the spring of the year. *n.*

Easter Bunny Eas·ter Bun·ny (ē⸴stər bun⸴ē) an imaginary animal
said to bring candy and eggs to children on Easter.
Suzie found the basket that she believed the Easter Bunny left for her.

Easter Bunny

Easter Sunday Eas·ter Sun·day (ē⸴stər sun⸴dē *or* sun⸴dā) the day that
Christians celebrate the rising from the dead of Jesus Christ.
We go to church at dawn on Easter Sunday.

eastern east·ern (ē⸴stərn) toward the direction of the sunrise.
Pennsylvania is an eastern state. *adj.*

Eastern Style East·ern Style (ē⸴stərn stīl) a kind of horse saddle
that is smaller than the Western Style.
English women used the Eastern Style saddle to ride horses.

easy eas·y (ē⸴zē) not difficult.
It is easy for Tony to learn to ride a bicycle.
adj. **easier, easiest** eas·i·er, eas·i·est

eat (ēt) to swallow food.
I love to eat candy. *v.* **ate, eaten, eating** eat·en, eat·ing

Eastern Style

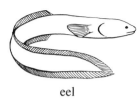

eel

egg

Cairo ●

Egypt

eaten eat·en (ēt⸗n) *v. pt. part.* See **eat.**

eating eat·ing (ēt⸗ing) *v. pres. part.* See **eat.**

eat up (ēt up) to swallow all of something.
   The bear will eat up the honey in the bee hive.
   v. **ate up, eaten up, eating up** eat·en up, eat·ing up

edge (ej) the line where something ends.
   The big tree touches the edge of the roof. *n. pl.* **edges** edg·es

Edinburgh Ed·in·burgh (ed⸗n·ber·ō) the capital city of Scotland.
   We found the Scottish hat in Edinburgh. *n.*

Edison, Thomas Alva Ed·i·son, Thom·as Al·va (ed⸗ə·sən, tom⸗əs
   al⸗və) inventor of the lightbulb, moving pictures
   and the phonograph.
   Edison invented the first talking baby doll. *n.*

editor ed·i·tor (ed⸗ə·tər) the person who corrects mistakes in
   newspapers, plays, books and movies.
   I want to be a newspaper editor. *n. pl.* **editors** ed·i·tors

eel (ēl) a long fish that looks like a snake.
   We saw an eel when we visited the aquarium. *n. pl.* **eels**

effect ef·fect (ə·fekt′) result.
   One bad effect of eating lunch late is not being hungry for dinner.
   n. pl. **effects** ef·fects

effective ef·fec·tive (ə·fek⸗tiv) able to do something well.
   She is effective at teaching math. *adj.*

effort ef·fort (ef⸗ərt) energy; work.
   It takes effort to ride a bicycle. *n. pl.* **efforts** ef·forts

egg (eg) a thin-shelled object made by a bird, reptile or fish, which
   is sometimes used as food.
   I will have an egg for breakfast. *n. pl.* **eggs**

egg white egg white (eg′hwīt) the clear part of an egg which
   becomes white when it is cooked.
   Lisa likes the egg white best, but I like the egg yolk.
   n. pl. **eggwhites** egg·whites

Egypt E·gypt (ē⸗jipt) a country in Africa; its capital is Cairo.
   The pyramids are in Egypt. *n.*

a	cat	**i**	sit	**oi**	oil	**ch**	chop	a in about
ā	ate	**ī**	lie	**ou**	out	**ng**	song	e in oven
ä	car	**o**	pot	**u**	cut	**sh**	she	ə = { i in pencil
e	set	**ō**	old	**u̇**	book	**th**	three	o in memory
ē	equal	**ô**	or	**ü**	blue	**ŦH**	there	u in circus
ėr	germ					**zh**	treasure	

Egyptian E·gyp·tian (i·jip′·shən) **1.** a person who lives in or who was born in Egypt.
> The Egyptian wears a veil. *n. pl.* **Egyptians** E·gyp·tians
> **2.** the language spoken by the people from Egypt.
> Abdul speaks Egyptian. *n. no pl.*
> **3.** having to do with the people or country of Egypt.
> The Egyptian pyramids are beautiful. *adj.*

elderberries

either ei·ther (ē′·ᴛʜər *or* ī′·ᴛʜər) **1.** one or the other of two things.
> There are two chairs so you may use either. *pron.*
> **2.** any one of two.
> You may sit on either side of your friend. *adj.*
> **3.** also; too.
> Jill is not going to the party so I will not go either. *adv.*

either ___ or ___ ei·ther ___ or ___ (ē′·ᴛʜər ___ ôr ___ *or* ī′·ᴛʜər ___ ôr ___) a choice of two things.
> You may have either cake or pie. *conj.*

elderberry el·der·ber·ry (el′·dər·ber·ē) a fruit that comes from a certain bush.
> The elderberry is dark purple and is used in pies, jellies and wines.
> *n. pl.* **elderberries** el·der·ber·ries

elderly eld·er·ly (el′·dər·lē) old.
> The elderly woman is in her eighties. *adj.*

elect e·lect (i·lekt′) to choose for an office or position of importance by voting.
> The city will elect a new mayor in June.
> *v.* **elected, elected, electing** e·lect·ed, e·lect·ing

elephant

electric e·lec·tric (i·lek′·trik) using energy that is made in a power plant by charging atoms.
> Turn on this switch to start the electric train. *adj.*

electrical e·lec·tri·cal (i·lek′·trə·kəl) having to do with energy that is made in a power plant by charging atoms.
> The lamp is electrical, but the candle is not. *adj.*

electricity e·lec·tric·i·ty (i·lek·tris′·ə·tē) the energy that is made in a power plant by charging atoms.
> Before the discovery of electricity, people used candles and oil lamps for light. *n. no pl.*

electron e·lec·tron (i·lek′·tron) the part of an atom that is used to make electricity.
> An electron is so small that we cannot see it with our eyes.
> *n. pl.* **electrons** e·lec·trons

elegant el·e·gant (el′·ə·gənt) very pretty; graceful.
> The woman looked elegant in the new gown. *adj.*

elevator

elf

elk

post office emblem

elephant el•e•phant (el′ə•fənt) a large, heavy animal with a long nose called a trunk and horns, called tusks, that come out of the mouth.
The baby elephant in the circus weighed 350 pounds.
n. pl. **elephants** el•e•phants

elevator el•e•va•tor (el′ə•vā•tər) a room or cage that moves up and down from one floor of a building to another floor.
The elevator stopped at each floor. *n. pl.* **elevators** el•e•va•tors

elf (elf) a small imaginary person who can do magic.
The story was about an elf who made shoes. *n. pl.* **elves**

elk (elk) a large deer with very large horns called antlers.
The elk walked through the snow and found the food. *n. pl.* **elk** *or* **elks**

else (els) other; different.
Is there anything else that you want to do today? *adj.*

elves (elvz) *n. pl.* See **elf.**

embarrass em•bar•rass (em•bar′əs) to make someone feel ashamed or shy.
You will embarrass me if you yell again. *v.* **embarrassed, embarrassed, embarrassing** em•bar•rassed, em•bar•rass•ing

embarrassed em•bar•rassed (em•bar′əst) **1.** ashamed or shy.
Mother felt embarrassed when her children screamed in the restaurant. *adj.*
2. *v. pt. t., pt. part.* See **embarrass.**

embarrassing em•bar•rass•ing (em•bar′ə•sing) *v. pres. part.* See **embarrass.**

emblem em•blem (em′bləm) a picture of something that means something else; a symbol of something.
The emblem on the man's shirt means that he works for the post office.
n. pl. **emblems** em•blems

emergency e•mer•gen•cy (i•mėr′jən•sē) **1.** an event that causes the need to do some activity quickly.
Operator, please get me the police; this is an emergency.
n. pl. **emergencies** e•mer•gen•cies
2. needing to do something quickly.
The little girl needed an emergency operation on her leg. *adj.*

a	cat	**i**	sit	**oi**	oil	**ch**	chop	ə =	a in about
ā	ate	**ī**	lie	**ou**	out	**ng**	song		e in oven
ä	car	**o**	pot	**u**	cut	**sh**	she		i in pencil
e	set	**ō**	old	**ů**	book	**th**	three		o in memory
ē	equal	**ô**	or	**ü**	blue	**ŦH**	there		u in circus
ėr	germ					**zh**	treasure		

emperor em·per·or (em‑pər·ər) a king or leader of a country.
Nero was an emperor in Rome many centuries ago.
n. pl. **emperors** em·per·ors

employer em·ploy·er (em·ploi‑ər) the person or business that pays
a person to do a job.
John's employer is the police department. *n. pl.* **employers** em·ploy·ers

empty emp·ty (emp‑tē) **1.** having nothing inside.
The school is empty in the summer.
adj. **emptier, emptiest** emp·ti·er, emp·ti·est
2. to take everything out of something.
Will you empty the garbage can for me?
v. **emptied, emptied, emptying** emp·tied, emp·ty·ing

empty

encephalitis en·ceph·a·li·tis (en·sef·ə·lī‑tis) a disease of the brain.
Doctors can cure encephalitis. *n. no pl.*

enchanted en·chant·ed (en·chan‑tid) being under a magic spell.
The enchanted frog became a prince when the girl kissed him. *adj.*

encourage en·cour·age (en·kėr‑ij) to give hope
or strength to someone.
Your friends will encourage you if you begin to feel sad.
v. **encouraged, encouraged, encouraging** en·cour·aged, en·cour·ag·ing

encyclopedia en·cy·clo·pe·di·a (en·sī·klə·pē‑dē·ə) a book or set of
books that gives many details about many things that are listed
in alphabetical order.
We used the encyclopedia to read about horses.
n. pl. **encyclopedias** en·cy·clo·pe·di·as

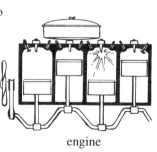
encyclopedia

end (end) **1.** the last part of something.
I did not like the end of the movie. *n. pl.* **ends**
2. to finish something.
We end a sentence with a period. *v.*
3. to stop something.
We must end this game before dinner.
v. **ended, ended, ending** end·ed, end·ing

enemy en·e·my (en‑ə·mē) people who fight each other or who do
not like each other.
Germany and the United States were enemies during World War II.
n. pl. **enemies** en·e·mies

energy en·er·gy (en‑ər·jē) strength; power; pep.
The little girl is full of energy. *n. pl.* **energies** en·er·gies

engine en·gine (en‑jən) a machine or motor.
The car will not start because there is something wrong with the engine.
n. pl. **engines** en·gines

engine

England
London

engineer en·gi·neer (en·jə·nir′) **1.** a person who designs machines.
My brother is an engineer for the Navy and designs airplanes. *n.*
2. a person who builds machines.
Her father is an electrical engineer, and he makes electrical machines.
n. pl. **engineers** en·gi·neers

England Eng·land (ing′glənd) a country in northern Europe that is also called Great Britain; its capital is London.
We went to England last summer. *n.*

English Eng·lish (ing′glish) **1.** the people who live in or who were born in England.
The English are very quiet people. *plural n.*
2. the language spoken in England, the United States, and many other countries.
We speak English in the United States. *n. no pl.*
3. about the people or country of England.
The boy from London is English. *adj.*

engraving en·grav·ing (en·grā′ving) a picture or drawing made on metal.
The man made an engraving on the silver button.
n. pl. **engravings** en·grav·ings

enjoy en·joy (en·joi′) to have fun, to be happy.
We will enjoy riding in the airplane.
v. **enjoyed, enjoyed, enjoying** en·joy·ed, en·joy·ing

enjoyable en·joy·a·ble (en·joi′ə·bəl) giving happiness; fun.
The visit to the zoo was enjoyable. *adj.*

enjoyment en·joy·ment (en·joi′mənt) pleasure; happiness.
Her enjoyment of the circus showed in her smiling face. *n. no pl.*

engraving

enlightenment en·light·en·ment (en·līt′n·mənt) knowledge of how to find peace and happiness.
Men have searched for enlightenment for centuries. *n. no pl.*

enormous e·nor·mous (i·nôr′məs) very large.
An elephant is enormous. *adj.*

enough e·nough (i·nuf′) as much as is needed.
We have enough food here to feed eighty men. *adj.*

enrober en·rob·er (in·rob′ər) a machine used for covering candy with chocolate.
The candymaker uses an enrober to cover his chocolates.
n. pl. **enrobers** en·rob·ers

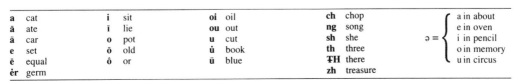

a	cat	i	sit	oi	oil	ch	chop		a in about
ā	ate	ī	lie	ou	out	ng	song		e in oven
ä	car	o	pot	u	cut	sh	she	ə =	i in pencil
e	set	ō	old	u̇	book	th	three		o in memory
ē	equal	ô	or	ü	blue	ŦH	there		u in circus
ėr	germ					zh	treasure		

enter en·ter (en′tər) **1.** to go into.
Enter the door on the left to go into the doctor's office. *v.*
2. to join in a race or contest.
You may enter the race if you are eighteen.
v. **entered, entered, entering** en·tered, en·ter·ing

entertain en·ter·tain (en·tər·tān′) to please someone or keep
someone interested.
The clown will entertain the children. *v.* **entertained, entertained,
entertaining** en·ter·tained, en·ter·tain·ing

entertainment en·ter·tain·ment (en·tər·tān′mənt) things that
people do to be happy, to be interested and to enjoy
themselves.
My favorite entertainment is going to the movies. *n. no pl.*

entrance en·trance (en′trans) **1.** a door into a building or room.
The entrance to the doctor's office is on the left.
n. pl. **entrances** en·tranc·es
2. having to do with the door into a building or room.
The entrance door is closed; we will need to use the exit. *adj.*

envelope en·ve·lope (en′və·lōp *or* än′və·lōp) the paper covering
for a letter, card or bill on which a person's name and
address are written.
The envelope had my name on it. *n. pl.* **envelopes** en·ve·lopes

enzyme en·zyme (en′zīm) a substance made and used by the body.
An enzyme is needed for every job that the body does, like digesting food.
n. pl. **enzymes** en·zymes

eohippus e·o·hip·pus (ē·ō·hip′əs) a small horse that lived on
Earth thousands of years ago.
The eohippus looked more like a dog than a horse and was only the
size of a cat. *n. pl.* **eohippuses** e·o·hip·pus·es

E Pluribus Unum E Plu·ri·bus U·num (ē plür′ə·bes yü′nəm)
Latin words stamped on United States coin money that means
"out of many, one."
"E Pluribus Unum" means that we are a united country, not divided
by differences.

equal e·qual (ē′kwəl) being the same as.
She gave us equal pieces of pie. *adj.*

equally e·qual·ly (ē′kwə·lē) in the same way; to be the same.
The pie was divided equally. *adv.*

equator e·qua·tor (i·kwā′tər) an imaginary line that goes around
the center of the Earth.
The United States is above the equator, and South America is
below the equator. *n. no pl.*

envelope

eohippus

equator

equipment e·quip·ment (i·kwip⁄mənt) tools; supplies.
We will need special equipment to climb that mountain. *plural n.*

eraser

erase e·rase (i·rās′) to take something away by rubbing or wiping.
The teacher asked Tony to erase the chalkboard.
v. **erased, erased, erasing** e·rased, e·ras·ing

eraser e·ras·er (i·rās⁄ər) the object that people use to erase something.
I use the eraser on my pencil often when I do math problems.
n. pl. **erasers** e·ras·ers

erode e·rode (i·rōd′) to slowly eat away the earth.
The wind and rain erode the mountains.
v. **eroded, eroded, eroding** e·rod·ed, e·rod·ing

erosion e·ro·sion (i·rō⁄zhən) the eating away of the earth by the wind and the rain.
We plant trees to stop the erosion of the soil. *n. no pl.*

erupt e·rupt (i·rupt′) to explode.
The volcano will erupt soon.
v. **erupted, erupted, erupting** e·rupt·ed, e·rupt·ing

eruption e·rup·tion (i·rup⁄shən) liquid flowing from the top of something.
We could see the eruption of the volcano. *n. pl.* **eruptions** e·rup·tions

escalator

escalator es·ca·la·tor (es⁄kə·lā·tər) moving stairs.
I like to ride an escalator better than riding an elevator.
n. pl. **escalators** es·ca·la·tors

escape es·cape (e·skāp′) **1.** to get away from.
The robbers will escape from the police if they can.
v. **escaped, escaped, escaping** es·caped, es·cap·ing
2. having to do with getting away.
The robber's escape plan was to lock the policeman in the cell. *adj.*

Eskimo

Eskimo Es·ki·mo (es⁄kə·mō) **1.** a person who lives in or who was born in the arctic (cold) areas of the world.
The Eskimo needs a dog sled to travel from place to place in the winter.
n. pl. **Eskimo or Eskimos** Es·ki·mo *or* Es·ki·mos
2. the language spoken by the people who live in the arctic.
I cannot understand the boy who is speaking Eskimo. *n. no pl.*
3. having to do with the people of the arctic.
The Eskimo house is called an igloo. *adj.*

a	cat	i	sit	oi	oil	ch	chop		a in about
ā	ate	ī	lie	ou	out	ng	song		e in oven
ä	car	o	pot	u	cut	sh	she	ə =	i in pencil
e	set	ō	old	u̇	book	th	three		o in memory
ē	equal	ô	or	ü	blue	ᵀH	there		u in circus
ėr	germ					zh	treasure		

especially es·pe·cial·ly (e·spesh⹁ə·lē) first of all; more than any other; just for.
I baked this cake especially for you. *adv.*

eucalyptus eu·ca·lyp·tus (yü·kə·lip⹁təs) **1.** a tree whose leaves are used in making medicines.
The eucalyptus has a very strong smell.
n. pl. **eucalyptuses** or **eucalypti** eu·ca·lyp·tus·es or eu·ca·lyp·ti
2. having to do with the tree that is used for making medicines.
The eucalyptus cough drops taste terrible. *adj.*

Europe Eur·ope (yur⹁əp) a continent west of Asia and east of the North Atlantic Ocean.
My family will go to Europe this summer. *n.*

European Eur·o·pe·an (yur⹁ə·pē·ən) **1.** a person who lives in or who was born in Europe.
Pierre was born in France, so he is both French and European.
n. pl. **Europeans** Eur·o·pe·ans
2. having to do with the people or the countries of Europe.
European people speak many different languages. *adj.*

even e·ven (ē⹁vən) **1.** despite.
Even with her fur coat the princess was cold. *adv.*
2. to a greater degree; more.
I have to study even more to get an A. *adv.*
3. indeed; in fact.
The sick man could not even stand up. *adv.*
4. flat; level.
The picture on the wall is not even. *adj.*

evening eve·ning (ēv⹁ning) **1.** the time of day between afternoon and night; between sunset and bedtime.
I like to watch TV in the evening. *n. pl.* **evenings** eve·nings
2. having to do with the time of day between afternoon and night.
I like to look at the evening stars. *adj.*

event e·vent (i·vent′) **1.** something that happens.
The discovery of America was a great event. *n.*
2. one activity in a program of things.
The boys' dance is the third event on the school program. *n. pl.* **events** e·vents

eventually e·ven·tu·al·ly (i·ven⹁chü·ə·lē) finally; in the end.
I am sure I will see that movie eventually. *adv.*

eucalyptus

Europe

evergreen trees

ever   ev·er (ev′ər)   **1.** at any time.
If I can ever help you with your math, give me a call. *adv.*
2. by any chance.
How did you ever lose so much weight? *adv.*

evergreen tree   ev·er·green tree (ev′ər·grēn trē)   a plant that has green leaves or needles all year.
The pine tree is an evergreen tree.

every   eve·ry (ev′rē)   each one.
Every boy and girl in the school will be happy to have school closed for the summer. *adj.*

everybody   eve·ry·bod·y (ev′rə·bud·ē *or* ev′rē·bod·ē)   each person.
Everybody who knows you thinks you are pretty. *pron.*

every day   eve·ry day (ev′rē dā)   daily, happening on each day.
I brush my teeth three times every day.

everyone   eve·ry·one (ev′rē·wun *or* ev′rē·wən)   each person.
Everyone who knows you thinks that you are pretty. *pron.*

everyone else   eve·ry·one else (ev′rē·wun els *or* ev′rē·wən els)   the other people in a group.
Everyone else was going to the dance, so I decided to go.

everything   eve·ry·thing (ev′rē·thing)   each thing; all things.
I like everything that is sweet. *pron.*

every time   eve·ry time (ev′rē tīm)   each time.
Every time I ride my bicycle I fall.

everywhere   eve·ry·where (ev′rē·hwer *or* ev′rē·hwar)   in each place; in all places.
I looked everywhere for that ring, but I can't find it. *adv.*

evidence   ev·i·dence (ev′ə·dəns)   something that shows people what is true; facts.
Fossils are evidence that certain animals once lived on Earth. *n. no pl.*

evil   e·vil (ē′vəl)   very bad.
The witch was an evil person. *adj.*

exact   ex·act (eg·zakt′)   right; correct.
I had the exact amount of money that I needed to pay for the doll. *adj.*

exactly   ex·act·ly (eg·zakt′lē)   correctly; precisely.
She got home exactly at 9:00. *adv.*

a	cat	i	sit	oi	oil	ch	chop		à in about
ā	ate	ī	lie	ou	out	ng	song		e in oven
ä	car	o	pot	u	cut	sh	she	ə =	i in pencil
e	set	ō	old	u̇	book	th	three		o in memory
ē	equal	ô	or	ü	blue	TH	there		u in circus
ėr	germ					zh	treasure		

examination ex·am·i·na·tion (eg·zam·ə·nā⸍shən) **1.** a check-up by a doctor.
> I went to see Dr. Smith for my examination. *n.*
> **2.** a test given by a teacher, school or college.
> I took my science examination yesterday.
> *n. pl.* **examinations** ex·am·i·na·tions

examine ex·am·ine (eg·zam⸍ən) to look at closely or carefully.
> The doctor will examine my ears.
> *v.* **examined, examined, examining** ex·am·ined, ex·am·in·ing

example ex·am·ple (eg·zam⸍pəl) something that is used to show how something else looks or works; a sample.
> The teacher put an example of the new math problem on the chalkboard.
> *n. pl.* **examples** ex·am·ples

examine

excellent ex·cel·lent (ek⸍sə·lənt) very, very good.
> Michael's dance was excellent. *adj.*

except ex·cept (ek·sept′) other than; but.
> Mary got all except one of the problems correct. *prep.*

exchange ex·change (eks·chānj′) **1.** a place where things are traded.
> We go to the book exchange every month.
> *n. pl.* **exchanges** ex·chang·es
> **2.** to trade something for another thing.
> I will exchange this dress for one that fits me.
> *v.* **exchanged, exchanged, exchanging** ex·changed, ex·chang·ing

excite ex·cite (ek·sīt′) to make happy.
> The new car will excite Dad.
> *v.* **excited, excited, exciting** ex·cit·ed, ex·cit·ing

excited ex·cit·ed (ek·sī⸍tid) **1.** very happy.
> Dad is excited about the new car. *adj.*
> **2.** *v. pt. t., pt. part.* See **excite.**

excitedly ex·cit·ed·ly (ek·sī⸍tid·lē) with great happiness.
> Dad waited excitedly for the man to bring the car keys. *adv.*

excitement ex·cite·ment (ek·sīt⸍mənt) a happy feeling.
> The new car caused a lot of excitement at our house. *n. no pl.*

exciting ex·cit·ing (ek·sī⸍ting) **1.** causing a happy feeling.
> Driving a new car is exciting. *adj.*
> **2.** *v. pres. part.* See **excite.**

exclaim ex·claim (ek·sklām′) to cry out or say something suddenly.
> "This new car is mine," he exclaimed.
> *v.* **exclaimed, exclaimed, exclaiming** ex·claimed, ex·claim·ing

excuse ___ ex·cuse ___ (ek·skyüz′ ___) a term of politeness said when asking for forgiveness for something that one did.
> The man said "excuse me" as he walked in front of me in the movie. *idiom*

exercise

exercise ex·er·cise (ek'sər·sīz) **1.** to do an activity that uses energy and makes the body stronger or healthier.
He will exercise for an hour every day.
v. **exercised, exercised, exercising** ex·er·cised, ex·er·cis·ing
2. an activity that uses energy and makes the body stronger.
The exercise that she taught me will strengthen my legs.
n. pl. **exercises** ex·er·cis·es
3. having to do with an activity that uses energy and makes the body stronger.
My exercise class meets every Tuesday. *adj.*

exhale ex·hale (eks·hāl') to let air out of the lungs.
The doctor said to take a deep breath and then exhale.
v. **exhaled, exhaled, exhaling** ex·haled, ex·hal·ing

exile ex·ile (eg'zīl *or* ek'sīl) to make someone leave a country.
The government may exile a person for very bad crimes.
v. **exiled, exiled, exiling** ex·iled, ex·il·ing

existence ex·ist·ence (eg·zis'təns) a fact that something is or was.
Fossils have proven the existence of dinosaurs. *n. no pl.*

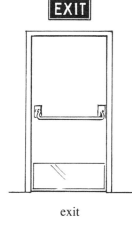

exit

exit ex·it (eg'zit *or* ek'sit) the way out of a building or a room.
The exit is in the back of the room. *n. pl.* **exits** ex·its

expect ex·pect (ek·spekt') to be almost sure that something will happen.
I expect to see my grandmother in July.
v. **expected, expected, expecting** ex·pect·ed, ex·pect·ing

expensive ex·pen·sive (ek·spen'siv) costing a large amount of money; worth a lot of money.
The new car was expensive. *adj.*

experience ex·per·i·ence (ek·spir'ē·əns) **1.** what we learn by doing or seeing something.
The experience of camping taught Tom to be careful in the forest. *n.*
2. a thing that happens to you.
Getting lost in the forest was a terrible experience.
n. pl. **experiences** ex·per·i·enc·es
3. to learn from doing or seeing something.
He experienced being alone in the forest.
v. **experienced, experienced, experiencing** ex·per·i·enced, ex·per·i·enc·ing

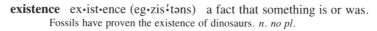

a	cat	i	sit	oi	oil	ch	chop		a in about
ā	ate	ī	lie	ou	out	ng	song		e in oven
ä	car	o	pot	u	cut	sh	she	ə =	i in pencil
e	set	ō	old	u̇	book	th	three		o in memory
ē	equal	ô	or	ü	blue	ŦH	there		u in circus
ėr	germ					zh	treasure		

experiment ex·per·i·ment (ek·sper'ə·mənt)   a test to discover
something, often done in science.
    The experiment is not dangerous if done carefully.
    n. pl. **experiments** ex·per·i·ments

explain ex·plain (ek·splān')   to tell about something.
    The teacher will explain how to do the math problem.
    v. **explained, explained, explaining** ex·plained, ex·plain·ing

explode ex·plode (ek·splōd')   to burst and be destroyed.
    The experiment can explode if you are not careful.
    v. **exploded, exploded, exploding** ex·plod·ed, ex·plod·ing

explode

explore ex·plore (ek·splôr' *or* ek·slpōr')   to search for or travel
through a place that is unknown to you or others.
    The boys will explore the cave together.
    v. **explored, explored, exploring** ex·plored, ex·plor·ing

explorer ex·plor·er (ek·slpôr'ər *or* ek·splōr'ər)   a person who
searches for or travels through a place that is unknown.
    Christopher Columbus was an explorer who came to America.
    n. pl. **explorers** ex·plor·ers

explosion ex·plo·sion (ek·splō'zhən)   the noise made when
something bursts.
    The chemical explosion was so loud that we heard it at school.
    n. pl. **explosions** ex·plo·sions

explosive ex·plo·sive (ek·splō'siv)   the thing that causes something
to burst and be destroyed.
    The chemical became an explosive when it became hot.
    n. pl. **explosives** ex·plo·sives

extinguish

export ex·port (ek'spôrt)   **1.** something that is sent to another
country and sold.
    Wheat is an export from the United States. *n. pl.* **exports** ex·ports
2. to send something to another country to be sold.
    We export wheat to Russia.
    v. **exported, exported, exporting** ex·port·ed, ex·port·ing

exposition ex·po·si·tion (ek·spə·zish'ən)   a fair or
display of things like paintings or machines.
    The exposition had many different electrical machines.
    n. pl. **expositions** ex·po·si·tions

express ex·press (ek·spres')   very fast.
    We took the express train to Chicago last summer. *adj.*

extinguish ex·tin·guish (ek·sting'gwish)   to stop a fire or
light from burning.
    The firemen will extinguish the fire.
    v. **extinguished, extinguished, extinguishing**
    ex·tin·guished, ex·tin·guish·ing

extinguisher

eye

eyebrow

extinguisher ex·tin·guish·er (ek·sting′gwish·ər) something that is used to stop a fire from burning.
The fire extinguisher is in the hall if you need it.
n. pl. **extinguishers** ex·tin·guish·ers

extra ex·tra (ek′strə) **1.** more than is needed at a certain time or for a specific thing.
We had extra food, so we asked the other campers to have dinner with us. *adj.*
2. more than usual.
Mother asked us to try extra hard to finish the painting. *adv.*

extremely ex·treme·ly (ek·strēm′lē) very much; much more than.
It is extremely hot in here this afternoon. *adv.*

eye (ī) the part of the face that can see.
I have something in my eye. *n. pl.* **eyes**

eyeball eye·ball (ī′bôl) the round part of the eye.
The eyeball will move when you watch something that is moving.
n. pl. **eyeballs** eye·balls

eyebrow eye·brow (ī′brou) the short hairs that are above the eye
She has beautiful black eyebrows. *n. pl.* **eyebrows** eye·brows

eyeglasses eye·glass·es (ī′glas·iz) things worn to help a person see better.
I need eyeglasses for reading. *plural n.*

eyesight eye·sight (ī′sīt) ability to see.
My eyesight is not good so I must wear eyeglasses. *n. no pl.*

eyeglasses

a cat	**i** sit	**oi** oil	**ch** chop		a in about		
ā ate	**ī** lie	**ou** out	**ng** song		e in oven		
ä car	**o** pot	**u** cut	**sh** she	ə =	i in pencil		
e set	**ō** old	**u̇** book	**th** three		o in memory		
ē equal	**ô** or	**ü** blue	**TH** there		u in circus		
ėr germ			**zh** treasure				

Ff

fabric   fab·ric (fab′rik)   material; cloth.
Velvet is a soft fabric, and satin is a shiny fabric. *n. pl.* **fabrics** fab·rics

fabulous   fab·u·lous (fab′yə·ləs)   wonderful; very good.
The ride on the airplane was fabulous. *adj.*

face   (fās)   **1.** the part of the head that is in front and has the eyes, nose and mouth.
I must wash my face and hands before dinner. *n.*
2. the front part of a watch or clock that has the numbers on it.
The face of my watch shines in the dark. *n. pl.* **faces** fa·ces
3. to turn toward or in the direction of.
Bill must face the class when he reads. *v.* **faced, faced, facing** fac·ing

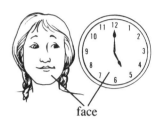
face

face cloth   (fās   klôth)   a piece of towel material that is used to clean the face.
We each have a face cloth in the bathroom. *n. pl.* **face cloths**

face to face   (fās   tü   fās)   looking at each other.
We have talked on the telephone but never met face to face. *idiom*

fact   (fakt)   true information about something.
It is a fact that two plus two equals four. *n. pl.* **facts**

factory   fac·tor·y (fak′tər·ē)   a place where things are made.
The factory on our street makes shoes. *n. pl.* **factories** fac·tor·ies

faint   (fānt)   to feel dizzy and pass out.
Mother will faint if she sees you in that tree.
v. **fainted, fainted, fainting** faint·ed, faint·ing

face cloth

fair   (fer *or* far)   **1.** a display of farm things like machines and food.
We won first prize at the fair for our apple pie. *n. pl.* **fairs**
2. right; just; honest.
It is not fair that my brother can go to the movie but I cannot. *adj.*
3. beautiful.
The man kissed the fair lady and she woke up.
adj. **fairer, fairest** fair·er, fair·est

fairground   fair·ground (fer′ground *or* far′ground)   a place where a farm display is held.
The fairground is near Grandmother's farm.
n. pl. **fairgrounds** fair·grounds

fairies   fair·ies (fer′ēz *or* far′ēz)   *n. pl.* See **fairy** (1).

fairly   fair·ly (fer′lē *or* far′lē)   **1.** average.
She is a fairly good ballplayer. *adv.*
2. in a just way or the right way.
Mother will divide the candy fairly. *adv.*

fairy   fair·y (fer′ē *or* far′ē)   **1.** an imaginary small person who can do magic.
The fairy appeared to Peter Pan. *n. pl.* **fairies** fair·ies
2. having to do with an imaginary small person.
The fairy godmother turned the pumpkin into a carriage. *adj.*

fairy

fairyland   fair·y·land (fer′ē·land *or* far′ē·land)   a make-believe or unreal place with magical things and people.
The parents decorated the gym to look like a fairyland.
n. pl. **fairylands** fair·y·lands

fall   (fôl)   **1.** the season of the year between summer and winter; the time of the year when the leaves change colors; autumn.
I think fall is the prettiest season of the year. *n. no pl.*
2. to drop towards the ground.
The picture will fall from the wall if you slam that door again.
v. **fell, fallen, falling** fall·en, fall·ing
3. having to do with autumn.
The fall air is cool. *adj.*

fall asleep   fall a·sleep (fôl ə·slēp′)   to begin a deep rest.
You must not fall asleep at school. *idiom*

fall in love with   (fôl in luv wiᴛʜ)   to have a deep liking for someone.
You will fall in love with my grandfather. *idiom*

fall off   (fôl ôf)   to drop from someplace or something.
The dish will fall off the shelf if you are not careful.
v. **fell off, fallen off, falling off** fall·en off, fall·ing off

fall over   fall o·ver (fôl ō′vər)   to drop to the ground; to drop to the side.
That vase will fall over if you bump the table.
v. **fell over, fallen over, falling over** fell o·ver, fall·en o·ver, fall·ing o·ver

false   (fôls)   not true; not real.
The story he told you was false. *adj.*

fame   (fām)   the public knowing who a person is.
The fame of TV and movie stars means that people know them everyplace they go. *n. no pl.*

a	cat	i	sit	oi	oil	ch	chop		a in about
ā	ate	ī	lie	ou	out	ng	song		e in oven
ä	car	o	pot	u	cut	sh	she	ə =	i in pencil
e	set	ō	old	u̇	book	th	three		o in memory
ē	equal	ô	or	ü	blue	ᴛʜ	there		u in circus
ėr	germ					zh	treasure		

147

familiar   fa·mil·iar (fə·mil‿yər)   well known; often seen.
> She looks familiar to me; maybe I have seen her here before. *adj.*

families   fam·i·lies (fam‿ə·lēz)   *n. pl.* See **family** (1).

family   fam·i·ly (fam‿ə·lē)   **1.** a group of people who are related;
mother, father, children, aunts, uncles, cousins
and grandparents.
> I have two brothers and one sister in my family. *n. pl.* **families** fam·i·lies
> **2.** having to do with a group of people who are related.
> It is a family custom to open one gift on Christmas Eve. *adj.*

famous   fa·mous (fā‿məs)   known by many people.
> The President of the United States is famous. *adj.*

fan   (fan)   **1.** a machine that blows air around the room.
> The fan blew the teacher's papers off her desk. *n.*
> **2.** a person who likes something or someone very much.
> Lisa is a baseball fan. *n. pl.* **fans**

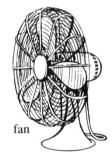
fan

fanciest   fan·ci·est (fan‿sē·əst)   *superl. adj.* See **fancy.**

fancy   fan·cy (fan‿sē)   elegant; decorated.
> Her new dress is fancy. *adj.* **fancier, fanciest** fan·ci·er, fan·ci·est

fang   (fang)   a long sharp tooth.
> The dog broke a fang eating the bone. *n. pl.* **fangs**

fantastic   fan·tas·tic (fan·tas‿tik)   wonderful.
> I think the new car is fantastic. *adj.*

fantasy   fan·ta·sy (fan‿tə·sē)   **1.** a dream.
> The trip to Hawaii is a fantasy that has come true. *n.*
> **2.** imaginary; not real.
> The story of Cinderella is a fantasy. *n. pl.* **fantasies** fan·ta·sies
> **3.** having to do with a dream or something that is imaginary.
> Cinderella is a fantasy story. *adj.*

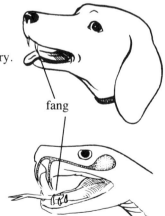
fang

far   (fär)   a long way, a great distance.
> We live far from my grandmother.
> *adv.* **farther** *or* **further, farthest** *or* **furthest**
> far·ther *or* fur·ther, far·thest *or* fur·thest

far away   far a·way (fär ə·wā′)   a long distance.
> Europe is far away from America.

fare   (fer *or* far)   the cost to ride a bus, cab, plane or train.
> The airplane fare is very expensive. *n. pl.* **fares**

farm

farmer

farm (färm) **1.** a place where animals are raised and food is grown.
We will visit my grandmother's farm. *n. pl.* **farms**
2. having to do with a place that raises animals and food.
The farm truck carries hay. *adj.*
3. to grow food and raise animals.
He will farm the land. *v.* **farmed, farmed, farming** farm·ing

farmer farm·er (färm′ər) a person who works on a place that raises animals and food.
The farmer has a large garden and many cows. *n. pl.* **farmers** farm·ers

farmhouse farm·house (färm′hous) the home for the people who raise animals and food.
The farmhouse is in the middle of the farm.
n. pl. **farmhouses** farm·hous·es

farming farm·ing (färm′ing) *v. pres. part.* See **farm** (3).

farther far·ther (fär′THər) to or at a greater distance.
Ben lives farther from school than I do. *comp. adj.* See **far.**

fascinating fas·ci·nat·ing (fas′n·āt·ing) very interesting; not boring.
The story I am reading is fascinating. *adj.*

fashionable fash·ion·a·ble (fash′ə·nə·bəl) being in style; the accepted way.
Wearing blue jeans to school is fashionable today. *adj.*

fast (fast) **1.** doing something quickly; in a short time.
Mother is a fast worker. *adj.* **faster, fastest** fast·er, fast·est
2. quickly.
I will work fast so that I can be finished in an hour. *adv.*
3. speedily.
The car was going fast when it hit the tree. *adv.*
4. to not eat.
Some people fast to lost weight. *v.* **fasted, fasted, fasting** fast·ed, fast·ing

fast asleep fast a·sleep (fast ə·slēp′) in a deep sleep; not awake.
Dad was fast asleep when we got home. *idiom*

fast moving fast mov·ing (fast mü′ving) quick; speedy.
The race car is fast moving.

a	cat	i	sit	oi	oil	ch	chop		a in about
ā	ate	ī	lie	ou	out	ng	song		e in oven
ä	car	o	pot	u	cut	sh	she	ə =	i in pencil
e	set	ō	old	ù	book	th	three		o in memory
ē	equal	ô	or	ü	blue	ŦH	there		ù in circus
ėr	germ					zh	treasure		

fat (fat) **1.** large; weighing many pounds.
You will get fat if you keep eating candy. *adj.* **fatter, fattest** fat·ter, fat·test
2. an oily substance that comes from animals.
Bacon has a lot of fat in it. *n. pl.* **fats**

father fa·ther (fä′THər) **1.** the male parent.
My father works in a grocery store. *n.*
2. Father, title of respect for a man of the church.
Father Thomas smiled at us as we walked into church.
n. pl. **fathers** fa·thers

fault (fôlt) **1.** mistake; reason for blame.
It was not my fault that the dish fell. *n.*
2. a break in the Earth's crust.
There is a large fault in California. *n. pl.* **faults**

feast

favorite fa·vor·ite (fä′vər·it) **1.** most liked.
You are my favorite friend. *adj.*
2. most liked.
I like all chocolate, but Snickers bars are my favorite.
n. pl. **favorites** fa·vor·ites

FDA (ef dē ā) Food and Drug Administration. *abbrev.*

fear (fir) **1.** to feel afraid.
I fear that you will get hurt. *v.* **feared, feared, fearing** fear·ing
2. a feeling of danger.
The fear of flying keeps me out of airplanes. *n. pl.* **fears**

fearless fear·less (fir′lis) not afraid; to have no
feelings of danger.
Superman is fearless. *adj.*

fearsome fear·some (fir′səm) something that causes fear.
The lion is fearsome. *adj.*

feast (fēst) a large meal with many different things to eat.
The king had a feast for the men who came back from war. *n. pl.* **feasts**

feather feath·er (feTH′ər) **1.** the growth that is on the skin of a bird.
A feather is light and fluffy. *n. pl.* **feathers** feath·ers
2. made of feathers.
My grandmother's feather bed is soft and comfortable. *adj.*

feather

feature fea·ture (fē′chər) **1.** part of the face.
My eyes are my best feature. *n.*
2. a part of something that makes it special or different.
The feature that describes an elephant is a long nose called a trunk.
n. pl. **features** fea·tures

fed (fed) *v. pt. t., pt. part.* See **feed** (1).

feed

felt-tip

federal fed·er·al (fed'ər·əl) having to do with the
government of a nation.
People can be exiled for breaking a federal law. *adj.*

fee (fē) the cost to join a club or to buy a service.
The fee for cable television is $25.00 a month. *n. pl.* **fees**

feed (fēd) **1.** to give food to an animal or a small baby.
It is time to feed the dog. *v.* **fed, fed, feeding** feed·ing
2. food that is given to an animal.
The chicken feed is in the barn. *n. no pl.*

feel (fēl) **1.** to touch something with a hand or other
part of the body.
The cat likes people to feel her fur. *v.*
2. to believe that something is true without facts or proof.
I feel she is telling the truth. *v.*
3. to have an emotion about someone or something.
I think I feel angry at him for breaking my doll. *v.*
4. to get the sense of being touched by someone or something.
The sun will feel warm today. *v.* **felt, felt, feeling** feel·ing

feeling feel·ing (fē'ling) **1.** emotion.
Love is a wonderful feeling. *n. pl.* **feelings** feel·ings
2. *v. pres. part.* See **feel.**

feel sorry for feel sor·ry for (fēl sor'ē fôr) to be sad about
someone; to have a sad emotion about someone; to have
sympathy for someone.
I feel sorry for the girl that lost the dog.

feet (fēt) *n. pl.* See **foot.**

fell (fel) *v. pt. t.* See **fall** (2).

fell asleep fell a·sleep (fel ə·slēp') See **fall asleep.**

fellow fel·low (fel'ō) a man or boy.
The fellow sitting next to me was my cousin. *n. pl.* **fellows** fel·lows

felt (felt) *v. pt. t., pt. part.* See **feel.**

felt-tip (felt-tip) the end of a pen that is made out of material
and not metal.
The felt-tip pen smells terrible. *adj.*

a	cat	i	sit	oi	oil	ch	chop		a in about
ā	ate	ī	lie	ou	out	ng	song		e in oven
ä	car	o	pot	u	cut	sh	she	ə =	i in pencil
e	set	ō	old	ů	book	th	three		o in memory
ē	equal	ô	or	ü	blue	ŦH	there		u in circus
ėr	germ					zh	treasure		

female fe·male (fē‧māl) **1.** a woman or a girl.
My mother is a female. *n. pl.* **females** fe·males
2. having to do with a woman or a girl.
The female baseball team will not let the men join the team. *adj.*

fence (fens) a wall that goes around a yard or a field.
The fence keeps the dog from running away. *n. pl.* **fences** fenc·es

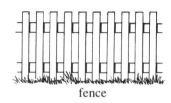

fence

fender fend·er (fen‧dər) the part of a horse saddle that hangs
between the stirrup strap and the horse.
The fender protects the horse from getting hurt by the rider's leg.
n. pl. **fenders** fend·ers

ferment fer·ment (fər·ment′) to change a liquid that has
sugar in it to alcohol.
The grapes will ferment in two months, and we will have wine.
v. **fermented, fermented, fermenting** fer·ment·ed, fer·ment·ing

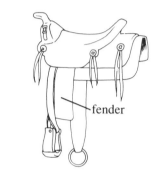

fender

fern (fėrn) a green plant with long stems and small leaves.
The fern under the tree needs water. *n. pl.* **ferns**

ferocious fe·ro·cious (fə·rō‧shəs) wild and mean.
A lion can be ferocious. *adj.*

ferociously fe·ro·cious·ly (fə·rō‧shəs·lē) in a wild and mean way.
The dog was ferociously eating the bone when we saw it. *adv.*

ferry fer·ry (fer‧ē) a boat that carries cars and people across water.
We took the ferry across the Ohio River. *n. pl.* **ferries** fer·ries

fertilizer fer·til·iz·er (fėr‧tl·ī·zər) food for plants that is put into
soil.
Dad gave the new apple tree some fertilizer. *n. pl.* **fertilizers** fer·til·iz·ers

fern

festival fes·ti·val (fes‧tə·vəl) a party celebrating something special.
The town is having a festival for Independence Day.
n. pl. **festivals** fes·ti·vals

fetlock fet·lock (fet‧lok) the back part of a horse's leg just above
the hoof.
The fetlock has hair on it for protection. *n. pl.* **fetlocks** fet·locks

fever fe·ver (fē‧vər) an abnormally high body temperature
caused by a sickness.
Mother gave the baby an aspirin because he had a fever.
n. pl. **fevers** fe·vers

ferry

few (fyü) **1.** not many; a small number.
We only have a few pieces of candy. *adj.* **fewer, fewest** few·er, few·est
2. not many; a small number.
A few of the students stayed to watch the game. *plural n.*
3. a small number of people or things.
Many people came to the dance, but only a few were
wearing costumes. *plural pron.*

fetlock

fiber fi·ber (fī'bər) a thin thread, string or hair.
She pulled a fiber from her sweater. *n. pl.* **fibers** fi·bers

fiction fic·tion (fik'shən) something that is not true; a story that
someone makes up.
The story of "Star Wars" is fiction. *adj.*

fictional fic·tion·al (fik'shə·nəl) not true; not real.
Spiderman is a fictional character. *adj.*

field (fēld) **1.** a piece of land or ground that has no woods or
buildings.
The farmer planted corn in his large field. *n.*
2. the part of a flag on which other parts are placed; the
background of the flag.
The American flag has white stars on a blue field. *n. pl.* **fields**

field glasses

field glasses field glass·es (fēld glas·iz) binoculars or glasses that
are used outdoors to make things look as if they are closer.
We used the field glasses to watch the deer run into the forest.
plural n.

field test (fēld test) to try a new product to see if it works.
The company will field test the hair dryer for two weeks.
v. **field tested, field tested, field testing** field test·ed, field test·ing

fierce (firs) very mean.
The dog can be fierce when he is angry.
adj. **fiercer, fiercest** fierc·er, fierc·est

fifth (fifth) after the fourth and before the sixth in a line or series.
I was the fifth person to cross the finish line. *adj.*

fight (fīt) **1.** to hit with one's fist in anger or in a contest.
The teacher does not want us to fight on the bus.
v. **fought, fought, fighting** fight·ing
2. a struggle with fists or an argument.
The boys had a fight on the bus yesterday. *n. pl.* **fights**

a	cat	i	sit	oi	oil	ch	chop		a in about
ā	ate	ī	lie	ou	out	ng	song		e in oven
ä	car	o	pot	u	cut	sh	she	ə =	i in pencil
e	set	ō	old	ù	book	th	three		o in memory
ē	equal	ô	or	ü	blue	TH	there		u in circus
ėr	germ					zh	treasure		

fighter   fight·er (fī´tər)   a person who takes part in a battle or physical combat.
The fighter has won six of his last seven fights.
n. pl. **fighters** fight·ers

figure   fig·ure (fig´yər)   **1.** small statue or form of a person.
The figure of a beautiful woman is on the table. *n.*
2. a number.
The figure on the food bill is wrong. *n. pl.* **figures** fig·ures
3. to think; to solve a problem.
I can figure the answer faster than you can figure it.
v. **figured, figured, figuring** fig·ured, fig·ur·ing

figure eight

figure eight   fig·ure eight (fig´yər   āt)   a design that looks like the number 8.
The girl made a figure eight on the ice with her skates.

figure out   fig·ure out (fig´yər   out)   to find the answer by thinking; to solve a problem.
Dad will figure out why the dryer is not working.
v. **figured out, figured out, figuring out** fig·ured out, fig·ur·ing out

Filipino   Fil·i·pi·no (fil·ə·pē´nō)   **1.** a person who lives in or who was born in the Philippine Islands (islands in the Pacific Ocean with the capital in Manila).
The dancer is a Filipino. *n. pl.* **Filipinos** Fil·i·pi·nos
2. having to do with the people of the Philippine Islands.
The Filipino boy has brown hair. *adj.*

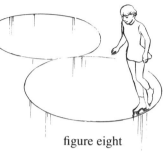
film

fill   (fil)   to put something into a container or space so that there is no room for more.
Please fill the water bottle. *v.* **filled, filled, filling** fill·ing

filled   (fild)   **1.** *v. pt. t., pt. part.* See **fill.**
2. having something inside.
The filled candy had chocolate inside of it. *adj.*

filling   fill·ing (fil´ing)   the material or ingredient put into something to fill up a hole.
The dentist put a filling in my tooth.
The filling in the pie is made with chocolate. *n. pl.* **fillings** fill·ings

film   (film)   **1.** the thin material put into cameras for taking pictures.
The film for the camera is in the bag. *n.*
2. a movie.
That was a funny film we saw at the movies last night. *n. pl.* **films**
3. to make a movie by taking pictures.
They will film the movie in our school. *v.* **filmed, filmed, filming** film·ing

filter   fil·ter (fil´tər)   **1.** something used to strain a liquid to get out solid pieces.
The coffee filter keeps the coffee beans out of the coffee pot. *n.*
2. a tool that is used to sift or sort things.
We have a filter on the clothes dryer to keep the lint off the clean clothes.
n. pl. **filters** fil·ters

filter

filth   (filth)   smelly dirt.
The pig was covered with filth. *n. no pl.*

filthy   filth·y (fil′thē)   very dirty.
The pig was filthy after rolling in the mud.
adj. **filthier, filthiest** filth·i·er, filth·i·est

fin

fin   (fin)   a part of a fish that looks like a wing and is used to move the fish through water.
The fish I caught has a torn fin. *n. pl.* **fins**

final   fi·nal (fī′nl)   last; coming at the end.
I passed my final exam in history. *adj.*

finally   fi·nal·ly (fī′nl·ē)   at last; after a long time.
The dog finally got a bath. *adv.*

find   (fīnd)   **1.** to discover; to learn.
Do you think we will find life on Mars? *v.*
2. to locate something that was lost.
I am still trying to find my ring.
v. **found, found, finding** find·ing

find out   (fīnd out)   to discover the cause of something; to learn the reason for something.
Can you find out why John did not come to school today?
v. **found out, found out, finding out** find·ing out

finger

fine   (fīn)   **1.** very good.
You did a fine job of cleaning the blackboard. *adj.*
2. elegant; very fancy.
Mother will use her fine china tonight. *adj.*
3. very small; tiny.
Sand is very fine stones. *adj.* **finer, finest** fin·er, fin·est
4. to charge a person money for breaking a law or a rule.
The teacher will fine you ten cents for throwing paper on the floor.
v. **fined, fined, fining** fin·ing
5. the money someone must pay for breaking a law.
Tom paid a $50.00 fine for speeding. *n. pl.* **fines**

finger   fin·ger (fing′gər)   a part of the hand.
I burned my finger on the stove. *n. pl.* **fingers** fin·gers

fingerprint   fin·ger·print (fing′gər·print)   the mark or design made by the end of a finger.
His fingerprint was on the glass. *n. pl.* **fingerprints** fin·ger·prints

fingerprint

a	cat	i	sit	oi	oil	ch	chop		a in about
ā	ate	ī	lie	ou	out	ng	song		e in oven
ä	car	o	pot	u	cut	sh	she	ə =	i in pencil
e	set	ō	old	u̇	book	th	three		o in memory
ē	equal	ô	or	ü	blue	ŦH	there		u in circus
ėr	germ					zh	treasure		

finish fin·ish (fin'ish) to do an activity to the end.
I will finish my homework before dinner.
v. **finished, finished, finishing** fin·ished, fin·ish·ing

finishing touch fin·ish·ing touch (fin'ish·ing tuch) the last detail of an activity.
Mother is adding the finishing touch to the birthday cake: the candle.

fiord (fyôrd *or* fyōrd) a finger-shaped bay of water near tall, rocky cliffs.
You can visit a fiord in Norway. *n. pl.* **fiords**

fireman

fire (fīr) **1.** the burning of something; flames.
We built a fire in the camp. *n. pl.* **fires**
2. having to do with something burning or something used to stop something from burning.
The fire hose reached the door of the burning house. *adj.*
3. to shoot a gun.
I will fire the gun to start the race. *v.*
4. to take away a person's job.
The store will fire John today. *v.* **fired, fired, firing** fir·ing

fire department fire de·part·ment (fīr di·pärt'mənt) **1.** a group of people who put out fires and work to stop things from burning.
There are fifteen people in our fire department.
2. a place where firemen and fire equipment are housed.
The fire department is near the school.

fireplace

fire drill (fīr dril) a practice of leaving a building when pretending that the building is on fire.
We have a fire drill every month at school.

fireman fire·man (fīr'mən) a person who works for the fire department and stops things from burning.
The fireman got the little girl out of the burning house.
n. pl. **firemen** fire·men

fire truck

fireplace fire·place (fīr'plās) a place built inside a house or in a yard where wood is burned.
The fireplace is full of burning wood. *n. pl.* **fireplaces** fire·plac·es

fire truck (fīr truk) a vehicle that firemen use to carry fire equipment to a place that is burning.
The fire truck was on the way to a fire when we saw it.

firewood fire·wood (fīr'wud) pieces of trees that are cut to be burned.
Father cut the firewood and carried it into the house. *plural n.*

firewood

first (fẻrst) **1.** before anyone else.
I was the first person at school this morning. *adj.*
2. the highest place; the winner.
I was the first of 200 in the spelling contest. *n. no pl.*
3. before others in time.
The person who finishes the test first is the winner. *adv.*

first name (fẻrst nām) what a person is called; name given to a child when born.
Her first name is Sally.

first place (fẻrst plās) the best in a contest or race.
He won first place in the bicycle race. *idiom*

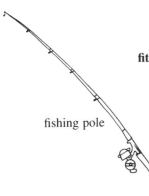

fish

fish (fish) **1.** an animal that lives in the water and uses fins to swim.
I have a goldfish in a glass bowl. *n. pl.* **fishes** *or* **fish** fish·es
2. to catch an animal that lives in the water.
I like to fish for trout. *v.* **fished, fished, fishing** fish·ing

fisherman fish·er·man (fish′ər·mən) a person who catches animals that live in the water.
My father is a good fisherman because he always catches many fish.
n. pl. **fishermen** fish·er·men

fishing pole fish·ing pole (fish′ing pōl) a long tool that is used to catch fish.
I took my fishing pole to the lake.

fish story fish stor·y (fish stôr′ē) a tale that has many imaginary details added to the facts.
Grandfather tells the best fish story I have ever heard.
idiom pl. **fish stories** fish stor·ies

fishing pole

fit (fit) **1.** in good health or condition.
The doctor said I was fit enough to play ball.
adj. **fitter, fittest** fit·ter, fit·test
2. to be the right size; not to be too big or too small.
The dress will fit me. *v.*
3. to be right for something or somebody.
My skills fit this job. *v.*
4. to go into.
The key will fit into the lock.
v. **fitted** *or* **fit, fitted** *or* **fit, fitting** fit·ted, fit·ting

a	cat	i	sit	oi	oil	ch	chop		a in about
ā	ate	ī	lie	ou	out	ng	song		e in oven
ä	car	o	pot	u	cut	sh	she	ə =	i in pencil
e	set	ō	old	u̇	book	th	three		o in memory
ē	equal	ô	or	ü	blue	ŦH	there		u in circus
ėr	germ					zh	treasure		

fix   (fiks)   **1.** to make a meal.
Mother will fix lunch for us. *v*.
2. to repair something that is broken or not working.
Dad can fix the dryer. *v*. **fixed, fixed, fixing** fix·ing

flag   (flag)   **1.** a cloth with a design or emblem on it that stands for a country, nation or club.
Each country has a special flag. *n. pl*. **flags**
2. having to do with a cloth with a design or emblem on it.
Our first flag maker was Betsy Ross. *adj*.

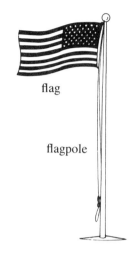

flag

flagpole

Flag Day   (flag dā)   the day Americans celebrate the designing of the flag; June 14.
We hang out our flag on Flag Day.

flagpole   flag·pole (flag′pōl)   the stick from which the flag hangs.
We put the flag up on the flagpole every morning and take it off the flagpole every night. *n. pl*. **flagpoles** flag·poles

flagstaff   flag·staff (flag′staf)   a flagpole.
The flagstaff on the ship had an American flag and a Navy flag flying on it. *n. pl*. **flagstaffs** flag·staffs

flame   (flām)   the heat and light that come from a fire.
The flame from the fire burned his finger. *n. pl*. **flames**

flammable   flam·ma·ble (flam′ə·bəl)   burns easily.
We must be careful with gas because it is flammable. *adj*.

flank

flank   (flangk)   the part of an animal between the ribs and the hips.
The fender of the saddle protects the horse's flank from the rider's legs.
n. pl. **flanks**

flap   (flap)   **1.** to move up and down.
The bird will flap his wings when he is ready to fly.
v. **flapped, flapped, flapping** flap·ping
2. something that looks like a wing and can be moved up and down.
The flap of the envelope must be closed when you mail it. *n. pl*. **flaps**

flash   (flash)   **1.** a quick, bright light.
The lightning flash made the sky bright. *n. pl*. **flashes** flash·es
2. to make a quick, bright light.
The camera will flash if it is dark in the room.
v. **flashed, flashed, flashing** flash·ing

flashcube   flash·cube (flash′kyüb)   the thing on a camera that makes a quick, bright light.
We need to use a flashcube if the room is dark.
n. pl. **flashcubes** flash·cubes

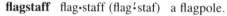

flashcube

flashlight

fleece

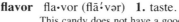

flight board

flashing light flash·ing light (flash′ing līt) a lamp or signal that turns light on and off very quickly.
The flashing light on the street means to be careful and look for cars.

flashlight flash·light (flash′līt) a lamp that can be carried outside to give light when you are walking or working in the dark.
Don't forget to take the flashlight with you tonight.
n. pl. **flashlights** flash·lights

flat (flat) smooth; not bumpy or bent.
The road in front of the school is flat. *adj.* **flatter, flattest** flat·ter, flat·test

flavor fla·vor (flā′vər) **1.** taste.
This candy does not have a good flavor. *n. pl.* **flavors** fla·vors
2. to give taste.
Jim used pepper to flavor the chicken.
v. **flavored, flavored, flavoring** fla·vored, fla·vor·ing

flavoring fla·vor·ing (flā′vər·ing) **1.** the ingredient in a food that gives it taste.
The lemon flavoring gives the chicken a sour taste.
n. pl. **flavorings** fla·vor·ings
2. *v. pres. part.* See **flavor** (2).

fleece (flēs) the hair of a sheep, used to make wool.
The fleece of the lamb is very soft. *n. pl.* **fleeces** fleec·es

fleet (flēt) a group of boats or ships.
We saw the Navy fleet in the harbor. *n. pl.* **fleets**

flew (flü) *v. pt. t.* See **fly** (1, 2, 3).

flies (flīz) **1.** *v. pres. t.* See **fly** (1, 2, 3).
2. *n. pl.* See **fly** (4).

flight (flīt) **1.** a ride in an airplane.
The flight to Chicago took three hours. *n.*
2. the act of flying.
The first flight for the baby bird was from the nest to the ground. *n. pl.* **flights**
3. having to do with flying.
The flight schedule said that the plane will arrive at 9:30. *adj.*

flight board (flīt bôrd) a sign at the airport that gives information about the airplanes that are coming into and going out of the airport.
The flight board said that Flight 66 was late and would not arrive until 10:00.

a	cat	i	sit	oi	oil	ch	chop		a in about
ā	ate	ī	lie	ou	out	ng	song		e in oven
ä	car	o	pot	u	cut	sh	she	ə =	i in pencil
e	set	ō	old	u̇	book	th	three		o in memory
ē	equal	ô	or	ü	blue	ŦH	there		u in circus
ėr	germ					zh	treasure		

flip (flip) **1.** to turn from one side to the other side.
Flip the pancake when you cook it. *v.*
2. to turn a switch on or off.
Please don't forget to flip off the lights when you leave the room.
v. **flipped, flipped, flipping** flip·ping

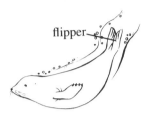
flipper

flipper flip·per (flip'ər) a flat foot or shoe that is used for swimming.
The seal has a flipper in the place of a tail. *n. pl.* **flippers** flip·pers

flirt (flèrt) to tease someone's feelings or emotions in a loving way.
The girl likes to flirt with the boys in her school.
v. **flirted, flirted, flirting** flirt·ed, flirt·ing

float (flōt) **1.** a decorated vehicle in a parade.
The best float in the parade was the one with Mickey Mouse
on it. *n. pl.* **floats**
2. to stay in the air without using wings or a motor.
A feather will float for a long time before it falls to the ground. *v.*
3. to stay on top of water.
I like to float on my back in the swimming pool.
v. **floated, floated, floating** float·ed, float·ing

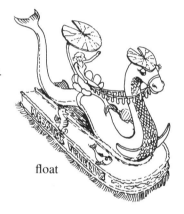
float

flock (flok) a group of birds.
Birds often fly together in a flock. *n. pl.* **flocks**

floe (flō) a piece of floating ice.
A large floe can damage a ship. *n. pl.* **floes**

flood (flud) **1.** to cover land with water.
The field will flood if the rain continues.
v. **flooded, flooded, flooding** flood·ed, flood·ing
2. an event that happens when water from a river or
rainfall covers land.
The breaking of the dam caused the flood. *n. pl.* **floods**

floor (flôr *or* flōr) **1.** the bottom of a room.
Your coat is on the floor. *n.*
2. a level of a building.
I live on the fourth floor of that building. *n. pl.* **floors**
3. the bottom of the ocean.
Many fish live on the floor of the ocean. *n. no pl.*
4. having to do with the bottom of a room.
The floor rug needs to be cleaned. *adj.*

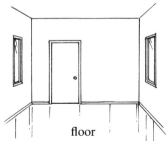
floor

floppy flop·py (flop'ē) moving easily; loose; without stiffness.
A rabbit has very floppy ears. *adj.* **floppier, floppiest** flop·pi·er, flop·pi·est

Florence Flo·rence (flôr'əns *or* flor'əns) a city in the
country of Italy.
We will visit Florence after we visit Rome. *n.*

flour

flower

fly

florist flo·rist (flôr'ist *or* flōr'ist *or* flor'ist) a person who grows or sells flowers.
The florist had very pretty roses today. *n. pl.* **florists** flo·rists

flour (flour) a powder made from grinding wheat or other grain.
Flour is used to make bread, pies, cookies and other foods. *n. no pl.*

flow (flō) **1.** the movement of water or other liquids.
The flow of the river is stopped by the dam. *n. no pl.*
2. to move or run like water.
The melted chocolate will flow out of the pan on to the ice cream.
v. **flowed, flowed, flowing** flow·ing

flower flow·er (flou'ər) the part of a plant or tree that is beautifully colored and has petals and a stem.
The plant had only one flower on it. *n. pl.* **flowers** flow·ers

flown (flōn) *v. pt. part.* See **fly** (1, 2, 3).

fluently flu·ent·ly (flü'ənt·lē) easily; smoothly.
He can speak English fluently. *adv.*

fluffy fluff·y (fluf'ē) light and soft.
The pillow on my bed is fluffy. *adj.* **fluffier, fluffiest** fluff·i·er, fluff·i·est

fluid flu·id (flü'id) **1.** a liquid; not a solid.
The fluid on the ground under the car is oil. *n. pl.* **fluids** flu·ids
2. a liquid; something that can flow or be poured.
The fluid hot chocolate spilled when Joe poured it too fast. *adj.*

fly (flī) **1.** to move in the air with wings.
The bird will fly away from the nest when he is hungry. *v.*
2. to take a ride in an airplane.
I will fly to Florida. *v.*
3. to wave in the air or be moved by the air.
The flag will fly from the flagpole. *v.* **flew, flown, flying** fly·ing
4. an insect with wings.
There is a fly in the kitchen. *n. pl.* **flies.**

fly ball (flī bôl) a baseball that is hit so that it flies high in the air before coming down.
Sarah caught the fly ball for the second out of the game.

foam (fōm) **1.** bubbles or suds.
The soap made a lot of foam. *n. no pl.*
2. to make bubbles or suds.
The ocean foams as it hits the land. *v.* **foamed, foamed, foaming** foam·ing

a	cat	**i**	sit	**oi**	oil	**ch**	chop	a in about
ā	ate	**ī**	lie	**ou**	out	**ng**	song	e in oven
ä	car	**o**	pot	**u**	cut	**sh**	she	ə = { i in pencil
e	set	**ō**	old	**u̇**	book	**th**	three	o in memory
ē	equal	**ô**	or	**ü**	blue	**ŦH**	there	u in circus
ėr	germ					**zh**	treasure	

foil   (foil)   **1.** a soft metal that can be folded.
Peter covered the dish with foil. *n. no pl.*
2. being made of a soft metal that can be folded.
The foil dish can go into the oven. *adj.*

fold   (fōld)   **1.** to bend something over.
Please fold your sweater and put it in the drawer.
v. **folded, folded, folding** fold·ed, fold·ing

foliage   fo·li·age (fō⸍lē·ij)   the leaves of a plant or tree.
In the fall the foliage is colored red, yellow and orange. *n. no pl.*

foliage

follow   fol·low (fol⸍ō)   **1.** to go behind someone or something.
My dog will follow me to your house. *v.*
2. to do what someone asks or tells you to do.
I will follow the directions that you gave me.
v. **followed, followed, following** fol·lowed, fol·low·ing

fond   (fond)   liking something or someone.
I am very fond of chocolate. *adj.* **fonder, fondest** fond·er, fond·est

fondant   fon·dant (fon⸍dənt)   a sugar paste used to make candy.
The fondant is made with sugar and lemon. *n. pl.* **fondants** fon·dants

food   (füd)   **1.** things we eat.
Chicken is my favorite food. *n. pl.* **foods**
2. having to do with things that we eat.
The food store was out of milk today. *adj.*

fool   (fül)   to trick or confuse someone.
The mask will fool everyone; they won't know who I am.
v. **fooled, fooled, fooling** fool·ing

foolish   fool·ish (fü⸍lish)   silly; stupid.
The boys are foolish if they think they can win this game. *adj.*

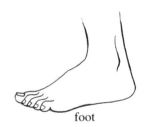
foot

foolishly   fool·ish·ly (fü⸍lish·lē)   doing something in a silly, stupid way.
The boys are acting foolishly. *adv.*

foot   (fůt)   **1.** the part of the body that is on the end of the leg and is used for standing and walking.
I stepped on a rock and hurt my foot. *n.*
2. a measurement that is twelve (12) inches long.
Twelve inches equals one foot. *n. pl.* **feet**

football   foot·ball (fůt⸍bôl)   **1.** a game played with an oval-shaped ball.
We play football every Saturday. *n. pl.* **footballs** foot·balls
2. the oval ball used to play the game of football.
Dad bought us a new football. *n.*
3. having to do with the game of football.
I am on the football team. *adj.*

football

footman foot·man (fùt⸝mən)   a person who helps people in and out of the doors of cars or carriages.
Cinderella's footman helped her into the carriage.
n. pl. **footmen** foot·men

footprint foot·print (fùt⸝print)   a mark or design made by a foot.
I can see my footprint in the mud. *n. pl.* **footprints** foot·prints

footprint

footstep foot·step (fùt⸝step)   **1.** the sound made by a foot on the floor.
I can tell your footstep from Dad's footstep. *n.*
2. a design or mark made by a foot.
I put my footstep into the wet cement. *n. pl.* **footsteps** foot·steps

footwear foot·wear (fùt⸝wer *or* fùt⸝war)   **1.** shoes or other coverings for the feet.
The shoe store had many different kinds of footwear. *n. no pl.*
2. having to do with shoes or coverings for the feet.
Footwear styles change every year. *adj.*

footwear

for   (fôr *or* fər)   **1.** to be used by or given to someone or something.
I made a cake for you. *prep.*
2. in place of something.
The children used buttons for the snowman's eyes. *prep.*
3. used at this time; for the purpose of.
Mother is using the fine china for dinner. *prep.*
4. at a meal.
We are having chicken for dinner. *prep.*
5. as long as; during this time.
We worked in the garden for three hours. *prep.*
6. purpose; reason.
I bought the roses for the centerpiece. *prep.*
7. compared with something.
The pants are too short for my legs. *prep.*
8. a feeling about someone.
I feel sorry for the little girl that lost her dog. *prep.*
9. because.
Bill went home, for he was too tired to work. *conj.*

forbid for·bid (fər·bid′)   not to let; not to allow.
Mother will forbid me to go to the movie if she knows that it is about monsters. *v.* **forbade** *or* **forbad, forbidden, forbidding** for·bade *or* for·bad, for·bid·den, for·bid·ding

a	cat	i	sit	oi	oil	ch	chop		a in about
ā	ate	ī	lie	ou	out	ng	song		e in oven
ä	car	o	pot	u	cut	sh	she	ə =	i in pencil
e	set	ō	old	ù	book	th	three		o in memory
ē	equal	ô	or	ü	blue	ŦH	there		u in circus
ėr	germ					zh	treasure		

force (fôrs *or* fōrs) **1.** power; strength.
The force of the wind was strong enough to turn over the car.
n. pl. **forces** forc·es
2. to use power or strength to make something happen.
I can force the door open. *v.*
3. to make someone do something.
I can force you to eat that food. *v.* **forced, forced, forcing** forc·ing

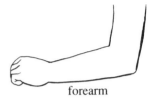
forearm

forearm fore·arm (fôr'ärm) the part of the arm between the elbow and the wrist.
I hurt my forearm playing tennis. *n. pl.* **forearms** fore·arms

forehead fore·head (fôr'id *or* for'id *or* fôr'hed) the part of the face above the eyes.
My hair covers my forehead. *n. pl.* **foreheads** fore·heads

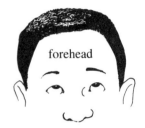
forehead

foreign office fo·reign of·fice (fôr'ən ô'fis *or* for'ən of'is) a government department that works with other countries' governments.
The foreign office controls the exports of America.

forelock fore·lock (fôr'lok *or* fōr'lok) the hair between the ears of a horse; the hair covering the forehead of a horse.
My horse's forelock is dark brown. *n. pl.* **forelocks** fore·locks

forest for·est (fôr'ist *or* for'ist) **1.** a large area covered by trees.
We will camp in the forest. *n. pl.* **forests** for·ests
2. having to do with a forest.
Weeds covered the forest path. *adj.*

forelock

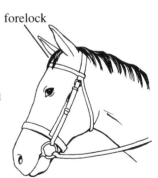

forested for·est·ed (fôr'ə·stid *or* for'ə·stid) having many trees.
The forested land helps to stop the wind from blowing the soil away. *adj.*

Forest Land For·est Land (fôr'ist *or* for'ist land) the name given to Labrador by the explorer Leif Ericson.
Leif Ericson's expedition discovered Labrador and named it Forest Land because of all the beautiful green trees.

forest ranger for·est rang·er (fôr'ist rān'jər) a person who works in a forest.
The forest ranger keeps the forest safe from fires.

forever for·ev·er (fər·ev'ər) **1.** a long, long time.
It took forever to travel from place to place before there were airplanes. *adv.*
2. with no end.
The mountains will last forever. *adv.*

forgave for·gave (fər·gāv') *v. pt. p.* See **forgive.**

forget-me-not

fork

fort

forget for·get (fər·get′) not to remember; to have facts leave your mind.
I will forget her telephone number, so I must write it down on paper.
v. **forgot, forgotten** *or* **forgot, forgetting**
for·got, for·got·ten *or* for·got, for·get·ting

forget-me-not for·get-me-not (fər·get′-mē-not) a small blue flower.
I will pick a forget-me-not for my teacher.
n. pl. **forget-me-nots** for·get-me-nots

forgive for·give (fər·giv′) to excuse someone for a mistake or an action.
I hope that Mother will forgive me for breaking the vase.
v. **forgave, forgiven, forgiving** for·gave, for·giv·en, for·giv·ing

fork (fôrk) **1.** a utensil or tool used for eating.
Be sure to put the fork on the left side of the dish. *n.*
2. the front part of a horse saddle.
The fork keeps the rider from falling forward. *n. pl.* **forks**

form (fôrm) **1.** the shape or design of something.
The carving was in the form of an old man. *n.*
2. a kind or type.
Dancing is a form of art. *n. pl.* **forms**
3. to shape or make something.
Mother will form a basket out of the clay.
v. **formed, formed, forming** form·ing

formation for·ma·tion (fôr·mā′shən) the making of something.
The formation of the mountains took hundreds of centuries. *n. no pl.*

former for·mer (fôr′mər) happening first; happening before; happening earlier; past.
My former teacher taught me how to paint. *adj.*

for once (fôr wuns) for the first time; for a change.
Will you listen to me for once?

for sale (fôr sāl) can be sold; can be bought.
The house is for sale.

fort (fôrt *or* fōrt) **1.** a place with walls all around it that is used to protect people from attacks.
The fort was built by the soldiers. *n.*
2. a place with walls all around it and used to play or hide in.
The children built a fort with the wood in the garage. *n. pl.* **forts**

a	cat	i	sit	oi	oil	ch	chop	ə =	a in about
ā	ate	ī	lie	ou	out	ng	song		e in oven
ä	car	o	pot	u	cut	sh	she		i in pencil
e	set	ō	old	u̇	book	th	three		o in memory
ē	equal	ô	or	ü	blue	ŦH	there		u in circus
ėr	germ					zh	treasure		

forth (fôrth) on to something else.
> The graduation speaker told the graduates to go forth and be
> good citizens. *adv.*

forward for·ward (fôr'wərd) in the direction of the front.
> The line is slowly moving forward. *adv.*

fossil fos·sil (fos'əl) the hardened skeleton or bone of an animal
that has been buried for many years.
> We found a fossil of a snail. *n. pl.* **fossils** fos·sils

fought (fôt) *v. pt. t., pt. part.* See **fight** (1).

found (found) **1.** *v. pt. t., pt. part.* See **find.**
> **2.** to start or set up an organization or club.
> We can found a club for girls only.
> *v.* **founded, founded, founding** found·ed, found·ing

founder foun·der (foun'dər) a person who starts a club, church,
country or other service.
> John Audubon was the founder of the Audubon Society.
> *n. pl.* **founders** foun·ders

fountain

fountain foun·tain (foun'tən) **1.** a jet or stream of water.
> We stood in front of the fountain and got wet. *n.*
> **2.** a device or machine that gives out water.
> The thirsty man got a drink from the water fountain.
> *n. pl.* **fountains** foun·tains

fox (foks) an animal that lives in the forest and has a pointed nose
and a bushy tail.
> I saw a red fox in the forest. *n. pl.* **foxes** fox·es

fraction frac·tion (frak'shən) a small part of something.
> Only a fraction of the class will go on the trip. *n. pl.* **fractions** frac·tions

fox

fragile frag·ile (fraj'əl) easily broken.
> The glass vase is very fragile. *adj.*

fragrant fra·grant (frā'grənt) having a nice, sweet smell.
> The roses are fragrant. *adj.*

frail (frāl) delicate; weak; not strong.
> The little girl is frail because she has been sick.
> *adj.* **frailer, frailest** frail·er, frail·est

frame (frām) **1.** a border made of wood or metal that
goes around a picture.
> I bought a frame for the picture so that I could hang it on the wall. *n.*
> **2.** one small picture on a roll of film.
> The first frame of the film is my favorite picture. *n. pl.* **frames**
> **3.** wooden; made of wood.
> The frame house was easy to build. *adj.*

frame

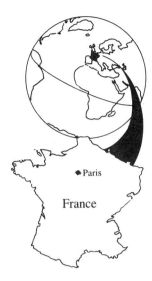

France

Franklin stove

France (frans) a country in the western part of Europe; its capital is Paris.
You can fly to France from here. *n.*

Franklin stove Frank·lin stove (frang'klən stōv) a heater that burns wood and that was designed by Benjamin Franklin.
We have a Franklin stove in our TV room.

frantically fran·ti·cal·ly (fran'tik·lē) in an excited, hurried way.
She was frantically looking for her lost ring. *adv.*

fraternal fra·ter·nal (frə·tèr'nl) twins who do not look exactly the same.
Joe and Jo Ann are fraternal twins. *adj.*

free (frē) **1.** not costing money.
The milk was free when I bought the cookies. *adj.*
2. without control by someone else.
America is a free country. *adj.*
3. loose; not tied or held.
The dog was free of his leash. *adj.* **freer, freest** fre·er, fre·est
4. to get loose; to get away from.
The dog will work to free himself from the chain.
v. **freed, freed, freeing** free·ing

freed (frēd) *v. pt. t., pt. part.* See **free** (4).

freedom free·dom (frē'dəm) the condition of being without limits; the condition of having the right to decide.
People in America have the freedom to make decisions for themselves without government control. *n. pl.* **freedoms** free·doms

free-form (frē'fôrm) without a design or pattern.
The painter created a free-form picture and no one knows what it is. *adj.*

freely free·ly (frē'lē) loosely; without controls; untied.
The dog ran freely. *adv.*

free time (frē tīm) unplanned time; time when nothing has to be done.
The teacher gives us ten minutes of free time every day.

freeze (frēz) to turn a liquid into ice by making it very cold.
We will freeze the orange juice in the ice cube tray.
v. **froze, frozen, freezing** fro·zen, freez·ing

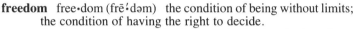

a	cat	i	sit	oi	oil	ch	chop		a in about
ā	ate	ī	lie	ou	out	ng	song		e in oven
ä	car	o	pot	u	cut	sh	she	ə =	i in pencil
e	set	ō	old	ù	book	th	three		o in memory
ē	equal	ô	or	ü	blue	TH	there		u in circus
èr	germ					zh	treasure		

freezer   freez·er (frē´zər)   a machine or part of a refrigerator that makes the water in food turn into ice.
The ice cream is in the freezer. *n. pl.* **freezers** freez·ers

French   (french)   **1.** the people who live in or who were born in France.
The French drink wine with their meals. *plural n.*
2. the language spoken by the people of France.
We are learning to speak French. *n. no pl.*
3. having to do with the people and the language of France.
I like to eat French food. *adj.*

frequently   fre·quent·ly (frē´kwənt·lē)   often; again and again.
The dog runs away frequently, but we always find him. *adv.*

freezer

fresh   (fresh)   **1.** newly grown; just picked from the plant or tree.
Fresh peas taste better than canned peas. *adj.*
2. new; still not used or touched.
The fresh snow made everything look white. *adj.*
3. not tired; feeling full of energy.
I felt fresh after my shower. *adj.* **fresher, freshest** fresh·er, fresh·est

freshly baked   fresh·ly baked (fresh´lē bākt)   just out of the oven.
The bread is freshly baked and still hot.

freshwater   fresh·wa·ter (fresh´wô·tər *or* fresh´wot·ər)   **1.** living in water that does not have salt in it; not living in ocean water.
Trout are freshwater fish. *adj.*
2. water that does not have salt in it; water that does not come from the ocean.
The river in the mountains is a freshwater river. *adj.*

friend   (frend)   a person that one likes, trusts, helps and enjoys.
Jean is a friend with whom I do many things and to whom I tell my secrets. *n. pl.* **friends**

friendly   friend·ly (frend´lē)   nice, kind and helpful.
The teacher is friendly with all the students.
adj. **friendlier, friendliest** friend·li·er, friend·li·est

friendship   friend·ship (frend´ship)   the feeling between two people who like, trust, help and enjoy each other.
My friendship with Jean is important to me. *n. pl.* **friendships** friend·ships

frog

frighten   fright·en (frīt´n)   to scare; to make afraid.
The lightning will frighten the dog if he is outside.
v. **frightened, frightened, frightening** fright·ened, fright·en·ing

frog   (frog *or* frôg)   an animal with webbed feet that lives in or near fresh water and that jumps.
The boys caught a green frog in the lake. *n. pl.* **frogs**

front page

from (from *or* frum *or* frəm) **1.** out of.
Milk comes from cows. *prep.*
2. apart from, because of distance.
My house is far from the school. *prep.*
3. beginning at a place.
We moved from the farm. *prep.*
4. off.
We picked the cherries from the tree. *prep.*
5. against.
The fort protected the soldiers from the Indians. *prep.*
6. after a certain time.
My birthday is two days from today. *prep.*
7. compared with.
My sister is different from me. *prep.*

from across from a·cross (from ə·krôs′) in the direction
of the other side.
We could hear her whispering from across the room.

front (frunt) **1.** the first part; not the back.
I was moved to the front of the room. *n. pl.* **fronts**
2. having to do with the first part, not the back.
I sat in the front seat with Dad. *adj.*

front page (frunt pāj) the first page of a newspaper.
My picture was on the front page.

frost (frôst) to put icing on a cake or other kind of dessert.
I will frost the cake with chocolate frosting.
v. **frosted, frosted, frosting** frost·ed, frost·ing

frosting frost·ing (frô′sting *or* fros′ting) icing or topping for a
cake or for cupcakes.
I like chocolate frosting better than vanilla frosting.
n. pl. **frostings** frost·ings

frown

frown (froun) a look of sadness, anger or disappointment.
The frown on his face meant that he was sad. *n. pl.* **frowns**

froze (frōz) *v. pt. t.* See **freeze.**

fruit (früt) **1.** a food that is the seed of a plant or tree with a covering
that is usually sweet.
My favorite fruit is the banana. *n. pl.* **fruits** *or* **fruit**
2. having to do with fruit.
The tree that they planted is a fruit tree. *adj.*

fruit

a	cat	i	sit	oi	oil	ch	chop		a in about
ā	ate	ī	lie	ou	out	ng	song		e in oven
ä	car	o	pot	u	cut	sh	she	ə =	i in pencil
e	set	ō	old	u̇	book	th	three		o in memory
ē	equal	ô	or	ü	blue	TH	there		u in circus
ėr	germ					zh	treasure		

fruit fly (früt flī) a small insect that lives on fruits and vegetables.
A fruit fly can damage a fruit tree.

fruit fly

frustrate frus·trate (frus⸱trāt) to make one feel useless and helpless.
Math problems frustrate me.
v. **frustrated, frustrated, frustrating** frus·trat·ed, frus·trat·ing

frustrating frus·trat·ing (frus⸱trāt·ing) **1.** *v. pres. part.*
See **frustrate.**
2. causing feelings of uselessness and helplessness.
Trying to keep our house clean is sometimes a frustrating job. *adj.*

fry bread (frī bred) a food made with corn and eaten
by the Indians.
We tasted the fry bread at the powwow.

frying pan fry·ing pan (frī⸱ing pan) a flat-bottomed pot with low
sides used for cooking foods in oil or butter.
Father made the eggs in his new frying pan.

fudge (fuj) a soft candy.
We made chocolate fudge last night. *n. pl.* **fudges** fudg·es

frying pan

fuel fu·el (fyü⸱əl) **1.** material burned for energy or heat.
The body uses food for fuel. *n. pl.* **fuels** fu·els
2. having to do with materials that are burned for
energy or heat.
We put gasoline in the car's fuel tank. *adj.*

full (fůl) **1.** filled to the top; not empty.
My glass is full of milk. *adj.* **fuller, fullest** full·er, full·est
2. using all; total.
We ran the machine at full speed. *adj.*

full moon (fůl mün) the moon during the time that all
its front side is lit.
The full moon made the night very bright.

fume (fyüm) to get angry and not tell anyone; to keep anger inside.
I fume about things for a long time before I calm down.
v. **fumed, fumed, fuming** fum·ing

full moon

fun (fun) **1.** a happy feeling; delight.
We had fun playing ball. *n. no pl.*
2. happy; playful; enjoyable.
The boy is fun to be around. *adj.*

funeral fu·ner·al (fyü⸱nər·əl) a ceremony done when a
dead person is buried.
I did not go to Aunt Helen's funeral. *n. pl.* **funerals** fu·ner·als

funnel

fur

furniture

fungus fun·gus (fung′gəs) a living thing that grows on plants. A mushroom is a fungus. *n. pl.* **fungi** *or* **funguses** fun·gi *or* fun·gus·es

fun-loving fun-lov·ing (fun-luv′ing) enjoyable; happy. Joe is a fun-loving person. *adj.*

funnel fun·nel (fun′l) a cone-shaped tool that is used for filling containers that have small openings. We used a funnel to pour the water into the jar. *n. pl.* **funnels** fun·nels

funnel cloud fun·nel cloud (fun′l kloud) a mass of water drops blowing in the air in the shape of a funnel. We saw a funnel cloud during the storm.

funniest fun·ni·est (fun′ē·est) *superl. adj.* See **funny.**

funny fun·ny (fun′ē) silly; causing a person to laugh. The clown is very funny. *adj.* **funnier, funniest** fun·ni·er, fun·ni·est

funny-looking fun·ny-look·ing (fun′ē-lùk·ing) appears odd or strange; different. A frog is a funny-looking animal. *adj.*

fur (fėr) **1.** the hair of an animal that covers the skin. The bear's fur is not soft. *n. pl.* **furs** **2.** made of the hair of an animal. I want a fur coat for winter. *adj.*

furious fu·ri·ous (fyùr′ē·əs) very angry. The teacher was furious with the class. *adj.*

furnace fur·nace (fėr′nis) a machine that burns fuel to make heat. The furnace keeps the house warm in the winter. *n. pl.* **furnaces** fur·nac·es

furniture fur·ni·ture (fėr′nə·chər) useful things in a room that make it ready for living, such as tables, chairs, dressers, beds and sofas. I have new furniture in my bedroom. *n. no pl.*

furry fur·ry (fėr′ē) covered with the hair of an animal; soft like fur. The furry rug was warm under my feet. *adj.* **furrier, furriest** fur·ri·er, fur·ri·est

further fur·ther (fėr′ᴛʜər) to or at a greater distance. I live further from school than you do. *comp. adj.* See **far.**

a	cat	i	sit	oi	oil	ch	chop	ə =	a in about
ā	ate	ī	lie	ou	out	ng	song		e in oven
ä	car	o	pot	u	cut	sh	she		i in pencil
e	set	ō	old	ù	book	th	three		o in memory
ē	equal	ô	or	ü	blue	ᴛʜ	there		u in circus
ėr	germ					zh	treasure		

fuss (fus)   a big complaint about something that is
not very important.
Joey made a fuss by screaming and yelling when Mom would
not let him have more candy. *n. no pl.*

fussy   fuss·y (fus′ē)   wanting things a certain way; hard to please.
I can be very fussy about the way my hair looks.
adj. **fussier, fussiest** fuss·i·er, fuss·i·est

future   fu·ture (fyü′chər)   **1.** a time to come; tomorrows.
We are never sure what will happen in the future. *n. no pl.*
2. in time to come.
In future years, you will remember only the good things about school. *adj.*

fuzzy   fuzz·y (fuz′ē)   covered with soft hair, thread or fibers.
The rabbit fur is fuzzy. *adj.* **fuzzier, fuzziest** fuzz·i·er, fuzz·i·est

fuzzy

Gg

galleon

gallon

gait (gāt) the way a person or animal walks or runs.
The horse's gait is slow and sure. *n. pl.* **gaits**

gale (gāl) a strong wind.
Last night's gale blew our apple tree down. *n. pl.* **gales**

galleon gal·le·on (gal′ē·ən *or* gal′yən) a kind of tall sailing ship that was used long ago.
The explorer sailed a galleon into unknown waters.
n. pl. **galleons** gal·le·ons

gallery gal·ler·y (gal′ər·ē) a place where pictures are displayed and sold.
The art gallery had many beautiful pictures, but they were very expensive.
n. pl. **galleries** gal·ler·ies

gallon gal·lon (gal′ən) a liquid measurement; four quarts.
We buy milk by the gallon. *n. pl.* **gallons** gal·lons

gallop gal·lop (gal′əp) **1.** the fast run of an animal with four legs.
The horse's gallop was very fast. *n. pl.* **gallops** gal·lops
2. to run fast.
My horse can gallop for miles.
v. **galloped, galloped, galloping** gal·loped, gal·lop·ing

gamble gam·ble (gam′bəl) to play a game for money.
He will gamble and lose his money.
v. **gambled, gambled, gambling** gam·bled, gam·bling

game (gām) **1.** a contest or competition with rules and players.
The boys played a game of football. *n.*
2. a way of playing; something that is played.
Let's play a game of tag. *n. pl.* **games**

game room (gām rüm) a special place in a house or a building where people can play.
We have a game room in our basement.

gander gan·der (gan′dər) a male goose.
The gander is taller than the goose. *n. pl.* **ganders** gan·ders

a	cat	**i**	sit	**oi**	oil	**ch**	chop	a in about
ā	ate	**ī**	lie	**ou**	out	**ng**	song	e in oven
ä	car	**o**	pot	**u**	cut	**sh**	she	ə = { i in pencil
e	set	**ō**	old	**u̇**	book	**th**	three	o in memory
ē	equal	**ô**	or	**ü**	blue	**ŦH**	there	u in circus
ėr	germ					**zh**	treasure	

Ganges River   Gan·ges Riv·er (gan⸍jēz   riv⸍ər)   a river in India.
　　The Ganges River is long and beautiful.

garage   ga·rage (gə·räzh′ *or* gə·räj′)   a place for keeping cars or a place that repairs cars.
　　We put our car in the garage every night. *n. pl.* **garages** gar·ag·es

garbage   gar·bage (gär⸍bij)   **1.** pieces of unwanted food, paper and other things that will be thrown out.
　　The garbage is put into a can in the back of the room. *n. no pl.*
　　2. having to do with things that will be thrown out.
　　Please empty the garbage can. *adj.*

garden   gar·den (gärd⸍n)   a place where plants, flowers and vegetables grow.
　　The farmer planted corn in his garden. *n. pl.* **gardens** gar·dens

gardening   gar·den·ing (gärd⸍n·ing)   the growing of plants.
　　Gardening is a hobby for many people. *n. no pl.*

gas   (gas)   **1.** a fuel that makes a vehicle run.
　　We use unleaded gas in our car. *n. pl.* **gases** gas·es
　　2. having to do with the fuel that is used in vehicles.
　　We buy our fuel from the gas station. *adj.*

gaskin   gas·kin (gas⸍kən)   the part of a horse's leg above the knee; the upper leg of a horse.
　　The gaskin is very strong. *n. pl.* **gaskins** gas·kins

gasp   (gasp)   to inhale quickly in excitement or fear.
　　The boy will gasp if he sees that bear. *v.* **gasped, gasped, gasping** gasp·ing

gate   (gāt)   **1.** a door in a fence.
　　Be sure to close the gate so the dog doesn't get out. *n.*
　　2. a door that leads from an airport to an airplane.
　　My airplane will leave from gate number eight. *n. pl.* **gates**
　　3. having to do with a door in a fence.
　　The gate post is broken. *adj.*

gather   gath·er (gaᴛʜ⸍ər)   bring together or come together into one place; to collect together in one place.
　　The teacher will gather the test papers before class ends.
　　v. **gathered, gathered, gathering** gath·ered, gath·er·ing

gave   (gāv)   *v. pt. t.* See **give.**

gaze   (gāz)   to look at for a long time; to stare.
　　Don't gaze at people, or they will think you are rude.
　　v. **gazed, gazed, gazing** gaz·ing

Ganges River

garage

garden

gaskin

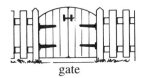

gate

gazelle

gear

genie

gazelle   ga·zelle (gə·zel′)   a small, fast animal that lives in Africa and Asia.
The gazelle can run very fast and is still graceful.
n. pl. **gazelles** *or* **gazelle** ga·zelles *or* ga·zelle

gear   (gir)   a wheel with teeth that is part of a machine.
My bicycle has only one gear. *n. pl.* **gears**

gee   (jē)   **1.** to direct a horse to turn to the right.
The rider said "gee," and the horse turned to the right.
v. **geed, geed, geeing** gee·ing
2. an exclamation of surprise.
"Gee!" the boy yelled, when he saw his new bicycle. *interj.*

geese   (gēs)   *n. pl.* See **goose** (1).

gelatin   gel·a·tin (jel′ə·tən)   a clear ingredient that has no taste and is used in making jellied salads and desserts.
Marshmallows have gelatin in them. *n. pl.* **gelatins** gel·a·tins

gem   (jem)   a valuable stone that is used in making jewelry.
That ring has a beautiful gem in it. *n. pl.* **gems**

gemstone   gem·stone (jem′stōn)   a valuable stone that is used in making jewelry; a gem.
A diamond is a gemstone. *n. pl.* **gemstones** gem·stones

general   gen·er·al (jen′ər·əl)   a person in the army, marines or air force that is the top leader of the soldiers.
The general told the soldiers to start the war. *n. pl.* **generals** gen·er·als

generation   gen·e·ra·tion (jen·ə·rā′shən)   people born about the same time.
My grandfather belongs to an earlier generation than I.
n. pl. **generations** gen·e·ra·tions

generous   gen·er·ous (jen′ər·əs)   willing to share with other people.
Her father is very generous. *adj.*

genie   ge·nie (jē′nē)   an imaginary person who can do magic.
The genie made the horse disappear. *n. pl.* **genies** *or* **genii** ge·nies *or* ge·ni·i

genius   gen·ius (jē′nyəs *or* jē′nē·əs)   a person who is very smart or very talented.
Thomas Edison was a genius with inventions. *n. pl.* **geniuses** gen·ius·es

Genoa   Gen·o·a (jen′ō·ə)   a city in Italy.
You can sail a boat to Genoa. *n.*

a	cat	i	sit	oi	oil	ch	chop		a in about
ā	ate	ī	lie	ou	out	ng	song		e in oven
ä	car	o	pot	u	cut	sh	she	ə =	i in pencil
e	set	ō	old	u̇	book	th	three		o in memory
ē	equal	ô	or	ü	blue	ᵀH	there		u in circus
ėr	germ					zh	treasure		

gentle   gen·tle (jen'tl)   kind; polite; tame.
> He is gentle with animals. *adj.* **gentler, gentlest** gen·tler, gen·tlest

gentleman   gen·tle·man (jen'tl·mən)   a polite, kind man who is well liked by other people.
> The gentleman has many friends. *n. pl.* **gentlemen** gen·tle·men

gently   gent·ly (jent'lē)   in a soft, kind, polite way.
> He gently placed the dog on the floor. *adv.*

germ   (jėrm)   a tiny plant or animal that causes disease or sickness.
> A germ is very small, and we cannot see it with our eyes. *n. pl.* **germs**

German   Ger·man (jėr'mən)   **1.** a person who lives in or who was born in Germany.
> The boy was born in Germany and is a German. *n. pl.* **Germans** Ger·mans
> **2.** having to do with the people or the language of Germany.
> The German cake is made with chocolate. *adj.*

German shepherd   Ger·man shep·herd (jėr'mən shep'ərd)   a kind of large, smart dog that often works with the police and blind people.
> The German shepherd is a smart and strong dog.

Germany   Ger·ma·ny (jėr'mə·nē)   a country in Europe that is divided into East Germany and West Germany.
> The capital of West Germany is Bonn, and the capital of East Germany is East Berlin. *n.*

germ-killer   germ-kill·er (jėrm-kil'ər)   something that damages the tiny plants and animals that cause diseases or sicknesses.
> Penicillin is a germ-killer. *n. pl.* **germ-killers** germ-kill·ers

get   (get)   **1.** to take hold of.
> John will get the dog. *v.*
> **2.** to pick up; to bring.
> I will get the paper. *v.*
> **3.** to become.
> What time will it get dark? *v.*
> **4.** to receive or be given something.
> I will get a dog for my birthday from my mother and father. *v.*
> **5.** to arrive someplace.
> I will get home before my brother.
> *v.* **got, gotten** *or* **got, getting** got·ten, get·ting

get away with   get a·way with (get ə·wā' wiᴛʜ)   to do something bad and not get caught or punished for doing it.
> He will not get away with hitting me. *idiom*

get into   get in·to (get in'tü)   to enter or go into.
> I will get into the house through the window.
> *v.* **got into, gotten into** *or* **got into, getting into**
> got in·to, got·ten in·to, get·ting in·to

German shepherd

East Berlin

• Bonn

Germany

get into

get into ___ head get in·to ___ head (get   in‛tü ___ hed)
to be stubborn about an idea.
She will get an idea into her head, and we will not be
able to talk her out of it. *idiom*

get off (get   ôf) **1.** to come down from the back of an animal.
I will get off the horse in the back of the barn. *v.*
2. to come out of a vehicle.
He will get off the train in Chicago.
v. **got off, gotten off** *or* **got off, getting off** got·ten off, get·ting off

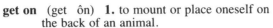

get on (get   ôn) **1.** to mount or place oneself on
the back of an animal.
I want to get on the elephant. *v.*
2. to go into a vehicle.
I will get on the train in Miami, Florida.
v. **got on, got on** *or* **gotton on, getting on** got·ten on, get·ting on

get out (get   out) **1.** leave quickly.
Please get out of here right now! *v.*
2. to take from someplace.
I will get out my book and read.
v. **got out, got out** *or* **gotten out, getting out** got·ten out, get·ting out

get out

get ready-set-go get read·y-set-go (get   red‛ē-set-gō)
words said to start a race.
We heard the man say "Get ready-set-go," and we began to run. *idiom*

get to (get   tü) to have time to begin something.
I want to read that book if I can ever get to it.
v. **got to, got to** *or* **gotten to, getting to** got·ten to, get·ting to

Gettysburg Get·tys·burg (get‛iz·bėrg) a city in the
state of Pennsylvania.
President Lincoln gave an important speech in Gettysburg. *n.*

get up (get   up) to awaken and move out of bed.
I will get up at eight o'clock on Saturday.
v. **got up, got up** *or* **gotten up, getting up** got·ten up, get·ting up

ghost (gōst) **1.** the spirit of a dead person.
The captain's ghost still walks on the ship. *n. pl.* **ghosts**
2. having spirits of dead people.
The ghost ship stays in the water. *adj.*

ghost

a cat	**i** sit	**oi** oil	**ch** chop		a in about
ā ate	**ī** lie	**ou** out	**ng** song		e in oven
ä car	**o** pot	**u** cut	**sh** she	ə =	i in pencil
e set	**ō** old	**u̇** book	**th** three		o in memory
ē equal	**ô** or	**ü** blue	**ŦH** there		u in circus
ėr germ			**zh** treasure		

giant gi·ant (jī'ənt) **1.** a very tall person.
The new basketball player is a giant. *n. pl.* **giants** gi·ants
2. very tall.
The redwood trees are giant trees. *adj.*

gift (gift) a present; something given to a person.
The new dog was a birthday gift from my parents. *n. pl.* **gifts**

gift

gigantic gi·gan·tic (jī·gan'tik) very large; huge.
The climber tried to climb the gigantic mountains in South America. *adj.*

giggle gig·gle (gig'əl) to laugh with short, high sounds.
The clown will make me giggle.
v. **giggled, giggled, giggling** gig·gled, gig·gling

gill (gil) the part of the fish that allows it to breathe.
The gill works as a lung for fish. *n. pl.* **gills**

Gimli Gim·li (jim'lē) a city in Canada.
Gimli is a small city on a lake in Canada. *n.*

gill

ginaca machine gin·a·ca ma·chine (jin'ə·kə mə·shēn')
a machine that cuts the tops off pineapples.
The ginaca machine makes cutting pineapples easy.

giraffe gi·raffe (jə·raf') an animal with long legs, a long
neck and spots on its skin.
The giraffe comes from Africa. *n. pl.* **giraffes** gi·raffes

girl (gėrl) a young female.
The girl bought a new dress. *n. pl.* **girls**

Gironde Gi·ronde (jə·rond' *or French* zhē·rônd') a city
in France, south of Paris.
We drove from Paris to Gironde. *n.*

give (giv) **1.** to put something into someone's hand.
I will give Tom the money. *v.*
2. to present a gift.
I will give Lisa a dress for her birthday. *v.*
3. to conduct; offer.
I will give Lisa cooking lessons this summer.
v. **gave, given, giving** giv·en, giv·ing

give a speech (giv ə spēch) to talk to a group of people.
I will give a speech to the P.T.A.

give birth (giv bėrth) to have a baby; to deliver a baby.
The dog will give birth to puppies this week.

give up (giv up) to stop trying; to surrender.
I will give up racing if I do not win on Saturday.
v. **gave up, given up, giving up** giv·en up, giv·ing up

giraffe

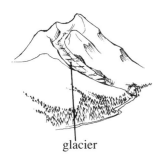

glacier

glacier gla·cier (glā′shər) a large area of ice that moves very slowly.
The hikers crossed the mountain glacier very carefully.
n. pl. **glaciers** gla·ciers

glad (glad) happy.
I am glad that school is finished for the summer.
adj. **gladder, gladdest** glad·der, glad·dest

glance (glants) to look quickly at someone or something.
I will glance at your homework later.
v. **glanced, glanced, glancing** glanc·ing

gland (gland) a part of the body that takes materials from the blood and changes them into something that the body uses or releases.
The liver is an important body gland. *n. pl.* **glands**

glass (glas) **1.** a container from which people drink.
I have milk in my glass. *n.*
2. an amount of liquid.
I want a glass of juice. *n. pl.* **glasses** glass·es
3. a hard, clear material that is easily broken.
The vase is made of glass. *n. no pl.*
4. made of a hard, clear material that is easily broken.
The glass vase was broken when we bought it. *adj.*

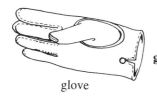

glass

glassworks glass·works (glas′wėrks) a place where glass is made.
I will buy some gifts at the glassworks. *plural n.*

gleam (glēm) a small flash of light.
The happy girl had a gleam in her eye. *n. pl.* **gleams**

glitter glit·ter (glit′ər) **1.** tiny dots of shiny material.
The girl wore glitter in her hair. *plural n.*
2. to shine or sparkle.
A diamond will glitter in the light.
v. **glittered, glittered, glittering** glit·tered, glit·ter·ing

glove

glove (gluv) a covering for the hand that has a separate place for each finger.
I lost my glove. *n. pl.* **gloves**

a	cat	i	sit	oi	oil	ch	chop		a in about
ā	ate	ī	lie	ou	out	ng	song		e in oven
ä	car	o	pot	u	cut	sh	she	ə =	i in pencil
e	set	ō	old	u̇	book	th	three		o in memory
ē	equal	ô	or	ü	blue	ŦH	there		u in circus
ėr	germ					zh	treasure		

glow (glō) **1.** a shine or sparkle.
The glow of the fire was bright. *n. pl.* **glows**
2. to shine or sparkle.
The candle will glow for a long time.
v. **glowed, glowed, glowing** glow·ing

glue (glü) **1.** a thick, sticky substance that is used to
hold two things together.
We used glue to fix the broken vase. *n. pl.* **glues**
2. to put things together with a thick, sticky substance.
Dad glued the broken chair together. *v.* **glued, glued, gluing** glu·ing

glue on (glü ôn) to put one thing on another thing with
a thick, sticky substance.
I will glue on the airplane wing.
v. **glued on, glued on, gluing on** glu·ing on

gnome (nōm) a short, imaginary person.
The gnome ran out of the tree. *n. pl.* **gnomes**

gnome

gnu (nü *or* nyü) an animal with a long tail and a head
like that of an ox.
The gnu comes from Africa. *n. pl.* **gnu** *or* **gnus**

go (gō) **1.** to move.
The train can go very fast. *v.*
2. to move to a certain place.
I will go to school tomorrow. *v.*
3. to be part of.
These checkers go with this game. *v.*
4. to make a sound.
The cow will go "moo." *v.*
5. to leave.
I will go home with you. *v.*
6. to happen; to take place.
Everything will go well today. *v.* **went, gone, going** go·ing

gnu

go ahead go a·head (gō ə·hed′) **1.** to have permission
to do something.
Mom said I could go ahead with the party. *idiom*
2. to do something anyway.
I will go ahead and give them the money, but I am
sure I paid that bill. *idiom*
3. to leave first.
I will go ahead, and you can meet me later.
v. **went ahead, gone ahead, going ahead**
went a·head, gone a·head, go·ing a·head

goat (gōt) an animal that has horns and a beard.
A goat looks like a sheep with a beard. *n. pl.* **goats**

go away go a·way (gō ə·wā′) to leave; to disappear.
Please go away, and don't come back.
v. **went away, gone away, going away**
went a·way, gone a·way, go·ing a·way

goat

go by (gō bī) to pass.
This month will go by quickly. *v.* **went by, gone by, going by** go·ing by

god (god) **1.** a spirit or thing believed to have great powers.
The Greeks believed that Cupid was the god of love. *n. pl.* **gods**
2. God; the spirit believed in most religions to have made the world and to rule over it.
They pray to God for help and forgiveness. *n. no pl.*

godmother god·moth·er (god'muᴛʜ·ər) an imaginary character who takes care of people and gives them wishes.
The fairy godmother turned the mouse into a horse.
n. pl. **godmothers** god·moth·ers

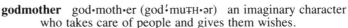

goggles

goggles gog·gles (gog'əlz) a clear covering worn against the eyes, used to keep things out of the eyes.
I wore goggles when I cut the wood. *plural n.*

gold (gōld) **1.** a yellow metal.
The dentist put gold in my tooth. *n. no pl.*
2. made of a yellow metal.
The gold chain on her neck is glittering. *adj.*

golden gold·en (gōl'dən) made of, or looking as if made of, the yellow metal gold.
Her hair looked golden in the sun. *adj.*

golf (golf *or* gôlf) a game played on grass with a small hard ball and clubs that have long handles.
I will learn to play golf this summer. *n. no pl.*

gone (gôn) *v. pt. part.* See **go.**

golf

good (gud) **1.** nice; pleasant.
The rose smells good. *adj.*
2. strong; able.
He is a good worker. *adj.*
3. high quality; useful.
He gave us some good ideas for making gifts. *adj.*
4. close; trusting.
We are good friends. *adj.*
5. successful; well paying.
He has a good job in the business. *adj.* **better, best** bet·ter

a	cat	i	sit	oi	oil	ch	chop		a in about
ā	ate	ī	lie	ou	out	ng	song		e in oven
ä	car	o	pot	u	cut	sh	she	ə =	i in pencil
e	set	ō	old	u̇	book	th	three		o in memory
ē	equal	ô	or	ü	blue	ᴛʜ	there		u in circus
ėr	germ					zh	treasure		

good-by *or* **good-bye** (gụd·bī′) farewell; words said
when leaving a person.
I forgot to say good-bye to Grandma before we left.
n. pl. **good-bys** *or* **good-byes**

good evening good eve·ning (gụd ēv′ning) words used to
say hello or good-bye at night.
The man tipped his hat and said "good evening" as he walked by us.

Good Friday Good Fri·day (gụd frī′dē) the day that Christians
remember as the day that Jesus Christ died.
We celebrate Good Friday three days before Easter.

good luck (gụd luk) **1.** words said to encourage someone.
The boys wished me good luck before I took the test.
2. having to do with giving someone encouragement or hope.
I have a good luck charm that I carry with me.

good-mannered good-man·nered (gụd-man′ərd) nice; polite.
Tom is good-mannered because he always says thank you. *adj.*

goodness good·ness (gụd′nis) a word said in surprise.
"Goodness, that was a fun ride!" *interj.*

goose

good night (gụd nīt) a good-bye said at night or
before going to sleep.
Good night and have sweet dreams.

good sport (gụd spôrt *or* gụd spōrt) a person who can
win and not brag or lose and not get angry.
She is fun to play with because she is a good sport.

goody good·y (gụd′ē) an exclamation of happiness or delight.
Goody! We are going to the circus! *interj.*

goofy goof·y (gü′fē) funny; silly.
He has a goofy look on his face. *adj.* **goofier, goofiest** goof·i·er, goof·i·est

go on (gō ôn) to happen.
What is going on in the kitchen?
idiom

goose (güs) a large bird that swims in water and looks
like a duck with a longer neck.
The goose ran after the little boy. *n. pl.* **geese**

go out (gō out) to stop burning.
The wind will cause the candle to go out.
v. **went out, gone out, going out** go·ing out

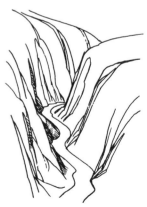
gorge

gorilla

gosling

gown

gorge (gôrj) a river valley that has high, rocky cliffs on both sides. They built a bridge over the gorge. *n. pl.* **gorges** gorg·es

gorilla go·ril·la (gə·ril′ə) a large, strong ape or monkey. We saw the gorilla in the zoo. *n. pl.* **gorillas** go·ril·las

gosling gos·ling (goz′ling) a baby goose. We watched the gosling waddle down to the stream. *n. pl.* **goslings** gos·lings

got (got) *v. pt. t.* See **get.**

got away got a·way (got ə·wā′) escaped; fled. The robber got away from the police. *idiom*

go to sleep (gō tü slēp) to fall asleep. I will go to sleep later.

go to work (gō tü wėrk) to start doing a job. I must go to work now, so I will call you back later.

go up (gō up) to go near; to approach. I will go up to the teacher and ask if I can go home early. *v.* **went up, gone up, going up** go·ing up

govern gov·ern (guv′ərn) to rule or lead a group of people, a city, state, country or nation; to set rules by which people live. Congress is one of the government branches that govern the United States. *v.* **governed, governed, governing** gov·erned, gov·ern·ing

government gov·ern·ment (guv′ərn·mənt *or* guv′ər·mənt) the people, rules, laws and offices that lead or guide the workings of a city, town, state, country or nation. The President is only one part of our government. *n. pl.* **governments** gov·ern·ments

governor gov·er·nor (guv′ər·nər *or* guv′nər) the person who is the leader in state government. The people of our state elect the governor. *n. pl.* **governors** gov·er·nors

gown (goun) a long, fancy dress. I wore a gown in my aunt's wedding. *n. pl.* **gowns**

grab (grab) to take something quickly. He will grab that from you if you do not move it. *v.* **grabbed, grabbed, grabbing** grab·bing

a	cat	i	sit	oi	oil	ch	chop		a in about
ā	ate	ī	lie	ou	out	ng	song		e in oven
ä	car	o	pot	u	cut	sh	she	ə =	i in pencil
e	set	ō	old	u̇	book	th	three		o in memory
ē	equal	ô	or	ü	blue	ŦH	there		u in circus
ėr	germ					zh	treasure		

graceful   grace·ful (grās′fəl)   moving smoothly; pleasing to look at.
> The girl was graceful as she walked down the stairs. *adj.*

gracefully   grace·ful·ly (grās′fəl·lē)   in a smooth way;
in a pleasing way.
> She walked gracefully. *adv.*

grade   (grād)   **1.** a level in school.
> I am in the eighth grade. *n.*
> **2.** a mark or rating on school work.
> I got a good grade on my math test. *n. pl.* **grades**
> **3.** to give a mark or rating.
> The teacher will grade our homework.
> *v.* **graded, graded, grading** grad·ed, grad·ing

gradually   grad·u·al·ly (graj′ü·ə·lē)   very slowly; a little at a time.
> The leaves gradually changed colors. *adv.*

graduate   grad·u·ate (graj′ü·āt)   to finish school and receive
a diploma for doing so.
> I will graduate from high school the same year that my brother
> will graduate from college.
> *v.* **graduated, graduated, graduating** grad·u·at·ed, grad·u·at·ing

graduation   grad·u·a·tion (graj·ü·ā′shən)   a ceremony that
celebrates a person's finishing school.
> We went to graduation last night. *n. pl.* **graduations** grad·u·a·tions

graduation

grain   (grān)   **1.** a seed or kernel of wheat, corn or oats.
> Sue found a grain of wheat in her shoe. *n. pl.* **grains**
> **2.** the seeds of wheat, corn or oats.
> We can grind the grain and make flour. *n. no pl.*
> **3.** having to do with the seeds of wheat, corn or oats.
> The grain bin is in the barn. *adj.*

grained   (grānd)   having little lines in it.
> This grained wood will make a beautiful table. *adj.*

grandchild   grand·child (grand′chīld)   a child of a
person's son or daughter.
> I am the only grandchild in the family.
> *n. pl.* **grandchildren** grand·chil·dren

granddaughter   grand·daugh·ter (grand′dô·tər)   the girl
child of a person's son or daughter.
> I am my grandmother's only granddaughter.
> *n. pl.* **granddaughters** grand·daugh·ters

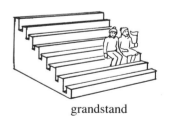
grandstand

grandfather   grand·fa·ther (grand′fä·ᴛʜər)   the father of a
person's mother or father.
> My mother's father is my grandfather. *n. pl.* **grandfathers** grand·fa·thers

grandma   grand·ma (grand′mä *or* gram′mä *or* gram′ə)   the mother
of one's father or mother; grandmother.
> My grandma is my mother's mother. *n. pl.* **grandmas** grand·mas

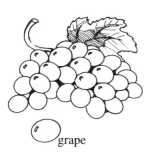
grape

grapevine

grass

grandmother   grand·moth·er (grand⸍muŦH·ər)   the mother of one's father or mother.
My grandmother is my father's mother.
n. pl. **grandmothers** grand·moth·ers

grandpa   grand·pa (grand⸍pä *or* gram⸍pä *or* gram⸍pə)
the father of one's father or mother; grandfather.
My grandpa is my father's father. *n. pl.* **grandpas** grand·pas

grandparent   grand·par·ent (grand⸍per·ənt)   the mother or father of a child's mother or father; grandmother or grandfather.
I have only one grandparent still alive. *n. pl.* **grandparents** grand·par·ents

grandson   grand·son (grand⸍sun)   the boy child of a person's son or daughter.
My brother is my grandmother's only grandson.
n. pl. **grandsons** grand·sons

grandstand   grand·stand (grand⸍stand)   the place where people sit in an arena or stadium.
The grandstand at the football stadium is very large.
n. pl. **grandstands** grand·stands

grant   (grant)   to give; to allow to have.
The bank will grant me a loan of $500.00.
v. **granted, granted, granting** grant·ed, grant·ing

grape   (grāp)   a fruit that grows on a vine and that is used in making wine, jelly and raisins.
I like a green grape better than a red grape. *n. pl.* **grapes**

grapevine   grape·vine (grāp⸍vīn)   the plant on which grapes grow.
We have a grapevine in our yard. *n. pl.* **grapevines** grape·vines

grass   (gras)   the plants that grow in a lawn, are green and have tiny stems or blades.
I cut the grass at home every week. *n. no pl.*

grass-eater   grass-eat·er (gras⸍ē·tər)   an animal that eats grass.
A cow is a grass-eater. *n. pl.* **grass-eaters** grass-eat·ers

grassland   grass·land (gras⸍land)   a field where grass grows and animals stay to eat the grass.
The cows feed on the grassland. *n. pl.* **grasslands** grass·lands

gratefully   grate·ful·ly (grāt⸍fəl·ē)   in a thankful way.
I gratefully hugged the man who found my dog. *adv.*

a	cat	i	sit	oi	oil	ch	chop		a in about
ā	ate	ī	lie	ou	out	ng	song		e in oven
ä	car	o	pot	u	cut	sh	she	ə =	i in pencil
e	set	ō	old	u̇	book	th	three		o in memory
ē	equal	ô	or	ü	blue	ŦH	there		u in circus
ėr	germ					zh	treasure		

185

grave (grāv) the place where a dead person or animal is buried.
We dug a grave for our dog. *n. pl.* **graves**

grave

gravel grav·el (grav′əl) small rocks or stones.
We have gravel in our driveway. *n. no pl.*

gravity grav·i·ty (grav′ə·tē) the natural force that
pulls things to the ground.
Gravity is the force that lets things fall down rather than up. *n. no pl.*

graze (grāz) to feed on grass.
The cows graze on the grasslands. *v.* **grazed, grazed, grazing** graz·ing

grease[1] (grēs) **1.** a thick oil used to protect things that are rubbing
together.
Father will put grease on the bicycle gears. *n.*
2. fat that comes from animals.
We fry foods in grease. *n. pl.* **grease**

gravel

grease[2] (grēs *or* grēz) to put oil on something.
Father will grease my bicycle. *v.* **greased, greased, greasing** greas·ing

great (grāt) **1.** wonderful; the best.
We played a great game of ball today. *adj.*
2. large; very big.
The great grandstand held hundreds of people.
adj. **greater, greatest** great·er, great·est
3. third generation past.
My great-grandmother was born in Italy. *adj.*

Great Britain Great Brit·ain (grāt brit′n) another name for
England, Scotland and Wales; an island country in Europe.
We will visit Great Britain.

Great Lakes

great-grandchild great-grand·child (grāt-grand′chīld)
a son or daughter of a grandson or granddaughter.
I am the great-grandchild of my mother's grandmother.
n. pl. **great-grandchildren** great-grand·chil·dren

great-grandfather great-grand·fa·ther (grāt-grand′fä·ᴛʜər)
the father of one's grandfather or grandmother.
My great-grandfather is 96 years old.
n. pl. **great-grandfathers** great-grand·fa·thers

Great Lakes (grāt lāks) the five huge lakes between
the United States and Canada.
The Great Lakes are Lake Ontario, Lake Erie, Lake Huron,
Lake Michigan and Lake Superior.

Greece (grēs) a country in southern Europe; its capital is Athens.
We took a boat from Italy to Greece. *n.*

Greenland

Godthaab

greedy greed·y (grḗdē) wanting more; wanting more than anyone else has.
We should not be greedy with food.
adj. **greedier, greediest** greed·i·er, greed·i·est

Greek (grēk) **1.** a person who was born in or who lives in Greece.
He was born in Greece so he is a Greek. *n. pl.* **Greeks**
2. the language spoken by the people of Greece.
He speaks Greek. *n. no pl.*
3. being about the people, language or customs of Greece.
Greek cookies are made with honey, not sugar. *adj.*

Greenland Green·land (grēńlənd *or* grēńland) a large island northeast of Canada; its capital is Godthaab.
Greenland belongs to Denmark. *n.*

greet (grēt) to say hello; to meet and welcome.
I will greet people as they come to the party.
v. **greeted, greeted, greeting** greet·ed, greet·ing

greeting greet·ing (grḗting) words of welcome or hello.
The letter had a warm greeting. *n. pl.* **greetings** greet·ings

grew (grü) *v. pt. t.* See **grow.**

grief (grēf) great sadness.
His grief is so great that he cannot eat. *n. no pl.*

grill (gril) **1.** a cooker used outside to cook food over a fire or over charcoal.
We cooked hot dogs on the grill last night. *n. pl.* **grills**
2. to cook meat over a fire or over charcoal.
We will grill hot dogs again tomorrow. *v.* **grilled, grilled, grilling** grill·ing

grill

grind (grīnd) to crush into very small pieces.
We grind the grain to make flour. *v.* **ground, ground, grinding** grind·ing

groan (grōn) a sound made that shows sadness or pain.
The groan of the sick girl woke me. *n. pl.* **groans**

groceries gro·cer·ies (grṓsər·ēz) different kinds of food that are for sale.
I will buy the groceries for Mom. *plural n.*

grocery gro·cer·y (grṓsər·ē) having to do with food that is for sale.
Will you stop at the grocery store for me? *adj.*

grocery

a	cat	**i**	sit	**oi**	oil	**ch**	chop
ā	ate	**ī**	lie	**ou**	out	**ng**	song
ä	car	**o**	pot	**u**	cut	**sh**	she
e	set	**ō**	old	**u̇**	book	**th**	three
ē	equal	**ô**	or	**ü**	blue	**ᵺH**	there
ėr	germ					**zh**	treasure

ə = { a in about / e in oven / i in pencil / o in memory / u in circus }

groom (grüm) a man who is getting married.
>The groom wore a white suit to the wedding. *n. pl.* **grooms**

ground (ground) **1.** dirt.
>The boy rolled on the ground and got dirty. *n. no pl.*
>**2.** grounds; the land around a building.
>The hospital needs three gardeners to take care of the grounds. *plural n.*
>**3.** the back part of a flag.
>We have white stars on a blue ground. *n. no pl.*
>**4.** *v. pt. t., pt. part.* See **grind.**

ground floor (ground flôr) the floor of a building at the same level as the ground or street.
>We live on the ground floor of that building. *adj.*

groom

group (grüp) **1.** things or people that are together.
>Our class is going to the movie in a group. *n.*
>**2.** things or people that are together because they are alike in some way.
>The girls in our group do not have their fathers living with them.
>*n. pl.* **groups**
>**3.** about things or people that are together.
>We will have a group party on Friday. *adj.*
>**4.** to put things or people together.
>Let's group together and go to the movie.
>*v.* **grouped, grouped, grouping** group·ing

grow (grō) **1.** to get bigger.
>Boys will grow to be men. *v.*
>**2.** to raise; to produce.
>The farmer will grow corn in his fields. *v.*
>**3.** to gradually appear.
>Ideas will grow in your mind. *v.* **grew, grown, growing** grow·ing

grower grow·er (grō′ər) a person who raises or grows plants.
>The grower of these pineapples is from Hawaii. *n. pl.* **growers** grow·ers

grow into grow in·to (grō in′tü) to become.
>The seed will grow into an apple tree.
>*v.* **grew into, grown into, growing into** grow·ing in·to

growl (groul) **1.** a low, rumbling sound that an animal makes.
>The dog's growl scared me. *n. pl.* **growls**
>**2.** to make a deep angry sound.
>The dog will growl if you try to get his food.
>*v.* **growled, growled, growling** growl·ing

grown (grōn) *v. pt. part.* See **grow.**

grown-up (grōn′up) an older person; an adult.
>There were two children and one grown-up in the car. *n. pl.* **grown-ups**

growth (grōth) **1.** how much something or someone grows.
The plant growth was almost two feet. *n. no pl.*
2. the act of growing.
The growth of children is slow. *n. no pl.*

grow up (grō up) to get older.
I want to grow up and become a painter.
v. **grew up, grown up, growing up** grow·ing up

gruff (gruf) mean; rough.
The gruff voice was scary. *adj.*

guard

grumble grum·ble (grum′bəl) a complaint said in a quiet voice.
The teacher heard Tony's grumble. *n. pl.* **grumbles** grum·bles

guarantee guar·an·tee (gar·ən·tē′) a promise.
The company gave us a guarantee that the dryer would work for five years.
n. pl. **guarantees** guar·an·tees

guard (gärd) **1.** to watch over something or someone; to protect something or someone from harm.
Soldiers guard our country.
v. **guarded, guarded, guarding** guard·ed, guard·ing
2. a person who watches over something or someone; a person who protects.
The guard at the bank protects the money. *n. pl.* **guards**

guardsman guards·man (gärdz′mən) a soldier who protects people.
My brother is a guardsman for a general in the Army.
n. pl. **guardsmen** guards·men

guava

guava gua·va (gwä′və) a small fruit that is yellow or red, grows on trees in the tropics and is used to make jelly or jam.
The guava was sweet tasting. *n. pl.* **guavas** gua·vas

guess (ges) **1.** to give an answer without knowing the facts; to predict the answer.
I sometimes guess the answers on a test. *v.*
2. to think or to have a feeling about without having facts.
I guess he is telling the truth. *v.* **guessed, guessed, guessing** guess·ing

guest (gest) a visitor.
We had a guest for dinner last night. *n. pl.* **guests**

a	cat	**i**	sit	**oi**	oil	**ch**	chop
ā	ate	**ī**	lie	**ou**	out	**ng**	song
ä	car	**o**	pot	**u**	cut	**sh**	she
e	set	**ō**	old	** u̇**	book	**th**	three
ē	equal	**ô**	or	**ü**	blue	**ŦH**	there
ėr	germ					**zh**	treasure

ə = { a in about / e in oven / i in pencil / o in memory / u in circus

guide (gīd) **1.** to help someone; to give directions; to lead.
I will guide you to the office. *v.* **guided, guided, guiding** guid·ed, guid·ing
2. a list of events or programs.
Ann looked in the TV guide to find a good movie. *n. pl.* **guides**

guilty guilt·y (gil⸍tē) having done something wrong or bad; being the person who is to blame for something.
He is guilty of breaking the window.
adj. **guiltier, guiltiest** guilt·i·er, guilt·i·est

guitar

guitar gui·tar (gə·tär′) a musical instrument with a long neck and strings that are played with the fingers.
Bruce plays the guitar and sings. *n. pl.* **guitars** gui·tars

Gulf of Mexico Gulf of Mex·i·co (gulf əv mek⸍sə·kō) a body of water that lies between Florida and Texas.
Many people fish in the Gulf of Mexico.

gum (gum) a sweet, sticky substance that people chew.
The dentist said that I should not chew gum. *n. no pl.*

Gulf of Mexico

gumdrop gum·drop (gum⸍drop) a sticky, sweet candy.
The gumdrop stuck to my teeth. *n. pl.* **gumdrops** gum·drops

gun (gun) **1.** a tool that is used to shoot bullets.
A gun is a dangerous weapon. *n. pl.* **guns**
2. having to do with a tool that shoots bullets.
The guard wears a gun belt. *adj.*

gun

gurgle gur·gle (gėr⸍gəl) to make a bubbling noise in the back of the mouth.
My baby brother will gurgle when he is happy.
v. **gurgled, gurgled, gurgling** gur·gled, gur·gling

guy (gī) a boy or a man.
Some guy wants to buy my car. *n. pl.* **guys**

gym (jim) a room where games or sports are played; gymnasium.
Our class goes to the gym for a half hour every day. *n. pl.* **gyms**

gypsy gyp·sy (jip⸍sē) a person who travels from place to place with a group of other people.
The gypsy had dark hair, dark eyes and dark skin. *n. pl.* **gypsies** gyp·sies

gym

Hh

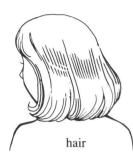

hair

habit   hab·it (hab′it)   something done often; a custom; a usual action.
I have a bad habit of biting my fingernails. *n. pl.* **habits** hab·its

had   (had *or* həd)   *v. pt. t., pt. part.* See **have.**

had better   had bet·ter (had bet′ər)   should; would be smart to.
We had better do our homework before we watch TV. *idiom*

had better not   had bet·ter not (had bet′ər not)   should not; would not be smart to.
We had better not eat too much pie. *idiom*

hail   (hāl)   small pieces of ice that fall from the clouds in a storm.
Hail fell and the wind blew during the storm last night. *n. no pl.*

hair   (her *or* har)   the thread-like growth that covers the head of people.
I brushed my hair before I went to school. *n. no pl.*

haircut   hair·cut (her′kut *or* har′kut)   the act of having one's hair made shorter.
I get a haircut at the barbershop once a month. *n. pl.* **haircuts** hair·cuts

hair-like   (her-līk)   something that looks like a hair.
The hair-like fur of the bear was very soft. *adj.*

hairy   hair·y (her′ē *or* har′ē)   covered with hair.
The gorilla is a hairy animal. *adj.* **hairier, hairiest** hair·i·er, hair·i·est

Haiti

Port-au-Prince

Haiti   Hai·ti (hā′tē)   a small country that is part of an island located between North America and South America, south of Florida; its capital is Port-au-Prince.
We sailed a boat from Florida to Haiti. *n.*

Haleakala   Ha·le·a·ka·la (hä·lā·ä·kä·lä′)   a volcano on the island of Maui in Hawaii.
Haleakala has not erupted for many years. *n.*

half   (haf)   one of two equal parts.
I ate half of the pie. *n. pl.* **halves**

a	cat	i	sit	oi	oil	ch	chop		a in about
ā	ate	ī	lie	ou	out	ng	song		e in oven
ä	car	o	pot	u	cut	sh	she	ə =	i in pencil
e	set	ō	old	u̇	book	th	three		o in memory
ē	equal	ô	or	ü	blue	ŦH	there		u in circus
ėr	germ					zh	treasure		

half-mast (haf-mast) the position of the flag when it is in the middle of the flagpole.
The flag was at half-mast because the soldier was killed. *n. no pl.*

half past (haf   past) 30 minutes past an hour.
I will pick you up at half past ten. *adj.*

half time (haf tīm) the break between the first part of a game and the second part of a game.
The band played during the half time at last night's football game.

halfway half·way (haf·wā′) in the middle; in the center.
The man ran halfway across the field. *adv.*

Halifax Hal·i·fax (hal′ə·faks) the capital of Nova Scotia, Canada.
We flew to Halifax, Canada. *n.*

hall (hôl) **1.** a narrow room or passage between rooms in a building or house.
Bob talked to me in the hall at school. *n.*
2. a very large room that is used for parties or meetings.
The church festival will be in the church hall. *n. pl.* **halls**

hallowed hal·lowed (hal′ōd) respected; honored as holy.
The church was built on hallowed ground. *adj.*

Halloween Hal·low·een (hal·ō·ēn′ *or* hol·ō·ēn′) a holiday celebrated on October 31 by children dressing up in costumes; "trick or treat" night.
I wore a monster costume on Halloween. *n.*

hallway hall·way (hôl′wā) a narrow room or passage between rooms in a house or building.
The hallway was dark, and I could not see where I was going.
n. pl. **hallways** hall·ways

halves (havz) *n. pl.* See **half.**

halyard hal·yard (hal′yərd) the rope used to raise a flag or a sail.
The soldier tied the halyard to the flagpole. *n. pl.* **halyards** hal·yards

ham (ham) the meat that comes from the top part of a pig's back leg.
We ate ham and potatoes for dinner last night. *n. pl.* **hams**

hamburger ham·burg·er (ham′bėr·gər) ground beef shaped flat and round, then cooked and made into a sandwich.
I ate a hamburger for lunch. *n. pl.* **hamburgers** ham·burg·ers

Hamel Ham·el (ham′əl) a small town in Germany.
The children of Hamel followed the man playing the horn. *n.*

half-mast

hamburger

hall

hall

hammer

hammock

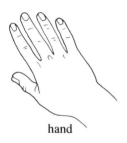

hand

handkerchief

hammer   ham·mer (ham′ər)   **1.** a tool used to pound nails into wood.
The house builder needs a hammer and nails. *n. pl.* **hammers** ham·mers
2. to pound nails with a tool.
I will hammer the nails into the wall.
v. **hammered, hammered, hammering** ham·mered, ham·mer·ing

hammock   ham·mock (ham′ək)   a bed made out of rope or canvas
that hangs between two poles or two trees.
We put a hammock between the trees in the backyard.
n. pl. **hammocks** ham·mocks

hand   (hand)   **1.** the part of the body at the end of an arm that has
four fingers and one thumb.
I write with my right hand. *n.*
2. a unit of measure equal to 4 inches used to measure the
height of horses.
My horse is 17 hands high. *n.*
3. the arm on a clock or watch that points to the numbers.
The little hand was on the one and the big hand was on the six. *n. pl.* **hands**
4. held in the hand; having the human body as
its energy source.
We used a hand saw to cut the wood for the fire. *adj.*
5. to give something to someone.
Please hand me the milk. *v.* **handed, handed, handing** hand·ed, hand·ing

handed   hand·ed (han′did)   *v. pt. t., pt. part.* See **hand** (5).

handful   hand·ful (hand′fùl)   as much as one hand can hold.
I took a handful of candy from the dish. *n. pl.* **handfuls** hand·fuls

handicapped   hand·i·capped (han′dē·kapt)   having difficulty in
learning, moving or thinking because of a problem with the
senses, the body or the mind.
Deaf people and blind people are often handicapped. *adj.*

handicraft   hand·i·craft (han′dē·kraft)   something that is made with
the hands by a skillful person.
A knitted sweater is a handicraft. *n. pl.* **handicrafts** hand·i·crafts

handkerchief   hand·ker·chief (hang′kər·chif)   a square piece of fine
material used to blow one's nose.
I always carry a handkerchief in my pocket.
n. pl. **handkerchiefs** hand·ker·chiefs

a	cat	**i**	sit	**oi**	oil	**ch**	chop		a in about
ā	ate	**ī**	lie	**ou**	out	**ng**	song		e in oven
ä	car	**o**	pot	**u**	cut	**sh**	she	ə =	i in pencil
e	set	**ō**	old	**ù**	book	**th**	three		o in memory
ē	equal	**ô**	or	**ü**	blue	**ŦH**	there		u in circus
ėr	germ					**zh**	treasure		

handle han·dle (han′dl) **1.** a part of something that is for the hand to grab or hold.
The handle on the pot is hot. *n. pl.* **handles** han·dles
2. to control with the hands; to manage.
I can handle the angry dog.
v. **handled, handled, handling** han·dled, han·dling

handle

handmade hand·made (hand′mād′) made with the hand and not by a machine.
The sweater I have on today is handmade. *adj.*

handsome hand·some (han′səm) good-looking; attractive in the way a person looks.
The gentleman standing near the door is handsome.
adj. **handsomer, handsomest** hand·som·er, hand·som·est

handsomely hand·some·ly (han′səm·lē) in a good-looking way; expensively.
He is handsomely dressed in a blue suit. *adv.*

handy hand·y (han′dē) easy to find; near to the hand.
The hammer is handy; I will get it for you.
adj. **handier, handiest** hand·i·er, hand·i·est

hang (hang) **1.** to hook something up high so it swings in the air.
I will hang the curtains. *v.* **hung, hung, hanging** hang·ing
2. to kill a person by hooking them up with a rope around the neck.
They will hang the man who shot the policeman.
v. **hanged, hanged, hanging** hang·ing

harbor

hang up (hang up) to put the telephone down on the base.
I will hang up the phone in ten minutes.
v. **hung up, hung up, hanging up** hang·ing up

happen hap·pen (hap′ən) to take place; to occur.
We do not know what will happen in the future.
v. **happened, happened, happening** hap·pened, hap·pen·ing

happier hap·pi·er (hap′ē·ər) *comp. adj.* See **happy.**

happily hap·pi·ly (hap′ə·lē) in a glad way.
The boy happily ran to his mother. *adv.*

happiness hap·pi·ness (hap′ē·nis) a good feeling; a joyfulness.
The girl's happiness showed on her face when she smiled. *n. no pl.*

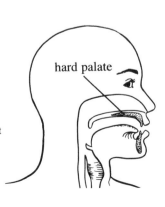

hard palate

happy hap·py (hap′ē) feeling good; glad.
I was happy to see her again. *adj.* **happier, happiest** hap·pi·er, hap·pi·est

happy ending hap·py end·ing (hap′ē en′ding) a good result; a good finish of a story or event.
The book had a happy ending.

harass har·ass (har′əs *or* hə·ras′) to bother; to tease; to be a pest.
Katie will harass you until you play ball with her.
v. **harassed, harassed, harassing** har·assed, har·ass·ing

harbor har·bor (här′bər) an area of water where boats
can safely stop and unload.
There are many boats in the harbor. *n. pl.* **harbors** har·bors

hard (härd) **1.** not soft; stiff; not able to move when touched.
The ice was hard. *adj.*
2. not easy; difficult.
Moving the sofa was hard work. *adj.*
3. strong; with much energy.
The man is a hard worker. *adj.* **harder, hardest** hard·er, hard·est

hard-boiled (härd-boild′) an egg that has been cooked so that both
the eggwhite and the yoke are firm.
We colored hard-boiled eggs for our Easter baskets. *adj.*

hardly hard·ly (härd′lē) just barely; not quite; almost cannot.
The boy is so small that he can hardly reach the doorknob. *adv.*

hard palate hard pal·ate (härd pal′it) the top of the mouth that
is above the tongue and is curved.
Peanut butter sticks to my hard palate.

hardware hard·ware (härd′wer) **1.** things made with metal,
such as nails, locks or tools.
We needed hardware for the door. *n. no pl.*
2. having to do with things made of metal.
We went to the hardware store to buy the lock for the door. *adj.*

hare (her *or* har) a large rabbit with long ears and long back legs.
The hare ran away from the dog. *n. pl.* **hares**

harmful harm·ful (härm′fəl) bad for the body; dangerous; wrong.
Cigarettes are harmful to a person. *adj.*

harness har·ness (här′nis) something with straps that is buckled
on to a person or an animal.
A parachute harness fits around the body of a person jumping
from an airplane. *n. pl.* **harnesses** har·ness·es

harsh (härsh) rough; cruel.
The man was very harsh to the dog.
adj. **harsher, harshest** harsh·er, harsh·est

hare

harness

a	cat	i	sit	oi	oil	ch	chop		a in about
ā	ate	ī	lie	ou	out	ng	song		e in oven
ä	car	o	pot	u	cut	sh	she	ə =	i in pencil
e	set	ō	old	u̇	book	th	three		o in memory
ē	equal	ô	or	ü	blue	ŦH	there		u in circus
ėr	germ					zh	treasure		

harshly harsh·ly (härsh′lē) in a rough way; in a cruel way.
>He treated the dog harshly. *adv.*

harvest har·vest (här′vist) **1.** the time when farmers gather or pick their crops.
>The harvest for corn is in September. *n. pl.* **harvests** har·vests
>**2.** to gather or pick ripe crops.
>We will harvest the corn in September.
>*v.* **harvested, harvested, harvesting** har·vest·ed, har·vest·ing

harvester har·vest·er (här′və·stər) a machine that gathers grain or other crops.
>We used a harvester to pick the corn. *n. pl.* **harvesters** har·vest·ers

has (haz *or* həz) *v. pres. t.* See **have.**

hasn't has·n't (haz′nt) has not.
>Dad hasn't come home yet. *contrac.*

harvester

hat (hat) a covering for the head.
>I will wear a hat today because it is cold outside. *n. pl.* **hats**

hatch (hach) to break out of a shell.
>The birds will hatch from the eggs in a few days.
>*v.* **hatched, hatched, hatching** hatch·ing

hate (hāt) **1.** to dislike greatly.
>The two men hate each other. *v.*
>**2.** to be unwilling; not to want to do something.
>We hate to go on a train. *v.* **hated, hated, hating** hat·ed, hat·ing

haul (hôl) to move from one place to another place by pulling, dragging or using a vehicle.
>We will haul the refrigerator to the basement.
>*v.* **hauled, hauled, hauling** haul·ing

hat

haunted haunt·ed (hôn′tid *or* hän′tid) full of ghosts.
>The old house is haunted. *adj.*

Havana Ha·van·a (hə·van′ə) the capital city of the island country of Cuba.
>We flew to Havana from Florida. *n.*

have (hav *or* həv) **1.** to own; to possess.
>I have a dog. *v.*
>**2.** to be part of.
>My new watch will have three hands. *v.*
>**3.** to eat.
>I will have a hamburger for lunch. *v.*
>**4.** to give birth.
>The dog will have her puppies any day now. *v.*
>**5.** to conduct; to hold; to lead.
>We will have a party for her birthday. *v.* **had, had, having** hav·ing

haven't have·n't (hav′ənt) have not.
I haven't eaten all day. *contrac.*

have to (hav tü) need to; must.
We have to do our homework before we watch TV. *aux.*

hay (hā) **1.** dried grass.
Horses eat hay. *n. no pl.*
2. having to do with dried grass.
We went into the hay field to play. *adj.*

hay

he (hē) the man or boy that a person is talking about.
John is so nice; he is a good friend. *pron.*

head (hed) **1.** the part of the body that has the eyes, ears, nose, mouth, hair and brain.
I put a hat on my head. *n.*
2. the top person or leader.
He is the head of our team. *n.*
3. something that is round like the top part of the body.
We picked a head of cabbage. *n.*
4. the part of a horse bridle that goes from the ears of the horse to the mouth bit.
We cannot use that bridle because a head is broken. *n.*
5. the top part of something.
The head of the letter had Mary's address written on it. *n. pl.* **heads**

head

head coach (hed kōch) the main person teaching a sport.
Mr. Wynn is the head coach at the high school.

head for (hed fôr) to go in the direction of something; to go to.
I will head for the ice cream store.
v. **headed for, headed for, heading for** head·ed for, head·ing for

heading head·ing (hed′ing) the first part of a letter.
I put my address in the heading of the letter. *n. pl.* **headings** head·ings

heal (hēl) to get well; to cure.
The cut on his arm will heal in a few days.
v. **healed, healed, healing** heal·ing

health (helth) the condition of a body; the physical state of the body.
I am in good health, but my brother is in poor health. *n. no pl.*

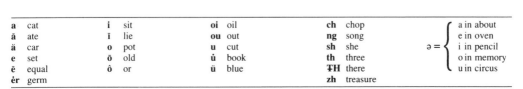

a	cat	**i**	sit	**oi**	oil	**ch**	chop	a in about
ā	ate	**ī**	lie	**ou**	out	**ng**	song	e in oven
ä	car	**o**	pot	**u**	cut	**sh**	she	ə = i in pencil
e	set	**ō**	old	**u̇**	book	**th**	three	o in memory
ē	equal	**ô**	or	**ü**	blue	**ŦH**	there	u in circus
ėr	germ					**zh**	treasure	

health resort health re·sort (helth ri·zôrt′) a place people go to
get over a disease or sickness or to get their bodies
in good physical condition.
The lady spent two weeks at the health resort and lost ten pounds.

healthy health·y (hel′thē) being in good physical
condition; being well.
I am not sick; I am healthy.
adj. **healthier, healthiest** health·i·er, health·i·est

hearing aid

hear (hir) **1.** to be aware of sounds; to use one's ears to
know there are sounds.
I can hear what you are saying. *v.*
2. to learn; to become aware of something.
I hear that you are going on vacation to Hawaii.
v. **heard, heard, hearing** hear·ing

heard (hėrd) *v. pt. t., pt. part.* See **hear.**

hearing hear·ing (hir′ing) **1.** *v. pres. part.* See **hear.**
2. the ability to listen to sounds; the ability to know
there are sounds.
My hearing is not very good. *n. no pl.*

hearing aid hear·ing aid (hir′ing ād) a tool that makes sounds
louder, used by people who do not hear well.
My hearing is not very good, so I wear a hearing aid.

hearing-ear dog hear·ing-ear dog (hir′ing-ir dôg) an animal
that is trained to alert deaf people to sounds.
My hearing-ear dog jumps at the door when someone knocks on it.

hearing impaired hear·ing im·pair·ed (hir′ing im·per′d)
having difficulty hearing; not being able to hear normally.
I am hearing impaired and do not hear all the sounds around me.

heart (härt) **1.** a body part that pumps the blood through the body.
The heart is a very important part of the body. *n.*
2. a shape that looks like the part of the body that pumps blood.
I drew my mother a heart on Valentine's Day. *n. pl.* **hearts**
3. love; kindness.
John has lots of heart. *n. no pl.*

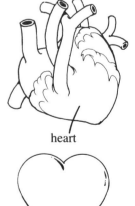

heart

heart attack heart at·tack (härt ə·tak′) a sudden sickness
that stops or slows the part of the body that pumps blood.
My father had a heart attack, but he is well now.

heartless heart·less (härt′lis) without love and kindness;
without feeling.
The stepmother was heartless and would not let Cinderella
go to the party. *adj.*

heater

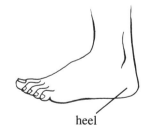

heather

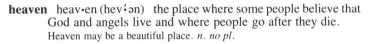

heel

heat (hēt) **1.** hot or warm air.
The heat from the fire warmed my hands. *n. no pl.*
2. the energy that keeps a building warm.
We pay fifty dollars a month for heat. *n. no pl.*
3. to warm something.
I will heat the chicken that is left from last night.
v. **heated, heated, heating** heat·ed, heat·ing
4. having to do with hot or warm air.
The heat vent in my room keeps the room warm. *adj.*

heater heat·er (hē′tər) a machine that makes warm air or that warms the air.
The heater in our house is electric. *n. pl.* **heaters** heat·ers

heather heath·er (heŦH′ər) a small bush with very small bell-shaped flowers.
Heather grows in Scotland. *n. pl.* **heathers** heath·ers

heave (hēv) to lift or pull something with difficulty; to lift and throw something with effort.
I will heave the box of books into the car.
v. **heaved, heaved, heaving** heav·ing

heaven heav·en (hev′ən) the place where some people believe that God and angels live and where people go after they die.
Heaven may be a beautiful place. *n. no pl.*

heavily heav·i·ly (hev′ə·lē) strongly; in large amounts; with great weight.
It rained heavily last night. *adv.*

heavy heav·y (hev′ē) **1.** being great in weight; not light.
The box of books is very heavy. *adj.*
2. hard; lasting a long time.
The rain was heavy last night. *adj.*
3. thick.
We painted on heavy paper. *adj.* **heavier, heaviest** heav·i·er, heav·i·est

Hebrew He·brew (hē′brü) a person in ancient times, from Israel.
Jesus Christ was a Hebrew. *n. pl.* **Hebrews** He·brews

hedge (hej) a row of bushes or trees that make a fence.
I will cut the hedge on Saturday. *n. pl.* **hedges** hedg·es

heel (hēl) the back part of the foot, below the ankle.
The new shoe hurt the heel of my right foot. *n. pl.* **heels**

a	cat	i	sit	oi	oil	ch	chop		a in about
ā	ate	ī	lie	ou	out	ng	song		e in oven
ä	car	o	pot	u	cut	sh	she	ə =	i in pencil
e	set	ō	old	u̇	book	th	three		o in memory
ē	equal	ô	or	ü	blue	ŦH	there		u in circus
ėr	germ					zh	treasure		

height (hīt) how tall something or someone is; the distance from the top to the bottom of something or someone.
The height of the basketball player is six feet three inches. *n. pl.* **heights**

held (held) *v. pt. t., pt. part.* See **hold.**

helicopter hel·i·cop·ter (hel′ə·kop·tər *or* hē′lə·kop·tər) a kind of airplane that has no wings and can fly straight up and down.
The propellers keep the helicopter in the air.
n. pl. **helicopters** hel·i·cop·ters

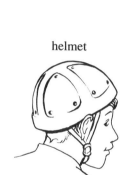
helicopter

hello hel·lo (he·lō′ *or* hə·lō′) word said when meeting someone; a greeting.
"Hello!" I said, when I walked into the room. *interj.*

helmet hel·met (hel′mit) a hat made from hard materials and worn to protect the head.
The boy wore a helmet when he raced his bicycle. *n. pl.* **helmets** hel·mets

help (help) **1.** to give aid; assistance.
I will help you with the dishes. *v.* **helped, helped, helping** help·ing
2. assistance; the act of aiding.
How can I thank you for the help you gave me? *n. no pl.*

helmet

helper help·er (hel′pər) a person who gives assistance or aid.
I was a teacher's helper today. *n. pl.* **helpers** help·ers

helpful help·ful (help′fəl) willing and able to give assistance or aid.
I was very helpful to the teacher. *adj.*

helpless help·less (help′lis) not having the ability to give assistance; not knowing how to give assistance.
My sister was helpless when I fell off the boat. *adj.*

helplessly help·less·ly (help′lis·lē) unable to give assistance or aid; not able to stop what is happening.
She helplessly watched me fall. *adv.*

help out (help out) to aid someone in doing something.
I will help out with the picnic lunch.
v. **helped out, helped out, helping out** help·ing out

help wanted (help won′tid) the part of a newspaper that lists jobs that are available.
I found my job in the help wanted section of last Sunday's paper.

Helsingor Hel·sing·or (hel′sing·ôr) a city in Sweden.
Helsingor has a beautiful harbor. *n.*

hen (hen) a female bird, especially a female chicken.
The hen laid an egg. *n. pl.* **hens**

hen

200

her (hėr *or* hər) **1.** belonging to a girl or a woman.
The girl had her hair cut by the barber. *adj.*
2. the girl or woman that one is talking about.
Jane is not here; I just saw her leave. *pron.*

herald her·ald (her′əld) a person who carries messages or who tells the news to a group of people.
The herald told the people in the hall that the war was over.
n. pl. **heralds** her·alds

herb (ėrb *or* hėrb) a plant that gives a certain taste to foods.
Mint is an herb. *n. pl.* **herbs**

Hercules Her·cu·les (hėr′kyə·lēz) a Greek god believed to be very strong and brave.
The Greek people believed that Hercules was half man and half god. *n.*

herbs

herd (hėrd) **1.** a large group of the same kind of animals.
The herd of cows moved under the tree when it started to rain. *n. pl.* **herds**
2. to move animals into a group.
We will herd the sheep together. *v.*
3. to make animals move from one place to another place.
We will herd the cows into the barn.
v. **herded, herded, herding** herd·ed, herd·ing

here (hir) in this place.
Mary left but she was here all day. *adv.*

heritage her·it·age (her′ə·tij) what is given to one family member by an older member; what is passed from generation to generation.
Traditions and customs are part of our heritage. *n. no pl.*

hero her·o (hir′ō) a brave and good man; a man who saves other people from danger or harm.
The firefighter who brought the girl out of the fire was a hero.
n. pl. **heroes** her·oes

heroine her·o·ine (her′ō·ən) a brave and good woman; a woman who saves other people from danger or harm.
The doctor who saved my father is a heroine to me.
n. pl. **heroines** her·o·ines

herd

herself her·self (hər·self′) that very same girl or woman that one is talking about.
The little girl hurt herself when she fell off the bicycle. *pron.*

a	cat	**i**	sit	**oi**	oil	**ch**	chop	a in about
ā	ate	**ī**	lie	**ou**	out	**ng**	song	e in oven
ä	car	**o**	pot	**u**	cut	**sh**	she	ə = { i in pencil
e	set	**ō**	old	**u̇**	book	**th**	three	o in memory
ē	equal	**ô**	or	**ü**	blue	**ŦH**	there	u in circus
ėr	germ					**zh**	treasure	

hey (hā)   a word that is used in calling to another person
or to show surprise.
"Hey! Where are you going with my bike?" the boy yelled. *interj.*

hi (hī)   hello; a word used when meeting or greeting another person.
"Hi," I said, as I passed the man on the street. *interj.*

hibernate   hi·ber·nate (hī′bər·nāt)   to sleep or not move
during the winter months.
The snake will hibernate all winter and wake up again when it is spring.
v. **hibernated, hibernated, hibernating** hi·ber·nat·ed, hi·ber·nat·ing

hibernation   hi·ber·na·tion (hī·bər·nā′shən)   the act of
sleeping through the winter.
The snake's hibernation will last three months. *n. no pl.*

hibernate

hibiscus   hi·bis·cus (hə·bis′kəs *or* hī·bis′kəs)   a bush that has
large bell-shaped flowers that may be red, pink or white.
My mother planted a hibiscus in her yard. *n. pl.* **hibiscuses** hi·bis·cus·es

hidden   hid·den (hid′n)   *v. pt. part.* See **hide** (1).

hide (hīd)   **1.** to put something in a place where no one can find it.
I will hide her gift until Christmas morning.
v. **hid, hidden** *or* **hid, hiding** hid·den, hid·ing
2. the skin of an animal.
We use the hide of a cow to make leather. *n. pl.* **hides**

hide-and-seek   (hīd′n-sēk′)   a game in which one player tries to
find the other players, who are hiding.
The children played hide-and-seek in the park. *n. no pl.*

hibiscus

high (hī)   **1.** far above the ground.
Mary hit the ball high into the air. *adv.*
2. above others.
The high school is across the street. *adj.*
3. above normal; more than before.
The temperature was high today. *adj.*
4. tall.
We rode the elevator in the high building. *adj.*
5. far above the ground.
The kite was high in the sky. *adj.*
6. expensive; costing much money.
Mike could not buy the car because the price was too high.
adj. **higher, highest** high·er, high·est
7. an excited feeling; a happy feeling.
I get a high watching the sun rise. *n. pl.* **highs**

high blood pressure   (hī blud′ presh·ər)   a bad health condition
that causes great pressure in the body's arteries.
My father has high blood pressure.

highchair

highchair high·chair (hī⸍cher *or* hī⸍char) a tall seat with a table that small children sit in to eat meals.
The little girl sat in her highchair to eat her breakfast.
n. pl. **highchairs** high·chairs

highly high·ly (hī⸍lē) very much; greatly.
People think highly of that gentleman. *adv.*

highness high·ness (hī⸍nis) a title of respect given to kings, queens, princes and princesses.
I bowed to the queen and said, "Good day, Your Highness."
n. pl. **highnesses** high·ness·es

high school (hī skül) the school children attend after elementary and junior high schools.
Grades 9 through 12 make up high school in some cities and grades 10 through 12 make up the high school in other cities.

hiker

hike (hīk) **1.** to take a long walk.
I like to hike in the forest. *v.* **hiked, hiked, hiking** hik·ing
2. a long walk.
Everyone was tired after the hike. *n. pl.* **hikes**

hiker hik·er (hīk⸍ər) a person who takes long walks.
The hiker climbed the mountain. *n. pl.* **hikers** hik·ers

hill (hil) a high part of the ground that is not as high as a mountain.
We rode our sleds down the hill. *n. pl.* **hills**

hillside hill·side (hil⸍sīd) the side of a hill.
We could see the whole hillside from the top of the hill.
n. pl. **hillsides** hill·sides

him (him) the boy or man that a person is talking about.
Joe is not here; I saw him leave an hour ago. *pron.*

himself him·self (him·self′) that very same boy or man that one is talking about.
The little boy hurt himself when he fell out of the tree. *pron.*

hind (hīnd) having to do with the back part of an animal.
Ham comes from the top part of a pig's hind leg. *adj.*

hinder hind·er (hin⸍dər) to slow something down; to hold something back; to get in the way of.
The rain will hinder our work in the garden.
v. **hindered, hindered, hindering** hin·dered, hin·der·ing

a	cat	i	sit	oi	oil	ch	chop		a in about
ā	ate	ī	lie	ou	out	ng	song		e in oven
ä	car	o	pot	u	cut	sh	she	ə =	i in pencil
e	set	ō	old	u̇	book	th	three		o in memory
ē	equal	ô	or	ü	blue	ᵀH	there		u in circus
ėr	germ					zh	treasure		

hip point (hip point) the part of a horse's body that is above a back leg.
> The rider hit the horse's hip point.

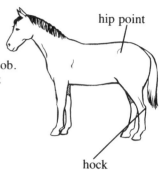

hip point

hock

hire (hīr) to pay someone to do a job; to give a person work or a job.
> The man will hire me to cut his grass. *v.* **hired, hired, hiring** hir·ing

hired hand (hīrd hand) a person who is paid to work on a farm or a ranch.
> I am a hired hand on my uncle's horse ranch.

his (hiz) belonging to a boy or a man.
> Jake found his shoes in the closet. *adj.*

hiss (his) **1.** the sound that a snake makes.
> We heard the hiss before we saw the snake. *n. pl.* **hisses** hiss·es
> **2.** to make a sound like the sound a snake makes.
> The people hissed because they did not like the play.
> *v.* **hissed, hissed, hissing** hiss·ing

historian his·to·ri·an (hi·stôr⁄ē·ən *or* hi·stōr⁄ē·ən) a person who studies or writes about past events.
> A historian loves to find out new facts about the past.
> *n. pl.* **historians** his·to·ri·ans

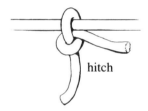

hitch

historical his·to·ri·cal (hi·stôr⁄ə·kəl *or* hi·stor⁄ə·kəl) known to be true in history; having to do with past events.
> The first walk on the moon was a historical event. *adj.*

history his·tor·y (his⁄tər·ē) **1.** the writings or record of things that happened in the past.
> If we study history, we learn what happened long ago and why it happened.
> *n. pl.* **histories** his·tor·ies
> **2.** having to do with studying the past.
> My history class is studying the Civil War. *adj.*

hit (hit) **1.** to strike with force.
> The boy will hit the ball with the bat. *v.*
> **2.** to reach with a force or a blow.
> The storm will hit the town at 4:30. *v.* **hit, hit, hitting** hit·ting
> **3.** a baseball that goes long and high enough that the player can reach a base before the ball is caught.
> Don got a hit in last night's baseball game. *n. pl.* **hits**

hit-and-run (hit⁄n-run′) having to do with striking someone or something and leaving before finding out if everything is all right; to run away after striking something.
> The dog was killed by a hit-and-run driver. *adj.*

hitter

hitch (hich) **1.** to tie or hook two things together.
> I will hitch the horse to the wagon. *v.* **hitched, hitched, hitching** hitch·ing
> **2.** a kind of knot that is used to tie sails.
> The hitch was easy to tie. *n. pl.* **hitches** hitch·es

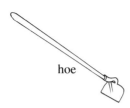

hoe

hole

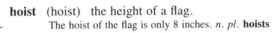

hitter   hit·ter (hit′ər)   the person who is at bat in a baseball game, the person who strikes the ball with the bat.
I was the fourth hitter to get on base in last night's baseball game.
n. pl. **hitters** hit·ters

hobby   hob·by (hob′ē)   something one likes to do in one's free time.
My hobby is reading, and my mother's hobby is painting.
n. pl. **hobbies** hob·bies

hock   (hok)   the joint of an animal's hind (back) leg.
The horse hurt its hock when it kicked the fence. *n. pl.* **hocks**

hoe   (hō)   a gardening tool that has a long handle and a thin, flat blade at the end of the handle.
We used a hoe to get the weeds out of the garden. *n. pl.* **hoes**

hoist   (hoist)   the height of a flag.
The hoist of the flag is only 8 inches. *n. pl.* **hoists**

hold   (hōld)   **1.** to have something in one's hand; to grasp.
I will hold your coat for you. *v.*
2. to support; to keep in the same place.
I will hold the ladder when you climb onto the roof.
v. **held, held, holding** hold·ing

holder   hold·er (hōl′dər)   a person or thing that keeps things together in one place.
The napkin holder is on the table. *n. pl.* **holders** hold·ers

hold on   (hōld ôn)   to grasp tightly.
Please hold on to the balloon so that it does not fly away.
v. **held on, held on, holding on** hold·ing on

hole   (hōl)   an opening; an empty spot in something.
The squirrel ran into the hole in the tree. *n. pl.* **holes**

holiday   hol·i·day (hol′ə·dā)   a special day; a day that celebrates a special event.
Christmas is a holiday. *n. pl.* **holidays** hol·i·days

Holland   Hol·land (hol′ənd)   the old name for a country in Europe that is now called the Netherlands.
We see windmills and tulips in Holland. *n.*

hollow   hol·low (hol′ō)   empty inside; having nothing on the inside.
A straw is hollow. *adj.*

a	cat	i	sit	oi	oil	ch	chop		a in about
ā	ate	ī	lie	ou	out	ng	song		e in oven
ä	car	o	pot	u	cut	sh	she	ə =	i in pencil
e	set	ō	old	u̇	book	th	three		o in memory
ē	equal	ô	or	ü	blue	ŦH	there		u in circus
ėr	germ					zh	treasure		

hollow out (hol'ō out) to empty the inside of something; to take out the insides of something.
> The Indians would hollow out logs and use them for canoes.
> *v.* **hollowed out, hollowed out, hollowing out**
> hol·lowed out, hol·low·ing out

holly berry hol·ly ber·ry (hol'ē ber'ē) the fruit of a holly bush, which is poisonous to eat.
> The holly berry is pretty, and people use it for decoration but not for food.

holy ho·ly (hō'lē) having to do with God and religion.
> Christmas is a holy day. *adj.* **holier, holiest** ho·li·er, ho·li·est

Holy Week Ho·ly Week (hō'lē wēk) the seven days before Easter.
> John goes to church every night during Holy Week.

holly berry

home (hōm) **1.** house; the place where one lives.
> That houseboat is my home. *n. pl.* **homes**
> **2.** having to do with one's house or place where one lives.
> I am having a home party tomorrow. *adj.*
> **3.** to the place where one lives.
> I want to go home now. *adv.*

home care (hōm ker) keeping a house in good condition.
> The book is about home care.

homecoming home·com·ing (hōm'kum·ing) a special game that a school's team plays and invites past students to attend.
> Our school's homecoming is on Saturday.
> *n. pl.* **homecomings** home·com·ings

homeland home·land (hōm'land) the country where a person lives or where a person was born.
> My grandmother's homeland is Italy. *n. pl.* **homelands** home·lands

homemade home·made (hōm'mād) made in the home and not in a factory.
> This is homemade jelly. *adj.*

home run (hōm run) a hit in a baseball game where the batter runs to all four bases and scores a point.
> I hit a home run in the baseball game yesterday.

homesick home·sick (hōm'sik) a feeling of missing one's home.
> I am homesick. *n. no pl.*

homespun home·spun (hōm'spun) woven cloth or material made at home and not in factories.
> The wool in the dress is homespun. *n. no pl.*

hood

home town (hōm toun) the city in which a person lives or was born.
> His home town is Chicago.

homework home·work (hōm′wėrk)   school work that students must do at home.
I finished my homework before dinner. *n. no pl.*

honest hon·est (on′ist)   truthful; not lying.
He is an honest person who never tells lies. *adj.*

honey hon·ey (hun′ē)   **1.** a sweet liquid that bees make for food.
We put honey on our bread. *n. pl.* **honeys** hon·eys
2. a nickname for someone you love.
Dad calls Mom "Honey" all the time. *n. no pl.*

honor hon·or (on′ər)   **1.** to show respect; to give credit for doing well.
The town will honor the soldiers with a parade on Independence Day.
v. **honored, honored, honoring** hon·ored, hon·or·ing
2. reward or special mention of a job well done.
The student with the best grades received the highest honor.
n. pl. **honors** hon·ors

hood (hůd)   **1.** a covering for the head.
My coat has a hood on it. *n.*
2. the part of the car that covers the motor.
The man opened the hood of the car to check the oil. *n. pl.* **hoods**

hoof (hůf *or* hüf)   the hard cover on the foot of some animals.
I cleaned the hoof of my horse. *n. pl.* **hoofs** *or* **hooves**

hook (hůk)   **1.** a piece of metal or wood that is curved and used to hold or hang things.
Put your coat on the hook behind the door. *n. pl.* **hooks**
2. to tie together or catch something with a piece of curved wood or metal.
I will hook the hammock to the tree.
v. **hooked, hooked, hooking** hook·ing

hooked (hůkt)   **1.** *v. pt. t., pt. part.* See **hook** (2).
2. needing something like drugs, tobacco or alcohol very badly.
My friend is hooked on chocolate and must have some every day. *adj.*

hoop (hůp *or* hüp)   a large wooden, metal or plastic ring or circle.
David put the basketball through the hoop. *n. pl.* **hoops**

hooves (hůvz *or* hüvz)   *n. pl.* See **hoof.**

hop (hop)   to jump on one foot.
I will hop to the chair. *v.* **hopped, hopped, hopping** hop·ping

hoof

hook

hoop

a	cat	**i**	sit	**oi**	oil	**ch**	chop		a in about
ā	ate	**ī**	lie	**ou**	out	**ng**	song		e in oven
ä	car	**o**	pot	**u**	cut	**sh**	she	ə =	i in pencil
e	set	**ō**	old	**ů**	book	**th**	three		o in memory
ē	equal	**ô**	or	**ü**	blue	**ŦH**	there		u in circus
ėr	germ					**zh**	treasure		

hope (hōp) **1.** to wish; to want.
I hope you like your gift. *v.* **hoped, hoped, hoping** hop·ing
2. a feeling that what one wants might happen.
My hope is that I can go to Hawaii this summer. *n. pl.* **hopes**

Hopi Ho·pi (hō´pē) **1.** a North American Indian tribe.
The Hopi live in Arizona. *plural n.*
2. a person who belongs to that tribe.
That Indian is a Hopi. *n. pl.* **Hopis** or **Hopi** Ho·pis or Ho·pi

horizontal ho·ri·zon·tal (hôr·ə·zon´tl or hor·ə·zon´tl)
flat; level; side to side.
We write on the horizontal lines on the paper. *adj.*

horizontally ho·ri·zon·tal·ly (hôr·ə·zon´tl·lē) from side to side.
The words on the page run horizontally. *adv.*

horn (hôrn) **1.** a hard, hollow growth on the head of some animals.
The bull broke a horn when he ran into the wall. *n.*
2. a musical instrument that a person plays by
blowing air into it.
Jill plays a horn in the school band. *n.*
3. the curved front part of a horse saddle.
The girl placed her hands on the saddle horn as she rode
the horse. *n. pl.* **horns**

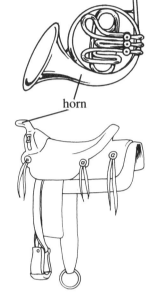

horn

horoscope ho·ro·scope (hôr´ə·skōp or hor´ə·skōp)
a chart for telling the future that uses the location of the
planets and the stars.
My horoscope said that I would win something today.
n. pl. **horoscopes** ho·ro·scopes

horrible hor·ri·ble (hôr´ə·bəl or hor´ə·bəl) terrible; very bad.
The fire was horrible. *adj.*

horror hor·ror (hôr´ər or hor´ər) scary; frightening.
I could not sleep after reading the horror story. *adj.*

horse (hôrs) a large animal with four legs and thick
hair on the neck and tail.
I can ride a horse. *n. pl.* **horses** hors·es

horse

horseback horse·back (hôrs´bak) a means of transportation;
going from place to place on a horse.
The man came to the farm on horseback. *n. no pl.*

horsefly horse·fly (hôrs´flī) an insect that bites animals,
especially horses.
The horse hit the horsefly with its tail. *n. pl.* **horseflies** horse·flies

horseman horse·man (hôrs´mən) a man who rides a horse.
The horseman rode very well. *n. pl.* **horsemen** horse·men

horsefly

208

horseshoe

hose

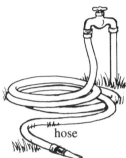

hot cross bun

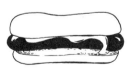

hot dog

horsemanship   horse·man·ship (hôrs′mən·ship)
the skill of riding horses.
His horsemanship is excellent. *n. no pl.*

horseshoe   horse·shoe (hôrs′shü *or* hôrsh′shü)   the metal covering
placed on a horse's hoof.
The horseshoe came off the horse's hoof. *n. pl.* **horseshoes** horse·shoes

horse stance   (hôrs   stants)   a Kung Fu position.
The Kung Fu teacher taught us the horse stance.

horse-training   horse-train·ing (hôrs-trā′ning)   teaching a horse.
Horse-training takes time and patience. *n. no pl.*

hose   (hōz)   a tube through which water runs and that one can move.
We used the hose to fill the baby's swimming pool. *n. pl.* **hoses** hos·es

hospital   hos·pi·tal (hos′pi·təl)   **1.** a building where sick people
are housed; a place where doctors and nurses
work with sick people.
I went to the hospital to have an operation. *n. pl.* **hospitals** hos·pi·tals
2. having to do with the building where sick people
go to get better.
I wore a hospital gown. *adj.*

hot   (hot)   very warm; not cold.
The soup was hot. *adj.* **hotter, hottest** hot·ter, hot·test

hot cake   (hot   kāk)   a pancake.
I want a hot cake for breakfast.

hot cross bun   (hot   krôs   bun)   a small sweet bread that has
a mark like a cross on it.
I had a hot cross bun with butter for lunch.

hot dog   (hot   dôg)   a kind of food made of meat shaped
into a long roll.
I ate a hot dog for lunch.

hotel   ho·tel (hō·tel′)   a large building with many bedrooms where
people stay when they are traveling.
We stayed in a hotel in Hawaii. *n. pl.* **hotels** ho·tels

hot-headed   hot-head·ed (hot′·hed·id)   easily angered;
having a bad temper.
Tom is so hot-headed that he is always fighting with someone. *adj.*

a	cat	**i**	sit	**oi**	oil	**ch**	chop	a in about
ā	ate	**ī**	lie	**ou**	out	**ng**	song	e in oven
ä	car	**o**	pot	**u**	cut	**sh**	she	ə = { i in pencil
e	set	**ō**	old	**u̇**	book	**th**	three	o in memory
ē	equal	**ô**	or	**ü**	blue	**TH**	there	u in circus
ėr	germ					**zh**	treasure	

hothouse   hot·house (hot⁄hous)   a building made of glass and used for growing flowers; a greenhouse.
> I bought the plants at the hothouse. *n. pl.* **hothouses** hot·hous·es

hour   (our)   a unit of time that equals 60 minutes.
> I can only stay for an hour. *n. pl.* **hours**

hourglass   hour·glass (our⁄glas)   a tool for measuring time that is made of glass and filled with sand.
> It takes one hour for the sand to run from the top part of the hourglass to the bottom part of the hourglass. *n. pl.* **hourglasses** hour·glass·es

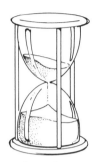

hourglass

hour hand   (our   hand)   the short arm on a clock or watch, which tells the hour.
> The hour hand was on the 1.

house   (hous)   **1.** a building in which a family lives.
> I live in the yellow house on this street. *n. pl.* **houses** hous·es

2. having to do with a place where a family lives.
> Dad bought red house paint. *adj.*

houseboat   house·boat (hous⁄bōt)   a boat on which people live; a house that floats on the water.
> Jim put his houseboat in the harbor. *n. pl.* **houseboats** house·boats

housefly   house·fly (hous⁄flī)   an insect that lives in and around houses.
> Mom used a spray to kill that big housefly. *n. pl.* **houseflies** house·flies

hour hand

household   house·hold (hous⁄hōld)   **1.** all the people who live in a certain home.
> We have two servants in our household. *n. pl.* **households** house·holds

2. having to do with a household.
> The household staff includes a maid and a butler. *adj.*

household cleaner   house·hold clean·er (hous⁄hōld   klē⁄nər)   chemicals that people use to wash things in a house.
> Dad used a household cleaner to clean the shower.

housework   house·work (hous⁄wėrk)   the jobs that people do to keep a home in good condition.
> My father and mother share the housework. *n. no pl.*

houseboat

how   (hou)   in what way; in what condition.
> How are you getting home from school? *adv.*

however   how·ev·er (hou·ev⁄ər)   but; yet; nevertheless.
> I want to go to the movie; however, Mother will not let me go. *adv.*

howl   (houl)   **1.** to laugh loudly.
> You will howl at the new movie. *v.* **howled, howled, howling** howl·ing

2. a long, loud moan or cry.
> The dog's howl woke me up last night. *n. pl.* **howls**

housefly

how many   how man·y (hou men⁄ē)   to what amount; in what quantity.
How many hot dogs can you eat?

huddle   hud·dle (hud⁄l)   to move close together; to bring the arms and legs close to the body.
I huddle in bed on cold mornings.
v. **huddled, huddled, huddling** hud·dled, hud·dling

huff   (huf)   to fill the lungs with air and blow the air out with great force.
The wolf will huff and puff and try to blow the straw house down.
v. **huffed, huffed, huffing** huff·ing

hug   (hug)   **1.** to hold something or someone in your arms.
I love to hug my doll. *v.* **hugged, hugged, hugging** hug·ging
2. a loving squeeze made with the arms.
Dad gave Mom a hug. *n. pl.* **hugs**

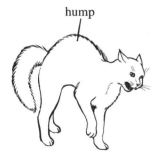

hug

huge   (hyüj)   very large in size or amount.
The giant is huge. *adj.* **huger, hugest** hug·er, hug·est

hum   (hum)   **1.** a singing sound made with the lips closed; a murmuring sound.
I heard Mother's hum and knew she was in a happy mood.
n. pl. **hums**
2. to make a singing sound with the lips closed.
Mother will hum when she is happy.
v. **hummed, hummed, humming** hum·ming

human   hu·man (hyü⁄mən)   a person; not an animal.
A person is a human. *n. pl.* **humans** hu·mans

hump

humid   hu·mid (hyü⁄mid)   a little bit wet; damp.
The air feels humid. *adj.*

humor   hu·mor (hyü⁄mər *or* yü⁄mər)   funny trait; the ability to see things as funny.
The story is full of humor. *n. no pl.*

hump   (hump)   **1.** a rounded lump or bump.
The dog found a hump of dirt to play on. *n. pl.* **humps**
2. to make an arch or curve in one's back.
The cat will hump its back when it is scared.
v. **humped, humped, humping** hump·ing

a	cat	i	sit	oi	oil	ch	chop		a in about
ā	ate	ī	lie	ou	out	ng	song		e in oven
ä	car	o	pot	u	cut	sh	she	ə =	i in pencil
e	set	ō	old	ù	book	th	three		o in memory
ē	equal	ô	or	ü	blue	ŦH	there		u in circus
ėr	germ					zh	treasure		

hung (hung) *v. pt. t., pt. part.* See **hang** (1).

hungrily hun·gri·ly (hung⁴grə·lē) in a manner showing a need or wanting.
> The dog looked hungrily at the bone. *adv.*

hungry hun·gry (hung⁴grē) needing or wanting food.
> I did not eat breakfast, so I am hungry now.
> *adj.* **hungrier, hungriest** hun·gri·er, hun·gri·est

hunt (hunt) **1.** the act of looking for something.
> The hunt for the lost child took all night. *n. pl.* **hunts**
> **2.** to look for someone or something.
> I will hunt for the letter. *v.*
> **3.** to look for and shoot animals.
> My father will hunt deer this week.
> *v.* **hunted, hunted, hunting** hunt·ed, hunt·ing

hunter hunt·er (hun⁴tər) a person who looks for and shoots animals.
> The hunter shot a deer. *n. pl.* **hunters** hun·ters

hunter

hurl (hèrl) to throw something by using great force or strength.
> I can hurl a rock across the river. *v.* **hurled, hurled, hurling** hurl·ing

hurricane hur·ri·cane (hèr⁴ə·kān) a storm with strong winds and heavy rain.
> The hurricane lasted all night. *n. pl.* **hurricanes** hur·ri·canes

hurried hur·ried (hèr⁴ēd) *v. pt. t., pt. part.* See **hurry.**

hurry hur·ry (hèr⁴ē) to go fast; to move quickly.
> I will hurry home if it is raining.
> *v.* **hurried, hurried, hurrying** hur·ried, hur·ry·ing

hurry off hur·ry off (hèr⁴ē ôf) to leave quickly.
> Please don't hurry off; stay and talk awhile.
> *v.* **hurried off, hurried off, hurrying off** hur·ried off, hur·ry·ing off

hurry up hur·ry up (hèr⁴ē up) to move faster.
> Hurry up; I can't wait forever.
> *v.* **hurried up, hurried up, hurrying up** hur·ried up, hur·ry·ing up

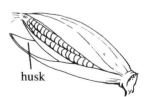

hurt (hèrt) **1.** to injure or harm something or someone.
> I do not want to hurt you. *v.*
> **2.** to cause pain or aches.
> A bee sting can hurt. *v.* **hurt, hurt, hurting** hurt·ing
> **3.** a pain or a feeling of sadness.
> The hurt from the burn was great. *n. pl.* **hurts**
> **4.** sad.
> Sue felt hurt when the class laughed at her. *adj.*

husk

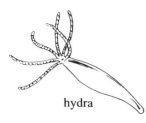

hydra

husband   hus·band (huz'bənd)   the man in a marriage, the man married to the wife.
The lady's husband is a dentist. *n. pl.* **husbands** hus·bands

husk   (husk)   the covering of an ear of corn.
You must take off the husk to eat the ear of corn. *n. pl.* **husks**

hydra   hy·dra (hī'drə)   **1.** Hydra; a monster in Greek stories who had nine heads.
Hercules killed Hydra. *n.*
2. a small animal that lives in fresh water and looks like a tube.
I did not see the hydra. *n. pl.* **hydras** or **hydrae** hy·dras or hy·drae

hydroelectric   hy·dro·e·lec·tric (hī·drō·i·lek'trik)   having to do with the making of energy with water power; having to do with making electricity by using the force of moving water.
The dam in the river makes hydroelectric power possible. *adj.*

hyena   hy·e·na (hī·ē'nə)   a wild animal that looks like a wolf, moves around at night and makes a terrible sound.
The hyena is from Africa. *n. pl.* **hyenas** hy·e·nas

hyena

a	cat	**i**	sit	**oi**	oil	**ch**	chop	a in about
ā	ate	**ī**	lie	**ou**	out	**ng**	song	e in oven
ä	car	**o**	pot	**u**	cut	**sh**	she	ə = { i in pencil
e	set	**ō**	old	** u̇**	book	**th**	three	o in memory
ē	equal	**ô**	or	**ü**	blue	**ŦH**	there	u in circus
ėr	germ					**zh**	treasure	

Ii

I (ī) me; the person speaking.
> I will read this book. *pron.*

ice (īs) frozen water.
> The ice will make the soda cold. *n. no pl.*

ice age (īs āj) a time when much of the Earth was covered with ice.
> The ice age lasted for centuries.

iceberg

iceberg ice·burg (īs′bėrg) a large piece of ice floating in the ocean.
> The ship hit the iceberg and sank. *n. pl.* **icebergs** ice·bergs

icecap ice·cap (īs′kap) a covering of ice that never melts.
> The icecap of the mountain can be seen all year. *n. pl.* **icecaps** ice·caps

ice chest (īs chest) a box that holds ice and keeps food cool or cold.
> We took the ice chest to the picnic to keep the soda cool.

ice cream (īs krēm) **1.** a cold dessert that is made with milk or cream.
> I like chocolate ice cream.
> **2.** having to do with the frozen dessert made with milk.
> I had an ice cream cone.

ice fish (īs fish) to fish on water that has ice on it.
> I like to ice fish in the winter.
> *v.* **ice fished, ice fished, ice fishing** ice fish·ing

ice chest

icehouse ice·house (īs′hous) a building where large pieces of ice are made; a building that holds large pieces of ice.
> We bought the ice for the ice chest from the icehouse.
> *n. pl.* **icehouses** ice·hous·es

Iceland Ice·land (īs′lənd) an island country in the North Atlantic Ocean; its capital is Reykjavik.
> Iceland is very cold. *n.*

ice cream

iceman ice·man (ī′sman) the name for a large animal-man that people have seen in the state of Minnesota.
> No one knows if the iceman is a real animal or not. *n. pl.* **icemen** ice·men

ice-skating ice-skat·ing (īs′skā·ting) a winter sport in which a person moves on a frozen body of water by using metal runners on the feet.
> I will go ice-skating this winter. *n. no pl.*

Iceland
Reykjavik

icy i·cy (ī'sē) covered with ice; slippery; very, very cold.
The streets get icy in the winter. *adj.* **icier, iciest** i·ci·er, i·ci·est

I'd (īd) **1.** I would.
I'd love a piece of cake. *contrac.*
2. I had.
I didn't join them for lunch because I'd eaten earlier. *contrac.*

idea i·de·a (ī·dē'ə) a thought; a solution to a problem.
I have an idea about how we can get money to go to the movie.
n. pl. **ideas** i·de·as

ideal i·de·al (ī·dē'əl) perfect; just right; the best.
This house is ideal for our family. *adj.*

identical i·den·ti·cal (ī·den'tə·kəl) the same; exactly alike.
The twins are identical. *adj.*

identification i·den·ti·fi·ca·tion (ī·den·tə·fə·kā'shən)
1. something used to show who a person is; something
used to identify a person.
A driver's license with a picture on it is a piece of identification. *n. no pl.*
2. having to do with showing what something or someone is.
The identification sign says that this is the waiting room. *adj.*

if (if) in case; on the condition that.
I will go to the movie if my parents allow me. *conj.*

igloo ig·loo (ig'lü) a house made of ice and snow.
The Eskimos built an igloo to live in. *n. pl.* **igloos** ig·loos

ignore ig·nore (ig·nôr' *or* ig·nōr') to pay no attention to; to
act as if a person were not near.
I will ignore what you just said.
v. **ignored, ignored, ignoring** ig·nored, ig·nor·ing

igloo

ill (il) sick; not well.
Tim has been ill for a week. *adj.* **worse, worst**

I'll (īl) I will *or* I shall.
I'll see you later. *contrac.*

illuminate il·lu·mi·nate (i·lü'mə·nāt) to make bright; to light up.
We will illuminate the room by turning on all the lamps.
v. **illuminated, illuminated, illuminating** il·lu·mi·nat·ed, il·lu·mi·nat·ing

a	cat	i	sit	oi	oil	ch	chop		a in about
ā	ate	ī	lie	ou	out	ng	song		e in oven
ä	car	o	pot	u	cut	sh	she	ə =	i in pencil
e	set	ō	old	u̇	book	th	three		o in memory
ē	equal	ô	or	ü	blue	ŦH	there		u in circus
ėr	germ					zh	treasure		

illusion il·lu·sion (i·lü′zhən) something that seems to be real but is not; a dream of something.
> Joe thought that he saw a ghost, but it was an illusion.
> *n. pl.* **illusions** il·lu·sions

I'm (īm) I am.
> I'm very hungry. *contrac.*

image im·age (im′ij) a picture in the mind; a vision; a picture on film.
> I have an image of what he will look like. *n. pl.* **images** im·ag·es

imaginary i·mag·i·nar·y (i·maj′ə·ner·ē) not real; pretend; made up in the mind.
> Cinderella is an imaginary character. *adj.*

imagination i·mag·i·na·tion (i·maj·ə·nā′shən) the ability to make up things; the ability to get ideas.
> I have a good imagination. *n. pl.* **imaginations** i·mag·i·na·tions

imagine i·mag·ine (i·maj′ən) to think; to make up; to create in your mind.
> I can imagine being older.
> *v.* **imagined, imagined, imagining** i·mag·ined, i·mag·in·ing

immediately im·me·di·ate·ly (i·mē′dē·it·lē) quickly; in no time.
> I want you to give me my doll immediately. *adv.*

immensely im·mense·ly (i·mens′lē) greatly; very much.
> I like chocolate immensely. *adv.*

immortal im·mor·tal (i·môr′tl) living forever; not capable of dying.
> I am not immortal, because someday I will die. *adj.*

impairment im·pair·ment (im·per′mənt) a reduction in strength; a problem; a difficulty; an injury.
> I have an impairment of my eyes. *n. pl.* **impairments** im·pair·ments

impatient im·pa·tient (im·pā′shənt) unable to wait; not willing to accept delay or problems.
> Joe is very impatient; he will not wait for me to get ready. *adj.*

impatiently im·pa·tient·ly (im·pā′shənt·lē) in a way that shows that a person is unable to wait.
> He is impatiently walking the floor. *adv.*

import im·port (im·pôrt′) to bring something into a country for the purpose of selling it or using it.
> The United States will not always import oil from Iran.
> *v.* **imported, imported, importing** im·port·ed, im·port·ing

importance im·por·tance (im·pôrt′ns) value; need.
> The teacher explained the importance of eating the right foods. *n. no pl.*

imagination

216

important im·por·tant (im·pôrt′nt) valuable; needed.
Good food is important to the body. *adj.*

importantly im·por·tant·ly (im·pôrt′nt·lē) in a serious way; in a valuable way; more needed.
He is acting importantly. *adv.*

impress im·press (im·pres′) to make someone think well of one.
I want to impress the boss.
v. **impressed, impressed, impressing** im·pressed, im·press·ing

impressed im·pressed (im·prest′) **1.** thinking well of someone or something.
I was impressed with the singer. *adj.*
2. *v. pt. t., pt. part.* See **impress.**

imprison im·pris·on (im·priz′n) to put in jail.
The police will imprison the robber.
v. **imprisoned, imprisoned, imprisoning** im·pris·oned, im·pris·on·ing

improve im·prove (im·prüv′) to make better.
I will improve my math skills.
v. **improved, improved, improving** im·proved, im·prov·ing

imprison

in (in) **1.** inside; within.
I put the cat in the box. *prep.*
2. within a time period; during this time.
I will visit my grandmother in June. *prep.*
3. on or within.
The bird is in the tree. *prep.*
4. from among; out of.
I want to be the best in spelling. *prep.*
5. near; within the area covered by.
I sat in the sun. *prep.*
6. at a location or place.
I live in California. *prep.*
7. into.
I went in the pool. *prep.*

in a hurry in a hur·ry (in ə hėr′ē) **1.** not having much time.
I am in a hurry so I can't stop and talk now.
2. quickly.
Joe finished his homework in a hurry.

in all (in ôl) totally; all together.
In all, there are ten of us going to the movie.

a	cat	**i**	sit	**oi**	oil	**ch**	chop		a in about
ā	ate	**ī**	lie	**ou**	out	**ng**	song		e in oven
ä	car	**o**	pot	**u**	cut	**sh**	she	ə =	i in pencil
e	set	**ō**	old	**u̇**	book	**th**	three		o in memory
ē	equal	**ô**	or	**ü**	blue	**ŦH**	there		u in circus
ėr	germ					**zh**	treasure		

in a row (in ə rō) lined up; one behind another.
 We stood in a row waiting to get in the movie.

in a spin (in ə spin) feeling confused; being in a hurry.
 There is so much to do I am in a spin. *idiom*

in back of (in bak əv) behind.
 The doghouse is in back of our house.

in bloom (in blüm) flowering; blooming.
 In the spring, those trees will be in bloom.

Inca In·ca (ing‹kə) a tribe of people that once lived in Peru
 (a country in South America).
 We are still learning things that the Inca knew hundreds of years ago.
 n. pl.

in case (in kās) if.
 In case I'm not here tomorrow, take notes for me.

inch (inch) a small unit of measure equal to ¹/₁₂ of a foot.
 The cake was one inch thick. *n. pl.* **inches** inch·es

in charge (in chärj) responsible; the boss.
 I am in charge when the teacher leaves the room. *idiom*

include in·clude (in·klüd′) to have as a part of; to have within it.
 I will include you in our next trip to the zoo.
 v. **included, included, including** in·clud·ed, in·clud·ing

increase in·crease (in·krēs′) to add to; to make larger.
 I will increase my study time to one hour.
 v. **increased, increased, increasing** in·creased, in·creas·ing

incredible in·cred·i·ble (in·kred′ə·bəl) unbelievable; amazing.
 The story he told is incredible. *adj.*

in danger in dan·ger (in dān′jər) at risk; near trouble.
 We are in danger of getting lost in the forest.

indeed in·deed (in·dēd′) surely; certainly; without a doubt.
 He is indeed my best friend. *adv.*

independence in·de·pend·ence (in·di·pen′dəns) freedom from
 others; freedom from control; a state of not needing
 anything from anyone.
 Because of the Revolutionary War, the United States obtained
 independence from Great Britain. *n. no pl.*

independent in·de·pend·ent (in·di·pen′dənt) free from others; free
 of control; not needing anyone else; not dependent on others.
 I will be independent when I have a job. *adj.*

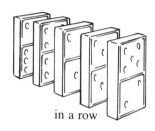

in a row

inch

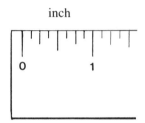

index

New Delhi

India

Indian Ocean

indoor plant

index in·dex (in′deks) an alphabetical list of what is in a book and where it can be found.
I used the index to find out which pages I should read to learn about the Civil War. *n. pl.* **indexes** *or* **indices** in·dex·es *or* in·di·ces

India In·di·a (in′dē·ə) a country in South Asia; its capital is New Delhi.
India has crowded cities. *n.*

Indian In·di·an (in′dē·ən) **1.** a person who lives or was born in the country of India.
The man from India is an Indian. *n.*
2. a person who is a member of any of the tribes of people that were living in America before Europeans arrived.
That Indian catches fish with a net. *n. pl.* **Indians** In·di·ans
3. having to do with Indians.
The Indian tribes fought the soldiers to keep their land. *adj.*

Indian Ocean In·di·an O·cean (in′dē·ən ō′shən) an ocean that is south of Asia, east of Africa and west of Australia.
The Indian Ocean is the third largest ocean in the world.

Indies In·dies (in′dēz) the islands that are north of the continent of Australia; the East Indies or the West Indies.
Columbus wanted to reach the Indies and to bring back gold and spices. *n.*

individual in·di·vid·u·al (in·də·vij′ü·əl) one person.
John is a kind individual. *n. pl.* **individuals** in·di·vid·u·als

indoor in·door (in′dôr) having to do with the inside of a building or a house.
I want to find an indoor hobby. *adj.*

indoor plant in·door plant (in′dôr plant) a plant that can grow inside a house or building.
I gave her an indoor plant for her bedroom.

indoors in·doors (in′dôrz *or* in′dōrz′) in a building or a house.
I must stay indoors today because I have a cold. *adv.*

industrial in·dus·tri·al (in·dus′trē·əl) having to do with factories.
This is the industrial part of the city. *adj.*

industry in·dus·try (in′də·strē) a business; a group of businesses.
Her father works in the food industry. *n. pl.* **industries** in·dus·tries

a	cat	**i**	sit	**oi**	oil	**ch**	chop
ā	ate	**ī**	lie	**ou**	out	**ng**	song
ä	car	**o**	pot	**u**	cut	**sh**	she
e	set	**ō**	old	**u̇**	book	**th**	three
ē	equal	**ô**	or	**ü**	blue	**₸H**	there
ėr	germ					**zh**	treasure

ə = { a in about / e in oven / i in pencil / o in memory / u in circus }

inexpensive in·ex·pen·sive (in·ik·spen′siv) not costing
much money; cheap.
The new coat was inexpensive. *adj.*

in fact (in fakt) really; truly.
In fact, he didn't come home from school yet.

infect in·fect (in·fekt′) to cause sickness; to give someone germs.
I could infect you with this cold.
v. **infected, infected, infecting** in·fect·ed, in·fect·ing

infection in·fec·tion (in·fek′shən) a sickness caused by germs.
I had an infection in my ear. *n. pl.* **infections** in·fec·tions

influence in·flu·ence (in′flü·əns) **1.** an effect on someone
or something; the power to affect what happens.
My father is a strong influence in my life. *n. pl.* **influences** in·flu·enc·es
2. to have an effect on something or someone.
He will greatly influence my life.
v. **influenced, influenced, influencing** in·flu·enced, in·flu·enc·ing

influential in·flu·en·tial (in·flü·en′shəl) having power to
make a change; well known; important.
Her father is very influential in the business world. *adj.*

inform in·form (in·fôrm′) to give facts to people; to tell
others what one has learned.
The newspaper will inform us about what is happening in the world.
v. **informed, informed, informing** in·formed, in·form·ing

information in·for·ma·tion (in·fər·mā′shən) facts; truths.
The encyclopedia gives us information about many different
things. *n. no pl.*

ingenious in·gen·ious (in·jē′nyəs) very smart; clever; inventive.
Thomas Edison was ingenious. *adj.*

ingredient in·gre·di·ent (in·grē′dē·ənt) something added
to a mixture.
Flour is one ingredient in bread. *n. pl.* **ingredients** in·gre·di·ents

ink

inherit in·her·it (in·her′it) to get something from your ancestors; to
get something from a person in your family after
the person dies.
I will inherit my mother's wedding ring.
v. **inherited, inherited, inheriting** in·her·it·ed, in·her·it·ing

initiate i·ni·ti·ate (i·nish′ē·āt) to start something;
to begin something.
I will initiate the discussion.
v. **initiated, initiated, initiating** i·ni·ti·at·ed, i·ni·ti·at·ing

injure in·jure (in′jər) to hurt; to cause pain; to harm.
I will not injure myself with the knife.
v. **injured, injured, injuring** in·jured, in·jur·ing

ink (ingk) the fluid or colored liquid used in pens and
to print newspapers.
The newspaper is printed with black ink. *n. pl.* **inks**

in line (in līn) standing in a row; one after the other.
Stay in line, or you will not get into the movie.

in order to in or·der to (in ôr′dər tü) so that; for the purpose of.
I am fixing the dryer in order to use it.

in other words in oth·er words (in uᴛʜ′ər wėrdz) to say
something another way; to explain further.
I can't go to the game. In other words, you will have
to find another ride.

in private in pri·vate (in prī′vit) alone; without anyone else.
I like to read in private.

in return in re·turn (in ri·tėrn′) exchange; as payment.
I will give you a dollar in return for your leaving me alone for an hour.

insect

insect in·sect (in′sekt) **1.** a small animal with six legs and
one or two pairs of wings.
A bee is an insect. *n. pl.* **insects** in·sects
2. having to do with small animals with six legs and wings.
The insect spray will keep the flies off you. *adj.*

insecticide in·sec·ti·cide (in·sek′tə·sīd) a chemical that kills
insects; an insect killer.
We used an insecticide on the grass to keep the fleas out of the lawn.
n. pl. **insecticides** in·sec·ti·cides

insect killer in·sect kill·er (in′sekt kil′ər) a chemical
that kills insects.
This insect killer is safe to use, but some are not.

inseparable in·sep·ar·a·ble (in·sep′ər·ə·bəl) always together;
cannot part.
The two friends are inseparable in the summer. *adj.*

insecticide

inside[1] in·side (in·sīd′) **1.** within; in or into a house or building.
I saw inside your house. *prep.*
2. indoors.
I stayed inside today. *adv.*
3. internally; in your mind.
I feel good inside today after giving blood. *adv.*

a	cat	**i**	sit	**oi**	oil	**ch**	chop	a in about
ā	ate	**ī**	lie	**ou**	out	**ng**	song	e in oven
ä	car	**o**	pot	**u**	cut	**sh**	she	ə = i in pencil
e	set	**ō**	old	**u̇**	book	**th**	three	o in memory
ē	equal	**ô**	or	**ü**	blue	**ᴛʜ**	there	u in circus
ėr	germ					**zh**	treasure	

inside² in·side (in´sīd) **1.** having to do with the
part within something.
The inside walls of the doghouse do not have paint on them. *adj.*
2. the interior.
The inside of the house is beautiful. *n. pl.* **insides** in·sides

inspector in·spec·tor (in·spek´tər) a person who checks for
mistakes or violations of the law.
Her uncle is a building inspector. *n. pl.* **inspectors** in·spec·tors

instance in·stance (in´stəns) example; illustration.
My grandparents, for instance, are still living in the town in which they
were born. *n. pl.* **instances** in·stanc·es

instantly in·stant·ly (in´stənt·lē) with no delay; immediately.
I can get the paper for you instantly. *adv.*

instead in·stead (in·sted´) in place of that; rather than that.
We wanted to go to the movie, but we had to go to church instead. *adv.*

instead of in·stead of (in·sted´ əv) in place of; rather
than; as an alternative to.
We went to church instead of the movie.

instinct in·stinct (in´stingkt) a natural reaction; an unlearned
action or behavior.
My instinct tells me that she is telling us the truth. *n. pl.* **instincts** in·stincts

institute in·sti·tute (in´stə·tüt *or* in´stə·tyüt) a type of school.
We are going to the dance institute. *n. pl.* **institutes** in·sti·tutes

instruction in·struc·tion (in·struk´shən) directions; order; teaching.
Follow my instruction, and you will learn how to make this pie.
n. pl. **instructions** in·struc·tions

instrument in·stru·ment (in´strə·mənt) **1.** a tool; a
device; a machine.
A hoe is a garden instrument. *n.*
2. a device used for making music.
A drum is an instrument that most bands have.
n. pl. **instruments** in·stru·ments

instrument

insult in·sult (in·sult´) to say something bad about someone.
Please do not insult my friends.
v. **insulted, insulted, insulting** in·sult·ed, in·sult·ing

insurance in·sur·ance (in·shùr´əns) a plan that protects against
loss in case of fire, theft or sickness.
The insurance on the car will help pay for the damage that happened
in the accident. *n. no pl.*

intelligent in·tel·li·gent (in·tel´ə·jənt) smart; very bright.
My father is very intelligent. *adj.*

intend in·tend (in·tend′) to plan; to set a goal; to aim;
   to have in mind.
   I intend to go to college when I finish high school.
   v. **intended, intended, intending** in·tend·ed, in·tend·ing

interest in·ter·est (in′tər·ist) **1.** to keep someone's attention;
   to give a person the feeling of wanting to learn.
   I hope to interest you in the Civil War.
   v. **interested, interested, interesting** in·ter·est·ed, in·ter·est·ing
   2. a hobby; a pleasing activity.
   My interest is growing plants. *n. pl.* **interests** in·ter·ests
   3. money made from an investment; money earned by saving
   money in the bank.
   I received $9.50 in interest from the bank. *n. no pl.*

interesting in·ter·est·ing (in′tər·ə·sting *or* in′tə·res·ting)
   1. *v. pres. part.* See **interest** (1).
   2. exciting; not boring.
   The book is interesting to me. *adj.*

intermediate in·ter·me·di·ate (in·tər·mē′dē·it) being in the
   middle; being at a middle level.
   I am an intermediate swimmer. *adj.*

international in·ter·na·tion·al (in·tər·nash′ə·nəl) between
   two or more countries; from one nation to another nation.
   The international airport allows planes from many countries
   to land there. *adj.*

interpret in·ter·pret (in·tėr′prit) to translate one language
   into another language.
   I will interpret what the Frenchman is saying.
   v. **interpreted, interpreted, interpreting** in·ter·pret·ed, in·ter·pret·ing

interpreter

interpreter in·ter·pret·er (in·tėr′prə·tər) a person who translates
   one language to another.
   The deaf girl watches the interpreter to learn what the teacher is saying.
   n. pl. **interpreters** in·ter·pret·ers

interruption in·ter·rup·tion (in·tə·rup′shən) a break in a
   conversation, program or meeting.
   The ringing telephone was a constant interruption of our meeting.
   n. pl. **interruptions** in·ter·rup·tions

interview in·ter·view (in′tər·vyü) a meeting where a person
   asks questions of one or more other people.
   I saw the interview on television. *n. pl.* **interviews** in·ter·views

a	cat	i	sit	oi	oil	ch	chop		a in about
ā	ate	ī	lie	ou	out	ng	song		e in oven
ä	car	o	pot	u	cut	sh	she	ə =	i in pencil
e	set	ō	old	u̇	book	th	three		o in memory
ē	equal	ô	or	ü	blue	₮H	there		u in circus
ėr	germ					zh	treasure		

into   in·to (in′tü)   **1.** move to the inside of something.
Dad went into the house to get the baby. *prep.*
2. move to a place.
We walked into the mountains. *prep.*
3. in the shape or form of.
We made the dough into small buns. *prep.*
4. against.
The bike smashed into the tree. *prep.*

introduce   in·tro·duce (in·trə·düs′ *or* in·trə·dyüs′)   to help
people meet each other; to tell the name of one person
to another person.
I will introduce you to my friend Diane.
   v. **introduced, introduced, introducing** in·tro·duced, in·tro·duc·ing

in two   (in tü)   into two pieces.
I broke the candy bar in two so that we each could have a piece.

invade   in·vade (in·vād′)   to go into a country with soldiers for the
purpose of taking control of the country.
They invaded the country with guns.
   v. **invaded, invaded, invading** in·vad·ed, in·vad·ing

invent   in·vent (in·vent′)   to make something that is new to the
world; to make something for the first time in the
history of man.
Thomas Edison worked hard to invent the light bulb.
   v. **invented, invented, inventing** in·vent·ed, in·vent·ing

invention   in·ven·tion (in·ven′shən)   something that is made for the
first time ever in the history of man; something that is
new to the world.
The phonograph was an invention of Thomas Edison's.
   n. pl. **inventions** in·ven·tions

inventor   in·ven·tor (in·ven′tər)   a person who makes things for the
first time in the history of man; a person who creates new
things for the world.
Thomas Edison was an inventor. *n. pl.* **inventors** in·ven·tors

invest   in·vest (in·vest′)   to use money to make more money; to buy
something at one price hoping that it can be sold at a higher
price; to put money in the bank to earn interest.
I will invest in the new company's stock.
   v. **invested, invested, investing** in·vest·ed, in·vest·ing

invisible   in·vis·i·ble (in·viz′ə·bəl)   cannot be seen.
Air is invisible. *adj.*

invitation   in·vi·ta·tion (in·və·tā′shən)   a request to do
something or go somewhere.
I got an invitation to Jill's party. *n. pl.* **invitations** in·vi·ta·tions

invitation

Iran

Ireland

invite in·vite (in·vīt′) to ask someone to do something or go somewhere.
I will invite Lisa to stay here tonight.
v. **invited, invited, inviting** in·vit·ed, in·vit·ing

Iran I·ran (i·ran′ *or* i·rän′) a country in Asia; its capital is Teheran.
Iran was once named Persia. *n.*

Ireland Ire·land (īr′lənd) an island in Europe that is divided into the Republic of Ireland and Northern Ireland.
Ireland is near England. *n.*

Irish I·rish (ī′rish) **1.** the people who live or were born in Ireland.
Some of the Irish still speak Gaelic. *plural n.*
2. having to do with the people and the country of Ireland.
The Irish war has continued for many years. *adj.*

iron i·ron (ī′ərn) **1.** a tool used to press wrinkles out of clothes.
I need the iron. *n. pl.* **irons** i·rons
2. a kind of metal that is silver in color and heavy.
Many tools are made of iron. *n. no pl.*
3. made of a heavy, silver metal.
The iron hammer is heavy. *adj.*

irrigate ir·ri·gate (ir′ə·gāt) to give water to plants with man-made streams of water.
We will irrigate the apple orchards.
v. **irrigated, irrigated, irrigating** ir·ri·gat·ed, ir·ri·gat·ing

is (iz) *v. pres. t.* See **be.**

iron

island is·land (ī′lənd) land that is surrounded by water.
Ireland is an island. *n. pl.* **islands** is·lands

islander is·land·er (ī′lən·dər) a person who lives on land surrounded by water.
The islander who owns this store has lived on Hawaii for five years.
n. pl. **islanders** is·land·ers

island

isn't is·n't (iz′nt) is not.
She isn't my cousin; she is my sister. *contrac.*

it (it) the thing about which a person is talking.
I got a bicycle for my birthday. It is red and white. *pron.*

a	cat	i	sit	oi	oil	ch	chop		a in about
ā	ate	ī	lie	ou	out	ng	song		e in oven
ä	car	o	pot	u	cut	sh	she	ə =	i in pencil
e	set	ō	old	u̇	book	th	three		o in memory
ē	equal	ô	or	ü	blue	ᵀH	there		u in circus
ėr	germ					zh	treasure		

Italian I·tal·ian (i·tal′yən) about the country, the people and the language of Italy.
Pizza is an Italian food. *adj.*

Italy It·a·ly (it′l·ē) a country in Europe that is shaped like a boot; its capital is Rome.
My grandmother is from Italy. *n.*

Italy

Rome

itch (ich) a feeling in the skin that makes a person want to scratch.
I have an itch on my arm. *n. pl.* **itches** itch·es

itchy itch·y (ich′ē) having a need to scratch; having many itches.
Every time I wear this dress, I feel itchy.
adj. **itchier, itchiest** itch·i·er, itch·i·est

item i·tem (ī′təm) a thing.
I am going to the store for an item or two. *n. pl.* **items** i·tems

its (its) belonging to a thing or animal.
The flower is blooming, and its blossom is bright red. *adj.*

it's (its) it is.
It's time to go home. *contrac.*

itself it·self (it·self′) that very same thing that one is talking about.
The turtle hides itself in its shell. *pron.*

itch

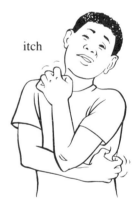

I. U. (ī′ū′) International Unit; a unit of measure of the amount of a vitamin or drug needed before the body is affected.
We eat 400 I.U. of meat a day. *abbrev.*

I've (īv) I have.
I've lived here for three years. *contrac.*

ivory i·vor·y (ī′vər·ē) a hard brownish-white material made from the tusks of elephants.
Ivory is very expensive. *n. pl.* **ivories** i·vor·ies

Jj

jacket

jacket   jack·et (jak′it)   a short coat.
The man's jacket was gray. *n. pl.* **jackets** jack·ets

jack of all trades   (jak əv ôl trādz)   a person who can do many things.
My father works as a carpenter, but he is a jack of all trades. *idiom*

jail   (jāl)   a place where people who have broken the law are housed as punishment; a prison.
The jail has iron bars on the windows and doors. *n. pl.* **jails**

jam   (jam)   fruit cooked with sugar until it is thick.
I like strawberry jam. *n. pl.* **jams**

Japan   Ja·pan (jə·pan′)   a country in Asia made up of many islands; its capital is Tokyo.
Japan is in the Pacific Ocean. *n.*

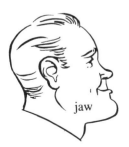

Japan

Tokyo

Japanese   Jap·a·nese (jap·ə·nēz′)   **1.** the people who live in or who were born in Japan.
The Japanese have a long history and an old culture. *plural n.*
2. having to do with the people, the language or the country of Japan.
I like Japanese food. *adj.*

jar   (jär)   a container with a large opening, usually made of glass.
We buy peanut butter in a jar. *n. pl.* **jars**

jaw   (jô)   the bottom part of the face; the bone that moves the bottom part of the face.
The jaw opens the mouth. *n. pl.* **jaws**

jaw

jealous   jeal·ous (jel′əs)   having a feeling of fear that someone may have something more or better than oneself.
I am jealous of my sister's curly hair. *adj.*

jealousy   jeal·ous·y (jel′ə·sē)   a dislike or fear of others; envy; wanting what other people have.
My jealousy about her hair does not stop me from liking her.
n. pl. **jealousies** jeal·ous·ies

a	cat	**i**	sit	**oi**	oil	**ch**	chop	
ā	ate	**ī**	lie	**ou**	out	**ng**	song	a in about
ä	car	**o**	pot	**u**	cut	**sh**	she	e in oven
e	set	**ō**	old	**u̇**	book	**th**	three	ə = i in pencil
ē	equal	**ô**	or	**ü**	blue	**ŦH**	there	o in memory
ėr	germ					**zh**	treasure	u in circus

jeans (jēnz) slacks or pants that are made of denim.
My new jeans are stiff. *plural n.*

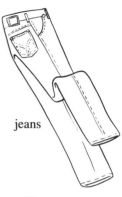

jeans

jeer (jir) to make fun of someone or something.
The boys will jeer my new haircut. *v.* **jeered, jeered, jeering** jeer·ing

jelly jel·ly (jel′ē) **1.** fruit cooked with sugar but without any seeds.
I like grape jelly. *n. no pl.*
2. a kind of candy with a soft, chewy center.
The strawberry jelly stuck to my teeth. *n. pl.* **jellies** jel·lies

jellybean jel·ly·bean (jel′ē·bēn) a kind of candy with
a soft, chewy center.
We always find a jellybean in the grass in the Easter basket.
n. pl. **jellybeans** jel·ly·beans

jellyfish jel·ly·fish (jel′ē·fish) a small sea animal whose body
looks like clear jelly.
The jellyfish may sting you if you bother it.
n. pl. **jellyfishes** or **jellyfish** jel·ly·fish·es

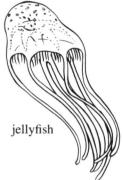

jellyfish

jerk (jėrk) to pull with a quick movement; to pull quickly.
Don't jerk the puppy's tail. *v.* **jerked, jerked, jerking** jerk·ing

Jesus Je·sus (jē′zəs) the person who started Christian religions,
called the Son of God; Jesus Christ.
Christmas is the celebration of the birth of Jesus. *n.*

jet (jet) a very fast airplane.
We took a jet to Chicago. *n. pl.* **jets**

jewel jew·el (jü′əl) a valuable stone or rock that is used in jewelry.
A diamond is a jewel. *n. pl.* **jewels** jew·els

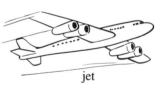

jet

jewelry jew·el·ry (jü′əl·rē) items that people wear on the body
as decoration or accessories.
Watches, rings, earrings, bracelets and necklaces are jewelry. *n. no pl.*

jingle jin·gle (jing′gəl) a happy song; a happy song that
advertises a product.
I heard that jingle on the radio. *n. pl.* **jingles** jin·gles

job (job) **1.** the work a person does to earn money.
Her father has a job in a department store. *n. pl.* **jobs**
2. having to do with work.
His job title is salesman. *adj.*

jockey jock·ey (jok′ē) **1.** the side part of the seat of a horse saddle.
A rider's leg rests on the jockey. *n.*
2. a person who rides a horse in a race.
The jockey is wearing red and green. *n. pl.* **jockeys** jock·eys

jewelry

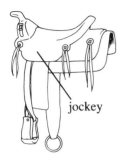

jockey

joust

join (join) **1.** to go with someone.
I am going to the movie; why don't you join me? *v.*
2. to tie or fasten together.
Dad will join the two pipes together. *v.*
3. to become a member of a group.
Ted will join the Boy Scout troop at school.
v. **joined, joined, joining** join·ing

joke (jōk) **1.** a funny story.
I laughed at Lee's joke. *n. pl.* **jokes**
2. to play a trick; to tell funny stories.
Lee will joke about many things. *v.* **joked, joked, joking** jok·ing

jolly jol·ly (jol′ē) full of joy; full of happiness.
Santa Claus is a jolly man. *adj.* **jollier, jolliest** jol·li·er, jol·li·est

journey jour·ney (jėr′nē) a trip; the action of going
from one place to another.
It is a long journey from New York to California. *n. pl.* **journeys** jour·neys

joust (joust *or* just) to fight on horseback with
spears or swords.
The knights would joust with each other for fun.
v. **jousted, jousted, jousting** joust·ed, joust·ing

joy (joi) happiness.
The joy of Christmas is giving gifts to people we like. *n. pl.* **joys**

judge (juj) **1.** the person who conducts or leads a trial.
The judge hit the desk with his gavel to quiet the courtroom. *n.*
2. the person who picks a winner in a contest.
The judge gave me a ribbon for my painting. *n. pl.* **judges** judg·es
3. to make a decision about something; to rate or evaluate
something or someone.
I will judge for myself if the movie is good.
v. **judged, judged, judging** judg·ing

juice (jüs) **1.** the liquid that comes from fruit.
I drink orange juice with my breakfast. *n. pl.* **juices** juic·es
2. having to do with the liquid that comes from fruit.
I broke my juice glass. *adj.*

juicy juic·y (jü′sē) full of the liquid that is in fruit.
The peach is juicy. *adj.* **juicier, juiciest** juic·i·er, juic·i·est

judge

a	cat	i	sit	oi	oil	ch	chop		a in about
ā	ate	ī	lie	ou	out	ng	song		e in oven
ä	car	o	pot	u	cut	sh	she	ə =	i in pencil
e	set	ō	old	u̇	book	th	three		o in memory
ē	equal	ô	or	ü	blue	ŦH	there		u in circus
ėr	germ					zh	treasure		

jump (jump) **1.** to move up off the ground; to leap.
Jack can jump high. *v.*
2. to move suddenly, as in fear.
When I see a spider, I jump. *v.* **jumped, jumped, jumping** jump·ing

jump rope (jump rōp) a piece of rope that has handles on both ends and that is used for jumping.
The girls played with the jump rope for an hour.

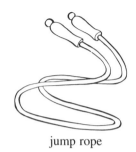
jump rope

Juneau Ju·neau (jü′nō) the capital city of Alaska.
It often rains in Juneau. *n.*

junior jun·ior (jü′nyər) younger than another; at a lower level than another.
I will be in junior high school next year. *adj.*

junk (jungk) **1.** old, unwanted things.
We cleaned the junk out of the garage. *n. no pl.*
2. having to do with old, unwanted things.
We took it to the junk store. *adj.*

junk

Juno Ju·no (jü′nō) a Roman goddess who was believed to be the protector of marriages.
Juno was the wife of Jupiter. *n.*

Jupiter Ju·pi·ter (jü′pə·tər) **1.** the biggest planet in our solar system.
Jupiter is eleven times bigger than Earth. *n.*
2. the Roman god believed to be the leader of the other gods.
The Romans believed that Jupiter was the king of the gods. *n.*

just (just) **1.** only.
There is just one piece of pie left. *adv.*
2. exactly; no more and no less.
There is just enough milk for the two of us. *adv.*
3. recently; a very little while ago.
We just got home from school when you called. *adv.*

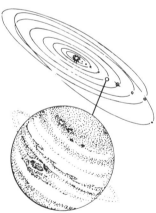
Jupiter

just then (just ᴛнen) at that time; at that moment.
I thought I heard footsteps, and just then Tom opened the door.

Jute (jüt) a member of a tribe of people who lived in Germany many centuries ago.
Some Jutes moved to England many years ago. *n. pl.* **Jutes**

Kk

Kalmar   Kal·mar (kal‿mär)   a city in the country of Sweden.
Kalmar is on the water and has a large harbor. *n.*

kangaroo   kan·ga·roo (kang·gə·rü′)   an animal that has long back legs, a large tail and a pouch or pocket for carrying its babies.
The kangaroo jumped around the field.
n. pl. **kangaroos** *or* **kangaroo** kan·ga·roos *or* kan·ga·roo

kangaroo

keep   (kēp)   **1.** to have something and not give it away or lose it.
I will keep your coat until you get back. *v.*
2. to cause something or someone to stay the same way as before.
This coat will keep you warm on cold days.
v. **kept, kept, keeping** keep·ing

keep a record of   keep a rec·ord of (kēp   ā   rek‿ərd   əv)   to write things down so that they can be remembered; to keep track of things.
I keep a record of how I spend my money.

keep ___ balance   keep ___ bal·ance (kēp ___ bal‿əns)   to stay up; not to fall.
I can keep my balance on a bicycle.

keeper   keep·er (kē‿pər)   a person who watches over other people, animals or things.
Mr. Allen is the keeper of the inn. *n. pl.* **keepers** keep·ers

keep from   (kēp   from)   to stop something from happening; to avoid.
I can keep from forgetting your number by writing it down.
v. **kept from, kept from, keeping from** keep·ing from

keep on   (kēp   ôn)   to continue.
Jan will keep on bothering you until you play ball with her.
v. **kept on, kept on, keeping on** keep·ing on

keep out   (kēp   out)   **1.** to stop someone from going into a place.
The man at the door will keep out people who do not have shoes on their feet.
v. **kept out, kept out, keeping out** keep·ing out

a	cat	i	sit	oi	oil	ch	chop		a in about
ā	ate	ī	lie	ou	out	ng	song		e in oven
ä	car	o	pot	u	cut	sh	she	ə =	i in pencil
e	set	ō	old	u̇	book	th	three		o in memory
ē	equal	ô	or	ü	blue	ᵀH	there		u in circus
ėr	germ					zh	treasure		

keep time (kēp tīm) to watch the time; to note the time passing.
People now keep time with watches and clocks.
v. **kept time, kept time, keeping time** keep·ing time

kelp (kelp) a kind of seaweed; a plant that grows in the ocean and is used in making some foods.
Kelp is used to make ice cream. *n. no pl.*

kept (kept) *v. pt. t., pt. part.* See **keep.**

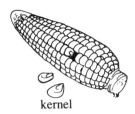
kernel

kernel ker·nel (kėr′nl) a seed; the food part of an ear of corn.
The kernel of corn is used to make popcorn. *n. pl.* **kernels** ker·nels

ketchup *or* **catsup** ketch·up (kech′əp) a sauce made from tomatoes that gives flavor to foods.
I put ketchup on my potatoes. *n. no pl.*

key

key (kē) the object that opens a lock.
I opened the door with the key. *n. pl.* **keys**

keyhole key·hole (kē′hōl) the place where a key fits into a lock.
Sometimes I leave my key in the keyhole. *n. pl.* **keyholes** key·holes

keyhole

kick (kik) **1.** to hit something with a foot.
I can kick the ball far. *v.* **kicked, kicked, kicking** kick·ing
2. a movement with the foot; the act of hitting something with the foot.
The horse's kick put a hole in the barn door. *n. pl.* **kicks**

kid (kid) **1.** a baby goat.
The kid ate the grass in the field. *n.*
2. a child.
I saw the kid who broke the window. *n. pl.* **kids**

kid

kidnap kid·nap (kid′nap) to steal a person; to take a person away without permission.
It is a crime to kidnap a person.
v. **kidnapped** *or* **kidnaped, kidnapped** *or* **kidnaped, kidnapping** *or* **kidnaping** kid·napped *or* kid·naped, kid·nap·ping *or* kid·nap·ing

kidney kid·ney (kid′nē) the part of the body that takes out unneeded things from the blood.
The kidney cleans the blood. *n. pl.* **kidneys** kid·neys

kill (kil) to cause someone or something to die; to take life from someone or something.
People kill animals for food. *v.* **killed, killed, killing** kill·ing

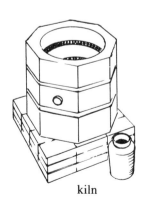

kiln (kil *or* kiln) a large brick oven or furnace that is used for baking things.
The pottery was baked in a kiln. *n. pl.* **kilns**

kiln

kitchen

kilogram kil·o·gram (kil′ə·gram) a unit of metric measurement that equals 1000 grams.
A kilogram is over two pounds. *n. pl.* **kilograms** kil·o·grams

kind (kīnd) **1.** nice; friendly; caring.
The new girl is kind. *adj.* **kinder, kindest** kind·er, kind·est
2. a type of something.
What kind of ice cream do you like? *n. pl.* **kinds**

kindergarten kin·der·gar·ten (kin′dər·gärt·n) school for children four and five years old.
I went to kindergarten before I started elementary school.
n. pl. **kindergartens** kin·der·gar·tens

king (king) the male leader or ruler of a country.
America does not have a king. *n. pl.* **kings**

kingdom king·dom (king′dəm) the land that is ruled by a certain king or queen.
The kingdom was ruled by a kind king. *n. pl.* **kingdoms** king·doms

kiss (kis) **1.** to touch with the lips to show love.
I will kiss Grandma good-bye. *v.* **kissed, kissed, kissing** kiss·ing
2. a touch with the lips to show love.
The baby's kiss was sticky. *n. pl.* **kisses** kiss·es

kitchen kitch·en (kich′ən) **1.** the room where food is cooked.
The kitchen smells of good food. *n. pl.* **kitchens** kitch·ens
2. having to do with the room where food is cooked.
The kitchen stove is hot. *adj.*

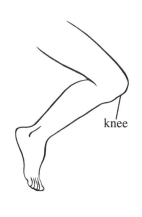
kite
knee

kite (kīt) **1.** a toy that floats in the air at the end of a string.
We flew the kite for an hour. *n. pl.* **kites**
2. having to do with a kite.
The kite tail was six feet long. *adj.*

kitten kit·ten (kit′n) a baby cat.
The kitten has not yet opened its eyes. *n. pl.* **kittens** kit·tens

knead (nēd) to press and pull on something in order to mix it together.
We knead bread dough before we bake it.
v. **kneaded, kneaded, kneading** knead·ed, knead·ing

knee (nē) the part of a person's or an animal's leg that bends.
The knee is bent when we walk or run. *n. pl.* **knees**

a	cat	i	sit	oi	oil	ch	chop		a in about
ā	ate	ī	lie	ou	out	ng	song		e in oven
ä	car	o	pot	u	cut	sh	she	ə =	i in pencil
e	set	ō	old	u̇	book	th	three		o in memory
ē	equal	ô	or	ü	blue	ŦH	there		u in circus
ėr	germ					zh	treasure		

knew (nü *or* nyü) *v. pt. t.* See **know.**

knife (nīf) a sharp tool that is used for cutting things.
Mother cut the meat with the knife. *n. pl.* **knives**

knight (nīt) a title for a man who fought for a king centuries
ago; a man who wore armor in battle.
The knight protected the king's kingdom. *n. pl.* **knights**

knit (nit) to make cloth or clothes using yarn and long needles.
Grandmother will knit me a new sweater.
v. **knitted** *or* **knit, knitted** *or* **knit, knitting** knit·ted, knit·ting

knives (nīvz) *n. pl.* See **knife.**

knob (nob) a handle or dial; something that one uses to
open a door or drawer.
The knob on the door is broken. *n. pl.* **knobs**

knock (nok) **1.** to hit with the fist.
I will knock on the door. *v.*
2. to hit and make fall.
I can knock the apple out of the tree.
v. **knocked, knocked, knocking** knock·ing
3. the sound made when something is hit with the fist.
I heard the knock on the door. *n. pl.* **knocks**

knot (not) the place where two pieces of rope or string
are tied together; the tie that holds two pieces of rope
or string together.
I learned to make a square knot. *n. pl.* **knots**

know (nō) to understand; to have facts; to learn facts.
I know how to tie a square knot. *v.* **knew, known, knowing** know·ing

koala ko·a·la (kō·ä′lə) a kind of animal that looks like a bear,
is gray, lives in trees and comes from Australia.
We saw a koala in the zoo. *n. pl.* **koalas** ko·a·las

Korea Ko·re·a (kô·rē′ə *or* kō·rē′ə) a country in Asia that is
divided into two countries, North Korea and South Korea.
The capital of North Korea is Pyongyang, and the capital of South
Korea is Seoul. *n.*

koala

Pyongyang

Seoul

Korea

Ll

label

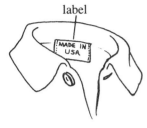

lace

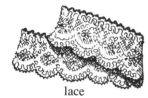

lacquer

label la·bel (lā′bəl) a piece of paper that is placed on something and tells what is in it, where it was made, where it is to go, of what it is made or to whom it belongs.
I put my name on the label of the coat. *n. pl.* **labels** la·bels

labor la·bor (lā′bər) **1.** work.
The flowers are the result of the gardener's labor. *n. pl.* **labors** la·bors
2. to work.
The gardener will labor in the garden for hours.
v. **labored, labored, laboring** la·bored, la·bor·ing

laboratory lab·o·ra·to·ry (lab′rə·tôr·ē) the place in which scientists conduct experiments; the place in which a scientist works.
The doctor sent the blood to the laboratory to be tested.
n. pl. **laboratories** lab·o·ra·to·ries

laborer la·bor·er (lā′bər·ər) a person who does hard work for money.
The laborer helped the builder of the house. *n. pl.* **laborers** la·bor·ers

labor-saving la·bor-sav·ing (lā′bər-sā′ving) making work easier; reducing or lessening the work.
The gardener uses labor-saving tools. *adj.*

Labrador Lab·ra·dor (lab′rə·dôr) the northeast part of Canada.
It gets very cold in Labrador. *n.*

labyrinth lab·y·rinth (lab′ə·rinth) a difficult and confusing path that goes in and out of places and makes one think one will not find the right way out; a maze.
The castle rooms were a labyrinth, and the knight became lost.
n. pl. **labyrinths** lab·y·rinths

lace (lās) **1.** a beautifully woven cloth or material with many small holes.
The dress was covered with white lace. *n. no pl.*
2. a shoestring.
The lace on my left shoe broke. *n. pl.* **laces** lac·es

lacquer lac·quer (lak′ər) a liquid that has no color that is put on things to make them shine.
We put lacquer on the door. *n. pl.* **lacquers** lac·quers

a	cat	**i**	sit	**oi**	oil	**ch**	chop		a in about
ā	ate	**ī**	lie	**ou**	out	**ng**	song		e in oven
ä	car	**o**	pot	**u**	cut	**sh**	she	ə =	i in pencil
e	set	**ō**	old	**u̇**	book	**th**	three		o in memory
ē	equal	**ô**	or	**ü**	blue	**ŦH**	there		u in circus
ėr	germ					**zh**	treasure		

ladder lad·der (lad′ər) a tool that a person climbs to
reach high places.
I used the ladder to reach the roof of the house. *n. pl.* **ladders** lad·ders

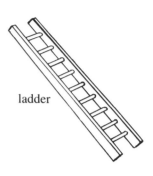

ladder

ladies la·dies (lā′dēz) *n. pl.* See **lady.**

lady la·dy (lā′dē) a woman with good manners.
The lady wore a lace dress. *n. pl.* **ladies** la·dies

laid (lād) *v. pt. t., pt. part.* See **lay.**

lake (lāk) a body of water that is surrounded by land.
We fished in the lake on the farm. *n. pl.* **lakes**

lamb (lam) **1.** a baby sheep.
We watched the lamb try to stand up. *n. pl.* **lambs**
2. the meat that comes from baby sheep.
We eat lamb on Easter Sunday. *n. no pl.*

lake

lamp (lamp) a device that gives light.
I have a new lamp in my bedroom. *n. pl.* **lamps**

land (land) **1.** to come down to the Earth.
The plane will land in ten minutes.
v. **landed, landed, landing** land·ed, land·ing
2. the part of the Earth that is made of dirt and rock.
The Earth is made of land and water. *n. no pl.*
3. an area of ground.
Dad bought the land near the river. *n.*
4. a country; a nation.
The land of Israel has a long history. *n. pl.* **lands**

landmark land·mark (land′märk) a thing on land that is easy to
see that helps one find a place.
The old tree by our driveway is a landmark. *n. pl.* **landmarks** land·marks

lamb

language lan·guage (lang′gwij) the system that a group of people
use to communicate ideas or share information.
The language of North America is different from the language of Japan.
n. pl. **languages** lan·guag·es

lanolin lan·o·lin (lan′l·ən) a kind of oil that comes from the wool
of sheep and that is used on a person's skin.
Lanolin will keep skin from becoming too dry. *n. pl.* **lanolins** lan·o·lins

lantern lan·tern (lan′tərn) a kind of lamp that is easy to move and
that burns oil or gas, not electricity.
A lantern can be carried from place to place. *n. pl.* **lanterns** lan·terns

lap (lap) the distance once around a racetrack, a football field
or the inside walls of a gym.
I ran one lap around the field before the coach stopped me. *n. pl.* **laps**

lamp

lantern

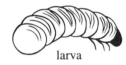

larva

large (lärj) very big.
The elephant is a large animal. *adj.* **larger, largest** larg·er, larg·est

larva lar·va (lärʹvə) the time in an insect's life when it looks like a worm.
A caterpillar is a larva of a butterfly.
n. pl. **larvae** *or* **larvas** lar·vae *or* lar·vas

last (last) **1.** being the one before this.
I saw Lisa last night. *adj.*
2. after all the others; the final one; at the end.
I came home last. *adv.*
3. to continue to happen; to go on for a time.
The movie will last for an hour. *v.* **lasted, lasted, lasting** last·ed, last·ing

lasting last·ing (lasʹting) staying for a long time.
I like the rose for its long lasting smell. *adj.*

late (lāt) **1.** after the right time; behind the time set by someone.
I was late for school this morning. *adj.*
2. beginning or lasting after the usual time.
We took the late bus home. *adj.* **later, latest** lat·er, lat·est
3. not early; after the start of something or some time period.
I arrived home late this morning. *adv.*

later lat·er (lātʹər) at a time after this time; at a time past.
Father will meet us at the store later. *adv.*

Latin Lat·in (latʹn) a language that the Romans used centuries ago.
Latin is an old language that most people do not speak today. *n.*

laugh (laf) **1.** to make happy sounds.
I laugh every time I see that clown.
v. **laughed, laughed, laughing** laugh·ing
2. a happy sound.
Her laugh makes me smile. *n. pl.* **laughs**

laughter laugh·ter (lafʹtər) the sound of people laughing and being happy.
The laughter in the next room kept me awake. *n. no pl.*

launch (lônch *or* länch) to push into the air; to start something moving.
I can launch the model airplane with this switch.
v. **launched, launched, launching** launch·ing

a	cat	i	sit	oi	oil	ch	chop		a in about
ā	ate	ī	lie	ou	out	ng	song		e in oven
ä	car	o	pot	u	cut	sh	she	ə =	i in pencil
e	set	ō	old	u̇	book	th	three		o in memory
ē	equal	ô	or	ü	blue	ŦH	there		u in circus
ėr	germ					zh	treasure		

laundry laun·dry (lôn′drē *or* län′drē) clothes that need to be washed or clothes that have been washed.
  Father does the laundry on Saturday. *n. no pl.*

lava la·va (lä′və *or* lav′ə) the melted rock that comes out of a volcano.
  You can find lava in Hawaii. *n. no pl.*

lavender lav·en·der (lav′ən·dər) a plant with small purple, sweet-smelling flowers that are used in making perfumes.
  The smell of lavender reminds me of my grandmother. *n. no pl.*

law (lô) a rule made by a nation or a state.
  They passed a law against driving after drinking too much alcohol.
  n. pl. **laws**

lawyer law·yer (lô′yər) a person who knows the rules made by nations and states; a person who helps people who have been arrested.
  I want to be a lawyer. *n. pl.* **lawyers** law·yers

lay (lā) **1.** to put or place something somewhere.
  I will lay the blanket over the baby. *v.*
  2. to make an egg.
  The chicken will lay one egg a day. *v.* **laid, laid, laying** lay·ing
  3. *v. pt. t.* See **lie** (3).

layer lay·er (lā′ər) a coating or covering; one covering or fold.
  Mother put a layer of suntan lotion on her arms before she went out into the garden. *n. pl.* **layers** lay·ers

lazily la·zi·ly (lā′zə·lē) without energy; in a way that shows that a person does not want to work.
  He lazily walked to the barn. *adv.*

lazy la·zy (lā′zē) not willing to work; without energy.
  He is lazy today. *adj.* **lazier, laziest** la·zi·er, la·zi·est

lead¹ (lēd) to show the way; to give directions.
  The general will lead the army to battle. *v.* **led, led, leading** lead·ing

lead² (led) **1.** a heavy, gray metal.
  The tips of these bullets are made of lead. *n. no pl.*
  2. being made of a heavy, gray metal.
  Grandpa gave me his lead soldiers to play with. *adj.*

leader lead·er (lē′dər) a person who guides other people; a person who shows the way to other people.
  The leader of our Boy Scout troop showed us how to tie knots.
  n. pl. **leaders** lead·ers

leaf (lēf) the thin green part of a tree or a plant.
  I watched a leaf fall off the tree. *n. pl.* **leaves**

laundry

lavender

leaf

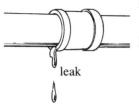

leak

leather tread

leak (lēk) a hole that lets a liquid or a gas get out.
We have a leak in the water pipe. *n. pl.* **leaks**

lean (lēn) **1.** to bend in the direction of something.
The plant will lean toward the sun. *v.*
2. to place something against something else for support.
You may lean your bicycle against the fence.
v. **leaned** *or* **leant, leaned** *or* **leant, leaning** lean·ing

leap (lēp) to jump high in the air.
I can leap over the fence.
v. **leaped** *or* **leapt, leaped** *or* **leapt, leaping** leap·ing

learn (lėrn) to put facts into the mind; to become able to do something; to come to know.
I will learn how to drive a car when I am sixteen.
v. **learned** *or* **learnt, learned** *or* **learnt, learning** learn·ing

learner learn·er (lėr'nər) a person who puts facts into his or her mind; a person who comes to know something.
I am a fast learner. *n. pl.* **learners** learn·ers

least (lēst) being the smallest amount or lowest in importance.
I have the least candy of anyone here. *adj.*

leather leath·er (leᴛн'ər) **1.** material made from animal skins.
Leather is a soft material but very strong. *n. no pl.*
2. made of the material that is made from animal skins.
My leather purse is gray. *adj.*

leather tread leath·er tread (leᴛн'ər tred) the bottom part of the stirrup on a saddle.
The leather tread helps to keep the foot in the stirrup.

leave (lēv) **1.** to go and not take something with you.
I will leave my bicycle at your house tonight. *v.*
2. to separate from; to go away from.
I will not leave this town. *v.*
3. to let remain.
Leave enough room on the paper for your name. *v.*
4. to go.
We will leave for school at eight o'clock. *v.* **left, left, leaving** leav·ing

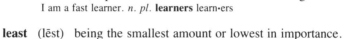

a	cat	**i**	sit	**oi**	oil	**ch**	chop	⎧ a in about
ā	ate	**ī**	lie	**ou**	out	**ng**	song	⎜ e in oven
ä	car	**o**	pot	**u**	cut	**sh**	she	ə = ⎨ i in pencil
e	set	**ō**	old	**u̇**	book	**th**	three	⎜ o in memory
ē	equal	**ô**	or	**ü**	blue	**ᵀʜ**	there	⎩ u in circus
ėr	germ					**zh**	treasure	

leaves (lēvz) *n. pl.* See **leaf.**

lecture lec·ture (lek‘chər) a talk on a specific topic or
    subject; a speech.
    I went to the lecture about Africa last night. *n. pl.* **lectures** lec·tures

led (led) *v. pt. t., pt. part.* See **lead** (1).

ledge (lej) a narrow shelf.
    I put the flower pot on the window ledge. *n. pl.* **ledges** ledg·es

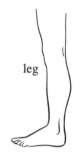
ledge

left (left) **1.** a direction that is opposite of right; a side
    that is opposite of right.
    I use my left hand to write and my right hand to eat. *adj.*
    2. *v. pt. t., pt. part.* See **leave.**

leftover left·o·ver (left‘ō·vər) a food that you still have after
    everyone has eaten all they want to eat.
    I will warm a leftover for my lunch. *n. pl.* **leftovers** left·o·vers

leg (leg) a part of a person or animal body that is used for
    walking and standing.
    I fell off the horse and broke my leg. *n. pl.* **legs**

leg

legend leg·end (lej‘ənd) a story that people have told
    for many years.
    The legend of Daniel Boone will be told for many more years.
    n. pl. **legends** leg·ends

lei (lā) a necklace made of flowers or a headband made of flowers.
    The woman gave me a lei when I got off the plane in Hawaii. *n. pl.* **leis**

lemon lem·on (lem‘ən) **1.** a yellow fruit that tastes sour.
    I put a piece of lemon in my tea. *n. pl.* **lemons** lem·ons
    2. made of the yellow, sour fruit.
    I put lemon juice on my fish. *adj.*

lei

lemonade lem·on·ade (lem·ə·nād′) a drink that is made
    with lemon juice.
    I drink a lot of lemonade in the summer. *n. pl.* **lemonades** lem·on·ades

lend (lend) to give something to someone for a short time.
    I will lend you $5.00 until next week. *v.* **lent, lent, lending** lend·ing

length (lengkth *or* length) the measurement of something from
    one end to the other end.
    The length of the hose is ten feet. *n. pl.* **lengths**

lemon

lens (lenz) the part of a camera that is made of a curved piece of
    glass and that makes things look closer than they really are.
    I broke the lens on my camera. *n. pl.* **lenses** lens·es

lens

lent (lent) **1.** *v. pt. t., pt. part.* See **lend.**
    2. Lent; the 40 days before Easter.
    I will not eat candy during Lent. *n.*

leopard leop·ard (lep'ərd) a large wild cat with black spots on its yellow fur.
    The leopard comes from Africa. *n. pl.* **leopards** leop·ards

less (les) a smaller amount; not as much.
    I have less money than you have. *adj.*

lesson les·son (les'n) **1.** something that a person is to learn; something that is taught to a person.
    I took a lesson in horseback riding. *n.*
    2. the time that someone is being taught.
    My dance lesson will start at one o'clock. *n. pl.* **lessons** les·sons

leopard

let (let) to allow; not to stop someone from doing something; to give permission.
    I will let you ride my bicycle. *v.* **let, let, letting** let·ting

let down (let doun) to lower; to move something toward the ground.
    She slowly let down the rope.
    v. **let down, let down, letting down** let·ting down

let go (let gō) to release hold of; to get rid of.
    If you let go of the string the balloon will fly away.
    v. **let go, let go, letting go** let·ting go

let's (lets) let us.
    Let's get some ice cream. *contrac.*

letter let·ter (let'ər) **1.** a written note or message.
    I wrote a letter to my grandmother. *n.*
    2. a mark that stands for a sound; a part of the alphabet.
    What letter is missing from this word? *n. pl.* **letters** let·ters

letter

lettuce let·tuce (let'is) **1.** a kind of green leafy vegetable.
    Rabbits eat lettuce. *n. no pl.*
    2. made from the green leafy vegetable.
    I had a lettuce salad for lunch. *adj.*

level lev·el (lev'əl) **1.** flat; even.
    Cows like to walk on level land. *adj.*
    2. a step or floor.
    I live on the first level of that building. *n. pl.* **levels** lev·els

lettuce

a	cat	**i**	sit	**oi**	oil	**ch**	chop	a in about
ā	ate	**ī**	lie	**ou**	out	**ng**	song	e in oven
ä	car	**o**	pot	**u**	cut	**sh**	she	ə = i in pencil
e	set	**ō**	old	**u̇**	book	**th**	three	o in memory
ē	equal	**ô**	or	**ü**	blue	**ŦH**	there	u in circus
ėr	germ					**zh**	treasure	

librarian li·brar·i·an (lī·brer⁴ē·ən) a person who works in the building or room where books are kept so that people can borrow or read them.
Our school librarian asked us not to talk in the library.
n. pl. **librarians** li·brar·i·ans

library li·brar·y (lī⁴brer·ē *or* lī⁴brar·ē) **1.** a building or a room where books are kept for people to borrow or to read there.
I borrowed two books from the library. *n. pl.* **libraries** li·brar·ies
2. having to do with the building or room where books are kept.
I have my own library card. *adj.*

lid

license li·cense (lī⁴sns) a piece of paper that shows that you have permission to do something.
A person cannot get a driver's license until he or she is sixteen years old.
n. pl. **licenses** li·cens·es

lid (lid) the covering of a pot, pan or jar.
Mother put the lid on the frying pan and steamed the chicken. *n. pl.* **lids**

lie (lī) **1.** an untrue statement; something said that is not true.
Jill told a lie when she said that she did not take the candy. *n. pl.* **lies**
2. to tell an untrue statement; to say something that is not true.
Jill should not lie. *v.* **lied, lied, lying** ly·ing
3. to put the body in a flat position.
I will lie on the bed for an hour. *v.* **lay, lain, lying** ly·ing

Vaduz
Liechtenstein

Liechtenstein Liech·ten·stein (lik⁴tən·stīn) a small country in Europe; its capital is Vaduz.
Liechtenstein is near Switzerland. *n.*

lieutenant lieu·ten·ant (lü·ten⁴ənt) an officer in the Navy, Army, Marines or Air Force.
My uncle is a lieutenant in the Navy. *n. pl.* **lieutenants** lieu·ten·ants

life (līf) the time a person or animal is alive; living or being alive.
Life is full of different experiences. *n. pl.* **lives**

life cycle life cy·cle (līf sī⁴kəl) the different stages a person, an animal, or a plant goes through when alive.
The life cycle of a person goes from baby to child to teenager to adult.

life jacket life jack·et (līf jak⁴it) a vest made of material that floats in water and that is worn to save a person from drowning.
Even a good swimmer should wear a life jacket when riding in a boat.

life jacket

life-sized (līf′sīzd) being as big as the real thing.
I made a life-sized picture of my dog for my wall. *adj.*

lifetime life·time (līf′tīm) the length of time that something is alive.
My grandmother has had a long lifetime. *n. pl.* **lifetimes** life·times

lift (lift) to raise up; to pick up.
I will lift the baby out of bed. *v.* **lifted, lifted, lifting** lift·ed, lift·ing

lift down (lift doun) to lower; to put down.
I will lift down the boxes from the attic.
v. **lifted down, lifted down, lifting down** lift·ed down, lift·ing down

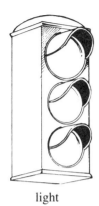

light

light (līt) **1.** a lamp that uses different colors to give directions to drivers; a traffic signal.
He stopped the car when the light turned red. *n.*
2. something that makes a place bright so that a person can see; a lamp.
Please put the light on. *n.*
3. a glow; a bright flash.
The flashbulb gave enough light to take the picture. *n. pl.* **lights**
4. not much color; not dark in color.
I have light brown hair. *adj.*
5. not much weight; not heavy; a small amount.
There is a light rain falling. *adj.* **lighter, lightest** light·er, light·est
6. to start something burning; to set fire to something.
Dad will light the barbecue. *v.* **lit, lighted** *or* **lit, lighting** light·ed, light·ing

lightning light·ning (līt′ning) **1.** a flash of brightness in the sky during a rainstrom.
Lightning is caused by electricity in the clouds. *n. pl.* **lightning**
2. having to do with a sudden flash in the sky.
The lightning storm lasted only a short time. *adj.*

lightning

lightning rod

lightning rod (līt′ning rod) a metal stick or rod that is put on a house or building to direct lightning into the ground.
The lightning hit the lightning rod on the barn, so the barn did not burn.

lightweight light·weight (līt′wāt) not having much weight; not heavy.
I wore a lightweight jacket to school today. *adj.*

like (līk) **1.** to enjoy; to feel good about.
I like reading in bed. *v.* **liked, liked, liking** lik·ing
2. similar to; almost the same as.
Sometimes my brother acts like a child. *prep.*

a	cat	**i**	sit	**oi**	oil	**ch**	chop	a in about
ā	ate	**ī**	lie	**ou**	out	**ng**	song	e in oven
ä	car	**o**	pot	**u**	cut	**sh**	she	ə = i in pencil
e	set	**ō**	old	**u̇**	book	**th**	three	o in memory
ē	equal	**ô**	or	**ü**	blue	**ŦH**	there	u in circus
ėr	germ					**zh**	treasure	

likeable like·a·ble (līʹkə·bəl) nice; enjoyable.
Amy is a likeable girl. *adj.*

likeness like·ness (līkʹnis) being alike; having some trait that is almost the same as someone or something else; a similarity.
The likeness shared between my brother and my father is the shape of their eyes. *n. pl.* **likenesses** like·ness·es

like to (līk tü) to enjoy.
I like to ride my bicycle. *v.* **liked to, liked to, liking to** lik·ing to

lily lil·y (lilʹē) a kind of flower that has large bell-shaped petals.
We have a white lily in our garden. *n. pl.* **lilies** lil·ies

lily

line (līn) **1.** a straight mark.
I put a line under my name. *n.*
2. a row of people or things.
We stood in line at the door. *n.*
3. the words that an actor in a movie or play says.
The actor forgot his lines. *n. pl.* **lines**

liner lin·er (līʹnər) a large ship that can carry hundreds of people from one place to another.
Mother and Father took a cruise on a large ocean liner. *n. pl.* **liners** lin·ers

liner

line up (līn up) to form a row of people.
The students must line up when they go to lunch.
v. **lined up, lined up, lining up** lin·ing up

lion li·on (līʹən) **1.** a large wild cat that has yellow fur and that comes from Africa.
The lion roared loudly and frightened my kitten. *n. pl.* **lions** li·ons
2. having to do with the large wild African cat.
The lion tamer walked into the lion cage very slowly. *adj.*

lion

lip (lip) one of the two outside parts of the mouth.
I cut my lip with the fork. *n. pl.* **lips**

liquid liq·uid (likʹwid) **1.** a substance that flows like water; a substance that is not solid.
Juice is a liquid. *n. pl.* **liquids** liq·uids
2. having to do with a substance that is not solid and that flows like water.
I poured the liquid chocolate on my ice cream. *adj.*

list (list) a series of names, numbers, words or things on a page.
I took the grocery list with me when I went to the store. *n. pl.* **lists**

listen lis·ten (lisʹn) to hear sounds; to pay attention to sounds.
I will listen to your story.
v. **listened, listened, listening** lis·tened, lis·ten·ing

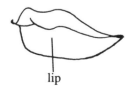
lip

litter

living room

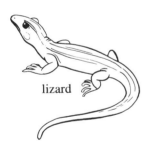

lizard

listener lis·ten·er (lis⸍n·ər) a person who hears what another person is saying; a person who pays attention to sounds.
A person can learn a lot if he is a good listener. *n. pl.* **listeners** lis·ten·ers

lit (lit) *v. pt. t., pt. part.* See **light** (6).

literature lit·er·a·ture (lit⸍ər·ə·chùr *or* lit⸍ər·ə·chər) written stories.
We will study literature in high school. *n. no pl.*

litter lit·ter (lit⸍ər) trash and garbage that is thrown on the land and not put in garbage cans.
The football field was covered with litter. *n.*

little lit·tle (lit⸍l) **1.** small; not big.
I want a little apple. *adj.*
2. small or young compared with another.
My little sister will be four years old tomorrow.
adj. **littler, littlest** lit·tler, lit·tlest

live[1] (liv) **1.** to have a home; to reside.
I live in that white house. *v.*
2. to be alive; to have life.
I want to live a long time. *v.* **lived, lived, living** liv·ing

live[2] (līv) alive; breathing.
I found a live turtle in the grass. *adj.*

lives (līvz) *n. pl.* See **life.**

living liv·ing (liv⸍ing) having life; not being dead.
The restaurant has a living plant on each table. *adj.*

living room liv·ing room (liv⸍ing rüm) the place in a house where the family spends a lot of time.
We have our television in our living room.

lizard liz·ard (liz⸍ərd) a reptile that has a long tail and a long body.
The green lizard ran out of the grass. *n. pl.* **lizards** liz·ards

a	cat	**i**	sit	**oi**	oil	**ch**	chop	a in about
ā	ate	**ī**	lie	**ou**	out	**ng**	song	e in oven
ä	car	**o**	pot	**u**	cut	**sh**	she	ə = i in pencil
e	set	**ō**	old	**u̇**	book	**th**	three	o in memory
ē	equal	**ô**	or	**ü**	blue	**ᵀH**	there	u in circus
ėr	germ					**zh**	treasure	

load (lōd) **1.** to put bullets in a gun.
The hunter will load his rifle in the forest. *v.*
2. to fill up something.
I will load the dishwasher. *v.*
3. to put things in a vehicle.
Father will load the dirt into the truck.
v. **loaded, loaded, loading** load·ed, load·ing
4. the things that are put into a vehicle; the things
that a person is carrying.
Mother has a big load of groceries. *n. pl.* **loads**

lobby lob·by (lob′ē) the first room inside a building; a waiting area.
The lobby of the hotel has many sofas and chairs in it.
n. pl. **lobbies** lob·bies

local lo·cal (lō′kəl) being close; living in the area;
not from far away.
Many local people use the park on Sunday afternoons. *adj.*

locker

locate lo·cate (lō′kāt) to find; to discover where something
or someone is.
I want to locate my grandmother.
v. **located, located, locating** lo·cat·ed, lo·cat·ing

location lo·ca·tion (lō·kā′shən) the place where something
or someone can be found.
I will ask the man for the location of the nearest store.
n. pl. **locations** lo·ca·tions

lock (lok) to close something with a key so that it
cannot be opened.
I will lock the door after you leave.
v. **locked, locked, locking** lock·ing

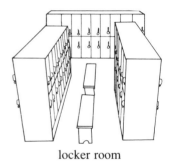
locker room

locker lock·er (lok′ər) a metal box or closet that can
be closed with a key.
I put my shoes in my school locker. *n. pl.* **lockers** lock·ers

locker room lock·er room (lok′ər rüm) a place where there are
many metal closets that can be closed with keys.
We change our clothes in the locker room.

lock up (lok up) to close with a key.
I will lock up my bicycle in the garage.
v. **locked up, locked up, locking up** lock·ing up

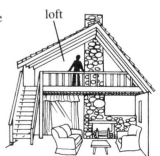
loft

loft (lôft *or* loft) a place that is just below the roof of a
building or a house; an attic.
We have a reading loft in our living room. *n. pl.* **lofts**

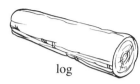

log

log (lôg *or* log) **1.** a piece of wood that still looks like
the trunk of a tree.
The log rolled down the hill. *n. pl.* **logs**
2. made of pieces of wood that still look like trunks of trees.
We have a log cabin in the forest. *adj.*
3. to cut trees for lumber.
The men will log the trees in this forest.
v. **logged, logged, logging** log·ging

logger log·ger (lô′gər *or* log′ər) a person who cuts trees
into logs; a lumberjack.
The logger cut the tree with an ax. *n. pl.* **loggers** log·gers

logger

loin (loin) the part of an animal's body between the ribs
and the hipbones.
The saddle does not touch the loin of the horse. *n. pl.* **loins**

London Lon·don (lun′dən) the capital city of Great Britain.
The Queen of England lives in London. *n.*

lonely lone·ly (lōn′lē) a sad feeling of being alone;
a sad feeling of being without other people.
I am lonely when my mother is not home.
adj. **lonelier, loneliest** lone·li·er, lone·li·est

long (lông *or* long) **1.** a great distance from one end to the
other end; not short.
The girl's hair is long. *adj.*
2. a great length of time.
I will have a long wait before I see the doctor.
adj. **longer, longest** long·er, long·est
3. for a great length of time.
Father will not be gone long. *adv.*
4. to want something badly; to greatly want something.
I long to have a dog of my own. *v.* **longed, longed, longing** long·ing

long ago long a·go (lông ə·gō′) many years past; a time
far in the past.
Long ago, knights fought to protect kingdoms.

loin

long-anticipated long-an·tic·i·pat·ed (lông-an·tis′ə·pā·tid) having
waited for something for a great length of time.
My brother's moving to another town was long-anticipated. *adj.*

a	cat	i	sit	oi	oil	ch	chop		a in about
ā	ate	ī	lie	ou	out	ng	song		e in oven
ä	car	o	pot	u	cut	sh	she	ə =	i in pencil
e	set	ō	old	u̇	book	th	three		o in memory
ē	equal	ô	or	ü	blue	ŦH	there		u in circus
ėr	germ					zh	treasure		

long-handled (lông-han⸴dld) having a long part that is used for gripping with the hand.
  We have a long-handled pan that we use for cooking on a campfire. *adj.*

longingly long·ing·ly (lông⸴ing·lē *or* long⸴ing·lē) with great wanting; with strong desire.
  He looked at the new car longingly. *adv.*

long-necked (lông-nek⸴t) having a long neck.
  The giraffe is a long-necked animal. *adj.*

long-handled

look (lùk) **1.** to see with the eyes; to try to find with the eyes.
  I often look at the stars at night. *v.*
  2. to appear; to seem to be.
  You look very happy. *v.* **looked, looked, looking** look·ing
  3. a view of something; a glance at something.
  The man climbed the ladder to get a closer look at the roof. *n. pl.* **looks**

look after (lùk af⸴tər) to take care of someone or something.
  I will look after your dog while you are gone.
  v. **looked after, looked after, looking after** look·ing af·ter

look around look a·round (lùk ə·round′) to quickly search an area or place; to scan with the eyes.
  I will look around the room for the book.
  v. **looked around, looked around, looking around** look·ing a·round

look for (lùk fôr) to try to find; to search for.
  I will look for the lost ring.
  v. **looked for, looked for, looking for** look·ing for

look forward to look for·ward to (lùk fôr⸴wərd tü) to wait with happiness; to anticipate with pleasure.
  I look forward to going to the circus.
  v. **looked forward to, looked forward to, looking forward to** look·ing for·ward to

look ___ in the eye (lùk ___ in ᴛнē ī) look straight at someone; to stare into another person's eyes.
  Please look me in the eye when you are talking.

look out (lùk out) to be careful; to watch out.
  I look out for broken glass when I walk without my shoes.
  v. **looked out, looked out, looking out** look·ing out

look up (lùk up) **1.** to direct the eyes at something in the air.
  If you look up, you can see the stars at night. *v.*
  2. to try to find something in a book of information.
  I will look up the definition in the dictionary.
  v. **looked up, looked up, looking up** look·ing up

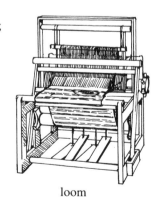

loom

loom (lüm) a machine that people use for weaving yarn or string into cloth.
  The settlers used a loom to make cloth. *n. pl.* **looms**

248

loop (lüp)   **1.** the part of a rope or string that is bent for tying.
The little boy has learned to make a loop with his shoelace. *n. pl.* **loops**
2. to move in a circle in the air.
The airplane will loop around and return to the same place.
v. **looped, looped, looping** loop·ing

loose (lüs)   not held tight; not fastened.
The tooth came out because it was loose.
adj. **looser, loosest** loos·er, loos·est

lord (lôrd)   a title given to a boss or a person who has power.
The knights always called the king "my lord." *n. pl.* **lords**

lose (lüz)   **1.** to no longer have; to not be able to find.
Please do not lose your gloves. *v.*
2. not to win a game; to be beaten in a game.
I think our team will lose the game tonight. *v.* **lost, lost, losing** los·ing

loser los·er (lü′zər)   the person or the team that did not
win the race, contest or game.
Our team was the loser in last night's game. *n. pl.* **losers** los·ers

loss (lôs)   not having what one once had; the action
of losing something.
I will feel a real loss when my friend moves to another city.
n. pl. **losses** loss·es

lost (lôst *or* lost)   **1.** cannot be found.
My ring is lost. *adj.*
2. *v. pt. t., pt. part.* See **lose.**

lot (lot)   a great amount; much.
I drank a lot of milk today. *n. pl.* **lots**

loud (loud)   not soft or quiet; making a big sound.
The balloon made a loud noise when it broke.
adj. **louder, loudest** loud·er, loud·est

loudly loud·ly (loud′lē)   not in a soft or quiet way.
The dog barked loudly when it saw the cat. *adv.*

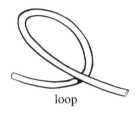
loop

a	cat	i	sit	oi	oil	ch	chop		a in about
ā	ate	ī	lie	ou	out	ng	song		e in oven
ä	car	o	pot	u	cut	sh	she	ə =	i in pencil
e	set	ō	old	u̇	book	th	three		o in memory
ē	equal	ô	or	ü	blue	ŦH	there		u in circus
ėr	germ					zh	treasure		

lounge (lounj) **1.** a place where people sit and rest.
I will meet you in the hotel lounge. *n. pl.* **lounges** loung·es
2. having to do with a place where people rest.
We sat in the lounge chairs. *adj.*

love (luv) **1.** to have strong feelings of liking
someone or something.
I love my sister. *v.*
2. to want very much; to have a strong desire.
I would love to have a dog. *v.*
3. to enjoy; to like.
I love to dance. *v.* **loved, loved, loving** lov·ing
4. a strong feeling of liking.
My love for my sister grows every day. *n. pl.* **loves**
5. having to do with strong feelings of liking.
The gentleman sent the lady a love letter. *adj.*

lounge

lovely love·ly (luv'lē) nice; pretty; good.
I had a lovely time visiting Grandmother.
adj. **lovelier, loveliest** love·li·er, love·li·est

lovingly lov·ing·ly (luv'ing·lē) in a way that shows
great feeling of liking.
He lovingly carried the baby to bed. *adv.*

low (lō) **1.** not high; near to the ground.
The water in the river was low. *adj.*
2. soft; not loud.
The music was very low. *adj.*
3. not hot; a cool temperature; a less than normal temperature.
The temperature was low yesterday. *adj.* **lower, lowest** low·er, low·est
4. not high; near to the ground.
The airplane flew low. *adv.*

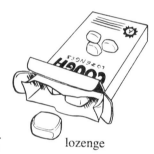

lozenge

lower low·er (lō'ər) **1.** to put down; to reduce; to lessen.
We will lower the window shades.
v. **lowered, lowered, lowering** low·ered, low·er·ing
2. *comp. adj.* See **low.**

lowest low·est (lō'ist) *superl. adj.* See **low.**

lozenge loz·enge (loz'inj) a small piece of hard candy or
a small medicine pill that is melted in the mouth.
The lozenge tasted like lemons. *n. pl.* **lozenges** loz·eng·es

luck (luk) fate; what happens by chance or without planning
or work; success that happens without work.
If luck is with me, I will pass the test. *n. no pl.*

luckily luck·i·ly (luk'ə·lē) happening without work,
planning or control.
Luckily, I found the cat before the dog did. *adv.*

lumber

lucky luck·y (luk′ē) having things happen by chance
or without work.
I am a very lucky person. *adj.* **luckier, luckiest** luck·i·er, luck·i·est

lumber lum·ber (lum′bər) pieces of wood; boards.
We will buy lumber to build the doghouse. *n. no pl.*

lumberjack lum·ber·jack (lum′bər·jak) a person whose job
is to cut down trees.
The lumberjack cut down the tree with an ax.
n. pl. **lumberjacks** lum·ber·jacks

lunch (lunch) the meal that we eat in the middle of the day;
the second meal of the day; the meal that we eat at noon.
I had lunch at school today. *n. pl.* **lunches** lunch·es

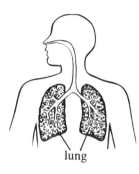

lung

lung (lung) a body part or organ that enables people and
animals to breathe air.
People can live with one lung, but people are born with two. *n. pl.* **lungs**

lute (lüt) a small musical instrument that looks like a
pear-shaped guitar.
The lute was used to play music for the king. *n. pl.* **lutes**

luxury lux·ur·y (luk′shər·ē) something that we have but that we
do not need; something that we do but that we do not
need to do to live.
A television is a luxury. *n. pl.* **luxuries** lux·ur·ies

lyceum ly·ce·um (lī·sē′əm *or* lī′sē·əm) a boys school in
Europe in the 1800s.
Lyceum is more difficult than school in America. *n. pl.* **lyceums** ly·ce·ums

lute

lying ly·ing (lī′ing) *v. pres. part.* See **lie** (2).

a	cat	i	sit	oi	oil	ch	chop		a in about
ā	ate	ī	lie	ou	out	ng	song		e in oven
ä	car	o	pot	u	cut	sh	she	ə =	i in pencil
e	set	ō	old	u̇	book	th	three		o in memory
ē	equal	ô	or	ü	blue	ŦH	there		u in circus
êr	germ					zh	treasure		

Mm

machine   ma·chine (mə·shēn′)   a thing with moving parts and gears that is used to make work easier; a device that has a use in some kind of work.
> Mom enjoys sewing with her new machine. *n. pl.* **machines** ma·chines

machine

mad   (mad)   angry.
> The dog was mad when the boy took the bone.
> *adj.* **madder, maddest** mad·der, mad·dest

made   (mād)   *v. pt. t., pt. part.* See **make.**

made of   (mād əv)   formed with; built from; produced with.
> The cake is made of flour, eggs, sugar and milk.

made up   (mād′ up)   not real; imaginary.
> The story I told was made up. *adj.*

magazine   mag·a·zine (mag·ə·zēn′ *or* mag′ə·zēn)   **1.** a book that has a soft cover, has different stories and is printed often.
> I read "Humpty Dumpty" magazine every month.
> *n. pl.* **magazines** mag·a·zines
> **2.** having to do with a book that has a soft cover and is printed often.
> The magazine cover has a picture of an egg with arms, legs and a face. *adj.*

magazine

magic   mag·ic (maj′ik)   the art of making things happen that cannot be explained; a mysterious power to do things that other people cannot do.
> Making the rabbit disappear is magic. *n. no pl.*

magical   mag·i·cal (maj′ə·kəl)   having to do with something that cannot be explained; having special powers.
> The witch's broom was magical. *adj.*

magician   ma·gi·cian (mə·jish′ən)   a person who does things that cannot be explained; a person who does magic.
> The magician made the tiger disappear. *n. pl.* **magicians** ma·gi·cians

magnificent   mag·nif·i·cent (mag·nif′ə·sənt)   **1.** wonderful; fantastic; grand; beautiful.
> The beach was magnificent. *adj.*
> **2.** handsome.
> The gentleman looked magnificent. *adj.*

magician

magnolia mag·nol·ia (mag·nō⸍lyə) **1.** a kind of tree with large flowers that have a strong, sweet smell.
The magnolia makes the whole yard smell sweet.
n. pl. **magnolias** mag·nol·ias
2. having to do with a kind of tree with strong, sweet-smelling flowers.
Magnolia flowers can be pink, purple, white or yellow. *adj.*

maiden maid·en (mād⸍n) a young woman who is not married.
The maiden waited for the knight to return from battle.
n. pl. **maidens** maid·ens

mailbox

mail (māl) **1.** letters, postcards or packages that a person who works for the post office brings to a house or building.
I will get the mail. *n. no pl.*
2. having to do with things that a postal worker brings.
The postman carries a mail bag. *adj.*
3. to send a letter, postcard or package to someone.
I will mail Grandmother a birthday card.
v. **mailed, mailed, mailing** mail·ing

mailbox mail·box (māl⸍boks) a metal or wooden container that people use for sending or getting cards, letters, postcards or packages.
I put the letter in the mailbox. *n. pl.* **mailboxes** mail·box·es

mailman mail·man (māl⸍man) a person working for the post office who brings letters, cards and packages to a house or building; the postman.
Our mailman brings the mail at ten o'clock every day.
n. pl. **mailmen** mail·men

mail pouch

mail pouch (māl pouch) a bag in which a postman carries letters, cards, postcards and packages.
The postman carries a mail pouch.

main (mān) largest; most important.
The principal is in the school's main office. *adj.*

mainland main·land (mān⸍land *or* mān⸍lənd) the largest part of a country; the part of a country that does not include the islands of the country.
Forty-eight states make up the mainland of the United States. Hawaii and Alaska are not part of the mainland. *n. pl.* **mainlands** main·lands

mailman

majestically ma·jes·ti·cal·ly (mə·jes⸍tik·lē) in a royal manner; like a king or a queen.
The lady walked majestically into the room. *adv.*

a	cat	**i**	sit	**oi**	oil	**ch**	chop
ā	ate	**ī**	lie	**ou**	out	**ng**	song
ä	car	**o**	pot	**u**	cut	**sh**	she
e	set	**ō**	old	**ú**	book	**th**	three
ē	equal	**ô**	or	**ü**	blue	**ŦH**	there
ėr	germ					**zh**	treasure

ə = { a in about / e in oven / i in pencil / o in memory / u in circus }

majesty maj·es·ty (maj′ə·stē) greatness; royal
appearance; grandeur.
The majesty of the mountains makes a person feel small.
n. pl. **majesties** maj·es·ties

major ma·jor (mā′jər) main; most important; greatest; largest.
The major job of a student is studying. *adj.*

make (māk) **1.** to create; to draw; to build.
He will make me a picture. *v.*
2. to put together; to produce.
He will make a table. *v.*
3. to cook.
Father will make dinner. *v.*
4. to perform; to do an action.
I will make a speech at the meeting. *v.*
5. to earn.
I will make three dollars for cutting the grass. *v.*
6. to cause someone to feel an emotion.
That movie will make you sad. *v.*
7. to force someone to do something that
they do not want to do.
You can't make me get into the car. *v.* **made, made, making** mak·ing

make a mistake make a mis·take (māk ə mə·stāk′)
to do something wrong.
I do not want to make a mistake on the math test.

make-believe make-be·lieve (māk′·bi·lēv)
pretend; not real; imaginary.
That is a make-believe castle. *adj.*

make fun of (māk fun əv) to tease; to make jokes about
someone or something.
The boys will make fun of my shoes.

make ___ into make ___ in·to (māk ___ in′tü) to
change something into another thing; to shape something
into a different form.
Mother will make the dough into small dinner rolls.
v. **made ___ into, made ___ into, making ___ into** mak·ing ___ into

makeup

make it (māk it) to be successful; to do what you wanted to do.
I want to be a lawyer. If I study hard, I can make it. *idiom*

maker mak·er (māk′ər) **1.** a machine that is used to do a
certain job; a machine that produces something.
The candy maker makes fudge. *n.*
2. a person who creates or produces something.
The saddle maker fixed my old saddle. *n. pl.* **makers** mak·ers

make the team (māk ᴛнə tēm) to be accepted as part of a team;
to be selected as a player on a team.
All the girls are trying to make the team. *idiom*

Kuala Lumpur

Malay Peninsula

make up (māk up) **1.** to create in the mind; to develop a story.
The teacher asked us to make up a story about a king. *v.*
2. to put on cosmetics; to put on lipstick, powder, etc.
I will make up my face. *v.* **made up, made up, making up** mak·ing up

makeup make·up (māk′up) lipstick, powder, rouge,
eye shadow, etc.; cosmetics.
I do not wear makeup. *n. no pl.*

makeup artist make·up ar·tist (māk′up är′tist) a person who
puts cosmetics on other people.
The makeup artist got the movie star ready for the pictures.

make up ___ mind (māk up ___ mīnd) to decide.
I cannot make up my mind about which dress to wear today. *idiom*

malaria ma·lar·i·a (mə·ler′ē·ə *or* mə·lar′ē·ə) a disease that
comes from the bite of a certain mosquito and that makes
a person have a fever and then chills.
The mosquitoes in America do not give people malaria. *n. no pl.*

Malay Ma·lay (mā′lā *or* mə·lā′) **1.** the people who live
on the Malay Peninsula.
The president of the company is a Malay. *n. pl.*
2. having to do with the people and the language of
the Malay Peninsula.
The Malay language is difficult to learn. *adj.*

male (māl) **1.** a man or a boy.
My father is a male. *n. pl.* **males**
2. having to do with boys or men.
The male baseball team will not let the girls join their team. *adj.*

mall (môl) a place with many different shops and stores;
a shopping center.
I bought my new shoes at the shoe store in the mall. *n. pl.* **malls**

mama ma·ma (mä′mə) mother; mom.
The baby wanted her mama. *n. pl.* **mamas** ma·mas

mamba

mamba mam·ba (mam′bə) a kind of snake whose bite
can kill a person.
A mamba can be found in Africa. *n. pl.* **mambas** mam·bas

mammal mam·mal (mam′əl) an animal that has hair and that
the female produces milk for its babies.
The horse is a mammal. *n. pl.* **mammals** mam·mals

a	cat	i	sit	oi	oil	ch	chop		a in about
ā	ate	ī	lie	ou	out	ng	song		e in oven
ä	car	o	pot	u	cut	sh	she	ə =	i in pencil
e	set	ō	old	u̇	book	th	three		o in memory
ē	equal	ô	or	ü	blue	ᵀHᵀ	there		u in circus
ėr	germ					zh	treasure		

man (man) **1.** a male adult.
> My father is a man. *n. pl.* **men**

2. all of the people on the Earth.
> New medicines can help man live longer. *n. no pl.*

manage man·age (man⸻ij) **1.** to be able to do something;
to arrange something.
> I can manage to get Mother a birthday card. *v.*

2. to control something; to direct someone.
> My mother will manage the new supermarket.
> *v.* **managed, managed, managing** man·aged, man·ag·ing

mandarin orange

manager man·ag·er (man⸻ə·jər) a person who is the boss of an
activity or a program; a person who controls something.
> The manager of the baseball team taught us how to throw the ball.
> *n. pl.* **managers** man·ag·ers

mandarin orange man·dar·in o·range (man⸻dər·ən   ôr⸻inj)
a small fruit that has an orange-colored skin.
> The mandarin orange is sweeter than the navel orange.

mane (mān) the thick hair that grows on the neck of some animals.
> The male lion has a mane around his face. *n. pl.* **manes**

mane

Manitoba Man·i·to·ba (man·ə·tō⸻bə) a province (state) in Canada;
its capital is Winnipeg.
> My uncle goes to Manitoba to fish every April. *n.*

manners man·ners (man⸻ərz) actions or behaviors.
> We are taught good manners so that we are not rude to people. *plural n.*

manservant man·serv·ant (man⸻sėr·vənt) a male person who
works in a house as a butler, cook or valet.
> The rich people in the big house have a manservant and a maid.
> *n. pl.* **menservants** men·serv·ants

manufacture man·u·fac·ture (man·yə·fak⸻chər) to make or build
things to be sold for money; to produce something to sell.
> Don plans to manufacture guitars. *v.* **manufactured, manufactured,**
> **manufacturing** man·u·fac·tured, man·u·fac·tur·ing

manufacturer man·u·fac·tur·er (man·yə·fak⸻chər·ər) the person or
business that produces things to be sold.
> Don will be a guitar manufacturer.
> *n. pl.* **manufacturers** man·u·fac·tur·ers

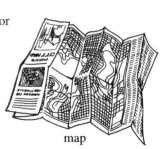

many man·y (men⸻ē) several; a great number; a lot.
> I ate many cookies at the party. *adj.* **more, most**

map (map) a drawing or picture that shows where places can
be found; a picture that is used for finding directions
in a city, country or state.
> I followed the map and found the library. *n. pl.* **maps**

map

marathon mar·a·thon (mar'ə·thon) a long race or contest.
My father ran in the marathon. *n. pl.* **marathons** mar·a·thons

marble

marble mar·ble (mär'bəl) a small ball made of stone, glass or clay; a toy.
I won his marble by hitting it with my marble. *n. pl.* **marbles** mar·bles

march (märch) **1.** to walk to a certain beat and in small steps.
I will march in the parade on Saturday.
v. **marched, marched, marching** march·ing
2. the action of walking to a certain beat and in small steps.
The parade march will start at ten o'clock. *n. pl.* **marches** march·es

mark (märk) a line, dot, or X that means something; a symbol.
I put a mark on the picture that I made. *n. pl.* **marks**

market mar·ket (mär'kit) **1.** a place where things are sold; a store.
I bought the broccoli at the farmer's market. *n. pl.* **markets** mar·kets
2. the place where stocks and bonds are bought, sold or traded.
The stock market is in New York City. *n. no pl.*

Mars

marriage mar·riage (mar'ij) the time when a man and a woman are married; the living together of a husband and a wife.
My mother and father have a good marriage. *n. pl.* **marriages** mar·riag·es

married mar·ried (mar'ēd) **1.** *v. pt. t., pt. part.* See **marry.**
2. being a wife or a husband.
My gym teacher is married, and my math teacher is single. *adj.*

marry mar·ry (mar'ē) to join together as husband and wife; to promise to live together as husband and wife.
The bride will marry the groom in a large wedding ceremony.
v. **married, married, marrying** mar·ried, mar·ry·ing

Mars (märz) **1.** one of the planets in the solar system.
Mars is the planet nearest the Earth in the solar system. *n.*
2. the Roman god of war.
People once believed that Mars decided the winner of war. *n.*

marshmallow

marshmallow marsh·mal·low (märsh'mal·ō *or* märsh'mel·ō)
a sweet candy or dessert that is made of sugar, gelatin and corn syrup.
We each cooked a marshmallow on the campfire.
n. pl. **marshmallows** marsh·mal·lows

a	cat	**i**	sit	**oi**	oil	**ch**	chop
ā	ate	**ī**	lie	**ou**	out	**ng**	song
ä	car	**o**	pot	**u**	cut	**sh**	she
e	set	**ō**	old	**ů**	book	**th**	three
ē	equal	**ô**	or	**ü**	blue	**ŦH**	there
ėr	germ					**zh**	treasure

ə = { a in about / e in oven / i in pencil / o in memory / u in circus

martial mar·tial (mär′shəl) having to do with fighting or with war.
Kung Fu is a martial art. *adj.*

marvelous mar·vel·ous (mär′və·ləs) wonderful; very good.
We had a marvelous time at the carnival. *adj.*

mask (mask) a covering that hides the face.
I wore a monster mask on Halloween. *n. pl.* **masks**

mask

mason ma·son (mā′sn) a person who builds things with
bricks; a bricklayer.
The mason used red brick to build our house. *n. pl.* **masons** ma·sons

mass (mas) a large number of people or things.
We jumped in the mass of leaves that the gardener had raked.
n. pl. **masses** mass·es

mass communication mass com·mu·ni·ca·tion
(mas kə·myü·nə·kā′shən) a way of getting information to a
large number of people.
People use radio, TV and newspapers to sell things through
mass communication.

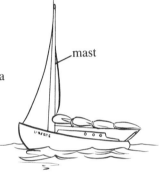

mast

mass media mass me·di·a (mas mē′dē·ə) ways of getting
information to a large number of people.
Radio and TV are mass media.

mass production mass pro·duc·tion (mas prə·duk′shən) making
things in large numbers; producing large amounts of things.
Cars are made in mass production.

mast (mast) **1.** the tall pole on a boat to which a sail is tied.
Father tied the front sail to the mast. *n.*
2. flagpole.
We hung the flag on the mast. *n. pl.* **masts**

mat

master mas·ter (mas′tər) **1.** a person who owns an animal;
a person who has control of an animal.
The dog's master taught it to sit and roll over when asked. *n.*
2. a person who owned and controlled slaves in the past.
Before the Civil War many black people were owned by a master.
n. pl. **masters** mas·ters

mat (mat) a small rug or piece of carpet on which one wipes
one's feet before going into a home.
The mat by the door says "Welcome." *n. pl.* **mats**

match (mach) **1.** a short stick with chemicals on one tip,
which starts a fire when it is rubbed on a rough surface.
Be careful not to burn yourself on the match. *n.*
2. a contest or a game.
The tennis match will start at ten o'clock. *n. pl.* **matches** match·es

match

Matterhorn

mate   (māt)   **1.** a partner; a husband or wife.
Some animals pick a different mate every year. *n.*
2. one of two things that make a set or a pair.
I lost the mate to my glove. *n. pl.* **mates**
3. to pick a partner; to pick a man or a woman with whom to have children.
Birds mate in the spring of the year.
v. **mated, mated, mating** mat·ed, mat·ing

material   ma·ter·i·al (mə·tir′ē·əl)   **1.** cloth or fabric.
Satin is a shiny material. *n.*
2. something that is used to make something else.
Wood is one material that people use to build a house.
n. pl. **materials** ma·ter·i·als

math   (math)   **1.** the school subject that teaches a person to work with numbers and measurements; mathematics.
Adding and subtracting numbers are part of math. *n. no pl.*
2. having to do with the school subject of working with numbers.
Tomorrow we will have a math test. *adj.*

matter   mat·ter (mat′ər)   a thing of importance; trouble.
I don't know what is the matter with Jill, but she is still crying.
n. pl. **matters** mat·ters

mattress

Matterhorn   Mat·ter·horn (mat′ər·hôrn)   a large mountain in the Alps (a mountain range in Europe).
The Matterhorn is between Italy and Switzerland. *n.*

mattress   mat·tress (ma′tris)   a cushion that is stuffed with material, placed on a bed frame and used for sleeping.
I have a hard mattress, but my brother has a soft mattress.
n. pl. **mattresses** mat·tress·es

may   (mā)   **1.** to give or have permission; to allow to.
You may have a cookie. *aux.*
2. to be possible; to be able to.
It may get very hot this afternoon. *aux. pt. t.* **might**

maybe   may·be (mā′bē)   perhaps; possibly.
Maybe I can go to the movie with you. *adv.*

mayonnaise   may·on·naise (mā·ə·nāz′)   a white ingredient or food that is made from egg yolk, oil and vinegar.
I like mayonnaise on my sandwich. *n. no pl.*

mayonnaise

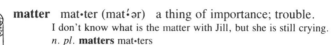

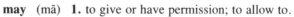

a	cat	i	sit	oi	oil	ch	chop		a in about
ā	ate	ī	lie	ou	out	ng	song		e in oven
ä	car	o	pot	u	cut	sh	she	ə =	i in pencil
e	set	ō	old	u̇	book	th	three		o in memory
ē	equal	ô	or	ü	blue	ŦH	there		u in circus
ėr	germ					zh	treasure		

mayor   may·or (mā‡ər)   the leader of a city; the person
who runs a city.
We will elect a new mayor in July. *n. pl.* **mayors** may·ors

me   (mē)   the person who is talking; I.
Please give me a cookie. *pron.*

meadow   mead·ow (med‡ō)   a large field of grass.
The farmer cut the grass in the meadow. *n. pl.* **meadows** mead·ows

meal   (mēl)   food eaten at a certain time of the day.
Breakfast is the most important meal of the day. *n. pl.* **meals**

mean   (mēn)   **1.** not nice; cruel; unkind.
The man was mean to the dog. *adj.* **meaner, meanest** mean·er, mean·est
2. to have an idea in mind; to intend to do something.
I mean to go with the big boys tonight.
v. **meant, meant, meaning** mean·ing

meadow

meaning   mean·ing (mē‡ning)   **1.** the definition of a word or phrase.
I looked up the meaning in the dictionary. *n. pl.* **meanings** mean·ings
2. *v. pres. part.* See **mean** (2).

meant   (ment)   *v. pt. t., pt. part.* See **mean** (2).

meanwhile   mean·while (mēn‡hwīl)   at the same time
but in another place.
I looked for my papers upstairs. Meanwhile, Mother was clearing
the table and found them in the kitchen. *adv.*

measure   meas·ure (mezh‡ər *or* mā‡zhər)   to find the length,
size or amount of something.
The man will measure my feet to see what size shoe I should wear.
v. **measured, measured, measuring** meas·ured, meas·ur·ing

meat   (mēt)   the part of an animal that people eat; food that
comes from an animal.
The meat of a cow is called beef; the meat of a pig is called pork.
n. pl. **meats**

meat

meat-eater   meat-eat·er (mēt-ēt‡ər)   a person or animal
that eats meat.
The lion is a meat-eater. *n. pl.* **meat-eaters** meat-eat·ers

meat-eating   meat-eat·ing (mēt-ēt‡ing)   having to do with eating
the meat of animals.
The meat-eating lion hungrily watched the bird. *adj.*

mechanic   me·chan·ic (mə·kan‡ik)   a person who fixes cars
or other machines.
The car mechanic fixed the brakes on father's car.
n. pl. **mechanics** me·chan·ics

medal

medicine

Mediterranean Sea

mechanical me·chan·i·cal (mə·kan'ə·kəl) having to do with machines; acting like a machine.
The mechanical robot walked toward the boy. *adj.*

medal med·al (med'l) a small piece of metal given as a prize or an award.
I won a medal in the race. *n. pl.* **medals** med·als

media me·di·a (mē'dē·ə) the means by which people learn what is happening in the world, such as newspapers, television, radio, magazines and journals.
The media helps citizens learn about the latest events. *plural n.*

medicine med·i·cine (med'ə·sən) **1.** pills or liquids that make sick people feel better; substances that cure diseases and sicknesses.
The doctor gave me some medicine for the flu.
n. pl. **medicines** med·i·cines
2. the science of treating sicknesses and diseases.
Doctors and nurses work in medicine. *n. no pl.*
3. having to do with things that treat sicknesses.
The medicine bottle had my name on it. *adj.*

meditate med·i·tate (med'ə·tāt) to think quietly.
I like to be alone so that I can meditate.
v. **meditated, meditated, meditating** med·i·tat·ed, med·i·tat·ing

meditation med·i·ta·tion (med·ə·tā'shən) the act of thinking quietly.
Some people spend one hour a day in meditation.
n. pl. **meditations** med·i·ta·tions

Mediterranean Sea Med·i·ter·ra·ne·an Sea (med·ə·tə·rā'nē·ən sē) the large body of water that separates the south of Europe from the north of Africa.
The Romans sailed across the Mediterranean Sea to fight in Africa.

medium me·di·um (mē'dē·əm) being between long and tall or between big and small; of an average size; not large or small.
My father is tall, but my mother is of medium height. *adj.*

meet (mēt) to come together with someone; to join something; to be introduced to someone for the first time.
We will meet the teacher at the school on Saturday.
v. **met, met, meeting** meet·ing

a	cat	i	sit	oi	oil	ch	chop		a in about
ā	ate	ī	lie	ou	out	ng	song		e in oven
ä	car	o	pot	u	cut	sh	she	ə =	i in pencil
e	set	ō	old	u̇	book	th	three		o in memory
ē	equal	ô	or	ü	blue	ŦH	there		u in circus
ėr	germ					zh	treasure		

meeting   meet·ing (mēt⸴ing)   **1.** *v. pres. part.* See **meet.**
2. an event when people get together to talk about
a special thing.
We are having a meeting at school tonight. *n. pl.* **meetings** meet·ings

melt   (melt)   to change from a solid to a liquid.
The ice will melt into water. *v.* **melted, melted, melting** melt·ed, melt·ing

member   mem·ber (mem⸴bər)   **1.** a person who belongs to
a club or a group.
I am a member of a book club. *n.*
2. a part of a body.
My thumb is a member of my hand. *n. pl.* **members** mem·bers

memorable   mem·or·a·ble (mem⸴ər·ə·bəl)   something that is
important and that people should remember.
Getting the medal was a memorable event in my life. *adj.*

memorial   me·mo·ri·al (mə·môr⸴ē·əl *or* mə·mōr⸴ē·əl)   **1.** something
that is a reminder of an important event, thing or person.
The Statue of Liberty is a memorial to the freedom of the people
in America. *n. pl.* **memorials** me·mo·ri·als
2. having to do with a reminder of an important event,
person or thing.
The memorial parade was held yesterday. *adj.*

memorial

Memorial Day   Me·mo·ri·al Day (mə·môr⸴ē·əl   dā)   a holiday
for remembering the soldiers and sailors who have died
while protecting our country.
Memorial Day is celebrated at the end of May.

memory   mem·or·y (mem⸴ər·ē)   **1.** the ability to remember things.
My memory is not very good; I am always forgetting things. *n.*
2. the thing that a person or animal remembers.
The memory of eating my grandmother's food still makes me smile.
n. pl. **memories** mem·or·ies

men   (men)   *n. pl.* See **man** (1).

mental   men·tal (men⸴tl)   having to do with the mind; having
to do with thinking.
Meditation is a mental process. *adj.*

Mercury

mental health   men·tal health (men⸴tl   helth)   how one
feels about oneself and others.
My mental health is good because I do not worry about things.

mention   men·tion (men⸴shən)   to talk about something for a
short time; to speak of briefly.
I forgot to mention that Linda is not meeting us.
v. **mentioned, mentioned, mentioning** men·tioned, men·tion·ing

menu men·u (men′yü) the list of the foods that a restaurant sells.
The menu had so many foods listed that I had trouble making up my mind.
n. pl. **menus** men·us

meow me·ow (mē·ou′) the sound that a cat or a kitten makes.
I can hear the meow of the cat but I cannot see her. *n. pl.* **meows** me·ows

merchant mer·chant (mėr′chənt) **1.** a person who sells things.
The merchant at the shoe store told me where to find the shoes I want.
n. pl. **merchants** mer·chants
2. having to do with buying and selling things.
The merchant ships sail to and from other countries. *adj.*

Mercury Mer·cur·y (mėr′kyər·ē) the planet in the solar system that is closest to the sun.
Mercury is the smallest planet in the solar system. *n.*

mermaid

mermaid mer·maid (mėr′mād) an imaginary creature whose lower body looks like a fish and whose upper body looks like a woman.
There was a movie about a mermaid who fell in love with a real man.
n. pl. **mermaids** mer·maids

merrymaking mer·ry·mak·ing (mer′ē·mā·king) having fun; laughing.
The prince's merrymaking angered the queen. *n. no pl.*

mess (mes) a group of things thrown together with no order; an untidy place.
The children's room was a mess. *n. pl.* **messes** mess·es

message mes·sage (mes′ij) words or ideas that one person sends to another person.
There is a message for you in the letter from Don.
n. pl. **messages** mes·sag·es

mess

messenger mes·sen·ger (mes′n·jər) a person who carries information, words or ideas from one person to another person.
The messenger brought the telegram to the office.
n. pl. **messengers** mes·sen·gers

met (met) *v. pt. t., pt. part.* See **meet.**

a	cat	i	sit	oi	oil	ch	chop	ə = {	a in about
ā	ate	ī	lie	ou	out	ng	song		e in oven
ä	car	o	pot	u	cut	sh	she		i in pencil
e	set	ō	old	u̇	book	th	three		o in memory
ē	equal	ô	or	ü	blue	ŦH	there		u in circus
ėr	germ					zh	treasure		

metal   met·al (met⸍l)   **1.** a material that is hard and shiny, is an element and can be melted to change its shape.
The metal in a penny is copper; the metal in a dime is silver.
n. pl. **metals** met·als
2. being made of a hard, shiny element that can be melted to change its shape.
The metal desk is very heavy. *adj.*

metal detector   met·al de·tec·tor (met⸍l di·tek⸍tər)   a device that can find things that are made of metal.
We used a metal detector to find coins buried under the sand.

metal detector

meter   me·ter (mē⸍tər)   a device that measures something.
The gas meter on the house measures how much gas you use.
n. pl. **meters** me·ters

method   meth·od (meth⸍əd)   a certain way of doing something; the steps that a person follows to get something done.
Father has a strange method of ironing his shirts. *n. pl.* **methods** meth·ods

me too   (mē   tü)   I agree; include myself.
Jim said, "I want some milk." I said, "Me too."

Mexican   Mex·i·can (mek⸍sə·kən)   coming from or having to do with the country of Mexico.
Tacos are my favorite Mexican food. *adj.*

Mexico   Mex·i·co (mek⸍sə·kō)   a country that is south of the United States; its capital is Mexico City.
Mexico is on the continent of North America. *n.*

mg   (mil⸍ə·gram)   *abbrev.* See **milligram.**

mice   (mīs)   *n. pl.* See **mouse.**

microphone   mi·cro·phone (mī⸍krə·fōn)   a device that carries sound from one place to another place.
The microphone in a hearing aid carries the sound from the air to the amplifier. *n. pl.* **microphones** mi·cro·phones

microscope   mi·cro·scope (mī⸍krə·skōp)   a tool or instrument that uses a lens to make small things look bigger.
We cannot see a germ with our eyes, but we can see it with a microscope.
n. pl. **microscopes** mi·cro·scopes

microscopic   mi·cro·scop·ic (mī·krə·skop⸍ik)   tiny; so small that it can only be seen with a microscope.
A germ is microscopic. *adj.*

microphone

microscope

middle mid·dle (mid′l) **1.** the center area; the place that is half way from the beginning and half way from the end.
I sat in the middle of my bed and read a book. *n. no pl.*
2. between two things.
I was the middle person in line to buy ice cream. *adj.*
3. between two people in age.
I am a middle child. My brother is older than I am, and my sister is younger than I am. *adj.*

Middle East Mid·dle East (mid′l ēst) the part of the world between Egypt and Iran.
Much of our oil comes from the Middle East.

Middle Way Mid·dle Way (mid′l wā) a way of living where a person only has as much as he needs, no more and no less.
Buddha taught people the Middle Way.

midget midg·et (mij′it) smaller than normal size.
I want a midget car so that I can learn to park it in small spaces. *adj.*

midnight mid·night (mid′nīt) the time when one day becomes another day; 12 o'clock at night.
The new year begins at midnight on December 31.
n. pl. **midnights** mid·nights

middle

Midwest Mid·west (mid·west′) the part of the United States that is east of the Rocky Mountains and west of the Appalachian Mountains.
Illinois is one of the states in the Midwest. *n.*

might (mīt) *aux. pt. t.* See **may.**

mighty might·y (mī′tē) strong; having great power.
Superman is mighty. *adj.* **mightier, mightiest** might·i·er, might·i·est

migrate mi·grate (mī′grāt) **1.** to move from one place to another place when the season changes.
The birds will migrate to the south before winter starts. *v.*
2. to move from one place to another.
The gypsy will migrate from one town to another town.
v. **migrated, migrated, migrating** mi·grat·ed, mi·grat·ing

mildew mil·dew (mil′dü *or* mil′dyü) a kind of mold or fungus that grows on things that are wet for a long time.
If you give the plant too much water, it will get mildew on it. *n. no pl.*

midget

mile (mīl) a distance that equals 5,280 feet.
I can walk a mile in fifteen minutes. *n. pl.* **miles**

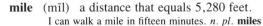

a	cat	**i**	sit	**oi**	oil	**ch**	chop		a in about
ā	ate	**ī**	lie	**ou**	out	**ng**	song		e in oven
ä	car	**o**	pot	**u**	cut	**sh**	she	**ə =**	i in pencil
e	set	**ō**	old	** u̇**	book	**th**	three		o in memory
ē	equal	**ô**	or	**ü**	blue	**ŦH**	there		u in circus
ėr	germ					**zh**	treasure		

mileage   mile·age (mī'lij)   the number of miles that a vehicle can go with only one gallon of fuel or gasoline.
The mileage of this new car is 39 miles per gallon.
n. pl. **mileages** mile·ag·es

miles per hour   (mīlz pər our)   a measurement of how fast a vehicle is going or traveling; how far a vehicle goes in one hour.
He drove the car at 70 miles per hour.

military   mil·i·tar·y (mil'ə·ter·ē)   **1.** people who protect a country; the Army, Navy, Air Force or Marines.
A general is an officer in the military. *n. no pl.*
2. having to do with the people that protect a country.
The military car led the parade. *adj.*

milk   (milk)   **1.** the white liquid that comes from a female animal and that is used to feed its children.
We drink the milk from the cow. *n. no pl.*
2. a white liquid that comes from some plants.
We drink coconut milk. *n. no pl.*
3. to take the white liquid from the inside of the animal.
The farmer will milk his cows early in the morning.
v. **milked, milked, milking** milk·ing

milk

mill   (mil)   **1.** a place where grain is ground into flour.
The farmers bring their wheat to the mill. *n.*
2. a place where things are made; a building used to manufacture things.
We bought the towels at the cotton mill. *n. pl.* **mills**

miller   mill·er (mil'ər)   a person who grinds grain into flour.
The miller will buy the wheat from the farmers. *n. pl.* **millers** mill·ers

milligram   mil·li·gram (mil'ə·gram)   a small unit of weight.
A milligram weighs less than an ounce. *n. pl.* **milligrams** mil·li·grams

millionaire   mil·lion·aire (mil·yə·ner' *or* mil·yə·nar')   a person who has one million dollars or more.
I would be a millionaire if I had a million dollars.
n. pl. **millionaires** mil·lion·aires

mime   (mīm)   **1.** to tell a story without words, only with gestures.
The man will mime the story of The Three Bears.
v. **mimed, mimed, miming** mim·ing
2. a person who tells a story without words, only with gestures.
The mime made us laugh when he played the bad wolf. *n. pl.* **mimes**

mime

mind   (mīnd)   the part of a person that knows, thinks, feels, wishes and decides.
John used his mind to make a good decision. *n. pl.* **minds**

miner

minute hand

mirror

mine (mīn) **1.** belonging to me; owned by me.
That red bicycle is mine. *pron.*
2. to take minerals out of the ground.
The men will mine the coal. *v.* **mined, mined, mining** min·ing
3. the place where minerals are taken out of the ground.
The mine is very deep. *n. pl.* **mines**

miner min·er (mī′nər) a person who takes minerals
from the ground.
The miner found the gold. *n. pl.* **miners** min·ers

Ming (ming) having to do with a royal dynasty that ruled
China from 1368 to 1644.
The Ming vase is very rare and very expensive. *adj.*

minute min·ute (min′it) a unit of time that equals 60 seconds; one
of 60 time units that make up an hour.
The timer on the stove rang after one minute. *n. pl.* **minutes** min·utes

minute hand min·ute hand (min′it hand) the long arm on the
face of a clock or watch that tells how many minutes have
passed since the hour started.
The minute hand goes around the face of the clock one time every hour.

miracle mir·a·cle (mir′ə·kəl) something that happens that cannot
be explained because it does not follow the rules of nature.
The doctor said that it is a miracle that Carol is walking again.
n. pl. **miracles** mir·a·cles

mirror mir·ror (mir′ər) a piece of glass that is covered with silver
and that reflects or shows what is in front of it.
I looked into the mirror to comb my hair. *n. pl.* **mirrors** mir·rors

mischief mis·chief (mis′chif) **1.** actions that make people mad
or that cause trouble or harm.
Tim is always causing mischief. *n. no pl.*
2. playful trouble; tricks; fun.
The campers will get into mischief this week. *n. no pl.*

mischievous mis·chie·vous (mis′chə·vəs) playful; full of
tricks; clever in playing tricks or pranks.
One of the mischievous things they will do is have a water fight. *adj.*

miserable mis·er·a·ble (miz′ər·ə·bəl) very unhappy; very
sad; feeling very bad.
Todd is miserable because his dog is lost. *adj.*

a	cat	i	sit	oi	oil	ch	chop		a in about
ā	ate	ī	lie	ou	out	ng	song		e in oven
ä	car	o	pot	u	cut	sh	she	ə =	i in pencil
e	set	ō	old	u̇	book	th	three		o in memory
ē	equal	ô	or	ü	blue	ŦH	there		u in circus
ėr	germ					zh	treasure		

misery mis·er·y (miz⸱ər·ē) an unhappy way of life;
  unhappy feelings.
> His misery will disappear when he finds the dog. *n. pl.* **miseries** mis·er·ies

misleading mis·lead·ing (mis·lē⸱ding) giving the wrong
  information or idea.
> The newspaper wrote a misleading story about the fire. *adj.*

miss (mis) **1.** to not get; to not hit.
> Please don't miss the ball. *v.*

2. to feel bad because someone is not present.
> I miss my friends. *v.*

3. to not reach; to let get away.
> My toy plane will miss the balloon. *v.*

4. to not meet; to arrive at the wrong time.
> I hope I do not miss my bus. *v.*

5. to not be present; to be absent from.
> If I am late I will miss history class. *v.* **missed, missed, missing** miss·ing

6. the act of not hitting.
> This was his second miss. *n. pl.* **misses** miss·es

7. Miss; the title or name given to a woman who is not married.
> My teacher is Miss Jones. *adj.*

8. an unmarried girl or woman.
> The young miss left her purse. *n. pl.* **misses** miss·es

mistletoe berry

missing miss·ing (mis⸱ing) not here; not present; absent; gone.
> The missing dog was found in the park. *adj.*

misspell mis·spell (mis·spel′) to not spell a word correctly.
> I always misspell the word "writing."
> *v.* **misspelled, misspelled, misspelling** mis·spelled, mis·spell·ing

mistake mis·take (mə·stāk′) an error; a wrong action or answer.
> I made only one mistake on the math test. *n. pl.* **mistakes** mis·takes

mitten

mistletoe berry mis·tle·toe ber·ry (mis⸱əl·tō ber⸱ē) the fruit
  of a mistletoe plant, which is harmful if eaten because
  it is poisonous.
> Do not eat the mistletoe berry.

mistress mis·tress (mis⸱tris) a female owner of a house.
> The mistress told the servants what to do to get ready for the party.
> *n. pl.* **mistresses** mis·tress·es

misunderstanding mis·un·der·stand·ing (mis·un·dər·stan⸱ding)
  a disagreement; a small fight or argument.
> We had a misunderstanding about who was to get the new bicycle.
> *n. pl.* **misunderstandings** mis·un·der·stand·ings

mobile home

mitten mit·ten (mit⸱n) a covering for the hand that does not have
  separate places for the fingers.
> The mitten was easy to put on the baby. *n. pl.* **mittens** mit·tens

mix (miks) **1.** dry ingredients that are already measured and blended together.
I used a cake mix to make this cake. *n. pl.* **mixes** mix·es
2. to blend or stir together.
I will mix the eggs and the flour. *v.* **mixed, mixed, mixing** mix·ing

mixed (mikst) **1.** not pure; being made of more than one thing.
The mixed breed dog was part collie and part German shepherd. *adj.*
2. not just men or just women; both men and women.
The mixed dances were fun. *adj.*
3. *v. pt. t., pt. part.* See **mix** (2).

moccasin

mixed up (mikst up) not sure about what you think; confused.
I am so mixed up that I can't decide what to do. *adj.*

mixture mix·ture (miks'chər) **1.** ingredients that have been stirred or blended.
I added milk to the egg and flour mixture. *n.*
2. a combination of things or people; a sample of many kinds of things or people.
There is a mixture of people living in America. *n. pl.* **mixtures** mix·tures

mobile mo·bile (mō'bəl) easy to move; having to do with moving things.
The mobile trailer is great for camping. *adj.*

mobile home mo·bile home (mō'bəl hōm) a house that can be moved; a house trailer.
The truck pulled the mobile home into the lot.

moccasin moc·ca·sin (mok'ə·sən) a soft shoe made of leather.
Indians made and wore moccasins. *n. pl.* **moccasins** moc·ca·sins

model mod·el (mod'l) **1.** a small copy of something.
We made a model of the airplane that Dad flew in the Air Force. *n.*
2. a person who poses for photographers; a person who is paid to have his or her picture taken.
The model waited for the camera to flash. *n. pl.* **models** mod·els
3. having to do with being a small copy of something.
The model airplane could really fly. *adj.*

model

modern mod·ern (mod'ərn) new; current; up to date; not old fashioned.
Some modern furniture is small and straight. *adj.*

a	cat	**i**	sit	**oi**	oil	**ch**	chop
ā	ate	**ī**	lie	**ou**	out	**ng**	song
ä	car	**o**	pot	**u**	cut	**sh**	she
e	set	**ō**	old	**u̇**	book	**th**	three
ē	equal	**ô**	or	**ü**	blue	**TH**	there
ėr	germ					**zh**	treasure

ə = {
a in about
e in oven
i in pencil
o in memory
u in circus
}

modified mod·i·fied (mod′ə·fīd) a little changed; slightly different.
The modified desk is shorter. *adj.*

Mohawk Mo·hawk (mō′hôk) a tribe of Indians who once lived
in the United States.
The Mohawk lived in the state of New York. *plural n.*

moist (moist) a little wet; damp; not dried.
The cake is moist. *adj.*

moisture mois·ture (mois′chər) wetness; the wetness in the
air or on the ground.
The moisture on the ground in warm weather is called dew; the
moisture on the ground in cold weather is called frost. *n. no pl.*

mollusk

mold (mōld) **1.** a fungus that grows on food and is
usually green in color.
The bread has mold on it. *n. pl.* **molds**
2. to shape or form something.
I will mold a horse out of the clay. *v.*
3. to get a fungus on something.
The bread will mold if it gets moisture on it.
v. **molded, molded, molding** mold·ed, mold·ing

mollusk mol·lusk (mol′əsk) any of a large group of animals that
have a soft body covered with a hard shell.
An oyster is a mollusk. *n. pl.* **mollusks** mol·lusks

molten mol·ten (mōlt′n) melted by heat; made liquid by heat.
Lava is molten rock. *adj.*

mom (mom) mother; mama.
My mom is making dinner. *n. pl.* **moms**

money

moment mo·ment (mō′mənt) a small period of time; a short time.
I know that John was here a moment ago. *n. pl.* **moments** mo·ments

mommy mom·my (mom′ē) mother; mama; mom.
The baby wanted her mommy. *n. pl.* **mommies** mom·mies

monarch mon·arch (mon′ərk) the ruler of a country;
a king or a queen.
Queen Elizabeth is the monarch of England. *n. pl.* **monarchs** mon·archs

monarchy mon·ar·chy (mon′ər·kē) a government that a king
or queen controls or rules.
England is a monarchy. *n. pl.* **monarchies** mon·ar·chies

money mon·ey (mun′ē) coins and dollar bills that people
use to buy and sell things.
I will use the money in my bank account for college.
n. pl. **moneys** *or* **monies** mon·eys *or* mon·ies

monkey

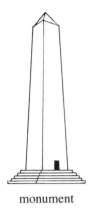

monument

moose

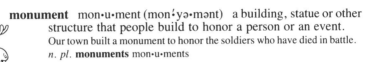

mop

money counter mon·ey coun·ter (mun⟋ē koun⟋tər) a person whose job is to count money.
The king's money counter did not see the clothes.

monkey mon·key (mung⟋kē) a kind of mammal that has a long tail, is covered with fur and walks on two legs.
The monkey wrapped his tail around the branch of the tree. *n. pl.* **monkeys** mon·keys

monster mon·ster (mon⟋stər) any imaginary animal that is mean and ugly.
The monster tried to catch the knight. *n. pl.* **monsters** mon·sters

month (munth) a measure of time that is about 30 days; one of the 12 parts of the year.
We went to see the desert last month. *n. pl.* **months**

monument mon·u·ment (mon⟋yə·mənt) a building, statue or other structure that people build to honor a person or an event.
Our town built a monument to honor the soldiers who have died in battle. *n. pl.* **monuments** mon·u·ments

moody mood·y (mü⟋dē) having changes in the way a person feels; emotionally changing.
Sue is a moody person. First she is happy, and then she is sad.
adj. **moodier, moodiest** mood·i·er, mood·i·est

moon (mün) a satellite of a planet.
The Earth's moon goes around the Earth in 29 days. *n. pl.* **moons**

moonlight moon·light (mün⟋līt) the shine or light from the moon.
The moonlight was so bright that we could see without a flashlight.
n. no pl.

moose (müs) an animal that looks like a large deer, is a mammal and lives in the forest.
The male moose has large antlers or horns. *n. pl.* **moose**

mop (mop) **1.** a tool that a person uses to clean the floor and that is made of cloth or sponge at the end of a long handle.
I rinsed the mop in the bucket. *n. pl.* **mops**
2. to clean the floor with a long-handled cleaning tool.
I will mop the kitchen floor for mother.
v. **mopped, mopped, mopping** mop·ping

a	cat	i	sit	oi	oil	ch	chop		a in about
ā	ate	ī	lie	ou	out	ng	song		e in oven
ä	car	o	pot	u	cut	sh	she	ə =	i in pencil
e	set	ō	old	u̇	book	th	three		o in memory
ē	equal	ô	or	ü	blue	ŦH	there		u in circus
ėr	germ					zh	treasure		

more (môr *or* mōr) **1.** *comp. adj.* See **many.**
    2. *comp. adj.* See **much.**
    3. additionally; further.
    She read the book once more. *adv.*
    4. a greater amount, degree or number of something.
    Tell me more about your trip. *n. no pl.*

morning morn·ing (môr⸴ning) the part of the day before 12 o'clock
    noon; the early part of the day.
    I woke up early this morning. *n. pl.* **mornings** morn·ings

morning star morn·ing star (môr⸴ning stär) a bright planet,
    Venus, that is seen in the sky just before sunrise.
    I saw the morning star when I woke up.

mortal mor·tal (môr⸴tl) not living forever; being able to die.
    Man is a mortal being. *adj.*

mortar mor·tar (môr⸴tər) the cement or paste that is between
    bricks to hold them together.
    The mortar will dry in a few hours. *n. no pl.*

mosquito

mosquito mos·qui·to (mə·skē⸴tō) a kind of insect that has
    two wings and whose bite causes itching.
    The female mosquito bites people to get blood to feed its eggs.
    n. pl. **mosquitoes** *or* **mosquitos** mos·qui·toes *or* mos·qui·tos

moss (môs *or* mos) small green or brown plants that
    grow close together.
    The moss is growing on the old apple tree. *n. pl.* **mosses** moss·es

most (mōst) **1.** *superl. adj.* See **many.**
    2. *superl. adj.* See **much.**
    3. the greatest amount or number; almost all.
    I ate most of the cookies. *n.*

most of the time (mōst əv ᴛнə tīm) often; usually.
    Most of the time I go right home after school.

moth (môth *or* moth) any of a family of insects that have
    wide wings and fly at night.
    The moth flew right into the light. *n. pl.* **moths**

moth

mother moth·er (muᴛн⸴ər) **1.** Mother; the name a child
    calls a female parent.
    I heard Lisa calling "Mother! Mother, where are you?" *n.*
    2. the female parent of a child or animal.
    The mother watched the baby bird learn to fly. *n. pl.* **mothers** moth·ers
    3. having to do with the female parent of a child or animal.
    The mother bird watched the baby bird learn to fly. *adj.*

Mother Nature moth·er na·ture (muᴛʜ⁄ər nā⁄chər)
the things around the world that people do not create or
control; the forces that keep the world going; the
non-changing laws of nature.
Mother Nature controls the amount of rain that the Earth gets.

motion picture mo·tion pic·ture (mō⁄shən pik⁄chər) **1.** a movie.
I saw the motion picture "E. T."
2. having to do with a movie or making a movie.
The motion picture company that made that movie was very smart.

mount (mount) **1.** to get on an animal.
I will mount the horse by myself. *v.*
2. to put something on something else; to attach something.
I will mount the horn on the bicycle.
v. **mounted, mounted, mounting** mount·ed, mount·ing
3. Mount; used before the name of a high hill or a mountain.
We will climb Mount Rainier. *n. pl.* **mounts**

mount

mountain moun·tain (moun⁄tən) **1.** a very tall hill or
mound of dirt and rocks.
We climbed the mountain and had lunch at the top.
n. pl. **mountains** moun·tains
2. having to do with a very tall hill.
The mountain road has many curves. *adj.*

mountain goat moun·tain goat (moun⁄tən gōt) a white goat
that lives in the high mountains.
The mountain goat is difficult to see in the winter.

mountain goat

mountain range moun·tain range (moun⁄tən rānj) a group of
mountains that are close to each other; a row of mountains.
The mountain range goes from the northern part of the state to
the southern part.

mountainside moun·tain·side (moun⁄tən·sīd) the slope or side
of the mountain below the top.
The mountainside is covered with wildflowers.
n. pl. **mountainsides** moun·tain·sides

mouse

mouse (mous) a small animal with a long, thin tail,
a pointed nose and fur.
The mouse is an animal that lives in fields or in houses.
n. pl. **mice**

a	cat	i	sit	oi	oil	ch	chop		a in about
ā	ate	ī	lie	ou	out	ng	song		e in oven
ä	car	o	pot	u	cut	sh	she	ə =	i in pencil
e	set	ō	old	u̇	book	th	three		o in memory
ē	equal	ô	or	ü	blue	ᴛʜ	there		u in circus
ėr	germ					zh	treasure		

mousetrap   mouse·trap (mous′trap)   a tool that people use
   to catch mice.
      There was a mouse in one mousetrap.
      n. pl. **mousetraps** mouse·traps

moustache   mous·tache (mus′tash *or* mə·stash′)   *n.* See **mustache.**

mouth   (mouth)   the part of the body that a person uses
   for taking in food.
      Please close your mouth when you are chewing food. *n. pl.* **mouths**

move   (müv)   **1.** to start in motion; to go.
      The bicycle will move when you pedal it. *v.*
      2. to change the place or position of something.
      I will move the bicycle out of the driveway. *v.*
      3. to change from one house to another house; to change from
      one place to another place.
      We will move to Chicago next month. *v.* **moved, moved, moving** mov·ing

movement   move·ment (müv′mənt)   the action of moving;
   the act of moving.
      We can see the movement of the hand on the clock.
      n. pl. **movements** move·ments

mover   mov·er (mü′vər)   a person who carries things from one
   house or place to another house or place.
      The mover took our furniture to the new house in Chicago.
      n. pl. **movers** mov·ers

movie   mov·ie (mü′vē)   pictures of people and things that are moved
   quickly through a projector and shown on a screen as a story
   with moving people and things; a motion picture; a film.
      I saw the movie "E. T." *n. pl.* **movies** mov·ies

movie house   mov·ie house (mü′vē   hous)   a place where films or
   motion pictures are shown; a theater.
      I like to go to the new movie house.

moving   mov·ing (mü′ving)   *v. pres. part.* See **move.**

moving stairway   mov·ing stair·way (mü′ving   ster′wā)
   steps that move; an escalator.
      The moving stairway took the shoppers to the second floor of the store.

moving truck   mov·ing truck (mü′ving   truk)   the vehicle
   that people use to take things from one place or house
   to another place or house.
      The moving truck will bring our furniture to the new house.

mph, m.p.h.   (mīlz pər our)   *abbrev.* See **miles per hour.**

Mr.   (mis′tər)   Mister; a title for an adult man used
   before his last name.
      Mr. Jones is married to my history teacher. *abbrev. pl.* **Messrs.**

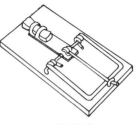

mousetrap

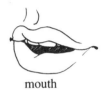

mouth

moving truck

Mrs. (mis‑iz) the title that comes before a married lady's name; the title given to a married woman.
Mrs. Jones is my favorite teacher. *abbrev. pl.* **Mmes.**

Ms. (miz) a title for an adult woman that is used before her last name.
Ms. Smith is the new math teacher. *abbrev. pl.* **Mses.**

Mt. (mount) *abbrev.* See **mount** (3). *pl.* **Mts.**

much (much) **1.** great in amount or number.
We do not have much time to get to the movie. *adj.* **more, most**
2. a great amount or number.
I did not eat much for lunch. *n. no pl.*
3. in a great degree.
My dog runs much faster than I do. *adv.*

much-loved (much‑luvd) liked greatly; liked by many.
The much-loved movie star waved to the fans. *adj.*

mud

mud (mud) wet dirt; soft and sticky wet dirt.
Please take the mud off of your shoes. *n. no pl.*

muddy mud·dy (mud‑ē) full of or covered with soft and sticky wet dirt.
The shoes are very muddy. *adj.* **muddier, muddiest** mud·di·er, mud·di·est

muffle muf·fle (muf‑əl) to cover sound or a source of sound so the sound is not loud; to soften sound.
I put the telephone under a pillow to muffle its ringing noise.
v. **muffled, muffled, muffling** muf·fled, muf·fling

mulch (mulch) a material such as straw, leaves or sawdust put around plants to keep the soil damp and to protect them from cold and heat.
We put mulch around the tree. *n. no pl.*

mule

mule (myül) an animal that is half horse and half donkey.
People say that a mule is very stubborn and will never do what it is told to do. *n. pl.* **mules**

multiply mul·ti·ply (mul‑tə·plī) to grow in number and amount; to reproduce.
The animals will multiply quickly.
v. **multiplied, multiplied, multiplying** mul·ti·plied, mul·ti·ply·ing

a	cat	i	sit	oi	oil	ch	chop		a in about
ā	ate	ī	lie	ou	out	ng	song		e in oven
ä	car	o	pot	u	cut	sh	she	ə =	i in pencil
e	set	ō	old	ů	book	th	three		o in memory
ē	equal	ô	or	ü	blue	̣TH	there		u in circus
ėr	germ					zh	treasure		

munch (munch) to make noise when eating; to eat noisily.
I will munch on these carrots.
v. **munched, munched, munching** munch·ing

muscle mus·cle (mus′əl) a meaty or fleshy part of the body that moves the other parts of the body.
I hurt a muscle in my back. *n. pl.* **muscles** mus·cles

muscular mus·cu·lar (mus′kyə·lər) having large muscles; being strong.
The carpenter is very muscular. *adj.*

museum mu·se·um (myü·zē′əm) a building where old or rare things are kept safe and displayed for people to see.
The museum of art has many old paintings. *n. pl.* **museums** mu·se·ums

mushroom

mushroom mush·room (mush′rüm *or* mush′rùm) a small fungus that is shaped like an umbrella and that grows quickly.
This mushroom is safe to eat, but some are not.
n. pl. **mushrooms** mush·rooms

music mu·sic (myü′zik) **1.** an arrangement or pattern of sounds that is pleasing or interesting to hear.
I like piano music. *n. no pl.*
2. having to do with the arrangement or patterns of sounds that are pleasing to hear.
I am taking music lessons. *adj.*

musical mu·si·cal (myü′zə·kəl) **1.** a movie or play that has lots of music in it.
I saw the musical "The Wizard of Oz." *n. pl.* **musicals** mu·si·cals
2. having to do with music.
The musical play had many people singing and dancing. *adj.*

mustache

music box mu·sic box (myü′zik boks) a case that has a small machine inside that plays music.
The music box plays "Whistle While You Work."

must (must *or* məst) **1.** need to.
People must eat to grow. *aux.*
2. should.
I must be going now. *aux.*
3. ought to.
You did a good job. You must have a reward. *aux.*

mustache mus·tache (mus′tash *or* mə·stash′) hair that grows between the nose and the mouth on a man's face.
My father grew a mustache. *n. pl.* **mustaches** mus·tach·es

mustang mus·tang (mus′tang) a small wild horse that lives in the western United States.
The man caught a mustang. *n. pl.* **mustangs** mus·tangs

mutt

mustard mus·tard (mus′tərd) a yellow food that is made from the seed of a plant and tastes hot or spicy.
I put mustard on my hot dog. *n. no pl.*

mutt (mut) a dog that is a mixture of breeds; a dog whose breed is not known.
His dog is a mutt, but it is cute. *n. pl.* **mutts**

muzzle muz·zle (muz′əl) the part of an animal's head that includes the mouth, nose and jaws.
The cat scratched the dog's muzzle. *n. pl.* **muzzles** muz·zles

muzzle

my (mī) belonging to me; mine.
I lost my ring. *adj.*

mydas fly my·das fly (mī′dəs flī) a kind of insect that is large and has an orange ring around its body.
A mydas fly will eat dead trees.

myself my·self (mī·self′) that very same person that is I.
I hurt myself on the bicycle. *pron.*

mysterious mys·ter·i·ous (mi·stir′ē·əs) full of secrets; something that cannot be explained; strange.
Magic is mysterious. *adj.*

mystery mys·ter·y (mis′tər·ē) something that is not known; a secret.
I do not know what happened to my ring. It is a mystery.
n. pl. **mysteries** mys·ter·ies

myth (mith) a story that tries to explain why something exists or how something in nature came to be.
The myth about Cupid tries to explain how love came to be on Earth.
n. pl. **myths**

mydas fly

a	cat	**i**	sit	**oi**	oil	**ch**	chop		a in about
ā	ate	**ī**	lie	**ou**	out	**ng**	song		e in oven
ä	car	**o**	pot	**u**	cut	**sh**	she	ə =	i in pencil
e	set	**ō**	old	**u̇**	book	**th**	three		o in memory
ē	equal	**ô**	or	**ü**	blue	**ᵀH**	there		u in circus
ėr	germ					**zh**	treasure		

Nn

nag (nag) to blame someone; to pester someone; to always find fault with someone.
> Mother will nag me until I take out the garbage.
> *v.* **nagged, nagged, nagging** nag·ging

nagging nag·ging (nag′ing) *v. pres. part.* See **nag.**

nail (nāl) **1.** a small piece of metal that has a point on one end and that is used to fasten two things together.
> Dad fixed the broken chair with a nail. *n.*
> **2.** the hard end of a finger or a toe.
> I broke a nail trying to open the can. *n. pl.* **nails.**
> **3.** to hang something or put two things together with a small piece of metal.
> I will nail the picture to the wall. *v.* **nailed, nailed, nailing** nail·ing

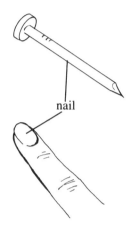

nail

name (nām) **1.** the word or words that tell what a thing is.
> The name for this insect is "spider." *n.*
> **2.** the identifying word for a person; a word that tells what a person is called.
> Her name is Lisa, and she is six years old. *n. pl.* **names**
> **3.** to give an identifying word to a person.
> Mother and Father decided to name the baby Susan. *v.*
> **4.** to give information; to tell facts.
> I can name all the states in the United States.
> *v.* **named, named, naming** nam·ing

nanny nan·ny (nan′ē) a person who takes care of a child and lives with the family.
> In England, some children have a nanny. *n. pl.* **nannies** nan·nies

nap (nap) a short sleep.
> I am very tired. I think I will take a nap. *n. pl.* **naps**

napkin

napkin nap·kin (nap′kin) a piece of paper or cloth that a person uses to clean the face and hands while eating food.
> I put a napkin on the left side of each plate. *n. pl.* **napkins** nap·kins

narrow nar·row (nar′ō) not wide; small in width.
> The paintbrush is narrow.
> *adj.* **narrower, narrowest** nar·row·er, nar·row·est

nasty nas·ty (nas′tē) not nice; mean; bad.
> That boy is nasty; he took my candy.
> *adj.* **nastier, nastiest** nas·ti·er, nas·ti·est

narrow

nation na·tion (nā′shən) a country.
> There are fifty states in our nation. *n. pl.* **nations** na·tions

naturalist

national na·tion·al (nash′ə·nəl) **1.** having to do with a
country or a nation.
Our national flag is red, white, and blue. *adj.*
2. having people from many different parts of the country.
The national car race was held in May. *adj.*

native na·tive (nā′tiv) **1.** one of the first people to live in a country.
The Indian is a native of America. *n.*
2. a person who was born in a certain country.
James was born in England. He is a native of England.
n. pl. **natives** na·tives

natural nat·ur·al (nach′ər·əl) **1.** having to do with nature; having
to do with the forces that make things happen on Earth.
The river made that natural bridge by eroding a hill of rocks. *adj.*
2. made by nature, not by man.
We only eat natural foods. *adj.*

natural gas nat·ur·al gas (nach′ər·əl gas) a form of energy that is
found under the ground in some parts of the world.
We use natural gas to heat our home.

naturalist nat·ur·al·ist (nach′ər·ə·list) a person who loves and
studies nature; a person who studies animals and places.
John Audubon was a naturalist. *n. pl.* **naturalists** nat·ur·al·ists

natural setting nat·ur·al set·ting (nach′ər·əl set′ing) the
place that is normal to a person or an animal; the place in
which an animal usually lives.
A forest is the natural setting for an owl.

nature na·ture (nā′chər) **1.** the things in the world that people do
not make or control; the forces that keep the world going and
that people cannot control or change.
Nature controls the weather. The weather is part of nature. *n. no pl.*
2. a characteristic or a trait; the way a person acts.
It is Virginia's nature to be quiet. *n. pl.* **natures** na·tures

naughty naugh·ty (nô′tē) bad; not pleasant.
You have been naughty all day.
adj. **naughtier, naughtiest** naugh·ti·er, naugh·ti·est

naughty

a	cat	i	sit	oi	oil	ch	chop		a in about
ā	ate	ī	lie	ou	out	ng	song		e in oven
ä	car	o	pot	u	cut	sh	she	ə =	i in pencil
e	set	ō	old	u̇	book	th	three		o in memory
ē	equal	ô	or	ü	blue	ŦH	there		u in circus
ėr	germ					zh	treasure		

navy   na·vy (nā:vē)   **1.** the part of a government that protects the country with sailors and large ships.
> Many countries have a navy. *n. pl.* **navies** na·vies
> **2.** the navy of a particular country.
> My cousin is a sailor in the United States Navy. *n. no pl.*
> **3.** a color that is dark blue.
> I wore a navy shirt today. *adj.*

near   (nir)   **1.** close by; not far away from.
> I live near the ocean. *prep.*
> **2.** within a short distance.
> He lives very near. *adv.*
> **3.** almost now; close in time; soon.
> In the near future we will use robots to do our work.
> *adj.* **nearer, nearest** near·er, near·est

nearby   near·by (nir:bī)   **1.** close; not far away.
> I live nearby so I will see you again. *adv.*
> **2.** close; not far.
> We are going to a nearby town for a picnic. *adj.*

nearly   near·ly (nir:lē)   almost; very close to.
> Jim is nearly 6 feet tall; he is 5 feet and 11½ inches tall. *adv.*

neat   (nēt)   not messy; clean and in order.
> Your room is always neat. *adj.* **neater, neatest** neat·er, neat·est

neatly   neat·ly (nēt:lē)   in a clean and orderly way.
> He neatly put the sweater in the drawer. *adv.*

necessary   nec·es·sar·y (nes:ə·ser·ē)   needed; something one must have or do.
> It is necessary that I get home quickly. *adj.*

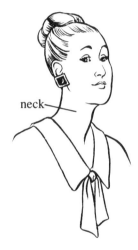

neck

neck   (nek)   the part of the body that joins the body to the head; the part of the body that joins the head to the shoulders.
> The giraffe's neck is long. *n. pl.* **necks**

necklace   neck·lace (nek:lis)   a decoration worn around the neck.
> I wore a necklace made of shells. *n. pl.* **necklaces** neck·lac·es

nectar   nec·tar (nek:tər)   juice that comes from flowers.
> Bees make honey from the flower's nectar. *n. pl.* **nectars** nec·tars

need   (nēd)   **1.** to want; to want to have.
> I need a new bicycle.
> *v.* **needed, needed, needing** need·ed, need·ing
> **2.** something that a person must have; something that a person cannot live without.
> Water is the most important need of the body. *n. pl.* **needs**

necklace

need to   (nēd   tü)   must; have to.
> I need to get home before it gets dark. *aux.*

nest

Negro Ne·gro (nē⸴grō) **1.** a person who was born in or whose family was born in Africa and who has dark brown skin.
The slave was a Negro. *n. pl.* **Negroes** Ne·groes
2. having to do with a person who has dark brown skin and whose family once came from Africa.
The Negro slaves were not treated well. *adj.*

neighbor neigh·bor (nā⸴bər) **1.** a person who lives near another person.
My neighbor mowed my grass when he mowed his.
n. pl. **neighbors** neigh·bors
2. being next to or near.
The neighbor countries of America are Canada and Mexico. *adj.*

neighborhood neigh·bor·hood (nā⸴bər·hùd) the area around a home or a building.
Our neighborhood has a park with a swimming pool.
n. pl. **neighborhoods** neigh·bor·hoods

neighboring neigh·bor·ing (nā⸴bər·ing *or* nā⸴bring) near; close.
The neighboring forest has many wild animals in it. *adj.*

neither nei·ther (nē⸴тнər *or* nī⸴тнər) not one or the other.
Joe and Pam like most food, but neither one likes beets. *adj.*

neither ___ nor ___ nei·ther ___ nor ___ (nē⸴тнər ___ nôr ___)
not one or the other; not either of the two.
Neither Lisa nor I look like my father. *conj.*

Neptune

Neptune Nep·tune (nep⸴tün *or* nep⸴tyün) a planet in the solar system that is the eighth one away from the sun.
Neptune is the fourth largest planet in our solar system. *n.*

nervous nerv·ous (nėr⸴vəs) scared; upset; excited; jumpy.
I was so nervous about the test that I forgot to put my name on my paper. *adj.*

nervously nerv·ous·ly (nėr⸴vəs·lē) in a scared, excited or upset way.
I nervously walked into the dark hall. *adv.*

nest (nest) a home for a bird or animal.
The bird's nest has one egg in it. *n. pl.* **nests**

net (net) a tool that is made out of a woven cloth with tiny holes in it and a handle.
Tom used a net to catch a butterfly. *n. pl.* **nets**

net

a	cat	i	sit	oi	oil	ch	chop		a in about
ā	ate	ī	lie	ou	out	ng	song		e in oven
ä	car	o	pot	u	cut	sh	she	ə =	i in pencil
e	set	ō	old	ù	book	th	three		o in memory
ē	equal	ô	or	ü	blue	ᴛʜ	there		u in circus
ėr	germ					zh	treasure		

neutral neu·tral (nü⸱trəl *or* nyü⸱trəl) taking no side in an
   argument or in a war; in the middle.
   Switzerland is a neutral country. *adj.*

never nev·er (nev⸱ər) at no time; not ever.
   I did not like the circus. I will never go to another one. *adv.*

nevertheless nev·er·the·less (nev·ər·ᴛʜə·les′)
   still; however; anyway.
   When someone is mean to you, you should be kind nevertheless. *adv.*

new (nü *or* nyü) **1.** not old; just opened or just bought.
   I have a new bicycle. *adj.*
   2. recent; up-to-date; modern; just invented.
   The new car is much smaller than the others. *adj.*
   3. one more; an additional one.
   Mother bought a new book for the library.
   adj. **newer, newest** new·er, new·est

New Brunswick New Bruns·wick (nü brunz⸱wik) a province
   (state) in the country of Canada; its capital is Fredericton.
   There is good fishing in New Brunswick. *n.*

Newfoundland New·found·land (nü⸱fənd·lənd *or* nü·found⸱lənd)
   a province (state) in the country of Canada; its capital
   is St. John's.
   It gets very cold in Newfoundland. *n.*

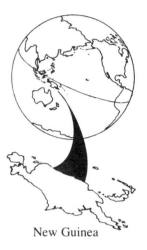
New Guinea

New Guinea New Guin·ea (nü gin⸱ē) an island country
   in the Pacific Ocean.
   New Guinea is near Australia. *n.*

news (nüz *or* nyüz) **1.** information; the most recent events
   or happenings in the world.
   The news of her death made me very sad. *n. no pl.*
   2. having to do with the latest information about
   what is happening.
   The news program said that the fire had stopped burning. *adj.*

newspaper news·pa·per (nüz⸱pā·pər *or* nyüz⸱pā·pər) **1.** sheets
   of paper that have information about what has happened
   printed on them.
   I read the front page of the newspaper every morning.
   n. pl. **newspapers** news·pa·pers
   2. having to do with the paper that has the news printed on it.
   The newspaper boy brings it early in the morning. *adj.*

newspaper

New Year's Eve (nü yirz ēv) the last day of the year; a holiday
   that celebrates the beginning of the new year.
   December 31 is New Year's Eve.

New Zealand

New Zealand New Zea·land (nü zē⸍lənd) an island country in the Pacific Ocean; its capital is Wellington.
New Zealand is near Australia.

next (nekst) **1.** nearest; closest.
Jerry lives in the next house. *adj.*
2. following in time; after this.
Next Monday is my birthday. *adj.*
3. following in time; coming after this.
We will visit the monkeys next. *adv.*

next door (nekst dôr) the house nearest this one; the home beside this one.
I live next door.

next to (nekst tü) nearest to; beside; closest to.
I stood next to Troy. *prep.*

nibble nib·ble (nib⸍əl) a very small bite.
I had a nibble of your sandwich. *n. pl.* **nibbles** nib·bles

nice (nīs) good; pleasant.
The new girl in school is very nice. *adj.* **nicer, nicest** nic·er, nic·est

nickel nick·el (nik⸍əl) a coin that equals five cents or five pennies.
I found a nickel. *n. pl.* **nickels** nick·els

nickelodeon nick·el·o·de·on (nik·ə·lō⸍dē·ən) one of the first movie houses, where the first films were shown.
It cost only five cents to get into a nickelodeon.
n. pl. **nickelodeons** nick·el·o·de·ons

nickel

niece (nēs) the daughter of a sister or a brother.
My brother's daughter is my niece. *n. pl.* **nieces** niec·es

night (nīt) **1.** the time of day between sunset and sunrise; the time of day when it is dark.
We can see the moon at night. *n. pl.* **nights**
2. having to do with the time of day between sunset and sunrise.
My brother is going to night school. *adj.*

Nightingale, Florence Night·in·gale, Flo·rence (nīt⸍n·gāl, flôr⸍əns) a nurse who made the job of nursing better and easier.
Florence Nightingale improved nursing.

a	cat	**i**	sit	**oi**	oil	**ch**	chop	a in about
ā	ate	**ī**	lie	**ou**	out	**ng**	song	e in oven
ä	car	**o**	pot	**u**	cut	**sh**	she	ə = { i in pencil
e	set	**ō**	old	**ù**	book	**th**	three	o in memory
ē	equal	**ô**	or	**ü**	blue	**ŦH**	there	u in circus
ėr	germ					**zh**	treasure	

nightly   night·ly (nīt′lē)   every evening; every night.
> I watch television nightly. *adv.*

nightshade   night·shade (nīt′shād)   a plant with red flowers and black berries that are poisonous.
> Belladonna is another name for nightshade.
> *n. pl.* **nightshades** night·shades

nighttime   night·time (nīt′tīm)   the time of day when it is dark; the time of day between sunset and sunrise.
> In the summer it gets cool in the nighttime. *n. pl.* **nighttimes** night·times

nightshade

no   (nō)   **1.** a command to stop; a command to not do something.
> No! Don't put your hand on the stove. *adv.*

2. not at all, not any.
> We have no more milk. *adv.*

3. an answer to a question meaning not doing, not going, not wanting, not agreeing, etc.
> Do you want more milk? No. *adv.*

4. not one; not any.
> No person can know everything. *adj.*

noble   no·ble (nō′bəl)   **1.** coming from a royal family; having a title.
> The noble prince loved the maiden. *adj.*

2. high-minded; good; ideal; showing greatness.
> It was a noble deed to try to stop the robber.
> *adj.* **nobler, noblest** no·bler, no·blest

nobody   no·bod·y (nō′bod·ē *or* nō′bə·dē)   not any person; no one; not one single person.
> Nobody knew the answer to the question. *pron.*

nod   (nod)   to lower the head and bring it up again, showing agreement.
> I will nod when I am ready to leave.
> *v.* **nodded, nodded, nodding** nod·ded, nod·ding

noisemaker

noise   (noiz)   any kind of sound, especially a loud or unpleasant one.
> The noise from the machines is very loud. *n. pl.* **noises** nois·es

noisemaker   noise·mak·er (noiz′mā·kər)   something that makes a sound that may not be nice to hear; something that makes sounds.
> We each got a noisemaker at the party. *n. pl.* **noisemakers** noise·mak·ers

noisily   nois·i·ly (noi′zə·lē)   in a way that makes a loud sound.
> He noisily opened the door to my room. *adv.*

noisy   nois·y (noi′zē)   making many loud sounds; full of noise.
> The children are noisy today. *adj.* **noisier, noisiest** nois·i·er, nois·i·est

none   (nun)   not any; not one; no person; no thing.
> None of the girls in my class are going to the party. *pron.*

nonfiction non·fic·tion (non·fik'shən) true; real; having facts.
The story of Thomas Edison is nonfiction. *adj.*

nonstop non·stop (non'stop') without a stop; going from one place to another without stopping.
We are taking a nonstop plane from San Francisco to New York. *adj.*

nonwhite non·white (non·hwīt') people who are not Caucasian (white-skinned).
The nonwhite population in Alaska is large. *adj.*

noon (nün) the middle of the day; 12 o'clock in the daytime.
We eat lunch at noon. *n. pl.* **noons**

no one (nō wun) not any person; not a single person.
No one came to the party. *pron.*

nor (nôr) and not.
We do not have the time nor the money to go on a vacation. *conj.*

normal nor·mal (nôr'məl) usual; like most things or times; not being different.
The normal time to eat lunch is noon. *adj.*

Norman-French Nor·man-French (nôr'mən-french') **1.** the people who live in the part of France called Normandy.
The Norman-French once fought with England. *n.*
2. having to do with the people that live in the part of France that is called Normandy.
The Norman-French man wore a red hat. *adj.*

north (nôrth) **1.** a direction that is opposite of south.
We rode north on our bicycles. *n. no pl.*
2. North; the part of an area that is above the south part on a globe.
The United States of America is in North America. *adj.*
3. North; the part of the country that fought to free the slaves in the Civil War.
The North won the war. *n. no pl.*

North America

North America North A·mer·i·ca (nôrth ə·mer'ə·kə) one of the seven continents of the world.
The United States, Canada and Mexico are in North America.

North Atlantic North At·lan·tic (nôrth at·lan'tik) the northern part of the Atlantic Ocean.
Newfoundland is in the North Atlantic.

a	cat	i	sit	oi	oil	ch	chop		a in about
ā	ate	ī	lie	ou	out	ng	song		e in oven
ä	car	o	pot	u	cut	sh	she	ə =	i in pencil
e	set	ō	old	u̇	book	th	three		o in memory
ē	equal	ô	or	ü	blue	ŦH	there		u in circus
ėr	germ					zh	treasure		

northeast north·east (nôrth·ēst′) being between the
  north and the east.
> New York is in the northeast part of the United States. *adj.*

northern north·ern (nôr′THərn) being toward the direction
  that is opposite of south.
> We took the northern road. *adj.*

North Pole (nôrth pōl) the most northern part of the world.
> Children believe that Santa Claus lives at the North Pole.

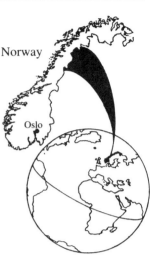

Norway

Oslo

North Star (nôrth stär) the bright star that is over the North Pole.
> Early sailors used the North Star to help them find directions.

northwest north·west (nôrth·west′) being between the
  north and the west.
> Oregon is in the northwest part of the United States. *adj.*

Norway Nor·way (nôr′wā) a country in Europe; its capital is Oslo.
> Norway is near Sweden. *n.*

Norwegian Nor·we·gian (nôr·wē′jən) **1.** a person from the
  country of Norway.
> Rob was born in Oslo and is a Norwegian. *n. pl.* **Norwegians** Nor·we·gians
  2. the language of the country of Norway.
> My grandmother speaks Norwegian. *n. no pl.*

nose (nōz) the part of the face or head of a person or animal that is
  above the mouth and that is used for smelling and breathing.
> My nose is cold. *n.*

nose

not (not) in no way.
> I am not going to school today. *adv.*

notebook note·book (nōt′bùk) a book of pages of paper that a
  person uses for writing notes or school lessons.
> I took my notebook to math class. *n. pl.* **notebooks** note·books

nothing noth·ing (nuth′ing) no thing; not any thing.
> Nothing exciting happened today. *n. no pl.*

notice no·tice (nō′tis) to see; to learn with the eye.
> You will notice that the house is clean.
> *v.* **noticed, noticed, noticing** no·ticed, no·tic·ing

nougat nou·gat (nü′gət *or* nü′gät) a kind of soft candy that is
  made of nuts and sugar.
> I had a chocolate nougat. *n. pl.* **nougats** nou·gats

notebook

novel nov·el (nov′əl) a long story or book that is imaginary.
> I read a novel this week. *n. pl.* **novels** nov·els

now (nou) **1.** at this time.
Now I am going to eat. *adv.*
2. a word used to start a sentence but that has no meaning to the sentence.
Now, what can you do? *adv.*

nowhere no·where (nō‧hwer *or* nō‧hwar) at no place; in no place.
We go nowhere without our dog. *adv.*

nuclear nu·cle·ar (nü‧klē·ər *or* nyü‧klē·ər) having to do with atoms or the energy made from atoms.
We live near the nuclear power plant. *adj.*

number num·ber (num‧bər) **1.** the marks or symbols that are dialed on a telephone.
Give me your number, and I will call you. *n.*
2. the marks or symbols that tell how many.
She lives at 5 Park Drive. *n.*
3. the word that tells how many.
Five is a number. *n.*
4. many; a great amount.
There were a number of people at the party. *n. pl.* **numbers** num·bers

numeral nu·mer·al (nü‧mər·əl *or* nyü‧mər·əl) a mark or symbol that means how many.
The numeral 5 means five. *n. pl.* **numerals** nu·mer·als

nurse (nėrs) **1.** a person who takes care of sick people; a person who follows the direction of a doctor when taking care of sick people.
My brother is an operating room nurse. *n.*
2. a person who lives with and takes care of a child.
Some rich people have a nurse for their children.
n. pl. **nurses** nurs·es
3. to take care of a sick person; to help a person get better.
I will nurse my mother. *v.*
4. to feed milk to a baby at the breast.
The cat will nurse her kittens for several weeks.
v. **nursed, nursed, nursing** nurs·ing

nurse

a	cat	i	sit	oi	oil	ch	chop		a in about
ā	ate	ī	lie	ou	out	ng	song		e in oven
ä	car	o	pot	u	cut	sh	she	ə =	i in pencil
e	set	ō	old	u̇	book	th	three		o in memory
ē	equal	ô	or	ü	blue	ŦH	there		u in circus
ėr	germ					zh	treasure		

nursery   nurs·er·y (nėr⸴sər·ē)   **1.** a room for a baby.
  The baby sleeps in the nursery. *n.*
  2. a place that grows and sells plants and flowers.
  We bought the apple tree at the nursery. *n. pl.* **nurseries** nurs·er·ies
  3. having to do with young children.
  My sister is in nursery school. *adj.*

nut   (nut)   a dry fruit or seed that grows on a tree and
  has a hard outer shell.
  A walnut is a nut. *n. pl.* **nuts**

nutrition   nu·tri·tion (nü·trish⸴ən *or* nyü·trish⸴ən)   food;
  something that gives energy to the body when it is eaten.
  Every living thing needs nutrition to grow. *n. no pl.*

nymph   (nimf)   a fairy; an imaginary small person.
  The Greek myth was about a nymph. *n. pl.* **nymphs**

nut

Oo

oak

oak (ōk) a kind of tree that grows tall, is very strong, and has nuts called acorns.
An oak will grow from an acorn. *n. pl.* **oaks**

oar (ôr *or* ōr) a tool that has a long handle and that a person uses to move a boat.
I will row the boat with this oar. *n. pl.* **oars**

oats (ōts) a grain that is the seed of a certain kind of grass.
Horses eat oats. *plural n.*

obelisk o·be·lisk (ob′ə·lisk) a kind of monument or stone that is tall and has four narrow sides with a point at the top.
The Washington Monument is an obelisk. *n. pl.* **obelisks** o·be·lisks

obey o·bey (ō·bā′) to do what a person says to do; to follow orders or directions.
I will obey the teacher. *v.* **obeyed, obeyed, obeying** o·beyed, o·bey·ing

object[1] ob·ject (ob′jikt *or* ob′jekt) anything that a person can see or touch.
Bill saw a shiny object lying in the grass. *n. pl.* **objects** ob·jects

object[2] ob·ject (əb·jekt′) to disagree with; to refuse to do; to say no to.
I will object to going to the zoo again.
v. **objected, objected, objecting** ob·ject·ed, ob·ject·ing

observation deck ob·ser·va·tion deck (ob·zər·vā′shən dek) a place from which to look.
We have an observation deck on our roof.

observatory ob·serv·a·to·ry (əb·zėr′və·tôr·ē *or* əb·zėr′və·tōr·ē) a place with a telescope used for looking at the stars; a place for looking at things.
The class went to the observatory. *n. pl.* **observatories** ob·serv·a·to·ries

observe ob·serve (əb·zėrv′) to look carefully at something; to watch.
We will observe the stars at the observatory.
v. **observed, observed, observing** ob·served, ob·serv·ing

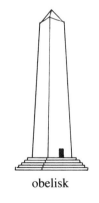

obelisk

a	cat	i	sit	oi	oil	ch	chop		a in about
ā	ate	ī	lie	ou	out	ng	song		e in oven
ä	car	o	pot	u	cut	sh	she	ə =	i in pencil
e	set	ō	old	u̇	book	th	three		o in memory
ē	equal	ô	or	ü	blue	ᵺH	there		u in circus
ėr	germ					zh	treasure		

obtain ob·tain (əb·tān′) to get; to work hard to get.
I will obtain my goal of going to college.
v. **obtained, obtained, obtaining** ob·tained, ob·tain·ing

occur oc·cur (ə·kėr′) to happen; to take place.
Lightning may occur during a rainstorm.
v. **occurred, occurred, occurring** oc·curred, oc·cur·ring

ocean o·cean (ō′shən) a large body of salt water; a sea.
The ocean is full of waves. *n. pl.* **oceans** o·ceans

ocean liner o·cean lin·er (ō′shən lī′nər) a large ship that crosses
an ocean; a large ship that carries people across an ocean.
The ocean liner can carry 400 people across the ocean.

ocean liner

o'clock (ə·klok′) by the clock; using the time shown on
a watch or clock.
It is one o'clock. *adv.*

octopus oc·to·pus (ok′tə·pəs) a sea animal that has eight
legs and a soft body.
The octopus lives on the bottom of the ocean.
n. pl. **octopuses** or **octopi** oc·to·pus·es or oc·to·pi

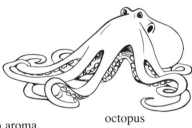

odor o·dor (ō′dər) a smell; an aroma; a scent.
I love the odor of roses. *n. pl.* **odors** o·dors

octopus

odorless o·dor·less (ō′dər·lis) without a smell; having no aroma.
Water is odorless. *adj.*

of (ov *or* uv) **1.** made of.
The book of paper is in the desk. *prep.*
2. containing; having inside.
The glass of milk is for Ray. *prep.*
3. belonging to.
The name of the new girl is Monica. *prep.*
4. from a group; among a group.
I had two kinds of ice cream in my cone. *prep.*

of course (əv kôrs) yes; surely; without a doubt.
Of course I will let you go to the movie. *idiom*

off (ôf *or* of) **1.** not on top of; from a place.
The cat knocked the vase off the table. *prep.*
2. away from; not with but near.
The car is parked off the road. *prep.*
3. not on.
Please turn the light off. *adv.*

offer of·fer (ô′fər *or* of′ər) to give to someone if they want it;
to present something that a person may take.
I will offer Mom some money, but she never takes any help.
v. **offered, offered, offering** of·fered, of·fer·ing

office of·fice (ôʹfis *or* ofʹis) **1.** a room where a person works at a desk; a workplace.
My father works in an office in that building. *n.*
2. a job or position of importance.
The man wants to be elected to a public office. *n. pl.* **offices** of·fic·es

officer of·fi·cer (ôʹfə·sər *or* ofʹə·sər) **1.** a person who has an important rank in the military or the police.
A general is an officer in the army. *n.*
2. a person who has a job or position in the government.
The mayor of the city is a public officer. *n. pl.* **officers** of·fi·cers

official of·fi·cial (ə·fishʹəl) a person who makes sure that the rules are followed or obeyed in a game or contest.
The football referee is an official. *n. pl.* **officials** of·fi·cials

off to the side (ôf tü ᴛʜə sīd) on one side of; not on or with, but near.
Chet waited off to the side of the other boys.

of ___ **own** (əv ___ ōn) belonging to the person talking or being talked about.
I want a room of my own.

ogre

often of·ten (ôʹfən *or* ofʹən) happening many times; frequently.
I visit her house often. *adv.* **oftener, oftenest** of·ten·er, of·ten·est

ogre o·gre (ōʹgər) a mean giant or monster who eats people.
The giant was an ogre. *n. pl.* **ogres** o·gres

oh (ō) a word that is said when a person is surprised, angry, hurt or happy.
Oh boy! A new bicycle! *or* Oh no! I dropped the glass of water! *interj.*

oil (oil) **1.** grease; a thick liquid that can burn and that will not mix with water.
I put salad oil on my lettuce. *n. pl.* **oils**
2. a fuel that is burned for heat or that is used to make things operate or go; petroleum.
There is a lot of underground oil in Texas. *n. no pl.*
3. having to do with a thick liquid that will burn and will not mix with water.
The oil can is empty now. *adj.*

oil

OK *or* **O.K.** (ōʹkāʹ) *abbrev.* See **okay.**

a	cat	**i**	sit	**oi**	oil	**ch**	chop	a in about
ā	ate	**ī**	lie	**ou**	out	**ng**	song	e in oven
ä	car	**o**	pot	**u**	cut	**sh**	she	ə = i in pencil
e	set	**ō**	old	**u̇**	book	**th**	three	o in memory
ē	equal	**ô**	or	**ü**	blue	**ᴛʜ**	there	u in circus
ėr	germ					**zh**	treasure	

okay o·kay (ō‗kā′) all right; fine.
It's okay with me if you want to go with us. *adj.*

Okinawa O·ki·na·wa (o·kə·nä‗wə) an island near Japan in
the Pacific Ocean.
We flew to Okinawa from Japan. *n.*

Okinawa

old (ōld) **1.** not new; belonging to someone for a long time.
Our house is old, but it is still nice. *adj.*
2. of age.
I am twelve years old. *adj.*
3. previous; former; the one before.
I liked my old house more than I like my new house.
adj. **older, oldest** old·er, old·est

old age (ōld āj) **1.** the time after a person becomes 65.
My grandmother is enjoying her old age.
2. living many years; a long life.
The man died of old age; he was 85 years old.

oleander o·le·an·der (ō·lē·an‗dər) an evergreen bush that has
flowers that are red, white or pink and that is harmful if eaten.
The oleander is poisonous. *n. pl.* **oleanders** o·le·an·ders

Olympics O·lym·pics (ō·lim‗piks) races, games and contests
of strength that happen every four years for athletes from
every country in the world.
We won several gold medals at the last Olympics. *plural n.*

on (ôn *or* on) **1.** atop of.
I sat on the wall. *prep.*
2. in a place.
I was on the farm yesterday. *prep.*
3. inside a bus, plane or other vehicle that one pays to ride.
I rode on a train. *prep.*
4. in; around; inside of.
She was on television yesterday. *prep.*
5. during a certain time.
On Tuesdays I go to piano lessons. *prep.*
6. by way of.
I talked on the phone with Lisa yesterday. *prep.*
7. participating with; active in.
I am on the baseball team. *prep.*
8. continuously.
Please read on to the end of the story. *adv.*
9. not off; working; going.
The light is still on. *adv.*

oleander

once (wuns) **1.** one time; one time only.
I once saw lightning hit a tree. *adv.*
2. in the past.
Once, horses were the only way to go from place to place. *adv.*

once more (wuns môr) again.
May I ride the horse once more?

once upon a time once up·on a time (wuns ə·pôn′ ə tīm)
at a time in the past.
Once upon a time, there was a king with a beautiful daughter. *idiom*

oncoming on·com·ing (ôn′kum·ing *or* on′kum·ing)
moving towards something.
The oncoming car was moving very fast. *adj.*

on display on dis·play (ôn dis·plā′) set out for people
to look at or to see.
My gold medal is on display in the principal's office.

one (wun) **1.** being a single thing or person.
You may have one cookie. *adj.*
2. a single person or thing.
Tom had several hot dogs, but I had only one. *pron.*

one by one (wun bī wun) one thing or one person at a time.
I counted the pennies one by one.

on fire (ôn fīr) burning.
The stove is on fire. *idiom*

onion

onion on·ion (un′yən) a vegetable that grows in the ground and
that is used to flavor cooking.
Every time I cut an onion I cry. *n. pl.* **onions** on·ions

only on·ly (ōn′lē) **1.** no other; nothing more; nowhere else.
We have only two eyes. *adv.*
2. just; not more than.
There are only two more days before Christmas. *adv.*
3. one and no more; just one.
My only dog was hit by a car. *adj.*

on the other hand on the oth·er hand (ôn ᴛHē uᴛH′ər hand)
the other side of a story or an idea; another way to look
at or think about something.
I really want to go to the party. On the other hand, I do not want to see Joe.
idiom

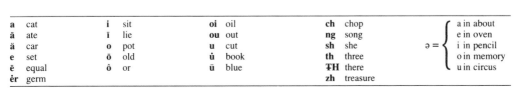

a	cat	i	sit	oi	oil	ch	chop		a in about
ā	ate	ī	lie	ou	out	ng	song		e in oven
ä	car	o	pot	u	cut	sh	she	ə =	i in pencil
e	set	ō	old	u̇	book	th	three		o in memory
ē	equal	ô	or	ü	blue	ᴛH	there		u in circus
ėr	germ					zh	treasure		

on time (ôn tīm) not late; at the right time.
> I was on time, but the bus was early. *idiom*

onto on·to (ôn⁀tü *or* on⁀tü) to; upon; on top of.
> The cat jumped onto the girl's lap. *prep.*

on top of (ôn top əv) at the highest point of something.
> I sat on top of the hill and ate an apple.

open o·pen (ō⁀pən) **1.** to move from a closed position;
to cause to be unclosed.
> I will open the door for you. *v.*

> **2.** to start a business.
> I will open a candy store. *v.* **opened, opened, opening** o·pened, o·pen·ing
> **3.** not shut; not closed.
> The door is open. *adj.*
> **4.** not closed in; without a fence.
> The backyard is open. *adj.*
> **5.** not covered.
> The open campfire burned for a long time. *adj.*

opening

open house o·pen house (ō⁀pən hous) a special time for visiting
and talking with people; an event where people visit.
> We are having an open house at school tonight.

opening o·pen·ing (ō⁀pə·ning) **1.** *v. pres. part.* See **open** (1, 2).
> **2.** a space.
> There is an opening through those bushes. *n.*
> **3.** a job that is unfilled; a job that has no one doing it.
> There is an opening at the grocery store. *n. pl.* **openings** o·pen·ings

open-minded o·pen-mind·ed (ō⁀pən-mīn⁀did) willing to
listen and learn; willing to try new things or to think
about other people's ideas.
> He listened to my idea because he is open-minded. *adj.*

operation op·e·ra·tion (op·ə·rā⁀shən) something done to the body
to make it better or healthier; the cutting open of the body by
a doctor to make it better.
> I had an operation on my broken arm. *n. pl.* **operations** op·e·ra·tions

opposite op·po·site (op⁀ə·zit) being straight across from something.
> Our houses are on opposite sides of Main Street. *adj.*

or (ôr) the other of two; a word used to show a choice of two.
> You may have pie or cake. *conj.*

orange o·range (ôr⁀inj *or* or⁀inj) **1.** a fruit that is yellow-red in
color, has a skin and is full of juice.
> I ate an orange after school. *n. pl.* **oranges** o·rang·es
> **2.** made from the yellow-red fruit.
> I like orange juice. *adj.*

orange

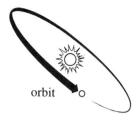

orbit

orchid

orbit or·bit (ôr� bit) **1.** to go around a planet.
The moon will orbit the Earth every 29 days.
v. **orbited, orbited, orbiting** or·bit·ed, or·bit·ing
2. the path of a rocket, plane or satellite around a planet or star.
The orbit of the Earth around the sun is oval. *n. pl.* **orbits** or·bits

orchid or·chid (ôr'kid) any of a family of plants that have
a very delicate flower with three petals.
The orchid is a beautiful flower. *n. pl.* **orchids** or·chids

order or·der (ôr'dər) **1.** to ask for food in a restaurant.
I will order a hot dog with mustard. *v.*
2. to command someone to do something.
The general will order the soldiers to go to war.
v. **ordered, ordered, ordering** or·dered, or·der·ing
3. the asking for food in a restaurant.
The waitress took our order. *n.*
4. a command to do or not do something.
I always obey any order that my parents give me. *n. pl.* **orders** or·ders
5. the way things are placed; the way one thing is placed near
or with other things.
The planets stay in the same order as they orbit the sun. *n. no pl.*

ordinary or·di·nar·y (ôrd'n·er·ē) **1.** normal; not special.
Today was an ordinary day. *adj.*
2. not beautiful; plain; average-looking.
She wore an ordinary dress to the party. *adj.*

ore (ôr *or* ōr) rock that has metal in it.
The miner looked for gold ore. *n. pl.* **ores**

organ or·gan (ôr'gən) a body part that has a separate
and special job.
The liver is a body organ. *n. pl.* **organs** or·gans

organization or·gan·i·za·tion (ôr·gə·nə·zā'shən) a group of people
who have a special purpose or reason to be a group.
The Red Cross is an organization that helps people who are in trouble.
n. pl. **organizations** or·gan·i·za·tions

organize or·gan·ize (ôr'gə·nīz) to plan; to put things in order.
I will organize the surprise party.
v. **organized, organized, organizing** or·gan·ized, or·gan·iz·ing

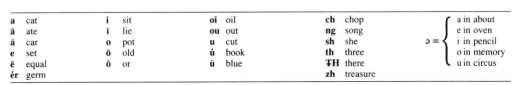

a	cat	i	sit	oi	oil	ch	chop		a in about
ā	ate	ī	lie	ou	out	ng	song		e in oven
ä	car	o	pot	u	cut	sh	she	ə =	i in pencil
e	set	ō	old	u̇	book	th	three		o in memory
ē	equal	ô	or	ü	blue	T̶H	there		u in circus
ėr	germ					zh	treasure		

Orient   O·ri·ent (ôr'ē·ənt *or* ōr'ē·ənt)   the area of the world that is Asia; the eastern part of the world.
China is part of the Orient. *n. no pl.*

origami   o·ri·ga·mi (ôr·ə·gä'mē)   the art of folding paper into decorations shaped like animals or flowers.
Origami was started in Japan. *n. no pl.*

original   o·rig·i·nal (ə·rij'ə·nəl)   the first; the one that was made before any other.
The original airplane carried only one man. *adj.*

Orion   O·ri·on (ô·rī'ən *or* ō·rī'ən)   a group of stars found over the equator that are shaped like a man wearing a sword.
Orion has a very bright star in it. *n.*

ornament   or·na·ment (ôr'nə·mənt)   a decoration; something that is pretty.
I put the new ornament on the Christmas tree.
n. pl. **ornaments** or·na·ments

ornament

ostrich   os·trich (ôs'trich *or* os'trich)   a large bird with long legs that runs fast and cannot fly.
The ostrich is from Africa. *n. pl.* **ostriches** os·trich·es

other   oth·er (uᴛʜ'ər)   **1.** the second of two; the one remaining.
The two boys were fighting. One boy hurt the other boy. *adj.*
2. different.
I know no other person named Chris. *adj.*

ouch   (ouch)   a word that a person yells when they feel pain.
He hit his finger and yelled "Ouch!" *interj.*

ounce   (ouns)   a small unit of weight; one of sixteen parts of a pound.
The new baby weighed six pounds and one ounce. *n. pl.* **ounces** ounc·es

our   (our *or* är)   belonging to us.
This is our school. *adj.*

ourselves   our·selves (our·selvz' *or* är·selvz')   the very same people that I am talking about, including me.
We bought ourselves candy bars. *plural pron.*

ostrich

out   (out)   **1.** not in; not inside.
I am going out to play ball. *adv.*
2. through.
I looked out the window and saw the snow. *prep.*

outdoors   out·doors (out·dôrz')   not in a building or a home; outside; not inside.
We cannot go outdoors when it rains. *adv.*

296

outing   out·ing (ou′ting)   a trip; a walk.
> The teacher took us on an outing to the fire department.
> *n. pl.* **outings** out·ings

outlaw   out·law (out′lô)   a person who has broken the law.
> The outlaw tried to run away from the police. *n. pl.* **outlaws** out·laws

outline   out·line (out′līn)   the line on the edge or the border of an object that shows the shape of the object.
> We drew an outline of the map. *n. pl.* **outlines** out·lines

out loud   (out   loud)   spoken; using one's voice.
> The teacher read the story out loud to the class. *idiom*

out of   (out   əv)   from.
> I ran out of the rain and into the house.

outline

out-of-doors   (out-əv-dôrz′)   outside; not inside.
> We had the party out-of-doors. *adv.*

outside[1]   out·side (out′sīd′)   **1.** not inside.
> I will play outside until it gets dark. *adv.*
> **2.** the part that is not on the inside.
> The outside of the candy bar is covered with chocolate.
> *n. pl.* **outsides** out·sides
> **3.** having to do with the area that is not inside.
> The outside wall of the garage is painted white. *adj.*

outside[2]   out·side (out′sīd′ *or* out·sīd′)   the other side; not in.
> I wonder what is outside the tent. *prep.*

oven   ov·en (uv′ən)   **1.** the part of the stove that bakes food; the inside part of a stove.
> I baked the bread in the oven for one hour. *n. pl.* **ovens** ov·ens
> **2.** having to do with the inside of a stove.
> The oven light is on. *adj.*

oven

oven cleaner   ov·en clean·er (uv′ən   klē′nər)   a chemical that a person uses to clean the inside of a stove.
> The oven cleaner has a bad smell.

a	cat	i	sit	oi	oil	ch	chop		a in about
ā	ate	ī	lie	ou	out	ng	song		e in oven
ä	car	o	pot	u	cut	sh	she	ə =	i in pencil
e	set	ō	old	u̇	book	th	three		o in memory
ē	equal	ô	or	ü	blue	ŦH	there		u in circus
ėr	germ					zh	treasure		

over o•ver (ō⋮vər) **1.** above.
There is a picture over the fireplace. *prep.*
2. above and across.
I jumped over the fence. *prep.*
3. on; into.
I poured the water over the flower. *prep.*
4. across; to the other side.
I walked over the bridge. *adv.*
5. more than.
I paid over three dollars for that ball. *prep.*
6. to here.
Do you want to come over to play? *adv.*
7. to; toward.
I walked over to the desk. *prep.*
8. finished; done; at the end.
The movie was over at ten o'clock. *adv.*
9. upside down.
I turned the egg over. *adv.*

overboard

over and over o•ver and o•ver (ō⋮vər ənd ō⋮ver) again and again; repeatedly.
I told you over and over not to get mud on your shoes. *adv.*

overboard o•ver•board (ō⋮vər•bôrd *or* ō⋮vər•bōrd) out of a boat; from the side of a ship and into the water.
The boy fell overboard, but his father caught him. *adv.*

overhand knot o•ver•hand knot (ō⋮vər•hand not) an easy knot that is made by taking one end of a rope or string and pulling it over the other end and through the loop.
The overhand knot is the easiest knot to tie.

overhand knot

overhead[1] o•ver•head (ō•vər•hed′) above; above or over the head.
A small airplane flew overhead. *adv.*

overhead[2] o•ver•head (ō•vər•hed′) being above or over the head.
The overhead light is too bright. *adj.*

overhear o•ver•hear (ō•vər•hir′) to listen to other people's conversation; to hear something that is private.
I can overhear the neighbors talking.
v. **overheard, overheard, overhearing** o•ver•heard, o•ver•hear•ing

overlap o•ver•lap (ō•vər•lap′) to go far enough to be on top of the next thing; to touch the top or the beginning of the next part; to last so long that the end of one thing happens at the same time that something else begins.
The dance contest will overlap the sewing contest.
v. **overlapped, overlapped, overlapping** o•ver•lapped, o•ver•lap•ping

overload o•ver•load (ō•vər•lōd′) to add too much weight or too many things.
When you overload the truck, things can fall out of it.
v. **overloaded, overloaded, overloading** o•ver•load•ed, o•ver•load•ing

owl

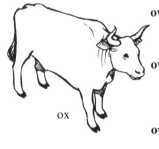

ox

oyster

overnight o·ver·night (ō·vər·nīt′) during the time of day that it is dark.
I will stay overnight and be back in the morning. *adv.*

overseas[1] o·ver·seas (ō·vər·sēz′) across the ocean.
Tina went overseas to England. *adv.*

overseas[2] o·ver·seas (ō′·vər·sēz) having to do with going or being across the ocean.
The overseas operator helped me call Tina in England. *adj.*

overturn o·ver·turn (ō·vər·tėrn′) to make something fall; to cause something to be upside down.
The truck will overturn if it is overloaded.
v. **overturned, overturned, overturning** o·ver·turned, o·ver·turn·ing

ow (ou) *interj. See* **ouch.**

owe (ō) to have to give money to someone for something; to have to pay someone for something; to be in debt to someone.
I owe Troy three dollars. *v.* **owed, owed, owing** ow·ing

owl (oul) a bird that has a big head and a rounded beak and that eats small animals.
The owl is a night bird. *n. pl.* **owls**

own (ōn) **1.** to have; to possess.
I want to own a red car. *v.* **owned, owned, owning** own·ing
2. belonging to a person; belonging to oneself or itself.
I have my own room. *adj.*

owner own·er (ō′·nər) the person to whom something belongs, the person who possesses something.
Mr. Drew is the owner of that red car. *n. pl.* **owners** own·ers

ox (oks) a kind of cattle that people use for farm work.
The ox pulled the plow across the field. *n. pl.* **oxen** ox·en

oxygen ox·y·gen (ok′·sə·jən) a colorless, odorless and tasteless gas that is in the air.
Plants, animals and people need oxygen to live. *n. no pl.*

oyster oys·ter (oi′·stər) an animal that lives in the ocean and that has a hard shell around it.
There was a pearl in the oyster. *n. pl.* **oysters** oys·ters

a	cat	i	sit	oi	oil	ch	chop		a in about
ā	ate	ī	lie	ou	out	ng	song		e in oven
ä	car	o	pot	u	cut	sh	she	ə =	i in pencil
e	set	ō	old	u̇	book	th	three		o in memory
ē	equal	ô	or	ü	blue	ŦH	there		u in circus
ėr	germ					zh	treasure		

Pp

pace (pās) to walk; to take slow steps; to walk back and forth.
I pace when I am nervous. *v.* **paced, paced, pacing** pac·ing

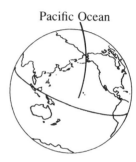

Pacific Ocean

pace the floor (pās тнǝ flôr) to walk back and forth many times.
I will pace the floor while I wait for you.

Pacific Pa·cif·ic (pǝ·sif⁀ik) the name of the ocean on the western
coast of the United States.
The state of Hawaii is in the Pacific. *n.*

pack (pak) **1.** to fill a container with things; to put
things in a suitcase.
I will pack for my trip tonight. *v.* **packed, packed, packing** pack·ing
2. a bag or soft case that is used for carrying things.
I put the food in the pack that I will carry. *n. pl.* **packs**

package pack·age (pak⁀ij) a box with things inside that is
wrapped with paper.
I mailed the package to her yesterday. *n. pl.* **packages** pack·ag·es

pad (pad) the soft cushion-like part of an animal's foot.
The pad protects the dog's foot when it walks on rocks or stones.
n. pl. **pads**

pack

padding pad·ding (pad⁀ing) a thick material that is used to protect
something; a thick lining or stuffing.
The padding in our shoes protects our feet from rocks or stones. *n. no pl.*

paddle pad·dle (pad⁀l) to row a canoe or boat with an oar.
I will paddle the boat around the lake.
v. **paddled, paddled, paddling** pad·dled, pad·dling

page (pāj) a piece of paper in a book, newspaper or magazine.
The teacher asked us to find the right page. *n. pl.* **pages** pag·es

package

paid (pād) *v. pt. t., pt. part.* See **pay.**

pain (pān) an ache; a feeling of hurt.
I have a pain in my leg. *n. pl.* **pains**

painful pain·ful (pān⁀fǝl) having much pain; hurting greatly.
Moving my leg is very painful. *adj.*

painfully pain·ful·ly (pān⁀fǝl·lē) with much hurt.
I painfully walked up the steps. *adv.*

paddle

paintbrush

pajamas

palace

paint (pānt) **1.** a liquid that is put on things to change their color.
I put white paint on the fence. *n. no pl.*
2. a substance that is used to draw or color pictures.
The little girl used the paint for her picture. *n. pl.* **paints**
3. to use a liquid to change the color of something.
I will paint the fence white.
v. **painted, painted, painting** paint·ed, paint·ing

paintbrush paint·brush (pānt′brush) a tool with hair-like bristles that is used to put colored liquid on things.
I used a big paintbrush when I painted the fence.
n. pl. **paintbrushes** paint·brush·es

painter paint·er (pān′tər) a person who puts colored liquid on things; a person whose job is painting.
The painter worked on the house today. *n. pl.* **painters** paint·ers

painting paint·ing (pān′ting) **1.** *v. pres. part.* See **paint** (3).
2. having to do with putting colored liquid on something.
The painting class was great fun. *adj.*
3. a picture made with paint; a valuable work of art.
I went to the gallery to see the new painting. *n. pl.* **paintings** paint·ings

pair (per *or* par) two things that go together or that match each other.
I have a pair of warm gloves to wear in the winter. *n. pl.* **pairs**

pajamas pa·ja·mas (pə·jä′məz *or* pə·jam′əz) a loose shirt and a pair of pants that a person wears when sleeping.
I have a new pair of pajamas. *plural n.*

palace pal·ace (pal′is) a large, beautiful house; a large house in which a king or queen lives.
Her house looks like a palace. *n. pl.* **palaces** pal·ac·es

palate pal·ate (pal′it) the roof of the mouth; the hard area over the tongue.
The toast hurt the palate of my mouth. *n. pl.* **palates** pal·ates

pale (pāl) having little color; light in color.
The dress is a pale pink. *adj.* **paler, palest** pal·er, pal·est

palomino pal·o·mi·no (pal·ə·mē′nō) a horse that is light in color with its mane and tail being even lighter.
I rode the palomino in the rodeo. *n. pl.* **palominos** pal·o·mi·nos

a	cat	i	sit	oi	oil	ch	chop		a in about
ā	ate	ī	lie	ou	out	ng	song		e in oven
ä	car	o	pot	u	cut	sh	she	ə =	i in pencil
e	set	ō	old	ů	book	th	three		o in memory
ē	equal	ô	or	ü	blue	ŦH	there		u in circus
ėr	germ					zh	treasure		

301

pan (pan) **1.** a container that is used for cooking food; a container that is not deep and has no cover.
I put some water in the pan. *n. pl.* **pans**
2. to use a container that is not deep and has no cover to look for gold in water.
I will pan for gold in North Carolina.
v. **panned, panned, panning** pan·ning

pan

pancake pan·cake (pan′kāk) a thin, flat cake made from flour, milk and eggs that is cooked on a flat pan or griddle; a hotcake.
I can eat only one pancake. *n. pl.* **pancakes** pan·cakes

panda bear pan·da bear (pan′də ber) an animal that looks like a bear and has black and white fur.
The panda bear came from China.

panic pan·ic (pan′ik) **1.** to run and scream in fear; to be so afraid that one has no control.
The little boy will panic if he cannot find his mother.
v. **panicked, panicked, panicking** pan·icked, pan·ick·ing
2. a sudden fear; a strong fear; a fear that causes a person to lose control.
The people in the burning building were in a panic. *n. no pl.*

pant (pant) having to do with clothing for the legs; having to do with trousers.
I caught my pant leg in the bicycle wheel. *adj.*

panda bear

pants (pants) clothing for the legs; trousers.
My new pants will keep my legs warm. *plural n.*

papa pa·pa (pä′pə *or* pə·pä′) father; dad; daddy.
The little girl called to her papa. *n. pl.* **papas** pa·pas

paper pa·per (pā′pər) **1.** a thin material made from trees that is used for writing, painting, drawing or wrapping.
A book is made from paper. *n. no pl.*
2. homework; a school assignment; something that is written.
I gave the teacher my history paper. *n. pl.* **papers** pa·pers
3. made from the material that is made from trees.
The paper doll will tear easily. *adj.*

paper bag pa·per bag (pā′pər bag) a sack or container made of paper and used for carrying things.
We put the groceries in the paper bag.

pants

paper-folding pa·per-fold·ing (pā′pər-fōl′ding) folding pieces of paper into shapes that look like birds, animals or flowers; origami.
Paper-folding is an old art. *n. no pl.*

paper towel

parachute

paper towel pa·per tow·el (pā⸐pər tou⸐əl) a piece of paper that is used to dry things or to clean things; a towel that is made of paper.
I used a paper towel to wipe up the milk I spilled.

parachute par·a·chute (par⸐ə·shüt) **1.** a cloth made of silk or nylon that slows a person or thing falling to the ground from great heights.
The man opened his parachute after he jumped from the airplane.
n. pl. **parachutes** par·a·chutes
2. to fall slowly to the ground from a great height hanging from a large, umbrella-shaped cloth.
The flier will parachute from the airplane.
v. **parachuted, parachuted, parachuting** par·a·chut·ed, par·a·chut·ing

parachuting par·a·chut·ing (par⸐ə·shü·ting)
1. *v. pres. part.* See **parachute** (2).
2. falling slowly to the ground hanging from a large, umbrella-shaped cloth.
Parachuting is dangerous. *gerund*

parade pa·rade (pə·rād′) **1.** an event in which many people, bands and floats march down the street.
We saw the Independence Day parade. *n. pl.* **parades** pa·rades
2. to march down the street in a group; to march in a group so that people can see you.
The people in the circus will parade down the street.
v. **paraded, paraded, parading** pa·rad·ed, pa·rad·ing

paralyze par·a·lyze (par⸐ə·līz) to make something or someone helpless or unable to move.
An accident can paralyze a person.
v. **paralyzed, paralyzed, paralyzing** par·a·lyzed, par·a·lyz·ing

parent par·ent (per⸐ənt *or* par⸐ənt) **1.** a mother or a father.
My father is a strict parent. *n. pl.* **parents** par·ents
2. having to do with being the source or the start of something.
The parent company is in Chicago; the other factory is in San Francisco. *adj.*

Paris Par·is (par⸐is) the capital of France.
Paris is a large city. *n.*

parish par·ish (par⸐ish) **1.** the area or people served by a church.
I am in a small parish. *n. pl.* **parishes** par·ish·es
2. having to do with the area or people served by a church.
The parish picnic is on Saturday. *adj.*

a	cat	**i**	sit	**oi**	oil	**ch**	chop	⎧ a in about
ā	ate	**ī**	lie	**ou**	out	**ng**	song	⎪ e in oven
ä	car	**o**	pot	**u**	cut	**sh**	she	ə = ⎨ i in pencil
e	set	**ō**	old	**u̇**	book	**th**	three	⎪ o in memory
ē	equal	**ô**	or	**ü**	blue	**ŦH**	there	⎩ u in circus
ėr	germ					**zh**	treasure	

park (pärk) **1.** land that is used for playing; land that is green and is used for keeping wild animals safe; land that is open to all people for relaxing, swimming, hiking, picnicking, etc.
I went to the park with grandmother. *n. pl.* **parks**
2. to drive a car, bike or other vehicle into a space and leave it.
I will park my bike and meet you inside the movie.
v. **parked, parked, parking** park·ing

parking lot park·ing lot (pär⸍king lot) a place where cars are driven into spaces and left.
The parking lot is full, so I will park the car on the street.

parking meter park·ing me·ter (pär⸍king mē⸍tər) a machine into which money is put so that a car can be left in a space for a certain amount of time.
I put a dime in the parking meter.

parking ticket park·ing tick·et (pär⸍king tik⸍it) a paper that tells how much a person must pay if the person leaves a car in the wrong space or if the time on the parking meter is gone before the person moves the car from the space.
I got a parking ticket for leaving the car in the parking lot too long.

parking meter

parliament par·lia·ment (pär⸍lə·mənt) **1.** the part of a government that makes the laws in some countries.
Canada is run by a parliament. *n. pl.* **parliaments** par·lia·ments
2. having to do with the government of some countries.
England's parliament building is in London. *adj.*

parrot par·rot (par⸍ət) a bird that lives in the tropics, has brightly colored feathers and can learn to talk.
I taught the parrot to say "No." *n. pl.* **parrots** par·rots

part (pärt) **1.** a piece of something; not the whole of something but some of it.
I want a part of that orange for lunch. *n. pl.* **parts**
2. to leave a person; to separate from a person.
I did not want to part from my sister.
v. **parted, parted, parting** part·ed, part·ing

partially par·tial·ly (pär⸍shəl·lē) in part; not all but some.
I was partially dressed when you called. *adv.*

particularly par·tic·u·lar·ly (pər·tik⸍yə·lər·lē) especially; to a high degree.
I was particularly interested in the part of the story about the horse race. *adv.*

parrot

party

part owner part own·er (pärt ō‘nər) a person to whom a part or piece of something belongs; one of many other owners.
My father is part owner of a store.

party par·ty (pär‘tē) **1.** a celebration; a festive event.
We had a party at school today. *n.*
2. a group of people who are together for political reasons.
The Democratic party nominated a person to run for President.
n. pl. **parties** par·ties
3. having to do with a celebration or a festive event.
We wore party hats. *adj.*

pass (pas) **1.** to go farther than one should have; to go beyond what is expected; to go by a place or a thing and not stop.
My father will pass that truck. *v.* **passed, passed, passing** pass·ing
2. a piece of paper that shows that a person has the right or permission to do something.
I got a pass to go to the swimming pool. *n. pl.* **passes** pass·es

passenger pas·sen·ger (pas‘n·jər) a person who rides in a vehicle but who is not the driver.
The student is a passenger on the school bus. *n. pl.* **passengers** pas·sen·gers

pastern

past (past) **1.** by and beyond.
I walk past the store every day. *prep.*
2. a time before; the years before this time.
In the past, people grew all the food that they ate. *n. no pl.*

pastern pas·tern (pas‘tərn) the part of a horse's foot that is above the hoof.
The horse hurt its pastern when it kicked the fence.
n. pl. **pasterns** pas·terns

pasteurization pas·teur·i·za·tion (pas·chər·ə·zā‘shən *or* pas·tər·ə·zā‘shən) a way of killing bacteria or germs in a liquid.
Pasteurization makes milk safe to drink. *n. no pl.*

pasture

pasteurize pas·teur·ize (pas‘chə·rīz *or* pas‘tə·rīz) to heat a liquid to kill bacteria or germs in it.
The dairy must pasteurize the milk before selling it.
v. **pasteurized, pasteurized, pasteurizing** pas·teur·ized, pas·teur·iz·ing

pasture pas·ture (pas‘chər) a field of grass that is for animals to eat.
The cows are in the pasture. *n. pl.* **pastures** pas·tures

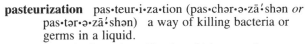

a	cat	i	sit	oi	oil	ch	chop		a in about
ā	ate	ī	lie	ou	out	ng	song		e in oven
ä	car	o	pot	u	cut	sh	she	ə =	i in pencil
e	set	ō	old	u̇	book	th	three		o in memory
ē	equal	ô	or	ü	blue	ŦH	there		u in circus
ėr	germ					zh	treasure		

pat (pat) to hit lightly; to touch lightly with the hand.
    I will pat you on the arm to wake you up.
    v. **patted, patted, patting** pat·ted, pat·ting

patch (pach) **1.** a small area of land; a small garden.
    We picked the watermelon from the melon patch. *n.*
    2. a small piece of cloth that covers a hole.
    Mother put a patch on my jeans. *n.*
    3. a small piece of cloth with a symbol or emblem on it.
    The boy earned his camping patch from the Boy Scouts.
    n. pl. **patches** patch·es

patch

patent pat·ent (pat′nt) to get a legal paper or document
that protects an invention from being copied or made by
someone else; to legally be the only person or company that
can make something.
    John needs to patent his invention.
    v. **patented, patented, patenting** pa·tent·ed, pa·tent·ing

path (path) a way through the woods; a trail; a walking lane.
    I followed the path to the river. *n. pl.* **paths**

patient pa·tient (pā′shənt) **1.** willing to wait; able to stand pain;
unaffected by waiting or pain.
    He will wait for me because he is very patient. *adj.*
    2. a person that a doctor takes care of; a person who is
in the hospital.
    My mother is a patient of Dr. Simpson's. *n. pl.* **patients** pa·tients

pattern pat·tern (pat′ərn) a design; the way marks are placed on
something; a repeated design on something.
    The wallpaper pattern has flowers and birds on it. *n. pl.* **patterns** pat·terns

path

paw (pô) the soft foot of an animal.
    The cat got a nail in its paw. *n. pl.* **paws**

pay (pā) to give money to someone who has worked for it; to give
money for something that a person buys.
    I will pay the paperboy for the newspaper. *v.* **paid, paid, paying** pay·ing

pay attention pay at·ten·tion (pā ə·ten′shən) to listen to
something or someone; to look at something or someone.
    Please pay attention to the teacher. *idiom*

paycheck pay·check (pā′chek) pay in the form of a note which the
worker takes to the bank and exchanges for money.
    I put my paycheck into the bank. *n. pl.* **paychecks** pay·checks

payment pay·ment (pā′mənt) money that someone pays for
something that has been bought.
    I made a payment on my new car. *n. pl.* **payments** pay·ments

paw

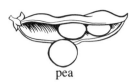

pea

pea (pē) a small, green, round vegetable that grows in a pod on a vine.
We ate a pea right off the vine. *n. pl.* **peas**

peace (pēs) a time when there is no war.
We all want peace, not war. *n. no pl.*

peaceful peace·ful (pēs'fəl) calm; quiet; without war.
The forest is peaceful at night. *adj.*

peacefully peace·ful·ly (pēs'fəl·lē) without fighting; very calm.
I walked peacefully through the forest. *adv.*

peach

peace treaty peace trea·ty (pēs trē'tē) a piece of paper that countries who are fighting each other sign to prove that they will stop the war.
All four countries signed the peace treaty that stopped the war.

peach (pēch) **1.** a fruit with a large seed and fuzzy skin.
I like to eat a peach at lunch. *n. pl.* **peaches** peach·es
2. made from the fruit that has a large seed and fuzzy skin.
I like peach pie. *adj.*

peak (pēk) the pointed top of a mountain or a hill.
You can see the snow on the mountain peak. *n. pl.* **peaks**

peak

peanut pea·nut (pē'nut) the nut-like seed of a plant that grows under the earth in a pod.
The peanut is used to make peanut butter. *n. pl.* **peanuts** pea·nuts

peasant peas·ant (pez'nt) a poor farmer in Europe.
A peasant does not make much money. *n. pl.* **peasants** peas·ants

peddler ped·dler (ped'lər) a person who sells things as he or she travels; a person who goes from place to place selling things.
The peddler came to the door of the house. *n. pl.* **peddlers** ped·dlers

peer (pir) someone who is in the same age group as another or is in the same kind of work.
My father is a salesman. Mr. Jones is a salesman. Mr. Jones is a peer of my father's. *n. pl.* **peers**

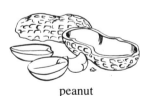

peanut

peer pressure peer pres·sure (pir presh'ər) an influence to do as friends do; a pushing to be like or to do as friends do.
Jan felt peer pressure to stay out late. *idiom*

a	cat	i	sit	oi	oil	ch	chop		a in about
ā	ate	ī	lie	ou	out	ng	song		e in oven
ä	car	o	pot	u	cut	sh	she	ə =	i in pencil
e	set	ō	old	u̇	book	th	three		o in memory
ē	equal	ô	or	ü	blue	ŦH	there		u in circus
ėr	germ					zh	treasure		

pence (pents) English pennies.
> The Englishman gave me eight pence. *plural n.*

pencil pen·cil (pen′səl) a tool with lead in it that is used for writing.
> I used a pencil to do my math problems. *n. pl.* **pencils** pen·cils

pencil

pendulum pen·du·lum (pen′jə·ləm *or* pen′dyə·ləm)
> a heavy weight that hangs from a point and swings back and
> forth; metal weight that hangs down from a clock and
> swings back and forth.
> The hands of the clock stopped when the pendulum stopped.
> *n. pl.* **pendulums** pen·du·lums

penicillin pen·i·cil·lin (pen·ə·sil′ən) a drug made from a mold that
> is used to treat sicknesses caused by bacteria.
> I take penicillin when I have an ear infection. *n. no pl.*

peninsula pe·nin·su·la (pə·nin′sə·lə *or* pə·nin′syə·lə) a piece of
> land that has water on three sides of it; a piece of land that
> sticks out into a body of water.
> San Francisco is on a peninsula. *n. pl.* **peninsulas** pe·nin·su·las

pendulum

pennant pen·nant (pen′ənt) a long, thin, triangular flag, sometimes
> with an emblem or symbol on it.
> Our school pennant has a bear on it. *n. pl.* **pennants** pen·nants

penny pen·ny (pen′ē) a coin made of copper that is worth one cent.
> I found a penny on the street. *n. pl.* **pennies** pen·nies

people peo·ple (pē′pəl) persons; men, women and children.
> There are many people in the United States. *plural n.*

pennant

pepper pep·per (pep′ər) a seasoning made from a berry of a tropical
> plant that has a hot, spicy taste.
> I put pepper on my eggs. *n. no pl.*

per (pər *or* pėr) for each; for every.
> The apples cost five cents per apple. *prep.*

percent per·cent (pər·sent′) one part of one hundred parts;
> a hundredth portion of something.
> I save ten percent of the money I earn. *n. pl.* **percents** per·cents

perch (pėrch) **1.** a pole or branch on which a bird sits.
> We put a perch in the bird cage. *n. pl.* **perches** perch·es
> **2.** to sit on the edge of something high or narrow.
> I will perch myself on this stool. *v.* **perched, perched, perching** perch·ing

Percheron Per·che·ron (pėr′chə·ron *or* pėr′shə·ron) a kind of
> large, strong horse used to pull vehicles.
> Grandfather has a Percheron to pull the wagon.
> *n. pl.* **Percherons** Per·che·rons

penny

perennial pe·ren·ni·al (pə·ren⸍ē·əl) a plant that lives a long time; a plant that will live for years.
The rose is a perennial. *n. pl.* **perennials** pe·ren·ni·als

perfect[1] per·fect (pėr⸍fikt) without a mistake or error; without a flaw.
Your speech was perfect. *adj.*

perfect[2] per·fect (pər·fekt⸍) to improve something; to make something better.
I want to perfect my tennis game.
v. **perfected, perfected, perfecting** per·fect·ed, per·fect·ing

perfectly per·fect·ly (pėr⸍fikt·lē) **1.** without a mistake.
She danced perfectly. *adv.*
2. completely; totally.
It was perfectly right for Helen to leave early. *adv.*

perform per·form (pər·fôrm⸍) to do; to act; to sing or dance.
The girl will perform a ballet.
v. **performed, performed, performing** per·formed, per·form·ing

performance per·form·ance (pər·fôr⸍məns) an act; a song or dance; a play, a show.
Her performance of the ballet was perfect.
n. pl. **performances** per·form·anc·es

perfume

perfume per·fume (pėr⸍fyüm *or* pər·fyüm⸍) a liquid that has the smell of flowers or something else that smells sweet.
I do not wear perfume. *n. pl.* **perfumes** per·fumes

perhaps per·haps (pər·haps⸍ *or* pə·raps⸍) maybe; possibly.
Perhaps I will find a perfume that I like. *adv.*

permission per·mis·sion (pər·mish⸍ən) **1.** needed approval; the okay to do something.
I asked permission to go to the library. *n. pl.* **permissions** per·mis·sions
2. having to do with the okay to do something.
The teacher gave me a permission slip to go to the library. *adj.*

person per·son (pėr⸍sən) an individual; a man, woman or child; a human.
There is a person at the door. *n. pl.* **persons** per·sons, *also* **people** peo·ple

a	cat	i	sit	oi	oil	ch	chop		a in about
ā	ate	ī	lie	ou	out	ng	song		e in oven
ä	car	o	pot	u	cut	sh	she	ə =	i in pencil
e	set	ō	old	u̇	book	th	three		o in memory
ē	equal	ô	or	ü	blue	ŦH	there		u in circus
ėr	germ					zh	treasure		

personal per·son·al (pėr′sə·nəl) having to do with a person; relating to only one person.
 Do not read my mail; it is personal. *adj.*

pest (pest) a person or thing that gives a person trouble; a bothersome person or thing; someone or something that is a nuisance.
 Katie can be a pest. *n. pl.* **pests**

pet (pet) **1.** an animal that a person or family keeps and loves.
 My dog is a pet. *n. pl.* **pets**
 2. having to do with an animal that is loved and kept by a family.
 The pet book tells you how to brush the dog. *adj.*
 3. to stroke or rub an animal or a person lovingly.
 The cat will purr when you pet it.
 v. **petted, petted, petting** pet·ted, pet·ting

petal

petal pet·al (pet′l) a part of a flower that is colored.
 This petal from the rose is red. *n. pl.* **petals** pet·als

pet store (pet stôr) a place that sells animals, fish and birds.
 I got my dog from the pet store.

petting zoo pet·ting zoo (pet′ing zü) a place where people can touch and pet animals.
 I like the petting zoo because you can get close to the animals.

phone

philatelist phi·lat·e·list (fə·lat′l·ist) a person who collects and sells postage stamps.
 The philatelist has many interesting stamps.
 n. pl. **philatelists** phi·lat·e·lists

philosophy phi·los·o·phy (fə·los′ə·fē) the study of knowledge and the truths that govern or control life and people.
 Philosophy is a difficult area of study. *n. no pl.*

phone (fōn) *abbrev. pl.* **phones.** See **telephone.**

phonograph pho·no·graph (fō′nə·graf) a machine that plays records; a record player.
 We will put records on the phonograph and dance to the music.
 n. pl. **phonographs** pho·no·graphs

phonograph

photo pho·to (fō′tō) *abbrev. pl.* **photos.** See **photograph.**

piano

pickaxe

pickle

photograph pho·to·graph (fō′tə·graf) **1.** a picture that is taken with a camera.
I took a photograph of the panda bear. *n. pl.* **photographs** pho·to·graphs
2. having to do with a picture taken with a camera.
The photograph album has many pictures in it. *adj.*

photographer pho·tog·ra·pher (fə·tog′rə·fər) a person who is paid to take pictures with a camera.
The photographer took a picture of our family.
n. pl. **photographers** pho·tog·ra·phers

photography pho·tog·ra·phy (fə·tog′rə·fē) having to do with taking pictures with a camera.
I took a photography class and learned how to use a new lens. *adj.*

physically phys·i·cal·ly (fiz′ə·kə·lē) of the body; bodily.
I am physically tired so I cannot play ball tonight. *adv.*

piano pi·an·o (pē·an′ō) a musical instrument with 88 keys that are black and white.
Chuck played my favorite song on the piano. *n. pl.* **pianos** pi·an·os

pick (pik) **1.** to select; to choose.
You may pick the movie that we will see. *v.*
2. to take flowers, fruits or vegetables from their trees or plants; to harvest a crop.
We will pick the corn tomorrow.
v. **picked, picked, picking** pick·ing

pickaxe pick·axe (pik′aks) a tool that has a heavy pointed metal bar at the end of a long wooden handle.
John used a pickaxe to dig a hole in the rocky ground.
n. pl. **pickaxes** pick·ax·es

pickle pick·le (pik′əl) to put food in a salty liquid so that it will not spoil.
I will pickle the corn. *v.* **pickled, pickled, pickling** pick·led, pick·ling

pick on (pik ôn) to tease; to pester; to bother.
Why do you always pick on me?
v. **picked on, picked on, picking on** pick·ing on

pick out (pik out) to select; to choose.
I want to pick out new shoes.
v. **picked out, picked out, picking out** pick·ing out

a	cat	**i**	sit	**oi**	oil	**ch**	chop		a in about
ā	ate	**ī**	lie	**ou**	out	**ng**	song		e in oven
ä	car	**o**	pot	**u**	cut	**sh**	she	ə =	i in pencil
e	set	**ō**	old	**ů**	book	**th**	three		o in memory
ē	equal	**ô**	or	**ü**	blue	**ŦH**	there		u in circus
ėr	germ					**zh**	treasure		

pick up   (pik   up)   **1.** to take hold of and lift.
Please pick up the baby. *v.*
2. to collect from different places; to put in a vehicle.
The man will pick up the letters from the mailboxes. *v.*
3. to hear; to locate sound; to find the place from
which a sound comes.
A horse can always pick up noises.
v. **picked up, picked up, picking up** pick·ing up

pickup truck

pickup man   pick·up man (pik‘up   man)   a person who helps a rider
get up off the ground at the rodeo.
The pickup man helped the rider while the clown got the bull to move.

pickup truck   pick·up truck (pik‘up   truk)   a vehicle that is open in
the back and that people use to collect or carry things.
Ed's pickup truck will be able to take the furniture to our new home.

picnic   pic·nic (pik‘nik)   **1.** an event when a person or people eat
outside; an event when people eat in a park-like area.
We had a picnic on Independence Day. *n. pl.* **picnics** pic·nics
2. having to do with eating outside or in a park.
The picnic basket has chicken and rolls in it. *adj.*

pie

Pict   (pikt)   a person from the oldest tribe of people in Scotland.
The picture of the Pict is in the history book. *n. pl.* **Picts**

picture   pic·ture (pik‘chər)   **1.** a drawing or a painting
of something or someone.
Mary will draw a picture of the school. *n.*
2. a photograph taken with a camera.
I took a picture of the waterfall. *n. pl.* **pictures** pic·tures
3. having to do with a drawing, painting or photograph.
The picture frame is on the table. *adj.*

pig

pie   (pī)   a food with a crust on the bottom and sides that
is filled with meat, fruit or other food.
Mother made a cherry pie. *n. pl.* **pies**

piece   (pēs)   **1.** a part of something; a portion of something.
I want a piece of cherry pie. *n.*
2. an item that is used in a game.
I won his checker piece in the game. *n. pl.* **pieces** piec·es

pied   (pīd)   having two or more colors in patches.
The dog was pied. *adj.*

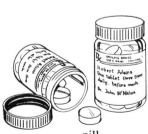

pill

pig   (pig)   a fat farm animal with a circular nose; a hog.
The pig lived on a farm. *n. pl.* **pigs**

pillow

pillowcase

pine

pineapple

pigpen   pig·pen (pig⸍pen)   the place on a farm where pigs are kept. The pigpen is always smelly and dirty. *n. pl.* **pigpens** pig·pens

pile   (pīl)   **1.** many things stacked up on each other; a heap of things; things placed on top of each other with no order. We jumped in the pile of leaves. *n. pl.* **piles**
2. to put things on top of each other without any order; to stack things on top of each other. I will pile my dirty clothes on this chair. *v.* **piled, piled, piling** pil·ing

pill   (pil)   a tablet of medicine. The penicillin is in the pill. *n. pl.* **pills**

pillow   pil·low (pil⸍ō)   a soft cushion for the head when a person is sleeping or resting; a bag filled with soft things, such as feathers, that is used for resting the head. I have a special pillow on which I sleep. *n. pl.* **pillows** pil·lows

pillowcase   pil·low·case (pil⸍ō·kās)   a cloth cover for a pillow. I put a clean pillowcase on the pillow. *n. pl.* **pillowcases** pil·low·cas·es

pilot   pi·lot (pī⸍lət)   a person who flies an airplane. The pilot flew the plane from Chicago to Florida. *n. pl.* **pilots** pi·lots

pin   (pin)   **1.** a sharp metal tool used to hold things together; a small piece of metal with a point on one end that fastens things together. I used a pin to close my coat. *n. pl.* **pins**
2. to use a small pointed piece of metal to hold things together. I will pin the dress hem. *v.* **pinned, pinned, pinning** pin·ning

pinch   (pinch)   to grab something with two fingers. Pinch the tomato and you can feel if it is ripe. *v.* **pinched, pinched, pinching** pinch·ing

pine   (pīn)   **1.** a kind of evergreen tree that has very thin pointed leaves called needles. The tall pine is ten years old. *n. pl.* **pines**
2. having to do with a kind of evergreen tree that has thin pointed leaves. The pine cone from the tree is very large. *adj.*

pineapple   pine·ap·ple (pī⸍nap·əl)   a fruit that grows on a plant in the tropics and that has a tough skin. The pineapple tastes sweet. *n. pl.* **pineapples** pine·ap·ples

a	cat	**i**	sit	**oi**	oil	**ch**	chop
ā	ate	**ī**	lie	**ou**	out	**ng**	song
ä	car	**o**	pot	**u**	cut	**sh**	she
e	set	**ō**	old	**u̇**	book	**th**	three
ē	equal	**ô**	or	**ü**	blue	**ŦH**	there
ėr	germ					**zh**	treasure

ə = { a in about / e in oven / i in pencil / o in memory / u in circus }

pioneer pi·o·neer (pī·ə·nir′) **1.** a person who goes first into an area and helps to start a city.
The pioneer went to places where no one had ever been before.
n. pl. **pioneers** pi·o·neers
2. having to do with the first people to go to an area and start a city.
Pioneer life was difficult and lonely. *adj.*

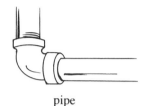
pipe

pipe (pīp) **1.** to blow into a bagpipe.
The man will pipe in the parade. *v.* **piped, piped, piping** pip·ing
2. a round tube that carries liquid or gas from one place to another place.
The water pipe in the kitchen broke and water went everywhere.
n. pl. **pipes**

piper pip·er (pī′pər) a person who plays a musical instrument by blowing into it; a person who plays a bagpipe.
The piper marched down the street in the parade. *n. pl.* **pipers** pip·ers

pirate pi·rate (pī′rit) **1.** a thief at sea; a person who robs things from ships.
The pirate took the gold coins from the king's ship. *n. pl.* **pirates** pi·rates
2. having to do with people who rob ships and boats.
The pirate ship flew a black flag on its mast. *adj.*

pirate

pit (pit) **1.** a work area at a racetrack.
The men sat in the pit waiting for the car to come in for repairs. *n.*
2. a deep hole in the ground.
The man dug a pit for cooking pigs. *n. pl.* **pits**

pitcher pitch·er (pich′ər) a container with a handle that a person uses for storing and pouring liquids.
There is orange juice in the glass pitcher.
n. pl. **pitchers** pitch·ers

pit crew (pit krü) the men who fix a race car at the racetrack.
The pit crew changed the tires in thirty seconds.

pitcher

pizza piz·za (pēt′sə) a food that is made from flat dough with tomato sauce, cheese and other things on top of it.
I like mushrooms on my pizza. *n. pl.* **pizzas** piz·zas

place (plās) **1.** to put something down; to put something in a certain position.
Place the centerpiece in the middle of the table.
v. **placed, placed, placing** plac·ing
2. a building, area, city or town.
There is a new place to eat on that street. *n.*
3. a location; a spot; a certain or specific spot.
I need a place to put my bicycle. *n. pl.* **places** plac·es

pizza

place mat (plās mat) a piece of cloth, paper or plastic that is placed under a plate and silverware on a table.
My place mat has a picture of a mountain on it.

place mat

plague (plāg) **1.** a dangerous disease that is passed from one person to another and that can kill people.
A plague happened in Europe many years ago. *n. pl.* **plagues**
2. to make something bad happen; to cause problems.
The rainy weather will plague the crops.
v. **plagued, plagued, plaguing** pla‑guing

plaid (plad) having a pattern of colored checks or stripes; a pattern of many colors of checks or stripes.
Joan wore a green and blue plaid skirt. *adj.*

plain (plān) **1.** not decorated; simple; without a pattern.
The jacket is plain.
adj. **plainer, plainest** plain‑er, plain‑est
2. flat land.
The cows eat the grass on the plain. *n. pl.* **plains**

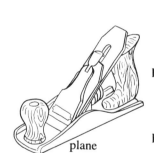

plaid

plan (plan) **1.** an idea of a way to do something; an idea to obtain a goal.
My plan is to go to college. *n.*
2. a drawing of how to build something; a drawing of something that is being made or built.
The plan has a large living room in the back of the house.
n. pl. **plans**
3. to organize; to think of a way to do something; to decide on an action.
I plan to find a job this summer.
v. **planned, planned, planning** plan‑ning

plane (plān) **1.** a tool that a person uses to even or flatten pieces of wood.
Dad used a plane to make the board smooth. *n. pl.* **planes**
2. *abbrev. pl.* **planes.** See **airplane.**

plane

planet plan‑et (plan′it) one of the large spheres that orbit the sun.
Earth is a planet.
n. pl. **planets** plan‑ets

plankton plank‑ton (plangk′tən) small plants and animals that float in large numbers on the surface of the ocean.
Many fish eat plankton. *n. no pl.*

a	cat	i	sit	oi	oil	ch	chop		a in about
ā	ate	ī	lie	ou	out	ng	song		e in oven
ä	car	o	pot	u	cut	sh	she	ə =	i in pencil
e	set	ō	old	u̇	book	th	three		o in memory
ē	equal	ô	or	ü	blue	ŦH	there		u in circus
ėr	germ					zh	treasure		

plant   (plant)   **1.** a living thing, not an animal, that has leaves, roots and a soft stem.
The plant under the window needs water. *n.*
2. a place where things are made; a factory.
Eric works at a steel plant. *n. pl.* **plants**
3. to put seeds into the ground; to put living things into the ground to grow.
I will plant a rosebush in the garden.
v. **planted, planted, planting** plant·ed, plant·ing

plant

plantation   plan·ta·tion (plan·tā′shən)   a large farm in the southern United States or in the tropics where food is grown.
We visited a pineapple plantation in Hawaii.
n. pl. **plantations** plan·ta·tions

plant-eater   plant-eat·er (plant-ē′tər)   an animal that eats plants.
The giraffe is a plant-eater. *n. pl.* **plant-eaters** plant-eat·ers

planter   plant·er (plan′tər)   a person who is paid to put seeds into the ground.
The man is a planter on the plantation.
n. pl. **planters** plant·ers

plaster   plas·ter (plas′tər)   a cement-like mixture that is used to cover walls and ceilings.
The plaster was put on the walls before they were painted. *n. no pl.*

plate

plastic   plas·tic (plas′tik)   **1.** a soft non-metal material made of minerals and rocks.
Many parts in a car are made of plastic.
n. pl. **plastics** plas·tics
2. made of a soft non-metal material.
The plastic bottle will not break when you drop it. *adj.*

plate   (plāt)   a flat dish.
I carried the plate to the table. *n. pl.* **plates**

plateau   pla·teau (pla·tō′)   land that is high and flat.
You can stand on a plateau and see the desert below.
n. pl. **plateaus** *or* **plateaux** pla·teaus *or* pla·teaux

platform   plat·form (plat′fôrm)   a little floor that is higher than the ground; a raised floor.
I gave a speech from the platform. *n. pl.* **platforms** plat·forms

platform

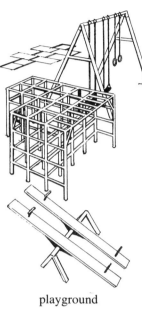

playground

playroom

play (plā) **1.** to have fun; to entertain oneself.
I will play outside. *v.*
2. to take part in a sport or a game.
Jim will play on the football team. *v.*
3. to make music on a musical instrument.
Doris can play the piano. *v.*
4. to perform or act in a show or story.
The man will play a pirate in the movie.
v. **played, played, playing** play·ing
5. a story that is acted out by actors and actresses;
a dramatic story.
She will be in the school play. *n. pl.* **plays**
6. the act of having fun.
I watched the little girl at play. *n. no pl.*

player play·er (plā′ər) a person who takes part in a sport or a game.
The short player threw the ball into the basket. *n. pl.* **players** play·ers

playful play·ful (plā′fəl) wanting to play; full of fun.
The new kitten is very playful. *adj.*

playground play·ground (plā′ground) a place where children can
go to have fun; a place with swings and slides for children.
I went to the playground after lunch. *n. pl.* **playgrounds** play·grounds

playroom play·room (plā′rüm *or* plā′rüm) a place in a house
or building where people have fun; a special room for playing.
We have a playroom in our cellar. *n. pl.* **playrooms** play·rooms

plead (plēd) to beg for something; to argue.
I will plead to go to the movie.
v. **pleaded** *or* **pled, pleaded** *or* **pled, pleading** plead·ed, plead·ing

please (plēz) **1.** a word used to ask for something politely.
May I please have a piece of candy? *adv.*
2. a word of politeness used to answer yes to a question.
"Do you want some more milk?" "Please." *adv.*
3. to make happy; to be agreeable.
The roses will please my mother.
v. **pleased, pleased, pleasing** pleas·ing

pleasure pleas·ure (plezh′ər *or* plā′zhər) fun; a good time.
It was a pleasure to go with you today. *n. pl.* **pleasures** pleas·ures

plenty plen·ty (plen′tē) more than enough; a large amount.
I had plenty of food at camp. *n. no pl.*

a	cat	**i**	sit	**oi**	oil	**ch**	chop		a in about
ā	ate	**ī**	lie	**ou**	out	**ng**	song		e in oven
ä	car	**o**	pot	**u**	cut	**sh**	she	ə =	i in pencil
e	set	**ō**	old	**ů**	book	**th**	three		o in memory
ē	equal	**ô**	or	**ü**	blue	**ŦH**	there		u in circus
ėr	germ					**zh**	treasure		

plot   (plot)   to put things and places on a map; to chart the
location of places on a map.
  The men will plot the locations of the icebergs on this map.
  v. **plotted, plotted, plotting** plot·ted, plot·ting

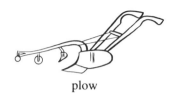
plow

plow   (plou)   **1.** a tool used on a farm to dig up the fields.
  The horse pulls the plow through the field. *n. pl.* **plows**
  2. to dig up and turn the dirt in a field.
  The farmer will plow the field after he picks the crops.
  v. **plowed, plowed, plowing** plow·ing

plum   (plum)   a dark red or purple fruit that grows on a tree,
tastes sweet and has a large seed in the center.
  I picked a plum from the tree and ate it. *n. pl.* **plums**

plumber   plumb·er (plum·ər)   a person who repairs broken
water pipes or sinks.
  The plumber fixed the leak in the kitchen sink. *n. pl.* **plumbers** plumb·ers

plus   (plus)   and; also; in addition to.
  She bought a skirt plus a matching sweater. *prep.*

Pluto   Plu·to (plü·tō)   a planet in the solar system.
  Pluto is the farthest planet from the sun. *n.*

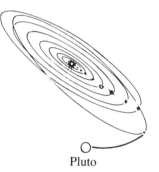
Pluto

pneumonia   pneu·mo·nia (nü·mō·nyə *or* nyü·mō·nyə)
a disease that causes a person to have liquid in the lungs so
that it is difficult to breathe.
  Pneumonia can make a person very sick. *n. no pl.*

pocket   pock·et (pok·it)   a piece of cloth that is sewn into clothes
or bags to hold things; the part of clothing in which things
are put and carried.
  I have a hole in my pocket so I lost my money. *n. pl.* **pockets** pock·ets

poem   po·em (pō·əm)   a story or an idea that is written in short
lines and that often has rhyming words at the end of each line.
  The teacher read us a poem before lunch. *n. pl.* **poems** po·ems

poet   po·et (pō·it)   a person who writes poems.
  The poet wrote about a sunset. *n. pl.* **poets** po·ets

poetry   po·et·ry (pō·i·trē)   poems or stories with short lines
written by a poet.
  Longfellow's poetry is so beautiful that you can imagine what
he is writing about. *n. no pl.*

poinsettia

poinsettia   poin·set·ti·a (poin·set·ē·ə *or* poin·set·ə)   a plant used
for decoration at Christmas that has a very small flower with
large red, white or pink leaves growing around it
that look like petals.
  The leaves of the poinsettia are dangerous to eat.
  n. pl. **poinsettias** poin·set·ti·as

318

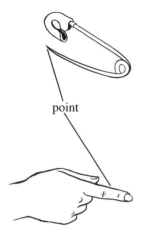

point

point (point) **1.** to show a certain location with the finger.
I will point to Chicago on the map. *v.*
2. to aim; to put something in the direction
of a place, person or thing.
I will point the gun at the target.
v. **pointed, pointed, pointing** point·ed, point·ing
3. points; a part of a car's ignition.
I changed the points in the car's motor. *plural n.*
4. a sharp tip or end of something.
The pin has a point on one end. *n.*
5. a measuring unit in a game or contest;
the things counted as a score in a game or contest.
I scored only one point in today's game. *n. pl.* **points**

point to (point tü)   to show with the finger; to give
the direction with the finger.
I will point to the right house.
v. **pointed to, pointed to, pointing to** point·ed to, point·ing to

poison poi·son (poi´zn) **1.** a gas, powder or liquid that can kill
or harm a person, plant or animal.
The skull and crossbones on the bottle means that there is
poison in the bottle. *n. pl.* **poisons** poi·sons
2. to kill or harm someone or something by using
a dangerous gas, powder or liquid.
The book is about a man planning to poison his boss.
v. **poisoned, poisoned, poisoning** poi·soned, poi·son·ing
3. having to do with a gas, powder or liquid that can kill
a person, plant or animal.
Carbon monoxide is a poison gas. *adj.*

poison gland

poison gland poi·son gland (poi´zn gland) a part of an
animal, insect or reptile that makes and stores a liquid that
will kill or hurt whatever it bites.
The black widow spider has a poison gland.

poisonous poi·son·ous (poi´zn·əs) made of a gas, powder
or liquid that can kill.
Carbon monoxide is poisonous. *adj.*

poke (pōk) to push into something with something pointed.
I will poke the fire. *v.* **poked, poked, poking** pok·ing

polar bear

polar bear po·lar bear (pō´lər ber) a big white bear that
lives near the North Pole.
The polar bear can easily hide in the snow at the North Pole.

a	cat	**i**	sit	**oi**	oil	**ch**	chop
ā	ate	**ī**	lie	**ou**	out	**ng**	song
ä	car	**o**	pot	**u**	cut	**sh**	she
e	set	**ō**	old	**u̇**	book	**th**	three
ē	equal	**ô**	or	**ü**	blue	**ŦH**	there
ėr	germ					**zh**	treasure

ə = { a in about / e in oven / i in pencil / o in memory / u in circus }

pole (pōl) a long, thin, round piece of wood or metal.
The street light is on a pole in front of our house. *n. pl.* **poles**

police po·lice (pə·lēs′) **1.** men and women whose job is
to make sure that people obey the law.
The police work to keep our town safe. *plural n.*
2. having to do with people who make sure that
people obey the law.
The police car went after the robber's car. *adj.*

policeman po·lice·man (pə·lēs′mən) a man who works for the
police; a male police officer.
The policeman gave the speeder a ticket. *n. pl.* **policemen** po·lice·men

police officer

police officer po·lice of·fi·cer (pə·lēs′ ô′fə·sər) a person
who makes sure that people obey the law; a policeman
or a policewoman.
The police officer stopped the car that was speeding.

policewoman po·lice·wom·an (pə·lēs′wùm·ən) a woman who
works for the police; a female police officer.
The policewoman stopped the robber from getting away.
n. pl. **policewomen** po·lice·wom·en

polite po·lite (pə·līt′) having good manners; acting
properly or correctly.
It is polite to say "please" and "thank you".
adj. **politer, politest** po·lit·er, po·lit·est

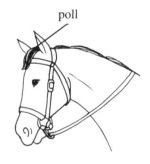

poll

politely po·lite·ly (pə·līt′lē) with good manners; properly
or correctly; in a polite way.
He politely thanked the man for his help. *adv.*

political po·lit·i·cal (pə·lit′ə·kəl) having to do with government.
The governor knows all the political groups in the state. *adj.*

politician pol·i·ti·cian (pol·ə·tish′ən) a person who is involved
in the running and the politics of a government.
The mayor is a good politician. *n. pl.* **politicians** pol·i·ti·cians

pommel

politics pol·i·tics (pol′ə·tiks) the workings of government;
the rules and operations of government.
People who vote must know about politics. *n. pl.* **politics** pol·i·tics

poll (pōl) the part of a horse's head between the ears;
the top of a horse's head where the forelock grows.
The horse's mane starts on its poll. *n. pl.* **polls**

pollen pol·len (pol′ən) a yellow dust that comes from flowers.
Pollen makes some people sneeze. *n. no pl.*

pommel   pom·mel (pum⁄əl *or* pom⁄əl)   the part on the front of a horse saddle that sticks up and out.
The cowboy grabbed the pommel when he mounted the horse.
n. pl. **pommels** pom·mels

Pomo   Po·mo (pō⁄mō)   an Indian tribe that lived in the western part of the United States.
The Pomo hunted the buffalo. *plural n.*

pond   (pond)   a small body of water; a small lake.
We went fishing in the pond on her grandfather's farm. *n. pl.* **ponds**

pony   po·ny (pō⁄nē)   a young horse; a small horse.
The pony is only four months old. *n. pl.* **ponies** pon·ies

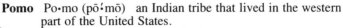
pool

pool   (pül)   **1.** a tank of water that is used for swimming.
We put clean water into the pool. *n.*
2. a small amount of liquid; a puddle.
Dick stepped into a pool of water when he got out of his car. *n. pl.* **pools**
3. a game that is played with balls and sticks on a table with six pockets.
We play pool in the recreation hall at camp. *n. no pl.*

poor   (pùr)   **1.** without money; having little money or value.
We give our used clothes to poor people. *adj.*
2. needing pity.
We should all help the poor child whose father died.
adj. **poorer, poorest** poor·er, poor·est

poorly   poor·ly (pùr⁄lē)   in a bad way; badly.
He is doing poorly in math this year. *adv.*

pop   (pop)   **1.** to break with a short, loud noise; to explode.
The balloon will pop if you put too much air into it.
v. **popped, popped, popping** pop·ping
2. a short, loud sound; an explosion.
We heard the pop of the bottle cap when she opened the bottle. *n.*
3. a soda; a liquid with bubbles that people drink.
I drank a bottle of pop at the circus. *n. pl.* **pops** *or* **pop**
4. having to do with a liquid with bubbles that people drink.
The pop bottle broke when she dropped it. *adj.*

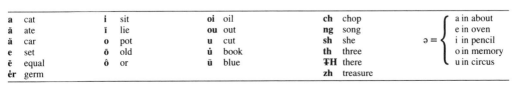
popcorn

popcorn   pop·corn (pop⁄kôrn)   a snack food that is made by heating the kernels of corn until they pop open.
We made some popcorn last night. *n. no pl.*

a	cat	i	sit	oi	oil	ch	chop		a in about
ā	ate	ī	lie	ou	out	ng	song		e in oven
ä	car	o	pot	u	cut	sh	she	ə =	i in pencil
e	set	ō	old	ù	book	th	three		o in memory
ē	equal	ô	or	ü	blue	ᴛʜ	there		u in circus
ėr	germ					zh	treasure		

pop into ___ head   pop in·to ___ head (pop in·tü ___ hed)
to suddenly think about something; to quickly
remember something.
The idea will pop into your head when you are not trying so hard. *idiom*

pop out   (pop out)   to come out fast; to come out suddenly.
The man will pop out of the box.
v. **popped out, popped out, popping out** pop·ping out

popper   pop·per (pop·ər)   a machine that heats kernels of
corn so that they pop open.
The popper makes the popcorn very quickly. *n. pl.* **poppers** pop·pers

popper

popular   pop·u·lar (pop·yə·lər)   **1.** liked by many people.
"E.T." was a popular movie. *adj.*
2. having many friends.
Lisa is a popular girl. *adj.*

population   pop·u·la·tion (pop·yə·lā·shən)   the number of people
in an area; the people in a city, state or country.
Our city has a population of 30,000. *n. pl.* **populations** pop·u·la·tions

porch   (pôrch *or* pōrch)   a raised floor with a roof, attached
to a house or building.
We have a large porch outside our back door. *n. pl.* **porches** porch·es

pork   (pôrk *or* pōrk)   the meat that comes from pigs.
Ham and bacon are pork. *n. no pl.*

porpoise   por·poise (pôr·pəs)   a sea animal that has a rounded
nose and is in the same family as the whale.
We saw the porpoise jump out of the ocean.
n. pl. **porpoises** *or* **porpoise** por·pois·es

porch

port   (pôrt *or* pōrt)   a place where boats are kept; a harbor.
We sailed into the nearest port. *n. pl.* **ports**

portable   port·a·ble (pôr·tə·bəl *or* pōr·tə·bəl)   able to be moved;
easily carried or moved.
We took the portable television camping with us. *adj.*

portrait   por·trait (pôr·trit *or* pôr·trāt *or* pōr·trit *or* pōr·trāt)
a picture of someone's face; a painted picture of a person.
An artist will paint my portrait. *n. pl.* **portraits** por·traits

position   po·si·tion (pə·zish·ən)   **1.** the place where a person
or thing is; the place in a line or a row.
I do not want to lose my position in line. *n.*
2. the way the body is placed; the body stance.
I am not sitting in a comfortable position. *n. pl.* **positions** po·si·tions

porpoise

possession   pos·ses·sion (pə·zesh·ən)   a thing that belongs
to a person; something that a person owns.
My bicycle is my favorite possession. *n. pl.* **possessions** pos·ses·sions

possum

REX RUBBON
October 31

poster

pot

possible pos·si·ble (pos⸗ə·bəl) able to happen; capable of being done.
It is now possible for man to walk on the moon. *adj.*

possum pos·sum (pos⸗əm) a small animal that carries its babies in a pocket or pouch, lives in trees and is most active at night; also, opossum (ə·pos⸗əm).
The possum pretends to be dead when it is afraid. *n. pl.* **possums** pos·sums

postage post·age (pō⸗stij) **1.** the cost of the stamps needed to mail a certain letter or a package.
The postage on the package was $2.64. *n. no pl.*
2. having to do with mail.
The postage stamp has a picture of a seashell on it. *adj.*

postcard post·card (pōst⸗kärd) a small piece of stiff paper on which people write a short message or note for mailing.
I got a postcard from my aunt who is visiting Italy.
n. pl. **postcards** post·cards

poster post·er (pō⸗stər) **1.** a large piece of paper with a message or a picture on it.
We put a poster from the zoo on the wall in the library.
n. pl. **posters** post·ers
2. having to do with a large piece of paper with a message or picture on it.
The poster board was knocked over by the wind. *adj.*

poster paint post·er paint (pō⸗stər pānt) a thick paint that people use for writing on posters.
The poster paint will not come off the sign easily.

post office (pōst ô⸗fis) a building where people sort mail before it is delivered to homes and businesses; a place where people bring letters and packages to be mailed; a place where stamps are sold.
I bought the stamps at the post office.

postpone post·pone (pōst·pōn′) to put off until another time.
I will postpone the party if it is raining.
v. **postponed, postponed, postponing** post·poned, post·pon·ing

pot (pot) a deep round pan or dish.
We put the soup in a pot. *n. pl.* **pots**

a	cat	**i**	sit	**oi**	oil	**ch**	chop
ā	ate	**ī**	lie	**ou**	out	**ng**	song
ä	car	**o**	pot	**u**	cut	**sh**	she
e	set	**ō**	old	**u̇**	book	**th**	three
ē	equal	**ô**	or	**ü**	blue	**TH**	there
ėr	germ					**zh**	treasure

ə = { a in about / e in oven / i in pencil / o in memory / u in circus }

potato po·ta·to (pə·tā′tō *or* pə·tā′tə) a kind of vegetable that grows under the ground and that has a thin skin on it.
I ate a baked potato for dinner. *n. pl.* **potatoes** po·ta·toes

potato

potato chip po·ta·to chip (pə·tā′tō chip) a snack food that is made by frying a thin piece of potato in oil.
It is difficult to eat only one potato chip.

potion po·tion (pō′shən) a liquid used for medicine, magic or poison.
The mean witch mixed a poison potion. *n. pl.* **potions** po·tions

pottery pot·ter·y (pot′ər·ē) dishes made of clay and heated to get hard.
This pottery was made by the Indians. *n. pl.* **potteries** pot·ter·ies

pottery

pouch (pouch) a pocket or bag.
The kangaroo has a pouch to carry her baby. *n. pl.* **pouches** pouch·es

pound (pound) **1.** a money unit in England.
A pound is worth more than a dollar. *n.*
2. a unit of weight that equals 16 ounces.
I gained a pound by eating all that food. *n. pl.* **pounds**
3. to hit or beat something hard several times.
I will pound the nail into the wood.
v. **pounded, pounded, pounding** pound·ed, pound·ing

pour (pôr *or* pōr) **1.** to make something (for example, a liquid) come out of a container in an even, steady way.
I will pour the hot water out of the pot. *v.*
2. to rain heavily.
The rain will pour out of the clouds. *v.* **poured, poured, pouring** pour·ing

pout (pout) **1.** to make a sad or angry face by pushing out the lower lip.
The baby will pout if he cannot go with his mother.
v. **pouted, pouted, pouting** pout·ed, pout·ing
2. a frown made with the lower lip pushed out.
Her pout makes you feel so sad. *n. pl.* **pouts**

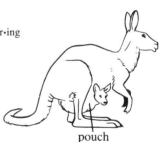

pouch

powder pow·der (pou′dər) a dust-like material that is made by crushing or grinding something solid.
We put powder on the baby's arms. *n. pl.* **powders** pow·ders

power pow·er (pou′ər) **1.** strength; energy; force.
Moving water has great power. *n. no pl.*
2. having to do with energy that does work or makes something work.
The power tools use electricity. *adj.*

powerful pow·er·ful (pou′ər·fəl) very strong; having lots of energy; being full of power.
Penicillin is a powerful drug. *adj.*

power plant

power plant pow·er plant (pou′ər plant) a place where energy is made; a place where electricity is made.
The power plant produces energy for the whole state.

powwow pow·wow (pou′wou′) an Indian meeting or ceremony.
There are many different kinds of food at a powwow.
n. pl. **powwows** pow·wows

practice prac·tice (prak′tis) **1.** to do something again and again to improve.
I will practice playing the piano for one hour a day.
v. **practiced, practiced, practicing** prac·ticed, prac·tic·ing
2. the way something is usually done.
It is my mother's practice to set the table before she starts to cook. *n.*
3. the act of doing something again and again so that you can learn to do it better; a drill.
We had band practice this afternoon. *n. pl.* **practices** prac·tic·es

prairie prair·ie (prer′ē) a large field of grass with few trees.
You can find a prairie in the midwestern part of the United States.
n. pl. **prairies** prair·ies

praise (prāz) **1.** to say good things to or about someone; to compliment someone.
I will praise her music. *v.* **praised, praised, praising** prais·ing
2. something good that is said about someone or something.
The movie received a lot of praise. *n. pl.* **praises** prais·es

pray (prā) to talk to God; to ask God for help and guidance.
We will pray before we eat. *v.* **prayed, prayed, praying** pray·ing

prayer (prer *or* prar) the words that people say when talking to God; the act of talking to God.
We say a prayer before we eat to thank God for the food. *n. pl.* **prayers**

preach (prēch) to speak about religion; to speak strongly about something.
The man will preach in church on Sunday.
v. **preached, preached, preaching** preach·ing

predict pre·dict (pri·dikt′) to tell what will happen before it happens; to know that something will happen before it happens.
The gypsy will predict your future.
v. **predicted, predicted, predicting** pre·dict·ed, pre·dict·ing

a	cat	**i**	sit	**oi**	oil	**ch**	chop		a in about
ā	ate	**ī**	lie	**ou**	out	**ng**	song		e in oven
ä	car	**o**	pot	**u**	cut	**sh**	she	ə =	i in pencil
e	set	**ō**	old	**u̇**	book	**th**	three		o in memory
ē	equal	**ô**	or	**ü**	blue	**ŦH**	there		u in circus
ėr	germ					**zh**	treasure		

prefer   pre·fer (pri·fer′)   to like one thing more than another;
    to like something better than anything else.
     I prefer chocolate ice cream to vanilla ice cream.
     v. **preferred, preferred, preferring** pre·ferred, pre·fer·ring

prepare   pre·pare (pri·per′ *or* pri·par′)   **1.** to get ready.
     I will prepare to go to camp. *v.*
    2. to make food.
     I will prepare dinner.
     v. **prepared, prepared, preparing** pre·pared, pre·par·ing

Presbyterian   Pres·by·ter·i·an (prez·bə·tir′ē·ən)   having to do
    with or belonging to a specific religious group whose church
    is operated by ministers and elders.
     My sister is marrying a Presbyterian minister. *adj.*

present[1]   pre·sent (prez′nt)   a gift; a thing that is given to someone.
     I gave her a present for her birthday. *n. pl.* **presents** pres·ents

present[2]   pre·sent (pri·zent′)   to give something to someone.
     I will present the gift to her.
     v. **presented, presented, presenting** pre·sent·ed, pre·sent·ing

present

preserve   pre·serve (pri·zėrv′)   to keep something so that it
    does not spoil; to keep safe.
     The museum will preserve the paintings.
     v. **preserved, preserved, preserving** pre·served, pre·serv·ing

president   pres·i·dent (prez′ə·dənt *or* prez′dənt)   **1.** the leader
    of the United States; the head of the American government.
     Abraham Lincoln was the president during the Civil War. *n.*
    2. the leader of a company, club or business.
     Her father is the president of the car company.
     n. pl. **presidents** pres·i·dents

press   (pres)   to push down on something with a great
    force; to push down hard.
     I will press the grapes until all the juice is out.
     v. **pressed, pressed, pressing** press·ing

pressure   pres·sure (presh′ər)   **1.** the pushing of a weight
    or a force; a feeling of heaviness.
     The horse can feel the pressure of the rider. *n. pl.* **pressures** pres·sures
    2. to force to do something; to make someone do something
    they do not want to do.
     The boy will pressure you to walk on the railroad tracks.
     v. **pressured, pressured, pressuring** pres·sured, pres·sur·ing

pretend   pre·tend (pri·tend′)   to make believe that something
    is real or true.
     I will pretend that I am a princess.
     v. **pretended, pretended, pretending** pre·tend·ed, pre·tend·ing

pretty   pret·ty (prit′ē)   pleasant to look at; nice-looking; attractive.
The girl in the picture is pretty. *adj.* **prettier, prettiest** pret·ti·er, pret·ti·est

prevent   pre·vent (pri·vent′)   to stop something from happening; to stop someone from doing something.
We can prevent forest fires by being careful with fire.
v. **prevented, prevented, preventing** pre·vent·ed, pre·vent·ing

prevention   pre·ven·tion (pri·ven′shən)   the act of stopping something from happening; the act of stopping someone from doing something.
The prevention of forest fires is everyone's job.
n. pl. **preventions** pre·ven·tions

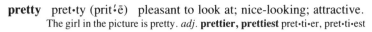

price tag

price   (prīs)   **1.** the amount of money for which something is sold; the cost of buying something.
The price of the ice cream cone was 50¢. *n. pl.* **prices** pric·es
2. having to do with the cost of something.
The newspaper had a price list of everything in that store. *adj.*

price tag   (prīs tag)   a small, stiff piece of paper that is on an item in a store and has the cost of the item written on it.
The price tag on the dress read $25.00.

prick   (prik)   to make a tiny hole in something with something that is sharp and pointed.
I will prick the balloon with this pin.
v. **pricked, pricked, pricking** prick·ing

priest   (prēst)   a minister in a church.
The priest taught us a new prayer. *n. pl.* **priests**

priest

prime minister   prime min·is·ter (prīm min′ə·stər)   the leader of a country.
The United States has a president, but Canada has a prime minister.

primitive   prim·i·tive (prim′ə·tiv)   very simple; coming from a much earlier time in the history of man; having to do with a time long ago.
The primitive men and women did not wear shoes. *adj.*

prince   (prins)   the son of a king and queen; the son of a country's ruler.
The prince was looking for a wife. *n. pl.* **princes** princ·es

a	cat	i	sit	oi	oil	ch	chop		a in about
ā	ate	ī	lie	ou	out	ng	song		e in oven
ä	car	o	pot	u	cut	sh	she	ə =	i in pencil
e	set	ō	old	u̇	book	th	three		o in memory
ē	equal	ô	or	ü	blue	ŦH	there		u in circus
ėr	germ					zh	treasure		

princess   prin·cess (prin⸍ses *or* prin⸍sis *or* prin·ses′)   the daughter
of a king and queen; the daughter of a country's ruler.
The princess was very beautiful. *n. pl.* **princesses** prin·cess·es

principal   prin·ci·pal (prin⸍sə·pəl)   the leader of a school;
the head of a school.
The principal helps the teachers in the school.
n. pl. **principals** prin·ci·pals

princess

print   (print)   **1.** to use a machine and ink to put pictures
and words on paper.
The editor will print the story in the newspaper. *v.*
2. to make letters that are not cursive or handwritten.
The teacher asked us to print our names on our papers.
v. **printed, printed, printing** print·ed, print·ing
3. having to do with using ink to put words
and pictures on paper.
The print shop smells like ink. *adj.*

printer   print·er (prin⸍tər)   a person who uses a machine
with ink to put words and pictures on paper.
The printer will make sure that the words on the paper
are clear. *n. pl.* **printers** print·ers

print

printing press   print·ing press (print⸍ing   pres)   a machine that
uses ink to mark words and pictures onto paper.
The printer uses a printing press to make books and magazines.

prison   pris·on (priz⸍n)   a building where lawbreakers
are kept; a jail; a building with bars on the windows
and doors so that people cannot get out.
The judge sent the robber to prison. *n. pl.* **prisons** pris·ons

privacy   pri·va·cy (prī⸍və·sē)   time alone or away from other people.
Everyone needs some privacy. *n. pl.* **privacies** pri·va·cies

private   pri·vate (prī⸍vit)   not open to everyone but to
only a few people; something not known to many
people; something kept to oneself.
We are having a private conversation that we do not want
the boys to hear. *adj.*

prize   (prīz)   **1.** something that a person earns by winning a game or
contest; an award; something that is given for good work.
I won first prize in the painting contest. *n. pl.* **prizes** priz·es
2. valuable; worthy of an award; good enough
to win an award.
She grows prize roses every year. *adj.*

probably   prob·a·bly (prob⸍ə·blē)   likely; having a great
chance of happening.
I will probably go to the movie tonight. *adv.*

printing press
(early)

problem   prob·lem (prob⸴ləm)   **1.** something that is difficult to do; a difficulty; something that needs to be solved or worked out.
I had a problem getting the dog out of the house. *n.*
2. a question that needs an answer; a school exercise.
I could not get the answer to the second math problem.
n. pl. **problems** prob·lems

proceed   pro·ceed (prə·sēd′)   to go on; to continue to do something that was stopped for a short time.
The car will proceed after the light turns green.
v. **proceeded, proceeded, proceeding** pro·ceed·ed, pro·ceed·ing

prison

process   proc·ess (pros⸴es *or* prō⸴ses)   **1.** the order of actions that must be done; the actions that are done to make something; a method with several steps.
There are six steps in the process of making fudge.
n. pl. **processes** pro·cess·es
2. to do something by a certain method; to treat something in a series of steps.
The man will process the film into pictures.
v. **processed, processed, processing** pro·cessed, pro·cess·ing

produce   pro·duce (prə·düs′ *or* prə·dyüs′)   to make something; to build something; to create something new.
I can produce a house from these toy logs.
v. **produced, produced, producing** pro·duced, pro·duc·ing

producer   pro·duc·er (prə·dü⸴sər *or* prə·dyü⸴sər)   a person who makes a movie.
He is the producer of "E.T." *n. pl.* **producers** pro·duc·ers

prize

product   prod·uct (prod⸴əkt)   something that is made by a company and sold; something that is made by people or by nature.
Coal is a product of nature, but steel is a product of humans.
n. pl. **products** prod·ucts

production   pro·duc·tion (prə·duk⸴shən)   the action of making things out of other materials.
Dad's factory is involved in the production of steel bars. *n. no pl.*

professor   pro·fes·sor (prə·fes⸴ər)   a person who teaches in a college.
Dr. Tyne is a history professor. *n. pl.* **professors** pro·fes·sors

a	cat	i	sit	oi	oil	ch	chop		a in about
ā	ate	ī	lie	ou	out	ng	song		e in oven
ä	car	o	pot	u	cut	sh	she	ə =	i in pencil
e	set	ō	old	u̇	book	th	three		o in memory
ē	equal	ô	or	ü	blue	ŦH	there		u in circus
ėr	germ					zh	treasure		

profit   prof·it (prof′it)   money that is left after all the bills for
services and materials are paid; money remaining after all
payments have been made.
The company had a $40,000 profit last year. *n. pl.* **profits** prof·its

program   pro·gram (prō′gram *or* prō′grəm)   list of events; a piece
of paper that lists the names of characters and acts in a play.
We gave each person a program. *n. pl.* **programs** pro·grams

project   pro·ject (prə·jekt′)   to make an image appear on a screen;
to make a picture appear on a screen.
The machine will project the picture.
v. **projected, projected, projecting** pro·ject·ed, pro·ject·ing

projector   pro·jec·tor (prə·jek′tər)   a machine that is used to show
a film or a movie on a screen; a machine that projects the
pictures of a movie onto a screen.
We put the film through the projector so that we could watch the movie.
n. pl. **projectors** pro·jec·tors

promise   prom·ise (prom′is)   **1.** to agree to do something or
to agree not to do something; to give one's word
about something.
I will promise not to be late tomorrow.
v. **promised, promised, promising** prom·ised, prom·is·ing
2. an oath not to do something; an agreement; a vow.
I made a promise not to be late tomorrow. *n. pl.* **promises** prom·is·es

projector

promote   pro·mote (prə·mōt′)   to advertise to sell something;
to tell what is good about something.
The commercial will promote the new toy.
v. **promoted, promoted, promoting** pro·mot·ed, pro·mot·ing

prong   (prông *or* prong)   a sharp point, such as those
on a spear or a fork.
He put the prong into his finger. *n. pl.* **prongs**

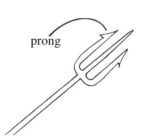

prong

proof   (prüf)   facts that prove that something is true; evidence.
The police looked for proof that the man was the killer. *n. no pl.*

property   prop·er·ty (prop′ər·tē)   things that a person owns;
land that a person owns.
The farm is my grandfather's property. *n. pl.* **properties** prop·er·ties

propose   pro·pose (prə·prōz′)   to suggest an idea; to offer
a new plan, system, idea or method.
I will propose that we have a candy sale instead of a bake sale.
v. **proposed, proposed, proposing** pro·posed, pro·pos·ing

prosperity   pros·per·i·ty (pro·sper′ə·tē)   wealth; success;
good fortune.
We wished the bride and groom good health and prosperity. *n. no pl.*

protest

protect pro·tect (prə·tekt′) to keep safe from harm; to keep
out of danger; to guard.
The dog will protect you at night.
v. **protected, protected, protecting** pro·tect·ed, pro·tect·ing

protection pro·tec·tion (prə·tek′shən) that which keeps something
safe from harm; something that guards; the act of keeping
something out of danger.
The dog is your protection. *n. pl.* **protections** pro·tec·tions

protest pro·test (prə·test′) to argue against something;
to say no; to refuse to do something.
I will protest the new rule about staying at school.
v. **protested, protested, protesting** pro·test·ed, pro·test·ing

proud (proud) satisfied with one's actions; happy
with something or someone; a feeling of liking oneself.
I am proud of my grades in math.
adj. **prouder, proudest** proud·er, proud·est

prove (prüv) to show what is true; to find
facts that show what is true.
I will prove that I did not take his money.
v. **proved, proved** *or* **proven, proving** prov·en, prov·ing

provide pro·vide (prə·vīd′) to give something that is needed;
to supply what is wanted by someone.
The teacher will provide the ice cream for the party.
v. **provided, provided, providing** pro·vid·ed, pro·vid·ing

province prov·ince (prov′əns) a division or part of a
country; a state.
Quebec is a province of Canada. *n. pl.* **provinces** prov·inc·es

public pub·lic (pub′lik) **1.** belonging to all the people, not
just a few; open for use by all the people; not private.
The library is a public building. *adj.*
2. all the people in an area; the population.
The meeting was open to the public. *n. no pl.*

publication pub·li·ca·tion (pub·lə·kā′shən) something that
is printed with ink and a printing press, such as a book,
newspaper or magazine.
My story was printed in the school's publication.
n. pl. **publications** pub·li·ca·tions

a cat	**i** sit	**oi** oil	**ch** chop		a in about
ā ate	**ī** lie	**ou** out	**ng** song		e in oven
ä car	**o** pot	**u** cut	**sh** she	ə =	i in pencil
e set	**ō** old	**u̇** book	**th** three		o in memory
ē equal	**ô** or	**ü** blue	**ŦH** there		u in circus
ėr germ			**zh** treasure		

publish pub·lish (pub′lish) to prepare something and have it printed for other people to read.
> The school will publish two newspapers every year.
> *v.* **published, published, publishing** pub·lished, pub·lish·ing

publisher pub·lish·er (pub′li·shər) a person or company that offers for sale things for other people to read, such as books, magazines or papers.
> Mr. Rose is the publisher of our newspaper. *n. pl.* **publishers** pub·lish·ers

pulp

puff (puf) to fill with air; to suck in air and get larger; to blow with short, quick breaths.
> I will puff up my cheeks and whistle. *v.* **puffed, puffed, puffing** puff·ing

pull (pùl) to move something toward oneself; to grab something and tug it toward you; to drag something.
> I will pull the wagon. *v.* **pulled, pulled, pulling** pull·ing

pull on (pùl ôn *or* pùl on) to tug something toward oneself; to grab hold of something and move it toward oneself.
> I will pull on the end of the rope.
> *v.* **pulled on, pulled on, pulling on** pull·ing on

pull out (pùl out) to move something from the inside of something else; to take from inside.
> Mother will pull out the piece of wood in my finger.
> *v.* **pulled out, pulled out, pulling out** pull·ing out

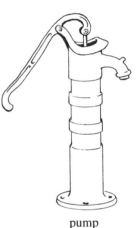
pump

pull up (pùl up) to come to the front of; to arrive.
> The bus will pull up to your front door.
> *v.* **pulled up, pulled up, pulling up** pull·ing up

pulp (pulp) the inside part of a fruit or vegetable; the meaty inside of a fruit or vegetable.
> The pulp of the orange is sour. *n. no pl.*

pump (pump) **1.** a tool that is used to move air or water from one place to another; a tool that is used to bring water up out of the ground.
> I got the water from the pump. *n. pl.* **pumps**
> **2.** to push air or water from one place to another.
> I will pump air into the tire.
> *v.* **pumped, pumped, pumping** pump·ing

pumpkin pump·kin (pump′kin *or* pung′kin) **1.** a round orange vegetable that is used for decoration at Halloween.
> I cut a scary face on the pumpkin.
> *n. pl.* **pumpkins** pump·kins
> **2.** made of round orange vegetables.
> I ate two pieces of pumpkin pie. *adj.*

pumpkin

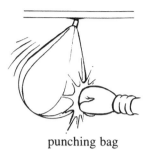

punching bag

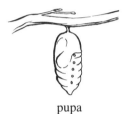

pupa

puppet

punch (punch) **1.** a drink made with fruit juices.
I drank a glass of punch. *n.*
2. a quick hit with the fist.
He has a powerful punch. *n. pl.* **punches** punch·es
3. to hit with the fist.
I will punch him if he hits me. *v.*
4. to make holes in something with a tool.
I will punch holes in this paper with the pencil.
v. **punched, punched, punching** punch·ing

punching bag punch·ing bag (pun′ching bag) a leather sack that
is filled with sand or air and used for boxing practice.
I hit the punching bag many times.

punch out (punch out) to remove or take out by first making holes.
We will punch out the pictures in the book.
v. **punched out, punched out, punching out** punch·ing out

punish pun·ish (pun′ish) to correct someone who has done
something wrong; to cause a loss or discomfort to someone
who has done something wrong.
I will punish Joe for breaking the light.
v. **punished, punished, punishing** pun·ished, pun·ish·ing

pupa pu·pa (pyü′pə) **1.** the stage of an insect's life between
being a larva and being an adult.
The larva turns into the pupa. *n.*
2. an insect that is in the second stage of life.
The pupa does not eat food but does drink water.
n. pl. **pupae** *or* **pupas** pu·pae *or* pu·pas

puppet pup·pet (pup′it) a doll that looks like a person or an animal
and has strings tied on it so that a person can move its
arms and legs.
Bert made the puppet dance across the stage. *n. pl.* **puppets** pup·pets

puppy pup·py (pup′ē) a baby dog.
I got a new puppy for my birthday. *n. pl.* **puppies** pup·pies

purchase pur·chase (pėr′chəs) **1.** a thing that
a person buys with money.
I made only one purchase at the store.
n. pl. **purchases** pur·chas·es
2. to buy something.
I will purchase a ball with my money.
v. **purchased, purchased, purchasing** pur·chased, pur·chas·ing

a cat	**i** sit	**oi** oil	**ch** chop		a in about
ā ate	**ī** lie	**ou** out	**ng** song		e in oven
ä car	**o** pot	**u** cut	**sh** she	ə =	i in pencil
e set	**ō** old	**ů** book	**th** three		o in memory
ē equal	**ô** or	**ü** blue	**ŦH** there		u in circus
ėr germ			**zh** treasure		

pure   (pyůr)   not mixed with anything else; clean; perfect; without a mistake.
The well water is pure. *adj.* **pur:r, purest** pur•er, pur•est

purr   (pėr)   to make a sound in the back of the throat; to make a sound like a cat.
The cat will purr when you pet it.
v. **purred, purred, purring** pur•ring

purse   (pėrs)   a bag in which people carry money, wallets, pictures and keys.
She put her wallet in her purse. *n. pl.* **purses** purs•es

purse

pus   (pus)   a white liquid that comes out of a sore or an infection.
The doctor took the pus out of the blister. *n. no pl.*

push   (půsh)   to move something away from you; to shove something away with your hands.
I will push open the door. *v.* **pushed, pushed, pushing** push•ing

push around   push a•round (půsh ə•round′)   to bully someone; to mistreat someone; to treat someone badly.
The boy will try to push around the little girl.
v. **pushed around, pushed around, pushing around**
push•ing a•round

pussy willow   puss•y wil•low (půs′ē   wil′ō)   a tree that has long, thin branches covered in early spring with soft, silky, fuzzy flowers.
We cut branches from the pussy willow and put them in a vase.

put   (půt)   to place something; to lay something down.
I will put the paper in the trash. *v.* **put, put, putting** put•ting

put away   (půt   ə•wā′)   to put a thing in its place; to return something to where it is kept.
I will put away the dishes.
v. **put away, put away, putting away** put•ting a•way

pussy willow

put down   (půt   doun)   to set something down; to place something in a lower place.
Grandma put down her knitting and picked up her book.
v. **put down, put down, putting down** put•ting down

put in   (půt   in)   to place inside; to deposit something inside something else.
The boy has a new bank, and his father put in $1.00 for him. *v.*

put on (pu̇t ôn) **1.** to get dressed; to place clothes on the body.
I will put on my new dress. *v.*
2. to do a play; to produce entertainment.
The school will put on a Christmas play. *v.*
3. to place together; to fasten.
I put on the diaper. *v.*
v. **put on, put on, putting on** put·ting on

put out (pu̇t out) to stop; to cause to stop or go out; to extinguish.
I will put out the candle. *v.* **put out, put out, putting out** put·ting out

puzzle

put ___ to sleep (pu̇t ___ tü slēp) to give an animal something so that it will die; to kill an animal gently.
The veterinarian will put the old dog to sleep. *idiom*

put ___ to the test (pu̇t ___ tü ᴛʜə test) to try out something; to test something to find out if it works.
I will put the new machine to the test.

put up (pu̇t up) to build; to erect.
We will put up a new doghouse.
v. **put up, put up, putting up** put·ting up

puzzle puz·zle (puz′əl) **1.** to confuse; to try to understand something difficult.
The problem will puzzle you for a short time.
v. **puzzled, puzzled, puzzling** puz·zled, puz·zling
2. a picture cut into many pieces that link together.
We put the puzzle together. *n.*
3. a game that people play by solving a question or finding an answer.
We had to find the hidden things in the puzzle. *n. pl.* **puzzles** puz·zles

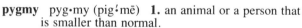

pygmy pyg·my (pig′mē) **1.** an animal or a person that is smaller than normal.
The whale is a pygmy. *n. pl.* **pygmies** pyg·mies
2. being smaller than normal.
The pygmy whale is only five feet long. *adj.*

python

python py·thon (pī′thon *or* pī′thən) a large snake that is not poisonous but that kills things by squeezing them.
The python is a dangerous snake. *n. pl.* **pythons** py·thons

a	cat	i	sit	oi	oil	ch	chop		a in about
ā	ate	ī	lie	ou	out	ng	song		e in oven
ä	car	o	pot	u	cut	sh	she	ə =	i in pencil
e	set	ō	old	u̇	book	th	three		o in memory
ē	equal	ô	or	ü	blue	ᴛʜ	there		u in circus
ėr	germ					zh	treasure		

Qq

quack (kwak) the sound made by a duck.
We heard the quack of the duck on the lake. *n. pl.* **quacks**

Quaker Quak·er (kwā‡kər) **1.** a person who belongs to the
Society of Friends church.
A Quaker does not believe in war. *n. pl.* **Quakers** Quak·ers
2. having to do with a person who belongs to the Society
of Friends.
My friend goes to a Quaker college. *adj.*

qualify qual·i·fy (kwol‡ə·fī) to become eligible to be part
of something; to be able to join something.
I can qualify to become a Boy Scout.
v. **qualified, qualified, qualifying** qual·i·fied, qual·i·fy·ing

quantity quan·ti·ty (kwon‡tə·tē) an amount;
a number; a large amount.
The quantity of corn in the box is listed on the front of the box.
n. pl. **quantities** quan·ti·ties

quarrel quar·rel (kwôr‡əl *or* kwor‡əl) to argue; to
have a fight with words.
The boys will quarrel about who rides the bicycle.
v. **quarreled** *or* **quarrelled, quarreled** *or* **quarrelled, quarreling** *or*
quarrelling quar·reled *or* quar·relled, quar·rel·ing *or* quar·rel·ling

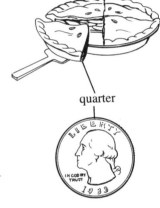
quarter

quarter quar·ter (kwôr‡tər) **1.** a coin that equals 25 cents.
The ice cream costs a quarter. *n.*
2. a part of an animal that includes one of the four legs.
The stone hit the rear quarter of the horse. *n.*
3. a fraction of something that equals one-fourth (¼).
I ate a quarter of the pie. *n. pl.* **quarters** quar·ters

quarter horse quar·ter horse (kwôr‡tər hôrs) a kind of horse that
is raised for racing and for riding in games.
The quarter horse can run very fast.

Quebec Que·bec (kwi·bek′) a province (state) of Canada; its capital
is the city of Quebec.
Quebec is in eastern Canada. *n.*

queen (kwēn) **1.** the wife of a king; the female ruler of a country.
The queen wore the Crown Jewels to the festival. *n. pl.* **queens**
2. having to do with a female ruler.
The queen bee does no work. *adj.*

Queen Elizabeth II

question ques·tion (kwes′chən) **1.** something that a person asks to get an answer or fact; an inquiry.
I asked the teacher a question about our homework.
n. pl. **questions** ques·tions
2. to wonder if something is right or true; to doubt the rightness of something.
I question whether he is telling the truth.
v. **questioned, questioned, questioning** ques·tioned, ques·tion·ing

questioningly ques·tion·ing·ly (kwes′chə·ning·lē) in a way that seems like a question; with a look of asking.
The teacher looked questioningly at me as I spoke. *adv.*

quick (kwik) **1.** smart; learning easily.
She has a quick mind and learned to read without difficulty. *adj.*
2. fast; speedy.
He is a quick runner. *adj.* **quicker, quickest** quick·er, quick·est

quickly quick·ly (kwik′lē) in a fast way; suddenly.
He quickly hid the candy from his sister. *adv.*

quilt

quiet qui·et (kwī′ət) **1.** having no sound; having no noise.
The library is a quiet place. *adj.* **quieter, quietest** qui·et·er, qui·et·est
2. the silence; the time when there is no noise.
I like the quiet of the library. *n. no pl.*

quietly qui·et·ly (kwī′ət·lē) in a silent way; with no noise; without sound.
I quietly walked up the steps. *adv.*

quilt (kwilt) a cover for the top of a bed; a bedspread that has padding inside of it.
My grandmother made a quilt for my bed. *n. pl.* **quilts**

quip (kwip) to say something funny; to make a joke.
The old man loves to quip with the children.
v. **quipped, quipped, quipping** quip·ping

quiver

quit (kwit) to stop; to play or work no longer.
I will quit and go home when it gets dark outside.
v. **quit** *or* **quitted, quit** *or* **quitted, quitting** quit·ted, quit·ting

quite (kwīt) very; to a great or high degree.
The soup was quite hot. *adv.*

quiver quiv·er (kwiv′ər) a container for arrows; a place to carry arrows for a bow.
The hunter filled the quiver before going hunting. *n. pl.* **quivers** quiv·ers

a	cat	i	sit	oi	oil	ch	chop		a in about
ā	ate	ī	lie	ou	out	ng	song		e in oven
ä	car	o	pot	u	cut	sh	she	ə =	i in pencil
e	set	ō	old	u̇	book	th	three		o in memory
ē	equal	ô	or	ü	blue	ŦH	there		u in circus
ėr	germ					zh	treasure		

Rr

rabbit rab·bit (rab⁴it) a small furry animal with long ears and a
short tail; a bunny.
> The rabbit hopped into the garden and ate the carrots. *n. pl.* **rabbits** rab·bits

rabbit

rabies ra·bies (rā⁴bēz) a disease that a person gets from the bite of
a very sick animal.
> The little boy was given shots to cure his rabies. *n. no pl.*

raccoon rac·coon (ra·kün′) a forest animal that has black spots
around its eyes and a long bushy tail with black rings.
> The raccoon lives near the lake. *n. pl.* **raccoons** rac·coons

race (rās) **1.** a contest to see who is the fastest;
a contest of speed.
> The race will start when the man shoots the gun. *n. pl.* **races** rac·es

2. to compete to see who can run or go the fastest; to
be in a contest of speed.
> The horses will race around the track. *v.* **raced, raced, racing** rac·ing

raccoon

racetrack race·track (rās⁴trak) the place where a contest of speed
is held; a road or a circular path that is used for racing.
> The horses ran around the racetrack. *n. pl.* **racetracks** race·tracks

racing rac·ing (rās⁴ing) **1.** a sport; a contest.
> Horse racing is fun to watch. *n. no pl.*

2. having to do with a sport or a contest.
> The racing car can go very fast. *adj.*

3. *v. pres. part.* See **race** (2).

rack

rack (rak) a wooden, plastic or wire frame that is
used to hold things.
> I put the dishes in the dish rack. *n. pl.* **racks**

radar ra·dar (rā⁴där) a tool that measures how fast something is
going or locates things like planes or ships.
> The weather watchers use radar to watch for storm clouds. *n. no pl.*

radiator ra·di·a·tor (rā⁴dē·ā·tər) a heater that works on
steam or hot water.
> The radiator in our classroom makes a lot of noise.
> *n. pl.* **radiators** ra·di·a·tors

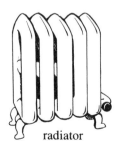
radiator

radio

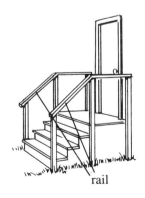

raft

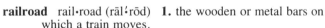

rail

radio   ra·di·o (rā′dē·ō)   **1.** an instrument that people use for sending and receiving messages through the air; a sound transmitter.
We listened to the news on the radio. *n. pl.* **radios** ra·di·os
2. having to do with sending sound through the air.
The radio set is not working. *adj.*
3. to send sound through the air.
The captain will radio for help.
v. **radioed, radioed, radioing** ra·di·oed, ra·di·o·ing

radio station   ra·di·o sta·tion (rā′dē·ō stā′shən)   a place where sound is sent through the air.
My father works at the radio station. *n. pl.* **radio stations** ra·di·o sta·tions

raft   (raft)   a flat boat with no sides.
We made a raft from the old logs. *n. pl.* **rafts**

rag   (rag)   an old piece of cloth.
I cleaned the floor with a rag. *n. pl.* **rags**

ragged   rag·ged (rag′id)   torn; tattered; looking like a rag.
The poor woman's dress was ragged. *adj.*

rail   (rāl)   a wooden or metal bar that is around a roof or porch or that is held when walking down stairs.
Grandpa holds onto the porch rail when he walks down the steps.
n. pl. **rails**

railroad   rail·road (rāl′rōd)   **1.** the wooden or metal bars on which a train moves.
Many people use the railroad to travel. *n.*
2. the trains, tracks, stations and workers that have to do with trains.
My father works for the railroad. *n. pl.* **railroads** rail·roads
3. having to do with trains.
I met her at the railroad station. *adj.*

railway   rail·way (rāl′wā)   having to do with trains.
The railway system has many miles of railroad tracks. *adj.*

rain   (rān)   **1.** the water that falls out of the clouds.
Flowers need rain to grow. *n. pl.* **rains**
2. to have water drops fall from the clouds.
It will rain tonight. *v.* **rained, rained, raining** rain·ing

rainbow   rain·bow (rān′bō)   a many-colored arch of light that sometimes appears in the sky after a rain.
You can see many colors in a rainbow. *n. pl.* **rainbows** rain·bows

a	cat	i	sit	oi	oil	ch	chop		a in about
ā	ate	ī	lie	ou	out	ng	song		e in oven
ä	car	o	pot	u	cut	sh	she	ə =	i in pencil
e	set	ō	old	u̇	book	th	three		o in memory
ē	equal	ô	or	ü	blue	ᵀH	there		u in circus
ėr	germ					zh	treasure		

raincoat   rain·coat (rān′kōt)   a piece of clothing that is worn
during the rain to keep a person dry.
>The raindrops roll off the raincoat. *n. pl.* **raincoats** rain·coats

rainfall   rain·fall (rān′fôl)   the amount of water that falls from the
clouds in a certain time and place.
>There is a lot of rainfall in a rain forest. *n. pl.* **rainfalls** rain·falls

rain forest   (rān   fôr′ist)   a place with many trees where
it rains often.
>There is a rain forest in the state of Washington.

rainy   rain·y (rā′nē)   having a lot of water fall from the
clouds; full of rain.
>I do not like rainy days. *adj.* **rainier, rainiest** rain·i·er, rain·i·est

raincoat

raise   (rāz)   **1.** to grow something.
>I will raise flowers in a garden. *v.*
>**2.** to take care of children until they grow up; to have and
to take care of animals.
>Grandpa wants to buy and raise horses. *v.*
>**3.** to move something higher; to move something up.
>We will raise the flag on the mast. *v.*
>**4.** to put up.
>I will raise my hand and ask a question. *v.* **raised, raised, raising** rais·ing

raise money   raise mon·ey (rāz   mun′ē)   to collect or earn
money for something.
>We will raise money by having a bake sale. *idiom*

raisin   rai·sin (rā′zn)   a dried grape.
>I am eating a raisin. *n. pl.* **raisins** rai·sins

rake   (rāk)   **1.** a tool with teeth-like things on one end
and a long handle on the other end that is used to gather
things on the ground.
>I used the rake to gather the leaves into a pile. *n. pl.* **rakes**
>**2.** to use a tool to gather things on the ground.
>I will rake the leaves into a pile. *v.* **raked, raked, raking** rak·ing

rake

rake up   (rāk   up)   to gather things on the ground into a pile.
>Please rake up the leaves. *v.* **raked up, raked up, raking up** rak·ing up

ran   (ran)   *v. pt. t.* See **run** (1, 2, 3).

ranch   (ranch)   **1.** a place where animals are raised; a large farm.
>My uncle has a horse ranch. *n. pl.* **ranches** ranch·es
>**2.** having to do with a large farm.
>The ranch workers feed and water the horses. *adj.*

rang   (rang)   *v. pt. t.* See **ring** (4).

rat

rattle

rattlesnake

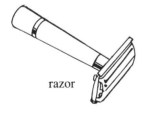

razor

range (rānj) a large group of mountains; a long row of mountains.
I can see the snow on the mountain range. *n. pl.* **ranges** rang·es

ranger rang·er (rān′jər) a person who works in a forest to protect it from fire and other dangers; a person who protects the land.
The ranger taught us how to put out a campfire safely.
n. pl. **rangers** rang·ers

rarely rare·ly (rer′lē *or* rar′lē) not often; very seldom; once in a long time; infrequently.
I rarely go to the library by myself. *adv.*

rat (rat) an animal with a long tail that looks like a large mouse.
The rat ran out of the old building. *n. pl.* **rats**

rather rath·er (raᴛʜ′ər) more willingly; with more desire; preferably.
I am going to the movie with Lisa, but I would rather go to the dance. *adv.*

rattle rat·tle (rat′l) a toy that has small seeds in it so that it makes noise when it is shaken; a baby's toy.
We brought the new baby a rattle. *n. pl.* **rattles** rat·tles

rattlesnake rat·tle·snake (rat′l·snāk) a poisonous snake with a rattle on the end of its tail that the snake shakes before attacking something.
A rattlesnake bit our pet rabbit. *n. pl.* **rattlesnakes** rat·tle·snakes

raw (rô) not cooked.
I cannot eat anything that is still raw. *adj.* **rawer, rawest** raw·er, raw·est

ray (rā) a thin line or stream of light.
A ray of sunlight came through the window. *n. pl.* **rays**

razor ra·zor (rā′zər) a tool with a sharp blade that people use for shaving hair from the face, body or legs.
I gave my father a new razor. *n. pl.* **razors** ra·zors

reach (rēch) **1.** to arrive at a place; to get somewhere.
I want to reach Chicago by Tuesday. *v.*
2. to stretch an arm to get something; to hold out a hand.
Can you reach the top shelf? *v.*
3. to put a hand in something.
I will reach into my pocket for the keys.
v. **reached, reached, reaching** reach·ing

a	cat	i	sit	oi	oil	ch	chop		a in about
ā	ate	ī	lie	ou	out	ng	song		e in oven
ä	car	o	pot	u	cut	sh	she	ə =	i in pencil
e	set	ō	old	ù	book	th	three		o in memory
ē	equal	ô	or	ü	blue	ᴛʜ	there		u in circus
ėr	germ					zh	treasure		

read (rēd) **1.** to look at printed words and get information from what is written; to understand written words.
I can read books and magazines. *v.*
2. to say the words that are printed on a page.
The teacher will read us a story. *v.* **read, read, reading** read·ing

reader read·er (rē′dər) **1.** someone who reads.
Katie is a good reader. *n.*
2. a book for learning to read.
David lost his reader. *n. pl.* **readers** read·ers

reading glasses read·ing glass·es (rē′ding glas′iz) lenses that are worn when someone is reading so that the person can see the words more clearly.
I must wear reading glasses.

reading glasses

read ___ mind (rēd ___ mīnd) to believe to know what someone is thinking.
I can look at her eyes and read her mind.
v. **read ___ mind, read ___ mind, reading ___ mind** read·ing ___ mind

ready read·y (red′ē) **1.** finished and able to be used or put on.
Your clothes are washed and ready to wear. *adj.*
2. prepared.
Dinner is ready. *adj.* **readier, readiest** read·i·er, read·i·est

real re·al (rē′əl *or* rēl) **1.** true; not fictional; not made up.
This is a real story. *adj.*
2. not a drawing; not a cartoon.
The story is about real people. *adj.*
3. genuine; not fake.
He is a real hero. *adj.*

realize re·al·ize (rē′ə·līz) to understand clearly and fully.
I realize how important school is.
v. **realized, realized, realizing** re·al·ized, re·al·iz·ing

really re·al·ly (rē′ə·lē *or* rē′lē) **1.** truly; genuinely; in a true way.
It is really happening to me. *adv.*
2. very; without any question.
That truck is really big. *adv.*

reaper reap·er (rē′pər) a machine that cuts and gathers grain.
The farmer bought a new reaper. *n. pl.* **reapers** reap·ers

reaper

reaping reap·ing (rē′ping) having to do with cutting and gathering grain.
The reaping machines make harvesting easier than it was before. *adj.*

reason rea·son (rē′zn) the cause for something; explanation.
The reason I will not be here is that I am going to visit my grandmother.
n. pl. **reasons** rea·sons

rebellious re·bel·lious (ri·bel⸍yəs) not wanting to do what is
 expected; not willing to do what one is told to do; going
 against the wishes of others.
 He is a rebellious student. *adj.*

rebound re·bound (rē⸍bound′) to bounce back after hitting
 something; in basketball, to bounce back after hitting the
 backboard or rim of the basket.
 The coach told the boys to catch the ball when it rebounds.
 v. **rebounded, rebounded, rebounding** re·bound·ed, re·bound·ing

rebound

rebuild re·build (rē·bild′) to remake something; to put something
 up again after it has been destroyed; to build again.
 We will rebuild the house after the flood.
 v. **rebuilt, rebuilt, rebuilding** re·built, re·build·ing

rebuilt (rē·bilt′) *v. pt. t., pt. part.* See **rebuild.**

receive re·ceive (ri·sēv′) to get something from someone;
 to be given something.
 I should receive the package today.
 v. **received, received, receiving** re·ceived, re·ceiv·ing

recently re·cent·ly (rē⸍snt·lē) in the near past; only a short
 time ago; not long ago.
 I recently went to the card shop. *adv.*

reception re·cep·tion (ri·sep⸍shən) a party where people can meet
 the host or guest of honor; a party after another event.
 The actors in the play were invited to a reception after the last show.
 n. pl. **receptions** re·cep·tions

recipe

recipe rec·i·pe (res⸍ə·pē) the directions for making some food; the
 list of ingredients and the step-by-step plan for making a food.
 I followed the recipe, but the cookies were not very good.
 n. pl. **recipes** rec·i·pes

recognize rec·og·nize (rek⸍əg·nīz) to see and know from
 having seen before; to look at something and remember what it
 is because you have seen it before.
 I will recognize her house when I see it.
 v. **recognized, recognized, recognizing** rec·og·nized, rec·og·niz·ing

a	cat	i	sit	oi	oil	ch	chop		a in about
ā	ate	ī	lie	ou	out	ng	song		e in oven
ä	car	o	pot	u	cut	sh	she	ə =	i in pencil
e	set	ō	old	u̇	book	th	three		o in memory
ē	equal	ô	or	ü	blue	ŦH	there		u in circus
ėr	germ					zh	treasure		

record[1]   rec·ord (rek′ərd) **1.** a paper that has information written on it; important information that is kept for future use.
I have a record of the money that I spent on the party. *n.*
2. a round plastic disc from which music is heard when played on a phonograph.
I want to hear your new record. *n. pl.* **records** rec·ords

record[2]   re·cord (ri·kôrd′) to write down important information; to write down things so people will remember them.
I will record the cost of the party hats.
v. **recorded, recorded, recording** re·cord·ed, re·cord·ing

record player

record player   rec·ord play·er (rek′ərd plā′ər) a machine that plays round plastic discs so that a person can hear music.
I put the record on the record player and listened to the music.

records keeper   rec·ords keep·er (rek′ərdz kē′pər) a person who keeps important information; a person who writes records.
The records keeper wrote the address of our new home in his book.

recreation room   rec·re·a·tion room (rek·rē·ā′shən rüm)
a room in which people play games.
We play table tennis in our recreation room.

rectangle   rec·tan·gle (rek′tang·gəl) a four-sided object with two longer sides, two shorter sides and four right angles.
Kathleen drew a rectangle. *n. pl.* **rectangles** rec·tang·les

rectangle

rectangular   rec·tan·gu·lar (rek·tang′gyə·lər) having four sides; shaped like a rectangle.
The classroom is rectangular. *adj.*

redwood   red·wood (red′wùd) having to do with a large evergreen tree that has red wood and grows in California and Oregon.
We have redwood furniture on our deck. *adj.*

reel   (rēl) a round frame that turns like a wheel and winds or lets out rope or fishing line.
I took my fishing pole and reel to the lake. *n. pl.* **reels**

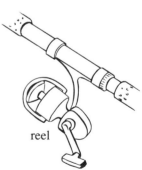

reel

refined   re·fined (ri·fīnd′) made pure; treated in a process that takes out things; purified.
We use refined sugar in our food. *adj.*

reflect   re·flect (ri·flekt′) **1.** to give back an image from a shiny surface.
The mirror will reflect how you look in the new clothes. *v.*
2. to show like a mirror.
His happiness will reflect in his face.
v. **reflected, reflected, reflecting** re·flect·ed, re·flect·ing

344

refrigerator

rein

reindeer

reflection re·flec·tion (ri·flek⌐shən) a picture or image that a person can see on a shiny, flat surface.
You can see your reflection in the water. *n. pl.* **reflections** re·flec·tions

refresh re·fresh (ri·fresh′) to make like new; to feel more energy; to feel strong and alert again.
A nap will refresh you.
v. **refreshed, refreshed, refreshing** re·freshed, re·fresh·ing

refrigerate re·frig·e·rate (ri·frij⌐ə·rāt) to make or keep cool; to put something in a cool place.
We will refrigerate the pie so it does not spoil.
v. **refrigerated, refrigerated, refrigerating**
re·frig·e·rat·ed, re·frig·e·rat·ing

refrigerator re·frig·e·ra·tor (ri·frij⌐ə·rā·tər) a machine that stores and cools food.
I put the milk in the refrigerator. *n. pl.* **refrigerators** re·frig·e·ra·tors

refuse re·fuse (ri·fyüz′) to say no; to decide not to do something; not to take something; to disagree.
I will refuse his money. *v.* **refused, refused, refusing** re·fused, re·fus·ing

regard re·gard (ri·gärd′) to think of something in a certain way; to consider something to be a certain way.
I regard your opinion highly and want to know what you really think.
v. **regarded, regarded, regarding** re·gard·ed, re·gard·ing

region re·gion (rē⌐jən) an area; a certain place.
I live in a farming region of the state. *n. pl.* **regions** re·gions

regular reg·u·lar (reg⌐yə·lər) **1.** common; normal; usual.
I will eat my regular breakfast. *adj.*
2. being done again and again at set times.
We will feed the animals at regular times every day. *adj.*

rein (rān) the part of a horse bridle that is used to control a horse.
If I pull the rein to the left, the horse will turn left. *n. pl.* **reins**

reindeer rein·deer (rān⌐dir) a large deer with large antlers (horns) that lives in cold regions of the world.
Santa Claus uses reindeer to pull his sled.
n. pl. **reindeer** rein·deer

a	cat	i	sit	oi	oil	ch	chop		a in about
ā	ate	ī	lie	ou	out	ng	song		e in oven
ä	car	o	pot	u	cut	sh	she	ə =	i in pencil
e	set	ō	old	u̇	book	th	three		o in memory
ē	equal	ô	or	ü	blue	ᵵH	there		u in circus
ėr	germ					zh	treasure		

rejoice re·joice (ri·jois′) to be very happy; to show great happiness; to be filled with joy.
We will all rejoice when the war is over.
v. **rejoiced, rejoiced, rejoicing** re·joiced, re·joic·ing

relative rel·a·tive (rel′ə·tiv) a person from the same family as another person.
Your uncle is your relative. *n. pl.* **relatives** rel·a·tives

relax re·lax (ri·laks′) to rest; to become less tense; to be comfortable.
I will sit here and relax before I start my homework.
v. **relaxed, relaxed, relaxing** re·laxed, re·lax·ing

relaxation re·lax·a·tion (rē·lak·sā′shən) the act of resting; the time when you are becoming less tense.
I like to read for relaxation. *n. no pl.*

relay[1] re·lay (rē′lā *or* ri·lā′) to carry a message or a thing from one place or person to another.
I will relay your message to Lisa.
v. **relayed, relayed, relaying** re·layed, re·lay·ing

relax

relay[2] re·lay (rē′lā) having to do with being carried from one place to another.
I watched the relay race. *adj.*

relay station re·lay sta·tion (rē′lā stā′shən) a place where travelers stopped when traveling in horse carriages; a place to rest and change horses.
The stagecoach stopped at a relay station every night.

reliable re·li·a·ble (ri·lī′ə·bəl) someone or something that a person can trust; dependable.
Because John is reliable, he will be here on time. *adj.*

relieve re·lieve (ri·lēv′) **1.** to make free of worry.
The good news will relieve John. *v.*
2. to take; to free.
I will relieve you of that heavy box.
v. **relieved, relieved, relieving** re·lieved, re·liev·ing

religion re·li·gion (ri·lij′ən) worship of God; belief in a superhuman power; a way of honoring or believing in God.
Many people have a religion that they practice. *n. pl.* **religions** re·li·gions

religious re·li·gious (ri·lij′əs) having to do with a belief in God and a way of honoring God.
A priest is a religious man. *adj.*

remain re·main (ri·mān′) **1.** to stay the same; to not change; to continue as before.
The inside of the house will remain the same, but we will paint the outside. *v.*
2. to stay; to not go; to not move.
I will remain here until you get home.
v. **remained, remained, remaining** re·mained, re·main·ing

remember re·mem·ber (ri·mem′bər) to keep in one's mind; to not forget; to put in one's memory.
I will always remember the fun we had at camp.
v. **remembered, remembered, remembering**
re·mem·bered, re·mem·ber·ing

remind re·mind (ri·mīnd′) to tell someone something that they have forgotten; to bring something to someone's attention; to cause someone to remember something.
I will remind Dad of his promise.
v. **reminded, reminded, reminding** re·mind·ed, re·mind·ing

remove re·move (ri·müv′) to take away; to take off.
I will remove the dishes from the table.
v. **removed, removed, removing** re·moved, re·mov·ing

repair

rename re·name (rē·nām′) to give something or someone a new or different title or name.
The principal will rename our school.
v. **renamed, renamed, renaming** re·named, re·nam·ing

renew re·new (ri·nü′ *or* ri·nyü′) to get again; to begin again; to take again.
I will renew my membership in the Boy's Club.
v. **renewed, renewed, renewing** re·newed, re·new·ing

rent (rent) to pay money to borrow something; to pay money to live in a house or apartment.
I will rent the piano for one month.
v. **rented, rented, renting** rent·ed, rent·ing

repair re·pair (ri·per′ *or* ri·par′) to fix or make work again.
Dad will repair the dryer.
v. **repaired, repaired, repairing** re·paired, re·pair·ing

repairs re·pairs (ri·perz′ *or* ri·parz′) the work that needs to be done to fix something or to make it work again.
The repairs on the burned house will cost a lot of money. *plural n.*

a cat	**i** sit	**oi** oil	**ch** chop		a in about
ā ate	**ī** lie	**ou** out	**ng** song		e in oven
ä car	**o** pot	**u** cut	**sh** she	ə =	i in pencil
e set	**ō** old	**u̇** book	**th** three		o in memory
ē equal	**ô** or	**ü** blue	**TH** there		u in circus
ėr germ			**zh** treasure		

repeat   re·peat (ri·pēt′)   to do or say again; to happen again.
The teacher asked us to repeat the poem.
v. **repeated, repeated, repeating** re·peat·ed, re·peat·ing

repetition   rep·e·ti·tion (rep·ə·tish′ən)   the doing or saying
of something again.
The repetition of the poem was not exciting. *n. pl.* **repetitions** rep·e·ti·tions

replace   re·place (ri·plās′)   **1.** to take the place of something else;
to give something for something else; to exchange.
I will replace the vase that I broke. *v.*
2. to put something back in the spot that it belongs;
to return something to its first location.
I will replace the book on the shelf.
v. **replaced, replaced, replacing** re·placed, re·plac·ing

report

reply   re·ply (ri·plī′)   **1.** to give an answer; to say or write something
after someone says or writes something to you.
I will reply to her letter tomorrow.
v. **replied, replied, replying** re·plied, re·ply·ing
2. something said or written as an answer.
My reply will be nice, but I will say no. *n. pl.* **replies** re·plies

report   re·port (ri·pôrt′ *or* ri·pōrt′)   **1.** a written record of something;
an account of something that happened.
I wrote a report on the Civil War. *n. pl.* **reports** re·ports
2. to give an account of something; to tell information.
I will report to the class about my visit to Washington, D.C. *v.*
3. to tell someone about an emergency.
I will report the fire.
v. **reported, reported, reporting** re·port·ed, re·port·ing

report card   re·port card (ri·pôrt′   kärd)   a written record or
listing of a student's grades in school.
I have three As on my report card.

reporter   re·port·er (ri·pôr′tər *or* ri·pōr′tər)   a person who
finds information and writes about it for a newspaper,
magazine, radio or television report.
The reporter wrote a story about the fire for the newspaper.
n. pl. **reporters** re·port·ers

reproduce   re·pro·duce (rē·prə·düs′ *or* rē·prə·dyüs′)
to make again; to have children.
People reproduce by having babies.
v. **reproduced, reproduced, reproducing** re·pro·duced, re·pro·duc·ing

reptile

reptile   rep·tile (rep′təl *or* rep′tīl)   a cold-blooded animal that crawls
on its belly or on short legs and that has scales on its body.
A snake is a reptile. *n. pl.* **reptiles** rep·tiles

require   re·quire (ri·kwīr′)   to ask or to insist that something be done; to demand; to order; to command.
The teacher will require that we do our homework every day.
v. **required, required, requiring** re·quired, re·quir·ing

reread   re·read (rē·rēd′)   to read something again.
The teacher told me to reread my book.
v. **reread, reread, rereading** re·read·ing

rescue   res·cue (res′kyü)   **1.** to save from danger or harm; to free from danger.
The fireman will rescue the man in the burning house.
v. **rescued, rescued, rescuing** res·cued, res·cu·ing
2. the act of saving something or someone from danger or harm.
The rescue was dangerous for the fireman. *n. pl.* **rescues** res·cues

rescue

research   re·search (ri·sėrch′ *or* rē′sėrch)   to look for and study information; to look for facts or evidence.
The scientists will research the treatment of cancer.
v. **researched, researched, researching** re·searched, re·search·ing

resent   re·sent (ri·zent′)   to feel hurt about something; to feel angry at someone; to dislike something that has been done.
I resent his going to talk to my teacher.
v. **resented, resented, resenting** re·sent·ed, re·sent·ing

reservation   res·er·va·tion (rez·ər·vā′shən)   **1.** land that belongs to a tribe of Indians.
Some Indians never leave the reservation. *n.*
2. an arrangement to hold a place for use at a later time; a promise that a person may use something later.
I have a plane reservation for next week. *n. pl.* **reservations** res·er·va·tions

resist   re·sist (ri·zist′)   **1.** to say no; to oppose.
I could not resist her invitation to have a piece of cake. *v.*
2. to work against something or someone.
The cloth may resist the dye.
v. **resisted, resisted, resisting** re·sist·ed, re·sist·ing

resistant   re·sis·tant (ri·zis′tənt)   working against something; not accepting something.
Lisa is resistant to the idea. *adj.*

a	cat	**i**	sit	**oi**	oil	**ch**	chop	a in about
ā	ate	**ī**	lie	**ou**	out	**ng**	song	e in oven
ä	car	**o**	pot	**u**	cut	**sh**	she	i in pencil
e	set	**ō**	old	**u̇**	book	**th**	three	o in memory
ē	equal	**ô**	or	**ü**	blue	**ŦH**	there	u in circus
ėr	germ					**zh**	treasure	

ə = {

resist-dyeing re·sist-dye·ing (ri·zist´-dī´·ing) a way of
coloring cloth by tying parts of the cloth so that the dye or
coloring agent will not soak in.
Tie-dyeing is a method of resist-dyeing. *n. no pl.*

resort re·sort (ri·zôrt´) a place that has entertainment where
people stay when vacationing.
The whole family is going to the resort for a week. *n. pl.* **resorts** re·sorts

respect re·spect (ri·spekt´) to admire someone; to think highly
of what another person says or thinks; to honor someone.
I respect my father's ideas and goals.
v. **respected, respected, respecting** re·spect·ed, re·spect·ing

respectively re·spec·tive·ly (ri·spek´·tiv·lē) in the same
order as mentioned.
On the map, the states of Virginia, West Virginia and Pennsylvania
are marked VA, WV and PA, respectively. *adv.*

resort

responsibility re·spon·si·bil·i·ty (ri·spon·sə·bil´·ə·tē)
something that a person must do; a duty; a person's job.
It is my responsibility to take out the garbage every day.
n. pl. **responsibilities** re·spon·si·bil·i·ties

responsible re·spon·si·ble (ri·spon´·sə·bəl) willing and able
to take care of something or someone; able to take care of
oneself without help; being the one to do something.
I am responsible for taking out the garbage. *adj.*

rest (rest) **1.** to stop working or playing.
I will rest after I finish mowing the lawn.
v. **rested, rested, resting** rest·ed, rest·ing
2. the act of stopping work or play; a time when a
person is not moving.
I took a short rest before I started mowing the lawn. *n. pl.* **rests**

restaurant res·tau·rant (res´·tər·ənt *or* res´·tə·ränt) **1.** a place to buy
meals; a place where people pay to eat food.
We ate dinner in a new restaurant. *n. pl.* **restaurants** res·tau·rants
2. having to do with a place where people pay to eat meals.
The restaurant menu had no prices on it. *adj.*

restaurant

restore re·store (ri·stôr´ *or* ri·stōr´) to return to an earlier
condition; to make like new again.
Mother will restore the old chair.
v. **restored, restored, restoring** re·stored, re·stor·ing

retire re·tire (ri·tīr´) to work no longer, especially
because of old age.
My father will retire when he is 65 years old.
v. **retired, retired, retiring** re·tired, re·tir·ing

retirement re·tire·ment (ri·tīr′mənt) the time when a person
no longer works to earn money.
My father will spend his retirement painting pictures for fun.
n. pl. **retirements** re·tire·ments

retreat re·treat (ri·trēt′) to move back from something;
to withdraw from something.
The army will retreat from a losing battle.
v. **retreated, retreated, retreating** re·treat·ed, re·treat·ing

return re·turn (ri·tėrn′) **1.** to come back to a starting point.
Bill will return home from college this month. *v.*
2. to give back to someone or something.
I will return the book to the library. *v.*
3. to put something back in its place; to put something back
in the spot where it is kept.
I will return the milk to the refrigerator.
v. **returned, returned, returning** re·turned, re·turn·ing

return

reverse re·verse (ri·vėrs′) to change something to the opposite
of what it started as; to put in the opposite direction or
way; to turn inside out.
I can reverse my decision and go to the party.
v. **reversed, reversed, reversing** re·versed, re·vers·ing

Revolutionary War Rev·o·lu·tion·ar·y War
(rev·ə·lü′shə·ner·ē wôr) the battles that the first colonies
in America fought against England for freedom from English
government and laws (1775-1783).
The colonies won the Revolutionary War, and America became free
of English rule.

revolve re·volve (ri·volv′) to turn in a circle; to move
around something.
The moon will revolve around the Earth in 28 days.
v. **revolved, revolved, revolving** re·volved, re·volv·ing

reward re·ward (ri·wôrd′) **1.** something given for doing a good
job or as thanks for an action.
The man gave me a reward for finding his dog. *n.*
2. money that is given to the person who catches a criminal
or a lawbreaker.
There is a $1,000.00 reward for catching the kidnapper.
n. pl. **rewards** re·wards

a	cat	i	sit	oi	oil	ch	chop		a in about
ā	ate	ī	lie	ou	out	ng	song		e in oven
ä	car	o	pot	u	cut	sh	she	ə =	i in pencil
e	set	ō	old	u̇	book	th	three		o in memory
ē	equal	ô	or	ü	blue	₮H	there		u in circus
ėr	germ					zh	treasure		

rhinoceros rhi·noc·er·os (rī·nos'ər·əs) a large animal with thick skin and one or two horns above its nose.
> The rhinoceros comes from Africa.
> *n. pl.* **rhinoceros** *or* **rhinoceroses** rhi·noc·er·os *or* rhi·noc·er·os·es

rhubarb rhu·barb (rü'bärb) a garden plant with large leaves whose stalks are used to make sauce and pies.
> I like to eat rhubarb. *n. pl.* **rhubarbs** rhu·barbs

ribbon rib·bon (rib'ən) **1.** a narrow strip of cloth.
> I put a ribbon in my hair. *n.*
> **2.** a narrow strip of something.
> There is a ribbon of metal around the case. *n. pl.* **ribbons** rib·bons

rice (rīs) the seed of a cereal grass that grows in warm areas.
> Rice is one of the main foods in China. *n. no pl.*

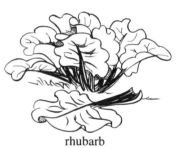
rhinoceros

rich (rich) **1.** having a lot of money or things.
> Her family is rich. *adj.*
> **2.** able to grow things; producing many plants.
> The soil is rich. *adj.*
> **3.** having a lot of butter, eggs or sugar.
> The cake is very rich. *adj.* **richer, richest** rich·er, rich·est

riches rich·es (rich'iz) things that are worth a lot of money; valuable things.
> The king has many riches. *plural n.*

rid (rid) to make free of something; to remove.
> The poison will rid the house of mice.
> *v.* **rid** *or* **ridded, rid** *or* **ridded, ridding** rid·ded, rid·ding

ridden rid·den (rid'n) *v. pt. part.* See **ride** (1, 2, 3).

rhubarb

ride (rīd) **1.** to move from place to place on an animal.
> I will ride the horse. *v.*
> **2.** to go from place to place in a car, bus or other vehicle.
> I want to ride in an airplane. *v.*
> **3.** to move on something; to travel over something.
> The new car rides the bumps smoothly.
> *v.* **rode, ridden, riding** rid·den, rid·ing
> **4.** a trip in a vehicle or on an animal.
> I took a ride on the horse. *n. pl.* **rides**

rider rid·er (rī'dər) a person who moves from place to place on an animal or in a vehicle.
> Jim is a good bicycle rider. *n. pl.* **riders** rid·ers

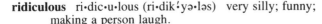
ribbon

ridiculous ri·dic·u·lous (ri·dik'yə·ləs) very silly; funny; making a person laugh.
> He wore a ridiculous hat. *adj.*

352

right (rīt) **1.** a direction that is opposite of left; on the side that is opposite of left.
I write with my right hand. *adj.*
2. correct; without a mistake.
I knew the right answer to the question. *adj.*
3. soon; in a short time; immediately.
Right after we eat we are going to the movie. *adv.*
4. something that is due a person; a legal claim.
We have a right to see the report of the accident. *n. pl.* **rights**

right away right a·way (rīt ə·wā′) immediately; as soon as possible.
I will get the book right away. *idiom*

right now (rīt nou) at this time; immediately; without waiting.
I want you to do your homework right now. *idiom*

ring

ring (ring) **1.** a round piece of jewelry that is worn on a finger.
The lady has a diamond ring. *n.*
2. a circle.
There is a ring of milk in the glass. *n.*
3. shaped in a circle.
There was a pineapple ring on the dish. *n. pl.* **rings**
4. to make a bell-like sound.
The telephone will ring in the office.
v. **rang, rung, ringing** ring·ing

ring out (ring out) to make a loud, bell-like sound.
The church bell will ring out at one o'clock.
v. **rang out, rung out, ringing out** ring·ing out

rinse (rints) to wash with water only; to wash something lightly.
I will rinse the dishes. *v.* **rinsed, rinsed, rinsing** rins·ing

rip (rip) to tear; to cut roughly.
The paper will rip if you pull it. *v.* **ripped, ripped, ripping** rip·ping

ripcord rip·cord (rip′kôrd) a string that is pulled to open a parachute.
As the skydiver fell, she pulled the ripcord and the parachute opened.
n. pl. **ripcords** rip·cords

ripcord

ripe (rīp) fully grown and ready to eat; ready.
Only pick the ripe apples. *adj.* **riper, ripest** rip·er, rip·est

ripen rip·en (rī′pən) to become fully grown and ready to eat.
The apple should ripen on the tree.
v. **ripened, ripened, ripening** ri·pened, ri·pen·ing

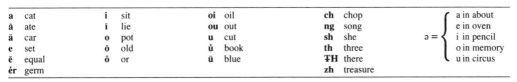

a	cat	i	sit	oi	oil	ch	chop		a in about
ā	ate	ī	lie	ou	out	ng	song		e in oven
ä	car	o	pot	u	cut	sh	she	ə =	i in pencil
e	set	ō	old	u̇	book	th	three		o in memory
ē	equal	ô	or	ü	blue	ŦH	there		u in circus
ėr	germ					zh	treasure		

rise (rīz) to move up; to get up; to move to a higher place.
The sun will rise at six o'clock.
v. **rose, risen, rising** ris•en, ris•ing

risk (risk) a chance; a danger.
It is a risk to drive a car too fast. *n. pl.* **risks**

river riv•er (riv´ər) a large stream of water that flows into
a lake, ocean or larger river.
The river flows past our city. *n. pl.* **rivers** riv•ers

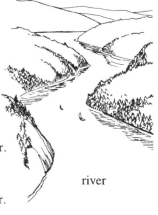
river

riverboat riv•er•boat (riv´ər•bōt) a large boat that travels on a river.
We can watch the riverboat move down the river.
n. pl. **riverboats** riv•er•boats

rivet riv•et (riv´it) a metal bolt that fastens heavy things together.
The builder put a rivet in the steel beams of the house. *n. pl.* **rivets** riv•ets

road (rōd) a path or street on which vehicles travel.
Turn right at the next road. *n. pl.* **roads**

roadblock road•block (rōd´blok) something put across a street or
road to stop all vehicles from continuing further.
The police put up a roadblock. *n. pl.* **roadblocks** road•blocks

road-making road-mak•ing (rōd-mā´king) having to do with
building streets and roads.
The road-making machine poured the tar onto the road. *adj.*

riverboat

roar (rôr *or* rōr) **1.** a loud, deep animal sound.
The lion's roar frightened me. *n. pl.* **roars**
2. to make a loud, deep noise like an animal; to growl.
The lion will roar if you get too close to him.
v. **roared, roared, roaring** roar•ing

roast (rōst) **1.** to cook with heat; to bake.
I will roast the hot dogs on the campfire.
v. **roasted, roasted, roasting** roast•ed, roast•ing
2. a piece of meat that has been baked in an oven.
We will have a roast for dinner. *n. pl.* **roasts**

robe

rob (rob) to take from someone; to steal; to take something
and not pay for it.
It is wrong to rob people. *v.* **robbed, robbed, robbing** rob•bing

robber rob•ber (rob´ər) a person who takes things without
paying for them; a person who steals.
The robber took all of her money. *n. pl.* **robbers** rob•bers

robin

robot

rocket

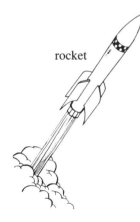

robe (rōb) a loose piece of clothing that a person wears in the house over night clothes or by itself.
I put on my robe and slippers before I sat down to watch television. *n. pl.* **robes**

robin rob·in (rob′ən) a dark bird with a reddish breast.
The robin returns here every spring. *n. pl.* **robins** rob·ins

robot ro·bot (rō′bot *or* rō′bət) **1.** a machine that looks like a person and does work; an electrical, mechanical machine that receives orders to do work.
The robot pushed the wagon for the man. *n. pl.* **robots** ro·bots
2. having to do with a mechanical person.
The robot arm can easily lift the sweeper. *adj.*

rock (rok) **1.** a kind of loud music.
I often listen to rock on the radio. *n. no pl.*
2. a large stone.
I threw the rock into the lake. *n. pl.* **rocks**
3. having to do with a stone or rock.
The rock machine smashes stones into small pieces of gravel. *adj.*
4. to move back and forth; to move from side to side.
I will rock the baby to sleep.
v. **rocked, rocked, rocking** rock·ing

rocket rock·et (rok′it) an engine with a long tube of fuel that is burned to push a spaceship up into space.
The rocket carried the spaceship to the moon. *n. pl.* **rockets** rock·ets

rocky rock·y (rok′ē) having many stones; full of stones.
The road was rocky.
adj. **rockier, rockiest** rock·i·er, rock·i·est

rode (rōd) *v. pt. t.* See **ride** (1, 2, 3).

rodeo ro·de·o (rō′dē·ō *or* rō·dā′ō) a festival that has contests of riding animals and roping cattle.
The rider roped a bull at the rodeo.
n. pl. **rodeos** ro·de·os

a	cat	i	sit	oi	oil	ch	chop		a in about
ā	ate	ī	lie	ou	out	ng	song		e in oven
ä	car	o	pot	u	cut	sh	she	ə =	i in pencil
e	set	ō	old	u̇	book	th	three		o in memory
ē	equal	ô	or	ü	blue	ŦH	there		u in circus
ėr	germ					zh	treasure		

roll (rōl) **1.** to move by turning over and over.
I will roll down the hill. *v.*
2. to turn something over and over to make a
round, tube-like shape.
I will roll the paper and make a spyglass. *v.*
3. to move along on wheels.
The bus will roll down the road. *v.*
4. to move something along on wheels.
We roll her around in the wagon. *v.*
5. to use a round, tube-like shape to make something flat.
We will roll the pie dough. *v.*
6. to make a long, deep, loud sound.
The thunder will roll through the sky.
v. **rolled, rolled, rolling** roll·ing
7. something wrapped around a tube.
I have a roll of paper. *n.*
8. a bread or cake made from rolled dough.
We had a sweet roll for breakfast. *n. pl.* **rolls**

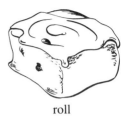

roll

roll over roll·over (rōl ō′vər) to change from one side to the other
side;
to turn to the other side.
I will roll over sometime in the night.
v. **rolled over, rolled over, rolling over** roll·ing o·ver

roll the film (rōl ᴛʜə film) to turn on a movie camera
and begin taking pictures on the moving film.
The producer began to roll the film. *idiom*

roof

roll up (rōl up) to turn something over and over into
a round, tube-like shape.
I will roll up the blanket. *v.* **rolled up, rolled up, rolling up** roll·ing up

Roman Ro·man (rō′mən) **1.** a person who lived in Rome
a long time ago or a person who lives in Rome, Italy, today.
Caesar was a Roman. *n. pl.* **Romans** Ro·mans
2. having to do with the people or city of Rome.
The Roman roads were made of stones. *adj.*

rooster

Rome (rōm) the capital of the country of Italy.
Rome is a very large city in Italy. *n.*

roof (rüf *or* rùf) the cover of a house or a building.
Our house has a flat roof. *n. pl.* **roofs**

room (rüm *or* rùm) **1.** a space in a house or building that
has walls separating it from other parts or spaces.
We have a living room and a dining room in our house. *n. pl.* **rooms**
2. enough space for something; space.
Do you have room in the car for me? *n. no pl.*

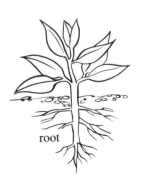

root

rooster roost·er (rü′stər) a male chicken.
The rooster crows loudly in the morning. *n. pl.* **roosters** roost·ers

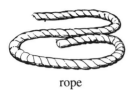

rope

rope strap

rose

root (rüt *or* rùt) the part of a plant that is under the ground.
The root of the plant drinks the water that the plant needs to grow.
n. pl. **roots**

rope (rōp) a strong string or cord that people use for
tying or pulling things.
We tied the rope around the tree. *n. pl.* **ropes**

rope strap (rōp strap) the part of a horse saddle that holds
a rope for catching cattle.
I put the rope on the rope strap.

rose (rōz) **1.** a flower that smells sweet and that has sharp
thorns on its stem.
I gave Mother a rose for her birthday. *n. pl.* **roses** ros·es
2. *v. pt. t.* See **rise.**

rosy ros·y (rō′zē) pinkish.
The sunset made the sky look rosy. *adj.* **rosier, rosiest** ros·i·er, ros·i·est

rotten rot·ten (rot′n) spoiled; bad; not fit to be eaten.
The apple was rotten, so we threw it away.
adj. **rottener, rottenest** rot·ten·er, rot·ten·est

rough (ruf) **1.** not smooth; bumpy; not even.
The sandpaper is rough. *adj.*
2. difficult; not gentle; liking to fight.
The bully was a rough boy. *adj.* **rougher, roughest** rough·er, rough·est

round (round) shaped like a circle or a ball.
The sun is round. *adj.* **rounder, roundest** round·er, round·est

round-up (round′up) having to do with gathering animals together.
Rodeos take place after round-up time each year. *adj.*

route (rüt *or* rout) a road or a path that leads to a place.
We took the northern route to the farm. *n. pl.* **routes**

row (rō) a line of people or things.
I sat in the back row at the movie. *n. pl.* **rows**

royal roy·al (roi′əl) having to do with a king or a queen.
The royal castle is the home of the king and queen. *adj.*

a	cat	i	sit	oi	oil	ch	chop		a in about
ā	ate	ī	lie	ou	out	ng	song		e in oven
ä	car	o	pot	u	cut	sh	she	ə =	i in pencil
e	set	ō	old	ù	book	th	three		o in memory
ē	equal	ô	or	ü	blue	ŦH	there		u in circus
ėr	germ					zh	treasure		

rub (rub) to press against something; to move back and
forth against something.
> Will you rub my back? *v.* **rubbed, rubbed, rubbing** rub·bing

rubber rub·ber (rub′ər) **1.** a material that stretches; a material
that will go back to its first place or position when pulled.
> This eraser is made of rubber. *n. no pl.*
> **2.** made of a material that stretches.
> The rubber stamp has my name on it. *adj.*

rubber band rub·ber band (rub′ər band) a circle made of
a stretchy material that people use to hold things together.
> I put a rubber band on the cards.

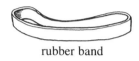

rubber band

ruby ru·by (rü′bē) a jewel that is deep red; a red gem.
> The ring has a ruby in it. *n. pl.* **rubies** ru·bies

rude (rüd) not polite; not using good manners.
> The man was very rude; he did not say thank you.
> *adj.* **ruder, rudest** rud·er, rud·est

rug (rug) a small carpet; a mat for the floor.
> My mother bought a new rug for my room. *n. pl.* **rugs**

ruin ru·in (rü′ən) to damage so it cannot be used again;
to make something unusable.
> The fire will ruin the house.
> *v.* **ruined, ruined, ruining** ru·ined, ru·in·ing

rule (rül) **1.** to govern or control.
> The President and Congress rule the United States.
> *v.* **ruled, ruled, ruling** rul·ing
> **2.** a law; a way to behave that a person must obey.
> We must follow the rule. *n. pl.* **rules**

ruler rul·er (rü′lər) **1.** a person who controls or governs.
> The ruler of England is the queen. *n.*
> **2.** a stick that people use to measure the length of things;
> a straight piece of wood or metal that shows how
> long something is.
> The ruler is 12 inches long. *n. pl.* **rulers** rul·ers

rug

rumbling rum·bling (rum′bling) a deep, low, long noise.
> The rumbling sound of the thunder woke me. *adj.*

run (run) **1.** to go fast on foot.
I will run around the field. *v.*
2. flow.
The water will run down the side of the house. *v.*
3. to work or operate a machine.
I can run the lawn mower. *v.* **ran, ran, running** run·ning
4. a score in a baseball game.
I hit in a run in last night's game. *n.*
5. exercise time; going very fast on foot for exercise.
I took the dog for a run. *n.*
6. a long race on foot.
Tomorrow's run is ten miles long. *n. pl.* **runs**

runaway run·a·way (run′ə·wā) having to do with escaping or leaving without permission or control.
The cowboy stopped the runaway horse. *adj.*

run away run a·way (run ə·wā′) to escape; to leave without telling someone where you are going; to go without permission.
The dog will run away if he is not tied.
v. **ran away, ran away, running away** run·ning away

run for (run fôr) to try to get elected to a political job or position.
The man next door will run for mayor.
v. **ran for, ran for, running for** run·ning for

runner run·ner (run′ər) a person who runs; a person who is in a long race on foot.
The runner ran past us. *n. pl.* **runners** run·ners

runner

runner-up run·ner-up (run′ər-up) the person who is second in a race or a contest; the second-place winner in a contest or a race.
Lisa was the runner-up in the spelling contest.
n. pl. **runners-up** run·ners-up

running run·ning (run′ing) **1.** having to do with fast exercise on foot.
The running shoes keep the runner from hurting his feet. *adj.*
2. *v. pres. part.* See **run** (1, 2, 3).

run out (run out) to have nothing left; to use all of something.
I hope we do not run out of milk before everyone has eaten.
v. **ran out, ran out, running out** run·ning out

run up to (run up tə) to go near; to go quickly in the direction of.
I will run up to the policeman.
v. **ran up to, ran up to, running up to** run·ning up to

a	cat	i	sit	oi	oil	ch	chop		a in about
ā	ate	ī	lie	ou	out	ng	song		e in oven
ä	car	o	pot	u	cut	sh	she	ə =	i in pencil
e	set	ō	old	u̇	book	th	three		o in memory
ē	equal	ô	or	ü	blue	ŦH	there		u in circus
ėr	germ					zh	treasure		

Russia

runway run·way (run′wā)   a long strip of land that planes use to take off and land.
  The plane sat on the runway waiting for its turn to take off.
  n. pl. **runways** run·ways

rush   (rush) **1.** to hurry; to move quickly.
  We will rush to catch the plane. *v.* **rushed, rushed, rushing** rush·ing
  2. a sudden movement; many people going somewhere or doing something in a hurry.
  The morning traffic rush causes many accidents. *n. pl.* **rushes** rush·es

Russia Rus·sia (rush′ə)   a large country in Europe and Asia; the common name for the Union of Soviet Socialist Republics (U.S.S.R.); its capital is Moscow.
  Some parts of Russia are very cold. *n.*

Ss

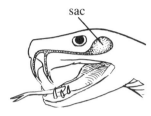

sac

sac (sak) a bag-like part of a plant, animal or person.
The spider has a poison sac in its body. *n. pl.* **sacs**

sack (sak) a bag or container made of cloth, paper or plastic that is used for carrying things.
We put the sand in the paper sack. *n. pl.* **sacks**

sad (sad) **1.** not happy; feeling bad.
A sad person does not laugh. *adj.*
2. feeling sorry.
He is sad that he broke your vase. *adj.* **sadder, saddest** sad·der, sad·dest

sack

saddle sad·dle (sad⸴l) a seat for a rider that goes on a horse's back.
I put the saddle on the horse. *n. pl.* **saddles** sad·dles

saddle horn sad·dle horn (sad⸴l hôrn) the front part of a horse saddle that sticks up.
The cowboy hung his rope on the saddle horn.

sadly sad·ly (sad⸴lē) with great sorrow; with much unhappiness.
The boy looked sadly at his dog as he left for school. *adv.*

sadness sad·ness (sad⸴nəs) an unhappy feeling; a sorry feeling.
I was filled with sadness when Grandmother left. *n. no pl.*

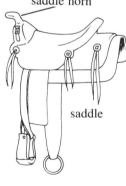

saddle horn

saddle

safe (sāf) **1.** protected; out of danger.
The bird is safe in the cage. *adj.*
2. free from danger.
It is safe to ride the bicycle on this street. *adj.* **safer, safest** saf·er, saf·est

safeness safe·ness (sāf⸴nəs) being free from danger; the feeling of being free from danger.
I like the safeness of my home. *n. no pl.*

safety safe·ty (sāf⸴tē) **1.** being free from danger, harm or worry.
Your safety is important to your parents. *n. no pl.*
2. having to do with being free from danger and harm.
I wear my safety belt when I am in a car. *adj.*

a	cat	**i**	sit	**oi**	oil	**ch**	chop		a in about
ā	ate	**ī**	lie	**ou**	out	**ng**	song		e in oven
ä	car	**o**	pot	**u**	cut	**sh**	she	ə =	i in pencil
e	set	**ō**	old	**u̇**	book	**th**	three		o in memory
ē	equal	**ô**	or	**ü**	blue	**TH**	there		u in circus
ėr	germ					**zh**	treasure		

saffron   saf·fron (saf′rən)   a plant that people use for cooking or for making an orange-yellow dye.
> Many people like the taste of saffron in their food. *n. pl.* **saffrons** saf·frons

sage   (sāj)   a very smart man; a wise man.
> The sage helped us to solve our problem. *n. pl.* **sages** sag·es

Sahara   Sa·har·a (sə·her′ə *or* sə·har′ə)   the world's largest desert, located in northern Africa.
> It is very hot and dry in the Sahara.

Sahara

said   (sed)   *v. pt. t., pt. part.* See **say.**

sail   (sāl)   **1.** to travel in a boat moved by the wind.
> We will sail in the harbor. *v.* **sailed, sailed, sailing** sail·ing
>
> **2.** a large piece of cloth that catches the force of the wind to move a boat in the water.
> We turned the sail so the wind could push against it. *n. pl.* **sails**

sailboat   sail·boat (sāl′bōt)   a kind of boat that the wind moves by pushing against a large piece of cloth or canvas.
> We went around the harbor in the sailboat. *n. pl.* **sailboats** sail·boats

sailing chart   sail·ing chart (sā′ling chärt)   a map of a body of water that shows where dangerous things are located.
> We used the sailing chart to sail safely into the harbor.

sail
sailboat

sailor   sail·or (sā′lər)   a person who sails a boat; a person who operates a boat.
> The sailor turned the boat around. *n. pl.* **sailors** sail·ors

saint   (sānt)   a very good person; a holy person.
> The Catholic Church named Joseph a saint. *n. pl.* **saints**

salad   sal·ad (sal′əd)   a mixture of cold vegetables such as lettuce, tomatoes, peppers and cucumbers.
> People often eat a salad with dinner. *n. pl.* **salads** sal·ads

salamander   sal·a·man·der (sal′ə·man·dər)   an animal that lives in damp, cool places, looks like a lizard and has smooth skin.
> We found a salamander near the pond. *n. pl.* **salamanders** sal·a·man·ders

sale   (sāl)   **1.** available to buy.
> My bicycle is for sale. *n. no pl.*
>
> **2.** an event where things cost less than their usual price.
> The toy store is having a sale on kites; they are only two dollars. *n. pl.* **sales**

salamander

salesclerk   sales·clerk (sālz′klėrk)   a person who works in a store and sells things to people.
> The salesclerk put the kite in a large bag. *n. pl.* **salesclerks** sales·clerks

saliva sa·li·va (sə·lī′və) the liquid in the mouth that keeps the mouth from getting dry.
The saliva rolled out of the baby's mouth. *n. no pl.*

salmon

salmon salm·on (sam′ən) **1.** a large fish with yellowish-pink meat.
The salmon swims against the current when moving to the place where it lays eggs. *n. pl.* **salmons** or **salmon** salm·ons
2. having to do with the large fish with yellowish-pink meat.
The salmon salad is very good. *adj.*

salmonella sal·mo·nel·la (sal·mə·nel′ə) bacteria that cause food poisoning.
Salmonella grows on foods that should be kept cold. *n. no pl.*

salt (sôlt) white grains found in seawater and in the ground that people put on food to give it flavor.
Joe always puts salt on his eggs. *n. no pl.*

salt water salt wa·ter (sôlt wô·tər *or* sôlt wot·ər) ocean water or seawater; water that has salt in it.
The salt water tastes salty.

salute

salty sal·ty (sôl′tē) being full of salt; tasting of salt.
The potato chip is salty. *adj.* **saltier, saltiest** salt·i·er, salt·i·est

salute sa·lute (sə·lüt′) **1.** to honor something or someone for something good.
I salute your efforts to learn math. *v.*
2. to raise a hand to the head in a greeting.
The soldier will salute the officer.
v. **saluted, saluted, saluting** sa·lut·ed, sa·lut·ing

same (sām) alike; identical.
Our clothes are the same size. *adj.*

same as (sām az) identical to; alike.
Her book is the same as mine.

same ___ as (sām ___ az) as much as; equal to.
The inside of the car is the same color as the outside of the car.

same time (sām tīm) simultaneously; happening together.
We got home at the same time.

a	cat	**i**	sit	**oi**	oil	**ch**	chop	a in about
ā	ate	**ī**	lie	**ou**	out	**ng**	song	e in oven
ä	car	**o**	pot	**u**	cut	**sh**	she	ə = { i in pencil
e	set	**ō**	old	**u̇**	book	**th**	three	o in memory
ē	equal	**ô**	or	**ü**	blue	**ŦH**	there	u in circus
ėr	germ					**zh**	treasure	

Samoa Sa·mo·a (sə·mō′ə) a country that is made up of several islands in the southern Pacific Ocean.
Samoa has some beautiful beaches. *n.*

sand (sand) very small pieces of rock that are near the ocean; the small grains of rock that are on a beach.
We put our towel on the sand. *n. pl.* **sands** *or* **sand**

sandal san·dal (san′dl) a shoe that is open on the top; a shoe with straps.
I lost my sandal in the sand. *n. pl.* **sandals** san·dals

sandal

sandman sand·man (sand′man) a fantasy character or person who makes children sleepy by putting sand on their eyes.
In the fairy tale, the sandman visited the children and made them sleepy. *n. pl.* **sandmen** sand·men

sandstorm sand·storm (sand′stôrm) a storm with high winds that picks up and carries sand.
The man got lost during the sandstorm. *n. pl.* **sandstorms** sand·storms

sandwich sand·wich (sand′wich) a food made of meats, cheeses or fillings that are put between two pieces of bread.
I ate a peanut butter sandwich for lunch. *n. pl.* **sandwiches** sand·wich·es

sang (sang) *v. pt. t.* See **sing.**

sank (sangk) *v. pt. t.* See **sink** (1).

sandwich

sapphire sap·phire (saf′īr) a jewel or gem that is blue.
She has a sapphire in her ring. *n. pl.* **sapphires** sap·phires

Sasquatch Sas·quatch (sas′kwäch) the Indian name for Bigfoot, a large animal creature believed to live in the northwestern United States.
The Indians say they have seen Sasquatch many times. *n.*

sat (sat) *v. pt. t., pt. part.* See **sit.**

sat down (sat doun) *v. pt. t., pt. part.* See **sit down.**

satin sat·in (sat′n) a smooth, soft shiny material.
My new dress is made of satin. *n. no pl.*

satisfied sat·is·fied (sat′i·sfīd) **1.** pleased with things; content; happy.
I am satisfied with my math grade. *adj.*
2. *v. pt. t., pt. part.* See **satisfy.**

satisfy sat·is·fy (sat′i·sfī) to meet a person's needs, wants or dreams; to obtain what a person needs or wants.
The pie will satisfy my hunger.
v. **satisfied, satisfied, satisfying** sat·is·fied, sat·is·fy·ing

Saturn

364

sausage

Saturn Sat·urn (sat′ərn) a planet in the solar system that has rings around it.
Saturn is close to Jupiter. *n.*

sausage sau·sage (sô′sij) **1.** meat that is cut into very small pieces and put into a skin-like tube.
I put the sausage in a sandwich. *n. pl.* **sausages** sau·sag·es
2. made of meat stuffed into skin-like tubes.
The sausage sandwich was very good. *adj.*

savanna sa·van·na (sə·van′ə) an area that gets a lot of rain and has a lot of grass with very few trees.
We walked through a savanna in Florida. *n. pl.* **savannas** sa·van·nas

save (sāv) **1.** to keep alive.
We will try to save the sick dog. *v.*
2. to keep for another time; not to use or give away.
I want to save this picture. *v.*
3. to take out of danger; to rescue.
The fireman will save the girl in the burning building.
v. **saved, saved, saving** sav·ing

saw

save the day (sāv ᵺə dā) to make a bad thing good; to change an event from bad to good.
Jim will save the day if he brings more food. *idiom*

saw (sô) **1.** *v. pt. t.* See **see**.
2. a tool with a blade that has sharp teeth for cutting wood or metal.
I used the saw to cut down the tree. *n. pl.* **saws**
3. to cut wood with a tool that has a blade with sharp teeth.
I will saw down the tree. *v.* **sawed, sawed** *or* **sawn, sawing** saw·ing

say (sā) to use the voice for speaking; to talk; to speak words.
I can say the poem. *v.* **said, said, saying** say·ing

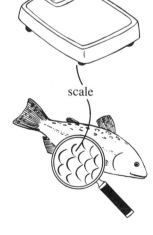
scale

scale (skāl) **1.** a flat, thin skin-like covering that is on the outside of a fish, snake or lizard.
Most fish have scales instead of skin. *n.*
2. a flat, thin covering on the hair of a sheep.
The scale on the wool cannot easily be seen. *n.*
3. a tool that people use to measure the weight of things.
I weighed myself on the scale. *n. pl.* **scales**

Scandinavia Scan·di·na·vi·a (skan·də·nā′vē·ə) the part of Europe that includes the countries of Norway, Sweden, Iceland and Denmark.
My family traveled all through Scandinavia last summer. *n.*

a	cat	i	sit	oi	oil	ch	chop		a in about
ā	ate	ī	lie	ou	out	ng	song		e in oven
ä	car	o	pot	u	cut	sh	she	ə =	i in pencil
e	set	ō	old	u̇	book	th	three		o in memory
ē	equal	ô	or	ü	blue	ᵺ	there		u in circus
ėr	germ					zh	treasure		

scarcely scarce·ly (skers⸴lē *or* skars⸴lē) barely; nearly; almost.
> We scarcely have enough time to get to the movie. *adv.*

scare (sker *or* skar) to frighten; to make afraid.
> The lightning will scare the dog. *v.* **scared, scared, scaring** scar·ing

scarecrow scare·crow (sker⸴krō *or* skar⸴krō) an ugly doll
that is made of old clothes and straw and used to frighten birds
away from a garden.
> We made a scarecrow for the garden. *n. pl.* **scarecrows** scare·crows

scare off (sker ôf *or* skar ôf) to frighten away; to
make run in fear.
> I will scare off the bear. *v.* **scared off, scared off, scaring off** scar·ing off

scarf (skärf) a long piece of material that people wear
on the head, neck or shoulders for warmth.
> I put the scarf around my neck. *n. pl.* **scarfs** *or* **scarves**

scarecrow

scarlet scar·let (skär⸴lit) having a bright red color.
> She wore a scarlet dress. *adj.*

scarlet fever scar·let fe·ver (skär⸴lit fē⸴vər) a sickness that causes
a red rash and a high fever.
> The little girl is very sick. She has scarlet fever.

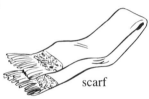

scarves (skärvz) *n. pl.* See **scarf.**

scary scar·y (sker⸴ē *or* skar⸴ē) frightening; causing
someone to be afraid.
> The picture of the monster is scary.
> *adj.* **scarier, scariest** scar·i·er, scar·i·est

scarf

scatter scat·ter (skat⸴ər) to throw things around an area;
to throw things in many directions.
> He will scatter the paper and not pick it up.
> *v.* **scattered, scattered, scattering** scat·tered, scat·ter·ing

scene (sēn) a view; what a person can see from a certain place.
> The scene from the top of the mountain is beautiful. *n. pl.* **scenes**

scenery scen·er·y (sē⸴nər·ē) **1.** the background in a play; the things
put on the stage to make it look like a certain place.
> The scenery for the play is made of paper. *n.*
> **2.** the countryside; the characteristics of a place.
> The winter scenery at the ski hotel is beautiful.
> *n. pl.* **sceneries** scen·er·ies

scenery

schedule sched·ule (skej⸴ùl) a listing of the times
that things will happen.
> The schedule says that the play will start at 7:30.
> *n. pl.* **schedules** sched·ules

scholar   schol·ar (skol′ər)   a person who studies and learns many things; a student.
Dr. Stephens is a scholar who has studied languages for many years.
n. pl. **scholars** schol·ars

school   (skül)   **1.** a building or place where people go to learn and study.
Our school is on this street. *n.*
2. a group of fish that swim together.
I saw a school of fish near the pier. *n. pl.* **schools**
3. having to do with learning and studying.
The school year begins in September. *adj.*

schoolhouse   school·house (skül′hous)   the building where people go to learn and study.
This schoolhouse has been here since 1896.
n. pl. **schoolhouses** school·hous·es

schoolroom   school·room (skül′rüm *or* skül′rûm)   a classroom; a room in a school where students and a teacher work.
My schoolroom is on the first floor of the school.
n. pl. **schoolrooms** school·rooms

schoolroom

schoolwork   school·work (skül′wèrk)   lessons that students learn in school; homework assignments; things that are taught or learned.
I did my schoolwork at home when I was sick. *n. no pl.*

science   sci·ence (sī′əns)   **1.** the study of nature; the facts and knowledge of the world and the things in it.
We learned about electricity in science. *n. no pl.*
2. having to do with the study of nature.
Our science class made a model of the solar system. *adj.*

scientific   sci·en·tif·ic (sī·ən·tif′ik)   having to do with the rules and facts in the study of nature; using the rules and facts in the study of nature.
Mr. Lang knows all the scientific facts about the weather. *adj.*

scientist   sci·en·tist (sī′ən·tist)   a person who studies nature; a person who does experiments.
The scientist made a scientific discovery. *n. pl.* **scientists** sci·en·tists

scissors

scissors   scis·sors (siz′ərz)   a tool that has two sharp blades and is used for cutting.
I used the scissors to cut the picture out of the book. *plural n.*

a	cat	**i**	sit	**oi**	oil	**ch**	chop	
ā	ate	**ī**	lie	**ou**	out	**ng**	song	a in about
ä	car	**o**	pot	**u**	cut	**sh**	she	e in oven
e	set	**ō**	old	**u̇**	book	**th**	three	ə = i in pencil
ē	equal	**ô**	or	**ü**	blue	**ŦH**	there	o in memory
ėr	germ					**zh**	treasure	u in circus

scold (skōld) to be angry and blame someone for doing something bad.
I will scold the boy for hitting you.
v. **scolded, scolded, scolding** scold·ed, scold·ing

score (skôr *or* skōr) **1.** the number of points made or won or earned in a game or a contest.
The score of the baseball game is 4 to 2. *n. pl.* **scores**
2. to gain a point in a game or contest.
I must score a point in the game. *v.* **scored, scored, scoring** scor·ing

scorpion scor·pi·on (skôr′pē·ən) a small poisonous animal that is in the spider family.
The scorpion does not look like a spider. *n. pl.* **scorpions** scor·pi·ons

scorpion

Scotland Scot·land (skot′lənd) a country that is part of Great Britain and that is north of England.
His grandfather came to America from Scotland. *n.*

Scottish Scot·tish (skot′ish) having to do with Scotland; being born in the country of Scotland.
The man is wearing a Scottish kilt and carrying a bagpipe. *adj.*

Scotland

Edinburgh

scout (skout) **1.** a boy or a girl in a club that teaches about camping.
She is a girl scout. *n.*
2. a person who goes before other people on a hike or a forest or jungle trip; the person who looks ahead.
We had a scout on our trip through the jungle. *n. pl.* **scouts**

scrap (skrap) small pieces of paper or cloth that are not needed and can be thrown away; leftover pieces of paper, cloth or wood.
I put the scrap of paper in the garbage. *n. pl.* **scraps**

scrape (skrāp) to take something off a surface or out of a container by using a sharp tool; to remove with something sharp.
I will scrape the skin off the carrots.
v. **scraped, scraped, scraping** scrap·ing

scratch (skrach) **1.** to dig into something with claws or nails.
The cat will scratch the chair with her claws. *v.*
2. to rub with the fingernail to stop something from itching.
I need to scratch my arm where the mosquito bit me. *v.*
3. to give someone or something a small cut; to give someone a cut that is not deep.
Do not scratch yourself on that nail.
v. **scratched, scratched, scratching** scratch·ing
4. a small cut that is not deep.
I got a scratch on my arm. *n. pl.* **scratches** scratch·es

scout

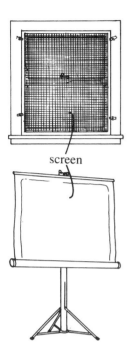

screen

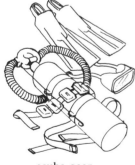

scuba gear

scream   (skrēm)   **1.** to shout; to yell; to speak very loudly.
I will scream if you hit me. *v.*
2. to yell in fear.
The woman will scream when she sees a mouse.
v. **screamed, screamed, screaming** scream·ing
3. a loud yell; a shout.
I heard her loud scream. *n. pl.* **screams**

screen   (skrēn)   **1.** a material made of wire with tiny holes;
a frame holding cloth made of woven wire that keeps insects
from passing through.
We put a screen in the window to keep the flies from coming
into the room. *n.*
2. a protective shield.
We have a screen in front of the fireplace to keep the sparks
from flying on to the rug. *n.*
3. a smooth cloth or surface on which movies or
pictures are shown.
We pulled the screen down so that we could show the film. *n. pl.* **screens**
4. something made of a woven wire material.
The screen door lets air into the house and keeps the flies outside. *adj.*

screenwriter   screen·writ·er (skrēn′rī·tər)   a person who writes
a story for a movie or television show.
The screenwriter wrote a great story. *n. pl.* **screenwriters** screen·wri·ters

scribble   scrib·ble (skrib′əl)   to write quickly so that it is difficult
to read what has been written; to make marks that
do not mean anything.
I will scribble my answer so the teacher cannot read it.
v. **scribbled, scribbled, scribbling** scrib·bled, scrib·bling

script   (skript)   the words in a movie or a play.
We are reading the script. *n. pl.* **scripts**

scriptwriter   script·wri·ter (skript′rī·tər)   a person who writes
a story for a play or a movie.
The scriptwriter wrote a play about an old man.
n. pl. **scriptwriters** script·wri·ters

scrub   (skrub)   to rub something very hard to clean it.
I will scrub the floor in the kitchen.
v. **scrubbed, scrubbed, scrubbing** scrub·bing

scuba gear   scu·ba gear (skü′bə gir)   the equipment or tools that
a person uses to dive underwater.
The scuba gear lets the diver breathe under the water.

a	cat	i	sit	oi	oil	ch	chop		a in about
ā	ate	ī	lie	ou	out	ng	song		e in oven
ä	car	o	pot	u	cut	sh	she	ə =	i in pencil
e	set	ō	old	u̇	book	th	three		o in memory
ē	equal	ô	or	ü	blue	ŦH	there		u in circus
ėr	germ					zh	treasure		

sculpture   sculp·ture (skulp'chər)   **1.** a figure or shape that is made by carving wood or cutting rock.
> The sculpture of a soldier is in the city park. *n. pl.* **sculptures** sculp·tures
2. the art of making figures from wood or rock.
> Leonardo da Vinci made sculpture. *n. no pl.*

S curve   (es kėrv)   a road that bends back and forth in the shape of an "S."
> There is an S curve on the mountain.

sculpture

scurvy   scur·vy (skėr'vē)   a disease caused by not eating enough vitamin C or not eating enough fruit or vegetables.
> People on long boat trips would get scurvy. *n. no pl.*

sea   (sē)   **1.** a large body of salt water; an ocean.
> The sea looks blue. *n. pl.* **seas**
2. having to do with a large body of water.
> The whale is a sea animal. *adj.*

seacoast   sea·coast (sē'kōst)   the place where the sea and the land meet; the land near the sea.
> I am going to the seacoast for the summer. *n. pl.* **seacoasts** sea·coasts

seal   (sēl)   **1.** an animal that lives in the ocean and that has flippers.
> The seal balanced the ball on its nose. *n.*
2. a special symbol or emblem.
> The governor has his own seal. *n.*
3. the part of an envelope that has glue on it.
> I wet the seal of the envelope before I closed it. *n. pl.* **seals**

S curve

sea level   sea lev·el (sē lev'əl)   the height of the sea; the level of the sea.
> We are 500 feet above sea level.

seamstress   seam·stress (sēm'stris)   a worker who sews things for money; a woman who works as a sewer.
> The seamstress made me a new dress. *n. pl.* **seamstresses** seam·stress·es

seaport   sea·port (sē'pôrt)   a town near the ocean; a harbor for ships.
> San Diego is a large California seaport. *n. pl.* **seaports** sea·ports

search   (sėrch)   **1.** to look for something or someone; to hunt for someone or something.
> I will search the playground for your ring.
v. **searched, searched, searching** search·ing
2. the act of looking for something or someone; the hunting for something or someone.
> The search for the ring took several hours. *n. pl.* **searches** search·es

seal

season sea·son (sē⁀zn) **1.** a time of the year that has a certain kind of weather.
Fall is my favorite season. *n.*
2. a time when something can happen; a time when something special takes place.
Today is the start of hunting season. *n. pl.* **seasons** sea·sons
3. to add flavor to food; to put ingredients into food to flavor it.
I will season the chicken with lemon.
v. **seasoned, seasoned, seasoning** sea·soned, sea·son·ing

seat belt

seat

seat (sēt) **1.** a chair; a place to sit.
I took the seat next to Lisa. *n.*
2. the part of a horse saddle where the rider sits.
It is not easy to stay in the seat when the horse is running. *n. pl.* **seats**

seat belt (sēt belt) a safety strap that keeps a person in place in a vehicle such as a car or an airplane.
I fastened my seat belt as soon as I sat in the car.

seaweed sea·weed (sē⁀wēd) a plant that grows in the ocean and is used as food by many sea animals.
Some people eat seaweed. *n. no pl.*

second sec·ond (sek⁀ənd) **1.** having to do with the one that comes after the first and before the third.
I came in second in the race. *adj.*
2. a short unit of time; one of the sixty units of time in a minute.
It will only take a second to get the book. *n. pl.* **seconds** sec·onds

second hand

second hand sec·ond hand (sek⁀ənd hand) the indicator on a clock or a watch that counts off the seconds.
The second hand makes a circle once each minute.

second-largest sec·ond-larg·est (sek⁀ənd-lär⁀jəst) not the biggest, but almost as big as the biggest.
Los Angeles is the second-largest city in the United States. *adj.*

secondly sec·ond·ly (sek⁀ənd·lē) for the second point; in the second place.
First I want to tell you about my trip, and secondly I want to hear about your trip. *adv.*

secret se·cret (sē⁀krit) **1.** something that a person should not tell to other people.
I have a secret, but I cannot tell you. *n. pl.* **secrets** se·crets
2. having to do with something that many people do not know.
I have a secret place for hiding my money. *adj.*

a	cat	i	sit	oi	oil	ch	chop		a in about
ā	ate	ī	lie	ou	out	ng	song		e in oven
ä	car	o	pot	u	cut	sh	she	ə =	i in pencil
e	set	ō	old	u̇	book	th	three		o in memory
ē	equal	ô	or	ü	blue	ŦH	there		u in circus
ėr	germ					zh	treasure		

secretary   sec·re·tar·y (sek′rə·ter·ē)   a person who writes letters, types and files reports for another person, a company, an office or a state.
My dad's secretary is a young man who is going to college.
n. pl. **secretaries** sec·re·tar·ies

secretly   se·cret·ly (sē′krit·lē)   without any other person knowing; in a secret way.
He secretly left the house. *adv.*

secret police   se·cret po·lice (sē′krit pə·lēs′)   police who do not wear uniforms so that people cannot tell that they are the police.
The secret police can go places other policemen cannot.

securely   se·cure·ly (si·kyûr′lē)   in a safe way; in a tight way.
I tied the dog securely to the gate. *adv.*

see   (sē)   **1.** to look with the eyes; to look at something.
I can see the ocean from my window. *v.*
2. to understand; to know.
I see what you are saying. *v.*
3. to know what things are by looking at them; the power to use the eyes.
I do not see well, so I wear glasses to read. *v.* **saw, seen, seeing** see·ing

seed

seed   (sēd)   **1.** the part of a plant that is used to start another plant.
I put the tomato seed in the ground to start a new tomato plant. *n. pl.* **seeds**
2. to put seeds into the ground.
I will seed the field with corn.
v. **seeded, seeded, seeding** seed·ed, seed·ing

Seeing Eye dog   see·ing eye dog (sē′ing ī dôg)   a dog that is trained to help a blind person move around without bumping into things.
Her Seeing Eye dog lets her know when it is safe to cross the street.

seem   (sēm)   to appear; to have the feeling of being something; to look like; to feel like.
I seem to be hungry all the time.
v. **seemed, seemed, seeming** seem·ing

seen   (sēn) *v. pt. part.* See **see.**

seldom   sel·dom (sel′dəm)   not often; only once in a while; rarely.
I seldom visit the library. *adv.*

Seeing Eye dog

select   se·lect (si·lekt′)   to pick one from a group of many; to choose something; to decide which thing a person wants.
I will select a new dress at the store.
v. **selected, selected, selecting** se·lect·ed, se·lect·ing

self-binder

selection se·lec·tion (si·lek′shən) **1.** the group of things from which a person chooses one thing; the things from which a person picks.
The selection of dresses is very large. *n.*
2. the thing that a person chooses from a group.
After looking at all of the dogs, the judge's selection for first prize was the poodle. *n. pl.* **selections** se·lec·tions

self-binder self-bind·er (self-bīn′dər) a reaping machine that both cuts and binds the wheat.
The self-binder was invented by Cyrus McCormick.
n. pl. **self-binders** self-bind·ers

self-defense self-de·fense (self-di·fens′) protection of one's own body or property; the ability to protect oneself and one's belongings.
If we know self-defense, no one can frighten us. *n. no pl.*

selfish self·ish (sel′fish) not being willing to share; not caring about anyone except oneself.
Joan is selfish; she would not help me with my problem. *adj.*

sell (sel) to take money for things; to exchange things for money.
I will sell my bicycle for thirty dollars. *v.* **sold, sold, selling** sell·ing

seller sell·er (sel′ər) a person who sells things.
The seller of the car wants too much money for it. *n. pl.* **sellers** sell·ers

senator sen·a·tor (sen′ə·tər) a person who is elected by the people of a state to work for them in the Senate of the United States.
We will elect a new senator in November. *n. pl.* **senators** sen·a·tors

send (send) to cause something to be moved from one place to another; to cause something to be carried from one place to another.
I will send this letter to Lisa. *v.* **sent, sent, sending** send·ing

senior sen·ior (sē′nyər) the fourth and last year in high school or college.
My brother is a senior and will graduate from college this May.
n. pl. **seniors** sen·iors

a	cat	i	sit	oi	oil	ch	chop		a in about
ā	ate	ī	lie	ou	out	ng	song		e in oven
ä	car	o	pot	u	cut	sh	she	ə =	i in pencil
e	set	ō	old	u̇	book	th	three		o in memory
ē	equal	ô	or	ü	blue	ŦH	there		u in circus
ėr	germ					zh	treasure		

sense (sens) **1.** the ability to feel and understand.
His sense of honesty is very good. *n.*
2. a power of the body to experience sensations from things outside the body.
My sense of smell is very good; I can tell what something is with my eyes closed. *n. pl.* **senses** sens·es
3. logic; intelligence; brains.
The boy will be all right; he has good sense. *n. no pl.*
4. to be able to feel and understand.
My dog can sense when I am angry at him.
v. **sensed, sensed, sensing** sens·ing

sensible sen·si·ble (sen′sə·bəl) logical; practical; showing good judgement.
She is very sensible. *adj.*

sent (sent) *v. pt. t., pt. part.* See **send.**

sentence sen·tence (sen′təns) a group of words that is correctly ordered to give meaning; a group of words that meets the rules of a language and makes a meaningful statement.
Please write a sentence using the word "right." *n. pl.* **sentences** sen·tenc·es

serpent

separate[1] sep·a·rate (sep′ər·it) having to do with things that are not connected or tied together; having to do with things that are apart.
My brother and I have separate rooms. *adj.*

separate[2] sep·a·rate (sep′ə·rāt) **1.** to move things apart; to put space between things; to make into two pieces.
I will separate the crayons for the two children. *v.*
2. to keep apart; to keep from joining.
I will separate the two boys.
v. **separated, separated, separating** sep·a·rat·ed, sep·a·rat·ing

serf (sėrf) a person who is owned by another person; a slave.
The serf was unhappy. *n. pl.* **serfs**

serfdom serf·dom (sėrf′dəm) the act of having serfs; slavery.
The Russians once believed in serfdom. *n. no pl.*

serious ser·i·ous (sir′ē·əs) not funny; intense; important.
We are having a serious talk about going to college. *adj.*

sermon ser·mon (sėr′mən) a speech; a lecture; a religious lecture; a serious talk.
The priest gave a sermon on being kind. *n. pl.* **sermons** ser·mons

serpent ser·pent (sėr′pənt) a snake.
The serpent bit the rabbit. *n. pl.* **serpents** ser·pents

servant serv·ant (sėr′vənt) a person who is paid money to do things for another person; a person who does things in another person's home for money.
Rich people have at least one servant. *n. pl.* **servants** serv·ants

servant

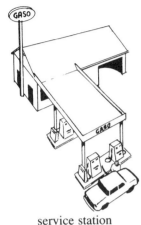

service station

set the table

serve (sėrv) **1.** to bring the food to a table in a restaurant.
The waiter will serve us our food. *v.*
2. to give help or assistance to someone.
How can I serve you? *v.*
3. to work in a government job; to be part of the military.
I will serve six years in the navy. *v.* **served, served, serving** serv·ing

service serv·ice (sėr´vis) **1.** a helpful action; the act of giving help or assistance to someone.
The service in that restaurant was not very good. *n. pl.* **services** serv·ic·es
2. having to do with helping someone.
The store has a service department that will fix your broken radio. *adj.*

service station serv·ice sta·tion (sėr´vis stā´shən) a place where people buy gas for their cars; a place where gas is sold.
We took the car to the service station.

set (set) **1.** a group of things that are alike or that go together.
I gave Mother a set of knives for the kitchen. *n. pl.* **sets**
2. to put something in its place; to position something.
I will set the sofa against the wall. *v.* **set, set, setting** set·ting

set free (set frē) to let go; to give freedom to an animal or person.
The slaves were set free after the Civil War.
v. **set free, set free, setting free** set·ting free

set off (set ôf) to start on a trip; to begin to go somewhere.
We will set off on the hike at dawn.
v. **set off, set off, setting off** set·ting off

set the table set the ta·ble (set ᴛнə tā´bəl) to put on a table the dishes and silverware that people use when eating a meal.
Mother will set the table for the children. *idiom*

setting set·ting (set´ing) **1.** the place where a person or thing lives; the place where something happens.
A giraffe can live only in a dry, warm setting. *n. pl.* **settings** set·tings
2. *v. pres. part.* See **set** (2).

settle set·tle (set´l) to make one's home in a certain place; to decide to stay in a place.
I think I will settle in California.
v. **settled, settled, settling** set·tled, set·tling

a	cat	i	sit	oi	oil	ch	chop		a in about
ā	ate	ī	lie	ou	out	ng	song		e in oven
ä	car	o	pot	u	cut	sh	she	ə =	i in pencil
e	set	ō	old	u̇	book	th	three		o in memory
ē	equal	ô	or	ü	blue	ᴛʜ	there		u in circus
ėr	germ					zh	treasure		

settlement set·tle·ment (set¹l·mənt) a small group of homes;
a place with a group of new homes.
The pioneers started a settlement in the mountains.
n. pl. **settlements** set·tle·ments

settler set·tler (set¹lər) a person who starts a new town or city; a
person who makes a home in a new place.
The settler moved his family to the new settlement. *n. pl.* **settlers** set·tlers

set up (set up) to build; to put in a place.
We will set up our tent. *v.* **set up, set up, setting up** set·ting up

several sev·er·al (sev¹ər·əl) some; more than a few; more than
one or two.
I have several pairs of shoes. *adj.*

severely se·vere·ly (sə·vir¹lē) deeply; extremely; to a great degree.
The boy was severely sick with a fever. *adv.*

sewing basket

sew (sō) to work with a needle and thread.
Donna will sew a new dress for Pat. *v.* **sewed, sewed, sewing** sew·ing

sewing sew·ing (sō¹ing) **1.** work that uses a needle and thread
to put pieces of fabric together.
Donna had a lot of sewing to do. *n. no pl.*
2. having to do with work that uses needles and thread
to put fabric together.
My sister is taking a sewing class. *adj.*
3. *v. pres. part.* See **sew.**

sewing basket sew·ing bas·ket (sō¹ing bas¹kit) a box or carton
that holds the things needed to sew fabric together,
such as needles, thread and scissors.
I found the red thread in the sewing basket.

sewing machine

sewing machine sew·ing ma·chine (sō¹ing mə·shēn′) a machine
that sews fabric together.
Mother fixed my pants on the sewing machine.

shade (shād) the darkness caused by something being in front
of the light source; the darkness that happens when the sun
cannot shine in a place.
I sat in the shade of the big tree. *n. no pl.*

shadow shad·ow (shad¹ō) the dark image made by a thing or
a person in front of a light source; the shade of something
or someone in front of the light.
I can see the shadow of the tree. *n. pl.* **shadows** shad·ows

shadow

shady shad·y (shā¹dē) out of the light of the sun; in the shadow
made by an object.
I like to read on the shady side of the porch.
adj. **shadier, shadiest** shad·i·er, shad·i·est

shaggy

shake hands

shaggy shag·gy (shag'ē) having long uncombed hair; covered with long hair that is not combed.
The shaggy dog ran in front of the car.
adj. **shaggier, shaggiest** shag·gi·er, shag·gi·est

shake (shāk) to move something quickly from side to side, up and down or back and forth.
Please shake the can of milk before opening it.
v. **shook, shaken, shaking** shak·en, shak·ing

shake hands (shāk hands) to hold another person's hand and move it up and down when meeting this person.
Remember to shake hands with the new people you will meet. *idiom*

shake up (shāk up) to move something from side to side or up and down quickly and forcefully.
I will shake up the bottle of pop.
v. **shook up, shaken up, shaking up** shak·en up, shak·ing up

shall (shal *or* shəl) surely will.
I shall go to college. *aux.*

shallow shal·low (shal'ō) not deep; having little height or depth.
The water in the lake is shallow.
adj. **shallower, shallowest** shal·low·er, shal·low·est

shame (shām) an embarrassment; a sad occurrence; a fact to feel sorry about.
It is a shame that he steals from other people. *n. no pl.*

shape (shāp) **1.** a form; a geometric form.
A circle is a shape. A square is a shape. *n.*
2. figures that are molded or formed.
The plastic shape was painted by the girl. *n.*
3. an outline of something; the way something looks or appears.
The shape of the shadow is the same as the object in front of the light. *n. pl.* **shapes**
4. to make something into a form; to make something into a geometric form.
I will shape the clay into a horse. *v.* **shaped, shaped, shaping** shap·ing

share (sher *or* shar) **1.** a person's part or piece of something.
Lisa may have my share of the pie. *n. pl.* **shares**
2. to cut up or divide into parts for several people; to give a part of something to someone.
I will share my candy with you. *v.* **shared, shared, sharing** shar·ing

a	cat	**i**	sit	**oi** oil	**ch** chop		a in about
ā	ate	**ī**	lie	**ou** out	**ng** song		e in oven
ä	car	**o**	pot	**u** cut	**sh** she	ə =	i in pencil
e	set	**ō**	old	**u̇** book	**th** three		o in memory
ē	equal	**ô**	or	**ü** blue	**ŦH** there		u in circus
ėr	germ				**zh** treasure		

shark (shärk) a meat-eating fish that lives in seawater.
    The shark attacked the diver. *n. pl.* **sharks**

shark

sharp (shärp) **1.** having a blade or a point that can cut
    something easily.
    The scissors are sharp. *adj.*
    2. having a point; not being rounded.
    The goat has a sharp horn. *adj.* **sharper, sharpest** sharp·er, sharp·est
    3. exactly.
    I will meet you at six o'clock sharp. *adv.*

sharpen sharp·en (shär'pən) to make into a point; to make sharp.
    I will sharpen your pencil.
    v. **sharpened, sharpened, sharpening** shar·pened, shar·pen·ing

shave (shāv) to take off hair with a sharp tool.
    My father will shave in the morning. *v.* **shaved, shaved, shaving** shav·ing

shave off (shāv ôf) to take off hair with a sharp tool.
    My brother will shave off his beard in the summer.
    v. **shaved off, shaved off, shaving off** shav·ing off

shawl

shaving cream shav·ing cream (shā'ving krēm) a foamy lotion or
    cream that is put on hair before shaving.
    My father puts shaving cream on his face before he shaves.

shawl (shôl) a piece of cloth that is put over the shoulders
    to keep them warm.
    My grandmother always wears a shawl. *n. pl.* **shawls**

she (shē) the girl or woman about whom a person is talking.
    Mary is having a birthday party. She will be nine years old. *pron.*

shear (shir) to cut off; to take the wool off sheep.
    I will shear the sheep. *v.* **sheared, sheared** *or* **shorn, shearing** shear·ing

shears

shears (shirz) large scissors; the tool that a person uses to take
    the wool off a sheep.
    I put the shears in the barn. *plural n.*

shed (shed) **1.** a small building that people use for storage
    or keeping things.
    We keep the lawn mower in the shed. *n. pl.* **sheds**
    2. to get rid of; to let fall; to fall off.
    The dog will shed his hair all summer. *v.* **shed, shed, shedding** shed·ding

sheep (shēp) a grown lamb; a farm animal with thick wool that
    is shaved and made into a warm fabric.
    We raise sheep for their wool. *n. pl.* **sheep**

sheet (shēt) large thin piece of wood, paper or cloth.
    The sail is made from a sheet of canvas. *n. pl.* **sheets**

sheep

sheet bend knot

shelf

shellfish

shield

sheet bend knot (shēt bend not) a kind of knot that ties together two different pieces of rope.
The scout leader made a sheet bend knot.

shelf (shelf) **1.** a flat board that holds things; a flat surface that holds things.
I put the book on the library shelf. *n.*
2. a flat extension or addition to something; a flat piece of rock or metal.
We found a rocky shelf in the ocean. *n. pl.* **shelves.**

shell (shel) a hard covering; something hard that protects the outside of something.
The turtle hides in its shell. *n. pl.* **shells**

she'll (shēl *or* shil) she will; she shall.
She'll call us when she gets home. *contrac.*

shellfish shell·fish (shel'fish) any animal that lives in the ocean and has a shell that protects it from harm.
An oyster is a shellfish. *n. pl.* **shellfishes** *or* **shellfish** shell·fish·es

shelter shel·ter (shel'tər) a place that is safe; a place that protects things or people.
A camping tent is a shelter. *n. pl.* **shelters** shel·ters

shelves (shelvz) *n. pl.* See **shelf.**

shepherd shep·herd (shep'ərd) a person who takes care of sheep.
The shepherd feeds the sheep. *n. pl.* **shepherds** shep·herds

Shetland pony Shet·land po·ny (shet'lənd pō'nē) a small horse that was first raised on the Shetland Islands.
I rode a Shetland pony at the state fair.

shield (shēld) **1.** a heavy piece of metal or wood that protects people or things.
The knight carried a shield and a sword. *n. pl.* **shields**
2. having to do with a heavy piece of metal or wood that protects.
There are many shield tiles on a rocket. *adj.*

shilling shil·ling (shil'ing) an old English coin that was worth 12 pennies.
The shilling is not used today. *n. pl.* **shillings** shil·lings

a	cat	i	sit	oi	oil	ch	chop		a in about
ā	ate	ī	lie	ou	out	ng	song		e in oven
ä	car	o	pot	u	cut	sh	she	ə =	i in pencil
e	set	ō	old	u̇	book	th	three		o in memory
ē	equal	ô	or	ü	blue	ŦH	there		u in circus
ėr	germ					zh	treasure		

shine (shīn) **1.** to glow; to give off light.
> The moon will shine brightly tonight. *v.*
> **2.** to make something bright; to polish.
> I will shine the shoes.
> *v.* **shined** *or* **shone, shined** *or* **shone, shining** shin·ing

shining shin·ing (shī'ning) *v. pres. part.* See **shine.**

shiny shin·y (shī'nē) bright; bright with light.
> The gold ring is shiny. *adj.* **shinier, shiniest** shin·i·er, shin·i·est

ship (ship) a large boat.
> The airplane landed on the ship. *n. pl.* **ships**

ship

shipworm ship·worm (ship'wėrm) a sea animal that is long
and worm-shaped, has a shell and digs into ships.
> We found a shipworm on the ship. *n. pl.* **shipworms** ship·worms

shipwreck ship·wreck (ship'rek) **1.** an accident that destroys
a boat or ship.
> An iceberg caused the shipwreck. *n. pl.* **shipwrecks** ship·wrecks
> **2.** to destroy a boat or a ship.
> If we hit the iceberg, we will shipwreck.
> *v.* **shipwrecked, shipwrecked, shipwrecking**
> ship·wrecked, ship·wreck·ing

shirt (shėrt) a piece of clothing that covers the chest, back
and arms of a person; a piece of clothing for the top
part of the body.
> Tom wore a blue shirt to school today. *n. pl.* **shirts**

shirt

shiver shiv·er (shiv'ər) to shake or tremble from cold or fear.
> She started to shiver from the cold air.
> *v.* **shivered, shivered, shivering** shiv·ered, shiv·er·ing

shock (shok) to scare someone or something suddenly;
to startle with fear.
> The spider will shock her. *v.* **shocked, shocked, shocking** shock·ing

shocked (shokt) **1.** having to do with a sudden scare; full of fear.
> I knew she was frightened by her shocked look. *adj.*
> **2.** *v. pt. t., pt. part.* See **shock.**

shoe (shü) **1.** a covering for the feet that is usually made of
leather or cloth.
> I broke the lace on my shoe. *n.*
> **2.** a metal covering for the bottom of an animal's hoof.
> We put a new shoe on the horse. *n. pl.* **shoes**
> **3.** having to do with a covering for the feet.
> I went to the shoe store. *adj.*

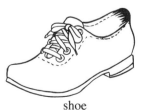

shoe

shoot

shoemaker   shoe·mak·er (shü′mā·kər)   a person who makes
or repairs shoes.
The shoemaker put a new sole on my shoe.
n. pl. **shoemakers** shoe·mak·ers

shone   (shōn)   *v. pt. t.* See **shine.**

shook   (shůk)   *v. pt. t.* See **shake.**

shoot   (shüt)   **1.** to pull the trigger of a gun; to fire a gun.
My father showed me how to shoot his rifle. *v.*
2. to try to throw a basketball through a hoop.
The player will shoot the ball toward the hoop.
v. **shot, shot, shooting** shoot·ing

shop   (shop)   **1.** a place where things are sold; a store.
I walked to the ice cream shop. *n. pl.* **shops**
2. to look in a store for things to buy; to buy things in a store.
I will shop for new shoes. *v.* **shopped, shopped, shopping** shop·ping
3. having to do with a store.
The shop owner helped me find the right shoes. *adj.*

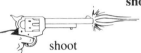

shoot

shoplift   shop·lift (shop′lift)   to take something from a store
without paying for it; to steal from a store.
It is a crime to shoplift.
v. **shoplifted, shoplifted, shoplifting** shop·lift·ed, shop·lift·ing

shoplifter   shop·lift·er (shop′lif·tər)   a person who steals
from a store; a person who takes things from a store
and does not pay for them.
They put the shoplifter in jail. *n. pl.* **shoplifters** shop·lift·ers

shopping center   shop·ping cen·ter (shop′ing sen′tər)   a
group of stores or shops.
The ice cream shop is in the shopping center.

shore   (shôr *or* shōr)   the place where the ocean meets the land;
the land near a sea, lake or ocean.
We will spend our vacation at the shore. *n. pl.* **shores**

short   (shôrt)   **1.** not tall; low in height.
The boy is short. *adj.*
2. not long; small in length.
We took a short walk after dinner.
adj. **shorter, shortest** short·er, short·est

shore

a	cat	i	sit	oi	oil	ch	chop		a in about
ā	ate	ī	lie	ou	out	ng	song		e in oven
ä	car	o	pot	u	cut	sh	she	ə =	i in pencil
e	set	ō	old	ů	book	th	three		o in memory
ē	equal	ô	or	ü	blue	ŦH	there		u in circus
ėr	germ					zh	treasure		

shortly   short·ly (shôrt′lē)   quickly; soon; in a small amount of time.
We will be home shortly. *adv.*

shot   (shot)   **1.** *v. pt. t., pt. part.* See **shoot.**
2. the sound of a gun being fired.
We heard the shot before we saw him run. *n.*
3. an injection from a doctor's needle.
The doctor gave me a shot in the arm. *n. pl.* **shots**

should   (shu̇d *or* shəd)   ought to.
I should help him with his homework. *aux.*

shoulder   shoul·der (shōl′dər)   **1.** the part of a person or animal where the arm joins the body.
He put his head on my shoulder. *n.*
2. the part of a horse where the front leg joins the body.
The rider hit the horse's shoulder with the rope. *n. pl.* **shoulders** shoul·ders

shoulder

shout   (shout)   **1.** to yell; to scream words; to say words loudly.
The boys shout at each other when they fight.
v. **shouted, shouted, shouting** shout·ed, shout·ing
2. words or sounds that are yelled or screamed.
I could hear his shout from next door. *n. pl.* **shouts**

shove   (shuv)   to push hard from behind or in back of something or someone.
I will shove the chair into the other room.
v. **shoved, shoved, shoving** shov·ing

shovel   shov·el (shuv′əl)   a long-handled tool that is used for digging.
I dug the hole with a shovel. *n. pl.* **shovels** shov·els

shovel

show   (shō)   **1.** a performance; a display; an exhibit.
We went to the art show. *n. pl.* **shows**
2. to point out; to point to.
The teacher will show us the new pictures. *v.*
3. to let see; to present to be seen.
I will show you my new dress.
v. **showed, showed** *or* **shown, showing** show·ing

show around   show a·round (shō ə·round′)   to take through a place; to point out different things about a place; to take on a tour of a place.
Let me show you around our school.
v. **showed around, showed around** *or* **shown around, showing around** show·ing a·round

shower   show·er (shou′ər)   a way of washing the body with water that falls on the body from above.
I like a bath better than a shower. *n. pl.* **showers** show·ers

shower

show off (shō ôf) to do something to get attention; to act up to get attention.
> Tony will probably show off at the party.
> *v.* **showed off, shown off** *or* **showed off, showing off** show·ing off

show up (shō up) to get to a place; to arrive; to appear.
> He will show up at any minute.
> *v.* **showed up, shown up** *or* **showed up, showing up** show·ing up

shriek (shrēk) to scream; to make a loud, sharp sound.
> The teacher will shriek if she sees the snake.
> *v.* **shrieked, shrieked, shrieking** shriek·ing

shrivel up shriv·el up (shriv′əl up) to become small and wrinkled; to get dry and full of wrinkles.
> The grape will shrivel up and become a raisin.
> *v.* **shriveled up** *or* **shrivelled up, shriveled up** *or* **shrivelled up, shriveling up** *or* **shrivelling up**
> shriv·eled up *or* shriv·elled up, shriv·el·ing up *or* shriv·el·ling up

shrug (shrug) to move the shoulders upward to show doubt or dislike.
> I often shrug when I do not understand the teacher.
> *v.* **shrugged, shrugged, shrugging** shrug·ging

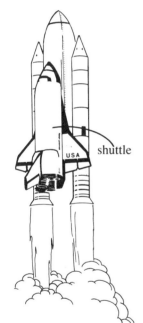

shuttle

shut (shut) **1.** to close something that is open.
> I will shut the window now that it is raining.
> *v.* **shut, shut, shutting** shut·ting
> **2.** closed; not open.
> The door is shut. *adj.*

shutter shut·ter (shut′ər) the part of a camera that opens and closes to allow light to reach the film.
> The shutter closes after each picture is taken. *n. pl.* **shutters** shut·ters

shuttle shut·tle (shut′l) **1.** a vehicle such as a bus, van or train that carries things or people and moves from one place to another and back to the first place many times each day.
> We will take the shuttle to the hospital every day this week. *n.*
> **2.** a rocket that goes into space and back again.
> Someday everyone will ride the shuttle to the moon.
> *n. pl.* **shuttles** shut·tles

shy (shī) not comfortable around people; timid and slightly afraid of people.
> The little girl is shy, so she will not talk to new people.
> *adj.* **shyer** *or* **shier, shyest** *or* **shiest** shy·er *or* shi·er, shy·est *or* shi·est

a	cat	i	sit	oi	oil	ch	chop		a in about
ā	ate	ī	lie	ou	out	ng	song		e in oven
ä	car	o	pot	u	cut	sh	she	ə =	i in pencil
e	set	ō	old	u̇	book	th	three		o in memory
ē	equal	ô	or	ü	blue	ŦH	there		u in circus
ėr	germ					zh	treasure		

sick   (sik)   not healthy; ill; having an illness or a disease.
> I did not go to school today because I am sick.
> *adj.* **sicker, sickest** sick·er, sick·est

sickly   sick·ly (sik′lē)   being ill often; not strong physically.
> The man has been sickly for many years.
> *adj.* **sicklier, sickliest** sick·li·er, sick·li·est

sickness   sick·ness (sik′nis)   a disease; an illness.
> His sickness makes him fall often. *n. pl.* **sicknesses** sick·ness·es

side   (sīd)   **1.** the surface or area of a thing or person that is not the front, back, top or bottom.
> The ingredients are printed on the side of the box. *n.*
> **2.** an area of a place, city or state.
> I grew up on the north side of this city. *n. pl.* **sides**

side by side   (sīd bī sīd)   next to each other.
> We sat side by side on the school bus. *idiom*

sidewalk   side·walk (sīd′wôk)   a paved, cement path for walking that is next to a street.
> I fell on the sidewalk in front of my house. *n. pl.* **sidewalks** side·walks

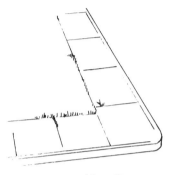
sidewalk

sigh   (sī)   to let out a long breath of air; to make a sad sound while letting out a long breath of air.
> She will often sigh when she is very tired.
> *v.* **sighed, sighed, sighing** sigh·ing

sight   (sīt)   **1.** the act of seeing; the power to see with the eyes.
> The boy lost his sight when he was young, so he is blind. *n. no pl.*
> **2.** a view; a vision.
> The sight from the top of the mountain was beautiful. *n.*
> **3.** the area that one can see; a person's line of vision.
> The camp was in sight of the scout. *n. pl.* **sights**
> **4.** to see; to look at with the eyes.
> I can sight the camp through the binoculars.
> *v.* **sighted, sighted, sighting** sight·ed, sight·ing

sightseeing   sight·see·ing (sīt′sē·ing)   **1.** going from place to place and looking at new places and things.
> Sightseeing in Europe can be fun and educational. *n. no pl.*
> **2.** having to do with going from place to place and looking at new places and things.
> We will take a sightseeing tour of Chicago. *adj.*

sign

sign   (sīn)   **1.** to put your name on something; to write your name.
> The whole class will sign the birthday card to the teacher.
> *v.* **signed, signed, signing** sign·ing
> **2.** a poster that has information written on it.
> There is a "For Sale" sign on the house next door to the school. *n.*
> **3.** a movement that tells something to someone.
> I will give you a sign when it is time to bring in the cake. *n. pl.* **signs**

signature

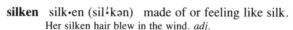

sign language

signal   sig·nal (sig′nəl)   some movement, light or sound that tells people something; a warning.
I gave Terry the signal to bring in the birthday cake. *n. pl.* **signals** sig·nals

signature   sig·na·ture (sig′nə·chər *or* sig′nə·chùr)   **1.** a person's name that is written by that person's own hand.
I put my signature next to the teacher's signature. *n.*
2. the part of a letter that has the writer's signed name.
The signature is the last part of a letter. *n. pl.* **signatures** sig·na·tures

sign language   sign lan·guage (sīn lang′gwij)   a system of communicating that uses movements of the hands, fingers and body for different words and phrases.
I learned sign language when I was at camp.

silence   si·lence (sī′ləns)   quiet; the absence of noise or sound.
I like the silence of the library. *n. pl.* **silences** si·lenc·es

silent   si·lent (sī′lənt)   without noise; without any sound.
The house was silent when I got home. *adj.*

silk   (silk)   **1.** the strings or threads of a spider's web.
The spider works hard to make the silk for his web. *n. no pl.*
2. the soft, thin threads in the tassel of an ear of corn.
We took the silk off the ear of corn. *n. no pl.*
3. a smooth thread that is taken from a certain caterpillar and made into a fine, beautiful material.
My dress is made of silk. *n. pl.* **silks**
4. made of a fine, beautiful material that is spun by silkworms.
I have a silk dress. *adj.*

silken   silk·en (sil′kən)   made of or feeling like silk.
Her silken hair blew in the wind. *adj.*

silkworm

silkworm   silk·worm (silk′wėrm)   a caterpillar that spins silk to make its cocoon.
The silkworm likes to eat mulberry leaves.
n. pl. **silkworms** silk·worms

silly   sil·ly (sil′ē)   funny; foolish.
He does some crazy things. He is so silly.
adj. **sillier, silliest** sil·li·er, sil·li·est

silly-looking   sil·ly-look·ing (sil′ē-lù′king)   having an appearance that is funny or ridiculous.
I made a silly-looking mask to make everyone laugh.
adj. **sillier-looking, silliest-looking** sil·li·er-look·ing, sil·li·est-look·ing

a	cat	i	sit	oi	oil	ch	chop		a in about
ā	ate	ī	lie	ou	out	ng	song		e in oven
ä	car	o	pot	u	cut	sh	she	ə =	i in pencil
e	set	ō	old	ù	book	th	three		o in memory
ē	equal	ô	or	ü	blue	ŦH	there		u in circus
ėr	germ					zh	treasure		

silver   sil·ver (sil′vər)   a grayish-white metal.
Silver is found in mines. *n. no pl.*

silversides   sil·ver·sides (sil′vər·sīdz)   a fish with a silver
stripe down its side.
I caught a silversides in the Atlantic Ocean. *n. pl.* **silversides**

silversides

similar   sim·i·lar (sim′ə·lər)   alike; almost the same.
We have similar bicycles. *adj.*

simple   sim·ple (sim′pəl)   not fancy; not decorated; not expensive.
The servants wore simple dresses.
adj. **simpler, simplest** sim·pler, sim·plest

simply   sim·ply (sim′plē)   only; merely.
The climber did not simply climb the high mountain; he was
the first ever to do it. *adv.*

since   (sins)   because.
I am wearing a hat since it is cold outside. *conj.*

sing   (sing)   to say words musically; to make musical sounds
with the voice.
I will sing in church on Sunday. *v.* **sang** *or* **sung, sung, singing** sing·ing

sing-along   sing-a·long (sing′ə·lông *or* sing′ə·long)   an event where
people sing together.
We had a sing-along at the party. *n. pl.* **sing-alongs** sing-a·longs

singer   sing·er (sing′ər)   a person who makes music with the
voice; a person who sings the words to music.
My aunt is a singer in a band. *n. pl.* **singers** sing·ers

singer

single   sin·gle (sing′gəl)   one; only one; lone; individual.
I made a sandwich out of a single piece of bread. *adj.*

single-seater   sin·gle-seat·er (sing′gəl-sēt′er)   something
that has only one place to sit.
My airplane is a single-seater, but my brother's airplane has two seats.
n. pl. **single-seaters** sin·gle-seat·ers

sink   (singk)   **1.** to go to the bottom; to go lower; to move
toward or to the ground.
The heavy rock will sink to the bottom of the lake.
v. **sank** *or* **sunk, sunk, sinking** sink·ing
2. a bowl or basin in which people wash themselves
or other things.
I put the dirty dishes in the sink. *n. pl.* **sinks**

sink

sip   (sip)   to drink a little bit of liquid; to drink a liquid slowly.
I will sip the orange juice. *v.* **sipped, sipped, sipping** sip·ping

sir   (sėr *or* sər)   a title of respect for a man.
Remember to say "yes, sir" when answering the teacher. *n. pl.* **sirs**

sister sis·ter (sis′tər) a female with the same mother and father as another.

My sister is eight years younger than I am.

n. pl. **sisters** sis·ters

sit (sit) to rest the lower part of the body on a piece of furniture; to rest the lower part of the body on something.

The teacher told me to sit in this seat.

v. **sat, sat, sitting** sit·ting

sit down (sit doun) to rest the lower part of the body on a piece of furniture; to rest the lower part of the body on something.

I will sit down next to Lisa.

v. **sat down, sat down, sitting down** sit·ting down

site (sīt) a location; a place.

This field is the site of the new shopping center. *n. pl.* **sites**

situation sit·u·a·tion (sich·ü·ā′shən) the way things are; the circumstance; the place or time of an event; the condition of things around.

We were locked in the room and that was a frightening situation.

n. pl. **situations** sit·u·a·tions

size (sīz) the bigness or smallness of someone or something; the height, length or weight of someone or something.

I am the same size as my sister. *n. pl.* **sizes** siz·es

skate

skate (skāt) to move across ice or wood with special sport shoes on the feet; to move on ice skates; to move on roller skates.

I will skate on the ice.

v. **skated, skated, skating** skat·ed, skat·ing

skateboard

skateboard skate·board (skāt′bôrd *or* skāt′bōrd) a board with four roller-skate wheels.

I can ride a skateboard. *n. pl.* **skateboards** skate·boards

skeptical skep·ti·cal (skep′tə·kəl) not believing; doubting the truth of something.

People were skeptical about the world being round. *adj.*

sketch (skech) to draw quickly; to make a picture or a drawing of someone or something.

I will sketch a picture of you.

v. **sketched, sketched, sketching** sketch·ing

a	cat	i	sit	oi	oil	ch	chop		a in about
ā	ate	ī	lie	ou	out	ng	song		e in oven
ä	car	o	pot	u	cut	sh	she	ə =	i in pencil
e	set	ō	old	u̇	book	th	three		o in memory
ē	equal	ô	or	ü	blue	ŦH	there		u in circus
ėr	germ					zh	treasure		

ski (skē) **1.** to move across water or snow with special
pieces of wood, metal or plastic attached to the feet.
I can ski on the snow but not on the water. *v.* **skied, skied, skiing** ski·ing
2. a long and narrow piece of sports equipment that
attaches to the foot.
I fell when the ski came off of my foot. *n. pl.* **skis** *or* **ski**
3. having to do with moving across snow or water while
wearing skis.
The ski shop is closed. *adj.*

ski

skier ski·er (skē⸱ər) a person who skis.
The skier was moving very fast down the snow-covered mountain.
n. pl. **skiers** ski·ers

skill (skil) an ability to do something.
I want to learn the skill of paper-folding. *n. pl.* **skills**

skilled (skild) being able to do something well; having the ability
to do something well; having knowledge; expert.
Father is a skilled painter. *adj.*

skillful skill·ful (skil⸱fəl) having the ability to do something
well; being talented.
The painter is creative and skillful. *adj.*

skirt

skin (skin) **1.** the thin covering on the body; the outside surface
of an animal or a person.
I cut the skin on my knee. *n. no pl.*
2. made from the outer covering of animals.
The sealskin coat is very warm. *adj.*

skirt (skėrt) the part of a horse saddle that hangs down along
the side of the horse.
The skirt is not very long. *n. pl.* **skirts**

skull (skul) the thick bone that forms the head of a person
or an animal; the bones of the head.
The miner found a skull of a cow when he was digging a hole. *n. pl.* **skulls**

skull and crossbones skull and cross·bones (skul and krôs⸱bōnz)
a symbol of poison or death that is a picture of a skull
above crossed bones.
The skull and crossbones are a signal of danger.

skull and crossbones

skunk (skungk) a black animal with a white stripe along its
back that sprays a smelly liquid when it is frightened.
We could smell the skunk before we could see it. *n. pl.* **skunks**

sky (skī) the space above the Earth; the air above the Earth; the
area where the clouds form.
The sky is very blue today. *n. pl.* **skies**

skunk

skydiver

skydive sky·dive (skī′dīv) to jump with a parachute from an airplane into the sky.
I want to learn to skydive.
v. **skydived** *or* **skydove, skydived** *or* **skydove, skydiving**
sky·dived *or* sky·dove, sky·div·ing

skydiver sky·div·er (skī′dīv·ər) a person with a parachute who jumps from an airplane.
We watched the skydiver fall to the ground. *n. pl.* **skydivers** sky·div·ers

skyline sky·line (skī′līn) the outline of a city or town with the sky in the background; the place where the outline of the Earth appears to meet the sky.
We can see the skyline from our window. *n. pl.* **skylines** sky·lines

slain (slān) killed with force.
The bodies of the slain cows were on the ground. *adj.*

slam (slam) to close with a loud noise.
Please do not slam the door. *v.* **slammed, slammed, slamming** slam·ming

slap (slap) **1.** to hit with a flat hand.
I will slap your hand if you throw that at her.
v. **slapped, slapped, slapping** slap·ping
2. the sound made when something is hit with a flat, open hand.
I heard the slap of her hand but did not see her hit him. *n. pl.* **slaps**

skyline

slave (slāv) **1.** a person whom another person owns; a person who works but is not paid.
The slave was not a free person and could not do many things. *n. pl.* **slaves**
2. having to do with people whom other people own.
The slave owner was often very cruel. *adj.*

slave catcher slave catch·er (slāv kach′ər) a person who hunted runaway slaves.
The slave catcher would beat the slaves that he caught.

slavery slav·er·y (slā′vər·ē) the act of keeping slaves; the condition of being a slave and not being free.
Slavery is against the law. *n. no pl.*

slay (slā) to kill a person or an animal with force.
The hunter will slay a deer. *v.* **slew, slain, slaying** slay·ing

a	cat	**i**	sit	**oi**	oil	**ch**	chop
ā	ate	**ī**	lie	**ou**	out	**ng**	song
ä	car	**o**	pot	**u**	cut	**sh**	she
e	set	**ō**	old	**u̇**	book	**th**	three
ē	equal	**ô**	or	**ü**	blue	**ŦH**	there
ėr	germ					**zh**	treasure

ə = { a in about, e in oven, i in pencil, o in memory, u in circus

sled (sled) **1.** a vehicle that has long, narrow boards or metal rods that slide on ice and snow.
    Children believe that Santa Claus brings toys in a sled. *n. pl.* **sleds**
2. having to do with a vehicle with long, narrow boards or metal rods that move on snow and ice.
    We took a sled ride down the long hill. *adj.*

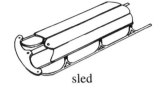
sled

sleep (slēp) **1.** to rest the body and mind; to close the eyes and rest.
    I can sleep through loud noises. *v.* **slept, slept, sleeping** sleep·ing
2. the time when one is resting the mind and body; a slumber.
    I had a good night's sleep. *n. no pl.*

sleepily sleep·i·ly (slē'pə·lē) in a resting, relaxing way; in a lazy way.
    He sleepily watched the television show. *adv.*

sleeping bag sleep·ing bag (slē'ping bag) a warm bag made of cloth in which a person sleeps when on a camping trip.
    We have a sleeping bag that is big enough for two people.

sleeping bag

sleeping pill sleep·ing pill (slē'ping pil) medicine that helps a person fall asleep; a pill that will put a person to sleep.
    Mother took a sleeping pill before going to bed.

sleepless sleep·less (slēp'lis) without resting; without sleep.
    I had a sleepless night. *adj.*

sleepy sleep·y (slē'pē) ready to rest; ready to go to sleep.
    I am very sleepy. I am going to bed.
    adj. **sleepier, sleepiest** sleep·i·er, sleep·i·est

sleeve (slēv) the part of clothing that covers the arm.
    I tore the sleeve on my coat. *n. pl.* **sleeves**

sleeve

slept (slept) *v. pt. t., pt. part.* See **sleep** (1).

slice (slīs) to cut off a thin piece of something.
    I will slice you a piece of fresh bread. *v.* **sliced, sliced, slicing** slic·ing

slid (slid) *v. pt. t., pt. part.* See **slide** (1).

slide (slīd) **1.** to move smoothly across a slippery surface.
    I will slide on the ice. *v.* **slid, slid** *or* **slidden, sliding** slid·den, slid·ing
2. a playground toy on which children move quickly and smoothly from the top to the bottom.
    I went on the slide. *n. pl.* **slides**

slightly slight·ly (slīt'lē) only a little; not much; to a small degree.
    I am slightly smaller than my sister. *adv.*

slide

slip

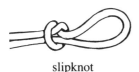

slipknot

slipper

slim (slim) thin; not fat; slender.
The woman in the picture is slim.
adj. **slimmer, slimmest** slim·mer, slim·mest

slip (slip) **1.** to slide by mistake on a smooth surface.
It is easy to slip on ice. *v.*
2. to come untied; to become loose.
The knot will slip if it is not tight. *v.*
3. to put something somewhere secretly.
I will slip the note under the door.
v. **slipped, slipped, slipping** slip·ping
4. an act of sliding by mistake.
I had a slip in the bathtub. *n. pl.* **slips**

slipknot slip·knot (slip´not) a kind of knot that can move
along the rope around which it is tied.
The cowboy pulled the slipknot tight around the calf's neck.
n. pl. **slipknots** slip·knots

slip out (slip out) to leave quietly and secretly.
I want to slip out of the meeting early.
v. **slipped out, slipped out, slipping out** slip·ping out

slipper slip·per (slip´ər) a light shoe with a soft bottom that
a person wears while at home resting.
I lost my slipper under the bed. *n. pl.* **slippers** slip·pers

slippery slip·per·y (slip´ər·ē) easy to slide on; slick.
Ice is very slippery.
adj. **slipperier, slipperiest** slip·per·i·er, slip·per·i·est

slope (slōp) the side of a mountain; rising or falling ground;
the side of a hill.
We will ski down the slope. *n. pl.* **slopes**

slow (slō) not fast; taking a long time.
Lisa is always late because she is a slow walker.
adj. **slower, slowest** slow·er, slow·est

slowly slow·ly (slō´lē) not in a fast way; not quickly.
The old dog walked slowly up the hill. *adv.*

slumber slum·ber (slum´bər) having to do with sleep or
resting; having to do with a light sleep.
I bought a new slumber suit. *adj.*

a	cat	**i**	sit	**oi**	oil	**ch**	chop	
ā	ate	**ī**	lie	**ou**	out	**ng**	song	a in about
ä	car	**o**	pot	**u**	cut	**sh**	she	e in oven
e	set	**ō**	old	**u̇**	book	**th**	three	ə = { i in pencil
ē	equal	**ô**	or	**ü**	blue	**ŦH**	there	o in memory
ėr	germ					**zh**	treasure	u in circus

slumber party slum·ber par·ty (slum⸍bər pär⸍tē) an event where people come together to sleep; an overnight stay and party.
>There were four girls at the slumber party.

small (smôl) little; not big; not much; not tall; not long.
>I want a small piece of cake. *adj.* **smaller, smallest** small·er, small·est

smart (smärt) being intelligent; being a good thinker; able to use one's brains; mentally bright.
>The girl got all As on her report card. She is very smart.
>*adj.* **smarter, smartest** smart·er, smart·est

smell (smel) **1.** to breathe in the odor or aroma of things; to use the nose to decide what something is.
>I can smell the fire. *v.*
>**2.** to have an odor or aroma.
>The cake will smell like chocolate when it is done.
>*v.* **smelled** *or* **smelt, smelled** *or* **smelt, smelling** smell·ing
>**3.** an odor or aroma.
>I like the smell of her perfume. *n. pl.* **smells**

smile

smile (smīl) **1.** a happy facial expression; a curve of the mouth that makes a person look happy.
>She has a pretty smile. *n. pl.* **smiles**
>**2.** to curve the mouth to look happy; to make a happy facial expression.
>The baby will smile when she sees her mother.
>*v.* **smiled, smiled, smiling** smil·ing

smoke (smōk) **1.** to breathe in the fumes of one's cigarette, pipe or cigar.
>It is dangerous to smoke. *v.*
>**2.** to preserve or flavor food by covering it with the fumes or gases of burning wood or other ingredients.
>The farmer will smoke the ham with hickory wood.
>*v.* **smoked, smoked, smoking** smok·ing
>**3.** the fumes or gases that rise from something that is burning.
>The smoke from the campfire burned my eyes. *n. no pl.*

smoke

smooth (smüтн) having no bumps or wrinkles; flat and even; having no movement.
>The water on the lake is very smooth today.
>*adj.* **smoother, smoothest** smooth·er, smooth·est

smoothly smooth·ly (smüтн⸍lē) without bumps or wrinkles; without jerky movements; evenly.
>That couple dances very smoothly together. *adv.*

snail

smorgasbord smor·gas·bord (smôr⸍gəs·bôrd *or* smôr⸍gəs·bōrd)
a meal or a restaurant that has many different things to eat
on a table; a buffet of many kinds of food.
I tasted everything at the smorgasbord.
n. pl. **smorgasbords** smor·gas·bords

snack (snak) a small meal; a light meal; not a full meal.
I always have a snack when I get home from school. *n. pl.* **snacks**

snail (snāl) a small animal with a soft body that has a hard
shell on its back.
The snail hid in its shell. *n. pl.* **snails**

snake (snāk) a long, thin animal that has no legs and slides
along the ground.
The snake is a reptile. *n. pl.* **snakes**

snake

snap (snap) the sound made by something thin and dry
when it breaks.
We could hear the snap of the branches as we walked on them. *n. pl.* **snaps**

snapshot snap·shot (snap⸍shot) a picture taken with a camera.
The snapshot of our party turned out very well. *n. pl.* **snapshots** snap·shots

sneak (snēk) to move very quietly; to be careful not to be
seen or heard; to take something quietly.
I will sneak into her room and get her book.
v. **sneaked, sneaked, sneaking** sneak·ing

sneak up on (snēk up ôn) to walk quietly behind someone
and then surprise them; to go near a person quietly.
Let's sneak up on Jerry and scare him.
v. **sneaked up on, sneaked up on, sneaking up on** sneak·ing up on

snapshot

sneeze (snēz) to blow air suddenly from the nose and mouth;
to make a sudden blow of air through the nose and mouth.
Pepper makes me sneeze. *v.* **sneezed, sneezed, sneezing** sneez·ing

sniff (snif) to smell quickly; to breathe in an odor quickly.
The dog will sniff the food before he starts to eat it.
v. **sniffed, sniffed, sniffing** sniff·ing

snore (snôr *or* snōr) **1.** to make a loud noise through the
mouth when sleeping.
I can hear Jim snore. *v.* **snored, snored, snoring** snor·ing
2. a loud noise made through the mouth when sleeping.
His snore woke me up. *n. pl.* **snores**

a	cat	i	sit	oi	oil	ch	chop		a in about
ā	ate	ī	lie	ou	out	ng	song		e in oven
ä	car	o	pot	u	cut	sh	she	ə =	i in pencil
e	set	ō	old	u̇	book	th	three		o in memory
ē	equal	ô	or	ü	blue	ŦH	there		u in circus
ėr	germ					zh	treasure		

snow (snō) tiny white flakes that fall from the clouds in the winter; frozen water that falls from the clouds.
I love to see snow. *n. no pl.*

snowball

snowball snow·ball (snō′bôl) a round ball made from snow.
My brother hit me with a snowball. *n. pl.* **snowballs** snow·balls

snow house (snō hous) a house made from snow; an igloo.
The Eskimos live in a snowhouse.

snow line (snō līn) the line on a mountain above which snow stays all year; the lowest place on a mountain where the snow never melts.
Many people ski above that mountain's snow line.

snowman snow·man (snō′man) a shape made of snow that looks like a man.
We made a snowman on the front lawn.
n. pl. **snowmen** snow·men

snowman

snowshoe snow·shoe (snō′shü) a light wooden frame that ties onto a shoe and makes walking in deep snow easier.
The hunter broke his snowshoe. *n. pl.* **snowshoes** snow·shoes

snowstorm snow·storm (snō′stôrm) a storm with lots of snow falling from the clouds.
The snowstorm lasted for five hours.
n. pl. **snowstorms** snow·storms

so (sō *or* sə) **1.** very; to a great degree.
I am so tired that I cannot walk fast. *adv.*
2. with the result that; for the reason that.
It was raining, so we opened the umbrella. *conj.*

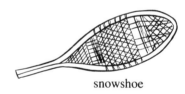
snowshoe

soak (sōk) to let stay in a liquid; to get very wet; to absorb a liquid.
We can soak the dirty clothes in water.
v. **soaked, soaked, soaking** soak·ing

soak up (sōk up) to take in a lot of liquid; to absorb a liquid.
The sponge will soak up the milk that you spilled.
v. **soaked up, soaked up, soaking up** soak·ing up

soap (sōp) a substance that is used for cleaning things and people.
Wash your hands with soap and water. *n. pl.* **soaps**

soap

soapy soap·y (sō′pē) being full of a substance that is used for cleaning; being full of foam or suds; being covered with soap.
His hands were still soapy when he came to the table.
adj. **soapier, soapiest** soap·i·er, soap·i·est

soar   (sôr *or* sōr)   to rise high above the ground; to rise high and fly smoothly or gracefully.
The airplane will soar into the clouds. *v.* **soared, soared, soaring** soar·ing

social   so·cial (sō′shəl)   **1.** having to do with people; having fun with people.
He is always with people. He is a social person. *adj.*
2. having to do with living in groups.
The ant is a social insect. *adj.*

sock

social life   so·cial life (sō′shəl   līf)   the time that a person is not working; the time a person spends having fun; a person's free time.
I have a busy social life.

social studies   so·cial stud·ies (sō′shəl   stud′ēz)   having to do with the learning about other people and places; having to do with the study of how people live.
I got an A on my social studies test.

society   so·ci·e·ty (sə·sī′ə·tē)   **1.** people of a certain time or place.
Society at the time of the pioneers was very strict. *n.*
2. a group of people who work together for a special reason; a group of people who live together.
This society does not accept people who steal. *n. pl.* **societies** so·ci·e·ties

sofa

sock   (sok)   a cloth covering for a foot.
I have a hole in my sock. *n. pl.* **socks**

sofa   so·fa (sō′fə)   a long piece of furniture on which people sit or lie; a couch.
We sat on the sofa to watch television. *n. pl.* **sofas** so·fas

soft   (sôft *or* soft)   **1.** not hard; mushy; bending easily.
The rabbit fur is very soft. *adj.*
2. quiet; not loud.
The music is soft and pleasant. *adj.* **softer, softest** soft·er, soft·est

soft-boiled

soft-boiled   (sôft′boild′ *or* soft′boild′)   cooked so that the inside is not hard.
We made soft-boiled eggs for breakfast. *adj.*

softly   soft·ly (sôft′lē)   quietly; not loudly.
Talk softly; do not yell. *adv*.

soil   (soil)   dirt; earth; loose ground.
I got soil on my knees when I crawled on the ground. *n. no pl.*

a	cat	i	sit	oi	oil	ch	chop		a in about
ā	ate	ī	lie	ou	out	ng	song		e in oven
ä	car	o	pot	u	cut	sh	she	ə =	i in pencil
e	set	ō	old	u̇	book	th	three		o in memory
ē	equal	ô	or	ü	blue	ŦH	there		u in circus
ėr	germ					zh	treasure		

solar so·lar (sō‑lər) having to do with the sun; coming from the sun.
We are using solar energy to heat the water in our house. *adj.*

solar collector

solar collector so·lar col·lec·tor (sō‑lər kə·lek‑tər) a device or machine that gathers the rays of the sun and uses them to make energy.
We have a solar collector on our roof.

solar system so·lar sys·tem (sō‑lər sis‑təm) the arrangement of the planets and their moons around the sun.
There are nine planets and the sun in our solar system.

sold (sōld) *v. pt. t., pt. part.* See **sell.**

soldier sol·dier (sōl‑jər) a person in the army; a person who fights for his or her country.
The soldier carried a gun into battle. *n. pl.* **soldiers** sol·diers

sole (sōl) the bottom part of a shoe; the part of a shoe on which the person walks.
I need a new sole on my shoe. *n. pl.* **soles**

soldier

solo so·lo (sō‑lō) **1.** alone; without other people.
He flew the airplane solo. *adv.*
2. having to do with being alone; having to do with being without other people.
The boy is solo sailing. *adj.*

some (sum *or* səm) **1.** a few; a number of things; an uncertain number of things.
I want some cookies. *adj.*
2. being an unknown person or thing.
Some boy took my cap. *adj.*
3. an unnamed number.
Most of the girls are going to the movie, but some will go to the game. *pron.*

somebody some·bod·y (sum‑bod·ē *or* sum‑bə·dē) an unknown person.
Does this hat belong to somebody? *pron.*

someday some·day (sum‑dā) at an uncertain time; on a day in the future.
Someday I will go to college. *adv.*

somehow some·how (sum‑hou) in an unknown way; by an unknown way.
I will get the money somehow. *adv.*

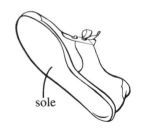
sole

someone some·one (sum‑wun *or* sum‑wən) an unknown person; an unnamed person.
Someone left the door open. *pron.*

something   some·thing (sum⸢thing)   **1.** an unknown thing or object; an unnamed object.
I found something in the bag. *pron.*
2. an unknown activity or action.
I want something to do. *pron.*

sometimes   some·times (sum⸢tīmz)   not often but once in a while; from time to time.
I sometimes go to her house to play ball. *adv.*

somewhat   some·what (sum⸢hwot)   partly; to a certain degree or amount; almost.
The boy is somewhat sad about leaving his home. *adv.*

somewhere   some·where (sum⸢hwer *or* sum⸢hwar)   an unknown place; an unnamed place.
We are going somewhere tonight. *adv.*

son   (sun)   a boy child of a parent.
My son is a good swimmer. *n. pl.* **sons**

song   (sông *or* song)   words that go with music; musical words; something that people sing.
We sing a song every morning. *n. pl.* **songs**

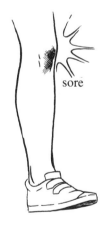

song

soon   (sün)   in a short time; before long.
Dad will be home soon. *adv.* **sooner, soonest** soon·er, soon·est

sooner   soon·er (sün⸢ər)   in a shorter time; more quickly.
He will be here sooner than you think. *adv.*

soothing   sooth·ing (sü⸢ŦHing)   calming; taking away fears; quieting; comforting.
The sound of the ocean is soothing. *adj.*

sore

sore   (sôr *or* sōr)   hurting; painful; causing hurt or pain.
I have a sore knee. *adj.* **sorer, sorest** sor·er, sor·est

sorrowful   sor·row·ful (sor⸢ə·fəl *or* sôr⸢ə·fəl)   full of sadness; feeling sorry or sad.
The little boy has a sorrowful look on his face. *adj.*

a	cat	**i**	sit	**oi**	oil	**ch**	chop		a in about
ā	ate	**ī**	lie	**ou**	out	**ng**	song		e in oven
ä	car	**o**	pot	**u**	cut	**sh**	she	ə =	i in pencil
e	set	**ō**	old	** u̇**	book	**th**	three		o in memory
ē	equal	**ô**	or	**ü**	blue	**ŦH**	there		u in circus
ėr	germ					**zh**	treasure		

sorry   sor·ry (sor′ē *or* sôr′ē)   feeling sad about something that
a person did or said; feeling sad about something that
happened; having sympathy for someone.
The girl was sorry that she hit the boy. *adj.*

sort   (sôrt)   to separate things into sets; to put like things together;
to go through things and put them into an order.
I will sort the cards and take out all the hearts.
v. **sorted, sorted, sorting** sort·ed, sort·ing

sort of   (sôrt əv)   in a small way; in almost the right
way; partly; somewhat.
He sort of hurt me but not badly. *idiom*

sound   (sound)   **1.** noise; what a person hears with ears.
I like to hear the sound of the bell. *n. pl.* **sounds**
2. to set off an alarm or siren; to make noise.
The bell will sound on the hour.
v. **sounded, sounded, sounding** sound·ed, sound·ing

sound wave

sound wave   (sound wāv)   the pattern a noise makes as it moves
in the air from the sound source to the sound receiver;
the movement of the air as sound moves.
The sound wave goes from the mouth of the speaker to
the ear of the listener.

soup   (süp)   a liquid food made from cooking meat, vegetables
or fish in water and adding other ingredients.
I like broccoli soup. *n. pl.* **soups**

sour   (sour)   **1.** a taste that is not sweet; a bitter taste.
A lemon tastes sour. *adj.*
2. spoiled; rotten; not fresh; not right in taste,
appearance or smell.
Do not drink the milk! It is sour. *adj.*

soup

south   (south)   **1.** in a direction that is opposite of north.
We drove south on the old road. *adv.*
2. being the geographical area of a place or town that
is opposite of north.
I live in the south part of town. *adj.*
3. South; the part of the United States that fought in the
Civil War for the right to have slaves.
The South lost the war. *n. no pl.*
4. the area that is the opposite of north.
In the south, the winters are warmer. *n. no pl.*

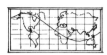

space center

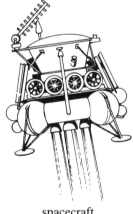

spacecraft

southern south·ern (suᴛʜ ́ərn) **1.** coming from the south.
A southern wind often brings rain. *adj.*
2. toward the south.
We took the southern route across the country. *adj.*

southwest south·west (south·west ́) being in the direction that is between the south and the west.
Arizona is in the southwest part of the United States. *adj.*

souvenir sou·ve·nir (sü·və·nir ́ *or* sü ́və·nir) something that a person keeps to help remember a place or an event.
I bought myself a souvenir of my trip to Hawaii.
n. pl. **souvenirs** sou·ve·nirs

space (spās) **1.** the area above the Earth; the huge area where the sun, stars and planets are; the sky above the clouds.
Astronauts fly in space. *n. no pl.*
2. an area; room.
I found a space for my bicycle. *n. pl.* **spaces** spac·es
3. having to do with the area above the Earth.
The space shuttle will take off tomorrow. *adj.*

space center space cen·ter (spās sen ́tər) the main offices of the people who put rockets into space; the place that controls the activities in space.
We heard the astronauts talking to the people at the space center.

spacecraft space·craft (spās ́kraft) any vehicle that carries people or things out into space.
A rocket is a spacecraft. *n. pl.* **spacecrafts** space·crafts

spaceflight space·flight (spās ́flīt) a trip into space.
The astronaut will be on her first spaceflight.
n. pl. **spaceflights** space·flights

spaceship space·ship (spās ́ship) a vehicle that goes into space.
The spaceship will return to Earth in two days.
n. pl. **spaceships** space·ships

a	cat	i	sit	oi	oil	ch	chop		a in about
ā	ate	ī	lie	ou	out	ng	song		e in oven
ä	car	o	pot	u	cut	sh	she	ə =	i in pencil
e	set	ō	old	u̇	book	th	three		o in memory
ē	equal	ô	or	ü	blue	ᴛʜ	there		u in circus
ėr	germ					zh	treasure		

space shuttle space shut·tle (spās   shut'l) a spaceship that astronauts fly into space and back to Earth.
The space shuttle has taken many trips to outer space.

spacesuit space·suit (spās'süt) the clothing that an astronaut wears when he or she is in space.
An astronaut must wear a spacesuit to walk on the moon.
n. pl. **spacesuits** space·suits

spacesuit

Spain (spān) a country in southern Europe; its capital is Madrid.
My neighbors once lived in Spain. *n.*

Spaniard Span·iard (span'yərd) a person who comes from the country of Spain.
The bullfighter is a Spaniard. *n. pl.* **Spaniards** Span·iards

Spanish Span·ish (span'ish) having to do with the people, the language or the country of Spain.
The boy was born in Madrid and is Spanish. *adj.*

spank (spangk) to hit with an open hand; to punish by hitting with the open hand.
Mother will spank Tom for coming home late.
v. **spanked, spanked, spanking** spank·ing

spanking (spang'king) **1.** the act of hitting with the open hand as a punishment.
I got a spanking for breaking the new vase.
n. pl. **spankings** spank·ings
2. *v. pres. part.* See **spank.**

spare (sper *or* spar) extra; something that is not in use.
I put the spare tire on the car after the other tire went flat.
adj. **sparer, sparest** spar·er, spar·est

sparkle spar·kle (spär'kəl) **1.** to give off a glitter or spark of light; to shine with flashes of light.
The stars will sparkle in the sky tonight.
v. **sparkled, sparkled, sparkling** spar·kled, spar·kling
2. a bright, quick light; something that gives off a quick light.
We knew she was excited when we saw the sparkle in her eyes.
n. pl. **sparkles** spar·kles

Madrid
Spain

spark plug (spärk   plug) a part of an engine that causes the gas to burn.
We need to change another spark plug in the car.

speak (spēk) to use the voice to say words; to talk; to say.
The man will speak to us about dinosaurs.
v. **spoke, spoken, speaking** spo·ken, speak·ing

spark plug

speaker

spear

speaker speak·er (spē⸍kər) a person who talks to a group of people; the person who is talking.
He is the speaker at the meeting. *n. pl.* **speakers** speak·ers

spear (spir) a weapon that is shaped like a long stick and has a sharp point at one end.
The cave man used a spear when hunting. *n. pl.* **spears**

spear-like (spir⸍līk) shaped like a spear; having a sharp point on one end.
The spear-like leaves of the pineapple plant will stick you if you are not careful. *adj.*

special spe·cial (spesh⸍əl) **1.** not ordinary; exceptional; not general; unusual; valuable.
Thanksgiving is a special day to give thanks for all the things we have. *adj.*
2. set apart; different from others.
We have a special place to keep the new puppies. *adj.*

specially spe·cial·ly (spesh⸍ə·lē) in a way that is different; in an exceptional way.
The baker specially decorated the cake for Susan's birthday. *adv.*

species spe·cies (spē⸍shēz) a group of animals or plants that are alike in certain ways; a specific kind of animal or plant.
The German shepherd is from the same species as the collie and the poodle.
n. pl. **species**

speck (spek) a small dot of something; a very small piece of something.
There is a speck of dust on the camera lens. *n. pl.* **specks**

spectator spec·ta·tor (spek⸍tā·tər *or* spek·tā⸍tər) a person who watches an event; a person who watches a game or a contest.
I am only a spectator at this game.
n. pl. **spectators** spec·ta·tors

speech (spēch) a talk about a subject; a lecture given to a group of people; a formal presentation of information.
I will give a speech to the social studies class.
n. pl. **speeches** speech·es

speechless speech·less (spēch⸍lis) not able to talk; being without words to say.
I was so scared that I was speechless. *adj.*

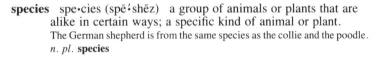

a	cat	i	sit	oi	oil	ch	chop		a in about
ā	ate	ī	lie	ou	out	ng	song		e in oven
ä	car	o	pot	u	cut	sh	she	ə =	i in pencil
e	set	ō	old	u̇	book	th	three		o in memory
ē	equal	ô	or	ü	blue	ᵺH	there		u in circus
ėr	germ					zh	treasure		

speed (spēd) the rate at which something moves; how
fast something moves.
The speed of the car was 70 miles an hour. *n. pl.* **speeds**

speedily speed·i·ly (spē′dl·ē) quickly; with great speed; very fast.
He speedily ran from the room. *adv.*

speeding speed·ing (spē′ding) moving very quickly; moving
faster than the law allows.
The speeding car raced through the stoplight. *adj.*

speeding ticket speed·ing tick·et (spē′ding tik′it)
a paper that a police officer gives to a person who drives
too fast, telling the person how much fine to pay.
The man got a speeding ticket for racing through the streets
at 70 miles per hour.

speed of sound (spēd əv sound) the rate at which sound waves
travel through the air.
The speed of sound is very fast.

speedway

speedway speed·way (spēd′wā) a racetrack; a place where
cars race at very fast speeds.
The cars may go fast on the speedway.
n. pl. **speedways** speed·ways

spell (spel) **1.** to name the letters in a word; to say or
write the letters in a word in the right order.
I can spell "encyclopedia."
v. **spelled** *or* **spelt, spelled** *or* **spelt, spelling** spel·ling
2. a magical event; a hex; a charm.
The fairy godmother put a spell on the mice and they
became horses. *n. pl.* **spells**

sperm whale

speller spell·er (spel′ər) a person who can say or write the
letters in words in the right order; a person who can name
the letters in a word.
I am the best speller in my class. *n. pl.* **spellers** spell·ers

spend (spend) **1.** to pay out.
I will spend this dollar in the candy store. *v.*
2. to use up.
You may only spend one hour outside tonight.
v. **spent, spent, spending** spend·ing

spent (spent) *v. pt. t., pt. part.* See **spend.**

sperm whale (spèrm hwāl) a large square-headed sea animal
that is killed for its oil.
The sperm whale is from the toothed whale species.

spice

spice (spīs) any part of a plant that people use to flavor
or season food.
Pepper is a spice. *n. pl.* **spices** spic·es

spider

spinning wheel

spider spi·der (spī′dər) an animal with eight legs that can spin a sticky thread to make a web.
The spider makes a web to catch insects. *n. pl.* **spiders** spi·ders

spiderling spi·der·ling (spī′dər·ling) a baby spider.
The spiderling came out of the spider egg. *n. pl.* **spiderlings** spi·der·lings

Spiderman Spi·der·man (spī′dər·man) a comic book and cartoon character that is part man and part spider.
Spiderman can make a web just like a spider can. *n.*

spill (spil) **1.** to cause a liquid to come out of its container by accident; to drop a liquid; to knock over something that has a liquid in it.
Please do not spill the milk on the table. *v.*
2. to cause things to fall; to make things come out of their container; to drop things.
Julie dropped the bag and all the candy spilled on the floor.
v. **spilled** *or* **spilt, spilled** *or* **spilt, spilling** spill·ing

spin (spin) **1.** to turn around and around quickly.
The toy top will spin for a long time. *v.*
2. to make thread or yarn by twisting wool.
The farmer will spin the wool into yarn. *v.* **spun, spun, spinning** spin·ning

spinning wheel spin·ning wheel (spin′ning hwēl) a device or machine that twists wool and makes it into thread or yarn.
The pioneer woman used a spinning wheel to make her yarn from the wool.

spirit spir·it (spir′it) **1.** a ghost; the soul of a person who was once alive.
My grandmother believes that the spirit of her mother is still in the house. *n.*
2. feeling; mood; a sensation of emotion.
We share in the spirit of peace. *n. pl.* **spirits** spir·its

spirited spir·it·ed (spir′ə·tid) being full of energy; lively; not lazy.
The horse was spirited. *adj.*

spirits spir·its (spir′its) a strong drink of alcohol.
The farmer asked for a glass of spirits. *plural n.*

spit (spit) to push saliva or food out of the mouth.
The baby will spit at you if she gets angry.
v. **spit** *or* **spat, spit** *or* **spat, spitting** spit·ting

a	cat	i	sit	oi	oil	ch	chop	ə =	a in about
ā	ate	ī	lie	ou	out	ng	song		e in oven
ä	car	o	pot	u	cut	sh	she		i in pencil
e	set	ō	old	u̇	book	th	three		o in memory
ē	equal	ô	or	ü	blue	ŦH	there		u in circus
ėr	germ					zh	treasure		

splash (splash) **1.** to make waves in the water.
The fish will splash around in the tank. *v.*
2. to hit something or someone with a liquid.
The puddle will splash all over you. *v.*
3. the sound made when a liquid hits something.
We can hear the rain splash against the window.
v. **splashed, splashed, splashing** splash·ing
4. a design or pattern made by throwing paint on a surface
or a piece of material.
We made a splash with the paint. *n. pl.* **splashes** splash·es

splash

splendid splen·did (splen′did) wonderful; grand; brilliant.
The view from the top of the mountain was splendid. *adj.*

split (split) to break into pieces or parts.
We split the logs for firewood. *v.* **split, split, splitting** split·ting

spoil (spoil) to go bad; to become rotten; to damage.
The milk will spoil if it is not in the refrigerator.
v. **spoiled** *or* **spoilt, spoiled** *or* **spoilt, spoiling** spoil·ing

spoke (spōk) *v. pt. t.* See **speak.**

spoon (spün) a tool that people use for eating that has
a rounded, bowl-like end and a handle.
We eat soup with a spoon. *n. pl.* **spoons**

spoon

sport (spôrt *or* spōrt) **1.** an organized game or contest.
Football is a sport. *n. pl.* **sports**
2. a person who can win and not brag or lose and
not get angry.
You must be a good sport even if you lose. *n. pl.* **sports**

sportsman sports·man (spôrts′mən *or* spōrts′mən) a
person who likes hunting, fishing, camping, hiking and
other outdoor activities.
My aunt likes to hunt and fish; she is quite a sportsman.
n. pl. **sportsmen** sports·men

spot (spot) **1.** a mark; a different-colored area.
Our dog has a white spot on his back. *n.*
2. a place or location.
I will meet you at the usual spot. *n. pl.* **spots**
3. to find in a crowd or a group.
I can spot Dad from here. *v.* **spotted, spotted, spotting** spot·ted, spot·ting

spotted spot·ted (spot′id) **1.** *v. pt. t., pt. part.* See **spot** (3).
2. having colored marks.
We have a spotted dog. *adj.*

spotted

sprain (sprān) to injure a part of the body by twisting it.
You can easily sprain your ankle when walking in shoes that do not fit.
v. **sprained, sprained, spraining** sprain·ing

sprang (sprang) *v. pt. t.* See **spring** (3).

spray

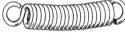

spring

spurs

spray (sprā) to put light drops of water or another liquid on something; to mist something with a liquid.
I will spray perfume on my neck. *v.* **sprayed, sprayed, spraying** spray·ing

spread (spred) **1.** to stretch out; to cover with something; to open.
The eagle will spread its wings and fly away. *v.*
2. to become known to others; to extend beyond this point.
The news will spread quickly. *v.* **spread, spread, spreading** spread·ing

spread the word (spred тнǝ wėrd) to tell other people about something; to make sure that other people hear the news.
We will spread the word about the surprise party.

spring (spring) **1.** a season of the year when things begin to grow; the season after winter and before summer.
The trees begin to bloom in the spring. *n.*
2. a tightly wound piece of metal that will go back into its first shape if it is pulled and let go.
The spring on the door closes the door quickly. *n. pl.* **springs**
3. to jump out suddenly; to leap.
We will spring out from behind the sofa and yell "Surprise!"
v. **sprang** *or* **sprung, sprung, springing** spring·ing

spring-cleaning spring-clean·ing (spring′klē′ning) a thorough cleaning that often is done in the spring of the year; an exceptionally good and complete cleaning.
I will give my room a spring-cleaning.
n. pl. **spring-cleanings** spring-clean·ings

sprint (sprint) having to do with short, fast runs.
The 100 yard dash is a sprint race. *adj.*

sprint car (sprint kär) a car that is specially built to race short distances at fast speeds.
The sprint car can go very fast but not for very long.

spun (spun) *v. pt. t., pt. part.* See **spin.**

spur (spėr) **1.** a wheel with many points that is attached to the heel of a horse rider's boot.
The spur does not hurt the horse. *n. pl.* **spurs**
2. to make a horse move by pricking it with the points of the small wheel on the horse rider's boot.
You can spur the horse to make him go faster.
v. **spurred, spurred, spurring** spur·ring

a	cat	**i**	sit	**oi**	oil	**ch**	chop		a in about
ā	ate	**ī**	lie	**ou**	out	**ng**	song		e in oven
ä	car	**o**	pot	**u**	cut	**sh**	she	ǝ =	i in pencil
e	set	**ō**	old	**u̇**	book	**th**	three		o in memory
ē	equal	**ô**	or	**ü**	blue	**тн**	there		u in circus
ėr	germ					**zh**	treasure		

spy (spī) **1.** to watch someone or something secretly.

I will spy on Tom and find out where he is going.

v. **spied, spied, spying** spy·ing

2. a person who secretly watches the actions of other people or countries.

I will be a spy and watch where Tom goes every day. *n. pl.* **spies**

square knot

square (skwer *or* skwar) a shape that has four sides of equal length with four equal corners or angles.

I cut a square out of the paper. *n. pl.* **squares**

square knot (skwer not) a kind of knot that ties two pieces or ends of cloth, rope or string together.

We made a square knot in the bandage.

squeak (skwēk) **1.** a short shrill sound; a tiny noise or sound.

We can hear the squeak of the door. *n. pl.* **squeaks**

2. to make a short shrill sound; to make a tiny noise or sound.

The door will squeak when you open it.

v. **squeaked, squeaked, squeaking** squeak·ing

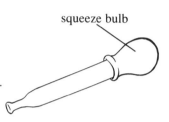
squeeze bulb

squeaky squeak·y (skwē'kē) making a short shrill sound.

The squeaky door needs oil.

adj. **squeakier, squeakiest** squeak·i·er, squeak·i·est

squeal (skwēl) to make a long shrill noise or sound.

The tires will squeal if you start out at a fast speed.

v. **squealed, squealed, squealing** squeal·ing

squealing squeal·ing (skwēl'ing) **1.** having a long shrill sound.

The squealing cat woke me. *adj.*

2. *v. pres. part.* See **squeal.**

squirrel

squeeze (skwēz) **1.** to press together with great force; to press tightly.

I will squeeze the toothpaste out of the tube. *v.*

2. to force through a small opening or hole.

I will squeeze through the hole in the fence.

v. **squeezed, squeezed, squeezing** squeez·ing

squeeze bulb (skwēz bulb) the round rubber part of a turkey baster that a person presses to force liquid out.

When you push the squeeze bulb, the liquid from the turkey fills the turkey baster.

stage

squirm (skwėrm) to wiggle; to move about because of not being comfortable.

I started to squirm when the teacher called my name.

v. **squirmed, squirmed, squirming** squirm·ing

squirrel squir·rel (skwėr'əl) a small land animal with a long bushy tail.

The squirrel lives in this tree and eats the seeds. *n. pl.* **squirrels** squir·rels

stagecoach

staircase

stall

S shape (es shāp) a form that looks like an "S."
Sue planted the flowers in an S shape.

S-shaped (es⸍-shāpt) having two bends; looking like an "S."
The hook is S-shaped. *adj.*

St.[1] (sānt) *abbrev.* See **saint.**

St.[2] (strēt) *abbrev.* See **street** (1).

stack (stak) **1.** to place things on top of each other;
to pile things one on top of another.
I will stack the dishes in the cupboard.
v. **stacked, stacked, stacking** stack·ing
2. a pile of things; things placed one on top of another.
I dropped the stack of papers all over the floor. *n. pl.* **stacks**

stage (stāj) **1.** a raised platform or deck on which people
give a performance or act.
We practiced the dance on the stage. *n.*
2. a phase or a time in the life of a plant or animal.
The egg is the first stage of a butterfly's life. *n. pl.* **stages** stag·es
3. having to do with the theater.
We used the stage door to get into the theater. *adj.*

stagecoach stage·coach (stāj⸍kōch) a wagon that horses pull
and that carries people from place to place.
The pioneer women often traveled in a stagecoach.
n. pl. **stagecoaches** stage·coach·es

stair (ster *or* star) a step; one of a series that let people
go from one level to another.
I broke the heel of my shoe on the stair. *n. pl.* **stairs**

staircase stair·case (ster⸍kās *or* star⸍kās) a set of steps;
the area of a house that has steps; a stairway.
Please do not run down the staircase. *n. pl.* **staircases** stair·cas·es

stairway stair·way (ster⸍wā *or* star⸍wā) a set of steps; a staircase;
the area with steps.
I fell down the stairway. *n. pl.* **stairways** stair·ways

stalk (stôk) the stem of a plant.
The stalk of this corn plant is very high. *n. pl.* **stalks**

stall (stôl) a separate part of a stable or barn for keeping an animal.
I put the horse in his stall. *n. pl.* **stalls**

a	cat	i	sit	oi	oil	ch	chop		a in about
ā	ate	ī	lie	ou	out	ng	song		e in oven
ä	car	o	pot	u	cut	sh	she	ə =	i in pencil
e	set	ō	old	u̇	book	th	three		o in memory
ē	equal	ô	or	ü	blue	ŦH	there		u in circus
ėr	germ					zh	treasure		

stamp (stamp) **1.** a small, sticky piece of paper that is put on a
letter or package to show that the cost of mailing has been paid.
The letter has a 22-cent stamp on it. *n. pl.* **stamps**
2. having to do with the sticky piece of paper that shows
that postage has been paid.
He put 25 cents in the stamp machine. *adj.*

stamp

stamp book (stamp bŭk) a book in which old or unusual stamps
are saved; a book that is about stamp collecting.
The stamp collector puts his old stamps in a stamp book.

stamp collector stamp col·lec·tor (stamp kə·lek′tər) a person
who gathers and saves old postage stamps.
The man at the store is a stamp collector.

stance (stants) a position in which the body is put;
the way a person stands; the posture of the body.
Her stance is like a man's. *n. pl.* **stances** stanc·es

stand (stand) **1.** to have the weight of the body on the feet;
to have the body in a straight position.
I will stand, but you may sit down. *v.*
2. to be built; to be located; to be in a place.
The statue will stand in the new playground area. *v.*
3. to endure; to cope with.
I will not stand his yelling at me. *v.* **stood, stood, standing** stand·ing
4. a small building or cart from which people sell things.
We bought the oranges from a fruit stand on the corner of the street. *n.*
5. a firm position or opinion; a strong belief.
The man wants a stoplight on the corner. He will not change his stand. *n.*
6. a small table or frame on which things can be placed.
The plant stand was once my grandmother's. *n. pl.* **stands**

stand

standing part stand·ing part (stan′ding pärt) the straight part
of a rope when a person makes a knot, not the loop or end.
Bill made a loop and then used the end to tie a knot around the standing
part of the rope.

stand up (stand up) **1.** to rise to one's feet; to get
up from a sitting position.
Please stand up and give me your answer. *v.*
2. to have the hair on the body point upward because of fear.
He will be so scared that his hair will stand up.
v. **stood up, stood up, standing up** stand·ing up

stapler

staple

staple   sta·ple (stā⸍pəl)   **1.** to put things together with a machine that pushes out U-shaped pieces of metal.
I will staple the papers together.
v. **stapled, stapled, stapling** sta·pled, sta·pling
2. a U-shaped piece of metal with pointed ends that is put into things to hold them together.
I got a staple in my finger. *n. pl.* **staples** sta·ples

stapler   sta·pler (stā⸍plər)   a machine or tool that pushes U-shaped pieces of metal into other things.
Use the stapler to fasten the wire to the fence. *n. pl.* **staplers** sta·plers

star   (stär)   **1.** a body of gas in the sky that gives off light.
Mother made a wish on the first star that she saw in the sky. *n.*
2. a shape that has five or six points.
We folded and cut the paper to make a five-pointed star. *n.*
3. a person who has the lead part in a movie, play or program; a person who is popular; a famous person.
She is the star of the movie. *n. pl.* **stars**

star

starch   (stärch)   a white powder that is used to make food stiff or thick; a white substance that is in many foods and that has no taste.
There is starch in flour and in spaghetti. *n. no pl.*

stare   (ster *or* star)   to look at something or someone and not look at anything else; to look at for a long time.
I can stare at the ocean for hours. *v.* **stared, stared, staring** star·ing

starfish   star·fish (stär⸍fish)   a sea animal whose arms reach out from the circular body so that it is shaped like a star.
The starfish holds on to things with its arms.
n. pl. **starfish** *or* **starfishes** star·fish·es

Stars and Stripes   (stärz ənd strīps)   the name of a song that is about the United States flag.
The band played "Stars and Stripes" as it paraded down the street.

starfish

start   (stärt)   to begin; to begin to move or go.
The car will not start. *v.* **started, started, starting** start·ed, start·ing

starting point   start·ing point (stär⸍ting point)   the place from which a race or a trip begins; the place where something begins.
Your house will be the starting point.

a	cat	i	sit	oi	oil	ch	chop		a in about
ā	ate	ī	lie	ou	out	ng	song		e in oven
ä	car	o	pot	u	cut	sh	she	ə =	i in pencil
e	set	ō	old	u̇	book	th	three		o in memory
ē	equal	ô	or	ü	blue	ᵮH	there		u in circus
ėr	germ					zh	treasure		

startle star·tle (stär'tl) to surprise; to frighten someone suddenly.
Please let me know when you are coming into the room or you
will startle me.
v. **startled, startled, startling** star·tled, star·tling

start off (stärt ôf) to begin; to begin to go.
We will start off on our trip at ten o'clock.
v. **started off, started off, starting off** start·ed off, start·ing off

start out (stärt out) to begin a trip.
We will start out from your house.
v. **started out, started out, starting out** start·ed out, start·ing out

starve (stärv) to die from not having food; to suffer
from lack of food.
A person can starve after not eating for seven days.
v. **starved, starved, starving** starv·ing

statehouse

state (stāt) **1.** an area that is one part of a country; a geographical
area that is governed by a legislature and a governor.
In what state do you live? *n. pl.* **states**
2. having to do with a geographical area that is a
part of a country.
The state roads are in very good condition. *adj.*

statehood state·hood (stāt'hùd) having to do with an area
becoming a state.
Abraham Lincoln signed the statehood papers making West
Virginia a state. *adj.*

statehouse state·house (stāt' hous) a building that
houses government offices of a state; the building that
houses state legislature.
The governor met our class in the statehouse.
n. pl. **statehouses** state·hous·es

statesman states·man (stāts'mən) a person who
has skills in politics; a person who knows how to
work well in government business.
Lincoln was a great statesman. *n. pl.* **statesmen** states·men

station sta·tion (stā'shən) a place where stagecoaches
stop for new horses; a place where trains or buses stop.
The stagecoach stopped at a different station each night.
n. pl. **stations** sta·tions

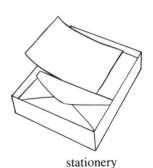

stationery

stationery sta·tion·er·y (stā'shə·ner·ē) paper things that people
use for writing; paper, cards and envelopes.
I bought some new stationery that has my name on it. *n. no pl.*

steam

steer

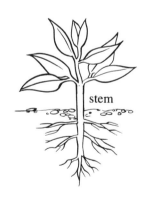
stem

statue stat·ue (stach′ü) a shape or likeness of a person or thing that is made of stone, metal or wood; a carving of a figure.
There is a statue of Abraham Lincoln in the park. *n. pl.* **statues** stat·ues

stay (stā) **1.** to remain in the same place; to not move away; to not go.
We will stay here for two weeks. *v.*
2. to not change; to remain the same way.
I hope that you will stay the way you are.
v. **stayed, stayed, staying** stay·ing

stay active stay ac·tive (stā   ak′tiv) to continue to work; to continue to erupt.
The volcano should stay active for many years.

steak (stāk) a good slice of meat, usually beef.
I had a small steak for dinner. *n. pl.* **steaks**

steal (stēl) to take something without paying for it; to take something without permission; to take something that belongs to some other person or a business.
The men wanted to steal the money from the grocery store.
v. **stole, stolen, stealing** sto·len, steal·ing

steam (stēm) **1.** the vapor that is made by boiling water; the heat that rises above things that are very hot.
I can see the steam above the hot cocoa. *n. no pl.*
2. to cook food with the vapor that is made by boiling water.
We can steam the broccoli in this pan.
v. **steamed, steamed, steaming** steam·ing
3. having to do with the vapor that is made by boiling water.
The steam engine pulled the train. *adj.*

steep (stēp) having a very sharp slope or slant; being almost straight up and down.
The mountainside is steep. *adj.* **steeper, steepest** steep·er, steep·est

steer (stir) a male from the cattle family.
Their steer is only two years old. *n. pl.* **steers**

stem (stem) the stalk of a plant; a small branch on which a flower grows.
The rose had a long stem. *n. pl.* **stems**

a	cat	i	sit	oi	oil	ch	chop		a in about
ā	ate	ī	lie	ou	out	ng	song		e in oven
ä	car	o	pot	u	cut	sh	she	ə =	i in pencil
e	set	ō	old	u̇	book	th	three		o in memory
ē	equal	ô	or	ü	blue	ŦH	there		u in circus
ėr	germ					zh	treasure		

step   (step)   **1.** a stair; one of the things that go up a staircase.
   I stood on the first step. *n.*
   2. a movement of the foot; a movement of the foot
   in a dance motion.
   Take one step forward and one step to the right side. *n.*
   3. an instruction; one of several instructions or directions.
   The first step is to mix the butter and sugar together. *n. pl.* **steps**
   4. to walk; to move one foot in front of the other foot.
   Please step into my office. *v.* **stepped, stepped, stepping** step·ping

stick

stepbrother   step·broth·er (step'bruᴛʜ·ər)   the son of a stepmother
   or stepfather.
   The son of my stepmother is my stepbrother.
   n. pl. **stepbrothers** step·broth·ers

stepmother   step·moth·er (step'muᴛʜ·ər)   the woman
   who has married a father but who is not the woman who
   gave birth to the child.
   My stepmother is very nice. *n. pl.* **stepmothers** step·moth·ers

step on   (step   ôn)   to put a foot on top of something;
   to walk on something.
   Please step on the ant.
   v. **stepped on, stepped on, stepping on** step·ping on

stepsister   step·sis·ter (step'sis·tər)   the daughter of a stepmother or
   stepfather.
   The daughter of my stepmother is my stepsister.
   n. pl. **stepsisters** step·sis·ters

stick candy

stick   (stik)   **1.** a small branch or piece of wood.
   I put the hot dog on a stick and cooked it over the campfire. *n. pl.* **sticks**
   2. to cling to something; to stay on or near something;
   to attach to something.
   The paper will stick to the glue. *v.* **stuck, stuck, sticking** stick·ing

stick candy   stick can·dy (stik   kan'dē)   a kind of hard candy in the
   shape of a stick that is made with syrup.
   Stick candy is easy to eat.

sticker   stick·er (stik'ər)   a small, sharp part of a plant; a thorn.
   The stem of the plant has a sticker on it. *n. pl.* **stickers** stick·ers

stick out   (stik   out)   to push out; to force out; to extend out.
   If you stick out your tongue again, I will put soap on it.
   v. **stuck out, stuck out, sticking out** stick·ing out

sticky   stick·y (stik'ē)   made of a material that attaches things to
   it; feeling like glue or paste.
   The tape is sticky. *adj.* **stickier, stickiest** stick·i·er, stick·i·est

sticker

stiff   (stif)   not able to bend easily.
   The cardboard is stiff. *adj.* **stiffer, stiffest** stiff·er, stiff·est

412

stifle

stifle sti·fle (stī′fəl) the front part of a horse's thigh.
The horse has a bruise on its stifle. *n. pl.* **stifles** sti·fles

still (stil) **1.** up to this time; yet; even to this time.
I am still living in the house in which I was born. *adv.*
2. without moving; without movement; calmly; without sound.
I have trouble sitting still. *adv.*

still picture still pic·ture (stil pik′chər) a photograph; a
picture that does not move.
Here is a still picture of the stars in that movie.

stinking stink·ing (sting′king) having a bad odor; smelling bad.
The stinking fish was rotten. *adj.*

stir

stir (stėr) **1.** to mix together; to blend with a spoon.
I will stir the eggs into the flour. *v.*
2. to move about with a spoon or a stick.
I will stir the paint before using it. *v.* **stirred, stirred, stirring** stir·ring

stir in (stėr in) to add and mix an ingredient to another
ingredient in a recipe.
I will now stir in the eggs. *v.* **stirred in, stirred in, stirring in** stir·ring in

stirrup stir·rup (stėr′əp *or* stir′əp) the part of a horse saddle
in which the rider places a foot.
I put my foot into the stirrup. *n. pl.* **stirrups** stir·rups

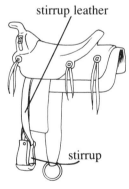

stirrup leather

stirrup

stirrup leather stir·rup leath·er (stėr′əp *or* stir′əp leᴛʜ′ər)
the strap of leather between the seat of a horse
saddle and the stirrup.
A person can make the stirrup leather shorter or longer.

stock (stok) **1.** a share or part ownership in a business.
My mother bought stock in the candy shop. *n. pl.* **stocks**
2. usual; without a change or modification; as made
by the manufacturer.
He bought a stock engine for his car. *adj.*

stock car (stok kär) a car that was not built for racing but
that is driven in a race; a car that has not been
changed from the way the manufacturer made it.
The stock car will be driven in the race.

a cat	**i** sit	**oi** oil	**ch** chop		a in about	
ā ate	**ī** lie	**ou** out	**ng** song		e in oven	
ä car	**o** pot	**u** cut	**sh** she	ə =	i in pencil	
e set	**ō** old	**u̇** book	**th** three		o in memory	
ē equal	**ô** or	**ü** blue	**ᴛʜ** there		u in circus	
ėr germ			**zh** treasure			

stockholder stock·hold·er (stok‘hōl·dər) a person who owns shares or stock in a business.
Mother is a stockholder in the candy shop.
n. pl. **stockholders** stock·hold·ers

stocking stock·ing (stok‘ing) a leg and foot covering for a woman; a woman's hose.
Mother got a tear in her stocking. *n. pl.* **stockings** stock·ings

stocking

stock market stock mar·ket (stok mär‘kit) the place where shares in businesses are bought and sold.
We have invested in the stock market.

stock report stock re·port (stok ri·pôrt') a record of how much a stock or a share in a business is worth; a record of the value of a stock.
Mother gets a stock report every month.

stole (stōl) *v. pt. t.* See **steal.**

stolen sto·len (stō‘lən) *v. pt. part.* See **steal.**

stomach stom·ach (stum‘ək) the part of a body that receives and digests food.
My stomach hurts. *n. pl.* **stomachs** stom·achs

stone (stōn) **1.** a rock; a hard material found in the earth.
I threw a stone in the lake. *n. pl.* **stones**
2. made of rocks.
The stone house is very cool in the summer. *adj.*

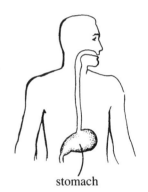
stomach

Stone Age (stōn āj) a time in the past when man first learned to make and use things made of stone.
This stone ax was made in the Stone Age.

stony ston·y (stō‘nē) having many rocks; full of rocks.
The river is stony. *adj.* **stonier, stoniest** ston·i·er, ston·i·est

stood (stůd) *v. pt. t., pt. part.* See **stand** (1, 2, 3).

stood to attention stood to at·ten·tion (stůd tü ə·ten‘shən) had the body in a straight position out of honor or respect.
We stood to attention while the band played the national anthem. *idiom*

stood up (stůd up) *v. pt. t., pt. part.* See **stand up.**

414

stop sign

stopwatch

storeroom

stop (stop) **1.** to go from moving or doing something to not moving or doing something.
Please stop hitting your sister. *v.*
2. to keep from moving or doing something; to prevent something from continuing.
I will stop the next car that tries to drive by. *v.*
3. to not continue.
We will stop reading at the end of the page.
v. **stopped, stopped, stopping** stop·ping

stop sign (stop sīn) a traffic sign that tells drivers to stop the vehicle and look for other vehicles.
The stop sign means that all cars must stop.

stopwatch (stop‘woch) a time-telling tool that has a second hand that a person can stop and start again by pressing down on a small button; a timer.
The coach used a stopwatch to measure how fast Jack ran from the start to the finish. *n. pl.* **stopwatches** stop·watch·es

store (stôr *or* stōr) **1.** a place where people can buy things; a shop.
He went to the store. *n. pl.* **stores**
2. to keep things; to put things away.
I will store the toys in the attic. *v.* **stored, stored, storing** stor·ing

storeroom store·room (stôr‘rüm *or* stôr‘ru̇m *or* stōr‘rüm *or* stōr‘ru̇m) a place in a building or house where things are kept for use in the future.
The old desk is in the school storeroom. *n. pl.* **storerooms** store·rooms

storm (stôrm) bad weather; wind with rain, snow or thunder and lightning.
We had a bad storm last night. *n. pl.* **storms**

storm window storm win·dow (stôrm win‘dō) a second window put on the outside of another window to keep out the winter cold.
The storm windows made our house warmer.

stormy storm·y (stôr‘mē) having wind with rain, snow or thunder and lightning; having great winds with other bad weather.
The night was stormy. *adj.* **stormier, stormiest** storm·i·er, storm·i·est

a	cat	**i**	sit	**oi**	oil	**ch**	chop	a in about
ā	ate	**ī**	lie	**ou**	out	**ng**	song	e in oven
ä	car	**o**	pot	**u**	cut	**sh**	she	ə = i in pencil
e	set	**ō**	old	**u̇**	book	**th**	three	o in memory
ē	equal	**ô**	or	**ü**	blue	**ŦH**	there	u in circus
ėr	germ					**zh**	treasure	

story sto·ry (stôr′ē *or* stōr′ē) **1.** a book; a tale; an account of what happened; an article in a newspaper or magazine.
I read a story about a soldier. *n.*
2. a level or floor of a building.
I live on the third story of the apartment house. *n. pl.* **stories** sto·ries
3. having to do with a tale or an account of something that happened.
The story title was "The Soldier." *adj.*
4. having to do with the levels or floors in a building.
I live in a four-story building. *adj.*

storybook

storybook sto·ry·book (stôr′ē·bůk) a book with one or more tales or accounts of things that happened.
Mother bought the baby a storybook. *n. pl.* **storybooks** sto·ry·books

storyteller sto·ry·tell·er (stôr′ē·tel·ər *or* stōr′ē·tel·ər) a person who tells tales or stories.
I listened to the storyteller at the library. *n. pl.* **storytellers** sto·ry·tell·ers

stove (stōv) an appliance in the kitchen on which people cook food.
The kettle is on the stove. *n. pl.* **stoves**

stove

straight (strāt) **1.** even; without a bend, curve or bump.
This street is straight. *adj.* **straighter, straightest** straight·er, straight·est
2. without a break or a rest; in a continuous line.
I worked for two hours straight. *adj.*

straightaway straight·a·way (strāt′ə·wā) the part of a racetrack that does not have a bend or a curve.
Car one passed car eleven on the straightaway.
n. pl. **straightaways** straight·a·ways

straighten straight·en (strāt′n) to take the bends or curves out of something; to put in correct condition.
Please straighten your tie. *v.* **straightened, straightened, straightening** straight·ened, straight·en·ing

straighten out straight·en out (strāt′n out) to unbend; to take the curves or bends out of something.
I can straighten out the hanger and use it as a stick. *v.* **straightened out, straightened out, straightening out** straight·ened out, straight·en·ing out

straighten up straight·en up (strāt′n up) to make neat; to make correct; to put in a good condition.
Please straighten up your bedroom. *v.* **straightened up, straightened up, straightening up** straight·ened up, straight·en·ing up

straightaway

strain (strān) **1.** to pour a liquid through a mesh or screen.
Mother will strain the seeds from the orange juice. *v.*
2. to pull to the tightest point; to make tight by pulling very hard.
Your weight may strain the hammock.
v. **strained, strained, straining** strain·ing

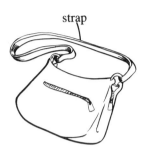

strap

straw

strawberry

strait　(strāt)　a narrow strip of water that joins or connects two large bodies of water.
There is a strand of hair in your face. *n. pl.* **straits**

The ship traveled through the strait to the ocean. *n. pl.* **straits**

strand　(strand)　a rope-like or thread-like piece of anything; a single long piece of something.
There is a strand of hair in your face. *n. pl.* **strands**

strange　(strānj)　**1.** unusual; not normal; different; odd.
I have a strange feeling. *adj.*
2. not known; never seen or heard before.
There is a strange man at the door.
adj. **stranger, strangest** strang·er, strang·est

strange-looking　strange-look·ing (strānj'·lùk'·ing)　having an odd or different appearance; not appearing normal.
That is a strange-looking dog. *adj.* **stranger-looking, strangest-looking,** strang·er-look·ing, strang·est-look·ing

stranger　stran·ger (strān'jər)　a person that you have never seen before; a person that you do not know.
Children should not talk to a stranger. *n. pl.* **strangers** stran·gers

strangle　stran·gle (strang'gəl)　to kill by squeezing the throat so breathing stops; to kill by choking or smothering.
The weeds can strangle little plants.
v. **strangled, strangled, strangling** stran·gled, stran·gling

strap　(strap)　a long narrow strip of leather.
I broke the strap on Mother's purse. *n. pl.* **straps**

straw　(strô)　**1.** dried stalks or stems of grain plants.
We gave the horse some straw to eat. *n. no pl.*
2. a small tube that people use for drinking liquid out of a container.
I drank the soda with a straw. *n. pl.* **straws**
3. made of dried stalks of grain plants.
The cabin has a straw floor. *adj.*

strawberry　straw·ber·ry (strô'·ber·ē *or* strô'·bər·ē)　**1.** a small red juicy fruit that grows on a low plant.
I picked a strawberry. *n. pl.* **strawberries** straw·ber·ries
2. having the flavor of the small red juicy fruit.
I want some strawberry ice cream. *adj.*
3. being made from the small red juicy fruit that grows on a small plant.
I ate a piece of strawberry pie. *adj.*

a	cat	**i**	sit	**oi**	oil	**ch**	chop	a in about
ā	ate	**ī**	lie	**ou**	out	**ng**	song	e in oven
ä	car	**o**	pot	**u**	cut	**sh**	she	ə = i in pencil
e	set	**ō**	old	**ù**	book	**th**	three	o in memory
ē	equal	**ô**	or	**ü**	blue	**ŦH**	there	u in circus
ėr	germ					**zh**	treasure	

straw-like (strô‑līk) looking like a small tube that people use for drinking liquid out of containers.
A mosquito has a straw-like nose. *adj.*

stream (strēm) a small channel of water that flows or moves; a creek.
The stream runs through the back of the farm. *n. pl.* **streams**

street (strēt) **1.** a paved road in a city or a town.
Remember to look both ways before crossing the street. *n. pl.* **streets**
2. having to do with a paved road.
The street sign is on the corner. *adj.*

stream

strength (strengkth *or* strength) the power that someone or something has.
The man lifted the car off the ground. He has great strength.
n. pl. **strengths**

streptomycin strep·to·my·cin (strep·tō·mī‑sn) a strong medicine that kills the bacteria that cause illnesses.
The doctor gave me some streptomycin for my sore throat. *n. no pl.*

stretch (strech) **1.** to pull to the full length; to extend fully; to reach as far as possible.
I can stretch to reach the top shelf. *v.*
2. to make longer by pulling; to make bigger by pulling.
We will stretch the taffy. *v.* **stretched, stretched, stretching** stretch·ing
3. the distance that something can reach, such as an arm or leg.
He has a long stretch. *n. pl.* **stretches** stretch·es

strict (strikt) having very rigid rules; being careful about following the rules; having many rules.
The teacher is strict. *adj.* **stricter, strictest** strict·er, strict·est

string (string) **1.** thick thread; thin wire; cotton yarn.
I tied the package with string. *n. no pl.*
2. a row of things tied in a line with thread.
I broke her string of beads. *n. pl.* **strings**
3. made of thick thread or cotton yarn.
The string picture has many colors in it. *adj.*

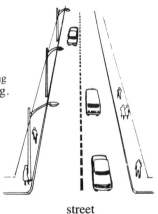
street

string art (string ärt) pictures made out of thick thread or cotton yarn.
I am learning to make string art.

strip (strip) a long narrow piece; something that is long and narrow.
I put a strip of paper in the book. *n. pl.* **strips**

stripe (strīp) a line or a band of color.
My shirt has a blue stripe on the sleeve. *n. pl.* **stripes**

string

striped (strīpt *or* strī‑pid) having long lines or bands of color.
A zebra is striped. *adj.*

stroke (strōk)   a sudden illness caused by a blood clot in the head.
My grandmother had a stroke last summer. *n. pl.* **strokes**

stroll (strōl)   to walk slowly.
I will stroll around the lake. *v.* **strolled, strolled, strolling** stroll·ing

strong (strông *or* strong)   having great strength; having great power; having the ability to hold or lift heavy things.
The man who moved the piano is strong.
adj. **stronger, strongest** strong·er, strong·est

struggle strug·gle (strug′əl)   to work hard; to work hard to get loose or to escape; to fight to get away.
The dog will struggle if you try to give him a bath.
v. **struggled, struggled, struggling** strug·gled, strug·gling

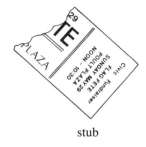

stub

stub (stub)   the end part of something; the end part of a ticket; a short piece of something.
The man took my ticket stub. *n. pl.* **stubs**

stubborn stub·born (stub′ərn)   not willing to change one's mind; having a strong opinion or idea; not open to new ideas.
Jim will not change his mind. He is very stubborn. *adj.*

stuck (stuk)   *v. pt. t., pt. part.* See **stick** (2).

student stu·dent (stüd′nt *or* styüd′nt)   **1.** a person who studies; a person who goes to school.
There is a new student in our class. *n. pl.* **students** stu·dents
2. having to do with people who study or who go to school.
The student desks are placed in rows. *adj.*

studio

studied stud·ied (stud′ēd)   *v. pt. t., pt. part.* See **study.**

studio stu·di·o (stü′dē·ō *or* styü′dē·ō)   a room or building in which an artist works.
The painter is in his studio. *n. pl.* **studios** stu·di·os

study stud·y (stud′ē)   to learn; to read and memorize; to work on school subjects.
I want to study French. *v.* **studied, studied, studying** stud·ied, stud·y·ing

a	cat	i	sit	oi	oil	ch	chop		a in about
ā	ate	ī	lie	ou	out	ng	song		e in oven
ä	car	o	pot	u	cut	sh	she	ə =	i in pencil
e	set	ō	old	u̇	book	th	three		o in memory
ē	equal	ô	or	ü	blue	ŦH	there		u in circus
ėr	germ					zh	treasure		

stuff (stuf) **1.** to fill the skin of an animal so that it can be kept as a trophy.
The man will stuff the head of the deer. *v.*
2. to fill to the fullest.
I will stuff the things in the drawer. *v.*
3. to fill a chicken or turkey with a bread mixture.
Mother will stuff the Thanksgiving turkey.
v. **stuffed, stuffed, stuffing** stuff·ing
4. things; belongings.
I have so much stuff in my room that I cannot find anything. *n. no pl.*

stuffing stuff·ing (stuf′ing) **1.** the material that is used to fill things.
The stuffing is coming out of the teddy bear. *n.*
2. the mixture of bread and eggs that is used to fill a chicken or turkey.
Mother makes good stuffing. *n. pl.* **stuffings** stuff·ings

stuffing

stump (stump) the remaining part of a tree or body part that has been cut; the part that remains after the biggest part has been removed.
The stump of the tree is still in the ground. *n. pl.* **stumps**

stupid stu·pid (stü′pid *or* styü′pid) not smart; dumb; not intellectually bright.
Sheep are very stupid animals.
adj. **stupider, stupidest** stu·pid·er, stu·pid·est

style (stīl) **1.** a design of clothes; a kind of clothing; fashion.
The man wears the cowboy style of pants. *n.*
2. a way of doing something; the manner in which something is done.
She has a great dancing style. *n. pl.* **styles**

stump

stylish styl·ish (stī′lish) to be up to date with the newest fashion or kind of clothes; to wear clothes in a special way.
The large hats are very stylish. *adj.*

subject sub·ject (sub′jikt *or* sub′jekt) something that is taught in school; something that is talked or read about.
Math is a school subject. *n. pl.* **subjects** sub·jects

substance sub·stance (sub′stənts) the material of which something is made.
Paste is a sticky substance. *n. pl.* **substances** sub·stanc·es

subtract sub·tract (səb·trakt′) to take something away.
I will subtract five from fifteen to get ten.
v. **subtracted, subtracted, subtracting** sub·tract·ed, sub·tract·ing

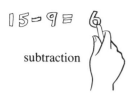

subtraction

subtraction   sub·trac·tion (səb·trak′shən)   **1.** the process of taking one amount away from another amount; the math process of taking one number away from another number.
I am very good at subtraction. *n. no pl.*
2. having to do with the process of taking one number away from another number.
I got an A on my subtraction test. *adj.*

succeed   suc·ceed (sək·sēd′)   to achieve; to win; to get what one wants or tries for.
If you study hard, you will succeed in this class.
v. **succeeded, succeeded, succeeding** suc·ceed·ed, suc·ceed·ing

success   suc·cess (sək·ses′)   a good result; an achievement.
The surprise party was a success. She was surprised.
n. pl. **successes** suc·cess·es

successful   suc·cess·ful (sək·ses′fəl)   **1.** having a good ending; being what was wanted or expected; having a good result.
The party was successful. *adj.*
2. having done something well; having a lot of money; being very well known.
My brother is successful. He has a good job and makes a lot of money. *adj.*

successfully   suc·cess·ful·ly (sək·ses′fə·lē)   with a good result; well.
I successfully finished the test. *adv.*

such   (such)   of a certain kind; to a great degree or extent; very.
There was such a bad storm that the river flooded. *adv.*

suck   (suk)   to pull in; to pull in through the mouth.
You make a lot of noise when you suck milk through your straw.
v. **sucked, sucked, sucking** suck·ing

sucker   suck·er (suk′ər)   a small new part of a plant; a shoot that starts on a plant and takes strength and food from the rest of the plant.
The farmer took the sucker off of the tomato plant. *n. pl.* **suckers** suck·ers

sudden   sud·den (sud′n)   quick; happening so fast that it was not expected.
We had a sudden storm last night. *adj.*

suddenly   sud·den·ly (sud′n·lē)   quickly; in a quick way.
The rain started suddenly. *adv.*

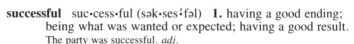

suck

sucker

a	cat	i	sit	oi	oil	ch	chop		a in about
ā	ate	ī	lie	ou	out	ng	song		e in oven
ä	car	o	pot	u	cut	sh	she	ə =	i in pencil
e	set	ō	old	u̇	book	th	three		o in memory
ē	equal	ô	or	ü	blue	ŦH	there		u in circus
ėr	germ					zh	treasure		

421

suffer   suf·fer (suf′ər)   to be in pain; to hurt for a long time; to feel hurt.
>The dog will not suffer if you put it to sleep.
>*v.* **suffered, suffered, suffering** suf·fered, suf·fer·ing

suffering   suf·fer·ing (suf′ər·ing)   **1.** feeling pain or hurt; having great pain.
>The suffering dog was howling. *adj.*
>**2.** *v. pres. part.* See **suffer.**

sugar   sug·ar (shŭg′ər)   **1.** a white, grainy substance that tastes sweet.
>I put sugar on my cereal. *n. no pl.*
>**2.** having to do with the white grains that taste sweet.
>The sugar bowl is on the table. *adj.*

sugar cane

sugar cane   sug·ar cane (shŭg′ər kān)   **1.** a tall plant with long flat leaves from which sugar is made.
>Sugar cane is grown in Hawaii.
>**2.** having to do with the plant from which sugar is made.
>We saw the sugar cane fields.

suggest   sug·gest (səg·jest′ *or* sə·jest′)   to give an idea; to offer help; to give advice.
>I will suggest that we go to a movie.
>*v.* **suggested, suggested, suggesting** sug·gest·ed, sug·gest·ing

suggestion   sug·ges·tion (səg·jes′chən *or* sə·jes′chən)   an idea that one person gives to another; a thought that people share.
>I made the suggestion that we should go to a movie.
>*n. pl.* **suggestions** sug·ges·tions

suit   (süt)   **1.** two pieces of clothing that go together; a set of clothes that are worn together.
>My father wears a suit to work every day. *n.*
>**2.** clothes that are worn for swimming.
>I put on my suit and went swimming in the lake. *n. pl.* **suits**

suit

suitcase   suit·case (süt′kās)   a bag in which clothes are packed for a trip; a piece of luggage.
>I packed my clothes in the suitcase. *n. pl.* **suitcases** suit·cas·es

suit of armour   suit of ar·mour (süt əv är′mər)   a set of metal clothing worn by a knight for protection.
>We saw the suit of armour in the museum.

sultan   sul·tan (sult′n)   the name for a king or ruler in a Moslem country.
>The sultan had many wives. *n. pl.* **sultans** sul·tans

summer   sum·mer (sum′ər)   **1.** the warm season of the year; the season that comes after spring and before fall.
>I do not go to school in the summer. *n. pl.* **summers** sum·mers
>**2.** having to do with the warm season of the year.
>We are having summer weather. *adj.*

suitcase

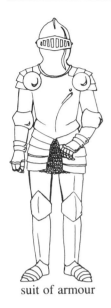

suit of armour

sundial

sunflower

summertime sum·mer·time (sum´ər·tīm) the time of year when it is warm and sunny; the season of summer.
I do not go to school in the summertime.
n. pl. **summertimes** sum·mer·times

sun (sun) **1.** the star in our solar system; the star around which the planets revolve (turn).
The sun gives the Earth warmth. *n. no pl.*
2. having to do with the rays from the star in our solar system.
I took a sun hat to the beach. *adj.*

sunburn sun·burn (sun´bėrn) red, burned skin caused by sitting too long in the sunlight.
I got a sunburn at the beach. *n. pl.* **sunburns** sun·burns

sunburst sun·burst (sun´bėrst) the pattern of light made by the sun; a pattern that looks like beams coming from the sun.
I put a sunburst on my shirt. *n. pl.* **sunbursts** sun·bursts

sundial sun·di·al (sun´dī·əl) a clock that uses the sun to make shadows and tell the time.
There is an old sundial in the park. *n. pl.* **sundials** sun·di·als

sundown sun·down (sun´doun) the time of day when the sun disappears from the sky; sunset.
The birds stop singing at sundown. *n. pl.* **sundowns** sun·downs

sunflower sun·flow·er (sun´flou·ər) a tall flower that has a brown center and yellow petals.
I picked a sunflower. *n. pl.* **sunflowers** sun·flow·ers

sunk (sungk) *v. pt. t., pt. part.* See **sink** (1).

sunken treasure sunk·en treas·ure (sung´kən trezh´ər) valuable things that have gone to the bottom of the ocean; underwater riches.
The diver is looking for sunken treasure.

sunlight sun·light (sun´līt) the light that the sun makes; the brightness of the sun.
The sunlight comes through my window in the morning. *n. no pl.*

sunny sun·ny (sun´ē) being bright; having the light of the sun; having a lot of sunshine.
Today is sunny. *adj.* **sunnier, sunniest** sun·ni·er, sun·ni·est

a	cat	**i**	sit	**oi**	oil	**ch**	chop		a in about
ā	ate	**ī**	lie	**ou**	out	**ng**	song		e in oven
ä	car	**o**	pot	**u**	cut	**sh**	she	ə =	i in pencil
e	set	**ō**	old	**u̇**	book	**th**	three		o in memory
ē	equal	**ô**	or	**ü**	blue	**ŦH**	there		u in circus
ėr	germ					**zh**	treasure		

sunrise sun·rise (sun⋅rīz) the time of day when the sun is first in the sky; the time when the sun appears to rise from the horizon; the beginning of the day.
The birds start to sing at sunrise. *n. pl.* **sunrises** sun·ris·es

sunroof sun·roof (sun⋅rüf *or* sun⋅r'uf) a window in the roof of a car made to let in the light of the sun.
We have a sunroof in our new car. *n. pl.* **sunroofs** sun·roofs

sunroof

sunset sun·set (sun⋅set) the action of the sun going below the horizon; the time when the sun disappears below the horizon.
I love to watch a beautiful sunset over the Pacific Ocean.
n. pl. **sunsets** sun·sets

sunshine sun·shine (sun⋅shīn) the light the sun makes; sunlight.
The sunshine comes through my window in the morning. *n. no pl.*

sunsuit sun·suit (sun⋅süt) a set of clothes that is worn when it is hot; a set of clothes that is worn to get a tan.
The little girl wore a blue sunsuit. *n. pl.* **sunsuits** sun·suits

suntan sun·tan (sun⋅tan) **1.** the dark skin caused by the rays of the sun.
I got a suntan this summer. *n. pl.* **suntans** sun·tans
2. having to do with the darkened skin made by the sun.
I put suntan lotion on her back. *adj.*

sunsuit

suntan oil sun·tan oil (sun⋅tan oil) an oily or greasy substance that people put on their bodies to help them get a suntan.
The suntan oil smells like coconuts.

super su·per (sü⋅pər) wonderful; great; the best.
We have a super time at the beach. *adj.*

Superman Su·per·man (sü⋅pər·man) a storybook, movie and cartoon character who is very strong and saves the world and people from harm.
Superman is a hero. *n.*

supermarket su·per·mar·ket (sü⋅pər·mär·kit) a big grocery store.
I went to the supermarket for my mother.
n. pl. **supermarkets** su·per·mar·kets

supervision su·per·vi·sion (sü·pər·vizh⋅ən) the watching over of something or someone; the act of managing something or someone.
The teacher is responsible for the supervision of the schoolroom. *n. no pl.*

supper sup·per (sup⋅ər) the last meal of the day; dinner.
We eat supper when Mother gets home from work. *n. pl.* **suppers** sup·pers

supplies sup·plies (sə·plīz′) things that are needed; materials that are stored away and used when needed.
We have all the supplies for the camping trip. *plural n.*

supply sup·ply (sə·plī′) to give things that are needed; to provide.
I will supply the hot dogs for the picnic.
v. **supplied, supplied, supplying** sup·plied, sup·ply·ing

suppose sup·pose (sə·pōz′) to think something; to consider as possible; to believe.
I suppose I could go to the store for you.
v. **supposed, supposed, supposing** sup·posed, sup·pos·ing

sure (shùr) **1.** certain; having no doubt; confident.
I am sure she will be here soon. *adj.* **surer, surest** sur·er, sur·est
2. a positive answer.
Sure, I'll go with you. *adv.*
3. certainly; without a doubt.
The apples sure were good. *adv.*

surfing

sure enough sure e·nough (shùr i·nuf′) certainly; as expected.
And sure enough, here she comes. *adv.*

surface sur·face (sėr′fis) **1.** the outside of something.
The surface of the door is smooth. *n.*
2. the outer layer of something.
The candy has a hard surface over a soft center. *n. pl.* **surfaces** sur·fac·es

surfing surf·ing (sėr′fing) the riding of the ocean waves; a sport where people use their bodies or small light boards to ride the ocean's waves.
Surfing can be fun if you are a good swimmer. *n. no pl.*

surprise sur·prise (sər·prīz′) **1.** an unexpected event or thing.
I got a surprise from my mother. *n. pl.* **surprises** sur·pris·es
2. having to do with an unexpected thing.
We are giving Lisa a surprise party. *adj.*
3. to do something unexpected; to do something without telling that it will happen.
I will surprise her with this gift.
v. **surprised, surprised, surprising** sur·prised, sur·pris·ing

a	cat	i	sit	oi	oil	ch	chop		a in about
ā	ate	ī	lie	ou	out	ng	song		e in oven
ä	car	o	pot	u	cut	sh	she	ə =	i in pencil
e	set	ō	old	ù	book	th	three		o in memory
ē	equal	ô	or	ü	blue	ŦH	there		u in circus
ėr	germ					zh	treasure		

surround   sur·round (sə·round′)   to form a circle around; to close all sides.

> We will surround the enemy so that they cannot escape.
> *v.* **surrounded, surrounded, surrounding** sur·round·ed, sur·round·ing

survey   sur·vey (sər·vā′)   **1.** to measure the length and width of a piece of land; to measure the size of land.

> The man will survey the farm. *v.*
> **2.** to look at something carefully; to oversee an activity.
> I will survey the work and report the result to you.
> *v.* **surveyed, surveyed, surveying** sur·veyed, sur·vey·ing

surveyor   sur·vey·or (sər·vā′·ər)   a person who measures the size of pieces of land.

> The surveyor measured the farm. *n. pl.* **surveyors** sur·vey·ors

swallow

swallow   swal·low (swol′·ō)   **1.** to move food or medicine from the mouth to the stomach.

> I cannot swallow pills.
> *v.* **swallowed, swallowed, swallowing** swal·lowed, swal·low·ing
> **2.** a small fast bird with long wings and a pointed, forked tail.
> The swallow lives in the barn. *n. pl.* **swallows** swal·lows

swallowtail   swal·low·tail (swol′·ō·tāl)   a flag that has two pointed tails on one side.

> The ship flew a swallowtail from its mast.
> *n. pl.* **swallowtails** swal·low·tails

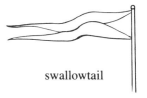

swallowtail

swam   (swam)   *v. pt. t.* See **swim** (1).

swamp   (swomp *or* swômp)   **1.** wet land; land that is soaked with water; a marsh.

> The crocodile lives in the swamp. *n. pl.* **swamps**
> **2.** having to do with land that is soaked with water.
> The swamp mud may have fossils in it. *adj.*

swan   (swon)   **1.** a large, graceful bird that has a long neck.

> The swan swam across the lake. *n. pl.* **swans**
> **2.** having to do with a large, graceful bird.
> Jim found a white swan feather. *adj.*

swan

sway   (swā)   to move back and forth; to swing from side to side.

> The tree branch will sway in the wind.
> *v.* **swayed, swayed, swaying** sway·ing

sweat   (swet)   the liquid that comes from a body when it is hot or when a person works hard.

> The man had sweat on his face. *n. no pl.*

Swede   (swēd)   a person who comes from or lives in Sweden.

> Lars is a Swede who was born in Sweden but lives in the United States.
> *n. pl.* **Swedes**

Sweden

Stockholm

Sweden Swe·den (swēd′n) a country in Europe; its capital is Stockholm.
Sweden is next to Norway. *n.*

sweep (swēp) to brush with a broom; to clean with a broom.
Please sweep the porch. *v.* **swept, swept, sweeping** sweep·ing

sweet (swēt) tasting like sugar; tasting like honey.
Candy is sweet. *adj.* **sweeter, sweetest** sweet·er, sweet·est

sweetheart sweet·heart (swēt′härt) a person's lover; a girlfriend or a boyfriend.
My brother has a sweetheart. *n. pl.* **sweethearts** sweet·hearts

sweetmeats sweet·meats (swēt′mēts) candies.
The candy store has many sweetmeats. *plural n.*

sweets (swēts) candies or other things made with sugar.
The dentist said that I should not eat many sweets. *plural n.*

sweet-smelling sweet-smell·ing (swēt-smel′ing) having a pleasant odor or aroma.
The peach tree is covered with sweet-smelling blossoms. *adj.*

sweet tooth (swēt tüth) a desire for something that tastes like sugar or honey; liking sweet things.
I have a sweet tooth all the time. *idiom*

swept (swept) *v. pt. t., pt. part.* See **sweep.**

swift (swift) very fast; very quick.
The runner is swift. *adj.* **swifter, swiftest** swift·er, swift·est

swiftly swift·ly (swift′lē) in a very quick manner.
The deer ran swiftly into the woods. *adv.*

swim (swim) **1.** to move in water; to use one's arms and legs to move in the water.
I am learning how to swim. *v.* **swam, swum, swimming** swim·ming
2. the act of moving in the water.
I took a long swim this afternoon. *n. pl.* **swims**
3. having to do with moving in the water.
My swim cap keeps my hair dry. *adj.*

swimmer swim·mer (swim′ər) a person who uses the arms and legs to move in the water; an animal that moves in the water.
A beaver is a good swimmer. *n. pl.* **swimmers** swim·mers

sweep

a	cat	i	sit	oi	oil	ch	chop		a in about
ā	ate	ī	lie	ou	out	ng	song		e in oven
ä	car	o	pot	u	cut	sh	she	ə =	i in pencil
e	set	ō	old	ů	book	th	three		o in memory
ē	equal	ô	or	ü	blue	ŦH	there		u in circus
ėr	germ					zh	treasure		

427

swimming hole swim·ming hole (swim′ing hōl) a place to
   swim; a small lake that people use for swimming.
   We have a great swimming hole on the farm.

swimming pool swim·ming pool (swim′ing pül) a large tank
   of water in which people swim.
   We are building a swimming pool in the backyard.

swimming suit swim·ming suit (swim′ing süt) clothes in which a
   person swims; clothes that a person uses for going into water.
   I bought a new swimming suit.

swimming team swim·ming team (swim′ing tēm) a group
   of people who have races and contests in the water;
   a group of people who have swimming races.
   I want to be on the swimming team.

swing (swing) **1.** to go back and forth in the air;
   to move back and forth on something that is hanging.
   We can swing on the hammock. *v.* **swung, swung, swinging** swing·ing
   2. a seat that is hanging from ropes or chains so that it
   can move back and forth.
   I sat in the swing and he pushed me. *n. pl.* **swings**

swirl (swėrl) to move in a circle; to turn around quickly.
   The water will swirl down the drain.
   v. **swirled, swirled, swirling** swirl·ing

swishing swish·ing (swish′ing) making a hissing sound.
   The tired boy fell asleep to the swishing sound of the trees. *adj.*

Swiss Alps (swis alps) high mountains in Switzerland;
   a mountain range in Switzerland.
   The Swiss Alps are beautiful.

switch (swich) **1.** a control knob; a dial that is used for turning
   a light, a machine or an appliance on and off.
   The switch on the bottom will turn the television on.
   n. pl. **switches** switch·es
   2. to change from one thing to another.
   May I please switch the television channel?
   v. **switched, switched, switching** switch·ing

Switzerland Swit·zer·land (swit′sər·lənd) a country in Europe;
   its capital is Bern.
   Many chocolate candies are made in Switzerland. *n.*

swollen swol·len (swō′lən) larger because of extra water;
   puffed up from water or pus.
   Her arm is swollen where the ball hit it. *adj.*

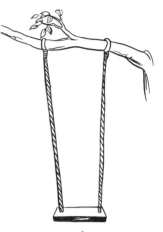

swing

switch

Switzerland

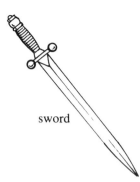

sword

syrup

swoop (swüp) to fly down quickly for an attack; to come down to the ground quickly.
The eagle will swoop to catch the rabbit.
v. **swooped, swooped, swooping** swoop·ing

sword (sôrd *or* sōrd) a weapon that has a long sharp blade.
The knight carried a sword and a shield. *n. pl.* **swords**

swung (swung) *v. pt. t., pt. part.* See **swing** (1).

symbol sym·bol (sim′bəl) something that is used to represent or stand for something else; an emblem.
The dove is a symbol of peace. *n. pl.* **symbols** sym·bols

sympathetic sym·pa·thet·ic (sim·pə·thet′ik) having sorry feelings for other people; sharing sad feelings with someone.
My friends are sympathetic about my losing my dog. *adj.*

sympathy sym·pa·thy (sim′pə·thē) a feeling of sorrow or sadness for someone else.
I have sympathy for the poor people in the world.
n. pl. **sympathies** sym·pa·thies

syrup syr·up (sir′əp *or* sėr′əp) a thick sweet liquid made with sugar and other ingredients.
I put maple syrup on my pancakes. *n. pl.* **syrups** syr·ups

system sys·tem (sis′təm) a way of doing things; an organized way of doing things; a process.
We have a good system for getting the work in the house finished.
n. pl. **systems** sys·tems

a	cat	**i**	sit	**oi**	oil	**ch**	chop	a in about
ā	ate	**ī**	lie	**ou**	out	**ng**	song	e in oven
ä	car	**o**	pot	**u**	cut	**sh**	she	ə = i in pencil
e	set	**ō**	old	**u̇**	book	**th**	three	o in memory
ē	equal	**ô**	or	**ü**	blue	**ŦH**	there	u in circus
ėr	germ					**zh**	treasure	

Tt

table ta·ble (tā′bəl) a piece of furniture with a flat top and legs.
I put the book on the table. *n. pl.* **tables** ta·bles

tablecloth ta·ble·cloth (tā′bəl·klôth) a piece of fabric or material that covers a table to protect or decorate it.
Mother always uses a tablecloth on the dining room table.
n. pl. **tablecloths** ta·ble·cloths

tablespoon ta·ble·spoon (tā′bəl·spün) a unit of measure in cooking.
I added a tablespoon of vanilla to the cake mix.
n. pl. **tablespoons** ta·ble·spoons

tablet tab·let (tab′lit) **1.** sheets of paper that are attached to each other on one side.
I bought a tablet for science notes. *n.*
2. a thin, flat piece of stone or metal on which people write.
The cave man drew pictures on this tablet. *n.*
3. a small pill.
The tablet was made of aspirin. *n. pl.* **tablets** tab·lets

table tennis ta·ble ten·nis (tā′bəl ten′is) a game that people play on a table using small wooden paddles and a small ball.
I won the game of table tennis.

tachina fly tach·i·na fly (tak′ə·nə flī) a kind of fly whose larvae (young) live on other insects.
The tachina fly was on the caterpillar.

tag (tag) a piece of paper or small card that hangs from something and has information written or printed on it.
The cost of the dress is on the tag. *n. pl.* **tags**

tail (tāl) the part of an animal that sticks out from the rear end of the animal.
A dog wags its tail when it is happy. *n. pl.* **tails**

tailor tai·lor (tā′lər) a person who makes men's clothing or a person who mends clothing.
The tailor made Father a new suit. *n. pl.* **tailors** tai·lors

take (tāk) **1.** to remove from a place and hold.
The mouse will take the cheese. *v.*
2. to carry with a person when going; to bring along.
I will take the camera to the zoo. *v.* **took, taken, taking** tak·en, tak·ing

take a bath (tāk ə bath) to wash in a tub; to sit in a tub and wash.
I will take a bath later. *idiom*

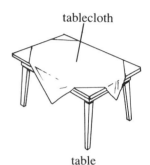
tablecloth

table

tablespoon

table tennis

tachina fly

take a seat (tāk ə sēt) to find a chair and sit.
  Please take a seat; the movie is going to start. *idiom*

take a walk (tāk ə wôk) to go outside and walk around.
  Susan decided to take a walk. *idiom*

take away take a•way (tāk ə•wā′) to remove; to get back.
  I will take away his toys if he is bad.
  v. **took away, taken away, taking away** tak•en a•way, tak•ing a•way

take care (tāk ker) to be careful; to stay safe.
  "Take care. I'll see you later." *idiom*

take ___ eyes off (tāk ___ īz ôf) to stop watching;
  to break one's glance.
  I will not take my eyes off of her all day. *idiom*

tag

take off (tāk ôf) to remove clothing; to remove things.
  Please take off your coat and relax.
  v. **took off, taken off, taking off** tak•en off, tak•ing off

take off for (tāk ôf fôr) to start out in the direction of;
  to leave to go to a place.
  I will take off for camp on Tuesday. *idiom*

take out (tāk out) to remove from the inside of something.
  Take out a piece of paper from the drawer.
  v. **took out, taken out, taking out** tak•en out, tak•ing out

take over take o•ver (tāk ō′vər) to begin being in control of
  something; to become the new boss; to become the new owner.
  Mother will take over the job next week. *idiom*

take pictures take pic•tures (tāk pik′chərz) to use a camera
  to get snapshots; to make photographs.
  I will take pictures at the party. *idiom*

take pictures

take place (tāk plās) to happen; to occur.
  The party will take place on Saturday. *idiom*

tale (tāl) a story, usually not a true story.
  The teacher will tell us the tale about the logger. *n. pl.* **tales**

a	cat	i	sit	oi	oil	ch	chop		a in about
ā	ate	ī	lie	ou	out	ng	song		e in oven
ä	car	o	pot	u	cut	sh	she	ə =	i in pencil
e	set	ō	old	u̇	book	th	three		o in memory
ē	equal	ô	or	ü	blue	ŦH	there		u in circus
ėr	germ					zh	treasure		

talent tal·ent (tal´ənt) skill; ability.
  The painter has talent. *n. pl.* **talents** tal·ents

talk (tôk) **1.** to use words to say things; to say words.
  We can talk later. *v.* **talked, talked, talking** talk·ing
  2. a conversation; a speech; a discussion.
  We had a nice talk. *n. pl.* **talks**

tangle

talk about talk a·bout (tôk ə·bout´) to say things about a person
  or things; to discuss something.
  Let's talk about college.
  v. **talked about, talked about, talking about**
  talked a·bout, talk·ing a·bout

talk to (tôk tü) to say words to a person; to speak to a person.
  I will talk to the teacher. *v.* **talked to, talked to, talking to** talk·ing to

talk with (tôk wiŦH) to have a conversation with;
  to speak together with.
  We will talk with the other girls.
  v. **talked with, talked with, talking with** talk·ing with

tall (tôl) **1.** not short; longer in height than is usual.
  The boy who plays basketball is tall. *adj.*
  2. exaggerated; having details added that are probably not true.
  He can tell some tall tales. *adj.* **taller, tallest** tall·er, tall·est

tank

tame (tām) **1.** gentle; not wild.
  The lion is tame now. *adj.* **tamer, tamest** tam·er, tam·est
  2. to become gentle; to change from wild to gentle; to
  cause to become gentle.
  The man will tame the tiger also. *v.* **tamed, tamed, taming** tam·ing

tan (tan) **1.** to make animal skin into leather.
  The man will tan the cow skin. *v.* **tanned, tanned, tanning** tan·ning
  2. skin darkened by the sun.
  She has a beautiful brown tan. *n. pl.* **tans**

tangle tan·gle (tang´gəl) a small, tight knot of hair or string; a mess.
  Mother combed out a tangle from my hair. *n. pl.* **tangles** tan·gles

tank (tangk) a large metal container used to hold liquids,
  gases or air.
  The diver wore an air tank. *n. pl.* **tanks**

tanner tan·ner (tan´ər) a person who makes animal
  skins into leather.
  The tanner made soft leather from the lambskin. *n. pl.* **tanners** tan·ners

tape

tape (tāp) a strip of material that is sticky on one or both sides.
  I used tape to put the picture on the wall. *n. no pl.*

tapering ta·per·ing (tā⸍pər·ing) becoming smaller at the end; narrowing at the end.
The dog has a tapering tail; the rabbit does not. *adj.*

tarantula ta·ran·tu·la (tə·ran⸍chə·lə) a large poisonous spider.
The tarantula at the zoo was black.
n. pl. **tarantulas** *or* **tarantulae** ta·ran·tu·las *or* ta·ran·tu·lae

tarantula

target tar·get (tär⸍git) the thing a person tries to hit when shooting a gun or arrow; the spot that should be hit.
I shot the arrow into the center of the target. *n. pl.* **targets** tar·gets

Tarzan Tar·zan (tär⸍zan *or* tär⸍zən) a fictional character in books and movies who lives with apes in the jungles of Africa.
Tarzan is a hero. *n.*

task (task) an assigned job; a chore; work.
I have a task to do before I can go out and play. *n. pl.* **tasks**

target

tassel tas·sel (tas⸍əl) a bunch of small threads found at the top of an ear of corn.
The deer is eating the tassel. *n. pl.* **tassels** tas·sels

taste (tāst) **1.** to determine the flavor of food.
I want to taste that ice cream. *v.*
2. to have a certain flavor.
The nuts taste salty. *v.* **tasted, tasted, tasting** tast·ed, tast·ing
3. a flavor.
The candy has a strawberry taste. *n. no pl.*
4. the liking of one thing more than others; the things a person prefers.
Her taste in music is different from mine. *n. pl.* **tastes**
5. having to do with a flavor.
The candy is a taste treat. *adj.*

tassel

taste bud (tāst bud) a bump on the tongue that determines the flavor of food.
We have more than one taste bud in our mouths.

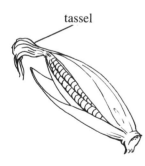

tasty tast·y (tā⸍stē) having lots of flavor; delicious; good tasting.
The cake is tasty. *adj.* **tastier, tastiest** tast·i·er, tast·i·est

taught (tôt) *v. pt. t., pt. part.* See **teach.**

a	cat	i	sit	oi	oil	ch	chop		a in about
ā	ate	ī	lie	ou	out	ng	song		e in oven
ä	car	o	pot	u	cut	sh	she	ə =	i in pencil
e	set	ō	old	u̇	book	th	three		o in memory
ē	equal	ô	or	ü	blue	ŦH	there		u in circus
ėr	germ					zh	treasure		

tax (taks) money people must pay to the government; money that the government uses to pay for the services that the government provides.
We pay tax on the money that we earn in our jobs. *n. pl.* **taxes** tax·es

tea (tē) **1.** the leaves of a certain bush, used to make a drink.
This tea is green, but that tea is black. *n. pl.* **teas**
2. a drink that is made from the leaves of a certain bush.
I had tea with my breakfast. *n.*
3. having to do with the drink or the leaves of a certain bush.
The tea bags are in the cabinet. *adj.*

tear

teach (tēch) to instruct; to help someone to learn; to direct the learning of someone; to give lessons.
Can you teach me how to ride a horse?
v. **taught, taught, teaching** teach·ing

teach ___ a lesson teach ___ a les·son (tēch ___ ə les´n) to prove a point; to show someone something about how to behave.
Because he broke the vase, he cannot have a cookie. That will teach him a lesson. *idiom*

teacher teach·er (tē´chər) a person who gives lessons; a person who helps someone to learn; a person who gives instructions.
My teacher taught me to paint. *n. pl.* **teachers** teach·ers

tear

teacup tea·cup (tē´kup) a small container that people use for drinking tea; a small cup.
I put the teacup on the table. *n. pl.* **teacups** tea·cups

team (tēm) a group of people who work together for the same goal; a group of people that play a game together against another group of people.
We have a good baseball team. *n. pl.* **teams**

teamster team·ster (tēm´stər) a person who carries things in a truck as a job; a person who drives a truck to earn money.
The truck driver is a teamster. *n. pl.* **teamsters** team·sters

tear[1] (ter *or* tar) to pull apart; to rip.
I will tear the paper into small pieces. *v.* **tore, torn, tearing** tear·ing

tear[2] (tir) a drop of liquid that comes from the eye.
She has a tear in her eye. *n. pl.* **tears**

tear down (ter doun) to take apart; to destroy.
We will tear down the sign now that the sale is over.
v. **tore down, torn down, tearing down** tear·ing down

tear off (ter ôf) to remove part of something by pulling hard; to rip part of a thing from the whole thing.
I will tear off the buttons on this old shirt.
v. **tore off, torn off, tearing off** tear·ing off

telephone pole

telephone

tear open   tear o·pen (ter ō′pən)   to pull apart so that something is not closed; to cause to come open by pulling.
I will tear open the bag of potato chips.
v. **tore open, torn open, tearing open** tear·ing o·pen

tears of joy   (tirz əv joi)   crying because one is happy; being so happy that tears fill the eyes.
He was so excited to see his mother that his eyes filled with tears of joy. *idiom*

tease   (tēz)   to play a joke on someone; to annoy someone; to bother with questions or requests.
She will tease you until you tell her what she wants to know.
v. **teased, teased, teasing** teas·ing

teeth   (tēth)   *n. pl.* See **tooth.**

telegram   tel·e·gram (tel′ə·gram)   a message sent by code over wires.
We sent our friends a telegram. *n. pl.* **telegrams** tel·e·grams

telegraph   tel·e·graph (tel′ə·graf)   **1.** a way of sending messages across wires by using a code.
I will use the telegraph to send Tom a message. *n. no pl.*
2. having to do with sending messages by code over wires.
The telegraph office is still open. *adj.*

telephone book

telephone   tel·e·phone (tel′ə·fōn)   **1.** a device that people use to talk to other people who are not in the same place; a phone.
I used the telephone to call the school. *n. pl.* **telephones** tel·e·phones
2. having to do with the tool that is used for calling people; having to do with a phone.
The telephone stand is in the corner. *adj.*

telephone book   tel·e·phone book (tel′ə·fōn bůk)   a book that lists the telephone numbers of the people in a city.
I found the number in the telephone book.

telephone pole   tel·e·phone pole (tel′ə·fōn pōl)   a tall wooden or metal pole that holds telephone wires above the ground.
There is a telephone pole on the corner.

telescope   tel·e·scope (tel′ə·skōp)   a device that a person looks through to see things that are far away; an instrument that makes things that are far away seem to be close.
The telescope made the moon look very big.
n. pl. **telescopes** tel·e·scopes

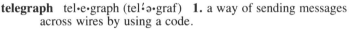
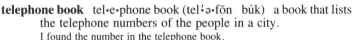
telescope

a	cat	i	sit	oi	oil	ch	chop		a in about
ā	ate	ī	lie	ou	out	ng	song		e in oven
ä	car	o	pot	u	cut	sh	she	ə =	i in pencil
e	set	ō	old	ů	book	th	three		o in memory
ē	equal	ô	or	ü	blue	ŦH	there		u in circus
ėr	germ					zh	treasure		

teletypewriter tel·e·type·writ·er (tel·ə·tīp′rī·tər) a device used by the deaf to type messages and send them over the telephone wires.
The deaf boy used the teletypewriter to talk to his grandfather.
n. pl. **teletypewriters** tel·e·type·writ·ers

television tel·e·vi·sion (tel′ə·vizh·ən) a device that brings pictures onto a screen; an instrument that lets people see pictures of things that are made in other places and sent through the air.
I watched a good program on the television last night.
n. pl. **televisions** tel·e·vi·sions

television

tell (tel) **1.** to give someone a message; to give information.
The book will tell us about the library. *v.*
2. to talk about a story; to relate a story or tale.
Will you tell me the story of Cinderella? *v.*
3. to find the difference in things; to discover a difference.
I can tell milk chocolate from dark chocolate.
v. **told, told, telling** tel·ling

tell ___ apart tell ___ a·part (tel ___ ə·pärt′) to know the difference between two things; to be able to distinguish one thing from another.
Can you tell the twins apart?
v. **told ___ apart, told ___ apart, telling ___ apart**
told ___ a·part, tell·ing ___ a·part

teller tell·er (tel′ər) **1.** a person who tells stories or tales.
My uncle is a wonderful teller of tales. *n.*
2. a person who works at a bank.
The teller gave me money for the check. *n. pl.* **tellers** tell·ers

teller

tell time (tel tīm) to look at a clock or a watch and give the time of day.
I learned to tell time when I was six years old. *idiom*

temperature tem·per·a·ture (tem′pər·ə·chər *or* tem′pər·ə·chür) the amount of heat or cold measured by a thermometer; the degree of heat or cold; how hot or cold it is.
The temperature is 62 degrees.
n. pl. **temperatures** tem·per·a·tures

temple tem·ple (tem′pəl) a church; a building in which religious ceremonies are held.
The people went to the temple to pray.
n. pl. **temples** tem·ples

temptation temp·ta·tion (temp·tā′shən) the feeling of wanting to do something that is wrong or that should not be done.
Candy is a temptation for people on a diet.
n. pl. **temptations** temp·ta·tions

tend (tend) to take care of something or someone.
I will tend the dog.
v. **tended, tended, tending** tend·ed, tend·ing

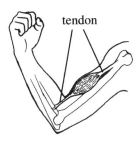
tendon

tendon ten·don (ten´dən) a band of tissue in a body that joins or
connects a muscle to a bone.
The horse pulled a tendon when he was running.
n. pl. **tendons** ten·dons

tension ten·sion (ten´shən) strain; a feeling of stress or pressure.
The tension in the school was high after the robbery. *n. no pl.*

tent (tent) a canvas shelter; a cloth building.
We slept in the tent. *n. pl.* **tents**

term (tèrm) the length of time a person works in an elected job;
an unchangeable amount of time.
The governor is elected to a term of two years. *n. pl.* **terms**

terminal ter·mi·nal (tèr´mə·nəl) **1.** a building or place where
people start and end a trip on a bus, train or plane.
I caught the bus at the terminal. *n. pl.* **terminals** ter·mi·nals
2. having to do with a place where people start and end trips.
We left the car in the terminal parking lot. *adj.*

tent

terrace ter·race (ter´is) a flat piece of land with sides that slope to
another piece of land.
The man planted the vines on the terrace of the mountain.
n. pl. **terraces** ter·rac·es

Terramycin Ter·ra·my·cin (ter·ə·mī´sn) a medicine that kills
bacteria that cause illnesses.
The doctor gave me Terramycin for my sore throat. *n. no pl.*

terrible ter·ri·ble (ter´ə·bəl) very bad; frightening; awful.
I had a terrible cold. *adj.*

terribly ter·ri·bly (ter´ə·blē) very much; to a great extent;
to a great degree.
The boy was terribly sad when his cat died. *adv.*

terraced hills

terrified ter·ri·fied (ter´ə·fīd) very afraid; scared;
filled with great fear.
The boy was terrified of the snake. *adj.*

a	cat	i	sit	oi	oil	ch	chop		a in about
ā	ate	ī	lie	ou	out	ng	song		e in oven
ä	car	o	pot	u	cut	sh	she	ə =	i in pencil
e	set	ō	old	u̇	book	th	three		o in memory
ē	equal	ô	or	ü	blue	ᵮH	there		u in circus
ėr	germ					zh	treasure		

terrify   ter·ri·fy (ter′ə·fī)   to make someone or something
   very afraid; to cause great fear.
   The snake will terrify the boy.
   v. **terrified, terrified, terrifying** ter·ri·fied, ter·ri·fy·ing

territory   ter·ri·to·ry (ter′ə·tôr·ē *or* ter′ə·tōr·ē)   an area; a region;
   an area of land or water that belongs to a government.
   Alaska was a territory of the United States before it became a state.
   n. pl. **territories** ter·ri·to·ries

test   (test)   a trial or examination; a group of questions to see if a
   person knows or can do something.
   I will put the new bicycle to a test. *n. pl.* **tests**

text   (tekst)   the words that are in a book, on a sign or in a magazine.
   The children looked at the pictures while the teacher read the text. *n. no pl.*

texture   tex·ture (teks′chər)   the look or feeling of a cloth or surface.
   The texture of silk is smooth. *n. pl.* **textures** tex·tures

Thailand   Thai·land (tī′land)   a country in Asia;
   its capital is Bangkok.
   Silk is made in Thailand. *n.*

than   (ᴛʜan *or* ᴛʜən)   compared with; in comparison with.
   My sister is taller than I am. *conj.*

thank   (thangk)   to say that one is pleased or that
   one appreciates something.
   I want to thank you for your help.
   v. **thanked, thanked, thanking** thank·ing

thankful   thank·ful (thangk′fəl)   pleased; full of appreciation
   and gratitude; feeling happy or relieved.
   I am thankful for your help. *adj.*

Thanksgiving   Thanks·giv·ing (thangks·giv′ing)   a holiday
   celebrated in November for the purpose of giving thanks for
   all the things or blessings that a person has.
   We will have turkey on Thanksgiving. *n.*

thank you note   (thangk yü nōt)   a letter sent to someone to thank
   them for a gift, a visit or a kind action.
   I sent my grandmother a thank you note for the sweater she sent me
   for my birthday.

thank you note

438

that   **1.** (ᴛʜat *or* ᴛʜət)   the thing about which a person is talking; the thing to which the speaker is pointing; a thing in the room but not close to the speaker.
I want some of that. *pron.*
That cupcake is the one I want. *adj.*
2. who; which.
The bicycle that I want is expensive. *relative pron.*
3. a word that begins a thought, wish or reason in a sentence.
I know that he will return. *conj.*

that'll   (ᴛʜat‘l)   that will.
I know that'll be a great gift for your mother. *contrac.*

that's   (ᴛʜats)   that is.
That's the boy who took the kite. *contrac.*

thaw   (thô)   to melt; to cause to melt.
The ice will thaw when it gets warm.
v. **thawed, thawed, thawing** thaw·ing

thaw

the   (ᴛʜə *or* ᴛʜi *or* ᴛʜē)   a certain thing or group of things; a certain person or group of people; a specific person or thing.
The boy is waving. *definite article*

theater   the·a·ter (thē‘ə·tər)   **1.** a building in which a movie is shown or a play is performed.
We went to the theater. *n. pl.* **theaters** the·a·ters
2. having to do with a building in which movies are shown or plays are performed.
The theater door is closed. *adj.*

theatre   the·a·tre (thē‘ə·tər)   British spelling of *theater.*
n. pl. **theatres** the·a·tres

theater

their   (ᴛʜer *or* ᴛʜar)   belonging to two or more people; belonging to them.
The family put their bicycles in their garage. *adj.*

them   (ᴛʜem *or* ᴛʜəm)   the people, things or animals about which a person is talking.
I saw them put the bicycles in the garage. *plural pron.*

themselves   them·selves (ᴛʜem·selvz′ *or* ᴛʜəm·selvz′)   these very same people, things or animals that one is talking about.
The boys hid themselves from the girls. *plural pron.*

a	cat	i	sit	oi	oil	ch	chop		a in about
ā	ate	ī	lie	ou	out	ng	song		e in oven
ä	car	o	pot	u	cut	sh	she	ə =	i in pencil
e	set	ō	old	u̇	book	th	three		o in memory
ē	equal	ô	or	ü	blue	ᴛʜ	there		u in circus
ėr	germ					zh	treasure		

then (ᴛHen) **1.** at that time.
It was difficult for the pioneers to travel because there
were no roads then. *adv.*
2. next in a line of things, instructions or events.
First she added the eggs, and then she added the milk. *adv.*

then and there (ᴛHen ənd ᴛHer) at that time and place;
immediately; without moving or waiting.
I decided then and there that I was not going with him. *adv.*

there (ᴛHer *or* ᴛHar *or* ᴛHər) **1.** in that place; at that location.
I went to the new shopping center. I found many nice things there. *adv.*
2. having to do with the existence of something.
There are many snakes in the forest. *pron.*

therefore there·fore (ᴛHer‹fôr *or* ᴛHar‹fôr) for that
reason; as a result.
1. I do not like to swim; therefore, I do not go to the pool. *conj.*
2. Bob lost his money and was therefore unable to go to the movies. *adv.*

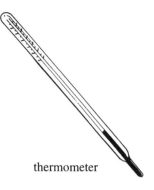

thermometer

there's (ᴛHerz *or* ᴛHarz) there is.
There's the boy who took the candy. *contrac.*

thermometer ther·mom·e·ter (thər·mom‹ə·tər) an instrument that
measures the temperature of the air or the body.
I put the thermometer in my mouth. *n. pl.* **thermometers** ther·mom·e·ters

thermos bottle ther·mos bot·tle (thėr‹məs bot‹l) a container that
keeps things at the same temperature as they were when placed
in the container; a container that keeps food hot or cold.
I took a thermos bottle filled with cold milk to the park.

thermostat ther·mo·stat (thėr‹mə·stat) the part of a heater or
cooler that controls the temperature.
If you turn the thermostat higher, the house will get warmer.
n. pl. **thermostats** ther·mo·stats

thermos bottle

these (ᴛHēz) the things, people or ideas about which a person is
talking; the things or people to which a person is pointing;
things that are close to the speaker.
1. These shoes are the ones that I want. *adj.*
2. I do not want these. *plural pron.* See **this** (1).

they (ᴛHā) the people about whom a person is talking.
Lisa and Tom are on vacation. They will be home next week. *plural pron.*

thick (thik) **1.** not thin; being very wide or deep.
That steak is very thick. *adj.*
2. being liquid but not pouring easily.
The maple syrup is thick.
adj. **thicker, thickest** thick·er, thick·est

thickly   thick·ly (thik′lē)   in a crowded manner; in a way that
has things close together.
The roses are thickly planted in the garden. *adv.*

thickness   thick·ness (thik′nis)   **1.** the distance between
two surfaces or layers.
The thickness of this wall is 18 inches. *n.*
2. the pouring state of a liquid.
Flour changes the thickness of the gravy. *n. pl.* **thicknesses** thick·ness·es

thief   (thēf)   a person who steals from other people;
a person who robs.
The thief broke into the house and took her television. *n. pl.* **thieves**

thief

thieves   (thēvz)   *n. pl.* See **thief.**

thigh   (thī)   the top part of a leg; the part of a leg between
the knee and the hip.
I hit my thigh on the chair. *n. pl.* **thighs**

thin   (thin)   **1.** not thick; not having much width; not fat.
The woman in the picture is thin. *adj.*
2. having little oxygen.
The air at the top of a high mountain is thin.
adj. **thinner, thinnest** thin·ner, thin·nest

thing   (thing)   an object; what a person can touch,
taste, smell, see, say or hear.
A chair is a thing. *n. pl.* **things**

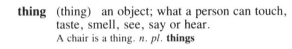

thigh

things   (thingz)   **1.** what a person owns.
I put all of my things in the closet. *plural n.*
2. life; a way of living.
Things change when a person gets older. *plural n.*
3. ideas; thoughts.
Write things down when you think of them. *plural n.*

think   (thingk)   to use the brain; to use the mind; to have ideas.
If you think hard, you can remember where you left your shoes.
v. **thought, thought, thinking** think·ing

thinker   think·er (thing′kər)   a person who uses his or her brain;
a person who invents or has ideas.
He solved the problem because he is a good thinker.
n. pl. **thinkers** think·ers

a	cat	**i**	sit	**oi**	oil	**ch**	chop	⎧ a in about
ā	ate	**ī**	lie	**ou**	out	**ng**	song	⎪ e in oven
ä	car	**o**	pot	**u**	cut	**sh**	she	ə = ⎨ i in pencil
e	set	**ō**	old	**u̇**	book	**th**	three	⎪ o in memory
ē	equal	**ô**	or	**ü**	blue	**TH**	there	⎩ u in circus
ėr	germ					**zh**	treasure	

think of (thingk əv) **1.** to remember; to bring to mind.
Can you think of her name? *v.*
2. to invent; to create; to have a new idea.
Lisa will think of a plan.
v. **thought of, thought of, thinking of** think·ing of

thinner thin·ner (thin′ər) *comp. adj.* See **thin.**

third (thėrd) being number three; coming after second and before
fourth; being next after second.
He was the third person to call about the car. *adj.*

thirsty thirst·y (thėr′stē) wanting a liquid to drink; needing water.
I am hot and thirsty. *adj.* **thirstier, thirstiest** thirst·i·er, thirst·i·est

this (ᴛʜis) the thing about which a person is talking; the
thing to which the speaker is pointing; a thing that
is close to the speaker.
1. This is the picture that I want. *pron. pl.* **these**
2. This picture is beautiful. *adj.*

this time (ᴛʜis tīm) on this occasion; at this event;
at this happening.
We will sing the song again; this time please do it right. *adv.*

this way (ᴛʜis wā) in this direction; in the direction
that something or someone is pointing.
I will walk this way, and you go that way. *adv.*

thong (thông *or* thong) a narrow strip of leather.
My sandal has a thong that goes between my large toe and the next toe.
n. pl. **thongs**

thong

thorax tho·rax (thôr′aks *or* thōr′aks) the middle part
of an insect body.
The thorax of the mosquito is the second part of its body.
n. pl. **thoraxes** *or* **thoraces** tho·rax·es *or* tho·ra·ces

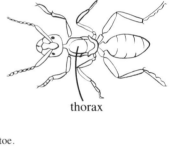
thorax

thorn (thôrn) a sharp, pointed growth on a plant; a sticker.
There is a thorn on the rose stem. *n. pl.* **thorns**

thorny thorn·y (thôr′nē) full of stickers; having
many sharp, pointed growths.
The rosebush is thorny. *adj.* **thornier, thorniest** thorn·i·er, thorn·i·est

thorn

Thoroughbred Thor·ough·bred (thėr′ō·bred) a breed or kind
of racehorse that started from the breeding of an English horse
with an Arabian horse.
The racehorse is a Thoroughbred. *n. pl.* **Thoroughbreds** Thor·ough·breds

those (ᴛʜōz) the things, people or ideas about which a person is
talking; the things or people to which a person is pointing;
things that are in the room but that are not close to the speaker.
1. Those are the shoes that I want. *plural pron.* See **that** (1).
2. Those shoes are very handsome. *adj.*

442

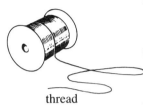

thread

thought (thôt) **1.** *v. pt. t., pt. part.* See **think.**
2. an idea; the thing about which a person thinks.
My thought was that we not go tonight. *n. pl.* **thoughts**

thoughtful thought·ful (thôt'fəl) being sensitive to
other people; thinking of other people.
The woman wanted to help me. She is a very thoughtful person. *adj.*

thread (thred) thin string.
I need red thread to sew the red dress.
n. pl. **threads** *or* **thread**

three-cornered three-cor·nered (thrē-kôr'nərd)
having three corners.
We made a three-cornered hat from a piece of newspaper. *adj.*

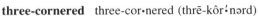

throat

three-story three-sto·ry (thrē-stôr'ē) having three
levels or floors.
We have a three-story house. *adj.*

threw (thrü) *v. pt. t.* See **throw.**

thrill (thril) **1.** to cause someone to be excited or happy.
The idea of going camping will thrill Mother.
v. **thrilled, thrilled, thrilling** thrill·ing
2. a shiver of excitement; an excited feeling.
It was a thrill to ride the roller coaster. *n. pl.* **thrills**

throat (thrōt) **1.** the passageway between the mouth and
the lungs; the front part of the neck.
I got a piece of candy caught in my throat. *n.*
2. the part of a horse between the head and the neck.
The fly landed on the horse's throat. *n. pl.* **throats**

throatlatch throat·latch (thrōt'lach) the strip of leather
on a bridle that goes under the throat of the horse.
The throatlatch tore.
n. pl. **throatlatches** throat·latch·es

throne

throne (thrōn) the chair of a king or a queen.
The king sits on the throne.
n. pl. **thrones**

a	cat	**i**	sit	**oi**	oil	**ch**	chop
ā	ate	**ī**	lie	**ou**	out	**ng**	song
ä	car	**o**	pot	**u**	cut	**sh**	she
e	set	**ō**	old	**ů**	book	**th**	three
ē	equal	**ô**	or	**ü**	blue	**ŦH**	there
ėr	germ					**zh**	treasure

ə = {
a in about
e in oven
i in pencil
o in memory
u in circus
}

through (thrü) **1.** in and out of the center of.
> The dog jumped through the hoop. *prep.*

2. by means of; by way of.
> He got well through taking medicine. *prep.*

3. from one side to the other of; over.
> The wagons drove through the mountains. *prep.*

4. across; from one end to the other of.
> The parade will march through the city. *prep.*

5. in one side and out the other of.
> I can see through the curtain. *prep.*

6. during the full time of.
> He slept through the movie. *prep.*

throughout through·out (thrü·out′) **1.** from the beginning
to the end of; during the whole of.
> He was frightened throughout the whole movie. *prep.*

2. over the whole area or location of.
> We searched throughout the house for her purse. *prep.*

throw

throw (thrō) to toss into the air; to send through the air.
> I will throw you the ball. *v.* **threw, thrown, throwing** throw·ing

throw away throw a·way (thrō ə·wā′) to get rid of;
to discard; to put into the garbage.
> I will throw away this old shirt.
> *v.* **threw away, thrown away, throwing away**
> threw a·way, throw·ing a·way

throwing throw·ing (thrō‿ing) tossing; sending through the air.
> Throwing a baseball takes a lot of strength. *gerund* See **throw.**

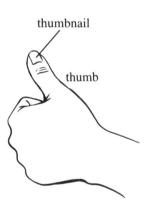

thumbnail

thumb

thud (thud) a dull sound made when something or someone
hits the ground; the sound of something hitting something else.
> The thud of the ball on the wall made me angry. *n. pl.* **thuds**

thumb (thum) the short, thick finger on the hand;
the finger that is not with the other fingers on the hand.
> I put my thumb into my glove. *n. pl.* **thumbs**

thumbnail thumb·nail (thum‿nāl) the hard covering on the
tip of the thumb.
> I broke my thumbnail by pulling on the tack.
> *n. pl.* **thumbnails** thumb·nails

thump (thump) **1.** the sound when something is pounded;
a pounding sound.
> The thump of the hammer on the wood awoke me. *n. pl.* **thumps**

2. to pound something hard.
> I will thump the nail with the hammer. *v.*

3. to make a noise or sound by pounding.
> The machine will thump all night and keep me awake.
> *v.* **thumped, thumped, thumping** thump·ing

thunder lizard
(brontosaurus)

thunder thun·der (thun⸳dər) the sound that is made during a storm; the sound that goes with lightning.
The thunder was very loud. *n. no pl.*

thunderclap thun·der·clap (thun⸳dər·klap) a single sound of thunder.
First I saw the lightning, and then I heard the thunderclap.
n. pl. **thunderclaps** thun·der·claps

thunder lizard thun·der liz·ard (thun⸳dər liz⸳ərd) a kind of dinosaur that made loud noises when it walked because it was so big and heavy.
The thunder lizard was very large.

thunderstorm thun·der·storm (thun⸳dər·stôrm) a rainstorm that has lightning and thunder with it.
The thunderstorm started just after sundown.
n. pl. **thunderstorms** thun·der·storms

ticket tick·et (tik⸳it) **1.** a piece of paper that a person buys to go into a show, movie or game.
I need to buy a ticket. *n.*
2. a piece of paper that a police officer gives to a person who has broken the law.
The speeder got a ticket from the police officer. *n. pl.* **tickets** tick·ets

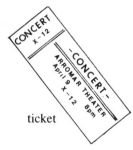

ticket

ticket window tick·et win·dow (tik⸳it win⸳dō) the place at a theater or arena where people can buy tickets.
I will go to the ticket window and buy our tickets to the game.

ticking tick·ing (tik⸳ing) the sound of a clock counting off the seconds of time; the noise of a clock marking the passing of seconds of time.
The ticking of the clock is soothing to hear. *gerund*

tide (tīd) the movement of the ocean; the rise and fall of the water level of the ocean on the shore.
The tide is going out to the ocean. *n. pl.* **tides**

tidy ti·dy (tī⸳dē) neat; clean; everything put in its place.
The room is tidy. *adj.* **tidier, tidiest** tid·i·er, tid·i·est

tidy up ti·dy up (tī⸳dē up) to clean up; to straighten things; to put things in their right places.
I will tidy up the television room.
v. **tidied up, tidied up, tidying up** ti·died up, ti·dy·ing up

a	cat	**i**	sit	**oi**	oil	**ch**	chop		a in about
ā	ate	**ī**	lie	**ou**	out	**ng**	song		e in oven
ä	car	**o**	pot	**u**	cut	**sh**	she	ə =	i in pencil
e	set	**ō**	old	**u̇**	book	**th**	three		o in memory
ē	equal	**ô**	or	**ü**	blue	**ŦH**	there		u in circus
ėr	germ					**zh**	treasure		

tie (tī) to put together with string, rope or ribbon; to fasten together string, rope or ribbon; to make a knot or bow.
I will tie a string around the box. *v.* **tied, tied, tying** ty·ing

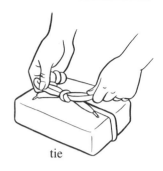
tie

tie-dye (tī'dī) to color cloth that has knotted areas, which will not get the color.
The teacher taught the class how to tie-dye.
v. **tie-dyed, tie-dyed, tie-dyeing** tie-dye·ing

tie-dyeing tie-dye·ing (tī'dī·ing) a way of coloring cloth in which part of the cloth is tied together.
Our class learned tie-dyeing. *n. no pl.*

tiger ti·ger (tī'gər) a large cat with yellow fur and black stripes.
You can find a tiger in Asia. *n. pl.* **tigers** ti·gers

tight (tīt) **1.** pulled together so that there is no room for movement; put together firmly; secure from movement.
He tied the rope so that it was tight. *adj.*
2. stretched; strained.
The boy's legs were tight from running.
adj. **tighter, tightest** tight·er, tight·est

tiger

tile (tīl) a flat piece of ceramic or baked clay that is used to cover surfaces for protection.
I broke a floor tile in the kitchen. *n. pl.* **tiles**

till (til) up to a certain time; until.
I will wait till Dad comes home before going to bed. *conj.*

timberline tim·ber·line (tim'bər·līn) the place on a mountain where trees stop growing because of the extremely cold weather above.
The snow line often starts at the timberline of a mountain.
n. pl. **timberlines** tim·ber·lines

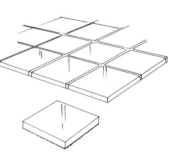

time (tīm) **1.** all the minutes, hours and days of life.
It takes time to build a house. *n. no pl.*
2. the specific minute and hour of the day.
The time is 9:30. *n. no pl.*
3. a specific minute, hour, day or period of time.
Many people dine during that time. *n. no pl.*
4. an amount of time.
The runner's time was 20 seconds. *n. no pl.*
5. an instance; an event; an occurrence.
We had fun the time that we went to that restaurant. *n. pl.* **times**
6. to measure the amount of time that a person does something.
I will time the speed at which you run.
v. **timed, timed, timing** tim·ing

tile

time flies (tīm flīz) the feeling that the minutes and the hours of the day are going quickly.
Time flies when you are having fun. *idiom*

timer

timer tim·er (tī′mər) a clock that measures the amount of time that has passed; a device that marks the amount of time that it takes to do something.
We started the timer when the runner began to run. *n. pl.* **timers** tim·ers

times (tīmz) multiplied by.
Six times three is eighteen. *prep.*

time stands still (tīm standz stil) the feeling that the minutes and the hours of a day are passing slowly.
When you are waiting for something to happen, time stands still. *idiom*

tin (tin) **1.** a soft, silver-colored metal.
This old can is made of tin. *n. no pl.*
2. made of a soft, silver-colored metal.
We put a tin roof on the tool shed. *adj.*

tinfoil tin·foil (tin′foil) a soft, silver-colored metal paper that is used to wrap food.
I took the tinfoil off of the food before I ate. *n. no pl.*

tiniest ti·ni·est (tī′nē·əst) *superl. adj.* See **tiny.**

tinker tink·er (ting′kər) to try to fix or repair something when you do not know how to fix it; to play at repairing something.
I want to tinker with the old car.
v. **tinkered, tinkered, tinkering** tink·ered, tink·er·ing

tin soldier

tinkle tin·kle (ting′kəl) **1.** a soft short ringing sound.
I can hear the tinkle of the bell. *n. pl.* **tinkles** tin·kles
2. to make a soft short ringing sound.
The bell will tinkle when the door opens.
v. **tinkled, tinkled, tinkling** tin·kled, tin·kling

tin soldier tin sol·dier (tin sōl′jər) a toy soldier that is made of tin.
I played with the tin soldier.

tiny ti·ny (tī′nē) very small.
The baby's fingers are tiny. *adj.* **tinier, tiniest** ti·ni·er, ti·ni·est

tip (tip) **1.** the end of a thing; the pointed end of something; a point.
We broke the tip of the pencil. *n. pl.* **tips**
2. to cause something to spill; to spill something; to knock something over.
Please do not tip the table.
v. **tipped, tipped, tipping** tip·ping

tip

a	cat	i	sit	oi	oil	ch	chop		a in about
ā	ate	ī	lie	ou	out	ng	song		e in oven
ä	car	o	pot	u	cut	sh	she	ə =	i in pencil
e	set	ō	old	u̇	book	th	three		o in memory
ē	equal	ô	or	ü	blue	ᵀH	there		u in circus
ėr	germ					zh	treasure		

tip over   tip o·ver (tip ō'vər)   to cause something to fall on its side or upside down.
Please do not tip over the vase.
v. **tipped over, tipped over, tipping over** tipped o·ver, tip·ping o·ver

tiptoe   tip·toe (tip'tō)   to walk quietly with the heels raised.
I will tiptoe into her room and get the book.
v. **tiptoed, tiptoed, tiptoeing** tip·toed, tip·toe·ing

tire   (tīr)   a rubber wheel.
I have a flat tire on my bicycle. *n. pl.* **tires**

tired   (tīrd)   being without energy; being sleepy; being exhausted from work or play.
I am so tired that I am going to bed early. *adj.*

tiredly   tired·ly (tīrd'lē)   in a sleepy, exhausted way; without energy.
The sick man walked tiredly to his bed. *adv.*

Titanic   Ti·tan·ic (tī·tan'ik)   a large ocean liner (cruise ship) that hit an iceberg and sank to the bottom of the ocean.
The Titanic was a very large, new ocean liner. *n.*

title   ti·tle (tī'tl)   the name of a book, play, television program or movie.
The title of my book is "Games." *n. pl.* **titles** ti·tles

to   (tü *or* tù *or* tə)   **1.** move toward; in the direction of.
I will go to the store. *prep.*
2. into; toward becoming.
The caterpillar will change to a butterfly. *prep.*
3. with; along with.
I talked to the teacher. *prep.*
4. until reaching the amount or limit of.
The boy grew to six feet. *prep.*
5. on; against.
The tape will stick to the picture. *prep.*
6. a word used to show the infinitive form of a verb (action word), for example, "to work," "to play."
I want to go with you.

toast   (tōst)   bread that has been browned by heating it; a piece of heated bread that is often eaten with breakfast.
I put peanut butter on my toast. *n. no pl.*

tobacco   to·bac·co (tə·bak'ō)   **1.** a plant whose leaves are used to make cigarettes and cigars.
Good tobacco makes good cigars.
n. pl. **tobaccos** *or* **tobaccoes** to·bac·cos *or* to·bac·coes
2. having to do with the leaves of a plant used in making cigarettes and cigars.
The tobacco jar smells sweet. *adj.*

tiptoe

toast

tobacco

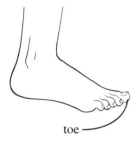

toe

today to·day (tə·dā′) **1.** during this day.
I want to go to the movie today. *adv.*
2. at this time in history.
Today every family has a car, yet only twenty years ago
that was not true. *adv.*
3. this present day; not yesterday or tomorrow.
Today is my birthday. *n. pl.* **todays** to·days

toe (tō) any one of the five parts at the end of the foot.
I hit my big toe on the table. *n. pl.* **toes**

toffee tof·fee (tô′fē *or* tof′ē) a kind of soft candy that is
difficult to chew; taffy.
I like chocolate toffee. *n. no pl.*

together to·geth·er (tə·geᴛʜ′ər) with someone or
something; not alone.
We will go to school together. *adv.*

toilet paper toi·let pa·per (toi′lit pā′pər) soft paper on a roll that
a person uses to clean the body after using the toilet.
The baby pulled the toilet paper around the bathroom.

toilet paper

told (tōld) *v. pt. t., pt. part.* See **tell.**

tomato to·ma·to (tə·mā′tō *or* tə·mä′tō) a red or yellow
fruit with seeds that is grown in a vegetable garden.
I put a tomato on my salad.
n. pl. **tomatoes** to·ma·toes

tombstone tomb·stone (tüm′stōn) a stone or marker that is
put on top of a person's grave.
The tombstone gave the day of birth and the day of death
of my grandfather.
n. pl. **tombstones** tomb·stones

tombstone

tomorrow to·mor·row (tə·môr′ō *or* tə·mor′ō) **1.** during
the day that comes after today.
I will see you tomorrow. *adv.*
2. the day that comes after today.
Tomorrow is a holiday.
n. pl. **tomorrows** to·mor·rows

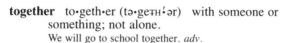

a	cat	**i**	sit	**oi**	oil	**ch**	chop	
ā	ate	**ī**	lie	**ou**	out	**ng**	song	
ä	car	**o**	pot	**u**	cut	**sh**	she	ə = { a in about
e	set	**ō**	old	**u̇**	book	**th**	three	e in oven
ē	equal	**ô**	or	**ü**	blue	**ᴛʜ**	there	i in pencil
ėr	germ					**zh**	treasure	o in memory
								u in circus

ton (tun) 2,000 pounds; a measure of weight that
equals 2,000 pounds.
That car weighs more than a ton. *n. pl.* **tons**

tongue (tung) the muscle on the floor of the mouth that
helps people talk and eat.
The taste buds are on the tongue. *n. pl.* **tongues**

tonight to·night (tə·nīt′) **1.** during the evening of this day;
on this night.
We are having chicken for dinner tonight. *adv.*
2. this evening; this night.
I will remember tonight forever. *n. pl.* **tonights** to·nights

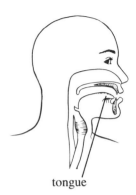

tongue

too (tü) **1.** also.
We are having potatoes too. *adv.*
2. more than enough; to a high degree.
There are too many people on this swing. *adv.*

too bad (tü bad) a response that means the speaker has no
feelings of sadness or pity about something.
Joe fell off his bike. Too bad! *idiom*

took (tük) *v. pt. t.* See **take.**

took pictures (tük pik′chərz) *v. pt. t.* See **take pictures.**

tooth

tool (tül) something that is used to make work easier;
something that a person uses to do work.
A hammer is a tool. *n. pl.* **tools**

too late (tü lāt) past the time that was agreed upon;
past the deadline.
It is too late to catch that bus. It has already left. *idiom*

tooth (tüth) one of the hard white things in the mouth
that are used for biting and eating.
I broke a tooth on the toffee. *n. pl.* **teeth**

toothbrush

toothbrush tooth·brush (tüth′brush) a tool that people use
to clean their teeth.
I keep my toothbrush near the bathroom sink.
n. pl. **toothbrushes** tooth·brush·es

toothed (tütht *or* tüŦHd) having teeth.
There are five kinds of toothed whales. *adj.*

toothpaste tooth·paste (tüth′pāst) a substance that is
put on a toothbrush and used to clean the teeth.
Our toothpaste tastes like mint.
n. pl. **toothpastes** tooth·pastes

toothpaste

top (top) the highest point; the part that is above the other parts; not the bottom.
I climbed to the top of the hill. *n. pl.* **tops**

topic top·ic (top′ik) the main idea of a book, movie, story or conversation; the subject about which a person is talking.
The topic of the man's speech was loving your neighbor.
n. pl. **topics** top·ics

top speed (top spēd) the fastest of many fast speeds; the fastest speed possible.
The racer won because his car had the top speed.

tore (tôr *or* tōr) *v. pt. t.* See **tear** (¹).

torn (tôrn *or* tōrn) **1.** having a rip or a tear; having a hole.
Her torn dress was mended by the seamstress. *adj.*
2. *v. pt. part.* See **tear** (¹).

tornado tor·na·do (tôr·nā′dō) a windstorm with a funnel cloud that moves in a circle and destroys things in its path.
The tornado wrecked the old barn.
n. pl. **tornadoes** *or* **tornados** tor·na·does *or* tor·na·dos

tornado warning tor·na·do warn·ing (tôr·nā′dō wôr′ning)
an advance announcement that a tornado is coming.
The radio gave the people in town a tornado warning.

tornado watch tor·na·do watch (tôr·nā′dō wôch)
an announcement that a tornado may be coming.
There was a tornado watch last night, but we did not have a tornado.

tornado

Toronto To·ron·to (tə·ron′tō) a large city in the country of Canada.
Toronto is on a large lake. *n.*

toss (tôs *or* tos) to throw in the air.
I will toss you the ball. *v.* **tossed, tossed, tossing** toss·ing

toss ___ about toss ___ a·bout (tôs ___ ə·bout′) to throw something around; to throw something from one place to another; to cause something to move from place to place.
The strong wind will toss the ship about.
v. **tossed ___ about, tossed___ about, tossing ___ about**
tossed ___ a·bout, toss·ing ___ a·bout

totally to·tal·ly (tō′tl·ē) fully; completely; entirely.
She was totally surprised by the party. *adv.*

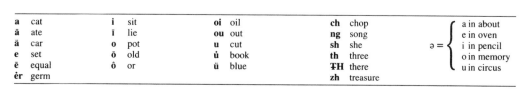

a	cat	i	sit	oi	oil	ch	chop		a in about
ā	ate	ī	lie	ou	out	ng	song		e in oven
ä	car	o	pot	u	cut	sh	she	ə =	i in pencil
e	set	ō	old	u̇	book	th	three		o in memory
ē	equal	ô	or	ü	blue	ȾH	there		u in circus
ėr	germ					zh	treasure		

totem pole   to·tem pole (tō′təm pōl) a wooden pole that has pictures and faces carved into it; a pole carved by Indians.
The totem pole stands in front of the chief's house.

touch   (tuch) **1.** to feel with the hand; to put a hand on something.
May I touch the cat? *v.*
2. to come into contact with; to meet.
We will walk so close together that your arm will touch mine.
v. **touched, touched, touching** touch·ing
3. a light pat; the act of putting the hand on something.
Her touch makes me feel safe. *n. pl.* **touches** touch·es
4. the sense of feeling or contacting the skin with something; the ability to feel the differences in textures.
Her sense of touch is very good. She can tell what is in the bag by feeling it. *n. no pl.*

totem pole

tough   (tuf) strong; able to be twisted but hard to tear.
Meat is tough and will not tear easily.
adj. **tougher, toughest** tough·er, tough·est

tour   (tùr) a journey; a trip that returns to the starting place.
My parents took me on a tour of America. *n. pl.* **tours**

tourist   tour·ist (tùr′ist) a person who is traveling to see a different place; a person who is on vacation in a new place.
The tourist took pictures of the city's museum.
n. pl. **tourists** tour·ists

tow   (tō) to pull something behind; to move something by pulling on it.
I will tow the wagon with my bicycle.
v. **towed, towed, towing** tow·ing

toward   to·ward (tôrd *or* tōrd *or* tə·wôrd′) in the direction of.
We are moving toward the right. *prep.*

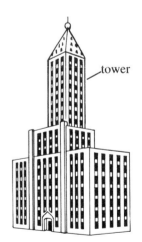

tower

towel   tow·el (tou′əl) a cloth that is used to dry water off things; a piece of soft paper that is used for drying things.
I dried my hands on the hand towel. *n. pl.* **towels** tow·els

tower   tow·er (tou′ər) a tall, narrow building or structure that is sometimes part of another building.
We walked to the top of the church's bell tower.
n. pl. **towers** tow·ers

town (toun) **1.** houses and buildings together in one area; a small city.
We moved from the farm into town. *n. pl.* **towns**
2. the shopping area of a city.
I am going to town to buy some shoes. *n. no pl.*
3. having to do with a small city.
The town library is on the main street. *adj.*

townspeople towns·peo·ple (tounz¦pē·pəl) the people who live in a certain town.
The townspeople work together to keep the streets pretty and clean. *plural n.*

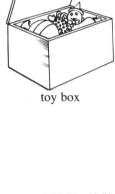

toy (toi) something that a child uses for play; a plaything.
A doll is a toy. *n. pl.* **toys**

toy box (toi boks) a place where toys are kept; a container for holding playthings.
I put the blocks in the toy box.

toy box

toymaker toy·mak·er (toi¦mā·kər) a person who builds things that children play with; a person who makes toys.
The toymaker made me a wooden puppet.
n. pl. **toymakers** toy·mak·ers

toymaking (toi¦mā·king) the making of children's playthings.
Toymaking is always fun. *gerund*

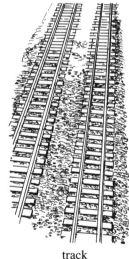

trace (trās) to draw a line around a pattern; to draw by using a pattern; to draw a line around something.
I will trace this picture onto another piece of paper.
v. **traced, traced, tracing** trac·ing

track (trak) **1.** the steel rails on which a train moves.
The man hit his toe on the track. *n.*
2. a road on which cars race; a racecourse.
The cars will race around the track. *n.*
3. a path around a sports field on which people walk or run.
The coach had the team run around the track. *n. pl.* **tracks**
4. having to do with a racecourse.
The track timer started the race. *adj.*
5. to hunt something or someone; to follow the footprints of something or someone.
We will track the deer.
v. **tracked, tracked, tracking** track·ing

track

a	cat	i	sit	oi	oil	ch	chop		a in about
ā	ate	ī	lie	ou	out	ng	song		e in oven
ä	car	o	pot	u	cut	sh	she	ə =	i in pencil
e	set	ō	old	u̇	book	th	three		o in memory
ē	equal	ô	or	ü	blue	ŦH	there		u in circus
ėr	germ					zh	treasure		

tractor trac·tor (trak'tər) a machine that farmers use to pull plows, wagons or other farm equipment.
I will learn to drive the tractor on Grandfather's farm.
n. pl. **tractors** trac·tors

trade (trād) **1.** to give one thing for another; to exchange things.
We will trade bicycles for today. You will ride mine, and I will ride yours.
v. **traded, traded, trading** trad·ed, trad·ing
2. the buying and selling of items.
Wheat is one of the items of trade in the United States. *n. pl.* **trades**

tractor

trader trad·er (trā'dər) a person who buys and sells items or who trades items.
The trader traded the trapper's pelts for flour and salt.
n. pl. **traders** trad·ers

trading post trad·ing post (trā'ding pōst) a store where pioneers could buy and sell or trade items.
The trader worked in the trading post.

tradition tra·di·tion (trə·dish'ən) a special action or habit of a country or a family; an activity that is always done to celebrate a special occasion; a custom.
Having lamb for Easter is a family tradition.
n. pl. **traditions** tra·di·tions

traditional tra·di·tion·al (trə·dish'ə·nəl) following a certain custom or tradition.
An early meal is traditional in our family. *adj.*

traffic traf·fic (traf'ik) **1.** the movement of people and vehicles on the street.
The traffic is busy in the afternoon. *n. no pl.*
2. having to do with the movement of people and vehicles on the streets.
The traffic light will turn green in a short time. *adj.*

trail (trāl) a marked path through woods, fields or mountains; a path.
The trail goes to the top of the mountain. *n. pl.* **trails**

trailer trail·er (trā'lər) a vehicle pulled by a car or truck that people use to carry things from one place to another.
We put the horse into the trailer and took him to the race track.
n. pl. **trailers** trail·ers

trailer

454

train

train (trān) **1.** a row of railroad cars that move together on railroad tracks; a locomotive.
The train stopped in the middle of the town. *n.*
2. the part of a dress that hangs down behind and drags on the ground.
The little girl carried the bride's train. *n. pl.* **trains**
3. having to do with a row of cars that move together on tracks.
I played with the toy train set. *adj.*
4. to practice a sport or a game.
The football team will train in the stadium. *v.*
5. to teach a person or an animal to do something.
We will train the dog to bring in the newspaper.
v. **trained, trained, training** train·ing

transfer[1] trans·fer (tran·sfėr′ *or* tran·′sfėr) to change from one vehicle to another; to change from one place or thing to another.
I will transfer to another school next year.
v. **transferred, transferred, transferring** trans·ferred, trans·fer·ring

transfer[2] trans·fer (tran·′sfėr) a piece of paper that gives permission to change to another bus or train.
I gave the bus driver my transfer. *n. pl.* **transfers** trans·fers

trap (trap) **1.** a device that people use to catch animals.
The man set a trap to catch a bear. *n. pl.* **traps**
2. to catch animals in a device that holds the animals in one place.
He wants to trap a black bear. *v.* **trapped, trapped, trapping** trap·ping

trapper trap·per (trap·′ər) a person who catches animals in traps.
The trapper sold the fur of the animals to the trader.
n. pl. **trappers** trap·pers

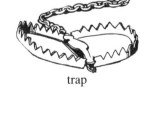

trap

travel trav·el (trav·′əl) to go to different places; to go from one place to another.
We will travel to England next year.
v. **traveled** *or* **travelled, traveled** *or* **travelled, traveling** *or* **travelling** trav·eled *or* trav·elled, trav·el·ing *or* trav·el·ling

traveler trav·el·er (trav·′ə·lər *or* trav·′lər) a person who goes to different places.
I am a happy traveler. *n. pl.* **travelers** trav·el·ers

travels trav·els (trav·′əlz) the action of going from one place to another.
His travels taught him new things in new places. *plural n.*

a	cat	i	sit	oi	oil	ch	chop		a in about
ā	ate	ī	lie	ou	out	ng	song		e in oven
ä	car	o	pot	u	cut	sh	she	ə =	i in pencil
e	set	ō	old	u̇	book	th	three		o in memory
ē	equal	ô	or	ü	blue	ŦH	there		u in circus
ėr	germ					zh	treasure		

tray (trā) a flat board with a low rim used to carry dishes or food.
 The waiter brought the tray of desserts to our table. *n. pl.* **trays**

treasure treas·ure (trezh′ər *or* trā′zhər) **1.** money and
 other valuable things that are stored away.
 The diver was looking for treasure. *n. pl.* **treasures** treas·ures
 2. having to do with money and other valuable things.
 The treasure chest was empty. *adj.*

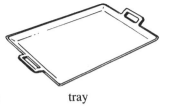

tray

treasury treas·ur·y (trezh′ər·ē *or* trā′zhər·ē) having to do with
 the money of a government.
 The treasury department gets money from our taxes to operate
 government services. *adj.*

treat (trēt) **1.** something special; a special food or snack.
 I am permitted one treat a day. *n. pl.* **treats**
 2. to deal with someone or something; to act in a certain way.
 We treat our friends as family. *v.*
 3. to give medicine or to give medical help.
 The doctor will treat the patient.
 v. **treated, treated, treating** treat·ed, treat·ing

treaty trea·ty (trē′tē) an agreement between two countries or
 two groups of people.
 The United States signed a treaty with the Indians. *n. pl.* **treaties** trea·ties

tree (trē) **1.** a large plant with a woody base and many
 branches and leaves.
 We planted an apple tree. *n. pl.* **trees**
 2. having to do with a large plant with branches and leaves.
 We built a tree house in our backyard. *adj.*

tree

tremendous tre·men·dous (tri·men′dəs) wonderful;
 amazing; great.
 The trip to Hawaii was tremendous. *adj.*

tremendously tre·men·dous·ly (tri·men′dəs·lē) in a
 wonderful way.
 We enjoyed the trip tremendously. *adv.*

triangle tri·an·gle (trī′ang·gəl) a shape with three straight sides.
 I folded the scarf into a triangle. *n. pl.* **triangles** tri·an·gles

triangular tri·an·gu·lar (trī·ang′gyə·lər) having three sides;
 shaped like a triangle.
 The triangular flag has three points. *adj.*

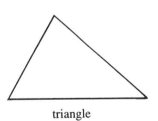

triangle

tribe (trīb) a group of people who share the same
 customs and ancestors.
 The Indian tribe still lives on the reservation. *n. pl.* **tribes**

trichinosis trich·i·no·sis (trik·ə·nō′sis) a disease that is caused by
 eating meat that is not cooked long enough.
 Trichinosis is a kind of food poisoning. *n. no pl.*

trip

troll

tropical fish

trick (trik) **1.** to play a joke on someone; to fool
or confuse someone.
Let's trick him by hiding. *v.* **tricked, tricked, tricking** trick·ing
2. a joke; a stunt.
We played a trick on Lisa. *n.*
3. a magical action; a skilled action.
The dog is learning to do a new trick. *n. pl.* **tricks**

tricky trick·y (trik′ē) able to fool or confuse people;
full of tricks or jokes.
The boy is tricky. I never know what he will do.
adj. **trickier, trickiest** trick·i·er, trick·i·est

tried (trīd) *v. pt. t., pt. part.* See **try.**

trip (trip) **1.** a traveling vacation; a journey from
one place to another.
We are taking a trip to Europe next year. *n. pl.* **trips**
2. to fall over something; to stumble.
Please pick up your toys or someone will trip over them.
v. **tripped, tripped, tripping** trip·ping

troll (trōl) an imaginary character that is a short man with a beard.
The troll in the story was very mean. *n. pl.* **trolls**

tropical trop·i·cal (trop′ə·kəl) having to do with any area near the
equator where it is very warm and often rains.
Hawaii is a tropical island. *adj.*

tropical fish trop·i·cal fish (trop′ə·kəl fish) any one of
the many fish that live in warm ocean waters.
We bought a tropical fish for our tank.

trot (trot) **1.** to move at a speed between a walk and a run.
The horse will trot around the track.
v. **trotted, trotted, trotting** trot·ted, trot·ting
2. a slow run.
The horse started his trot when he reached the straightaway. *n. pl.* **trots**

trouble trou·ble (trub′əl) **1.** a problem; a bad situation.
She is having trouble with her boyfriend. *n.*
2. something that is difficult to do.
The trouble I have in school is learning math. *n. pl.* **troubles** trou·bles

trousers trou·sers (trou′zərz) pants that cover the whole leg.
My father spilled coffee on his trousers. *plural n.*

a	cat	**i**	sit	**oi**	oil	**ch**	chop
ā	ate	**ī**	lie	**ou**	out	**ng**	song
ä	car	**o**	pot	**u**	cut	**sh**	she
e	set	**ō**	old	**u̇**	book	**th**	three
ē	equal	**ô**	or	**ü**	blue	**ŦH**	there
ėr	germ					**zh**	treasure

ə = { a in about / e in oven / i in pencil / o in memory / u in circus }

truck (truk) **1.** a large vehicle that is used for carrying things from place to place.
We loaded the furniture into the truck. *n. pl.* **trucks**
2. having to do with a large vehicle that carries things.
The truck driver drove for many miles. *adj.*

true (trü) real; not made up; having the real facts; not false.
This is a true story about a soldier. *adj.* **truer, truest** tru·er, tru·est

truly tru·ly (trǘlē) in a real way; exactly as it happened or was told; really; in fact.
I truly liked the gift she gave me. *adv.*

trunk (trungk) **1.** a large box with a lid; a large suitcase.
People store and keep things in trunks. *n.*
2. the thick, bottom part of a tree; the stem of a tree.
The bark on the trunk is falling off. *n.*
3. the long nose of an elephant.
The elephant picked up the straw with its trunk. *n. pl.* **trunks**

trust (trust) to believe in someone; to have faith in someone; to depend on someone.
I can trust my mother because she loves me.
v. **trusted, trusted, trusting** trust·ed, trust·ing

truth (trüth) the real fact; the honest fact; not a lie.
He always tells the truth. *n. pl.* **truths**

truthfulness truth·ful·ness (trüth́fəl·nis) honesty; the quality of telling the truth.
I never question his truthfulness. *n. no pl.*

try (trī) to attempt to do something; to make an effort to do something; to test the skill at doing something.
I will try to reach the book on the top shelf. *v.* **tried, tried, trying** try·ing

try on (trī ôn) to put on some piece of clothing to see if it fits or looks right.
I want to try on this blue shirt. *v.* **tried on, tried on, trying on** try·ing on

try out (trī out) to use something to see if you like it or want it; to test the way something works; to experiment with something.
I want to try out the red bicycle.
v. **tried out, tried out, trying out** try·ing out

tryout try·out (trī́out) a test to see if one can be a part of something; an audition.
I went to the football tryout today. *n. pl.* **tryouts** try·outs

T-shirt (tḗshėrt) a knit shirt with no collar and short sleeves that is worn for play or under another shirt.
His T-shirt has a picture of Superman on it. *n. pl.* **T-shirts**

trunk

trunk

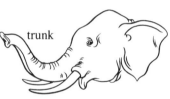

trunk

T-shirt

TTY (tē tē wī) *abbrev. pl.* **TTYs.** See **teletypewriter.**

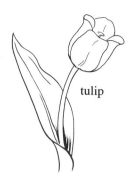

tulip

tub (tub) **1.** a large container that has no lid or cover.
We put the apples from the tree in a large tub. *n.*
2. the large container in a bathroom in which people bathe or wash their bodies; a bathtub.
I like to sit and read in the tub. *n. pl.* **tubs**

tube (tüb *or* tyüb) something round and hollow that is used to hold or carry liquids.
Toothpaste comes in a tube. *n. pl.* **tubes**

tuberculosis tu·ber·cu·lo·sis (tü·bėr·kyə·lṓsis *or* tyü·bėr·kyə·lṓsis) a disease of the lungs that is not easy to cure.
Many years ago people died from tuberculosis. *n. no pl.*

tulip tu·lip (tǘlip *or* tyǘlip) a flower that has petals in the shape of a cup.
The tulip will bloom in the spring. *n. pl.* **tulips** tu·lips

tuna

tumble out tum·ble out (tuḿbəl out) **1.** to flow freely without stopping.
Words tumble out of the baby when she is happy. *v.*
2. to fall or roll out of something.
Sit down, or you may tumble out of the boat.
v. **tumbled out, tumbled out, tumbling out** tum·bled out, tum·bling out

tuna fish tu·na fish (tǘnə fish) a kind of ocean fish that is caught for food.
We had tuna fish for lunch.

tune-up (tüńup *or* tyüńup) the testing and fixing of an engine.
The car needs a tune-up. *n. pl.* **tune-ups**

turkey

tunnel tun·nel (tuńl) a hole in rock or earth through which people, animals or vehicles can travel.
The men built a tunnel through the mountain. *n. pl.* **tunnels** tun·nels

turkey tur·key (tėŕkē) **1.** a large brown or white bird that people raise for food.
The farmer raised the turkey for his Thanksgiving dinner.
n. pl. **turkeys** tur·keys
2. having to do with a large brown or white bird that is eaten.
We always have a turkey dinner on Thanksgiving. *adj.*

a	cat	**i**	sit	**oi**	oil	**ch**	chop
ā	ate	**ī**	lie	**ou**	out	**ng**	song
ä	car	**o**	pot	**u**	cut	**sh**	she
e	set	**ō**	old	**ù**	book	**th**	three
ē	equal	**ô**	or	**ü**	blue	**ŦH**	there
ėr	germ					**zh**	treasure

ə = { a in about / e in oven / i in pencil / o in memory / u in circus }

turn (tėrn) **1.** to change direction; to move toward something.
I will turn to the right. *v.*
2. to change from one side to the other; to move part way around.
I will turn my head so I cannot see you. *v.*
3. to change; to become.
I hope I will turn brown from the sun. *v.*
4. to make go in a circle; to go in a circle; to move in a circle.
If you turn fast many times you may get dizzy.
v. **turned, turned, turning** turn·ing
5. a bend; a place in something where it changes direction.
There is a sharp turn in the road. *n.*
6. a chance to play; a player's time to play.
It is Jill's turn now, and then it will be your turn. *n. pl.* **turns**

turn

turn a page (tėrn ə pāj) to go to the next page in a book, newspaper or magazine.
We will each turn a page as the teacher reads the book to us.

turn around turn a·round (tėrn ə·round′) to make the body go in a circle; to put one's back to something; to look behind oneself.
I will turn around and count to ten while you hide. *v.* **turned around, turned around, turning around** turned a·round, turn·ing a·round

turn away turn a·way (tėrn ə·wā′) to move from something; to put one's back to a person or thing.
I will turn away from the snake. *v.* **turned away, turned away, turning away** turned a·way, turn·ing a·way

turn into turn in·to (tėrn in′tü) to become something else; to change from one thing to another.
The caterpillar will turn into a butterfly.
v. **turned into, turned into, turning into** turned in·to, turn·ing in·to

turn off (tėrn ôf) to stop a machine; to put out something that is lighted; to shut off.
Please turn off the light. *v.* **turned off, turned off, turning off** turn·ing off

turn on (tėrn ôn) to start a machine or tool; to put on; to make flow.
Please turn on the light. *v.* **turned on, turned on, turning on** turn·ing on

turn over turn o·ver (tėrn ō′vər) to change from one side to the other; to move the back to the front.
I will turn over the card.
v. **turned over, turned over, turning over** turned o·ver, turn·ing o·ver

turn tail (tėrn tāl) to run away from something; to run away.
The boys will be so afraid that they will turn tail and run. *idiom*

turn tail

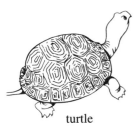

turtle

turn up (tėrn up) **1.** to increase the loudness; to raise the volume.
Please turn up the radio. I cannot hear it. *v.*
2. to appear; to arrive.
Joe is not here, but he may turn up soon.
v. **turned up, turned up, turning up** turn·ing up

turtle tur·tle (tėr'tl) an animal that moves slowly and that has a hard shell on its body.
The turtle hides in its shell. *n. pl.* **turtles** tur·tles

tusk (tusk) a very long, pointed tooth on an animal, which sticks out when the mouth is closed.
The elephant has a broken tusk. *n. pl.* **tusks**

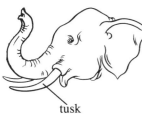

tusk

tutor tu·tor (tü'tər *or* tyü'tər) a person who helps a student with difficult lessons; a person who helps a student with schoolwork outside of the school.
I have a tutor for math. *n. pl.* **tutors** tu·tors

TV (tē vē) *abbrev. pl.* **TVs.** See **television.**

twice (twīs) two times.
I have only been in that house twice. *adv.*

twig (twig) a very small branch.
The bird sat on the twig. *n. pl.* **twigs**

twig

twin (twin) one of two children that are born at the same time from the same mother.
Her twin looks just like her. *n. pl.* **twins**

twine (twīn) very thin or fine rope; heavy string.
I put twine on the package. *n. no pl.*

twist (twist) to turn; to wind things together; to put things together by turning.
I will twist the threads together.
v. **twisted, twisted, twisting** twist·ed, twist·ing

twisty twist·y (twis'tē) full of turns; having many bends.
The mountain road is twisty. *adj.* **twistier, twistiest** twist·i·er, twist·i·est

twine

tying ty·ing (tī'ing) **1.** putting two things together with string or rope; joining the ends of a length of string or rope with a knot or bow.
Tying the legs of a steer together is a difficult rodeo event. *gerund*
2. *v. pres. part.* See **tie.**

a	cat	i	sit	oi	oil	ch	chop		a in about
ā	ate	ī	lie	ou	out	ng	song		e in oven
ä	car	o	pot	u	cut	sh	she	ə =	i in pencil
e	set	ō	old	ů	book	th	three		o in memory
ē	equal	ô	or	ü	blue	ŦH	there		u in circus
ėr	germ					zh	treasure		

type (tīp) **1.** to put letters on paper by using a machine such as a typewriter or a computer printer.

I can only type 40 words per minute. *v.* **typed, typed, typing** typ·ing

2. raised letters that are used in a machine for printing written materials.

Not many printers use type today. *n. no pl.*

3. kind; sort; class.

What type of candy do you like? *n. pl.* **types**

typewriter type·writ·er (tīp′rī·tər) a machine that people use to print words on a piece of paper.

Ann writes letters with an electric typewriter.

n. pl. **typewriters** type·writ·ers

typewriter

typhoid ty·phoid (tī′foid) having to do with a kind of disease that bacteria in food causes.

Typhoid fever is a dangerous kind of food poisoning. *adj.*

Uu

ugly

ugly ug·ly (ug′lē) not nice to look at; not pretty; unpleasant to the eye.
She drew an ugly picture. *adj.* **uglier, ugliest** ug·li·er, ug·li·est

unable un·a·ble (un·ā′bəl) not able to do something; not having the skill or talent to do something.
I am unable to sew. *adj.*

unbaked un·baked (un·bākt′) not baked; not cooked.
Mother put the unbaked bread on the table to rise. *adj.*

unbelieving un·be·liev·ing (un·bi·lē′ving) doubting; showing no belief; showing doubt.
He looked at me with unbelieving eyes when I said he could have more pie. *adj.*

uncle un·cle (ung′kəl) the brother of a mother or a father.
My Uncle Lee is my father's brother. *n. pl.* **uncles** un·cles

uncomfortable un·com·fort·a·ble (un·kum′fər·tə·bəl *or* un·kumf′tə·bəl) not feeling comfortable; not feeling good; not feeling relaxed; uneasy.
I was uncomfortable in that chair. *adj.*

unconscious un·con·scious (un·kon′shəs) not awake; not aware of what is going on around you; not alert; in a deep sleep or a coma.
The boy was unconscious when he got to the hospital. *adj.*

uncontrolled un·con·trolled (un·kən·trōld′) wild; without control.
The fire was uncontrolled until the firemen used some chemicals on it. *adj.*

uncooked un·cooked (un·kůkt′) not cooked; raw.
Eating uncooked meat is dangerous. *adj.*

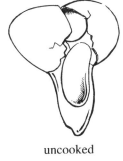

uncooked

under un·der (un′dər) beneath; below; lower than.
Your shoes are under the table. *prep.*

undergravel filter un·der·grav·el fil·ter (un′dər·grav·əl fil′tər) a cleaner that is put under the gravel in a fish tank.
The undergravel filter will keep the water in the fish tank clean for two weeks.

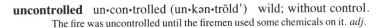

a	cat	**i**	sit	**oi**	oil	**ch**	chop
ā	ate	**ī**	lie	**ou**	out	**ng**	song
ä	car	**o**	pot	**u**	cut	**sh**	she
e	set	**ō**	old	**ů**	book	**th**	three
ē	equal	**ô**	or	**ü**	blue	**ŦH**	there
ėr	germ					**zh**	treasure

ə = {
a in about
e in oven
i in pencil
o in memory
u in circus
}

underground[1]   un·der·ground (un·dər·ground)
   1. being below the top of the earth; buried;
   being below the level of the ground.
   Some mines have underground tunnels. *adj.*
   2. being a place that is not known by many, that is
   secret or where secret things are done.
   The underground railroad secretly took slaves from the South. *adj.*

underground[2]   un·der·ground (un·dər·ground′)   below
   the top of the earth.
   Some animals live underground. *adv.*

underground

underneath   un·der·neath (un·dər·nēth′)   beneath; below;
   lower than; covered by.
   Your shoes are underneath the sofa. *prep.*

understand   un·der·stand (un·dər·stand′)   **1.** to know the feelings
   of others; to feel sympathy for the feelings of others.
   I understand how you feel. *v.*
   2. to have the facts and know what they mean; to know
   the meaning of something.
   I understand how to do these problems. *v.*
   3. to hear what someone is saying and to know what they
   mean; to know the meaning of what is said.
   I understand what the teacher is talking about. *v.* **understood,
   understood, understanding** un·der·stood, un·der·stand·ing

underwater   un·der·wa·ter (un·dər·wô·tər *or* un·dər·wot·ər)
   below the surface of the water; beneath the water.
   The diver dove underwater to find the treasure. *adv.*

underwater

undress   un·dress (un·dres′)   to take off the clothes.
   I will undress the baby and give her a bath.
   v. **undressed, undressed, undressing** un·dressed, un·dress·ing

uneven   un·e·ven (un·ē·vən)   not flat; not even; not level;
   out of balance.
   The table is uneven, and everything slides off it. *adj.*

unfair   un·fair (un·fer′ *or* un·far′)   unjust; not right.
   It is unfair for him to get more candy than I get.
   adj. **unfairer, unfairest** un·fair·er, un·fair·est

unfinished   un·fin·ished (un·fin·isht)   not complete; not done;
   not finished.
   My test was unfinished, but I gave it to the teacher. *adj.*

unfold   un·fold (un·fōld′)   to open from a folded position or shape.
   I will unfold my sweater and put it on a hanger.
   v. **unfolded, unfolded, unfolding** un·fold·ed, un·fold·ing

unforgettable   un·for·get·ta·ble (un·fər·get·ə·bəl)   something that is
   remembered forever; something that cannot be forgotten.
   The trip to Hawaii was unforgettable. *adj.*

uniform

unfriendly un·friend·ly (un·frend′lē)   not nice; not willing to make friends; not friendly.
The children in the new school are unfriendly. *adj.*

ungrateful un·grate·ful (un·grāt′fəl)   not full of thanks; not thankful; not appreciative.
I gave her some candy, but she was ungrateful for the gift. *adj.*

unhappiness un·hap·pi·ness (un·hap′ē·nis)   sadness; sorrow.
There is really no reason for your unhappiness. *n. no pl.*

unhappy un·hap·py (un·hap′ē)   not happy; sad.
She is unhappy because she cannot go shopping.
adj. **unhappier, unhappiest** un·hap·pi·er, un·hap·pi·est

unhook un·hook (un·hük′)   to take something off a hook; to take something down from a curved piece of metal or wood.
I will unhook the fish you caught.
v. **unhooked, unhooked, unhooking** un·hooked, un·hook·ing

uniform u·ni·form (yü′nə·fôrm)   clothes of a special kind that are worn by all the people who are members of a certain group.
Policemen wear uniforms. Soldiers also wear uniforms.
n. pl. **uniforms** u·ni·forms

Union Army Un·ion Ar·my (yü′nyən är′mē)   the soldiers who fought for the North during the Civil War.
The Union Army wore blue uniforms.

unique u·nique (yü·nēk′)   different from others; one of a kind; unusual.
This picture is unique because there is no other one like it. *adj.*

united u·nit·ed (yü·nī′tid)   joined together; acting as one.
The doctors are united in their fight against cancer. *adj.*

United States U·nit·ed States (yü·nī′tid stāts)   America; a country in North America with 50 states; its capital is Washington, D.C.
I live in the United States.

unity u·ni·ty (yü′nə·tē)   the action of working together; the act of being united.
The unity of the class members is easily seen by their work. *n. no pl.*

universe u·ni·verse (yü′nə·vėrs)   all things that exist; everything in the solar system.
The universe is endless. *n. no pl.*

Washington D.C.

United States

a	cat	i	sit	oi	oil	ch	chop		a in about
ā	ate	ī	lie	ou	out	ng	song		e in oven
ä	car	o	pot	u	cut	sh	she	ə =	i in pencil
e	set	ō	old	u̇	book	th	three		o in memory
ē	equal	ô	or	ü	blue	ŦH	there		u in circus
ėr	germ					zh	treasure		

465

university u·ni·ver·si·ty (yü·nə·vėr′sə·tē) a large college; an educational system that is made of many colleges.
I am going to the state university when I finish high school.
n. pl. **universities** u·ni·ver·si·ties

unknown un·known (un·nōn′) not known; strange; not familiar.
The writer of this story is unknown. *adj.*

unless un·less (ən·les′ *or* un·les′) if not that; except that.
Do not eat that candy unless you want to stay in your room all night. *conj.*

unlock un·lock (un·lok′) to open a lock.
Please unlock the door.
v. **unlocked, unlocked, unlocking** un·locked, un·lock·ing

unmanned un·manned (un·mand′) not having people; empty of people.
The unmanned spaceship was sent into space first. *adj.*

unmarried un·mar·ried (un·mar′ēd) having no husband or wife; not being married.
The new teacher is unmarried. *adj.*

unroll

unnaturally un·nat·ur·al·ly (un·nach′ər·ə·lē) strangely; not normally; not in the usual way.
I knew something was wrong because she was acting unnaturally. *adv.*

unpleasant un·pleas·ant (un·plez′nt) not nice; mean; bad.
The woman was very unpleasant when she answered my question. *adj.*

unpopulated un·pop·u·lat·ed (un·pop′yə·lā·tid) not having many people; being without people.
The island is still unpopulated. *adj.*

unroll un·roll (un·rōl′) to roll flat from a curled position or shape.
I will unroll the sleeping bag.
v. **unrolled, unrolled, unrolling** un·rolled, un·roll·ing

unsafe un·safe (un·sāf′) not free from danger or harm; not safe.
This cave is unsafe. *adj.* **unsafer, unsafest** un·saf·er, un·saf·est

unselfish un·self·ish (un·sel′fish) very giving; willing to share.
She loaned me her coat. She is unselfish. *adj.*

untie

unsweetened un·sweet·ened (un·swēt′nd) having no sugar; bitter.
The tea is unsweetened. *adj.*

untie un·tie (un·tī′) to loosen a knot; to open something that is tied together; to undo a knot.
You may untie the ribbon and open the gift.
v. **untied, untied, untying** un·tied, un·ty·ing

unwrap

until un·til (ən·til′ *or* un·til′) **1.** up to the time of.
Father will not be home until seven o'clock. *prep.*
2. up to the time when.
You will not go outside until you finish your homework. *conj.*

unused un·used (un·yüzd′) never used before; not being used.
The shed is unused since we sold the tools. *adj.*

unusual un·u·su·al (un·yü′zhü·əl) different from most others;
odd; not normal.
That is an unusual picture. *adj.*

unwind un·wind (un·wīnd′) to unroll from a curled position
or shape; to relax from a tight position; to take some off a roll.
I will unwind the string and tie it to the kite.
v. **unwound, unwound, unwinding** un·wound, un·wind·ing

unwrap un·wrap (un·rap′) to take off the covering;
to take the cover off.
Please unwrap my gift first.
v. **unwrapped, unwrapped, unwrapping** un·wrapped, un·wrap·ping

up (up) **1.** to the top; to a higher place.
The monkey climbed up the tree. *prep.*
2. to the beginning; to or near the top or start of something.
We sailed up the river. *prep.*
3. ended; finished; gone.
The time is up; you must give me your test. *adj.*
4. above the Earth; in the sky.
The sun will come up at six o'clock. *adv.*
5. not lying down; upright.
We will get up early and go fishing. *adv.*
6. to a higher place; into the air.
The boy threw the ball up. *adv.*

up and down

up and down (up ən doun) **1.** from the ground to the air
and back to the ground.
The children jumped up and down. *adv.*
2. from one place to another and back again; from the top
to the bottom and back to the top.
We walked up and down the street. *adv.*

upper up·per (up′ər) toward the top part of something.
I live on an upper floor of the building. *adj.*

a	cat	**i**	sit	**oi**	oil	**ch**	chop	a in about
ā	ate	**ī**	lie	**ou**	out	**ng**	song	e in oven
ä	car	**o**	pot	**u**	cut	**sh**	she	i in pencil
e	set	**ō**	old	**u̇**	book	**th**	three	o in memory
ē	equal	**ô**	or	**ü**	blue	**ŦH**	there	u in circus
ėr	germ					**zh**	treasure	

ə =

upright up·right (up'rīt) standing tall and straight; erect; not bent or curved.
People first used an upright pole to tell the time. *adj.*

upset up·set (up·set') worried; excited; bothered; disturbed.
Mother was upset when she saw the broken window. *adj.*

upside down up·side down (up'sīd doun) with the top turned to the bottom.
The boy is standing upside down; his head is on the floor, and his feet are in the air. *adv.*

upside down

upstairs up·stairs (up'sterz *or* up'starz) on the floor above; on the next level up.
My bedroom is upstairs, and my brother's is on this floor. *adv.*

uptown up·town (up'toun') to the north part of town; to the upper part of town; away from the main business part of town.
I am going uptown to shop. *adv.*

upward up·ward (up'wərd) to a higher place; toward the top.
The elevator is moving upward now. *adv.*

uranium u·ra·ni·um (yů·rā'nē·əm) a mineral ore that is found in the ground and that gives off electromagnetic energy, called radiation.
Uranium is a valuable and dangerous mineral. *n. no pl.*

Uranus Ur·a·nus (yůr'ə·nəs) a large planet in our solar system.
Uranus is far from the sun. *n.*

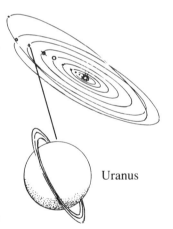

Uranus

us (us *or* əs) the people who are talking; the person who is talking and one or more other people.
They gave us their pictures. *pron.*

use[1] (yüz) to put to action; to put to work; to do work with.
I will use the rake. *v.* **used, used, using** us·ing

use[2] (yüs) a way of working with something.
I found a new use for my bat. *n. pl.* **uses** us·es

used (yüzd) not new; having been worked with or worn before.
My father bought a used car, not a new car. *adj.*

used to (yüst tü) did in the past; did in a time before now; formerly did.
I used to go to that school. *aux.*

useful use·ful (yüs'fəl) helpful; having many uses.
The broom is useful when cleaning the attic. *adj.*

usher

usher ush·er (ush′ər)   a person who shows people to their seats in a theater or a stadium.
The usher lead us to our seats. *n. pl.* **ushers** ush·ers

usual u·su·al (yü′zhü·əl)   common; not different; ordinary; normal; being the same as before.
I will meet you in our usual place. *adj.*

usually u·su·al·ly (yü′zhü·ə·lē)   most often; in a way that is not different; most of the time.
I usually have lunch in the cafeteria. *adv.*

a	cat	i	sit	oi	oil	ch	chop		a in about
ā	ate	ī	lie	ou	out	ng	song		e in oven
ä	car	o	pot	u	cut	sh	she	ə =	i in pencil
e	set	ō	old	u̇	book	th	three		o in memory
ē	equal	ô	or	ü	blue	ᴛ̵ʜ	there		u in circus
ėr	germ					zh	treasure		

Vv

vacation va·ca·tion (vā·kā′shən) **1.** a trip; a time when you do not work or go to school.
We are going to the beach on a vacation. *n. pl.* **vacations** va·ca·tions
2. to go on a trip; to travel for pleasure.
We will vacation in Europe.
v. **vacationed, vacationed, vacationing** va·ca·tioned, va·ca·tion·ing
3. having to do with a trip for pleasure.
We have a vacation home by the beach. *adj.*

vaccinate vac·ci·nate (vak′sə·nāt) to give a shot so a person will not get a sickness.
The doctor will vaccinate me against measles.
v. **vaccinated, vaccinated, vaccinating** vac·ci·nat·ed, vac·ci·nat·ing

vaccination vac·ci·na·tion (vak·sə·nā′shən) a shot that a doctor or nurse gives so a person will not get a disease or sickness.
The doctor gave me a vaccination. *n. pl.* **vaccinations** vac·ci·na·tions

vacuum cleaner

vacuum vac·u·um (vak′yü·əm *or* vak′yūm) to use a machine to clean the floor or the rug.
I will vacuum the stairs.
v. **vacuumed, vacuumed, vacuuming** vac·u·umed, vac·u·um·ing

vacuum cleaner vac·u·um clean·er (vak′yü·əm klē′nər) a machine that picks up dirt off the floor or a carpet.
I will run the vacuum cleaner on the rug.

vain (vān) having too much pride in the way you look or in your skills and talents.
He is vain; he thinks he is the best at everything. *adj.*

valentine val·en·tine (val′ən·tīn) **1.** a card that tells how much you like a person; a card sent on a holiday in February.
I sent my mother a beautiful valentine. *n. pl.* **valentines** val·en·tines
2. Valentine; a saint who was a priest that preached of love and loving and who was killed by a Roman emperor.
Valentine was named a saint because of his teachings of love.

valentine

Valentine's Day Val·en·tine's Day (val′ən·tīnz dā) a holiday celebrated on February 14 in memory of St. Valentine; the day people send cards to people they love.
I gave her candy on Valentine's Day.

van

valley val·ley (val⁴ē) the land between two mountains; the low land between the mountains.
The valley is green from the rainwaters of the mountain.
n. pl. **valleys** val·leys

Valley Forge Val·ley Forge (val⁴ē fôrj) a town in the state of Pennsylvania where George Washington and his army stayed during the Revolutionary War.
Valley Forge has a monument to George Washington. *n.*

valuable val·u·a·ble (val⁴yü·ə·bəl *or* val⁴yə·bəl) having great worth; expensive; important; well thought of.
The diamond is very valuable. *adj.*

van (van) a covered truck that people use to carry things.
The furniture was loaded into the moving van. *n. pl.* **vans**

Vancouver Van·cou·ver (van·kü⁴vər) a large city in Canada.
It rains often in Vancouver. *n.*

vandal

vandal van·dal (van⁴dl) a person who breaks or destroys things that belong to other people.
A vandal broke the windows in the classroom. *n. pl.* **vandals** van·dals

vandalism van·dal·ism (van⁴dl·iz·əm) the act of breaking and destroying things that belong to other people.
The school was ruined by vandalism. *n. no pl.*

vanish van·ish (van⁴ish) to disappear; to be gone.
The magician made the rabbit vanish.
v. **vanished, vanished, vanishing** van·ished, van·ish·ing

vanish into thin air van·ish in·to thin air (van⁴ish in⁴tü thin ər) to be gone; to disappear without a trace; to vanish; to be not seen.
Sometimes I wish I could vanish into thin air. *idiom*

vase

vanity van·i·ty (van⁴ə·tē) great pride in the way one looks or in one's skills.
I do not like him because of his vanity. *n. pl.* **vanities** van·i·ties

variety va·ri·e·ty (və·rī⁴ə·tē) a type or kind.
A rose is one variety of flower; a tulip is another variety.
n. pl. **varieties** va·ri·e·ties

vase (vās) a pretty holder for flowers.
I put the rose in the glass vase. *n. pl.* **vases** vas·es

a	cat	i	sit	oi	oil	ch	chop		a in about
ā	ate	ī	lie	ou	out	ng	song		e in oven
ä	car	o	pot	u	cut	sh	she	ə =	i in pencil
e	set	ō	old	u̇	book	th	three		o in memory
ē	equal	ô	or	ü	blue	ᴛH	there		u in circus
ėr	germ					zh	treasure		

vast (vast) large; covering a large area.
The desert is vast. *adj.*

vegetable veg·e·ta·ble (vej⁴ə·tə·bəl *or* vej⁴tə·bəl) **1.** a plant the parts of which some people eat as food.
My favorite vegetable is broccoli. *n. pl.* **vegetables** veg·e·ta·bles
2. having to do with the plants whose parts people use as food.
We have a vegetable garden where we grow peppers, onions, corn and lettuce. *adj.*

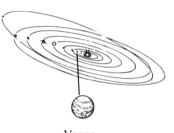
vegetables

vegetation veg·e·ta·tion (vej·ə·tā⁴shən) the plants that grow in an area.
The vegetation in the desert is different from the vegetation in the mountains. *n. no pl.*

Venice Ven·ice (ven⁴is) a city in the country of Italy.
People travel on water canals in Venice. *n.*

Venus Ve·nus (vē⁴nəs) a planet in our solar system.
Venus is easy to see from Earth. *n.*

verse (vėrs) lines that are grouped together in a poem.
I learned the first verse of a poem yesterday. *n. pl.* **verses** vers·es

vertical ver·ti·cal (vėr⁴tə·kəl) going up and down; running from top to bottom; upright.
I drew a vertical line on the paper. *adj.*

Venus

vertically ver·ti·cal·ly (vėr⁴tə·kə·lē) in an upright position; in an up-and-down or top-to-bottom manner.
The mast stands vertically on the boat. *adv.*

very ver·y (ver⁴ē) greatly; extremely; to a large degree.
The stove is very hot. *adv.*

vessel ves·sel (ves⁴əl) a small tube in the body that carries blood.
I broke a blood vessel when I hit my arm. *n. pl.* **vessels** ves·sels

veterinarian vet·er·i·nar·i·an (vet·ər·ə·ner⁴ē·ən *or* vet·ə·ner⁴ē·ən) a doctor who takes care of animals.
The veterinarian gave my dog a shot. *n. pl.* **veterinarians** vet·er·i·nar·i·ans

vice-president vice-pres·i·dent (vīs-prez⁴ə·dənt *or* vīs-prez⁴dənt) the person who is under the president in power; the second person in control of the country.
We do not pick the vice-president; the president selects the vice-president. *n.*

vertical

victory vic·tor·y (vik⁴tər·ē) a win in a contest, race or battle.
Winning the spelling contest was a great victory. *n. pl.* **victories** vic·tor·ies

viewfinder

view (vyü) **1.** to look at; to see.
We will view the ocean from the top of the hill.
v. **viewed, viewed, viewing** view·ing
2. a scene; something that is looked at.
The view from the mountain was breathtaking. *n.*
3. a thought; an opinion; a person's idea of things.
His view is that we should not vote for Tom. *n. pl.* **views**

viewer view·er (vyǘər) a person who watches; an observer.
I am a television viewer. *n. pl.* **viewers** view·ers

viewfinder view·find·er (vyǘ·fīn·dər) the part of a
camera into which a person looks before taking a picture.
I looked into the viewfinder and then took the picture.
n. pl. **viewfinders** view·find·ers

Viking Vi·king (vī́·king) **1.** one of the men who sailed large,
open ships from Sweden, Denmark and Norway between
the years 700 and 1000.
It is believed that the Vikings were the first Europeans to
discover North America. *n. pl.* **Vikings** Vi·kings
2. the name of a spaceship sent to study Mars.
The Viking was unmanned. *n. no pl.*

village vil·lage (viĺ·ij) **1.** a small town; a small group
of houses and buildings.
There is an old Indian village on the river. *n. pl.* **villages** vil·lag·es
2. having to do with a small town.
The village store is very small. *adj.*

vine

villager vil·lag·er (viĺ·i·jər) a person who lives in a small town.
The villager likes the quiet. *n. pl.* **villagers** vil·lag·ers

vine (vīn) any plant with a long stem that grows up things.
The vine is growing up the side of the house. *n. pl.* **vines**

vinegar vin·e·gar (viń·ə·gər) a sour liquid made by
fermenting apples or wine.
I put vinegar on my salad. *n. no pl.*

vineyard vine·yard (viń·yərd) a place where grapes are grown;
a place where grapevines are grown.
We drove through the vineyard. *n. pl.* **vineyards** vine·yards

violent vi·o·lent (vī́·ə·lənt) having to do with a strong force;
having a strong force; terribly strong.
He has a violent temper. *adj.*

vinegar

a	cat	**i**	sit	**oi**	oil	**ch**	chop	a in about
ā	ate	**ī**	lie	**ou**	out	**ng**	song	e in oven
ä	car	**o**	pot	**u**	cut	**sh**	she	ə = i in pencil
e	set	**ō**	old	**u̇**	book	**th**	three	o in memory
ē	equal	**ô**	or	**ü**	blue	**ŦH**	there	u in circus
ėr	germ					**zh**	treasure	

violet vi·o·let (vī′ə·lit) a small, dainty flower that is light purple.
I put a violet in my hair. *n. pl.* **violets** vi·o·lets

virus vi·rus (vī′rəs) a living substance that causes a
sickness or disease.
A virus causes a cold. *n. pl.* **viruses** vi·rus·es

vision vi·sion (vizh′ən) **1.** the act of seeing with the eyes;
the ability to use the eyes to see.
My vision is good, so I do not wear glasses. *n. no pl.*
2. a dream; an imagined thing.
The woman had a vision about something that will happen in the future.
n. pl. **visions** vi·sions

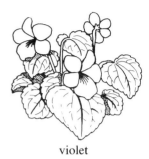

violet

visit vis·it (viz′it) **1.** time spent with another person; the act
of going to see someone or someplace.
I had a nice visit with my aunt. *n. pl.* **visits** vis·its
2. to go to see someone or someplace.
I will visit the museum tomorrow.
v. **visited, visited, visiting** vis·it·ed, vis·it·ing

visitor vis·i·tor (viz′ə·tər) a person who goes to see another person.
We had a surprise visitor in the classroom today. *n. pl.* **visitors** vis·i·tors

vitamin vi·ta·min (vī′tə·mən) **1.** a substance in food that
the body needs to grow and to stay healthy.
What vitamins are in an orange? *n. pl.* **vitamins** vi·ta·mins
2. having to do with a certain or specific nutrient
or substance in food.
The orange is full of vitamin C. *adj.*

voice (vois) the sound made in the throat when speaking or singing.
The teacher has a pretty voice. *n. pl.* **voices** voic·es

visit

volcano vol·ca·no (vol·kā′nō) an opening in the earth
from which hot, steaming lava comes.
There is a volcano on the island of Hawaii.
n. pl. **volcanoes** *or* **volcanos** vol·ca·noes *or* vol·ca·nos

volleyball vol·ley·ball (vol′ē·bôl) having to do with
a game between two teams using a ball and a high net.
We watched the volleyball game. *adj.*

volunteer vol·un·teer (vol·ən·tir′) to give without being asked
to give; to offer without being asked to offer.
I will volunteer to tell a story to the baby.
v. **volunteered, volunteered, volunteering** vol·un·teered, vol·un·teer·ing

vote (vōt) **1.** to indicate who or what a person wants in an election;
to complete a ballot in an election.
I will not vote for him. *v.* **voted, voted, voting** vot·ed, vot·ing
2. a choice in an election; an indication of who or what
a person wants in an election.
She has my vote. *n. pl.* **votes**

volcano

voter

voter   vot·er (vō‹tər)   a person who chooses in an election; a person who votes.
The voter put his ballot in the box. *n. pl.* **voters** vot·ers

voyage   voy·age (voi‹ij)   a trip on the water; a sailing trip; a cruise.
We are taking a voyage on a large ocean liner. *n. pl.* **voyages** voy·ag·es

Voyager   Voy·ag·er (voi‹i·jər)   one of two spacecrafts.
Voyager 1 explored Jupiter, and Voyager 2 explored Uranus. *n.*

a	cat	i	sit	oi	oil	ch	chop		a in about
ā	ate	ī	lie	ou	out	ng	song		e in oven
ä	car	o	pot	u	cut	sh	she	ə =	i in pencil
e	set	ō	old	u̇	book	th	three		o in memory
ē	equal	ô	or	ü	blue	ᵺH	there		u in circus
ėr	germ					zh	treasure		

wade (wād) to walk through water that is not very deep.
I like to wade in the children's pool.
v. **waded, waded, wading** wad·ed, wad·ing

wading pool wad·ing pool (wā'ding pül) a large container holding water that is not deep.
The neighbors have a wading pool in their yard.

wading pool

wag (wag) to move back and forth; to move from side to side.
The dog will wag his tail when he sees you coming.
v. **wagged, wagged, wagging** wag·ging

wagon wag·on (wag'ən) a large cart; a four-wheeled vehicle.
I have a red wagon. *n. pl.* **wagons** wag·ons

waist (wāst) the part of the body between the chest and the hips; the middle of the body.
The lady has a small waist. *n. pl.* **waists**

wait (wāt) **1.** to stay in one place until something happens.
My dog will wait on the porch until I come home. *v.*
2. to not do something until a certain time.
I will wait until I am eighteen to learn to drive. *v.*
3. to not start an action until something happens.
I will wait to cook dinner until Dad comes home.
v. **waited, waited, waiting** wait·ed, wait·ing

wag

waiter wait·er (wā'tər) a man who takes the order and brings the food to the table in a restaurant.
I asked the waiter for a glass of water. *n. pl.* **waiters** wait·ers

wait for (wāt fôr) to not do something until someone arrives; to give a person time to arrive.
I will wait for you at the store. *v.* **waited for, waited for, waiting for** wait·ed for, wait·ing for

waitress wai·tress (wā'tris) a woman who takes the order and brings the food to the table in a restaurant.
The waitress gave the bill to me. *n. pl.* **waitresses** wai·tress·es

wagon

wake (wāk) to stop sleeping; to cause to stop sleeping.
I cannot wake Dad, and he is supposed to leave early.
v. **woke, woken, waking** wo·ken, wak·ing

wake up (wāk up) to stop sleeping; to cause to stop sleeping.
I will wake up Dad.
v. **woke up, woken up, waking up** wo·ken up, wak·ing up

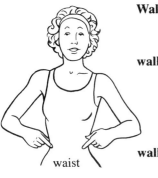

waist

Wales (wālz) a country in Europe that is part of Great Britain; its capital is Cardiff.
We will visit Wales after we visit England. *n.*

walk (wôk) **1.** to use the feet to move the body.
We should walk into a room, not run into a room. *v.*
2. to take an animal for exercise.
I will walk the dog. *v.* **walked, walked, walking** walk·ing
3. the act of moving the body with the feet.
I took a walk around the lake. *n. pl.* **walks**

walk over walk o·ver (wôk ō′vər) to go toward someplace or something by foot.
I will walk over to her house.
v. **walked over, walked over, walking over** walked o·ver, walk·ing o·ver

wall (wôl) **1.** one of the four sides to a room; a brick or rock fence that encloses an area.
I hung her picture on the wall. *n. pl.* **walls**
2. having to do with one of the four sides of a room; having to do with a brick or rock fence that encloses an area.
I have a wall clock in my bedroom. *adj.*

Wales

Cardiff

wallet wal·let (wol′it *or* wôl′it) a flat case in which people carry money, credit cards and pictures.
I put the five dollar bill in my wallet. *n. pl.* **wallets** wal·lets

wallpaper wall·pa·per (wôl′pā·pər) decorated paper that people paste on walls.
Mother put wallpaper on the walls in the kitchen.
n. pl. **wallpapers** *or* **wallpaper** wall·pa·pers

wand (wond) a stick that a magician uses.
The magician waved the wand over the hat. *n. pl.* **wands**

wander wan·der (won′dər) to walk without knowing where you are going; to move without having a special place to go.
I will wander through the shopping center.
v. **wandered, wandered, wandering** wan·dered, wan·der·ing

wand

want (wont *or* wônt) to have a wish for something; to desire something.
I want a new baseball. *v.* **wanted, wanted, wanting** want·ed, want·ing

a	cat	**i**	sit	**oi**	oil	**ch**	chop
ā	ate	**ī**	lie	**ou**	out	**ng**	song
ä	car	**o**	pot	**u**	cut	**sh**	she
e	set	**ō**	old	**u̇**	book	**th**	three
ē	equal	**ô**	or	**ü**	blue	**T̶H**	there
ėr	germ					**zh**	treasure

ə = { a in about / e in oven / i in pencil / o in memory / u in circus }

want to (wont tü) to have a wish to do something.
I want to go with you to the shopping center.
v. **wanted to, wanted to, wanting to** want·ed to, want·ing to

war (wôr) **1.** a violent fight between two countries, nations
or groups of people.
A war started when the settlers broke the treaty with the Indians. *n. pl.* **wars**
2. having to do with a violent fight between two countries
or groups of people.
I like to read war stories. *adj.*

warden ward·en (wôrd'n) a person who works to enforce the
law and rules; a person who protects things.
The game warden in the park makes sure people follow the park
rules about the animals. *n. pl.* **wardens** ward·ens

warehouse ware·house (wer'hous *or* war'hous) a large building
in which a business keeps or stores things.
There are hundreds of boxes of food in the grocer's warehouse.
n. pl. **warehouses** ware·hous·es

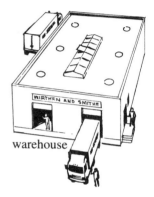
warehouse

warm (wôrm) **1.** a little hot; not cool; between cool and hot.
The water in the swimming pool is warm. *adj.*
2. friendly and welcoming.
She has a warm smile. *adj.* **warmer, warmest** warm·er, warm·est
3. to heat; to change from cool to hot.
I will warm the soup. *v.* **warmed, warmed, warming** warm·ing

warm-blooded warm-blood·ed (wôrm'blud'id) animals whose
blood temperature stays about the same no matter what
the temperature around them.
People are warm-blooded. *adj.*

warmly warm·ly (wôrm'lē) in a warm way; in a friendly way.
She warmly met the new girl. *adv.*

warm up (wôrm up) **1.** to heat; to change from cool to warm.
I will warm up the soup. *v.*
2. to get ready to exercise; to prepare to exercise.
I want to warm up before class.
v. **warmed up, warmed up, warming up** warm·ing up

warn (wôrn) to tell someone that there is danger.
Please warn her that the step is broken.
v. **warned, warned, warning** warn·ing

warring war·ring (wôr'ing) having to do with fighting or
being in a battle.
Custer was killed by the warring Indians. *adj.*

wash

warrior   war·ri·or (wôr′ē·ər *or* wor′ē·ər)   a person who fights in a war; a strong fighter; a soldier.
The Indian warrior watched for the enemy.
n. pl. **warriors** war·ri·ors

warship   war·ship (wôr′ship)   a large boat that has many guns and cannons and is used in a war.
The warship sank in the battle. *n. pl.* **warships** war·ships

was   (woz *or* wuz *or* wəz)   *v. pt. t.* See **be.**

wash   (wosh *or* wôsh)   **1.** to clean with soap and water; to clean.
I will wash the windows. *v.*
2. to clean oneself.
I forgot to wash. *v.* **washed, washed, washing** wash·ing

washer

wash-and-wear   (wosh′-ən-wer′ *or* wosh′-ən-war′ *or* wôsh′-ən-wer′ *or* wôsh′-ən-war′)   a kind of material from which clothes are made that has been treated so that it does not need to be ironed after it is washed.
I have a wash-and-wear shirt that never looks wrinkled. *adj.*

washer   wash·er (wosh′ər *or* wô′shər)   a machine that washes clothes.
Father put the laundry in the washer. *n. pl.* **washers** wash·ers

George Washington

Washington, George   Wash·ing·ton, George (wosh′ing·tən,   jôrj)   the first president of the United States.
George Washington fought in the Revolutionary War.

washtub   wash·tub (wosh′tub *or* wôsh′tub)   a large container that people use to wash clothes; a large metal container in which things are washed.
Father washed the dog in the washtub. *n. pl.* **washtubs** wash·tubs

wash up   (wosh up)   to clean the face and hands with soap and water.
Please wash up before you come to the dinner table.
v. **washed up, washed up, washing up** wash·ing up

waste   (wāst)   to not use properly so that some must be thrown away; to not use something in the fullest possible way; to throw away things that a person could use.
Please do not waste the poster paper.
v. **wasted, wasted, wasting** wast·ed, wast·ing

a	cat	i	sit	oi	oil	ch	chop		a in about
ā	ate	ī	lie	ou	out	ng	song		e in oven
ä	car	o	pot	u	cut	sh	she	ə =	i in pencil
e	set	ō	old	u̇	book	th	three		o in memory
ē	equal	ô	or	ü	blue	ŦH	there		u in circus
ėr	germ					zh	treasure		

wastebasket   waste·bas·ket (wāst′bas·kit)   a container for things that are thrown away.
> Put the scrap pieces of paper in the wastebasket.
> *n. pl.* **wastebaskets** waste·bas·kets

wasting time   wast·ing time (wā′sting tīm)   not using time properly; not doing what a person should be doing; playing instead of working.
> Stop wasting time and get to work on your homework.

wastebasket

watch   (woch *or* wôch)   **1.** a clock that a person wears, usually on the wrist; a timepiece.
> I got a watch for my birthday. *n. pl.* **watches** watch·es
> **2.** to look at; to look carefully.
> I will watch you, and then I will try to do it. *v.*
> **3.** to guard; to protect.
> The guard will watch the robber. *v.*
> **4.** to take care of; to supervise.
> I will watch the baby while you shop.
> *v.* **watched, watched, watching** watch·ing

watchful   watch·ful (woch′fəl *or* wôch′fəl)   looking very carefully; attentive; alert to problems.
> The teacher is very watchful and sees everything the students do. *adj.*

watch

watch out   (woch out)   to be careful.
> Please watch out for the ball.
> *v.* **watched out, watched out, watching out** watch·ing out

water   wa·ter (wô′tər *or* wot′ər)   **1.** a clear, odorless, tasteless liquid; the liquid from the faucet that people drink; the liquid that comes from rain or snow and fills the lakes, rivers, oceans and ponds.
> I will have a glass of water. *n. no pl.*
> **2.** having to do with the clear, odorless, tasteless liquid that people drink.
> I can see the water tower from the mountain. *adj.*

waterfall   wa·ter·fall (wô′tər·fôl *or* wot′ər·fôl)   a place where water from a river or a creek falls down over rocks.
> We visited a waterfall in Hawaii. *n. pl.* **waterfalls** wa·ter·falls

watering can   wa·ter·ing can (wô′tər·ing kan)   a container used to pour water onto plants.
> Karen used a watering can to water the flowers.

waterfall

water lily

water lily wa·ter lil·y (wô⁺tər lil⁺ē) a plant that floats on top of the water in a lake or pond and has a sweet-smelling flower.
The ducks swam by the white water lily.

waterway wa·ter·way (wô⁺tər·wā *or* wot⁺ər·wā) a body of water through which ships and boats may go; a channel of water.
The Mississippi River is a large waterway. *n. pl.* **waterways** wa·ter·ways

wave (wāv) **1.** to move the hand in a gesture of greeting or good-bye; to give a signal with the hand or something held in the hand.
I will wave to you from the train. *v.* **waved, waved, waving** wav·ing
2. the movement of the ocean; a swell or crest of water made by the ocean.
The wave knocked her down into the ocean. *n. pl.* **waves**

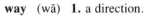

wave

way (wā) **1.** a direction.
You go this way, and I will go that way. *n.*
2. a path; a course.
I found a way through the forest that is very pretty. *n.*
3. method of doing something; means of doing.
I like my way of combing my hair. *n.*
4. a custom; a tradition.
Our family's way of celebrating Christmas is really fun. *n. pl.* **ways**

way of life (wā əv līf) the customs and habits that one practices; the manner in which a person deals with experiences.
Fishing for their food is a way of life for the Eskimo people.

we (wē) the person speaking and one or more other people.
They are going to the store, but we are not. *plural pron.*

weak (wēk) not having much power; not strong.
The child is weak and cannot lift the heavy box.
adj. **weaker, weakest** weak·er, weak·est

wealth (welth) much money and many belongings; riches.
The man has wealth and can buy anything he wants. *n. no pl.*

wealthy wealth·y (wel⁺thē) having much money and many belongings.
The man who has ten cars is wealthy.
adj. **wealthier, wealthiest** wealth·i·er, wealth·i·est

a	cat	**i**	sit	**oi**	oil	**ch**	chop
ā	ate	**ī**	lie	**ou**	out	**ng**	song
ä	car	**o**	pot	**u**	cut	**sh**	she
e	set	**ō**	old	**u̇**	book	**th**	three
ē	equal	**ô**	or	**ü**	blue	**TH**	there
ėr	germ					**zh**	treasure

ə = { a in about / e in oven / i in pencil / o in memory / u in circus }

weapon weap·on (wep′ən) an object or tool that people use in fighting.
A gun can be a weapon. *n. pl.* **weapons** weap·ons

wear (wer *or* war) to put on the body; to have on the body.
I will wear a new shirt today. *v.* **wore, worn, wearing** wear·ing

wear away wear a·way (wer ə·wā′) to reduce the size of something through use; to get smaller slowly.
The rocks will wear away as the river flows over them.
v. **wore away, worn away, wearing away** wear·ing a·way

wear down (wer doun) to become smaller slowly from use or wear; to reduce the size of.
He can wear down the heels of his shoes very fast.
v. **wore down, worn down, wearing down** wear·ing down

weary wear·y (wir′ē) tired; without energy.
I felt weary after the long walk home. *adj.*

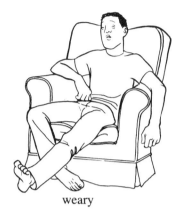

weary

weather weath·er (weᴛʜ′ər) the condition of the outside air; the things that cause the condition of the outside air.
We are having great weather today; it is sunny and warm. *n. no pl.*

weave (wēv) to form cloth from thread or string; to put fibers together to form cloth.
My mother can weave pretty material from sheep's wool.
v. **wove, woven, weaving** wo·ven, weav·ing

web (web) the net-like structure that a spider makes.
The spider wove its web from one tree to the other. *n. pl.* **webs**

wedding wed·ding (wed′ing) **1.** a ceremony in which two people get married.
The wedding was in the new church. *n. pl.* **weddings** wed·dings
2. having to do with a marriage ceremony.
There were many wedding pictures of the bride and groom. *adj.*

weed (wēd) an unwanted plant that grows in a garden or a lawn; a plant that does not have a use.
I pulled the weed out of the flowerpot. *n. pl.* **weeds**

web

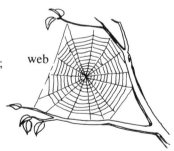

weedkiller weed·kill·er (wēd′kil·ər) a chemical that makes unwanted plants in the garden die.
We will put weedkiller on the lawn to kill the dandelions.
n. pl. **weedkillers** weed·kill·ers

week (wēk) seven days; the time from Sunday to Saturday.
I will be on vacation for one week. *n. pl.* **weeks**

weekend week·end (wēk′end) the two days at the end of the work week or school week; Saturday and Sunday.
I like to play with my dog on the weekend. *n. pl.* **weekends** week·ends

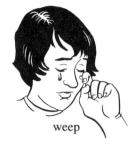

weep

weigh

weep (wēp) to cry quietly.
She will weep when we leave. *v.* **wept, wept, weeping** weep·ing

weigh (wā) to measure how heavy something is; to put on a scale that measures pounds.
I will weigh the baby on the scale.
v. **weighed, weighed, weighing** weigh·ing

weight (wāt) **1.** a heavy thing that is lifted for exercise.
I can lift a 50-pound weight. *n.*
2. the number of pounds and ounces that something or someone weighs; how heavy something or someone is.
The baby's weight is 22 pounds. *n. pl.* **weights**

weird (wird) strange; unusual; not normal.
She has a weird haircut. *adj.*

welcome wel·come (wel′kəm) **1.** to greet someone; to give someone a warm greeting.
She will welcome the visitor into her home.
v. **welcomed, welcomed, welcoming** wel·comed, wel·com·ing
2. "you are welcome;" a polite answer to "thank you."
I said "you are welcome" when she thanked me for the gift. *adj.*

well (wel) **1.** good; right; with skill or talent.
She sings well. *adv.*
2. a word said when sighing; a word of acceptance or surprise.
"Well, I don't know what to say!" *interj.*
3. a deep hole where water is found.
I put the bucket in the well. *n. pl.* **wells**
4. in good health; not sick.
I was sick for two days but I am well now. *adj.*

we'll (wil *or* wēl) we will; we shall.
We'll meet you there. *contrac.*

well-educated well-ed·u·cat·ed (wel′ej′ə·kā·tid) having gone to the best schools; having gone to school for a long time; having had much schooling.
He is a well-educated person. *adj.*

well-known (wel′nōn′) famous; known by many people; familiar to many people.
The well-known movie star waved to the crowd. *adj.*

a	cat	i	sit	oi	oil	ch	chop		a in about
ā	ate	ī	lie	ou	out	ng	song		e in oven
ä	car	o	pot	u	cut	sh	she	ə =	i in pencil
e	set	ō	old	u̇	book	th	three		o in memory
ē	equal	ô	or	ü	blue	ᵺH	there		u in circus
ėr	germ					zh	treasure		

well-trained (wel⸍trānd′) having received good instructions or lessons; having received a good education or schooling; being good-mannered and having good control.
The well-trained horse obeyed the rider. *adj.*

Welsh (welsh *or* welch) having to do with the people or country of Wales.
The Welsh people are very warm and friendly. *adj.*

wet

went (went) *v. pt. t.* See **go.**

wept (wept) *v. pt. t., pt. part.* See **weep.**

were (wėr *or* wər) *v. pt. t., pt. part.* See **be.**

west (west) the direction that is opposite of east; the direction in which the sun sets.
We will travel to the west. *n. no pl.*

western west·ern (wes⸍tərn) coming from, being in or going toward the west.
The western wind comes from the Pacific Ocean. *adj.*

west side (west sīd) the part of a town on the side opposite the east side.
I play baseball on the west side.

wet (wet) full of water; not dry.
The wet dog cannot come into the house.
adj. **wetter, wettest** wet·ter, wet·test

we've (wēv) we have.
We've just arrived. *contrac.*

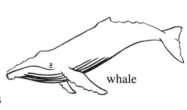
whale

whale (hwāl) a large ocean animal shaped like a fish that is killed for the oil in its body.
We watched the whale come above the water for air. *n. pl.* **whales**

whalebone whale·bone (hwāl⸍bōn) **1.** having to do with a kind of whale that has a stiff substance for its teeth; baleen.
The whalebone whale has no teeth. *adj.*
2. the stiff substance that is in the mouth of some whales instead of teeth.
People once used whalebone to make women's clothing. *n. no pl.*

what (hwot *or* hwut *or* hwət) **1.** a question word that asks "which thing?"
What is for breakfast? *pron.*
2. a question word that asks "which one?"
What time are we leaving? *adj.*

whatever what·ev·er (hwot·ev⸍ər) anything or everything; nothing specific.
You may have whatever you want from the bakery. *pron.*

wheat

what's (hwots *or* hwuts) **1.** what is.
What's the number? *contrac.*
2. what has.
What's he done now? *contrac.*

wheat (hwēt) **1.** a grain that people use to make flour.
The farmer has several fields of wheat. *n. no pl.*
2. made from the grain that is used to make flour.
I had a wheat muffin for breakfast. *adj.*

wheel (hwēl) **1.** a round object that turns around its center.
We put the tire on the front bicycle wheel. *n. pl.* **wheels**
2. to roll something that has wheels.
I will wheel the wagon into the garage.
v. **wheeled, wheeled, wheeling** wheel·ing

wheelchair wheel·chair (hwēl⸍cher *or* hwēl⸍char)
a seat with wheels that is used by people who cannot walk
or who have difficulty in walking.
She uses a wheelchair to get from one place to another.
n. pl. **wheelchairs** wheel·chairs

wheel

when (hwen) **1.** a question word that asks "what time?"
or "what day?"
When will we eat? *pron.*
2. at the time that.
I will go when you go. *conj.*
3. at any time that; whenever.
The dog barks when a stranger gets close to the house. *conj.*

whenever when·ev·er (hwen·ev⸍ər *or* hwən·ev⸍ər) at
any time; at whatever time.
I am ready whenever you are ready. *conj.*

where (hwer *or* hwar) a question word that asks "at what
place?" or "to what place?"
Where are we going? *adv.*

wherever wher·ev·er (hwer·ev⸍ər *or* hwar·ev⸍ər) at, to
or in any or every place.
You may go wherever you want on your birthday. *conj.*

wheelchair

a	cat	**i**	sit	**oi**	oil	**ch**	chop
ā	ate	**ī**	lie	**ou**	out	**ng**	song
ä	car	**o**	pot	**u**	cut	**sh**	she
e	set	**ō**	old	**u̇**	book	**th**	three
ē	equal	**ô**	or	**ü**	blue	**ŦH**	there
ėr	germ					**zh**	treasure

ə = { a in about / e in oven / i in pencil / o in memory / u in circus

whether   weth·er (hweᴛʜ'ər)   if.
He wants to know whether we are going or not. *conj.*

which   (hwich)   **1.** a question word that asks "what certain one or ones?"
Which shirt should I wear? *adj.*
2. that.
She finally found a dress which pleases her. *relative pron.*

whipped cream

while   (hwīl)   during the time that.
I watched while Lisa danced. *conj.*

whine   (hwīn)   to complain in a high, sad, childish voice; to make a long sad cry.
The baby will whine if he does not get his way.
v. **whined, whined, whining** whin·ing

whip   (hwip)   to hit or beat with a flexible stick or strap.
I will whip the rug to get it clean.
v. **whipped, whipped, whipping** whip·ping

whip-like   (hwip'līk')   looking or working like a flexible stick; being long and bendable.
The baleen whales have whip-like shapes in their mouths. *adj.*

whipped cream   (hwipt krēm)   the soft, sweet, white topping that people put on desserts.
I put whipped cream on my apple pie.

whiskers

whisker   whisk·er (hwis'kər)   a hair that grows on the face.
The shaver missed a whisker near his mouth. *n. pl.* **whiskers** whisk·ers

whisper   whis·per (hwis'pər)   to talk in a quiet voice; to talk softly.
If we whisper, Mother will not hear us talking.
v. **whispered, whispered, whispering** whis·pered, whis·per·ing

whistle   whis·tle (hwis'əl)   **1.** to make a shrill sound with the lips and the tongue.
I will whistle for the dog.
v. **whistled, whistled, whistling** whis·tled, whis·tling
2. a tool that is used to make a shrill sound.
I blew the whistle and the dog ran to me. *n. pl.* **whistles** whis·tles

whistle

who   (hü *or* ü)   a question word that asks "what person?"
Who will help me find the dog? *pron.*

whoa   (hwō *or* wō)   word a person uses to stop a horse.
I pulled on the reins and said "Whoa!" *interj.*

who'd   (hüd)   who would.
Who'd want to buy that ugly shirt? *contrac.*

whole (hōl) not broken; being in one piece; complete; being all of something; not being divided.
I ate the whole pie. *adj.*

whom (hüm) the person spoken about; which person.
I know whom I will call for help. *relative pron.*

whooping cough whoop·ing cough (hüp'ing kôf) a child's disease that makes a person cough and have trouble breathing.
My brother has whooping cough, so I cannot play with him.

whose (hüz) **1.** a question word that asks "belonging to who or what?"
Whose shoes are in the living room? *adj.*
2. someone's; belonging to someone.
The shoes belong to my friend, whose name is Jean. *relative pron.*
The teacher will give an F to any student whose homework is not finished. *relative pron.*

why (hwī) a question word that asks "for what reason?"
Why did you not go to the movie? *adv.*

wicked wick·ed (wik'id) evil; cruel; mean.
The man was wicked. He always whipped his dog. *adj.*

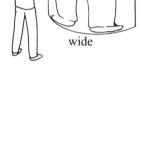
wide

wide (wīd) **1.** broad from side to side; having a large distance from one side to the other side; not narrow.
Our street is wide. *adj.*
2. great in size or scope; extensive; great in number.
We have a wide variety of candy in the store.
adj. **wider, widest** wid·er, wid·est

widen wid·en (wīd'n) to make larger from one side to the other side; to become larger.
Her eyes will widen when she sees the new bicycle.
v. **widened, widened, widening** wid·ened, wid·en·ing

widespread wide·spread (wīd'spred') covering a large area; used by many people.
Television reaches a widespread audience. *adj.*

widow wid·ow (wid'ō) a woman whose husband has died.
My aunt is a widow; my uncle died last year. *n. pl.* **widows** wid·ows

a	cat	i	sit	oi	oil	ch	chop		a in about
ā	ate	ī	lie	ou	out	ng	song		e in oven
ä	car	o	pot	u	cut	sh	she	ə =	i in pencil
e	set	ō	old	u̇	book	th	three		o in memory
ē	equal	ô	or	ü	blue	ᴛʜ	there		u in circus
ėr	germ					zh	treasure		

width (width *or* witth) the measurement from one side to the other side; the distance across something.
> The width of my new belt is 2½ inches. *n. pl.* **widths**

wife (wīf) a married woman; a woman who has a husband.
> My brother's wife is very pretty. *n. pl.* **wives**

wig (wig) fake or false hair; a covering for the head made of hair.
> I wore a red wig with my Halloween costume. *n. pl.* **wigs**

wig

wiggle wig·gle (wig'əl) to move or twist back and forth with short, quick movements.
> I will wiggle out of the sleeping bag.
> *v.* **wiggled, wiggled, wiggling** wig·gled, wig·gling

wild (wīld) uncontrollable; not tame; free; not in a cage.
> The lion is wild. *adj.* **wilder, wildest** wild·er, wild·est

wildlife wild·life (wīld'līf) animals and plants that live without the help of people; untamed animals and plants.
> Deer are part of the wildlife of the forest. *n. no pl.*

wildly wild·ly (wīld'lē) in a violent way.
> The angry woman shouted wildly. *adv.*

will (wil *or* wəl) to be doing something in the future.
> I will go to school but not today. *aux. pt. t.* **would.**

wiggle

willing will·ing (wil'ing) ready to help; eager to help.
> I am willing to do that for you. *adj.*

win (win) **1.** to not lose; to succeed; to obtain what is wanted.
> No one was sure that the colonists would win their fight with the British. *v.*
> **2.** to be first in a game or a fight.
> Our team will win the game. *v.* **won, won, winning** win·ning

wind¹ (wind) **1.** the movement of the air; moving air.
> The wind is strong today. *n. pl.* **winds**
> **2.** having to do with moving air.
> A kite uses wind power to fly. *adj.*

wind² (wīnd) to roll or turn something around an object or around itself.
> I will wind the film for your camera. *v.* **wound, wound, winding** wind·ing

windless wind·less (wind'lis) without having moving air.
> It is a windless day, so I cannot fly the kite. *adj.*

windmill wind·mill (wind'mil) a machine that uses moving air for its energy; a machine that makes energy from the wind.
> There was an old windmill in Holland. *n. pl.* **windmills** wind·mills

windmill

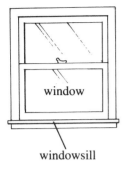

window

windowsill

window win·dow (win′dō) an opening in the wall of a building, usually covered by glass.
I broke a window in the garage. *n. pl.* **windows** win·dows

windowsill win·dow·sill (win′dō·sil) the ledge or shelf at the bottom of the opening in a wall.
I put the pot of flowers on the windowsill. *n. pl.* **windowsills** win·dow·sills

windy wind·y (win′dē) having a lot of air moving; full of air movements.
It is windy and a good day to fly a kite.
adj. **windier, windiest** wind·i·er, wind·i·est

wine (wīn) an alcoholic drink made by fermenting grapes or other fruit.
Mother drinks white wine. *n. pl.* **wines** *or* **wine**

winemaker wine·mak·er (wīn′mā·kər) a person who makes wine by smashing and fermenting grapes or other fruit.
The winemaker smashed the grapes to make wine.
n. pl. **winemakers** wine·mak·ers

winemaking wine·mak·ing (wīn′mā·king) the process of smashing and fermenting grapes or other fruit to make an alcoholic drink.
Many people enjoy learning about winemaking. *n. no pl.*

wing

wing (wing) **1.** the arm of a bird or an insect; the part of a bird or insect that is used to fly.
The bird broke its wing. *n.*
2. the part of an airplane that helps it fly.
The wing of the airplane is broken. *n. pl.* **wings**
3. having to do with the part of a plane that helps it fly.
The pilot lowered the wing flaps. *adj.*

wingspread wing·spread (wing′spred) the width of a bird's wings; the distance from the tip of one wing to the tip of the other wing on a bird or airplane.
The eagle has a large wingspread. *n. pl.* **wingspreads** wing·spreads

wink

wink (wingk) to close one eye as a signal.
I will wink at you when it is time to leave.
v. **winked, winked, winking** wink·ing

wink of sleep (wingk ov slēp) a tiny bit of sleep.
It was so noisy that I did not get a wink of sleep. *idiom*

a	cat	i	sit	oi	oil	ch	chop		a in about
ā	ate	ī	lie	ou	out	ng	song		e in oven
ä	car	o	pot	u	cut	sh	she	ə =	i in pencil
e	set	ō	old	u̇	book	th	three		o in memory
ē	equal	ô	or	ü	blue	ŦH	there		u in circus
ėr	germ					zh	treasure		

winner win·ner (win′ər) a person who is first in a game or contest; a person who wins.
The winner of the race was a nine-year-old boy. *n. pl.* **winners** win·ners

winter win·ter (win′tər) **1.** the coldest time of the year; the season that comes after autumn and before spring.
I enjoy the snow in the winter. *n. pl.* **winters** win·ters
2. having to do with the coldest season of the year.
Winter roads are often slippery. *adj.*

wipe (wīp) to clean or dry by rubbing with a soft material; to clean or dry by rubbing.
Please wipe your feet before coming into the house.
v. **wiped, wiped, wiping** wip·ing

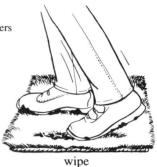
wipe

wire (wīr) **1.** thin metal string.
We tied the tree to the fence with wire. *n. pl.* **wires** *or* **wire**
2. having to do with thin metal string.
We used the wire cutters to open the fence. *adj.*

wise (wīz) very smart; having good skills in making decisions.
Father will help me to decide. He is very wise.
adj. **wiser, wisest** wis·er, wis·est

wisely wise·ly (wīz′lē) in a smart way; in a way that shows good judgment.
He wisely decided not to go. *adv.*

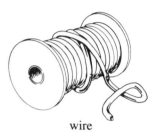
wire

wish (wish) **1.** to want; to desire; to say what you want.
I wish I could go to the park today. *v.* **wished, wished, wishing** wish·ing
2. a thing that someone wants or desires; the act of asking for what one wants or desires.
I made a wish and blew out the candles on my birthday cake.
n. pl. **wishes** wish·es

witch (wich) a woman who is mean and can do magic.
The witch turned the prince into a frog. *n. pl.* **witches** witch·es

with (wiŦH *or* with) **1.** using.
I swept with the broom. *prep.*
2. in the company of; in addition to.
I want to go with you. *prep.*
3. to.
I enjoy talking with the new boy at school. *prep.*
4. having; possessing.
The boy with the broken arm played with me. *prep.*
5. against.
We played with the football team at school. *prep.*
6. carrying; holding.
He came with a gift. *prep.*

witch

withers

withdraw with·draw (wiꜰʜ·drô′ *or* with·drô′) to take back; to remove; to take away.
I will withdraw my money from the bank.
v. **withdrew, withdrawn, withdrawing**
with·drew, with·drawn, with·draw·ing

withdrawn with·drawn (wiꜰʜ·drôn′ *or* with·drôn′)
v. pt. part. See **withdraw.**

withers with·ers (wiꜰʜ′ərz) the high point on the back of the horse, between the shoulders.
Horses are measured from the ground to the withers. *n. pl.* **withers** with·ers

within with·in (wiꜰʜ·in′ *or* with·in′) inside of; not more than a certain time or amount.
Your guess of my weight must be within five pounds. *prep.*

wolf

without with·out (wiꜰʜ·out′ *or* with·out′) not having; lacking something.
The girl went outside without a coat. *prep.*

wives (wīvz) *n. pl.* See **wife.**

woke up (wōk up) *v. pt. t.* See **wake up.**

wolf (wu̇lf) **1.** a wild animal that looks like a dog and that eats meat.
The wolf lives in the forest. *n. pl.* **wolves**
2. having to do with the wild animal that looks like a dog.
The wolf hunters set the animal traps. *adj.*

wolf spider wolf spi·der (wu̇lf spī′dər) a kind of large spider.
The wolf spider lives for three years.

wolves (wu̇lvz) *n. pl.* See **wolf.**

woman wom·an (wu̇m′ən) an adult girl; a lady; a female person.
My teacher is a woman. *n. pl.* **women** wom·en

won (wun) *v. pt. t., pt. part.* See **win.**

wonder won·der (wun′dər) to think about; to question.
I wonder what airplanes will look like in twenty years.
v. **wondered, wondered, wondering** won·dered, won·der·ing

wonderful won·der·ful (wun′dər·fəl) great; very good.
I had a wonderful time at the zoo. *adj.*

woman

a	cat	i	sit	oi	oil	ch	chop		a in about
ā	ate	ī	lie	ou	out	ng	song		e in oven
ä	car	o	pot	u	cut	sh	she	ə =	i in pencil
e	set	ō	old	u̇	book	th	three		o in memory
ē	equal	ô	or	ü	blue	ꜰʜ	there		u in circus
ėr	germ					zh	treasure		

wondering won·der·ing (wun'dər·ing) thinking about something; questioning things that may happen.
He spends his time wondering what space travel will be like in the future. *gerund*

won't (wōnt *or* wunt) will not.
I won't do the dishes if he won't help. *contrac.*

wood (wud) the material that comes from trees; the hard part of a tree under the bark.
Our house is made of wood. *n. no pl.*

wood

woodcarver wood·carv·er (wud'kär·vər) a person who uses tools to make figures out of wood; a person who carves pictures in wood.
The woodcarver made a puppet. *n. pl.* **woodcarvers** wood·carv·ers

woodcutter wood·cut·ter (wud'kut·ər) a person who cuts down trees or who chops trees into logs or smaller pieces of wood.
The woodcutter cut the tree into logs for the fireplace.
n. pl. **woodcutters** wood·cut·ters

wooden wood·en (wud'n) made of the material that comes from trees; made of wood.
The woodcarver made a wooden puppet. *adj.*

woodcarver

woods (wudz) a small group of trees; a forest.
There are deer in the woods near the lake. *plural n.*

woodworking wood·work·ing (wud'wer·king) making things from wood.
The young girl is skilled at woodworking. *n. no pl.*

wool (wul) **1.** the hair of a sheep.
The farmer shaved the wool from the sheep. *n. no pl.*
2. the cloth that is made from the hair of sheep.
She will weave the wool on the loom. *n. no pl.*
3. having to do with the hair of sheep or the material made from the hair of sheep.
This is a wool sweater. *adj.*

woodcutter

woolen wool·en (wul'ən) made from the hair of sheep; made from the material that comes from the hair of sheep.
I have a woolen coat that is very warm. *adj.*

wool

word (werd) a group of letters or sounds that have a meaning; a meaningful group of written symbols.
Can you find the word "encyclopedia" in the dictionary? *n. pl.* **words**

word of mouth (werd əv mouth) a way of getting or spreading information by people telling each other but not writing it.
I learned through word of mouth that we are having a test in math today. *idiom*

wore (wôr *or* wōr) *v. pt. t.* See **wear.**

work (wėrk) **1.** to use energy to do something; to do labor; to get paid for doing a job.
I will work in the pet store this summer. *v.*
2. to operate; to function.
The light will work if you turn the top switch to the "on" position. *v.*
3. to cause to happen; to manipulate something to operate.
You will work the stage lights in the theater.
v. **worked, worked, working** work·ing
4. the act of using energy to do something; labor.
Painting pictures is not hard work. *n. no pl.*
5. the result of using energy; something that is done.
He does good work. *n. no pl.*
6. a job; the thing a person gets money to do.
A doctor's work is to make sick people better. *n. no pl.*
7. having to do with doing labor.
Tom bought himself a new pair of work pants. *adj.*

worker work·er (wėr′kər) **1.** a person who uses energy to do a job; a person who is paid to do a job.
He is a worker in the shoe factory. *n.*
2. an ant whose job is to get the food for the colony; an insect that works for the colony.
The worker is busy all the time. *n. pl.* **workers** work·ers
3. having to do with people or insects that work.
The worker ant must bring food to the other ants. *adj.*

workout

workman work·man (wėrk′mən) a person who works with his hands; a person who works.
The workman put a new roof on the garage. *n. pl.* **workmen** work·men

work out (wėrk out) to exercise.
I will work out in the gymnasium.
v. **worked out, worked out, working out** work·ing out

workout work·out (wėrk′out) an exercise session; the act of exercising.
I had a good workout today. *n. pl.* **workouts** work·outs

workshop work·shop (wėrk′shop) **1.** a place to work with tools; a place where tools are stored.
Dad built a table in his workshop. *n.*
2. a teaching session; a class for learning new things.
I took a workshop on bicycle repair. *n. pl.* **workshops** work·shops

workshop

a	cat	i	sit	oi	oil	ch	chop		a in about
ā	ate	ī	lie	ou	out	ng	song		e in oven
ä	car	o	pot	u	cut	sh	she	ə =	i in pencil
e	set	ō	old	u̇	book	th	three		o in memory
ē	equal	ô	or	ü	blue	ŦH	there		u in circus
ėr	germ					zh	treasure		

world   (wėrld)   **1.** the planet Earth; the globe.
Asia is the largest continent in the world. *n. no pl.*
2. having to do with the Earth.
The world population is always growing. *adj.*

worm   (wėrm)   a small animal that is thin and round, has no
legs and crawls on the ground.
The worm came out of the dirt. *n. pl.* **worms**

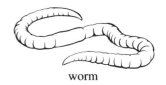
worm

worm-like   (wėrm‑lῑk)   looking like the thin, round animal
that crawls on the ground.
A caterpillar is worm-like. *adj.*

worn   (wôrn)   *v. pt. part.* See **wear.**

worn down   (wôrn   doun)   *v. pt. part.* See **wear down.**

worried   wor·ried (wėr‑ēd)   **1.** *v. pt. t., pt. part.* See **worry.**
2. concerned; anxious.
The worried look on his face told me something was wrong. *adj.*

worrier   wor·ri·er (wėr‑rē·ər)   a person who is always concerned
about things; a person who gets anxious.
I will call Mother and tell her I will be late. She is a worrier and
will be concerned. *n. pl.* **worriers** wor·ri·ers

worry   wor·ry (wėr‑ē)   to feel concern; to become frightened;
to become anxious.
She will worry if I am late.
v. **worried, worried, worrying** wor·ried, wor·ry·ing

worship

worse   (wėrs)   more bad; less good.
I am still sick today. I feel worse than I did yesterday.
comp. adj. See **bad** and **ill.**

worship   wor·ship (wėr‑ship)   to take part in a religious ceremony;
to honor and love God or other religious leaders.
The Buddhists worship Buddha, and the Christians worship Christ.
v. **worshiped** *or* **worshipped, worshiped** *or* **worshipped, worshiping** *or*
worshipping wor·shiped *or* wor·shipped, wor·ship·ing *or* wor·ship·ping

worst   (wėrst)   most bad; least good.
He is the worst cook I have ever met. *superl. adj.* See **bad** and **ill.**

worth   (wėrth)   the value of something; the importance of something;
the cost of something.
The diamond ring is worth many dollars. *adj.*

would   (wụd *or* wəd)   *aux. pt. t.* See **will.**

would like   (wụd   lῑk)   to want; to desire.
I would like to be a teacher. *idiom*

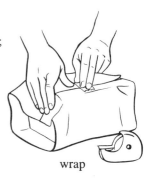
wrap

wouldn't   would·n't (wụd‑n't)   would not.
I wouldn't want to go there. *contrac.*

wreath

would've (wùd‑əv) would have.
> We would've gone too, but Lisa was sick. *contrac.*

wound (wünd) to cause an injury; to hurt.
> The knife can wound a person.
> *v.* **wounded, wounded, wounding** wound‑ed, wound‑ing

woven wo‑ven (wō‑vən) made of interlaced threads or strings.
> I have a woven skirt. *adj.*

wow (wou) a word used to show surprise or great pleasure;
> an exclamation of delight.
> Wow! That is a beautiful dog! *interj.*

wrap (rap) to cover something on all sides with paper or cloth;
> to put something around a thing.
> I will wrap the birthday present.
> *v.* **wrapped, wrapped, wrapping** wrap‑ping

wrapped (rapt) **1.** covered on all sides by something.
> The wrapped box sat on the table for two days. *adj.*
> **2.** *v. pt. t., pt. part.* See **wrap.**

wreck

wreath (rēth) a circle made of flowers or leaves that is
> used for decoration.
> We put a Christmas wreath on the front door. *n. pl.* **wreaths**

wreck (rek) **1.** something that has been damaged; a ship or
> car that has been in an accident.
> The wreck of the ship was found in the ocean. *n. pl.* **wrecks**
> **2.** to damage or ruin; to have an accident that damages or ruins.
> You will wreck your bicycle if you are not careful.
> *v.* **wrecked, wrecked, wrecking** wreck‑ing

wrestle wres‑tle (res‑əl) to fight and try to throw a person
> to the ground; to struggle with a person.
> He will wrestle with the champion.
> *v.* **wrestled, wrestled, wrestling** wres‑tled, wres‑tling

wrestling wres‑tling (res‑ling) a sport where players try
> to throw each other to the ground.
> You must be strong to participate in wrestling. *n. no pl.*

wrestle

wriggle wrig‑gle (rig‑əl) to turn and twist; to wiggle.
> Sometimes a fish will wriggle off the hook after I catch it.
> *v.* **wriggled, wriggled, wriggling** wrig‑gled, wrig‑gling

a	cat	i	sit	oi	oil	ch	chop		a in about
ā	ate	ī	lie	ou	out	ng	song		e in oven
ä	car	o	pot	u	cut	sh	she	ə =	i in pencil
e	set	ō	old	ù	book	th	three		o in memory
ē	equal	ô	or	ü	blue	ŦH	there		u in circus
ėr	germ					zh	treasure		

wriggler   wrig·gler (rig′lər)   a mosquito larva.
  The wriggler twists and turns to get food into its mouth.
  n. pl. **wrigglers** wrig·glers

wring   (ring)   to twist something to get water or other liquid out of it.
  I will wring the wet towel and then hang it on the clothesline.
  v. **wrung, wrung, wringing** wring·ing

wring

wrinkle   wrin·kle (ring′kəl)   **1.** to make creases or folds in things;
  to cause to have creases or folds.
  My pants will wrinkle if I sit down.
  v. **wrinkled, wrinkled, wrinkling** wrin·kled, wrin·kling
  2. a fold or crease.
  I put a wrinkle in my pants when I sat down. *n. pl.* **wrinkles** wrin·kles

wrinkly   wrin·kly (ring′klē)   full of wrinkles; having many
  creases or folds in it.
  The blouse is wrinkly and needs to be ironed.
  adj. **wrinklier, wrinkliest** wrin·kli·er, wrin·kli·est

write   (rīt)   **1.** to use a pencil or pen to put words on paper;
  to use chalk to put words on a board.
  I will write my name on my book. *v.*
  2. to make up a story and put it on paper; to be an author.
  I will write a story about our vacation.
  v. **wrote, written, writing** writ·ten, writ·ing

write down   (rīt doun)   to put words on paper; to make a
  note of something to be remembered; to put ideas or
  thoughts into writing.
  I will write down the address of the store. *v.* **wrote down, written
  down, writing down** writ·ten down, writ·ing down

wrinkle

write in   (rīt in)   to put words into an empty space on a paper;
  to fill in an empty space with words.
  I will write in the names of the countries on this map.
  v. **wrote in, written in, writing in** writ·ten in, writ·ing in

writer   writ·er (rī′tər)   a person who makes up or creates
  stories or reports; an author.
  The reporter is a writer for the newspaper. *n. pl.* **writers** writ·ers

written   writ·ten (rit′n)   *v. pt. part.* See **write.**

wrong   (rông *or* rong)   **1.** not right; not as usual; not normal.
  There is something wrong with the television. *adj.*
  2. not right; not correct.
  I gave the wrong answer to the first question. *adj.*

write

wrote   (rōt)   *v. pt. t.* See **write.**

Xx

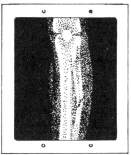

x-ray

x-ray (eks′rā) **1.** a picture through the walls of something to show what is inside, taken with a machine that uses special rays of light.
I saw the x-ray of my leg bone. *n. pl.* **x-rays**
2. having to do with pictures of the inside of things taken with special machines.
The x-ray machine in the airport can find hidden metal weapons. *adj.*

a	cat	**i**	sit	**oi**	oil	**ch**	chop	
ā	ate	**ī**	lie	**ou**	out	**ng**	song	
ä	car	**o**	pot	**u**	cut	**sh**	she	
e	set	**ō**	old	**u̇**	book	**th**	three	
ē	equal	**ô**	or	**ü**	blue	**ŦH**	there	
ėr	germ					**zh**	treasure	

ə = { a in about / e in oven / i in pencil / o in memory / u in circus }

Yy

yak (yak) a long-haired ox.
The yak comes from Asia. *n. pl.* **yaks**

Yankee Yan·kee (yang′kē) a person who plays baseball for the New York Yankees; a member of the New York baseball team.
Babe Ruth was a Yankee for many years. *n. pl.* **Yankees** Yan·kees

yard (yärd) **1.** the area outside a house; the ground outside a house.
I will play in the yard and not in the driveway. *n.*
2. the area inside a fence.
We cannot go into the yard with the zebras. *n. pl.* **yards**

yarn (yärn) soft thread that is made from wool.
Mother uses yarn to make sweaters. *n. pl.* **yarn** *or* **yarns**

yeah (ye *or* ya *or* ye′ə) slang way of saying yes.
Yeah, I want to go with you. *adv.*

year (yir) twelve months; 365 days.
I will learn to drive in one year. *n. pl.* **years**

yearly year·ly (yir′lē) every year; every 365 days; every twelve months.
I visit my doctor for a checkup yearly. *adv.*

yell (yel) **1.** to shout; to say loudly; to get angry and talk meanly.
The teacher will yell if we forget to bring our homework.
v. **yelled, yelled, yelling** yell·ing
2. a shout; words said loudly.
Her yell frightens me. *n. pl.* **yells**

yellow fever yel·low fe·ver (yel′ō fē′vər) a disease that a certain kind of mosquito can give to a person.
A mosquito bit the man, and he got yellow fever.

Yellow Pages Yel·low Pag·es (yel′ō pā′jəz) the part of the telephone directory in which businesses are listed by category or kind of thing.
I looked in the Yellow Pages to find a new toy shop.

Yellowstone Yel·low·stone (yel′ō·stōn) a large national park mostly in the state of Wyoming that has a famous geyser named "Old Faithful."
The ranger told us about the geysers at Yellowstone. *n.*

yes (yes) a word used to show agreement or to give a positive answer; not no.
I asked if I could go, and Mother said yes. *adv.*

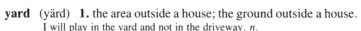

yak

yarn

Yellowstone

yesterday yes·ter·day (yes′tər·dē *or* yes′tər·dā)
the day that was before today; one day ago.
Today is Monday, so yesterday was Sunday. *n. pl.* **yesterdays** yes·ter·days

yet (yet) up to now.
Father has not come home from work yet. *adv.*

yogurt yo·gurt (yō′gərt) a food that is made of milk
and certain bacteria.
I put berries in my yogurt. *n. pl.* **yogurts** yo·gurts

yogurt

you (yü *or* yu̇) the person or persons to whom one is talking.
I want you to come to my party. *pron.*

you'd (yüd *or* yu̇d) **1.** you would.
You'd love my grandmother; she is very kind and gentle. *contrac.*
2. you had.
You'd better go to bed now. *contrac.*

young (yung) having little age; not old.
The baby is eleven months old. He is young.
adj. **younger, youngest** young·er, young·est

your (yu̇r *or* yər) belonging to the person or persons to whom
one is talking.
This is not my pencil. It must be your pencil. *adj.*

you're (yu̇r) you are.
You're coming with us, right? *contrac.*

yours (yu̇rz) belonging to you; belonging to the person or persons
to whom one is talking.
This pencil is yours. *pron.*

yourself your·self (yu̇r·self′ *or* yər·self′) that very same person or
persons to whom one is talking.
You should help yourself to the food. *pron. pl.* **yourselves** your·selves

young

yum (yum) a word used to say how good something tastes or smells.
Yum! That pie smells delicious. *interj.*

a	cat	i	sit	oi	oil	ch	chop		a in about
ā	ate	ī	lie	ou	out	ng	song		e in oven
ä	car	o	pot	u	cut	sh	she	ə =	i in pencil
e	set	ō	old	u̇	book	th	three		o in memory
ē	equal	ô	or	ü	blue	₮H	there		u in circus
ėr	germ					zh	treasure		

Zz

zebra ze·bra (zē⸍brə) an animal with thick black stripes on its body that looks like a horse or donkey.
The zebra comes from Africa. *n. pl.* **zebras** *or* **zebra** ze·bras *or* ze·bra

zip code (zip kōd) the number at the end of an address that tells to which post office the mail is to go.
Please put the zip code on the letter.

zoo (zü) a place where animals are kept for people to see and learn about; an animal park.
We will visit the zoo. *n. pl.* **zoos**

zookeeper zoo·keep·er (zü·kē⸍pər) a person who takes care of the animals in the zoo.
The zookeeper feeds the animals every day. *n. pl.* **zookeepers** zoo·keep·ers

zoologist zo·ol·o·gist (zō·ol⸍ə·jist) a person who studies animals.
The zoologist learned about the animals in the desert.
n. pl. **zoologists** zo·ol·o·gists

zoom (züm) to go very fast.
The jet will zoom past the clouds. *v.* **zoomed, zoomed, zooming** zoom·ing

zebra

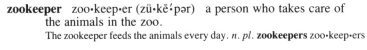

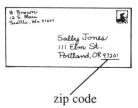

zip code